Inuit Women

Inuit Women

Their Powerful Spirit in a Century of Change

JANET MANCINI BILLSON AND KYRA MANCINI

ROWMAN & LITTLEFIELD PUBLISHERS, INC.
Lanham • Boulder • New York • Toronto • Plymouth, UK

ROWMAN & LITTLEFIELD PUBLISHERS, INC.

Published in the United States of America
by Rowman & Littlefield Publishers, Inc.
A wholly owned subsidiary of The Rowman & Littlefield Publishing Group, Inc.
4501 Forbes Boulevard, Suite 200, Lanham, Maryland 20706
www.rowmanlittlefield.com

Estover Road, Plymouth PL6 7PY, United Kingdom

British Library Cataloguing in Publication Information Available

Library of Congress Cataloging-in-Publication Data Available

ISBN-13: 978-0-7425-3596-1 (cloth : alk. paper)
ISBN-10: 0-7425-3596-7 (cloth : alk. paper)
ISBN-13: 978-0-7425-3597-8 (pbk. : alk. paper)
ISBN-10: 0-7425-3597-5 (pbk. : alk. paper)

Printed in the United States of America

♾™ The paper used in this publication meets the minimum requirements of American
National Standard for Information Sciences—Permanence of Paper for Printed Library
Materials, ANSI/NISO Z39.48-1992.

For Qatsuq
and the women of
Pangnirtung

This book is dedicated to
James Clifford Ramey
beloved brother and dear uncle
1946–1999

and to Clifford Earle Ramey
beloved father and grandfather
1918–2005

ABOUT THE COVER ARTIST

Lypa Pitsiulak (1943–)

"If there had been a writing system a long time ago, we would have been able to read and hear many touching stories about the Inuit way of life. Even though they didn't have a writing system, the Inuit stories were kept alive by telling them to others by memory. The Inuit had such stories and memories in their minds for a long time. I can do the same thing."

Born at Illutalik camp, Lypa moved to Pangnirtung in 1967 and became a successful printmaker and sculptor. In 1977, he moved his family to an outpost camp, where he makes a living today as an artist and hunter.

His print "Disguised Archer" appeared on a Canadian stamp in the 1980s and several of his carvings have been sold to prestigious galleries. Two of the tapestries on display at the Carleton University Art Gallery were inspired by Lypa's drawings depicting epic myths from Inuit oral history. Lypa is a visual storyteller *par excellence*.

His wife Annie, also a well known artist, sells her art works through the Uqqurmiut Centre for Arts and Crafts in Panniqtuuq and had one of her drawings chosen for that group's logo.

Japanese film crews documented life at the camp in the 1980s and in 2000. In 1988, the National Film Board produced a film about his life and work called *Lypa*.

CONTENTS

PREFACE

Inuit Women has been several years in the making, and has come to fruition shortly after Nunavut—a new territory carved out of traditional Inuit homelands in the Canadian North—goes into effect. We focus on the challenges facing Inuit women as they enter the twenty-first century, placed into the broader historical context of a complex past and a rapidly changing present. We draw on the memories of Inuit elder women to draw a picture of their lives in the whaling period of the late nineteenth century and how they have since changed. We also use early accounts written by whaler's wives, missionaries, and anthropologists, but temper those with the comments of contemporary Inuit women as they struggle to clarify their own history.

As the heart of this book, Inuit females from 14 to 100 years old portray their lives in their own voices. Feminists have criticized traditional social science methodology for creating and perpetuating myths that inhibit our understanding of women's experiences and position in society. Marybelle Mitchell argues that "the lack of reliable observations concerning precontact relations between men and women" makes it impossible to document change. Eighteenth and nineteenth century observations were made by males, most of them untrained in the social sciences: "...the majority of non-Inuit who recorded Inuit oral literature were male missionaries and male anthropologists who had no interest in or access to the female domain."[1] For that reason, we have interviewed many elder women and have made use of the few extant observations by nineteenth century women (such as Margaret Penny in Chapter 1) who traveled to the Arctic with their seafaring husbands.

We expand this discourse with our own limited analysis (superimposed, explanatory frameworks such as a feminist sociological perspective, conflict-functionalist analysis, social impact-social vitality analysis, and theories of marginality, social change, and identity).[2] For comparative purposes, we refer to findings from twentieth century studies of similar aboriginal groups.

To help us avoid the pitfalls of "outsider research," we developed the Progressive Verification Method (PVM) an approach grounded in feminist theory. Involving Inuit women as full participants in a flexible, responsive research process helped us address the myths of researcher authority; objectivity; historical and cultural abstraction; non-interference; and a single, androcentric society.[3] We hope to counterbalance the relative inattention to women's issues and lives that characterizes so much of the otherwise valuable work on the Inuit.

The Myth of Researcher Authority

Traditional social science has established the researcher as "authority," an expert who can describe, predict, and control social reality even if the objects of research are ignorant of or disagree with the study's existence and findings. While systematic observation of the human condition is facilitated by adherence to the canons of "the scientific method," data stand a better chance of being valid if we view people as "subjects" rather than objects and as expert witnesses about their own lives. Carolyn Fluehr-Lobban argues that "ethically conscious" anthropological research involves relating on a par with "subjects" rather than conducting research from above. She calls for "more participatory, more egalitarian models."[4] Maria Mies contends that we must reconstruct the research process to include the concerns of women who do not have the luxury of conducting research on women.[5] A feminist methodology implies a "non-hierarchical, non-authoritarian, non-manipulative, humble relation to the 'subject.'"[6] It also implies that "valid distinctions based on race, ethnicity, region, language, or age should not override the commonalities women share."[7]

In taking this wisdom to heart, our objective as outsiders trying to understand another culture was to see that culture as much as possible through the eyes of the women who live in it. We could not discard our personae as white, female social scientists from southern Canada and the United States, but we wanted to relate to Inuit women in a collaborative mode of inquiry that would bring us closer to doing research *with rather than on women*. We hoped that the Progressive Verification Method would diminish the chances that we would distort, make invisible, or misinterpret diverse life experiences, as so much research has done in the past.[8]

To that end, we used focus group and individual interviews (conducted in Pangnirtung between 1988 and 2000) as our primary data-gathering technique. We consciously defined interviewees as "consultants" and equal participants in the process. As sociologists, we preferred to use intensive, structured group interviews (as opposed to oral histories or the non-structured interviews of anthropology) because they afford systematic questioning and involvement of a broad spectrum of community members.

As a primary research tool, the focus group method worked exceptionally well for Inuit women,[9] since gathering in small groups punctuates their routine daily life in Pangnirtung. Although we arranged some group interviews more formally, often we were invited to ask our questions during a "natural gathering" over tea and bannock. We asked the same questions in all interviews, and then inserted probes to explore emergent material more deeply. The questions guided women as they reflected upon the status and role of women—in both traditional and contemporary times—by asking them to recall memories of their parents, grandparents, and great-grandparents. We also invited them to talk about contemporary gender relationships and to describe how they are socializing their daughters and sons for the future. Group sessions stimulated debate, multiple descriptions of reality, and various explanations of causality.[10] They also helped women to overcome structural isolation and to realize that their individual sufferings may be rooted in social forces that affect other women as well. Co-author Mancini transcribed the taped interviews, which ranged in length from one to four hours.

We invited more than twenty male informants to answer parallel questions, primarily to flesh out women's descriptions of men's roles and power (past and present), but also to ascertain their views of issues currently facing men and women together. Men's responses resembled women's views regarding major problems in gender relations (including battering and substance abuse) and the differential status and role of males and females. Our study and methodology focus on the experiences of women, however, echoing Margrit Eichler's concern that feminist research must "start from a female perspective which may or may not need to be modified when men are taken into consideration."[11]

Although we did not interview a statistically random or especially large number of women, we made concerted efforts to talk with a broad sample of women across age and status groups. Rather than employing the "snowball" or reputational technique (whereby people are asked to refer someone who might know about a particular question or fit a particular category), we asked participants to give us the names of other women who might have a *different* experience, history, or viewpoint. This technique worked extremely well, as the women seemed to understand that we did not want to record the voices only of women leaders, or women from one extended family, or from one original camp. The surnames of those interviewed indicate that, in fact, a wide range of families was included. Similarly, we took care to interview teenage girls as well as elders, homemakers as well as women in wage-paying jobs, and women who had little or no formal education as well as high school graduates or college students.

At the end of each interview, we asked participants to reflect on the position of Inuit women. They enjoyed contributing to a self-reflexive discussion of what they had learned and engaged in an interpretive analysis of the strengths, problems, and needs of women in their community. Conceptualization extended to dialogues in the natural setting as well. As the project moved toward completion, our collaborative analysis was presented to the next interviewees, refined again and again, thus becoming "progressively verified." When conflicting or contradictory material emerged, we restated the perceptions of previous interviewees: "Someone told us such-and-such—what is your perception?" We asked them to explain why women might not agree on a common analysis. When we started hearing the same analyses and no new material was emerging other than personal anecdotes, we knew it was time to step back, write, and re-enter with a draft manuscript for community reflection. In our quest for a broad-based analytical consensus, the PVM helped diminish the authority structure between researcher and researched and, we believe, rendered a more accurate, realistic document. In addition, the PVM helped us broach the gaps inevitably created by the fact that a universe of discourse exists in every culture that is not readily penetrable by participant observation or direct observation.

The Myth of Objectivity

Dorothy Smith argues that the norm of objectivity actually mystifies rather than explains human relationships and alienates the "object" of research through anonymous and impersonal methods. Detachment, she believes, is *not* a condition of science: "Taking sides, beginning from some position with some concern does not destroy the 'scientific' character of the enterprise.... Indeed, in sociology there is no possibility of detachment."[12] If nothing else, social science cannot be value-neutral because society is not yet neutral on such issues as gender, race, or sexual preference. Nor can researchers remove all traces of bias or values from our perceptual lenses.

While the objectification linked with surveys, polls, analysis of secondary statistical data, and other quantitative methods has its place—for example, in comparing female wages or employment rates to male data for large population samples—it has limited utility. However, understanding *why* such differentials exist or *how* they affect women tends to be facilitated through interactive research techniques.

Although we were firmly committed to working with Inuit women as consultants, we lived in the community as human beings, as women, and as feminists. We recorded daily life through our own cultural and gender "lenses." We saw social phenomena that Inuit women did not always articulate. We encountered the land and the sea through our own senses. For all of these reasons, our presentation cannot be wholly "objective" (as much social science in the past has pretended to be). We used the participant observation traditions of sociology and anthropology but, because outsiders to any culture can never grasp its full complexities, we kept our experiences and perceptions separate in the fieldnotes that open each chapter. These entries are frankly subjective and anecdotal, and represent another way of communicating what we learned in Pangnirtung.

As many ethnographers have pointed out, certain advantages accrue to the role of "the stranger"—sometimes people find it easier to talk to someone they do not have to live with on a daily basis. A major report on crime in Baffin Island communities makes this point: "Many of the Inuit community residents interviewed by non-Inuit members of the project team specifically stated that they were participating in the interview *precisely because the team member was from outside* [the community]."[13] We hope that has been true in this case, but should also note that Inuit women openly supported each other in being frank in our presence. They embraced the intent and process of our study, and worked hard to help all of us "tell the truth."

Including our subjective experiences does not imply, however, that we abdicated our role as outsider, stranger, or "other." As social scientists, we initiated the study, began to define questions, and inadvertently or purposely imposed a foreign interpretive framework. We have a responsibility to elaborate what we see. Sometimes we thought we heard an underlying current of oppression in gender relations that Inuit women or men seemed to ignore or gloss over. Because we are trained observers, we recorded data that might support (or fail to support) our interpretation of oppression. Then, as a critical part of the PVM, we made our assumptions, hypotheses, and tentative conclusions open not just to our colleagues and reviewers, but also to the Inuit consultants. We revised the manuscript after careful discussions with Inuit women about the discrepancies in our viewpoints, and offer throughout the book their explanations as well as our own. We also offer possible solutions to problems they have defined as important but that have not been a part of Inuit culture up to this point.

Our research process involved extensive participation from the community, including permission to enter the community for a research purpose, full knowledge and approval of the research agenda and questions, help with recruiting women into the focus group discussions, interpreting and other data gathering assistance, involvement in the on-going process of data analysis, and critical review of each chapter.

By the same token, our Inuit consultants did not always agree with each other, which we accept as evidence that "subjectivity" reigns on the side of experts as well. Even in a community of 1,400 people, experiences and views differed according to age, socioeconomic status, extended family membership, and being descended from one "band" or another before moving to Pangnirtung. While we have tried to make sense of some of the seemingly contradictory statements, on the other hand, we assume that any people who have lived through a period of great and rapid change will sometimes have difficulty "making sense" of what they know to be true for themselves and for their neighbors.

The Myth of Historical and Cultural Abstraction

The Progressive Verification Method self-consciously employs the case study approach in order to help avoid the myth of historical and cultural abstraction. Creating a research process in which women can discuss their individual views and social contexts mitigates the errors of abstraction. Analysis of the social structure in which women exist is an integral part of grounding inquiry, says Eichler.[14] As Westkott points out, "The idea of grounding inquiry in concrete experience rather than in abstract categories is reflected in women's historical identification with the concrete, everyday life of people and their survival needs."[15] The case study approach seemed to us especially relevant for Inuit women because their contexts differ significantly from community to community, era to era. Notions of causal relations that float in a vacuum, tethered to neither time nor place, render social science unrealistically abstract and uselessly ahistorical, Dorothy Smith argues.[16] Linda Archibald and Mary Crnkovich emphasize the importance of "seeing things in context," especially in trying to understand women cross-culturally.[17]

Accounts by white male explorers, archeologists, police, traders, and government workers added to a sometimes distorted picture of "Inuit life." Assumptions of universal patriarchy; devaluation of women; male control of the material base of daily life; woman as outsider, deviant, and alienated are inextricably bound to the narrow context of white social science—and all these assumptions have been made about Inuit women. It is for these reasons that we used interviews and participant observation (within a case study approach) to bring the voices of Inuit women to readers who live miles away, both literally and figuratively.

The case study approach has both pluses and minuses, however. On the plus side, by focusing on one community's experience during the past century, we could "breathe life" into more abstract, historical, or statistical observations on the Inuit in general. We could track down a "community memory" of the major historical events of the recent past (e.g., the whaling period, which some elders recalled) and the resettlement period, which anyone over 30 or 35 could remember. Had we tried to study women's changing roles in a series of communities, the unique historical events might have confused the picture.

Another important plus was that we could ask interviewees about the experience of "women in their community" (of which they have direct knowledge). This allowed them to generalize on the basis of real life data (thereby uncovering patterns), but also to avoid revealing their own personal experiences if they so chose. We considered this latter factor to be extremely important in interviewing women and teenagers, who might want to discuss typical issues that face women everywhere (such as abortion, pregnancy, single parenthood, child abuse, spousal assault, or divorce) without jeopardizing their own privacy. For example, we asked questions in public rather than personal terms ("What do Inuit women here see as the major problems facing them today?"). Maintaining emphasis on "public issues" rather than "personal troubles" provided women with a way of grasping the social relations that organize their worlds through active participation in an analytical and self-reflective dialogue. It is also in keeping with a feminist sociological approach and what Robin McGrath claims is the preferred mode of communication for Inuit women: "According to Inuit women, it is proper to recall the 'learning years,' to show themselves as children or young girls who make mistakes and accept correction, but it is improper to boast or attract attention as adults. For women to draw attention to themselves overtly is to invite ridicule."[18] If Inuit women write about themselves, they do so in fictionalized terms or wait until they become elders.

The elegance of the PVM is that it provides subjects with a way of "grasping the social relations organizing the worlds of their experience" through active participation in an analytical and self-reflective dialogue.[19] Our purpose was to uncover collaboratively how the status and roles of Inuit women have changed over time, not to extricate individual life histories. As Smith clarifies, a specific "case" is only a point of entry into a larger social and economic process.

The case study method entailing the use of interviews and participant observation also allowed us to use a third research technique (thus generating "triangulation" of methodologies). We integrated historical and other data specifically relevant to this community, although we consider the accounts of contemporary women to be our primary source material and our first responsibility. After reviewing relevant social science literature, history, and demographic data (using the U. S. Library of Congress and university and civic libraries in Canada), we contacted community leaders. Although Reinharz advocates *not* undertaking an extensive literature search before an investigation,[20] in order to avoid self-fulfilling prophecies, we found it essential to have a basic awareness of the geography, history, and social context prior to making contact with people in the communities. The Inuit perceived this as an expression of courtesy and respect. As we worked with women in Pangnirtung, they suggested books, articles, pictures, and letters of which they were aware, sometimes giving them to us for later reading. In addition, we visited the Angmarlik Cultural Centre in Pangnirtung and libraries there and in Iqaluit that contain materials unavailable elsewhere. As we have worked through a series of drafts, inevitably we have uncovered or been referred to other very useful materials. In this sense, "data gathering in the experiential mode is not exclusively data creating, but can really be 'gathering up' what is already there."[21] After completing our fieldwork, we conducted a secondary literature review targeting questions that remained unresolved. And, doing a case study allowed us to incorporate "key informant" data from elders and those who work in high-contact positions in the community (for example, social workers, nurses, RCMP officers and constables, and cultural center staff).

On the negative side, a case study always runs the risk of presenting life in one community as though it could be generalized to *all* similar communities. To some extent, this is possible, because the Inuit who live in Pangnirtung have many cultural, social, and economic similarities to other Inuit living in Nunavut. For that reason we have cited studies of other Inuit settlements, and incorporated a few interviews with women in comparable communities to explicate points made by Pangnirtung women. We have also chosen to explore the possible implications of Nunavut in the last chapter, which will affect not just Pangnirtung, but all of Nunavut's hamlets. Life in Pangnirtung is unique, however, as is life in any of the 27 communities that make up Nunavut. Each was exposed to different outside forces, different personalities among its own leaders, and singular historical and climactic events. We believe that many of our findings could easily be replicated in other Baffin Island communities such as Pond Inlet, Cape Dorset, or Broughton Island. Yet, very different outcomes might be obtained in a place such as Iqaluit (the new capital of Nunavut and also on Baffin Island), which, at over 4,000 people, has a much more' diverse population and southern-oriented lifestyle.

We are certain, also, that we were not allowed to see into Inuit lives further than our consultants felt comfortable letting us see. Gwen Reimer, who conducted interviews in Pangnirtung during the early 1990s, acknowledges that a prominent family served as her guide, and therefore she heard "one side of women's story." She concludes, "ethnography is always partial—both in terms of it always being incomplete and in terms of it never being free from bias," a conclusion we share.[22]

Finally, although we have ventured to make some interpretive analyses of our own, we have tried to let the analyses of Inuit women prevail. In Chapter 19, we offer the "academic overlay" of three theoretical frameworks that seem to fit closely what the Inuit of Pangnirtung have told us: Conflict and functional theory; social vitality theory; and marginality theory. Undoubtedly, we could have imposed many other frameworks instead, but we felt that these three best encapsulated the main issues raised by our consultants. Even these frameworks, however, fall woefully short of reflecting the complicated past, transition, and future experienced by Inuit women.

The Myth of Non-Interference

Positivism traditionally assumes that the research process is (and should be) non-interfering—care should be taken to record social reality factually without changing it. The feminist perspective, by contrast, asks "knowledge for what?" In some cases, measuring is not the end of the researcher's job. Stimulating awareness or applying knowledge for positive social change may also be involved in the research process.

This is more than an activist critique. It is also a logical one. The Heisenberg principle of physics, which states that the very act of measuring a phenomenon alters it at least infinitesimally, translates into a social scientific equivalent, the Hawthorne Effect. We cannot measure a social phenomenon without affecting it, even if only to raise people's awareness of it. To engage subjects in a reasoned, analytical discussion of the sources and consequences of gender stratification in their community, for example, is a matter of degree of interference, rather than interference versus the alleged non-interference of "objective" methods like surveys.

For example, Mies describes her experience of conducting life history interviews with German women. When women listened to each other's stories, they "were struck by the similarity of their experiences, i.e., the commonness and monotony of the everyday violence."[23] We observed (and felt ourselves) the same similarities during our interviews and observations. Often, Inuit women asked us about issues faced by other women with whom we had conducted research (i.e., the Blood, Chinese, Iroquois, Jamaican, Mennonite, and Ukrainian women interviewed for Keepers of the Culture). Feminist methodology acknowledges rather than denies research that raises consciousness, which in turn may lead to political strategies and/or personal change. On the other hand, we exerted extreme care in not offering advice, taking sides of a debate, or proposing solutions to problems Inuit women addressed.

Interference, however subtle and unavoidable, involves risks and perplexities. We tried to be aware of our biases, values, and the ways in which our research approach might affect the Inuit by discussing these issues on a daily basis. As anthropologist Nicole-Claude Mathieu argues, the boundaries of cultures are complex and the position of women in many cultures may render them "other." She believes that the exploration of oppression in its many forms worldwide, however problematic, is a legitimate focus of our research.[24] We are, as female researchers, "other" in our own cultures; we must be self-reflective about our own positions. To observe, record, and document oppression is to refuse to abdicate our position as women and as researchers.

The methodological corollary to this principle is that, as Smith argues, "the sociological inquirer herself [is] a member of the same world she explores, active in the same relations as those for whom she writes. Like Jonah, she is inside the whale."[25] In Pangnirtung, reminded of Smith's comment by the real whales in the waters nearby, we recognized our simultaneous inherent status as "insiders." Although our cultural context differs on one level, on another level we are deeply embedded in the same everyday contexts of being female. This truth was expressed several times as Inuit women said to each other and to us as we tried to make sense out of gender relations and women's issues, "we are really sisters."

The Myth of a Single Androcentric Society

Finally, but perhaps most importantly, Marcia Millman and Rosabeth Moss Kanter have pointed out that traditional social science assumes that a monolithic, single society exists: If we have described men, we can generalize to women.[26] Insofar as women are isolated, marginal, and dependent, it is inevitable that others will speak for them; in the case of social science, historically it has been men who have attempted to do that speaking. This type of social science "concentrates on the distortion and misinterpretation of women's experience"[27] either through ignoring it, measuring it only in masculine terms as the abstract deviation of essential humanity, or by defining it in terms of women's relationship to men, which becomes the source of female stereotypes.

The androcentric, patriarchal bias of most social science methods "has rendered women not only unknown, but virtually unknowable."[28] We have tried in this research to bring women to the foreground, a difficult task in that the vast majority of literature we encountered focused on Inuit male activities such as whaling, camp leadership, hunting, trapping, or trading as though they represented the Inuit experience. However, because most fieldwork until recently was conducted by male ethnographers, who tended to gain more access into male worlds (especially hunting) than into female worlds, this led to a "typically skewed and male oriented" view of women's role and power.[29] In addition, that fieldwork was conducted among informants born in the late nineteenth century, at the height of commercial whaling, so accounts of "traditional" life focused on that period. Feminism "implies assuming a perspective in which women's experiences, ideas and needs are valid in their own right."[30] If most women have been socialized into patriarchal social contexts—and that is certainly true for nineteenth and twentieth century Inuit women whose lives were touched so deeply by missionaries and whalers—structurally controlled by men and culturally devalued, then social science must break out of the traditional non-gendered perspective in order to study those contexts.

The Progressive Verification Method used in *Inuit Women* brings us one step closer to apprehending the social forces surrounding changes in women's status and roles. Use of intensive interviews, the Informed Consent Agreement, and the right to give feedback on a draft analysis of data all contribute to separating our cultural bias from the portrait of this community. No final interpretation of data is valid for all time or will satisfy everyone, but the book will add Inuit voices to those that have tried to describe and understand "the people" who have lived in these lands for the past few thousand years. Our goal was to write "an adequate interpretation which is endorsed by participants, confirmed by readers and cognitively satisfying [to] the researcher."[31] We hope that our most critical readers, the women of Pangnirtung, will feel that goal has been achieved.

Notes

1 McGrath, "Circumventing the Taboos," p. 226. The approach is also broadly consistent with the position that sociologists should focus on "public issues" rather than "personal problems." See C. Wright Mills, *The Sociological Imagination* (New York: Oxford University Press, 1959).

2 Louis-Jacques Dorais makes this distinction in *Quaqtaq: Modernity and Identity in an Inuit Community* (Toronto: University of Toronto Press, 1997), p. 115. He says that in his study, he considered himself a "premodern" anthropologist, "one who contents himself with a clear and…honest description of the people he is studying." We aspire to that goal as well, but have tried to keep our descriptions separate from those of our consultants, especially by using the technique of introducing each section with interleaves based on our fieldnotes.

3 Full explication of the Progressive Verification Method appears in Janet Mancini Billson, "The Progressive Verification Method: Toward a Feminist Methodology for Studying Women Cross-Culturally," *Women's Studies International Forum,* 14, 3 (1991): 201-215; and the appendix of Billson's *Keepers of the Culture: The Power of Tradition in Women's Lives* (Lexington Books, 1995/Ottawa: Penumbra Press, 1999/Rowman & Littlefield, 2006). *Keepers* also includes a chapter on Inuit women, "Daughters of Sedna," short segments of which have been adapted for this book.

4 Carolyn Fluehr-Lobban, ed., *Ethics and the Profession of Anthropology: Dialogue for a New Era* (Philadelphia: University of Pennsylvania Press, 1990).

5 Maria Mies, "Towards A Methodology for Feminist Research," in *Theories of Women's Studies* (London: Routledge and Kegan Paul, 1983), p. 123.

6 Liz Stanley and Sue Wise, "'Back into the Personal' or: Our Attempt to Construct 'Feminist Research,'" in *Theories of Women's Studies*, p. 181.

7 Janet Mancini Billson, "'Challenging Times': Complexities of Feminism and the Women's Movement." Review Essay of *Challenging Times: The Women's Movement in Canada and the United States,* edited by Constance Backhouse and David Flaherty. [Montreal: McGill-Queen's University Press, 1992] in *Canadian Review of American Studies* [special issue, "Reinterpreting the American Experience: Women, Gender, and American Studies," Part II] (1992): 317-325.

8 See Marcia Westkott, "Feminist Criticism of the Social Sciences, *Harvard Educational Review* 49, 4 (November 1979): 422-430; and Du Bois, "Passionate Scholarship."

9 For a discussion of conducting focus groups in cross-cultural and international settings, see Janet Mancini Billson, *The Power of Focus Groups for Social and Policy Research: A Training Manual,* 4th edition (Barrington, RI: Skywood Press, 2005).

10 Alfred Schutz, "On Multiple Realities," in *Collected Papers I* (The Hague: Martinus Nijhoff, 1962).

11 Margrit Eichler, "Sociology of Feminist Research in Canada," *Signs*, 3, 2 (1977), p. 410.

12 Dorothy Smith, "Institutional Ethnography: A Feminist Method," *Resources for Feminist Research*, 6-13 (May, 1986), p. 12.

13 Curt Taylor Griffiths, Evelyn Zellerer, Darryl S. Wood, and Gregory Saville, *Crime, Law, and Justice among Inuit in the Baffin Region, N.W.T., Canada* (Burnaby, BC: Criminology Research Centre, Simon Fraser University, 1995), p. 10.
14 Eichler, "Sociology of Feminist Research in Canada," p. 419.
15 Westkott, "Feminist Criticism of the Social Sciences," p. 426.
16 Dorothy Smith, "Women's Perspective as A Radical Critique of Sociology," *Sociological Inquiry* (44, 1974): 7-13.
17 Linda Archibald and Mary Crnkovich, "Intimate Outsiders: Feminist Research in a Cross-Cultural Environment," in *Changing Methods: Feminists Transforming Practice*, edited by Sandra Burt and Lorraine Code (Peterborough, ON: Broadview Press, 1995).
18 Robin McGrath, "Circumventing the Taboos: Inuit Women's Autobiographies," in *Undisciplined Women: Tradition and Culture in Canada*, edited by Pauline Greenhill and Diane Tye (Montreal: McGill-Queen's University Press, 1997), p. 224.
19 Smith, "Institutional Ethnography: A Feminist Method," p. 6.
20 Reinharz, "Experiential Analysis," in *Theories of Women's Studies*, edited by Gloria Bowles and Renate Duelli Klein. London: Routledge and Kegan Paul, 1983, p. 175.
21 Reinharz, "Experiential Analysis," p. 179.
22 Reimer, "Female Consciousness," p. 97.
23 Mies, "Towards A Methodology for Feminist Research," pp. 134-35. Qualitative research relies on three basic ways of knowing: Archival (People's artifacts); Narrative (people's stories); Observational (people's behaviors), according to Kathleen Bennett deMarrais, ed., in *Inside Stories: Qualitative Research Reflections* (Mahwah, NJ: Lawrence Erlbaum Associates, 1998), p. xi. The three approaches often overlap.
24 Nicole Claude Mathieu, "'Woman' in Ethnology: The Other of the Other, and the Other of the Self," *Feminist Issues*, 8, 1 (1988): 3-14.
25 Dorothy Smith, "The Everyday World as Problematic: A Feminist Methodology," in Dorothy Smith, *The Everyday World as Problematic* (Boston: Northeastern University Press, 1987), p. 142.
26 Marcia Millman and Rosabeth Moss Kanter, eds., *Another Voice: Feminist Perspectives on Social Life and Social Science* (New York: Anchor Books, 1975), p. xiii.
27 Westkott, "Feminist Criticism of the Social Sciences," p. 423.
28 Du Bois, "Passionate Scholarship," p. 107.
29 J. Matthiasson, *Living on the Land: Change among the Inuit of Baffin Island* (Peterborough, ONT: Broadview Press, 1992), p. 74. Barbara Bodenhorn also makes this point in "'I Am Not a Great Hunter, My Wife Is': Inupiat and Anthropological Models of Gender," *Études/Inuit/Studies* 14, 1-2 (1990): 66.
30 Renate Duelli Klein, "How to Do What We Want to Do: Thoughts about Feminist Methodology," in *Theories of Women's Studies*, p. 89.
31 Shulamit Reinharz, "Experiential Analysis," p. 175.

ACKNOWLEDGMENTS

In the pages that follow, we present the voices of Inuit women (and some men) as the "experts" on the topic of the changing roles and status of women in Pangnirtung, Baffin Island. When we began this study in 1988, they lived in Canada's Northwest Territories (N.W.T.). As this book goes to press, the Inuit live in a new Canadian territory, Nunavut (see Chapter 19). Our efforts to describe and understand the transformation of Inuit life during the past century have been made possible by many organizations and individuals, and we want to express our appreciation to all of them here.

As a research site, Pangnirtung is unique in having had early, prolonged, and intense contact with Anglo-Europeans, compared to other Eastern Arctic communities. As Chapter 1 details, Cumberland Sound and the region around what later came to be known as Pangnirtung was visited by explorers seeking the Northwest Passage; anthropologists; Scottish and American whalers; and many other white people before the 20th century. In this century, archeologists, anthropologists, psychologists, ethnographers, and other scientists have continued to explore the area. This contact may have made the community more self-reflective (for example, several interviewees referred to the studies of Knud Rasmussen and Jean Briggs), but also more suspicious toward the conclusions that outsiders draw about their lives. Certainly, as the Inuit we interviewed clearly expressed, some of the contact with white southern or European culture has had a negative impact on the Inuit. On the other hand, the legacy of cooperative, mutually productive relationships established during the whaling period also laid the groundwork for this type of research. For example, as outlined in the *Preface*, the Inuit of Pangnirtung facilitated data gathering and tackled the arduous process of reviewing draft manuscripts very seriously, indeed. We say thank you—*kujannamik*—to them for making this book stronger, and apologize for any remaining errors or misinterpretations.

Pangnirtung Hamlet Council granted permission to hold group discussions with women and men, and the Scientific Institute of the N.W.T. in Yellowknife licensed the entire project (the equivalent Nunavut body, the Nunavut Research Institute, now would license similar research). Former Pangnirtung Mayor Johnny Mike and Senior Administrative Officer, the late Allan Angmarlik, graciously brought our proposal to the Hamlet Council during the spring of 1988, arranged for our initial transportation and housing, and immediately put us in touch with women from the *kitaq* (women's group). Allan Angmarlik died in the crash of a light aircraft en route to Iqaluit in 2000, before *Their Powerful Spirit* was completed. Sadly, he never saw the final manuscript of a project he had so generously supported. We wish to express our sincerest thanks to them and to all the people of "Pang" for allowing us to enter their world in 1988 and subsequent field visits.

We also extend our appreciation to Annie Shoapik Bowkett, Sheila Qappik Oolayou, Peeona Shukulaq, and Leesee Karpik for their sensitivity in interpreting interviews with elders and others who felt more comfortable speaking Inuktitut. Without their talents and the help of Rosie and Pauloosie Veevee, Peterosie and Leah Qappik, Peepeelee Qappik, and the Reverend Loie Mike, we could never have made our way through the complexities of Inuit life. For shelter, heart-stopping seal hunting trips, weekends camping in exquisite solitude "out on the land," and introductions to dozens of Inuit women and men, we are deeply grateful to them.

Through the generosity of Mary Crnkovich, formerly of the Canadian Arctic Resources Committee and editor of *Gossip: A Spoken History of the North*, we have also been able to integrate information from interviews conducted with Inuit women during 1988-89 by Angela Bernal in the Baffin Island communities of Cape Dorset, Pond Inlet, Spence Bay, and Broughton Island. The perspectives voiced in these interviews were similar to those found among Pangnirtung women and serve to broaden the scope of this study. The interviews were transcribed by Mancini and preliminarily edited by Billson for *Gossip*. Two articles by Billson also appeared in *Gossip*, and have been excerpted or adapted in part for this book: "Changing Role of Inuit Women and Their Families: New Choices for a New Era" and "Violence toward Inuit Women and Children," in *Gossip: A Spoken History of Women in the North*, edited by Mary Crnkovich, Ottawa: Canadian Arctic Resources Committee, 1990.

Inuit women who agreed to be listed here as consultants, and whom we wish to recognize as the true experts on Inuit lives in Pangnirtung, are: Apea Akpalialuk, Meleah Akpalialuk, Anna Akulukjuk, the late Malaya Akulujuk, Margaret Akulujuk, Becky Kilabuk Akulukjuk, Theresa Alikatuktuk, Eena Alivaktuk, Jeannie Alivaktuk, Leetia Alivaktuk, Meeka Alivaktuk, Tina Angmarlik, Evie Anilniliak, Elizabeth Arnakaq, Mary Arnakaq, Meeka Arnakaq, Annie Shoapik Bowkett, the late Qatsuq Eevik, Anna Etuangat, Vera Evic, the late Martha Kakee, Jukeepa Kanayuk, Leesee Karpik, Annie Martha Keenainak, Raygelee Keenainak, Geela Keenainak, Diana Kilabuk, Reepa Kilabuk, Peah Kisa, Rita Kisa, Saila Kisa, Sheila Kunilusie, Eena Kullualik, Bertha Kunilusie, Geela Maniapik, Geetee Maniapik, Rebecca Mearns, Dianne Metuq, Lena Metuq, Loie Mike, Mona Mike, Leona Nakashuk, Sowdloo Nakashuk, Susie Nakashuk, Tina Nowdlak, Sally Nowdluk, Malaya Nowyuk, the late Annie Okalik, Aitainaq Oshutapik, the late Kudloo Pitsiulak, Annie

Pitsiulak, Leah Qappik, Peepeelee Qappik, Sheila Qappik Oolayou, Susa Qappik, Lizzie Ryan, Mary Shukulaq, Peeona Shukulaq, Geela Sowdluapik, Naiomi Veevee, and Rosie Veevee. Many others participated, but chose to remain anonymous.

Inuit men interviewed in Pangnirtung, who elaborated on men's traditional and contemporary roles and powers, include: Roposie Alivaktuk, Abraham Arnakaq, the Reverend Ben Arreak, Jolly Atagoyuk, Andrew Dialla, Tim Dialla, Jaco Ishuluktaq, Simeonie Keenainak, Daniel Kilabuk, Jonah Kilabuk, the late Billy Kunilusie and his son, Charlie, Manasie Maniapik, Iola Metuq, Lucas Nowdlak, Aisa Papatsie, Jooeelee Papatsie, Peterosie Qappik, Guyasie Veevee, Pauloosie Veevee, and William Veevee. *Qallunaat* (white) residents of Pangnirtung who gave first-hand views on policing, education, health, and business issues include: Mary Bender, the Reverend Roy Bowkett, Lynn Cameron, Nancy Edell, Glenn Hanna, Chamberlain Jones, Irene Jones, Ed McKenna, Corol McKillican, Rick McKillican, Joanne McKinnon, Geoff Ryan, Peter Walker, and others.

In order to protect their identities, we have intermingled the voices of those who participated in the research project and have altered their names, number of children, occupations, and ages. In terms of content and substance, however, we have allowed their voices to flow virtually unaltered throughout the book. The only exception to anonymity occurs in field notes at the beginning of each chapter where, if names are used, they are correct and used with permission.

Several Inuit women and men read and discussed a working draft during the summer of 1993. This review process, to which the authors were committed from the outset (see Billson 1990) was made possible through the efforts of Lori Colomeda, Department of Nursing, Salish-Kootenai College in Montana. Colomeda brought the next draft to three women initial and key contacts in Pangnirtung: Sheila Qappik, Loie Mike, and Geela Maniapik. The women discussed the book and clarified or added material where necessary. In 1994, the Reverend Ben Arreak and Allan Angmarlik took the time to read the manuscript carefully and to update it as needed. Billson took the penultimate draft back to Pangnirtung, accompanied by a sociologist-colleague and friend who shares our love of the Arctic and its people, Margaret Brooks Terry of Baldwin-Wallace College. She lent a third set of eyes and ears to our perceptions, and diligently took invaluable fieldnotes on new developments. Several group and individual interviews updated original data and explored Inuit expectations regarding the new territory, Nunavut, which was launched in 1999.

Billson returned in the winter of 1997 to conduct focus groups with women students at the Pangnirtung branch of Nunavut Arctic College and women of the *kitaq* to gather their reactions to the manuscript and to add new data on the key issues facing Inuit women in Pangnirtung. During that visit, Mary Bender, Annie Shoapik Bowkett, and others completed invaluable readings of chapters in which they had special expertise. Final interviews took place in early April 1999, during the celebrations of the new territory, Nunavut. The manuscript was updated in Pangnirtung during August 2000 and 2001, after gathering initial reactions to the realities of Nunavut's first year.

Judith Varney Burch, a specialist in Inuit art whose own travels have taken her to most Nunavut communities, read the final manuscript. Her dedication to the project was critical to producing a viable manuscript and their feedback has been integrated throughout. We are also grateful to Rowman & Littlefield's external readers for their incisive and very helpful comments. The book has been given wings by a supportive editorial staff at Rowman & Littlefield, especially our editor, Jessica Gribble. We appreciate her faith in the book.

One of the joys in life for a writer is to belong to a writer's group. Special thanks go to Marie Schwartz and other members of the Women's Research Group at the University of Rhode Island, who gave sensitive readings to parts of this book.

The following organizations paved the way for this research with generous support: The Canadian Embassy, Washington, DC (Faculty Research Grants); Rhode Island College (Faculty Research Grants and a Summer Research Stipend); and, for housing, the Rev. David Sissmore (1988) and the Rev. Roy Bowkett (1996, 1997, 1999, 2000), Principals, Arthur Turner Training School, Pangnirtung. Without their assistance, we could not have conducted this study. In Ottawa, aunt and uncle, Dorothy and Gordon Johnston, and many friends (Victor Konrad and Aili Curtis, Katherine and Dick Seaborn, and Richard Martin and Daniele Drolet) provided waystations to and from the Arctic. Chris and Lydia (Hayes) Curtis of Kelston, England, shared their home as a peaceful haven for writing the penultimate draft—a gift of immeasurable value.

Kathleen Ramey and the (the late) Clifford Ramey of London, Ontario (parents and grandparents) hosted our many visits to the University of Western Ontario library—we are grateful for their encouragement and help over the years. The love of reading, writing, and learning started back in the 1940s in their home in Hagersville Army Camp, Ontario, and continues to be nourished as our explorations of the world continue.

We are grateful for having had the opportunity to work together as mother and daughter, first by sharing weeks of living with and interviewing the Pangnirtung women and men, and later as we waded through the data analysis, writing, and revising process. It is a special moment, indeed, when a strong familial bond between two women becomes a strong intellectual bond as well.

Last, but certainly not least, we both wish to express our gratitude to Norman T. London, husband and stepfather respectively, who joined us for a four-day hike into Aiyuittuq National Park, just north of the hamlet, and lent his support throughout the project. In so many ways, he has walked with us every step of this extraordinary journey to the edge of the Arctic Circle.

Janet Mancini Billson   Kyra Mancini

I

INTRODUCTION

It's the same all over the world, that women have problems with their culture. I don't think it's just the Inuit or the white people. It's the whole world.

—Eena

Photo 1.1 Pangnirtung Fiord, leading to Pangnirtung Pass.

1

1

"The People"

When I think about things—so many changes! My four children haven't had a glimpse of what I saw in my life, because everything changed so fast. Sometimes I wonder, how did I cope with it?

—Meeka

Lessons from Knud Rasmussen

Photo 1.2 Rainbow, Pangnirtung.

3

We come across an Inuk working on his boat, scraping away layer upon layer of crackled old paint with deliberate patience. At first, he seems reluctant to talk, but then he mentions that Knud Rasmussen wrote a good book on the Inuit.[1] After sizing us up, he begins to talk about drugs and family violence, alcohol and suicide, slowly revealing layer upon layer of information. Still, we feel that he is holding back.

The next day, as we happen to walk by his house, he beckons us to visit. He has described our conversation to his wife. She wants to meet us, he murmurs, but after greeting us with an air of vague recognition, she refuses to discuss even minor matters, more out of shyness than lack of interest. Later, in a group of women, she will speak openly.

We all sit quietly watching the couple's three young sons careen around the living room on various toy vehicles. One rides a small bike with training wheels that squeak so much even his older brother protests, "That's driving me nuts!" As is typical of Inuit culture (*illiqusiq* or "ways and habits"),[2] the parents do not ask the child to stop so we can converse. The man says that Inuit are perfectly comfortable sitting for hours without making small talk, punctuating the silence with an occasional grunt, joke, or grin.[3] He adds that we, on the other hand, come from a culture that views silence as "dead space"—a concept that makes us uneasy and overly talkative or inquisitive.

Finally, he crosses the room to the television set. There, laid as casually as a comic book, is the Knud Rasmussen volume published in 1908. He is extremely proud of it, and says that someone told him he should wear gloves when he reads it. This prize possession symbolizes the ability to bridge the chasm between Inuit and *Qallunaat* (white people, literally, people with "bushy eyebrows").[4] "The Inuit trusted *him*," the man says pointedly. "He told the truth...what he wrote rings true." We gingerly leaf through a few pages that verge on crumbling. We take his carefully selected words to mean that it would be difficult for us to learn about Inuit culture but not impossible. This well-read man speaks about trusting writers—or not—and the fact that virtually all social scientists, government agents, and journalists publish in English, not in the Inuit language, Inuktitut ("the Inuit way").[5]

We share his concerns and describe our commitment to ask people in the community to read our final draft. He volunteers to be a reader, and opens up even more after we mention that many elders have spent days talking with us. He looks at the old book again and says softly, "We Inuit hold our thoughts inside. I don't know why. Then you just get a part of our life. The rest we hold back." His words echo in our ears as we sit again in silence. We realize that he has already accomplished his goal in inviting us into their home. It was to share his warning and to give us a model—the old Danish explorer who ventured among the Netsilik and Igloolik Inuit almost 100 years ago and stayed close in his writings to the people's words. As we walk back through the settlement, we marvel at both the subtlety and the directness of this lesson. Like the man's work on his boat, we have much patient scraping and chipping ahead of us.[6]

ℭ

This story is a poignant one. It is a story of people caught in the vise-grip of a rapid and dramatic cultural metamorphosis that is complex in its causes and far-reaching in its consequences. Inuit—"the people"—of Baffin Island live in the Arctic and sub-Arctic regions of Canada.[7] They experienced spectacular and disconcerting changes during the twentieth century, a period of major transition for aboriginal peoples in North America and throughout the world. In one brief generation, they were resettled from a hunting and gathering economy based on sharing, reciprocity, and cooperation to a post-industrial society based on wages, accumulation of resources, welfare, and competitive norms.[8] In the words of Malachi Arreak, a negotiator for the Inuit land claims, "We've gone from basically the Stone Age to the Space Age in just three generations, which is why some people are having trouble now."[9] This book will trace the Inuit from what we call the Late Traditional Period through the Resettlement and Transitional Periods, and into the Early Nunavut Period.

From the Late Traditional Period to Resettlement

The Inuit are riding the waves of cultural transformation out of an ancient past into a modern present that often brings anguish along with hope. Less than 50 years ago, the Inuit (who were then known as Eskimos) pursued a nomadic life, roaming in search of subsistence at the top of the North American continent in a post-contact but still traditional era. Today, the Inuit own an airline that ferries tourists up from the "south" and a television network that broadcasts images of a lifestyle that only those over 40 have experienced first-hand.

Many factors triggered this metamorphosis, but resettlement during the mid-twentieth century into tiny hamlets—after thousands of years of wandering on the land—embodied the most powerful elements of change. During the Resettlement Period (approximately 1950 to 1970), the Canadian government brought people from more than 700 tiny camps into approximately forty communities, a phenomenon that approximated urbanization because it disturbed the customary interpenetration of economic and social relations. Traditional lifestyles and values still shape contemporary gender roles and social relations to some extent, but the amalgamation of old and new also caused confusion.

The term "resettlement" implies managed or coerced relocation of Native peoples from their traditional lands and camps into newly created population centers. Knowledge of the old life pulled the Inuit toward the land; the promise of a better life pulled them toward the settlements. The dilemma tore at the very heart of Inuit families. While some Inuit came into the settlements voluntarily on the wave of government-induced momentum and trading incentives, many believe that the process was *more* the effect of social policy than of individual choice. Many observers have agreed:

> [Resettlement] symbolizes how...the Canadian state controlled Inuit life in fundamental ways. Many Inuit did not settle in these communities willingly; they were coerced by the government to move into central locations so as to facilitate the delivery of public services such as health and education and also so that they could be assimilated into southern Canadian ways."[10]

The resettlement process was a wrenching one, albeit the government undertook it for ostensibly good reasons. Illness, death, and imminent starvation led to relocation; relocation often resulted in dislocation. Families were splintered when children were sent away to residential schools or tuberculosis victims were kept in southern Canada for medical treatment. Extended periods of hospitalization had the same devastating effect as residential schooling on family life and individual identity.[11]

In the Late Traditional Period, the Inuit lived in a world that seldom touched the formal social, political, or economic institutions of southern Canada. During the Resettlement Period, they existed on the economic, geographic, and political fringe of Canadian society. Culturally, they forged a creative amalgam of "traditional" Inuit and "modern" southern lifestyles that has inspired many observers to comment on their flexibility and adaptability—as well as their astonishing tenacity.[12] Socially, the Inuit held a classically marginal position, straddling two cultures but belonging fully to neither.[13] That was about to change.

From the Transitional Period to Nunavut

Aboriginal people make up about 3.7 percent of the Canadian population. Among aboriginals only about 5 percent identify themselves as Inuit of "single" or "mixed" origin.[14] Most of Canada's Inuit lived in the former Northwest Territories (NWT), which stretched from Baffin Island on the east coast to the Yukon Territory in the west. Even within that context, the Inuit constituted a clear minority—only about 10 percent of the NWT population.[15] With a small population and the impacts of resettlement, the Inuit were faltering.

The Transitional Period began when Inuit children *born* in the settlements grew up going to school, speaking English, and envisioning a time when they might have a more secure and less marginal existence. It ended on April 1, 1999, with the official creation of a new territory, *Nunavut*—"our land"—out of the old NWT. Now the Inuit dominate an enormous chunk of the Canadian landmass that stretches far above the tree line from the Saskatchewan-Manitoba border almost to the North Pole (Map 1.1). Of the 27,000 residents of Nunavut in

1999, about 80 percent or almost 22,000 were *Nunavummiut* –Inuit residents of Nunavut. Going from a minority to a majority of the voting population within the territory offers the promise of steering the ship of Inuit destiny from the helm rather than the stern.

   Nunavut includes all of Canada north of 60° N and east of the tree line, and the islands in Hudson Bay, James Bay, and Ungava Bay that do not belong to Manitoba, Ontario, or Québec (see Chapter 18 for an in-depth discussion of the new territory and the land settlement that created it).[16] This unique area of over 770,000 square miles contains more wildlife than people, and its people are young compared to other cultural groups in Canada: more than half of all Inuit in Nunavut are under 25 years of age because of a relatively high birth rate.[17] Peter Jull graphically described the creation of Nunavut:

> A hunter-gatherer people with a stubborn sustainable development philosophy
> and no visible modern industrial economy are taking over one-fifth of the world's
> second largest nation-state. Or, a vast area without trees, covered with snow and
> ice for most of the year, is being transformed into a full modern society with
> computers and parking tickets under the control of a people known to the world
> largely through cartoons of fur parkas, domed snowhouses, and polar bears.[18]

Map 1.1 Nunavut in Canada

Source: Natural Resources Canada (http://atlas.gc.ca, 2002)

We trace gender relations from "the time before," when Inuit lived "out on the land," to the creation of Nunavut, with its unique challenges. Although marginality and the residual impacts of rapid social change on a fragile but persistent culture remain, the Inuit are working to make the twenty-first century their own.

A Case Study of Pangnirtung
"The gathering place of the bull caribou"

A British clerk referred to the southeastern part of Baffin Island as "this distant and unsurveyed country," cut off as it was from Canada's mainland by the deep waters and treacherous icebergs of Cumberland Sound. For all but three brief months a year, the Baffin coastline is jammed with ice, but nineteenth century whalers from Scotland and New England managed to slip in during the summer months, winter over, and sail home the following summer. This was the case for the *Lady Franklin,* a whaling ship captained by William Penny that arrived in 1857 and left in 1858. Margaret Penny, a Scottish "petticoat whaler" who accompanied her husband, was the first white woman to winter over in the frigid whaling grounds.[19] During her sojourn, Margaret Penny had time to socialize with the "kind-hearted" Inuit women. She kept a journal of her contacts with the Baffin Inuit that year, recording observations of Inuit life and absorbing the beauty of the land and seascapes.[20] In spite of the initial language barrier, Penny wrote that the Inuit "are really a most interesting people, particularly the females." The women presented her with small skins, made her tea, and took her for long walks across the tundra to teach her about flowers, berries, and birds. In turn, virtually every night on shipboard, the captain's wife made tea for numerous Inuit guests who visited her ice-bound home.

This part of the Canadian North has since been well surveyed, but it remains distant and inaccessible except by ship or airplane. Over the years, we have flown via jet from Ottawa into Iqaluit on Frobisher Bay. From there we continued almost due north on the "workhorse of the Arctic," an old Twin Otter plane that dropped us onto a gravel runway in Pangnirtung. This small hamlet perches alongside magnificent Pangnirtung Fiord, which cuts north toward the Arctic Circle on the northeastern side of Cumberland Sound (Map 1.2). Mountains reaching almost 2,200 meters (7,150 feet) high stand guard on either side of the fiord. No highways connect Pangnirtung to the rest of the world; the only way in and out by land is to take a sled or skidoo across country from other Baffin Island communities that lie hundreds of miles away.

One of four Baffin communities that exceed 1,000 souls,[21] Pangnirtung, pronounced "Pangniqtuuq" in Inuktitut, reflects the massive changes experienced by the other twelve Baffin communities. To the translation of Pangnirtung, which means "the usual gathering place of the bull caribou," Inuit add "but they don't come here anymore," as a way of underscoring the changes the region has seen since Penny's time. The emergence of a tiny settlement here in the 1920s drove out caribou and other game herds. The early establishment of a hospital in Pangnirtung, and the early presence of white whalers, Anglican missionaries, and traders make this an ideal community for a case study of social change.

Map 1.2 Nunavut

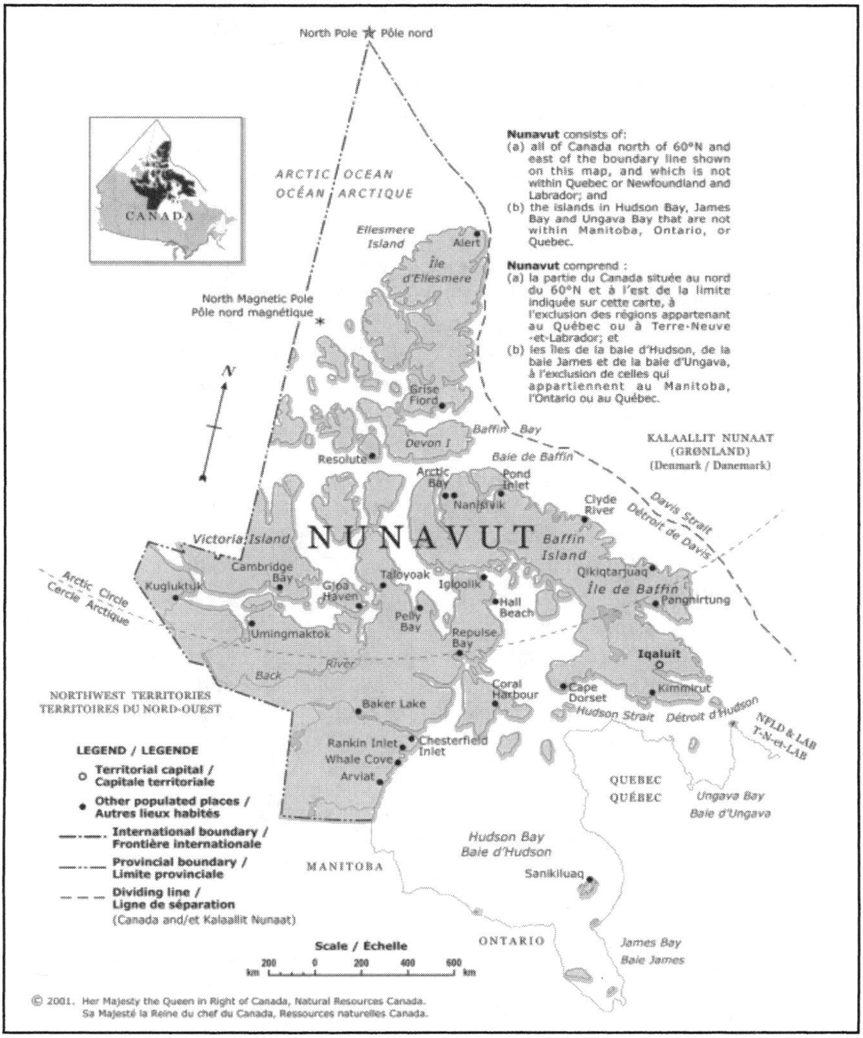

Source: www.atlas.gc.ca/site/english/maps/reference/provincesterritories/nunavut

Our purpose was to document the impact of these changes, especially on gender roles and the balance of power in female/male relationships. For more than a decade, we conducted interviews, read oral histories and studies by other researchers, visited cultural centers, attended community events, lived with Inuit families, and observed daily life in the "land of the midnight sun."[22] We explored how life for Inuit women has altered since the mid-1800s, and in keeping with Inuit tradition, we conducted most interviews in small groups over tea. Like Margaret Penny, we conversed with women during long walks along the Duval River, which leaps with falls and rapids through rocky gorges down from Mt. Duval, just behind the village. Some women were interviewed individually, as schedules and other considerations prevailed. Families took us out on the land with them for days at a time to the old camps they called home until the 1950s or 1960s. These boat trips always involved seal hunting along the way and fishing for Arctic char at midnight where icy, crystal rivers meet treacherous but spectacular fiords.

Females from thirteen to 100 years old reminisced about the past, spoke of the present, and tried to puzzle out the future. Informally, we learned from young girls, who interpreted for their parents and grandparents, and who seemed to relish the task of showing us how to catch lemmings among the rocks or how to extract an egg gingerly from a bird's nest. They taught us several words of Inuktitut and how to count in their language.

Although we focus on the relations between women and men, and the changing roles of women, they are inextricably intertwined with the broader framework of Inuit life. In order to learn more about traditional and contemporary male roles, and to recognize diversity of perspectives while focusing on women, we also held several formal and informal interviews with Inuit men. As Hamilton and Barrett argue, "Since gender relations also entangle men in diverse ways, amongst themselves and with women, men also can contribute to the debate."[23] We also interviewed Qallunaat female and male social service workers, police officers, medical staff, teachers, church leaders, and hamlet officials. Women and men, Inuit and Qallunaat alike spoke of hope and loss, optimism and despair, joy and confusion.

The Inuit engaged with us in a dialogue of interpretation and analysis. Together we tried to answer several broad questions: What are the most important sources and consequences of social change in their community? What are their strengths as aboriginal women? What special issues mark the relationships between women and men? How do the Inuit go beyond adapting to or coping with often trying circumstances? How are they shaping an age-old culture that is at once fading—and evolving toward southern lifestyles—and regenerating? What difference will the creation of Nunavut make for their future? Their answers to these and many other questions fill the pages of this book.

Since we used a case study approach to documenting social change, the voices cannot represent all Inuit, nor all Inuit of Baffin Island, nor all Qikirtarmiut or Umanaqjuarmiut[24] (Cumberland Sound Inuit), nor even all Pangnirtarmiut (women and men of Pangnirtung). Inuit customs, beliefs, and lifestyles vary, sometimes dramatically, from group to group.[25] Nevertheless, these voices help us understand the common threads of Inuit life throughout Nunavut.[26]

The Collision of Cultures
"That really hurts the old way of life"

The Inuit lived in virtual isolation for thousands of years in a succession of related cultures: Pre-Dorset (Tunit), Dorset, Thule, and Central or Modern Eskimo. Long ago, they ventured from Asia across a frozen land bridge over the Bering Sea into Alaska. As they moved eastward across the top of what is now Canada, the Thule settled above the tree line; this prehistoric, maritime group relied heavily on whale hunting.[27] Contact with the "people of the forests," the Dene Indians, was relatively rare, especially for the people of Baffin Island.[28] The Thule developed into today's Central Eskimo (including Baffin Inuit).

The history of Qallunaat penetration into the Eastern Arctic and sub-Arctic is a long and complicated one. The Vikings may have made contact with the people living on the eastern shores of "Baffin Land," closest to Greenland, between 1000 AD and the 1400s, but the first recorded "discovery" occurred in 1576 when Martin Frobisher explored Baffin Island while searching for the elusive Northwest Passage.[29] Frobisher's English compatriot, John Davis, probed Cumberland Sound in 1585 and 1587.[30] In 1616, William Baffin explored the eastern side of the Island, but the isolated waters of Cumberland Sound were not disturbed again until Scotsman William Penny sailed into them in 1840. In the same decade, Sir John Franklin was lost while exploring the region.[31] Other expeditions by Baffin, Robert Bylot, and Henry Hudson traced new bays and islands on seventeenth and eighteenth century maps.[32] While contact occurred during these earlier traditional eras, the consequences did not alter the core of Inuit culture or gender relations.

The Late Traditional Period

Then came Europeans and Euro-Canadians—*Qallunaat*—in search of adventure, whales, wealth, or souls. The collision of cultures that began with explorers and continues through the invisible waves of television today has created both havoc and hope. Problems started when white people brought guns, new forms of disease, and alcohol. Drugs followed, as did attempts by non-Native animal activists to redefine the meaning of hunting among Native groups.[33] While life expectancy was relatively short before contact with Qallunaat, and Inuit died from hunting accidents and starvation, the people were free of major contagious disease. In fact, according to Diamond Jenness, infectious disease was "virtually unknown between Coronation Gulf and the magnetic pole" until contact with white traders, missionaries, Royal Canadian

Mounted Police (RCMP), whalers, and anthropologists.[34] These visitors from southern Canada, the United States, or Europe brought waves of tuberculosis, influenza, measles, venereal disease, and other debilitating or fatal sicknesses against which the Inuit had no natural immunity.

The north offered riches. For instance, the impressive bowhead whale choked the Arctic waters, growing to over 60 feet long. In the early 1800s, American whalers scrambled along Baffin's east coast (Davis Strait) for whale oil and baleen, the latter used in making women's corsetry. In a given winter, thirty or more whaling ships would work in the area. The Inuit negotiated with the whalers to establish more "permanent and predictable" relations in order to counterbalance resource shortages brought on by an unstable climate and poor caribou harvests. Especially in the 1830s and 1840s, whalers who returned to the east Baffin stations in summer found the communities decimated by a long winter of starvation. The whaling ships offered the promise of relief and opportunity as the Inuit engaged in trading whale baleen and seal meat for metal, needles, bread, and molasses: "Throughout the 1830s, they tried to bring the ships into Cumberland Sound by showing the captains what a rich whaling ground it was.[35]

By 1860, Captain Penny and others had established more whaling stations along Cumberland Sound at Kekerten (Kikitaet), Blacklead Island, and Cape Haven.[36] These whalers from warmer climates enlisted the help of the Inuit, who not only hunted with harpoons along the floe edge and wrestled the great carcasses into manageable pieces but also helped ensure the whalers' survival through long, trying winters. Inuit women worked at the whaling stations, processing whale meat, rendering tons of blubber into oil, cooking and cleaning for both Inuit and Qallunaat crews, and tending to the makeshift camps: "Women also joined the whaling workforce, as professional seamstresses, laundresses, provisioners, and tanners." [37] Most encounters between Qallunaat and the Inuit were cordial but not all ended happily. Some whaling captains introduced alcohol, "cheated local people when they could, and made no attempt to restrain their crews from conduct that was considered immoral by most people in both European and Inuit societies. Liaisons with Inuit women were commonplace."[38]

While whaling provided economic opportunity for the Inuit, Baffin Inuit fell prey to diseases brought by whites: "In spite of the almost continuous arrivals of people from other parts of Baffin Island looking for work with the fleet, the population dropped from an estimated 1000 souls in 1840 to about 350 in 1857."[39] And, by 1870, when Baffin Island became part of the young Dominion of Canada,[40] the bowhead whale had been hunted almost to extinction. By the early 1880s, whaling had declined, but limited commercial hunting of beluga whales persisted until the 1920s, making for almost a century of this type of contact with Americans and Europeans.

The second half of the nineteenth century brought a steady but small stream of distinguished scientists, including naturalist Ludwig Kumlien and anthropologist Franz Boas, who recorded Inuit life.[41] William Wakeham, A. P. Low, Bernhard Hantzsch, and others sponsored by the Canadian government tried to map the vast and difficult interior lands. An American Geographical Society search for evidence of Sir John Franklin's disastrous 1845 voyage into northern waters brought many Inuit into contact with whites during the 1870s. Assorted traders influenced Inuit economies by developing Arctic white fox trapping (previously unknown to the Inuit) and, later, a sealskin trade.[42]

In 1921, the Hudson's Bay Company built its first post in Pangnirtung, followed two years later by the first RCMP detachment.[43] By 1940, the Canadian government had brought the Arctic Archipelago under its authority and control. Along with the whalers, traders, and police came the missionaries. In tents and *igloos* (snow houses), missionaries taught "reading, then writing, simple progressive arithmetic, hygiene, morals and the Bible study."[44] The Reverend E. J. Peck, based as of 1894 at Blacklead Island whaling station, invented the Inuktitut syllabic writing system for a language that had been strictly oral up to that point.[45] The Anglican mission moved into Pangnirtung in 1926, and established St. Luke's Hospital there in 1929-30 under the leadership of Dr. Lesley Livingstone. In 1970, the mission created the Arthur Turner Training School (ATTS) to train Inuit men (and later, women) for ordained full-time positions in the Anglican ministry.[46] Along with education and health care, missionaries imported a powerful belief system that struck at the most delicate of human emotions: guilt, spiritual longing, and plausible explanations of life's tragedies. The Inuit sometimes felt hostile toward the missionaries, says an Inuk minister: "They said, 'your traditional beliefs [shamanism] are no longer valid. These are the beliefs you will now adopt.'" One report issued on the hospital at Pangnirtung said that the "Eskimo were pagan, and often made it very difficult for the Missionaries to treat the patients properly in their tents and snow huts."[47] The shock ran deep, but the Inuit greatly respected the teachings of the early missionaries.

Because of Pangnirtung's relatively large size compared to the other emerging Baffin settlements, and the hamlet's economic role in support of white activities, the impact of contact might have been amplified. This observation was made as early as 1936 by a government agent, who noted that a few Inuit had already settled around Pangnirtung. They were employed by the Hudson's Bay Company during whaling and as servants at the mission and hospital. Those at Blacklead Island devoted all their time to hunting, in contrast, and did not "gather in large numbers as they do here in Pangnirtung. They have not the feeling that they are living close to the whiteman."[48]

While being near the hospital also afforded this handful of Inuit better medical care, it also exposed them routinely to *Qallunat* ways. As an RCMP liaison observes, white people brought more than "booze and disease" with them:

The RCMP, Hudson's Bay Company, and the government itself have imposed their ways on the Inuit people and destroyed their culture. Before whites came, Inuit were living off the land. They were quite capable out there with their traditional ways. The Bay exploited them for the furs and everything else they had.

Then Canadian law was put on them. Whereas the Bay came into the North strictly for trade and business, the police came during the early 1920s to help the government secure Canadian sovereignty in the North. They were to serve as an arm of social control, "to enforce the laws and do every other government duty."

The RCMP played a large part in the process of bringing Inuit into the twentieth century and under the domination of white, paternalistic institutions, a role they had played as Canadian government liaison to Indians during the crucial treaty period. When the people lived out on the land, the "Mounties" flew to various camps to conduct medical and other emergency evacuations.

The Resettlement Period was prefigured by government actions in the early decades of the twentieth century. According to Eric Alden Smith, "In the early 1930s, several families were moved from Inujjuaq to Pangnirtung...under rather obscure circumstances."[49] As of 1948, the Inuit began to receive the Canadian family allowance or "baby bonus" of $6 to $8 per month per child: "This made up a considerable portion of Inuit monetary income at first."[50] When the hospital was built in 1925-26, the first wave of Inuit moved into Pangnirtung.

By the end of the 1930s, "most Canadian Inuit had been drawn into the capitalist mode of production. Their economy, now based on commercial hunting (with guns) and trapping—rather than being autarkic—was ruled, for a good part, by European and Canadian merchants established in Montreal, London, or Paris. Even if the Inuit still lived a nomadic life (except in Labrador), their dominant social relations were those of petty commodity production."[51] Although subsistence hunting and fishing continued, Inuit livelihoods were enmeshed in southern economic institutions by the end of the Late Traditional Period.

The Resettlement Period

The Inuit see themselves as aboriginal people, not Indians, but legally their status changed in 1939 when the Supreme Court of Canada ruled that the term "Indians" used in the 1867 British North America Act should include Inuit as well. This meant that the Inuit became an official federal responsibility, although little action occurred in this regard until after World War II and Inuit did not win the right to vote until 1962, during the height of the Resettlement Period. Government policy written in 1955 by Jean Lesage, then minister of northern affairs and national resources, reveals the underlying assimilationist attitudes:[52]

The objective of Government policy is relatively easy to define. It is to give the Eskimo the same rights, privileges, opportunities and responsibilities of all other Canadians: in short, to enable them to share fully in the national life of Canada. It is pointless to consider whether the Eskimo was happier before the white man came, for the white man has come and time cannot be reversed. The only realistic approach is to accept the fact that the Eskimo will be brought evermore under the influences of civilization to the south. The task, then, is to help him adjust his life and his thoughts to all that the encroachment of this new life must mean.[53]

Resettlement (carried out by a central government without much consultation with those affected) is not the same process as immigration (usually engaged in by individuals or families as a matter of personal choice), nor does it have the same consequences for cultural stability. The Inuit were to be modernized by a successive wave of southern institutions. Armitage characterized such assimilationist policies toward aboriginal peoples in Australia, Canada, and New Zealand as being indicative of racism and colonialism (in other words, imperialism).[54] The Inuit can be included among indigenous groups that Nuttall refers to as "ethnic minorities being sedentarised by the state and who are, in the process, losing traditional means of subsistence such as herding and trading" (in this case, hunting and gathering).[55]

The resettlement of Inuit into Pangnirtung typifies the dramatic upheavals that have shocked both Canadian Inuit and American Eskimos. Since World War II, "all Eskimo groups have been under mounting pressure to modernize" after centuries of sporadic contact with whites.[56] The collision of cultures that reverberated across the Eastern Arctic intensified after the Canadian government brought the Inuit from scattered camps into small hamlets during the late 1950s and early 1960s.[57] An Inuk elder explains that a camp might be 40 or 50 people: "A few families—they never go beyond 50. When we come into communities, it suddenly becomes 200 or 300 people. The culture and our way of living started to change then."

In the late 1950s, Northern Service staff and welfare officers conducted resource surveys for the Department of Northern Affairs, which decided "it was more convenient to group all Inuit in a few settled communities" than to try to administer services to a scattered population. As Dorais pointed out, "In fact, sedentarization had already begun ten years before. The schools, nursing stations, administrative headquarters, trading posts, and even missions had become the core of permanent villages, where the snow-house/tent type of habitation had rapidly been replaced by makeshift wood and cardboard shacks."[58] In spite of the core amenities and growing dependency on government transfer payments, fewer than 100 Inuit lived in Pangnirtung during the post-war period.

The pull of the land was strong. Table 1.1 shows that growth was very slow until the canine encephalitis epidemic of 1962, which severely hampered hunting with train dogs and resulted in government-initiated resettlement to Pangnirtung. Then, the hamlet grew dramatically to almost 600 people. Many of our consultants had lived in a camp called Nunatta (and still visit the old camps there during the summer months); they moved into Pangnirtung in 1965. In May of 1966, residents of camps at Abraham Bay, Toakjuak, Avatuktoo, and Nowyakbik arrived.[59]

Table 1.1 Population Shift from the Land to Pangnirtung

Year	Total # Inhabitants of Cumberland Sound Region	Population Of Pangnirtung
1840	1,500 (Franz Boas)[60]	--
1857	300 (Franz Boas)[61]	--
1910[62]	168	--
1925 (hospital)	350	54 (Inuit only)
1944	454[63]	45 (Inuit only)
1951	461[64]	75 (Inuit only)[65]
1956	N/A	94 (Inuit only)
1961	542-559[66]	98 (Inuit only)
1962 (dog epidemic)	N/A	600 (Inuit only)
1966	594-603[67]	340 (Inuit only)
1981	N/A	790 (840 total)
1996	N/A	(1,243 total)
1997	N/A	(1,400 total)
2000	N/A	(1,500 total)

Source: Except where otherwise footnoted, this table is based on McElroy, *Alternatives in Modernization*; Dorais, "The Canadian Inuit and Their Language," pp. 188-189; and Harper, reporting the 1996 Census of Canada data in "Pangnirtung," p. 345.

By late 1966, however, only 340 Inuit remained in the settlement, the rest having returned to the land because of lack of adequate housing and a burning desire to live the traditional life style. "Outpost camps" (a southern term that implies that "post" living should be the norm) have attracted a few families who determinedly stayed on the land during the Resettlement Period. A few more families returned to the land in the 1970s when the NWT territorial government established its Outpost Camp Programme (later subsumed under the Community Harvester Assistance Programme of the Department of Renewable Resources). The Inuit created some new camps and reactivated many traditional camps. Another way to visualize the shift from the land to the settlements is through looking at the percentage of Inuit living in each situation in 1966, comparing Pangnirtung to Clyde River, also on Baffin Island (figure 1.1).

According to Brian and Cherry Alexander, before 1975, only three Inuit camps remained on Baffin Island. The figure climbed to 29 by 1986 and to 34 by 1995.[68] By then, throughout the Inuvik (western), Kiktikmeot (central), and Baffin (eastern) Arctic regions, 54 permanent camps and about the same number of temporary sites dotted the more remote parts of the landscape, serving as home to about 1,200 Inuit.[69] As the government added housing and brought more children into the schools, the population steadily climbed to present levels.

Pangnirtung has more than quadrupled since the initial Resettlement Period, to over 1,500 in 2000—an unimaginably large community by the standards of a bygone era but now typical among Canadian Arctic hamlets.

**Figure 1.1 Population Shift from the Land
to Pangnirtung and Clyde River, 1966**

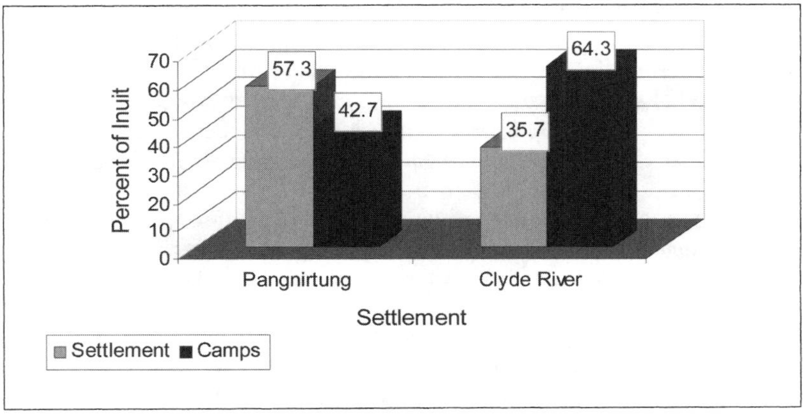

Source: Haller, et al, *Baffin Island—East Coast*, p. 154.

In the early days of resettlement, once again the Mounties acted as the primary link for key social services and benefits. The RCMP enforced federal law, investigated crimes, provided relief and medical aid, and brought people south for treatment or trial. They took chest X-rays with portable machines during the tuberculosis epidemic and they counted the census (hospital ships such as the *CGS Nascopie* and the *C.D. Howe* also x-rayed the Inuit through the mid-twentieth century). They "often stirred political controversy and even exercised considerable influence on the government's programs and policies" with their observations and reports.[70] Stern and Condon argue that both the RCMP and the missionaries were feared and respected: "The former had the ability to admonish and arrest, while the latter had the force of a powerful deity *and* government laws behind their admonitions."[71]

Resettlement spawned both confidence and uncertainty as Inuit created new identities and navigated unfamiliar challenges. It also advanced economic and political marginalization. As the population ballooned, welfare dependency and the generation gap expanded. Ottawa or Yellowknife (the capital of the former Northwest Territories) made key decisions, which created political dependency. Even with the late twentieth century decision to carve Nunavut out of the old Northwest Territories, the Inuit lack full control of their resources or political future (see Chapter 19). The challenge for the twenty-first century will be to redefine culture in a way that affords Inuit maximum control over their destiny within the context of a highly multicultural Canadian family.

Dagenais and Piché argue that the social construction of gender relations interacts with imperialism, including internal colonization, to shape the dominant ideologies of development.[72] In this sense, the economic, governmental, political, and legal institutions of Canada inevitably molded the future of women within the emerging context of Inuit life. With the decline of traditional Inuit culture since resettlement, clearly defined gender roles also faded. Contact with Qallunaat changed life for Inuit women, who watched their men adopt increasingly patriarchal attitudes toward women. Yet, life changed for Inuit men, who found their role as providers greatly impeded by life in the settlements. Now, Inuit men face chronic unemployment and diminished hunting opportunities; they must find new ways to feed their families. Many Inuit women resist marriage and worry about their expanding role as principal providers for their children. Unfortunately, as in other communities, rates of violence between intimate adults have skyrocketed in men's desperate attempt to rebalance roles.

The composite of memories and reflections in this book takes us back to the eras before resettlement. It also brings us forward to an examination of contemporary challenges in Inuit communities, and affords a glimpse of what the twenty-first century might bring for "the people." Throughout, the "powerful spirit" of Inuit women and men defines their story.

Notes

1 "Inuk" is the singular form of "Inuit." Knud Rasmussen, *People of the Polar North: A Record* (Philadelphia: Lippincott, 1908). See also his edited collection, *Eskimo Songs and Stories* (New York: Delacorte Press, 1973 [1908]); *Intellectual Culture of Hudson Bay Eskimos. Report of the Fifth Thule Expedition 1921-24* (Volume I: Observations on the Intellectual Culture of the Iglulik Eskimos, 1928, Volume II: Observations on the Intellectual Culture of the Caribou Eskimos, 1930, and Volume III: Iglulik and Caribou Eskimos, 1930), (Copenhagen: Nordisk Forlag); and *The Netsilik Eskimos: Cultural Life and Spiritual Culture. Report of the Fifth Thule Expedition 1921-24*, 8, 1-2:1-542 (Gyldendalske Boghandel, Nordisk Forlag, 1931). Also, Cornelius H. W. Rémie, "Flying Like a Butterfly, or Knud Rasmussen among the Netsilingmiut," *Études/Inuit/Studies* 12 (1988): 101-27.

2 Ann Meekitjuk Hanson distinguishes between *illiqusiq,* ways and habits of Inuit life, and *isomainaqiijutiit,* or culture that involves entertainment ("things to make us relax when chores have been completed"). "Inuit Culture: The Baffin Region," *The Nunavut Handbook* (Iqaluit, NWT: Nortext, 1998), p. 70.

3 Dorais described the related Quaqtamiut of Northern Québec as "sober in their speech. They do not talk when they have nothing to say, but when they do, they are not afraid to speak their minds." Louis-Jacques Dorais, *Quaqtaq: Modernity and Identity in an Inuit Community* (Toronto: University of Toronto Press, 1997), p. 90.

4 The word Qallunaat (sometimes spelled *Qallunat, qadlunat,* or *kabloonat*) refers to whites (plural form) and can mean "people with beautiful manufactured material." Odette Leroux, Marion E. Jackson, and Minnie Aodla Freeman, eds., *Inuit Women Artists: Voices from Cape Dorset* (Vancouver: Douglas & McIntyre/Canadian Museum of Civilization and University of Washington Press, 1994), p. 16.

5 Louis-Jacques Dorais, "The Canadian Inuit and Their Language," in *Arctic Languages: An Awakening*, edited by Dirmid R. F. Collis (Paris: UNESCO, 1990), p. 186.

6 Cornelius H. W. Rémie raises the question of whether the Rasmussen accounts were as accurate as many Inuit and scholars seem to assume. In the case of the Arviligjuarmiut culture of Pelly Bay, also in the Eastern Arctic, Rémie said that Rasmussen depicted a "traditional" culture that had already changed substantially and was marred by strife. He names exploration of the Arctic as one source of change that had already occurred by the time Rasmussen arrived: "Ermalik and Kukigak: Continuity and Discontinuity in Pelly Bay, Northwest Territories, Canada," in *Continuity and Discontinuity in Arctic Cultures*, edited by Cunera Buijs (Leiden: Universiteit Leiden, Centre of Non-Western Studies, 1993) and "Shifting Cultural Identities: Case Materials from Pelly Bay, NWT," in *Arctic Identities: Continuity and Change in Inuit and Saami Societies*, edited by Jarich G. Oosten and Cornelius H. W. Rémie.

7 Brody believes that *Inuit* best translates as "persons" rather than "people," but most scholars use the latter interpretation. Hugh Brody, *The Other Side of Eden: Hunters, Farmers, and the Shaping of the World* (New York: North Point Press, 2000), p. 303. We use the term "Arctic" throughout to refer to the Arctic and sub-Arctic climatic and ecological environment in which the Inuit live. Although the majority of Inuit live below the Arctic Circle, their existence is "arctic," as Kaj Birket-Smith described in *The Eskimos* (Caribou Inuit) during the 1930s: "The limit of Arctic climate is not a parallel of latitude, but may be defined approximately by a line drawn through those places where the mean temperature in the warmest month is 10 degrees C (50 degrees F). Almost everywhere...we find this Arctic climate with long, severe winters and short, cool summers. Tree growth is inhibited by the cold, and the eye encounters only endless moss and lichen-covered tundras, barren, rocky plains, or, at best, stern heather moors and low willow thickets." (London, New York: Methuen, 1971 [1959, 1936]).

8 This is documented in Janet Mancini Billson, "Social Change, Social Problems, and the Search for Identity: Canada's Northern Native Peoples in Transition," *American Review of Canadian Studies* 18, 3 (1988): 295-316. Obviously, permafrost and short summers precluded the horticultural or agricultural periods that many other societies have moved through before industrialization; many societies have not industrialized to any significant extent, nor should industrialization be assumed as a natural or optimal stage in human history. See also Gerhard Lenski and Jean Lenski, *Human Societies: An Introduction to Macrosociology*, 3rd ed. (New York: McGraw-Hill, 1978).

9 Quoted in Mary Williams Walsh, "Canada's Inuit Reclaiming Ancestral Land," *Los Angeles Times* (September 15, 1992), p. C4. The point is made also by Curt Taylor Griffiths, Evelyn Zellerer, Darryl S. Wood, and Gregory Saville in *Crime, Law, and Jus-*

tice among Inuit in the Baffin Region, NWT, Canada (Burnaby, BC: Criminology Research Centre, Simon Fraser University, 1995), p. 15: "It is often said that the Inuit went from the Stone Age to Space Age in 40 years. The cultural aftershocks...are still being felt...As one resource worker...stated, 'they stepped right out of igloos and right into rocket ships.'"

10 Hicks, "The Nunavut Land Claim and the Nunavut Government," p. 44. "The Canadian Inuit and Their Language," p. 210.

11 See, for example, David Omar Born, *Eskimo Education and the Trauma of Social Change* (Ottawa: Department of Indian and Northern Affairs, 1970); and Charles W. Hobart, "Some Consequences of Residential Schooling of Eskimos in the Canadian Arctic," *Arctic Anthropology* 6 (1970): 123-135.

12 George W. Wenzel warns of idealizing traditional Inuit life or assuming that Inuit accommodation to "modern" trappings (such as government-subsidized houses, motorized canoes, or rifles) means that non-material cultural values have shifted. This surfaces in relationship to the seal hunting controversy: "To Inuit, tradition and subsistence are their present reality, while to those opposed to sealing, they refer to an idealized Inuit way of life of five hundred years ago." *Animal Rights, Human Rights Ecology, Economy and Ideology in the Canadian Arctic* (Toronto: University of Toronto Press, 1991), pp. 57-59.

13 See Asen Balikci, "Ethnic Relations and the Marginal Man in Canada: A Comment," *Human Organization* (1960): 170-171, and Janet Mancini Billson, "No Owner of Soil: Redefining the Concept of Marginality," in *Marginality and Society: Issues in Class, Race, and Gender,* edited by Rutledge Dennis (Newbury Park, CA: Sage Publications, forthcoming). Compared to some other Inuit groups, the Baffin Inuit came into settlements relatively late. For example, according to Dorais, "By 1875, all Labrador Inuit were living in permanent sedentarized villages, each with a Moravian church, school and store." Some Inuit were in regular contact with the Royal Canadian Mounted Police as early as 1904. Dorais, "The Canadian Inuit and Their Language," p. 203.

14 For 1990s data, see Thomas Isaac, "Land Claims and Self-Government Developments in Canada's North," in *A Passion for Identity: An Introduction to Canadian Studies,* edited by David Taras and Beverly Rasporich (Toronto: ITP Nelson, 1997), p. 475. For 1980s data, see Mary Jane Norris, "The Demography of Aboriginal People in Canada," in *Ethnic Demography: Canadian Immigrant, Racial and Cultural Variations,* edited by Shiva S. Halli, Frank Trovato, and Leo Driedger (Ottawa: Carleton University Press, 1990), p. 35.

15 Canadian Embassy, "Nunavut Joins Canadian Federation on April 1," *Canada Quarterly* 7, 2 (April 1999): 1-2.

16 For a comprehensive discussion of Nunavut and the history of the agreement, see Jack Hicks, "The Nunavut Land Claim and the Nunavut Government: Political Structures of Self-Government in Canada's Eastern Arctic," in *Dependency, Autonomy, Sustainability in the Arctic,* edited by Hanne K. Petersen and Birger Poppel (Aldershot, ONT: Ashgate, 1999).

17 Canadian Embassy, "Nunavut Joins Canadian Federation on April 1," p. 1.

18 Peter Jull, "Nunavut Abroad," *Northern Perspectives* 21, 3 (1993): 15.

19 W. Gillies Ross, *This Distant and Unsurveyed Country: A Woman's Winter at Baffin Island, 1857-1858* (Montréal: McGill-Queen's University Press, 1997), p. xvi.

Captain Penny was requesting a land grant for a whaling station (which he eventually received).

20 Ross, *This Distant and Unsurveyed Country*, p. 29. Several American whaling wives accompanied their husbands on whaling trips, but Ross said that the practice never became popular among the British (pp. xxv-xxvi). See also Ross: "Commercial Whaling and Eskimos in the Eastern Canadian Arctic 1819-1920," pp. 242-266 in *Thule Eskimo Culture: An Anthropological Retrospective*, edited by A. P. McCartney, National Museum of Man Mercury Series, Archaeological Survey of Canada, Paper 88 (Ottawa: National Museum of Man, 1979); *Whaling and the Eskimos: Hudson Bay 1860-1915* (Ottawa: Publications in Ethnology 10, National Museum of Canada, 1975); and "Whaling, Inuit, and the Arctic Islands," pp. 33-50 in *A Century of Canada's Arctic Islands, 1880-1980*, edited by Morris Zaslow (Ottawa: The Royal Society of Canada, 1981).

21 The communities ranged in size from 130 to Iqaluit's 4,000 in 1997.

22 Other recent studies include Pauktuutit, *The Inuit Way: A Guide to Inuit Culture*, edited by David Boult (Ottawa: Inuit Women's Association, 1991). David Morrison *et al* have produced an illustrated book on recent Inuit history and lifestyles, based on the writings and collections of anthropologist/archaeologist Diamond Jenness: *Inuit: Glimpses of an Arctic Past* (Ottawa: Canadian Museum of Civilization, 1995).

23 Robert Hamilton and Michele Barrett, cited in Arlene Tigar McLaren, *Gender and Society: Creating a Canadian Women's Sociology* (Toronto: Copp Clark Pitman, 1988), p. 21.

24 Eight main Inuit groupings exist in Canada: the Labrador, Ungava, Baffin, Iglulik, Caribou, Netsilik, Copper, and Western Arctic (Inuvialuit) Inuit. The Inuvialuit descended from relatively recent immigrants from Alaska. They took the place of the Mackenzie Inuit, who were virtually extinguished by smallpox and influenza at the turn of the century. The Sadlermiut of northwestern Hudson Bay died out following contact with whites during the same period. Culturally, Canadian Inuit are related to the Inupiat of Alaska, the Katladlit of Greenland, and the Yuit of Siberia, among others. See *The Canadian Encyclopedia Plus*. Anthropologists such as Franz Boas designated the Caribou, Copper, Netsilik, Iglulik, and Baffin Island Inuit as "Central Eskimo," although the Baffin Inuit clearly live in the Eastern Arctic of Canada. (The Cumberland Sound Inuit, as Baffin Island Inuit, would also have been considered by Boas as Central Eskimo.) They are composed of two major groupings, the Qikirtarmiut, who lived on Kekerten Island (which includes two groups formerly known as the Kinguamiut and the Kingnaimiut—or what Boas called the Kingnaitmiut) and the Umanaqjuarmiut (formerly known as the Talirpingmiut). Boas said that the Kingnaitmiut had lived near Pangnirtung and on Miliaqdjuin, a nearby island; ironically, after their service on Kekerten Island during the whaling period, many were resettled to Pangnirtung. See Boas, *The Central Eskimo* (Lincoln: University of Nebraska Press, 1964 [originally published by the Bureau of American Ethnology, 6th Annual Report, Washington, DC, 1888]), p. 29. In the nineteenth century, many more groupings existed in the Cumberland Sound area. See Marc G. Stevenson, *Inuit, Whalers, and Cultural Persistence: Structure in Cumberland Sound and Central Inuit Social Organization* (Toronto: Oxford University Press, 1997), pp. xvii, 116-117. One informant also referred to the local Inuit in Pangnirtung as Kitimiut. Generically, based on their current residence in Pangnirtung, they can also be called Pangnirtarmuit.

25 David Damas, "The Diversity of Eskimo Societies," pp. 111-117 in *Man the Hunter*, edited by R. E. Lee and I. DeVore (New York: Aldine, 1979). Stevenson says that "Inuit in Pangnirtung still distinguish themselves today on ...whether they are, or are descended from, Qikirtarmiut or Umanaqjuarmiut. *Inuit, Whalers, and Cultural Persistence*, p. 117.

26 Evidence of parallel experiences in other Canadian Inuit communities, as they shifted to settlements, can be found in: Nelson H. Graburn, *Eskimos without Igloos: Social and Economic Development in Sugluk* (Boston: Little Brown, 1969); Harold W. Finkler, "North of 60: Inuit and the Administration of Criminal Justice in the Northwest Territories—The Case of Frobisher Bay [Iqaluit]" (Ottawa: NRD 76-3, 1976); Nelson H. H. Graburn, *General Introduction to Lake Harbour, Baffin Island* (Ottawa: Northern Coordination and Research Centre, 1963) and *Lake Harbour, Baffin Island: An Introduction to the Social and Economic Problems of a Small Eskimo Community* (Ottawa: Northern Co-ordination and Research Centre, 1963); Donald B. Marsh and Winifred Marsh, *Echoes into Tomorrow: A Personal Overview of a Century of Events and Endeavours Affecting the History of Canada and the Inuit* (Three Hills, AB: Prairie Graphics, 1991) [Pond Inlet]; Ann McElroy, *Alternatives in Modernization: Styles and Strategies in the Acculturative Behavior of Baffin Island Inuit*, Vols. I, II, and III (New Haven, CT: Human Relations Area Files, Ethnography Series, 1977 [Pangnirtung]); Heather Myers and Scott Forrest, "While Nero Fiddles: Economic Development in Pond Inlet 1987-97," paper presented at the Third International Congress of Arctic Social Sciences, Copenhagen, Denmark, May 21-23 1998; George W. Wenzel, *Clyde Inuit Adaptation and Ecology: The Organization of Subsistence* (Canadian Ethnology Service, Paper No. 77, National Museum of Man Mercury Series, Ottawa: National Museums of Canada, 1981) [Clyde River]; Richard G. Condon, *Inuit Behavior and Seasonal Change in the Canadian Arctic*, Studies in Cultural Anthropology, No. 2 (Ann Arbor: UMI Research Press, 1981) and *Inuit Youth: Growth and Change in the Canadian Arctic* (New Brunswick, NJ: Rutgers University Press, 1987); Charles J. Hanley, "Tomorrow Slowly Encroaches on Harsh, Scenic Arctic" [Pond Inlet], *Los Angeles Times* (October 11, 1987), pp. 2ff; Colin Irwin, "Lords of the Arctic, Wards of the State: The Growing Inuit Population, Arctic Resettlement, and Their Effects on Social and Economic Change—A Summary Report," *Northern Perspectives* 17, 1 (1989) 2-12; Barry Brown, "Future Bleak As Winter for Arctic Town," *Baltimore Sun*, January 6 (1988), p.2 [Broughton Island]; Priit J. Vesilind, "Hunters of the Lost Spirit," *National Geographic* 163, 2 (1983): 151-197; Asen Balikci, "Anthropological Field Work among the Arviligjuarmiut of Pelly Bay, NWT," *The Arctic Circular* 14 (1961); and Doug Struck, "Among the People" (Series), *The Baltimore Sun*, January 13-17 (1985). Resettlement as a tool of modernization has caused complications for many Native communities. For example, Inuit were moved from Port Burwell on Killiniq Island, NWT, to northern Québec in 1978 because of "deteriorating economic and social conditions." In 1988, the Canadian Government negotiated an agreement with the Inuit Makivik Corporation to pay former Port Burwell residents $2.5 million in exchange for dropping their lawsuit against the government for personal damages. The suit alleged that Inuit had been "forcibly removed" from their traditional community, to which they now wish to return. Similarly, Inuit were gathered from their camps to create the new settlement of Pond Inlet during the 1950's, "to combat epidemic and famine."

27 Kenn Harper, *Pangnirtung* (published by the author, 1972), pp. 3-5. In about 1000 AD, Thule ancestors, who originated in northern Alaska, started to migrate eastward along the coast of the Arctic Ocean; the Dorset culture lived 2,000-3,000 years earlier; archeologists speculate that all Inuit originated from the same stock of Asian people who migrated across the Bering Straits land bridge to Alaska between 9,000 and 8,000 B.C. See Dorais, "The Canadian Inuit and Their Language," and James V. Wright, *A History of the Native People of Canada, Vol. 1: 10,000-1,000 BC* (Hull, Québec: Canadian Museum of Civilization, 1995); and Peter Schledermann, *Crossroads to Greenland: 3,000 Years of Prehistory in the Eastern High Arctic* (Calgary: The Arctic Institute of North America, 1990). Farley Mowat describes in *The Farfarers* his theory that, long before the Vikings explored the Canadian coastline (around 1000 A.D.), another people called the Albans visited the High Arctic and the coasts of Labrador and Newfoundland (Toronto: Key Porter, 1998). Excerpted as "Farley's Version" in *Canadian Geographic* 118, (September 1998), pp. 65-82.

28 One of the earliest and most comprehensive anthropological studies of the Inuit (then known as the Canadian Eskimo) was conducted by Franz Boas: "The Eskimo of Baffin Land and Hudson Bay," *Bulletin of the American Museum of Natural History* XV (1901). George Sabo III estimates that Inuit hunters and gatherers lived along the south coast of Baffin Island for at least 800 years; see his *Long Term Adaptations among Arctic Hunter-Gatherers: A Case Study from Southern Baffin Island* (New York: Garland, 1991), p. 4. Other archaeologists such as Therkel Mathiassen date the movement from Alaska to the Eastern Arctic to 1,000 years ago. For a recent estimate of time lines, see Robert McGhee, who places the Dorset period from AD 500-1000 and the Thule period from AD 1000-1600, with an Intermediate period from 1600-1771 and the Historic period from 1771-1921: *Ancient People of the Arctic* (Vancouver: University of British Columbia Press/Canadian Museum of Civilization [Ottawa]), 1996, p. 22.

29 William W. Fitzhugh and Jacqueline S. Olin, eds., *Archeology of the Frobisher Voyages* (Washington, DC: The Smithsonian Institution Press, 1993).

30 See Pierre Berton, *The Arctic Grail: The Quest for the Northwest Passage and the North Pole, 1819-1909* (New York: Viking, 1988); Farley Mowat, *Ordeal by Ice: The Search for the Northwest Passage, Vol. 1, The Top of the World Trilogy* (McClelland and Stewart, 1960), and *Tundra: Selections from the Great Accounts of Arctic Land Voyages* (Toronto: McClelland and Stewart, 1977); Edward Struzik and Mike Beedell, *Northwest Passage: The Quest for an Arctic Route to the East* (Toronto: Key Porter, 1991); and Nortext, *The Baffin Handbook* (Iqaluit, NWT: Nortext Publishing, 1993), pp. 42-43.

31 Harper, *Pangnirtung,* pp. 10-11; Heinrich Kutschak, *Overland to Starvation Cove: With the Inuit in Search of Franklin 1878-1880* (Toronto: University of Toronto Press, 1987); and Fitzhugh and Olin, *Archeology.* American explorer Charles Francis Hall also searched for evidence of Franklin's fate, but found instead the site of Frobisher's 16th century mines and base camp on Baffin Island (*Life with the Esquimaux: A Narrative of Arctic Experience in Search of Survivors of Sir John Franklin's Expedition* (Edmonton: Hurtig, [1865] 1970).

32 For a broad overview of northern exploration, see Daniel Francis, *Discovery of the North: The Exploration of Canada's Arctic* (Edmonton: Hurtig, 1986).

33 For example, Joel S. Savishinsky describes the stress created by anti-hunting groups in *The Trail of the Hare: Environment and Stress in a Sub-Arctic Community*

(Langhorne, PA: Gordon & Breach, 1994). The effects of contact with whites are far-reaching, as documented by William W. Fitzhugh in *Cultures in Contact: The European Impact on Native Cultural Institutions in Eastern North America A.D. 1000-1800* (Washington: Anthropological Society of Washington Series, 1985).

34 Richard G. Condon, *The Northern Copper Inuit: A History* (Norman: University of Oklahoma Press, 1996), p. 137. This does not mean that the Inuit were free of non-contagious diseases such as parasites, insect bites, trichinosis, pneumonia, chronic otitis media, and dental disease. There is no conclusive evidence for pre-contact tuberculosis in the Canadian Arctic; evidence suggests infection via nineteenth century European whalers. James B. Waldram, D. Ann Herring, and T. Kue Young, *Aboriginal Health in Canada: Historical, Cultural, and Epidemiological Perspectives* (Toronto: University of Toronto Press, 1995), pp. 36-38.

35 Renee Fossett, *In Order to Live Untroubled: Inuit of the Central Arctic, 1550-1940* (Winnipeg: University of Manitoba Press, 2001), pp. 167-168.

36 Harper, *Pangnirtung,* pp. 12-19.

37 Fossett, *In Order to Live Untroubled,* p. 169.

38 Fossett, *In Order to Live Untroubled,* p. 169.

39 Fossett, *In Order to Live Untroubled,* p. 170.

40 The people became Canadian citizens in 1869, however, when the Canadian Parliament passed legislation that provided temporary government for "Rupert's Land and the North-western Territory." The rest of the Arctic Archipelago was added in 1880. John S. Matthiasson, *Living on the Land: Change among the Inuit of Baffin Island* (Peterborough, ONT: Broadview Press, 1992), p. 27.

41 With his trip to Baffin Island in 1883-84, Franz Boas left as a geographer but "returned as a cultural anthropologist" whose *The Central Eskimo* "can quite rightly be called the first published ethnographic monograph of the modern era...." Edward J. Hedican, *Applied Anthropology in Canada: Understanding Aboriginal Issues* (Toronto: University of Toronto Press, 1995), p. 23. See Franz Boas, "A Journey in Cumberland Sound and on the West Shore of Davis Strait in 1883 and 1884," *American Geographical Society Bulletin* 26 (1884): 242-272; and Boas [Ludger Muller-Wille, ed.], *Franz Boas among the Inuit of Baffin Island, 1883-1884* (Toronto: University of Toronto Press, 1998).

42 Kenn Harper, *Pangnirtung* (published by the author, 1972).

43 Kenn Harper, "Pangnirtung," in *The Nunavut Handbook: 1999 Commemorative Edition,* edited by Marion Soublière (Iqaluit, NT: Nortext Multimedia, 1998), p. 347. The establishment of a trading post usually resulted in a small gathering of Inuit who worked for the traders or missionaries, long before resettlement began. This was certainly true for Pangnirtung. See J. Matthiasson, *Living on the Land,* p. 42. Men supplied the trader's needs and women performed housekeeping and (according to Matthiasson) sometimes provided sexual services. See also Alan Cooke's exploration of a complicated relationship in "The Eskimos and the Hudson's Bay Company," pp. 209-223 in "Le peuple esquimau aujourd'hui et demain," *Quatrième Congrès international de l Fondation française d'études nordique, Bibliothèque arctique et antarctique,* edited by J. Malaurie (Paris: Mouton, 1973); and David Damas, "Shifting Relations in the Administration of the Inuit: The Hudson Bay Company and the Canadian Government," *Études/Inuit/Studies* 17, 2 (1993): 5-28.

44 Marsh and Marsh, *Echoes into Tomorrow*, p. 210.

45 All Canadian Inuit speak one language, but several dialects of Inuktitut exist. Dorais, "The Canadian Inuit and Their Language." The Reverend E. J. Peck kept records of his contact with the Inuit: *The Eskimo* (Anglican Church of Canada General Synod Archives, Peck Papers, M56-1 Series, 1922).

46 Marsh and Marsh, *Echoes into Tomorrow,* pp. 229-238.

47 Quoted in Waldram, Herring, and Young, *Aboriginal Health in Canada*, p. 165.

48 PAC RG85/815, file 6954 [3], 14 September 1936, MacKinnon to Turner, NWT and Yukon Branch.

49 Eric Alden Smith, *Inujjuamiut Foraging Strategies: Evolutionary Ecology of an Arctic Hunting Economy* (New York: Aldine de Gruyter, 1991), p. 122.

50 Smith, *Inujjuamiut Foraging Strategies*, p. 122.

51 Dorais, "The Canadian Inuit and Their Language," p. 203.

52 Helm and Damas refer to the early 1960s as the "contact-traditional" period in Inuit history, when the influence of Euro-Canadian institutions intensified because of illness, starvation, and resettlement but traditional Inuit culture was still very much alive. Judith Helm and David Damas, "The Contact-Traditional All-Native Community of the Canadian North," *Anthropologica* 5 (n.d.): 9-21. We prefer to use the term "resettlement period," as regular contact with whites occurred for Cumberland Sound Inuit more than 100 years before resettlement.

53 Cited in J. Matthiasson, *Living on the Land*, pp. 94-95, and explored in R. Duibaldo, *The Government of Canada and the Inuit 1900-1967* (Ottawa: Research Branch, Corporate Policy, Department of Indian and Northern Affairs, Canada, 1985).

54 Andrew Armitage, *Comparing the Policy of Aboriginal Assimilation: Australia, Canada, and New Zealand* (Vancouver: University of British Columbia, 1995). For other interpretations of Canadian government and white southern actions and attitudes toward the Inuit as a form of [perhaps sometimes unconscious] colonialism, see Ken W. Barger, "Inuit and Cree Adaptation to Northern Colonialism," in *Contemporary Political Organization of Native North Americans*, edited by E. L. Schusky (Washington: University Press of America, 1980); Thomas R. Berger, *A Long and Terrible Shadow: White Values, Native Rights in the Americas, 1492-1992* (Vancouver and Toronto: Douglas & McIntyre, 1991); Kenneth Coates, *Canada's Colonies: A History of the Yukon and Northwest Territories,* (Toronto: James Lorimer, 1985); Kenneth Coates and Judith Powell, *The Modern North: People, Politics, and the Rejection of Colonialism* (Toronto: James Lorimer, 1989); Robert Paine, *The Nursery Game—Colonisers and Colonised in the Canadian Arctic, Études/Inuit/Studies* 1 (1977): 5; and Robert Paine, ed., *Patrons and Brokers in the East Arctic* (St. John's, NFLD: Institute of Social and Economic Progress, Memorial University of Newfoundland, 1971) and *The White Arctic: Anthropological Essays on Tutelage and Ethnicity* (Toronto: University of Toronto Press, 1977).

55 Mark Nuttall, *Protecting the Arctic: Indigenous Peoples and Cultural Survival* (Amsterdam: Harwood Academic, 1998), p. 128.

56 Victor F. Valentine and Frank G. Vallee, eds., *Eskimo of the Canadian Arctic* (Toronto: Macmillan, 1978), p. xii.

57 Hugh Brody, *The People's Land: Eskimos and Whites in the Eastern Arctic* (Markham, ONT: Penguin Books, 1975).

58 Dorais, "The Canadian Inuit and Their Language," p. 209. Settlements of 200 or more have a nursing station. The nursing station in Pangnirtung had only one nurse (and no doctors) for 800 people in the late 1970s. See Duffy, *The Road to Nunavut*, p. 65. The situation has since improved, but the doctor still visits only once a month.

59 Haller, et al, *Baffin Island—East Coast*, p. 63.

60 Haller, et al, said that Boas might have overestimated the 1840 figure, but no other records exist; Boas attributed the sharp decline to the introduction of several diseases by whalers in the mid-1800s. A. A. Haller, D. C. Foote, and P. D. Cove [edited by G. Anders], *Baffin Island—East Coast: An Area Economic Survey* (Ottawa: Department of Indian and Northern Affairs, 1967), p. 57.

61 Franz Boas, *The Central Eskimo*, p. 18.

62 Hantzsch undertook this census as a matter of interest. He counted "38 married couples, 12 widows or wives separated from their husbands, and 80 children and young people" in 39 tent-dwellings; he found no men living by themselves. The number of children ranged from one to six, and customary adoption was common. Bernhard Hantzsch, *My Life among the Eskimos: Baffin Journeys in the Years 1909 to 1911,* edited and translated by L. G. Neatby, Institute of Northern Studies, Mawdsley Memoir 3 (Saskatoon: University of Saskatchewan, 1977), p. 39.

63 Based on Haller, et al, *Baffin Island—East Coast*, p. 150.

64 Based on Haller, et al, *Baffin Island—East Coast*, p. 157.

65 Based on Haller, et al, *Baffin Island—East Coast*, p. 156.

66 Based on Haller, et al, *Baffin Island—East Coast*, pp. 150, 156.

67 Based on Haller, et al, *Baffin Island—East Coast*, pp. 150, 156.

68 Bryan Alexander and Cherry Alexander, "The Inuit of the Canadian Eastern Arctic: Out on the Land," in *The Vanishing Arctic*, edited by Bryan Alexander and Cherry Alexander (London: Blandford Cassell, 1996), p. 142.

69 *The Canadian Encyclopedia Plus.*

70 R. Quinn Duffy, *The Road to Nunavut: The Progress of the Eastern Arctic Inuit since the Second World War* (Montréal: McGill-Queen's University Press, 1988), p. 12. For a detailed analysis of the RCMP role, see Harwood Steele, *Policing the Arctic: The Story of the Conquest of the Arctic by the Royal Canadian (formerly North-West) Mounted Police* (London: Jarrolds, 1995).

71 Pamela R. Stern and Richard G. Condon, "A Good Spouse is Hard to Find: Marriage, Spouse Exchange, and Infatuation among the Copper Inuit," in William Jankowiak, ed., *Romantic Passion: A Universal Experience?* (New York: Columbia University Press, 1995), p. 210.

72 Huguette Dagenais and Denise Piché, eds. *Women, Feminism, and Development/Femmes, Féminisme et Dévèloppement* (Montréal: McGill-Queens University Press, 1999).

II

LIFE OUT ON THE LAND

My great-grandmother taught my mother and grandmother how to do everything.
                                                                    —Geela

Photo 2.1 Ruins of a traditional qarmaq made of whale jawbone, stones, sod, and skins.

2

Traditional Roles:
Gender and Survival[1]

I was born in a little camp about 60 miles from here, in Shark Fiord. My whole family goes there every year—not to sleep over—just to get it back in mind, in memories.

—Rosie

Jagging for Fish

Photo 2.2 Fishing for Arctic char in a rock pool at midnight.

On our first evening out on the land with Peter and Leah Qappik, we put up our tent and nap briefly after the long, cold boat ride from Pangnirtung to Shark Fiord. Leah calls us at midnight to join the family on a fishing expedition. With tea and bannock warming our blood, we don our hiking boots. The weak August sun casts an eerie light across the hills that embraced this couple when they, as children, lived out on the land. We set off across the spongy tundra, inadvertently crushing tiny wildflowers under our feet. Like a proud leader of old, Leah goes first. She carries the "jagging stick"—an old hockey stick that Peter has equipped with a bent nail for hooking fish. Little Mary, clutching a miniature fishing pole, slips her tiny hand into her mother's. Following Leah a few paces behind, Susa steps in the same crannies her mother instinctively finds in the gloom. We follow with Sheila and the others who have come to live on the land, if only for a few days.

The air feels so unimaginably clean in this place far from the toxic vapors of urbanization that we climb the gentle slopes almost effortlessly. Eventually we come to a place where the river meets the fiord.[2] Here we will find the delicate, salmon-like Arctic char. Peter stops by the shore but Leah motions us to step onto a circle of rocks in the middle of the river. Many years ago, someone strategically placed these stones to trap the unsuspecting fish for a few critical seconds during their migration upstream to the glacial lakes.

The mothers slip into the center of the stone ring. High rubber wading boots shield their legs from the bone-numbing water. The girls take their places standing on the rocks, where they can see the fish with the advantage of height. For almost an hour, with quiet chatting and much laughter, the women try to spear the char as the girls point, "There! There! Over there!" We squint into the clear water, tinted amber by the feeble light, and try to see the fish darting and swishing around the rocks. Even when our eyes adjust to the shadows, we cannot see the char quickly enough to be of any use. The girls laugh at us and we laugh at ourselves. As a team, they have already spotted and caught dozens of fish.

Soon, Leah tires of jagging, passes the spear to one of her daughters, and, with an impish smile, reaches under a large rock with her gloved hand. Within seconds she pulls out a surprised char and flings it up to the riverbank, where her husband swiftly guts the prize and piles it with the other cleaned fish. Showing the adeptness of her maturity, Leah strips off her gloves and gropes with bare hands for another fish and yet another and another. Her face glows in the pallid light: "This is a good place," she grins.

Leah remembers going to a fishing camp when she was only six years old, but the fish frightened her. Then, too, women used to make a circle of rocks to keep the char from escaping into the river: "My mother put me right next to that place, and I remember the fish flopping around in the water. I was very, very scared. I cried my head off! My mother put me in another spot. I watched them catch those fish, so now I am a good fisher, by hook or by spear or by hand, because I watched them from the time I was very small." Within two hours, this small but accomplished fishing party has landed seventy large Arctic char, all of which have been cleaned, rinsed, and placed neatly into plastic bags for the walk back to camp. This one night of collaborative fishing will feed the families for weeks to come. Other work has been done, too—the reinforcement of kinship bonds and the practicing of ancient skills.[3]

As we rise the next morning, we notice that our friends have already filleted, scored, and hung the char on wooden racks scattered throughout the encampment. The long drying process has begun. A whole, cleaned fish arrives at our tent. Grilled on an open fire, it provides our lunch and dinner for three days. The flavor of fresh fish taken from crystalline waters reminds us of the bounty of land and sea, and of the people's wealth.

ᔆ

W e begin with a portrait of life out on the land, the undulating tundra punctuated by majestic but forbidding mountains, sparkling rivers, and glacial moraines. Home to the Inuit for thousands of years, this treacherous environment dictated the imperative for sheer survival which, in turn, shaped traditional gender roles. The Inuit vehemently deny that social problems they confront now in the settlements also marred life out on the land. Generally, they insist, life out on the land was "good" and families seemed happier, even in the face of crushing hardships.

A Nomadic Life
"There was no easy going"

I nuit women and men reveal a keen sense of loss when they speak of life out on the land. Not that it was an easy life; in many ways, it was excruciatingly hard. Yet, their stories accentuate the closeness that came from successfully meeting the fierce challenges that attended nomadic life in a harsh climate.[4] The Inuit constructed their society on the basis of the family, Jenness observed in the early part of the twentieth century.[5] Living on the land meant that families had to work together, both within their immediate family and within the community of families:

> For Inuit, the basis of secure, successful subsistence is the social relatedness of one person to another, rather than individual prowess or special equipment. And the only means of establishing these extended, long-lasting relations is through kinship. Social relatedness…becomes a means of redressing the unpredictability of the environment. As a result, subsistence is more than a means of

survival. It is a set of culturally established responsibilities, rights and obliga-
tions that affect every man, woman and child each day.[6]

That relatedness, assured by overlapping and complicated social networks, was
obvious in the summer when families took their meals in communal fashion.
Each family took its turn preparing dinner, which women served after the men
returned from hunting. Mime performances, chatting, gambling, playing ball, or
dancing completed the evening:

> The day before it is her turn to cook, the woman goes to the hills to fetch shrubs
> for the fire...the kettle is placed on the top of it and the fire is fed with shrubs
> and blubber. When the meal is ready the master of the house stands beside it,
> crying "Ujo! Ujo! (boiled meat) and everybody comes out of the hut.... The
> dish is carried to a level place and the men sit down around it in one circle,
> while the women form another.[7]

Geela, 38, remembers living in a *qarmaq* (small hut) made of sod (Arctic
heather) and seal or caribou skins layered over a framework of whale jawbones
or ribs.[8] This construction style emanated from the Thule, who built substantial
winter houses: "[The Thule] brought the basic style from Alaska but in the
wood-scarce Canadian Arctic had to substitute whale ribs and jaws for
driftwood logs...walls were of stone, with rafters of whalebone supporting the
roof, which was formed of hides covered with a thick layer of turf."[9] Later, the
houses in this area were made of canvas, bits of wood left by ships, and
cardboard. Women made summer tents of sealskin and lined them with moss,
which the RCMP in Pangnirtung considered "sufficient" for human habitation.
Snow houses had disappeared by 1958 because they were considered by the
Inuit as inferior, less prestigious, too cold for southern clothing, and too small.[10]

Geela and her family traveled every summer to a different place as a break
from the main camp: "Out on the land the Inuit had to work hard every day.
Even the children had to work. There was no easy going." Both men and women
had fewer choices. Survival was the common goal around which life turned, day
after day, winter after winter. Adding to exigencies of weather, game
movements were unpredictable, as Franz Boas pointed out in 1888:

> The number of deer [caribou] on Cumberland Peninsula is so variable that the
> result of the hunt is often unsatisfactory. Although in some seasons numerous
> herds are met, in others scarcely enough animals are killed to afford a sufficient
> stock of skins for the winter clothing.[11]

Food was scarce because the Inuit had also been distracted from their usual pattern of migration, hunting, and fishing in order to work in the nineteenth century
whaling industry. An account by Brother Warmow, a Moravian missionary who
accompanied the Penny whaling expedition to Blacklead Island and Kekerten,
vividly portrays domestic life in an *igloo* in 1857-1858, beyond the stretch of
individual memory for today's Inuit. The lamp he refers to is the woman's

qulliq, which she used for cooking, heating, and lighting. It was her responsibility to keep the flame burning in the flat, oblong vessel that she filled with whale or seal oil. This helped her family survive all but the most adverse conditions:[12]

> Imagine an entire family, old and young, in such an abode. The whole furniture consists of a lamp, often very dim and scarcely burning, and a few well-worn reindeer-skins [caribou]. Upon these latter, the members of the family sit, in a posture similar to that which the ptarmigan assume in very cold weather, namely with the head drawn down between the shoulders. The mistress of the house is engaged trimming the wick of the lamp, and carefully dropping it on the scanty supply of oil, lest the light should be altogether extinguished—a piece of frugality of which they know nothing, when better times come. Beside her sits another female member of the family, chewing at a skin, destined to be made into boots or clothing, a domestic employment which is here perhaps akin to washing clothes with us. The master, if not out hunting or fishing, occupies a place beside his wife, and is busy trimming some of his implements, or boring holes in the pieces of a broken stone-vessel, in order to repair it—an operation which he will perform very skilfully [sic]. They have nothing to eat, except occasionally a handful of seaweed, which they dip in hot water and consume with a good appetite, unsuitable for food as it may appear to us. With all this poverty, we must not imagine discontented looks. In such circumstances, many Europeans would murmur against God and man. But these people are quite contented, and seem to know nothing of misery.... If I take a present out of my pocket [e.g., tobacco], they receive it with smiling faces.

Boas adds to the imagery of living on the land a hundred years ago in his description of "home life":

> While in times of plenty the home life is quite cheerful, the house presents a sad and gloomy appearance if stormy weather prevents the men from hunting. The stores are quickly consumed, one lamp after another is extinguished, and everybody sits motionless in the dark hut. Nevertheless, the women and men do not stop humming their monotonous *amna aya* and their stoicism in enduring the pangs of hunger is really wonderful. At last, when starvation is menacing the sufferers, the most daring of the men resolves to try his luck. Though the storm may rage over the icy plain, he sets out to go sealing. For hours he braves the cold and stands waiting and watching at the breathing hole until he hears the blowing of the seal and succeeds in killing it.... The sledge is unloaded, the seal dragged into the house, and every one joyfully awaits his share. The animal is cut up, every household receiving a piece of meat and blubber. The gloomy huts are again lighted up and the pots, which had been out of use for some days, are again hung up over the lamps.[13]

Flexibility and inventiveness helped the Inuit survive in seemingly overwhelming conditions. Like other hunter-gatherers, the Inuit adapted inventively to long-term and short-term fluctuations in resources and climate. A 1968 film by Asen Balikci shows the Netsilik Inuit creating sled runners out of caribou hide in the absence of wood: They cut "their summer tent of caribou hide in half, wetting the pieces, wrapping each half around a line of fish laid together with crossbars of caribou antler, lashed with thongs of sealskin. In the spring, when the sled thawed, they took it apart, ate the fish, sewed the tent back together, and moved in."[14] The strong ethos that underscored mutual support and sharing amplified the power of ingenuity. Residential flexibility paralleled organizational flexibility, as bands moved across the land to maximize hunting and fishing, always seeking to support the whole community rather than the individual.[15]

Maata Pudlat of Cape Dorset tells a story familiar to Baffin women of the transitional generation—those who were born on the land and brought into the settlement at an early age:

"WE WOULD SHARE"

I was born in a camp with my twin brother. At that time we were still pretty much Inuit and we had no southern things to get mixed up with. We were living in huts, we travelled by dog team, and we slept overnight in an igloo [*igluvigaq*] when we had to. I lived with all my brothers and sisters. We used to have very large families, even though we were struggling, maybe because the more we struggled, the closer we got. We seemed to have most things that we needed. We don't depend on each other like that anymore. We're close now, but not as close as we were before.... [Our children]...have most things that they need, whereas before, in my childhood, we didn't have very much. We would share. We would find love and comfort by helping others. [16]

Sometimes the burdens seemed more than a single human could carry, even in collaboration with others, but the lives and contributions of the Inuit cannot be demarcated simply in terms of survival and hard labour. Many women, especially those over 30, say that going out on the land was the happiest time for them. One woman's eyes filled with tears as she speaks: "I will never forget the good times we had then." Mary, 45, who grew up in a camp and still likes to go out on the land on weekends, adds: "Maybe it was harder. There were no skidoos. They used dog teams. But there was also much happiness, especially in the summertime, when there was good caribou hunting out at the summer camps." Says an elder of their trips to a distant lake: "I can still see a large herd of caribou on the side of the hills. We were in a boat and, because we didn't have motors in those days, we were very slow—we paddled or used a sail."[17] Life was hard but "it was always fun."

Sometimes, Inuit women say, the still night air was filled with men's drum dancing and women's guttural throat singing, vanishing art forms that a few Inuit have faithfully retained. They remember playing a sticks and spindle game that fascinated old and young alike. Older women speak sentimentally of walking into the hills to pick flowers and berries just for the sheer joy of being at one with nature. They learned how to dance and play the accordion during the whaling period, as Margaret Penny observed firsthand: "Some of them sing very sweetly. The whole of them are fond of music and think it a great treat to get down to the cabin to hear the accordion played by the second mate...."[18]

Leeta, 72, remembers life out on the land: "People used to walk a lot; we used to do everything, even sew. We made *kamiks* [*kamiit* or boots] and *amautiit* [hooded parkas]. When the sealskin boots wore out, we repaired them. Now, I don't make *kamiks* anymore." Leeta learned to sew by watching her grandmother and sister. Now she sews dresses with a sewing machine, when she has time after taking care of grandchildren while her daughter works outside the home: "We used to go out with the dog teams, but now I don't do anything much. Back then, some things were fun but some things were not. We didn't have other people around. It was mostly our own people." Life was good in spite of the constant need to prepare against nature.

Many of the contemporary problems caused or exacerbated by alcohol abuse and unemployment were non-existent when virtually everyone lived in small camps of a few families each. This comparison of traditional simplicity versus modern complexity pervades our conversations with older Inuit women and men. Now many families still spend time out on the land, hunting and fishing, clam digging or berry picking, as the seasons dictate. They go out of necessity, for few families can afford to feed themselves solely through wage employment and buying from the northern stores. They go for pleasure, for rekindling family unity or harmony between Inuk and nature—and they go for remembering a time when male and female roles seemed clearly delineated and parents had more control over their children.[19]

The Inuktitut expression for being out on the land, *maqainniq,* encompasses hunting, fishing, gathering, and all the camping activities that now help the Inuit recapture a time when they seemed to live more in harmony with nature and with each other.[20]

The Gender Calculus
"A man is the hunter his wife makes him"

Many classical studies of hunter-gatherer societies emphasized "man the hunter," but the roles of Inuit men and women carefully intermeshed in the old hunting, fishing, and gathering culture: "Marriage was not an option, but a matter of life and death, the union of a hunter and a seamstress. Neither could live without the contribution of the other."[21] Gender roles fell into two clearly demarcated spheres. Men hunted *tuktu* (caribou), *natsiq* (seal), and other game, sometimes for their own use and later for the burgeoning fur trade,[22] trying to provide a wealth of skins and meat to feed the camps. Typically, men hunted cooperatively because of the demands of a harsh environment.[23] They made the tools for hunting and sewing, from *qajaq* (kayak) frames to the *qamutik* (*komatik* or sled) to the *ulu* (the woman's U-shaped knife). They built the family's *igloo*, constructed the whale jawbone frames for the caribou skin houses, drove the sled dogs, and carved children's toys and dolls. They tracked wildlife and managed resources, and protected their families.

Inuit oral history portrays women as competent across a wide range of activities that included sewing and processing of skins. Women managed childbirth, nurtured the children, and nursed the sick and the elderly. They preserved or cooked the meat and fish. When it was time to move camp, the women carried bundles of the family possessions down to the water, and then rowed their *umiaks* ("the woman's boat, round and made of skins) filled with people, skins, and gear, while the men steered.[24] When the wind chill takes temperatures down to 80 degrees below zero, a human face can freeze in 60 seconds and a person can die within fifteen short, agonizing minutes, so women worked very hard to keep the family in warm clothing. Women transformed the caribou hides that men brought home into the "second skin" that would keep the hunters alive next time around. Women made and repaired the *kamiks* that kept the family from freezing to death or losing their toes to frostbite. They supplied drinking water, gathered fuel for fire, tended the lamps, gave birth to children, and kept the camp running. Jenness described a similar division of labor among the Copper Inuit (also considered Central Eskimo):

> [Men] do most of the hunting, build the snow huts, and erect the heavy deerskin tents that are used in the spring and the fall.... During migrations, the man does all the loading of the sled, his wife handing him the household goods through the doorway or through a hole in the wall. She helps him, however, to lash up the sled, while the children...harness the dogs.... All the cooking and sewing fall on the women. In summer, this often includes the gathering of fuel, though the children are usually sent out for this purpose.[25]

Matthiasson characterizes the coupling of male-female roles among the Inuit of another Baffin Island community, Pond Inlet:

> In both traditional and contact-traditional Tununermiut, the men were the hunters, and hunting skills were both highly valued and the basis for the acquisition of overt political authority and influence. However, once an animal had been killed and skinned, the processing of the hide and carcass usually became the responsibility of the wife. If the animal was to be cached, it would be buried "on the trail" by the hunter, after the skin had been cut off. If it was brought back to the camp, the hunter would skin it and then cut away the thick fatty tissue just under the skin, which the wife would then render into fat for cooking and heating.[26]

Usually, women distributed the seal or caribou bounty, reinforcing kinship and communal ties with wisdom and generosity. Women made tents for summer camping, painstakingly sewing the skins with treasured ivory needles and strands of sinew. (Today, they sit on the living room floor, surrounded by a sea of white duck canvas, and sew the store-bought material with prized electric sewing machines.) A young girl learned to sew by making clothes for tiny soap-stone dolls carved by her father *[ataata]*.

The gender calculus was elegantly simple: If the woman lacked skill in making warm clothing, the man would freeze to death on the hunt. If the man did not hunt well, the woman could not make clothing to protect herself and her family from the elements. In an unforgiving climate and terrain, men needed women's skills as processors of food and skin as much as women needed the raw materials from which they created nutritious meals and protective clothing. The common Inuit saying that a man who lost his wife could not function alone encapsulated the critical role of women. Both partners were essential—neither was peripheral or marginal to the tasks of survival. Conditions were so severe in eight to ten months of winter that that everyone had to marry and almost every task was a male task or a female task. Thus, men and women developed a cooperative model that enabled them to withstand the cold and protect their children. Men and women had to work together in order to survive. Bilby observed women and children filling in the cracks of *igloo* snow blocks that the men had carefully laid in ever decreasing circles; the women spread heather over the sleeping benches fashioned by the men, and so forth.[27] Mainah, 46, recalls her childhood in the camp:

> My mother always looked after sealskins, scraping off the blubber, drying them, stretching them, and making them into things like *kamiks*. In the sum-mertime, when the skins were dry enough, my mother gathered them and sewed them together to make a tent. In the wintertime, when the men were hunting caribou, she dried the skins and made clothing out of them. She made parkas and something that looked like pants—using the caribou leg skins—and she made mittens out of sealskin.

Women hung the wet fur clothes above the lamp when the family went to bed, raised themselves several times a night to turn them or fluff them to prevent brittleness, and rose first in the morning to complete the task. Men provided women with tools for cleaning, sewing, and preparing hides. This arrangement called for a sharp delineation between "men's skills" and "women's skills,"[28] yet most Inuit elders believe that men and women enjoyed a virtually equal relation-ship. Reciprocity characterized the division of labour and the exercise of power.[29] Men viewed women not as inferior but as having a "different job." The skills of one balanced the skills of the other.

The Inuit do not describe these role differences in terms of nature or biology but of necessity and workability. Thus, it was a gendered rather than a sexual division of labour.[30] The ever-essential hunt dominated the cycle of life: "The ideology of pre-contact Inuit served to ensure reproduction of the indigenous mode of production by supporting the chief economic activity, the hunt."[31] As Mitchell notes, "each person had to be skilled in all the tasks appropriate to his or her gender if the group was to function as a self-sufficient unit."[32] Bodenhorn argued that the whole set of subsistence activities, "both technical and symbolic," underscored the fundamental interdependence of women and men.[33] Bilby, in his twelve years living on Baffin Island in the early part of the twentieth century—before the Inuit moved into hamlets—describes a situation that our elder Inuit women and men also recall:

> There seems to be a happy sort of sex equality among these people, or perhaps it should rather be said that a mutually agreeable division of equally essential labours cause the men and women to live more on a common footing than they do among many other [groups]. [34]

Thomsen saw among both Baffin and Greenland Inuit that women's activities and organizations have always been "complementary, rather than conflictual" in relationship to men's activities (especially in leadership and politics).[35] By specializing women and men both contributed essential work to the family's well being, but they created a synergy that benefited both genders far beyond what either could do alone. "Work," Guemple found among Belcher Island Inuit, was defined as "something one does *for* someone of the opposite gender."[36] Hunting (or, later, carving) was central to male self-esteem: "For an Inuit hunter, being a good provider is everything. His status, his prestige, his whole identity is around being a good provider. It was shameful not to be a good hunter. It was excruciatingly painful to somebody not being able to provide for a family."[37] If the man failed, he broke the circle of complementarity that linked him so closely to his female partner.

As marriage occurred without a formal ceremony, so, too, divorce occurred when either person chose to end the union (rarely after the birth of the first child). Women were not considered chattels or slaves; they owned their tools and implements (ulus, scrapers, sewing utensils, cooking pots and the lamp, drying racks, other furnishings, and perhaps some of the dogs and the spring tent).[38] Children stayed with their mother when a couple separated. Divorce created great hardships for both men and women, which helps explain why it occurred so seldom in pre-settlement days.

Gender Roles in the Whaling Period

Whaling was always a central part of Baffin Inuit life. Boas wrote that the Inuit "pursued the monstrous animal in all waters with their imperfect weapons, for a single capture supplied them with food and fuel for a long time."[39] However, when the Scottish and American whalers arrived in Cumberland Sound in the mid-1800s, traditional life took on a new face at the whaling stations. Although the gender division of labour remained essentially the same, the decision of where to live and when to relocate shifted toward a new model. So did the hierarchies governing economic productivity. With the establishment of the whaling stations, men now engaged in fishing and hunting activities under the direction of a whaling master for commercial purposes and with a broader reward system:

> On his first wintering whaling voyage in 1853, Captain Penny had hired Eskimo men to hunt during the winter, to drive dogsleds during the spring, and to man whaleboats during the summer. This set a precedent for all subsequent wintering voyages. Because the native men could perform useful tasks in all seasons, it became normal for the ships' captains to employ them for the entire duration of their sojourn in Cumberland Sound. Consequently, Eskimos had to move with their families to the winter harbour selected by a captain and to reside there for the better part of a year. To compensate the Eskimos for the reduction of the time available for their own subsistence hunting, a whaling master had to assume some responsibility for feeding the men and their families while they were working for his vessel. And, of course, he had to pay them for their services by providing them with goods such as used whaleboats and whaling gear, guns and ammunition, tools and implements, metal and wood, clothes and cloth.[40]

Inuit women continued to sew clothing, but instead of producing garments only for their families, they began to sew for the whalers as well, taking advantage of the needles and cloth that they traded for fresh meat and ivory.[41] Women gathered berries in the summer and dried them to feed the men during fall hunting.[42] Margaret Penny (who raved about the warm sealskin clothing Inuit women made for her) described the "great abundance" of berries at the whaling station on Kekerten Island in 1857:

> I had a pail full of delicious blue berries gathering from the hills. They are covered with them [August 1857].[43] The weather is very warm and the female natives seem to amuse themselves in little excursions to gather the berries that have been buried under the snow all winter. I have had many presents of them and find them very good and fresh [May 1858].[44]

After contact with whalers, making duffel wool socks or boot liners—sometimes with delicate embroidered figures dancing around the tops—lengthened Inuit women's long list of talents. Generations of women continue to teach these skills, mother to daughter. By the time she reached puberty, a girl understood how to prepare skins and the basics of clothing construction. Caribou skin parkas, fur boots, and mittens were her stock in trade. She also learned the art of gathering shellfish in cold, dangerous waters.

Boys worked beside their fathers, especially when they took the dog teams and sleds out hunting. Pauloosie, 40, recalls that life consisted of hunting and surviving: "The men hunted for food and my mom looked after us, made the clothing, made suppers to eat, looked after the house. I was happy." Qatsuq, whom we interviewed when she was 98, was a child during the late nineteenth century. She lived at the Kekerten whaling station (and then later moved into the new settlement of Pangnirtung). Qatsuq remembers clearly how gender roles played out in the cycle of life; her memories closely parallel the cycle of life presented by anthropologists, including George Sabo, shown in Table 2.1. Sabo did not distinguish between male and female activities, nor did he chart female productive activities such as processing skins. These additional activities are shown in table 2.2.

Figure 2.1 The Annual Cycle of Hunting, Fishing, and Gathering[a]

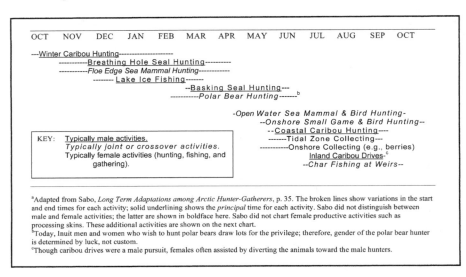

[a]Adapted from Sabo, *Long Term Adaptations among Arctic Hunter-Gatherers*, p. 35. The broken lines show variations in the start and end times for each activity; solid underlining shows the *principal* time for each activity. Sabo did not distinguish between male and female activities; the latter are shown in boldface here. Sabo did not chart female productive activities such as processing skins. These additional activities are shown on the next chart.
[b]Today, Inuit men and women who wish to hunt polar bears draw lots for the privilege; therefore, gender of the polar bear hunter is determined by luck, not custom.
[c]Though caribou drives were a male pursuit, females often assisted by diverting the animals toward the male hunters.

"WE DID A LOT OF HARD WORK"

In early autumn, the women started getting ready for the winter. We made tents and sealskin clothes for the men first, and their *kamiks*, before clothes for the ladies and the children. We started the caribou skin for men before everybody, because we were so used to it. We did that every year—making the clothes for different seasons. We used a *tasiqqut* [a scraper made from metal and wood] to make it easier to sew the hides. That time, we didn't use underwear, but we made baby clothes from rabbit fur. We made the man's parka from *tuktu* [caribou].

When it was wintertime and all ice, the men went hunting by dog team. When the spring came around, in March or April, they went by foot on the floe edges so they could have an igloo, and hunted for baby seals. Sometimes men made *qamutiik* (sleds) that just fit in the boat so they could hunt down by the floe edge. Every male went except for the elders and the children. When the men were gone, then women went hunting too, by dog sled. We would catch some seals, but we didn't go very far.

They brought us skin from a ring seal that you can blow up to carry water. We scraped the fur off the skin. When we sewed it, we always kept it wet so it would be easier to sew. We braided the thread before we started sewing it. Every time the thing got old, it would tinkle! Then we all went back to Keker-ten and lived in our permanent houses.

Once we had the baby sealskins, we started making them into clothes for the summer. The meat is good, too. I love eating boiled seal meat!

Men did not eat all day while they were out hunting, so when they were to be back any day, we started boiling some seal meat with our *qulliq* [lamp]. There were not any camp stoves at that time. When we started living in Pang-nirtung, we started seeing camp stoves.

When we started the *qulliq*, we would hammer the fat so it wasn't just one big piece of blubber. We used Arctic willow to crush the blubber so it was easy to burn. We set up metal legs so the lamp didn't touch the ground. We made some tea and boiled some seal meat, then put all the oil back in and started an-other fire. We used a very little [short] light if the tent was too hot, and if the tent was too cold, we used a long fire.

After the men were at the floe edge trying to catch some whales, they went back to Kekerten and got ready to go hunting again for walrus. When we got some walrus, we took the blubber to a big pot. Then we would say, "That's the end of the hunting for the year." By then, we had enough food for the whole year. We would stay at the camp and take our time cleaning our stuff, and maybe get ready to go caribou hunting again. We would not use the big boats that we used for whale hunting; we would go by different boats and bring along a *qajaq*. As you can see, we worked hard at that time!

By using Qatsuq Eevik's account of women's activities during the late 1800s and into the Resettlement Period of the mid-twentieth century, as well as other accounts cited in this chapter, we were able to reconstruct the Annual Cycle of Processing, Sewing, and Other Female Productivity (Table 2.2)—activities that were often missing from male-oriented accounts of "the cycle of life." Ann Meekitjuk Hanson remembers the care that Inuit women took in handling the seal:

I remember, when my father or brother-in-law would bring home a seal, it was my mother's responsibility to butcher the animal. Before she skinned the seal, however, she would put out a small piece of freshwater ice—a message to all the other seals swimming under the ice that they would not be thirsty. Inuit re-spected all animals and cruelty was not accepted.[45]

The woman's kitbag of tools included a *takhut* (stone or wooden tamper) for tending the flickering flame of the oil lamp. She made the lamp wick from a fine moss mixed with the fuzzy part of the Arctic willow, which spreads lazily across the tundra, a low, horizontal tree of life. When preparing seal or caribou skins, she or her husband sliced the thicker layers of fat away with a *saligut*, a straight-edged knife with a wooden handle. Then, using a skinning board angled prop-erly to ease her job, she scraped away the layers closest to the skin with the curved blade of her *ulu* knife. Next, she softened the skin with her scoop-like stone or metal *tasiqqut* (scraper). She would also have a whetting stone to keep her tools razor-sharp, drying racks for skins and clothing, strong caribou sinew thread, and a thimble. Her skills created the man's *qulituk* (parka) and his *kaliktuktu* ("pants of caribou"). This description by contemporary women is supported and augmented by Margaret Penny's keen observations in 1857 (original spelling and grammar are retained):

> [To clean the sealskins is] a tedious process. Every [female] has as part of her establishment some fifty wooden pins about six inches long. With them, she pins skins tight out in winter on the frozen snow. As the oil oses [oozes] out of the skins she scrapes it off with her half moon knife [*ulu*]. This generaly takes three or four days if keen frosty weather. After this date they are rolled up. If coarse they are kept for a summer tent, which requires 15 skins, as they generaly have a new tent every year, the old tent being taken to line the inside of the snow eddloo [*igloo*] or hut.... If sealskins are used for atagois [*amautiit*, or parkas] or trowsers the prosiss is more tedious, has to be scraped and softened with their [teeth] untill they become as pliable as doe skin.[46]

Indeed, the Inuk woman in times past (and even now to some extent) used her teeth as a portable tool that stayed with her into old age, as this elder explains:

> Another important thing was our teeth...we had to chew skins before we made them into things, and after some things were made—like *kamiks*—we continued to chew them every night until they wore out and we had to make another pair. See my teeth? They are only half worn down. My mother's teeth were almost flat to her gums.... The making of clothing was a lifelong thing and, even so, a woman took pride in what she made.[47]

With her skills and tools, and the mutual help of the men in her family, the Inuk woman fed her family. To the staples of seal, caribou, fish, and berries, she added the bannock and tea that Inuit adopted from the Scottish whalers.[48] *Maktak*, the raw skin of the beluga, narwhal, or Greenland whale, was a delicacy that also prevented scurvy. Women added herbs, buds, roots, seeds, grasses, seaweed, birds, ducks, duck and goose eggs, mussels, and clams to the Inuit food supply. The Hudson's Bay Company ship brought tea and other southern staples. When they ran out of tea, the women used leaves from the land as a substitute. (They could still use the plant for tea now, "But all we can think is to go and buy tea from the Bay.") When food was low, sometimes the Inuit cut up the tail of a whale and boiled it.[49] Every Saturday the whalers gave out biscuits to the women and tobacco and other supplies to the men. In Inuktitut, the word for Saturday is *Xsivatarvik,* "the day we get the biscuits." When the whalers wintered over, the Inuit women would board the ships for a "Saturday-night dance with the sailors."[50] Rosie, 50, says she "will never forget the old times." Life was better in many ways, although she and the other women used to feel tired from the arduous physical labour. She traded skins at the Bay for "a lot of money."

Figure 2.2: The Annual Cycle of Processing, Sewing, and Other Female Productivity

OCT	NOV	DEC	JAN	FEB	MAR	APR	MAY	JUN	JUL	AUG	SEP	OCT

--Cooking, cleaning, cleaning household equipment/gear, caring for children, sick/elderly, moving camp, finding water---
--Scraping, Cleaning, Drying Caribou Skins (Winter Drive)-----
--Scraping, Cleaning, Drying Seal Skins---------
--Sewing Caribou Parkas for Men--
---------Sewing Sealskin Tents--
--Sewing Sealskin Clothing and Boots for Men, Women, and Children--------------------------
--Sewing Rabbit Fur Baby Clothes--
--Freezing or Drying Fish---
--Scraping, Cleaning, Drying Baby Seal Skins-------
--Sewing Summer Clothing from Baby Seal Skins--------
--Making Household Items---------------------------------
-Processing Small Game and Birds-----------------------------
--Scraping Cleaning, Drying Caribou Skins (Inland)
--Gathering Fuel (e.g., Arctic Willow)-----
------Processing Shellfish---------
---------Drying Berries---------------
-----Rendering Whale/Walrus Blubber----

Crossing Role Boundaries

The Inuit did not delineate gender roles as precisely as some have reported, which, in turn, had a profound effect on the balance of power. Generally, the heavier tasks fell to the men, but both women and men braved the elements to protect their families. Contrary to popular images of nomadic life, females crossed over into "male" territory when it was necessary for survival. They fished and helped with communal caribou drives.[51] Men built rows of stone cairns for summer hunting: "Women and children tried to scare the animals, in order to drive them towards the men who hid behind the cairns, shooting at the caribou with their bows and arrows when the herd passed by."[52] Giffen acknowledges the important assistance women and even children proffered during caribou hunting: "The women...surround the deer and drive them toward the narrow defile where the men lie in ambush ready to shoot them. This practice obtains in practically the entire Eskimo territory, with the exception of the Polar region where the men stalk the animals."[53] When necessary, women fished, helped with construction, and hunted. Similarly, although women counted food preparation and cooking as a central part of their role, men crossed into the woman's territory of preparing food and mending clothes when they lived on the land for extended periods while hunting or fishing. If necessary, males helped scrape hides, gather fuel for cooking, or engaged in other tasks commonly thought of as falling within the woman's routine. Williamson observed men using *amautiit* for carrying young children when their spouses were sick, in hospital, or deceased.[54]

This phenomenon, which we call "role crossover," has been noticed by many observers of pre- and post-settlement Inuit life. For example, Bodenhorn's research with the Inupiaq women of Barrow, Alaska, indicates that husbands consider their wives hunters because the women "ritually attract the animals":[55]

> Men and women [were] not thought to be somehow congenitally incapable of doing something generally assigned to a member of the opposite sex…going out in the whale boat was considered a man's job. If there was a labor shortage, however, women were immediately recruited…."[56]

Gwen Reimer, who interviewed Pangnirtung women during the 1990s, notes that "Inuit women maintain a strong relationship with the land: some women have been and are known as skilled hunters. Likewise, Inuit men maintain a strong relationship with the family and community: male midwives were and are not unknown."[57] Margaret Penny recorded several instances of Inuit women at Kekerten whaling station performing typically male roles. In one incident, the small whaleboats went perilously adrift in the ice floes, stranding both Inuit and Scottish men. The Inuit women formed a successful rescue party: "They were no sooner told [about the crisis] than they set off, old and young, to lend their aid."[58] In June, when the men were busy with the whale hunt, Penny witnessed Inuit women dragging whale carcasses back from the floe edge (usually an Inuk male activity) and slicing whale blubber on board the whaling ship (usually a Scottish male activity).[59] Widows might need to teach their boys about game, weather, and hunting. Similarly, Jenness observed that a man would occasionally engage in "women's work":

> Occasionally, in summer, he will cook a pot of meat if his wife is engaged for the moment in some other occupation, such as dressing skins, and he himself has nothing to do. The men often help their wives to scrape the skins, especially in the fall, when the daylight is short and new clothes are urgently needed for the approaching winter. Sometimes too they do little sewing on their own account.[60]

Jenness described an elder male who made himself a pair of water-boots in 1915: "The women were quite surprised at the excellence of his sewing, and talked about it for a long time afterwards." He observed an elder male teaching his young stepdaughter to seal, and described two women who went sealing, "leaving their husbands to mind the huts, and they often taunted the men with this afterwards."[61] Women fished with sticks (as they still do today) and occasionally killed a seal near the floe edges when the men were away, as Saila, 44, reports:

In my childhood, the women had to become hunters when all the men hiked to the mainland for caribou. If an animal arrived at the camp, they would shoot it. The men always left a gun behind for them. Women would trap or hunt seals not far from camp, perhaps on one of the nearby islands.

Rachael Uyarasuk remembers: "Our husbands …would soften caribou skins for us. Our husbands would be our helpers and we would help each other. That's how we were husband and wife before we get store-bought items."[62] Higilaq was the oldest in her family. Her father used to let her go caribou hunting by boat in summer. She killed caribou "many times." Like other women, she killed seals by cutting an air hole in the ice and waiting with clubs for the seals to come up for air. Men hunted with arrows but she used them only to play. In 1930, Giffen wrote, "though there are occasional instances of women engaging in procuring animals on land or ice, they are no doubt exceptional." [63] Giffen said that such hunting would have involved "less important animals" such as birds, fawns, foxes, marmots, and other small game that might involve working traps.[64]

By contrast, older women who participated in this study said that they hunted regularly for survival purposes when the men were away from camp. Although caribou drives were a male pursuit, females often assisted by diverting the animals toward the male hunters Certainly, their hunting included small game and lending assistance to the male hunting activities, but our consultants paint a much more complex picture. Women speak of killing seals when the men were away and helping men land seals. Many elderly and middle-aged women like Saila remember their husbands or fathers taking them hunting when they were young girls:

My older sister and I used to go with Dad. The women were hunters, too, at that time—if the women were young and strong. My father would hike up to the glacier area to hunt caribou. My mother usually stayed behind with my sisters and other families. Some girls, like my sister, went out with my father once in a while. They were using guns then, but the women did not do too much hunting. They would just follow and help.

When she was a small child, Qatsuq's father took her to Nettilling Lake, across Cumberland Sound, for caribou hunting and seal hunting—even whaling. The people would have to hike up the mountains to find caribou. Because that would take a long time, when Qatsuq was a young mother she never went hunting with her husband: "I had to raise my children." The moment her daughter was old enough, though, she returned to hunting:

I didn't go in the wintertime, but I went in the summertime. We used to catch seals on the ice, when it was breaking in the spring. The women went hunting with harpoons because at that time we didn't have any rifles. We used to hunt in the seal hole. We always had happy times when we were hunting. All the men would be at the floe edge hunting very big whales, something like killer whales, and all the women would be on the ice hunting for seals. That time we only had four boats and many men.

One woman says that being an Inuk was not really that hard. She liked hunting for seals or caribou: "When I was little, I went out by dog team with my father and I killed a caribou with a gun. I was shaking! Life seems harder looking back on it now, but back then it was easier." Sudloo, 80, loved hunting with her husband. Martha, an elder, started hunting as a child, and stopped only when her husband died. At the very least, women who accompanied the men on hunting expeditions cared for provisions and clothing, freeing the men up for the hunt itself. Even at home, Martha says, Inuit women confronted their share of polar bears:

> I'm so scared of polar bears! One time there was a polar bear that close! I never moved because every time I moved, the polar bear moved. I was holding my kid in my right hand and a cigarette and lighter in my left hand. That polar bear was standing on a very thin rock shaped like an oil lamp. He was ready to jump on me. His feet were together, ready! I just stood there. Finally, a boat came and my son killed that polar bear with a rifle, even though no one was supposed to kill polar bears then. It landed right in front of me! He had no choice but to save me—it was really going after me!

Indeed, some elder women say that the one thing they dislike most about living in the settlement is not being able to go hunting anymore. Today, Inuit men and women who wish to hunt polar bears draw lots for the privilege; gender of the polar bear hunter is determined by luck, not custom. Collaboration and role crossover in traditional Inuit life had important consequences for the balance of power between males and females.

Notes

1 Segments of this chapter appeared in an earlier version by Janet Mancini Billson as "New Choices for a New Era," pp. 43-59 in *Gossip: A Spoken History of Women in the North*, edited by Mary Crnkovich (Ottawa: Canadian Arctic Resources Committee, 1990).

2 The use of stone weirs is common throughout the Eastern Arctic, especially when the ice breaks up in late June and during late August, and the fish migrate to inland lakes. See Rémie, "Ermalik and Kukigak."

3 Wenzel makes this point: "In these activities, participants are socially joined to one another, these kinship ties structure the activity, and the activity reinforces interpersonal bonds." *Animal Rights, Human Rights Ecology, Economy and Ideology in the Canadian*

Arctic, p. 62. D. Lee Guemple found among the Qikirtarmiut of the Belcher Islands (southeastern Hudson Bay) that "all members of the local hunting camp or the regional hunting band are 'relatives' provided that they maintain some kind of regular contact with one another and cooperate according to the traditional rules" of generalized exchange. "Teaching Social Relations to Inuit Children," pp. 131-139 in *Hunters and Gatherers, 2: Property, Power and Ideology*, edited by T. Ingold, D. Riches, and J. Woodburn (Oxford: Berg, 1988), p. 133. Others, such as Franz Boas, argue that this principle operates especially under circumstances of scarcity. For a detailed discussion of Inuit kinship systems, see Nelson H. H. Graburn and B. Stephen Strong, *Circumpolar Peoples: An Anthropological Perspective* (Pacific Palisades, CA: Goodyear, 1973), pp. 156-160, and David Damas, *Igluligmiut Kinship and Social Groupings: A Structural Approach* (Ottawa: National Museum of Canada, Bulletin No. 196, 1963), pp. 180-212.

4 Canadian explorer Vilhjalmur Stefansson argued that the image of a harsh climate in the Arctic is exaggerated and that eking out a living is not as difficult as some might expect. The Inuit consultants for this book, however, stressed the essential interconnectedness of the people in surviving the long, dark Arctic winters. See Stefansson's *The Friendly Arctic: The Story of Five Years in Polar Regions* (New York: Macmillan, 1943); also, Eugene Y. Arima, "Views on Land Expressed in Inuit Oral Tradition," Hugh Brody, "Land Occupancy—Inuit Perceptions," and William B. Kemp, "Inuit Land Use in South and East Baffin Island," in *Inuit Land Use and Occupancy Project I-III*, edited by Milton M. R. Freeman (Ottawa: Department of Indian and Northern Affairs, 1976-77).

5 Diamond Jenness, *The Life of the Copper Eskimos: A Report of the Canadian Arctic Expedition 1913-18, Part A, Vol. XII* (New York: Johnson Reprint Corporation, [1922] 1970), p. 83.

6 Wenzel, *Animal Rights, Human Rights Ecology, Economy and Ideology in the Canadian Arctic*, p. 60.

7 Reported in Boas, *The Central Eskimo*, pp. 169-170. We did not observe such segregation of sexes during similar communal dinners in contemporary Pangnirtung.

8 *Qammat* is the singular form (one hut). Margaret Penny recorded in her diary of 1957-58 that some Inuit lived in larger dwellings that held two or three families. In Ross, *That Distant and Unsurveyed Country*, p. 98.

9 Alan D. McMillan, *Native Peoples and Cultures of Canada: An Anthropological Overview* (Vancouver: Douglas & McIntyre, 1995), p. 247. Duffy notes that these houses were dark inside, "rather dirty in some instances, restricted in size, heated by seal-oil lamps, but fairly well suited to the needs of...hunting and trapping." *The Road to Nunavut*, p. 26.

10 Duffy, *The Road to Nunavut*, p. 26.

11 Boas, *The Central Eskimo*, p. 30.

12 Matthau Warmow, *Extract from Br. M. Warmow's Journal of his Residence in Cumberland Inlet, During the Winter of 1857-58, Periodical Accounts Relating to the Missions of the Church of the United Brethren Established among the Heathen* 23 (1858): 91-92.

13 Boas adds that if the hunter fails to bring back a seal and the storm does not subside in time, famine strikes: "If the worst comes cannibalism is resorted to.... In such cases children particularly are killed and eaten. Fortunately, however, such occurrences are very rare." *The Central Eskimo*, p. 166.

14 Jean L. Briggs, "Expecting the Unexpected: Canadian Inuit Training for an Experimental Lifestyle," *Ethos* 19 (1991): 259-287 (p. 263).

15 This point was made by Sabo in *Long Term Adaptations among Arctic Hunter-Gatherers*, p. 2. Sabo's study centered on the Lake Harbour area. He attributes the high level of adaptability to far-reaching bilateral kinship networks.

16 From Maata Pudlat, "Boy, Have Things Changed," in Crnkovich, ed., *Gossip*, p. 17. The interview was conducted by Angela Bernal and transcribed for *Gossip* by Kyra Mancini; the authors are grateful for editor Crnkovich's permission to use this interview.

17 Stuart Hodgson, ed., *Stories from Pangnirtung* (Edmonton: Hurtig, 1976), p. 83.

18 Ross, *This Distant and Unsurveyed Country*, p. 82.

19 Naomi Musmaker Giffen discusses traditional roles in *The Roles of Men and Women in Eskimo Culture* (Chicago: University of Chicago Press, 1930); see also Eleanor Burke Leacock, "Relations of Production in Band Society," in Eleanor Burke Leacock and Richard Lee, eds., *Politics and History in Band Societies*, (New York: Cambridge University Press, 1982); and John S. Matthiasson, "Northern Baffin Island Women in Three Cultural Periods," *Western Canadian Journal of Anthropology* 6, 3 (1976): 201-212.

20 Dorais, *Quaqtaq*, p. 88-89.

21 David Morrison and Georges-Hébert Germain, *Inuit: Glimpses of an Arctic Past* (Hull, Québec: Canadian Museum of Civilization, 1995), p. 28. An example of the emphasis on male production in hunter-gatherer societies was the "Man the Hunter" symposium held in Chicago in April 1966; see Alan Barnard and James Woodburn, "Property, Power and Ideology in Hunter-Gathering Societies: An Introduction," in *Hunters and Gatherers*, edited by Tim Ingold, David Riches, and James Woodburn (Oxford: Berg, 1988), p. 5.

22 See, for example, Shepard Krech III, ed., *The Subarctic Fur Trade: Native Social and Economic Adaptations* (Vancouver: University of British Columbia Press, 1984); and A. Stevenson, "Then Came the Traders," *Inuit Women in Transition* (Ottawa: Department of Indian and Northern Affairs, 1975).

23 Wenzel, *Animal Rights, Human Rights Ecology, Economy and Ideology in the Canadian Arctic*, p. 60.

24 *The Canadian Encyclopedia Plus*; National Geographic Society, *The World of the American Indian* (Washington, DC: National Geographic Society, 1979), pp. 92-93, 95; Zebedee Nungak and Eugene Arima, *Inuit Stories/Légendes Inuits: Povungnituk* (Seattle: University of Washington Press, 2001). According to Sabo, men also used the *umiak* for whale hunting, because they were more stable than the *kayaq* (*Long Term Adaptations among Arctic Hunter-Gatherers*, p. 42.

25 Jenness, *The Life of the Copper Eskimos*, pp. 88-89.

26 J. Matthiasson, *Living on the Land*, p. 76.

27 Julian W. Bilby, *Among Unknown Eskimo: An Account of Twelve Years Intimate Relations with the Primitive Eskimo of Ice-Bound Baffin Land, with a Description of Their Ways of Living, Hunting, Customs and Beliefs* (London: Seeley Service, 1923; later published as *Among Unknown Eskimos: Twelve Years in Baffin Island*. Philadelphia: J. B. Lippincott, 1923), pp. 79, 81.

28 The more male-dominant relationship was portrayed by Jean Briggs: "Eskimo Women: Makers of Men," in Carolyn J. Matthiasson, ed., *Many Sisters: Women in Cross-Cultural Perspective* (New York: Free Press, 1974), and Briggs, *Never in Anger: Portrait of an Eskimo Family* (Cambridge, MA: Harvard University Press, 1970). Briggs' field-

work for *Never in Anger* centered on the Utkuhikhalingmiut ("Uktu") of Chantrey Inlet in the Central Canadian Arctic. She also did research among the Qipisamiut of Pangnirtung. Boas referred to the "tribes" and "subtribes" of Cumberland Sound collectively as the Oqomiut. Boas, *The Central Eskimo*, p. 32. Giffen reported that women rowed during seasonal migrations, but men crewed while on hunting expeditions. Men used paddles and women used oars for these "women's boats." *Men and Women in Eskimo Culture*, p. 4.

29 The norm of reciprocity characterized Inuit life on the land. See, for example, George W. Wenzel, "*Niniqtuq:* Resource Sharing and Generalized Reciprocity in Clyde River, Nunavut," *Geographische Zeitschrift* 84 (1995): 130-42.

30 For a discussion of a similar feminist position, see Margaret L. Andersen. *Thinking about Women: Sociological Perspectives on Sex and Gender*. Boston: Allyn & Bacon, 1997, pp. 8-9.

31 Marybelle Mitchell, *From Talking Chiefs to a Native Corporate Elite: The Birth of Class and Nationalism among Canadian Inuit* (Montréal: McGill-Queen's University Press, 1996), p. 30.

32 Mitchell, *From Talking Chiefs to a Native Corporate Elite*, p. 34.

33 Barbara Bodenhorn. "'I Am Not a Great Hunter, My Wife Is': Inupiat and Anthropological Models of Gender," *Études/Inuit/Studies* 14, 1-2 (1990): 55-74. She cites evidence that the Inupiat classify sewing, butchering, and sharing (what anthropologists might call "women's work") as part of "hunting skills."

34 Bilby, *Among Unknown Eskimos*, p. 103.

35 Marianne Lykke Thomsen, *Ethnicity and Feminism: Inuit Women in Greenland and Canada* (Montréal: McGill-Queens University Press, 1999).

36 Bodenhorn, "'I Am Not a Great Hunter, My Wife Is'," p. 59.

37 Paul Gessell, "The Art of the Matter: Inuit Art Marks 50-Year Milestone along the Rocky Road to Recognition," *The Citizen's Weekly* (March 28, 1999), p. C4, citing Maria von Finckenstein, curator of contemporary Inuit art for the Canadian Museum of Civilization.

38 Morrison and Germain, *Inuit*, p. 29.

39 Boas, *The Central Eskimo*, p. 32. Boas observed that in Cumberland Sound the Inuit caught whales in all the fiords and narrow channels. See also Tom Lowenstein, *Ancient Land, Sacred Whale: The Inuit Hunt and its Rituals* (New York: Farrar, Straus, and Giroux, 1994) for a detailed description of Inuit whaling practices and the meaning of whaling to Inuit culture; also, W. Barron, *Old Whaling Days* (Hull, Québec: Hull Press, 1895); David Boeri, *People of the Ice Whale: Eskimos, White Men, and the Whales* (New York: E. P. Dutton, 1983); and Daniel Francis, *Arctic Chase: A History of Whaling in Canada's North* (St John's, NFLD: Breakwater Books, 1984).

40 Ross, *This Distant and Unsurveyed Country*, pp. 87-88.

41 Robin McGrath, *Canadian Inuit Literature: The Development of a Tradition*, Canadian Ethnology Service Paper No. 94 (Ottawa: Natural Museums of Canada [National Museum of Man, Mercury Series], 1984), p. 5; and "Inuit Write about Illness: Standing on Thin Ice," *Arctic Medical Research* 50 (1991): 30-36.

42 Giffen, *Men and Women in Eskimo Culture*, p. 10.

43 Ross, *This Distant and Unsurveyed Country*, p. 40.

44 Ross, *This Distant and Unsurveyed Country*, p. 168.

45 Peter Ernerk, "Inuit Culture: The Kivalliq Region," in *The Nunavut Handbook* (Iqaluit, NWT: Nortext, 1998), p. 77.

46 Ross, *This Distant and Unsurveyed Country*, p. 135.

47 Quoted in Norman Hallendy, "Reflections, Shades and Shadows," *Collected Papers on the Human History of the Northwest Territories*, *Occasional Paper No. 1*, Prince of Wales Northern Heritage Centre, 1982, p. 11.

48 Dorothy Eber, *When the Whalers Were up North: Inuit Memories from the Eastern Arctic* (Montréal: McGill-Queen's University Press, 1990).

49 Ross, *This Distant and Unsurveyed Country*, p. 132.

50 Ross, *This Distant and Unsurveyed Country*, p. 87.

51 Based on reports of our consultants, plus descriptions of nineteenth century life by Boas, *The Central Eskimo*, pp. 171-173. See also Janet Mancini Billson, *Keepers of the Culture: The Power of Tradition in Women's Lives* (Lexington Books, 1995/Ottawa: Penumbra Press, 1999/Rowman & Littlefield, 2006); Billson, "New Choices for a New Era"; Hugh Brody, *Living Arctic: Hunters of the Canadian North* (Vancouver: Douglas and MacIntyre, 1987); Fred Bruemmer, et al., *The Arctic World* (Toronto: Key Porter, 1985); D. L. Guemple, "Men and Women, Husbands and Wives: The Role of Gender in Traditional Inuit Society," *Études/Inuit/Studies* 10, 1-2 (1986): 9-24; Dorothy Eber and Peter Pitseolak, *People from Our Side* (Edmonton: Hurtig, 1975); Hugh McCullum and Karmel McCullum, *This Land Is Not for Sale: Canada's Original People and Their Land—A Saga of Neglect, Exploitation, and Conflict* (Toronto: Anglican Book Centre, 1975); Morrison and Germain, *Inuit*; and Doug Wilkinson, *Land of the Long Day* (New York: Henry Holt, 1965).

52 Dorais, *Quaqtaq*, p. 17.

53 Giffen, *Men and Women in Eskimo Culture*, p. 5. Boas also describes women and children frightening seals away from holes (using sticks), thereby driving them to holes where the men waited with harpoons: *The Central Eskimo*, p. 455.

54 Robert G. Williamson, *Eskimo Underground: Socio-Cultural Change in the Canadian Central Arctic* (Uppsala, Sweden: Institutionen for Allman Och Jamforande Etnografi Vid Uppsala Universitet [Occasional Papers II—on Rankin Inlet], 1974), p. 51.

55 Bodenhorn, "'I Am Not a Great Hunter, My Wife Is'," p. 58.

56 Bodenhorn, "'I Am Not a Great Hunter, My Wife Is'," p. 60.

57 Gwen D. Reimer, "Female Consciousness: An Interpretation of Interviews with Inuit Women," *Études/Inuit/Studies* 20, 2 (1996), p. 81.

58 Ross, *This Distant and Unsurveyed Country*, p. 183.

59 Ross, *This Distant and Unsurveyed Country*, p. 183.

60 Jenness, *The Life of the Copper Eskimos*, p. 88.

61 Jenness, *The Life of the Copper Eskimos*, p. 88.

62 Rachael Uyarasuk, "Rachael Uyarasuk (Inuit)," in *In the Words of Elders: Aboriginal Cultures in Transition*, edited by Peter Kulchyski, Don McCaskill, and David Newhouse (Toronto: University of Toronto Press, 1999), p. 258.

63 Giffen, *Men and Women in Eskimo Culture*, p. 3.

64 Giffen, *Men and Women in Eskimo Culture*, p. 7. She offers an extremely detailed description of the division of labor and its variability depending upon circumstance, especially when it came to hunting, dragging large mammals to shore, fishing, curing fish, flensing seals, and caching food supplies.

3

Traditional Power:
A Delicate Balance

Most women I have known were very strong in helping create order in the camp, in shaping the future.

—Jeannie

The Woman of the Waves

Photo 3.1 Leaving with the tide in a "chestnut boat."

As carver and outfitter Jaco Ishulutaq revs up the inboard motor, Arctic terns eye us with mild interest as they follow the small chestnut boat out of a narrow inlet into Pangnirtung Fiord. The early morning sky is such a soft, velvety gray that it feels as though one could stroke it, like the belly of an old walrus lying on sunlit rocks. Only the slenderest streaks of lavender and teal tinge the margins where the sky meets the mountains.

After an hour of chugging along in early morning silence, it is time for a "land break," to empty bladders behind a boulder and to warm ourselves with tea and bannock while the sun climbs higher. Mists rise on either side of the channel as the boat glides softly into a sheltered bay. Squat charcoal rocks seem to spring from the sea like giant whales, too old and tired to thrash at us. Vaporous wraiths curl around the rocks, veiling the ragged shoreline. Real whales, small and vigilant, dive parallel to the shore beyond our boat. Jaco draws the creaky old craft close to a rock. Our companion, Peah, motions us to climb ashore. The respite lasts less than fifteen minutes, and then we set off again.

Finally, we head into Cumberland Sound. A cloying fog envelops our view for a few harrowing moments. Where are we going? The rock sentinels that warned of shoreline disappear. Then the mists magically lift, revealing an iceberg that looks like a perfectly sculpted giant wave captured off the wild Atlantic coast and frozen for eternity in glassine crystal. Then we pass an "iceberg dragon" swimming lazily in a shimmering expanse of water. The spirits must have carved the spiny ridges and long tail of the iceberg, Jaco says. We want to draw nearer but the currents around this mammoth chunk of frozen sea make it too dangerous. We will ply on toward Kekerten Island to see the remnants of the old whaling station.[1]

Peah begins to speak softly about a female being, "The Woman of the Waves," who lives beneath the icy waters. Sedna, whose real name was Sanna, she says, lived a long time ago. She was a beautiful young woman who rejected all suitors until a handsome stranger appeared in her parents' camp. He promised her a beautiful home and plenty of food: "Your lamp shall always be filled with oil, your pot with meat." They married and she followed him to a wild and foreboding land, where the "man" removed his hood and goggles to reveal himself as a spirit in the form of a fulmar or large seabird.

Rachel Attituq Qitsualik says that this was the "hateful *tuurngaq*, twisting and leering from the depths of the dwarfish and malformed mass that served as a head."[2] Sedna sent word to her father about her miserable marriage, asking him to take her home. After a time, her father and mother pursued Sedna, lured there by a rival bird-spirit, and tried to rescue her. The fulmar followed them to the shore and caused a heavy storm to frighten them. Sedna's mother, who had shamanistic powers, subdued the *tuurngaq*, but the young men who rowed the rescue boat panicked when they saw the ugly bird-spirit. They threw Sedna into the water as her parents stood helplessly by. Qitsualik, an Inuit folklorist, offers this version:

> The father wheeled about upon hearing the anguished cry of his child, and saw that the young men had thrown her overboard. And yet he was paralyzed, watching but lifting no hand in assistance, even while his daughter begged and pleaded, desperately clinging to the boat in white-knuckled desperation. She would be sacrificed, he knew then, to spare the rest of them.
>
> But still the spirit came on, writhing through the air with the speed of an arrow — for the girl still clung tightly to the boat. The monster's vengeance would have been wreaked upon them within moments if one of the youths had not lifted his oar high overhead, to bring it crashing down upon the girl's knuckles.
>
> Immediately, the other rowers followed his example, so that the girl's cries of fear and agony were quickly drowned out by the repeated blows of oars upon her now mangled hands. And still she clung, until at last her hands came apart under those blows—first the fingertips, then pieces of second digits, the flesh of which disappeared into the waters.
>
> And only when all of her fingers were completely gone, did she herself fall away from the *umiaq*. Her father met her gaze at this moment, seeing that her eyes reflected not fear any longer, but only the wisdom that comes with disillusionment and betrayal. And this was the last he saw of his daughter, this gaze that would haunt him ever after, before she slid beneath the sea, and the rowers carried him home.
>
> Yet she did not die. But she would never know her home, or family, or the surface world, ever again.[3]

Sedna sank into the deep as her tormented father watched. Her fingertips became the whales and walruses, the fishes and the seals that would feed her people abundantly forever. If the Inuit did not propitiate the souls of seals, Sedna would punish them by causing a failure in hunting and subsequent famine.[4] Sedna's mother, Lumaajuq, "was transformed into a narwhal, her long braided hair becoming the tusk borne by this species of whale." Now, Sedna lives in a lower world in a house of stone and whale ribs, guardian of the souls of sea mammals. If human behaviour displeases her, she can warn the sea mammals away when hunters try to kill them: "If this happened, no hunter—regardless of skill—could catch a single seal, upon which most Inuit depended."[5] The one thing that Sedna could not do in her watery home, though, was to comb her tangled hair. Thus, the shamans of old could use their powers to comb her hair in order to appease her and bring favor to the sea hunters.

Many versions of this story exist. One is that her father *wanted* her to marry the fulmar, instead of a human—a logical version in the days of arranged marriages and rebellious daughters. The version reported by Qitsualik is similar to the one recorded by Boas over a hundred years ago, but Boas reported that the father cut Sedna's fingers off in order to appease the spirit-bird (and save his own life).[6] In every version, the subtext of a father and daughter in conflict over her marriage—and the father sacrificing his daughter to the sea—remains the same. In 1901, Boas wrote that Sedna became the "principal deity of the Central Eskimo" and "has supreme sway over the destinies of mankind." Qitsualik maintains that, contrary to Boas' report, Sedna was never considered a goddess by the Inuit but rather as the mother of all sea mammals who deserved their respect. In any case, Inuit women still derive from Sedna a sense of power because of her defiance, resoluteness, and strong will. She still holds a central place in the ways of the people as giver of food.

Peah finishes her story: "So, women are the source of life for Inuit." She watches our expressions as she tells this ancient Inuit legend, and adds in a whisper: "Maybe the icebergs are her tears." As we write this, a defiant but peaceful Sedna, carved from black soapstone streaked with filaments of gold, watches us from her place on the desk.

ɔ꒟

Many outsider reports of traditional Inuit culture depict a decidedly male-dominant pattern. Men made the decisions; women obeyed orders. Men hunted; women stayed close to the camp. Friedl contended that "women were completely dependent on the men for their very survival."[7] Movement in the public sphere gave men the opportunity to earn reputations as hunters and to establish trading relationships with outsiders. As hunters and traders, men enjoyed opportunities for achievement, social prominence, and power, from which they excluded women: "Labour was divided between men as keepers of the land and women as keepers of the camp,"[8] underscoring the dominance of males in the public sphere and females in the private or domestic sphere.

The literature often suggests "an image of chauvinistic male hunters dominating their women and trading them back and forth as if they were property."[9] While many historical accounts portrayed Inuit women as relatively powerless compared to men, we asked consultants for this book (the oldest of whom were also born in the late nineteenth century) to remember not only their own lives but also those of their great-grandparents and grandparents. These elder women and men paint a more complex picture of female-male relations than had been reported earlier. In fact, the Inuit depict relatively balanced, if not egalitarian, power relations during the period before European contact.[10]

Pauktuutit, the Inuit Women's Association headquartered in Ottawa, has contended that men and women in pre-contact Inuit society were equal partners, with women being publicly deferential and privately influential in decision making."[11] Woman's mastery in "things female" gave her a certain kind of authority. The influence of European-style patriarchal values came with contact and, as in other societies, these values passed through "inherited" culture and socialization of children.[12] Jean Briggs made the case that "acute interdependence between husbands and wives mitigated patriarchy to give a relation nearer equality," emanating from clearly defined gender roles.[13] Elder women say rather matter-of-factly that the man was "the boss"—but they also agree that male and female jobs were equally important to the functioning of the community.[14] The disparity may lie in the fact that even the oldest women interviewed during the end of the twentieth century were born and raised 70 to 100 years earlier, when the patriarchal influence of white male explorers, traders, whalers, missionaries, and police had already permeated Inuit culture. In contrast, anthropologist John Murdoch's nineteenth century work with the Inupiaq of Barrow, Alaska, indicated that males and females shared power: "Women appear to stand on a footing of perfect equality with men in both the family and the community." Much of the work done by Arctic social scientists in the twentieth century reported "male dominance" among the Inuit but that may well have been the result of deeper cultural intrusions by southern white institutions than was the case during Murdoch's time.

According to a contemporary historian, Marybelle Mitchell, although "publicly deferential and privately influential, Inuit women probably wielded considerable informal power, which they have recently begun to exercise more overtly."[15] In any case, the concept of power involves many closely interrelated factors—played out in both household and community arenas—such as authority, influence, autonomy, social prominence, estimations of strength and skills, and differential valuations of gender role and social identity. When all of these factors are included in analysis of power relations between Inuit women and men, the picture becomes much more complicated than turn-of-the-century reports of male domination would have suggested. The unique structure of Inuktitut reflects these complexities.

Definitions of Male and Female
"More man-like...more woman-like"

Because survival was a shared responsibility, the Inuk woman's power derived from her art, her skill, and her centrality in the band's ability to endure. Males held ultimate decision-making priority, but because women's skills were equally important for survival of the family and band, women, especially elder women, enjoyed considerable respect. The woman developed competence in certain essential tasks; the man took pride in tasks that he knew best. Men realized that if women did not do all the sewing and cooking and taking care of children, men would not have life. Most did not take the woman's role for granted. Importantly, the resources of the older generation did not fall only to male offspring. Rather, a man's eldest son inherited his equipment and property, and the woman's property went to her eldest daughter.[16]

As Inuk leader Ann Meekitjuk Hanson notes, one key to male-female roles and power relations lies in the language of Inuktitut: "The word for man means the one *more man-like*, and the word for woman means the one *more woman-like*."[17] Inuktitut contains the idea that man-like and woman-like characteristics exist in every person. People expect a woman to learn sewing, but if she wants to develop "man's skills" such as hunting, "that's identified as being a part of her character rather than as something strictly linked to her sex." Hanson believes that freedom to be an individual forms an essential strength of Inuit culture: "The individual may express her character in whatever way she wishes. Whether she wants to learn her father's skills, like fixing skidoos, or to take on female skills, it is her choice and her interest."

Traditional Power Relations
"Both men and women were the leaders"

The flexible definition of male and female spills over into power relations between the sexes. The Inuit provide an excellent example of a culture in which clear division of labour based upon gender can exist side by side with flexibility and shared power. Women may not have had *precisely* an equal voice, especially after contact with whites, but their expertise in things female constituted the basis for a certain indisputable authority. Greenlandic Inuk Karla Williamson has concluded that the notion of pre-contact Inuit women as subservient to men needs debunking.[18]

The shape of traditional power relations is complex. Life *was* hard for the Inuk woman, as one elder recalls: "She was the first to rise and the last to sleep. Her husband was always right—she could be punished by her parents for not pleasing her husband." In terms of power distribution, the husband was clearly the head of the family: "He had the final word, and that's just the way it was." The Inuit tended to accept the principle of ultimate male authority, as an elder recalls: "The man was the boss...all the men." Ultimate *male authority* in matters such as moving to new hunting areas or settling intergroup disputes did not necessarily translate into impenetrable *male dominance*, however.[19] Consensus was more workable than dictatorial stances in a tiny band of nomads. Some women remember their grandmothers talking about "boss women."

Rosie argues that "the father was the boss" in the camps, while the mother enacted her critical roles in cooking and sewing. Men made decisions about when and where to move, because men were the acknowledged experts in game movements and climate changes. Jeannie agrees that men were more powerful because, if they had to move to another camp, men would choose the new site. Boas observed in the 1880s "a kind of chief in the settlement [camp], whose acknowledged authority is, however, very limited."[20] The headman was known as the *pimain* (he who knows everything best) or *issumautang* (or *isumaitoq*, one who thinks). This person was typically one whom others felt most comfortable with and "who were able to manage others to do different tasks."[21] It was usually a middle-aged man with high prestige based on excellent hunting skills and other abilities who guided rather than governed.[22] Male or female leadership was usually limited to kin-based communities; sometimes headmen were chosen to deal with special situations or crises but their tenure was short-lived.[23] When a disagreement arose, "adults together would discuss and try to fix things up, not only men but women were involved."[24] Occasional stories told of exceptional women leaders. For example, Marc Stevenson documents a female leader or "matriarch" named Soudlu at Avatuktoo, who was raised as a hunter and "father's assistant," an elder (Malukaitok) who "reputedly maintained 'despotic matriarchal power over a large settlement,'" and three women, Nuneeaguh, Kowna, and Kivitoo, who ran small trading operations.[25]

Briggs noticed that *isuma* or good judgment is a signpost of maturity and allows others to treat a person—male or female—as an "autonomous...self-governing individual whose decisions and behavior should not be directed, in any way, outside the limits of the role requirements to which one is expected to conform."[26] This has profound consequences for women's identity and autonomy as well as for the nature of leadership. Minnie Aodla Freeman recalls the role of her grandfather, Weetaltuk, as headman in pre-settlement days:

> On Cape Hope Island, he was the leader of the people, his sons and daughters and in-laws. He chose where the seasons would be spent. He performed the church services, did baptisms and burials, and divided the animals that were killed. When freeze-up came he was the first one to test the ice to see it if was safe to travel. His supply of Qallunaat goods—sugar, tea, and flour—was always plentiful.... His house was the centre of every activity: dances, church and feasting. He lacked no equipment of any sort, whether Inuk man's tools or Qallunaat tools.[27]

While not every headman had such prosperity or broad scope of powers, typically he could at least make the decision to move to another place or suggest that some men hunt for seal while others hunt for caribou. Yet, no obligation existed to obey the "orders." Other men in the camp could simply refuse to follow the headman, although for the most part they respected his wisdom and insight: "They had no ultimate control over their fellows, as anyone was at any time free to pack up and move to another camp, but they could be highly autocratic and get away with it if their prestige remained high enough."[28] Briggs has documented this in her study of Pangnirtung families:

> The senior man—who was the grandfather, grandfather-in-law, or father-in-law of all but one of the men in camp—was recognized as "leader" by almost all these young men. In everyday matters of whether or not to hunt and where and when, the elder exercised authority only over his own household members. But in long-range decisions, such as whether to move to Pangnirtung or not, the people deferred to his wishes, and when he moved his household to a new seasonal campsite, others tended to follow...."[29]

Whatever authority the headman held did not emanate from ritual or traditional titles but from the fact that virtually everyone in a camp was connected to each other—*nuatkattait*—and "this bond of relationship...keeps the people united and maintains peace and harmony in the community."[30]

Women "always had to listen to the men," Lena recalls, perhaps echoing the authority accorded the special place of headman: "If the men felt it was time to move to another area to hunt, the whole family had to follow. They didn't complain." In spite of male authority based in survival issues, elder Inuit women insist that the couple shared authority in the *ilagiit* (traditional extended family), which was defined broadly to include people linked genealogically or through social relations and the division of labor.[31] Lena insists that "mother and father, not just one, were equally respected and sometimes feared." In a similar vein, Balikci found that the father was "the recognized head of the family, responsible for all the major decisions," but his female partner enjoyed autonomy *in her sphere of responsibilities* and could influence the male's decisions.[32]

According to some women, a head couple shared leadership of the camps. Martha supports this notion: "Men and women were equal because both the girl and the boy were taught by their parents through their childhood until they reached their teens. A girl learned the man's way and the boy learned the woman's way, so it was equal." As Lepowsky found in her study of the Vanatinai of Micronesia, "respect for individual autonomy, role overlap, and public participation of women in key subsistence and prestige domains of social life" support the achievement of gender equality.[33] According to Morrison and Germain, the Inuk woman came close to full equality in traditional society, especially because she could become an *angakkuq* (shaman):

> A woman owned property independently of her husband, and was ultimately a free individual able to make her own choices. She was mistress in her own house, where her authority was complete. Her husband was bound to discuss all important matters with her, such as proposed camp moves or plans on where to spend the summer. Her opinion was heard in the dance house when deliberations were in progress, and even on the hunting field when caribou were sighted and a drive was to be organized. After menopause, some women became sha-

mans, and thus obtained considerable spiritual influence within the community. The position of women was probably highest during the summer, when people were living in small, intimate camps and behavior was less formal, less governed by the roles of male pride than during the winter.[34]

Although Inuit men might have held sway in decisions affecting the entire community, an "ethic of respect" infused daily life. Qaida, 42, remembers "the women's side":

> My grandfather was "captain of the community"—he shared that with my grandmother. They would look after the whole camp together. My grandmother delivered the babies. Both men and women were the leaders, because men couldn't look after the women in those days, or still now. My grandfather couldn't deliver the babies, sew for his family, or help other families. The woman was more looking after the women's side. She would teach us how to sew, how to make things, how to cook, how to survive, how to scrape the hides, to dry them the proper way. All those were things that men could not do. He *could*, but in those days they didn't!

Qaida believes that women earned respect for their skills and knowledge, which people viewed as essential to the survival of the band. This notion supported significant women's power. Kudloo, 86, also recalls that the husband was boss in her family—"It's always like that." Men respected women for their work, however, contributing to the balance of power: "They would respect women. Whenever I made something, I would tell my husband to be happy about it. When I was a young woman, people would talk about me—I was really good in sewing; I was a fast runner. I didn't really like it because I didn't want people talking about me, but I would talk about it to my husband. I would tell him to be happy about the things I made."

Sudloo's wedding ceremony included words about the man being the leader: "Every time my husband went hunting or camping for the year, I would go with him because my husband was the boss of the house." Yet, they were equal in their work because each had unique roles and they sometimes worked as a team. Rosie also makes this distinction: Men may have been the ultimate and legitimate authorities, but women were *equal to* men. Men may have had superior physical strength and musculature, but women were strong in other ways and balanced the male roles. Meena, a seamstress in her 40s, remembers her father's mother: "At that time, each camp had its own boss. My father and another man seemed to control the camp. Women seemed to know better than the men did—even though men seemed to be the boss. Men had more *control* over everything." Just as a man was boss for the whole camp, so within each couple male opinion took precedence. Iola describes how men have defined their power relationship with women over time:

Although they would consult with each other on crucial matters, the wife would have to agree. In the camp, we usually had one leader, but everybody had a say—even the women. We never really ignored the women or left them out of the decision-making. The men always went to the women for what size hut they want to make. The father and the mother would build the hut together, but he would ask the mother where she would like it, what shape, how they want to do it.

Qatsuq describes her father, the great Angmarlik, as the "leader for men." Qatsuq's mother worked for the wife of an American whaler, "for her place to be clean." Qallunaat used to go to the camps by small ships. "*They* used to be the boss during the whaling days," says Qatsuq. Maata agrees: "Our parents had no powers. In the old days, white man was somebody *big* with a lot of power.... Always giving and never receiving anything from them—that's what made them so powerful, I guess."[35]

Sometimes the whalers' wives became powerful leaders among the Inuit women. They employed the Inuit as guides, whalers, and processors. Among the Inuit, however, Qatsuq remembers that the men seemed to be stronger than the women and told women what to do. Women were stronger, she believes, only as cleaners: "At that time we didn't have soap, so with an *ulu* we would scrape the dirty ones [homes, skins, etc.]." The community's norms allowed men to expect women to take orders from men, but "the man was not commanding his wife all the time," recalls Iola. It depended on the couple: "If the man was really harsh on his wife, he would make a lot of commands. He was really the boss. But not all men did that, even in the old days." Males expressed power by beating women on rare occasions. An elder woman says that women should be respected for what they do and for being head of the house: "They know more about it—cleaning and all the other things they do in the house, how they care for it and the people in the family. It should be equal, the man and the woman being bosses." She fails to understand why men "are always being called the head," reflecting her own sense of empowerment from generations gone by. Women were far from docile, nor did they hesitate to use "sharp verbal attacks" to express their wifely power. As Matthiasson said of his observations among another Inuit group, "If all did not go well for a Tununermiut wife, everyone else in her camp soon knew about it."[36]

Females figure significantly in the world of Inuit religion, myths, and legends. Sedna, as we saw earlier, was a pivotal Inuit mythological figure, reflecting women's prominence in spiritual matters. All versions of the Sedna story credit her with creating the sea life that has nourished the Inuit for centuries. Her place as protector of the sea animals has earned her a place in Inuit mythology and religion forever.[37] The female represents "Creativity and...the life-giving powers of the cosmos."[38] Women exchanged stories and ideas with other women as they worked, and perpetuated genealogical, kinship, and folkloric knowledge.

Female shamans gave crucial "magical performances, with the purpose of insuring good luck to the men in the hunt":

> A common ceremony is that of the wife of a hunter placing a piece of blubber on his *qajaq* when he departs. Bears are thought to be especially susceptible to charms, and certain measures must be taken by the wife to insure pleasing the spirit of the Polar bear, so that more of the same species may be taken.[39]

Jenness wrote of two powerful female shamans who lived in the early 1900s:

> Two shamans, a man and a woman, began to hold a séance, but in the midst of it they drank a little of the blood of the deer, although this had been prohibited to them. The man…lost all his shamanistic powers. The woman…walked away towards the sun up the side of a ridge. Suddenly she disappeared into the ground, and a moment afterwards a dog sprang out from the same spot; then the dog disappeared and the woman took its place again. This occurred three or four times in the sight of all the people.[40]

Sometimes couples shared the shaman role in their camp: "Ilatsiak's wife, who was a shaman like her husband, put her fingers into her mouth on one occasion; gradually her hands became the feet of a wolf, then her head and body began to change and finally only her legs remained human."[41] As Qatsuq recalls in *Stories from Pangnirtung*, people thought women had special healing powers:

"A SHAMAN HELPED HER"

For each camp, there were many medicine women. They didn't use plants. They did it by eating food. At that time, they did not believe in God. My mother was bleeding for a long time until one of the ladies who was a "magic"—a shaman—helped her. Sick people had a ghost in them. She was the only one who could cure her, by driving out the ghost. When my mother was bleeding, the rest of the people wanted her to get pregnant, so she did. That is why she had me. That cured the bleeding and I am still living now.

When my parents returned to Kikitaet [Kekerten] from Oomanayoak, they saw that the people had changed from their old ways of life into bad and evil ways and worshipped a false god they called Sanah [Sanna, now Sedna]. My mother wanted the people to turn back. So, in the summer my mother got some women together to make caribou clothes. The clothes were at least two times as big as the ones Eskimos wore or maybe bigger than anybody could use on earth. My mother cut out the patterns and the women sewed them together. They made everything—the parka, the *kamiks*, the mittens, the pants—the whole works! After they finished, they threw everything into the water because that is what my mother wanted them to do. They made those clothes so that they could throw them into the water and no longer be followers of this god!

But even after this incident, the people remained evil. My mother tried to tell them to turn from their evil ways but because she was a woman, they didn't listen. When my father helped her, then the people listened.

> Three women were witch doctors [shamans] in those days and they, too, gave up their witchcraft to follow Sanah. The witch doctors I remember were Ookaetok, Inumah, Alevattah, and Ashoeetok. I never knew others. Since I was a small girl, people have turned from their old way of believing that there was a god that helped them in hunting, a god that was on earth, and one that the witch doctors saw.[42]

Another elder tells of being born during winter in an igloo when women had their babies alone. She says she "never heard of Jesus or true God," but she remembers about Sedna. She clarifies the relationship between shamanism and power. The man was boss in the camps, but occasionally "a woman was boss":

> Great-grandmother Asivak was a shaman who also was camp boss. She had a great power. I heard this from other people [Etuongat told her—her family never talks about it]. My great-grandmother had so much power! My grandmother used to tell me before she died, every time they would go to something in another tent, my grandmother wasn't allowed to go because it was too scary. One time she peeked in the tent and they were doing scary things. The women served as healers for sick people.

During the missionary period ("before we became religioned"), this elder tried to become Anglican. Her husband rejected the idea, so they separated for a year. The clash between the old beliefs and the new religion tore some couples apart.

Orchestrating the Family Structure
"Inuit women were the planners"

As in similar cultures, the man's extended absences from home fortified the woman's position.[43] Women created small associations as they lived in camps and "looked after everything" while the men were hunting. The Inuk woman made the day-to-day decisions while at the same time respecting her husband's authority. Ann Meekitjuk Hanson explains: "Inuit women were the planners. They look after the future with their children and their grandchildren. All the men did was bring the food, most of the time, and the women planned everything for their life ahead."

Spousal Exchange and Adoption Decisions

Women may have held ultimate sway in running the household and organizing family activities, but men traditionally orchestrated the family structure with decisions that affected girls and women in the most intimate of ways. Men organized spousal exchange and adoptions, although some men consulted their wives on such matters.[44] Women explain these practices in terms of the men's greater ability, because of their travels, to understand the complex relations among bands that wandered in irregular patterns across the North and lived miles apart when they settled in for winter. Men had to knit together the loose threads of Inuit society in ways that cut across unraveled loyalties and convoluted lineages.

Conferring with his wife was particularly important long ago with regard to the Inuit custom of institutionalized spouse exchange. "This form of socially sanctioned extramarital sexual and procreative activity—apparently devoid of jealousy—is difficult [for Qallunaat] to comprehend," according to Pamela Stern and Richard Condon, and accounts of it tend to leave the impression that Inuit couples lack strong emotional bonds to each other.[45] Stern and Condon argue the opposite: Mutual dependency often combined with both affection and passion. Although spouse exchange may have been useful for economic and family alliance reasons, women recall that husbands usually consulted their wives and seldom took the practice lightly. Spouse exchange always occurred on a temporary basis (lasting a few days to a few weeks) and usually required the consent of all partners, including the wives. In fact, sometimes one or both women initiated the exchange,[46] because it represented a type of marriage that permanently linked the couples and their offspring.[47] Generally, the practice took place to help forge kinship bonds between unrelated families and did not involve promiscuity,[48] although it might have served to "diffuse sexual tension and jealousy" and "provided a legitimate avenue for the expression of sexual attraction."[49] Stern and Condon hypothesized that spouse exchange "provided a reciprocal and egalitarian method for extramarital sex that neither threatened the critical marriage bond nor led to its dissolution."

Although spouse exchange may have performed that latent, unintended function, we have not found evidence that this was the manifest, intended function of the practice. Jenness speculated that in some cases of spouse exchange "lust seemed to be the only motive,"[50] although other motives might have been hidden from him as an outsider. Jenness reported that jealousy created conflict between husbands and wives but did not necessarily lead to divorce.[51] Birket-Smith believed that "husbands in these cases are so far from being jealous of one another that the exchange of wives is, on the contrary, considered to be one of the most effective means of emphasizing *and* strengthening a friendship."[52] In addition to "exchange marriages," trial marriages were common. Both polygamy and polyandry occurred occasionally, although RCMP were known to break up such unions by deporting co-wives to other camps.[53]

Women did not always have the right to make their own choices about child bearing and adoption (see chapter 13). If a man wanted to adopt a child out to someone he knew wanted a baby, he could make that decision unilaterally: "Back some years ago, men would do that. The lady didn't have any right to say no or yes. Even if the wife says no, if the husband says yes, that's it." (Now, both parents are likely to decide together, with the woman's decision taking precedence if they differ.) Apphia Agalakti Awa tells this story of how her father forced her mother to give Apphia to her mother's uncle:

> She didn't have a baby sister, and she was desperate to keep me because I was a girl and I was her first child...my father didn't want to keep me. He was hoping for a son...my mother was not a very bossy woman and she was having a hard time at that point, so she had to listen to her husband. He was so much older than her. She couldn't say no to him even though she was crying so much inside at the thought of having to leave me... She told me later that on her way to Repulse Bay she had a really hard time. She had been breast-feeding, so her breasts were swollen and filled with milk.[54]

Female Infanticide

Female infanticide, present in a handful of Inuit societies when missionaries arrived in the Canadian Arctic during the mid-nineteenth century, furnishes another arena of possible male dominance in previous eras. Most Inuit women who remember the practice (or heard stories of it) believe that men had the deciding voice in whether or not to kill a baby at birth. The practice was not spread evenly throughout regions or camps, and may not have been as prevalent among the ancestors of Inuit in present-day Pangnirtung as it was in other areas. For example, Guemple pointed out that, while female infanticide was a "pan-Arctic method of disposing of children," the rates varied from low in Igloolik to high in Pelly Bay and Spence Bay, "where all female children not betrothed at birth or adopted by some couple are ordinarily disposed of in this manner."[55] Oopik, in her 60's, had not even heard of killing infant girls: "We are just starting to realize that in those days people in different camps lived different ways of life."

Contrary to some journalistic reports, the Inuit practiced infanticide against male as well as female babies. Rita contends that it mattered little whether you gave birth to a male or a female in the old days: "If you had six sons, you wanted a daughter; or if you had lots of daughters, you wanted a son." Numbers of children and gender balance counted more than the infant's sex *per se*. (Certainly, that remains true today in the case of adoption). Anthropologist Balikci thought that male and female infanticide was a way to control the size of the population in the face of ecological pressures.[56] He said that either parent, the grandfather, or a widowed grandmother could decide to kill a child, but sometimes it was simply the strongest personality in the household that made the fateful decision.[57] Balikci also believed that Inuit used female infanticide specifically to control the composition of the population so that the female/male ratio would be even at marriageable age. He cites Rasmussen's count in Pelly Bay of 66 boys to 36 girls (indicating a higher rate of female than male infanticide) but a much more evenly balanced ratio of 73 males and 67 adults (indicating a higher male death rate from natural causes, hunting accidents, suicide, and so forth). In the days before Inuit moved into settlements, the male mortality rate certainly surpassed that of females, which may have reduced the differential impact of female infanticide.[58]

Burch believed that abandoning an infant to die of exposure was actually an attempt to save an older child's life when the family was migrating and resources were extremely low; the infant was simply the youngest of either sex.[59] Others have countered that female infanticide constituted a blatant expression of male dominance over women: Males were simply more valuable in an era when the Inuit depended on men's superior upper body strength to hunt and drag home the heavy caribou or whale carcasses—comparatively "unproductive" baby girls were smothered or left to die of exposure. Yet, Inuit women interviewed for this study explained infanticide as a form of achieving gender balance, not as an expression of hostility toward females.[60] Remie finds no empirical evidence for either gender balance or population control arguments in his study of another Baffin community further north (Pelly Bay). Rather, he speculates that the intrusion of white influences into the Eastern Arctic (especially among the Netjilingmiut and Arviligjuarmiut, whose rates of infanticide seemed very high compared to other bands) forced a migration to the Repulse Bay and Chesterfield Inlet areas, leaving an imbalanced sex ratio in its wake.[61]

An accurate picture of the extent of female infanticide and its role in the balance of power between men and women remains murky because (as mentioned in the Preface) anthropological and missionary records of the time suffered from distortion based on competing cultural values and male bias: "…the majority of non-Inuit who recorded Inuit oral literature were male missionaries and male anthropologists who had no interest in or access to the female domain" or problems.[62] Additionally, few elders are able or willing to talk about the subject definitively. Guemple speculates that the relatively balanced male-female adoption rates in contemporary Inuit society may reflect the disappearance of female infanticide.[63] Improved health care and the decline of both infant and maternal mortality rates would also support balanced adoption in more recent times.

Arranged Marriages

In order to ensure that every male of marriageable age would have a partner, arranged marriages became customary out on the land. Arranged marriages functioned to ensure that all marriageable adults found partners during the childbearing years—an important concern for small populations in a harsh climate. Arranged marriages also protected bloodlines against intermarriage, linked bands with each other, and, according to some older women, served as a buffer against prostitution, promiscuity, or early pregnancy without the stability of a relationship. Balikci's study of the Netsilik Inuit indicated a preference for arranged marriage with a cousin or more distant relative.[64] However, Inuit who lived around Cumberland Sound forbade that practice as incestuous, as Boas recorded: "Marriages between relatives are forbidden: cousins, nephew and niece, aunt and uncle, are not allowed to intermarry."[65] Occasionally, a man broke the monogamous pattern by taking a second wife—it simply was too difficult to support more than one family.[66]

The spousal promise was usually made after a girl's birth or even before birth, conditional upon the baby's gender. This practice was common throughout the Canadian Arctic, including in Cumberland Sound. Sometimes, the males grew tired of waiting for a girl to reach maturity (usually defined by her first period) and married someone else, leaving the girl open to other suitors.

Although mothers and grandmothers often arranged these unions, men were also instrumental in arranging marriages, as Meeka, in her early 50's relates: "I had a boyfriend, but my grandfather on my mother's side arranged a marriage with a different guy because he was related to us. He wanted him to be with me. I didn't really want to marry him, but I had no choice." Sometimes a mother would write to another woman about her son's interest in the other's daughter. Before the days of writing, "If the son wanted to be with her daughter, he would go to the camp and be with her. The fathers would agree." Jeannie, 50, entered a marriage arranged by her fiancée's father: "I minded, but I was expected to go along with it." She likes that women today can choose their own husbands.

Martha, in her 90s, recalls that, "when a man wanted someone for a wife, he would get her from another settlement. The parents would give her to the man for marriage." Formal marriage followed a period of living together and the birth of the first child. Most married out of their camp. The couple would then move to the camp of whichever family needed them most, but in Baffin this almost always meant the woman's family: "Usually the young couple must begin housekeeping with the young wife's family and the young man, if he belongs to a strange tribe, must join that of his wife." [67] (Boas noted that the man then cannot truly be "master of his own actions" until his wife's parents have deceased.) On the positive side, the young couple helped her parents during this period, to ensure that they knew all the skills essential for surviving in their own household. If the couple lived with his parents, the groom would pay a bride price. If the relationship dissolved during the trial period, the bride's parents would have to return the gift. Otherwise, either male or female could abandon this "trial marriage" without penalty.[68] Lucy, 39, shares memories of arranged marriages:

> People from different camps used to gather in Pangnirtung. That's when I met my husband-to-be. Parents have to say "yes" if they wanted him for a son-in-law. Women didn't know their husband when they became husband and wife. That's the part where women seemed smaller than men. The parents would say yes and that's it. Even if the girl didn't want him, they went through with it. [How long did these marriages last?] Forever.

Both the onset of menses and the arranged relationship with a man marked a girl's transition into adulthood. Similarly, as soon as the male married or lived with a woman, he entered adulthood. Iola explains: "Now you've got your own way and you can handle it—raise your family! No more dependence on your parents." The community expected the man to provide for his pregnant woman. (Now, an expectant mother will often stay with her parents and depend on them for support.) "Before, when they started living together, they had to move from the parents' house. If they lived within it, the man had to provide everything. That was *his* responsibility."

Sometimes marriages occurred between older men and young teenaged girls, as Apphia Agalakti Awa remembers in *Saqiyuq: Stories from the Lives of Three Inuit Women*: "My mother…was just a girl, not even fit to have a husband. Her family gave her to a man who was old enough to be her father."[69] Marriage occurred without benefit of a formal ceremony until after the advent of missions, although sometimes the man presented a gift to the woman's mother. The camp leader married older couples. Women vaguely remember saying a few words to each other that included "one man, one woman." Martha recalls: "They would talk and make promises to each other." Kudloo looks back: "My mother arranged my marriage; we were never married by a minister, though." Sudloo simply lived with her husband, and enjoyed hunting and fishing with him.

When missionaries began to filter into the region during the late 1800s, marriage ceremonies in the Christian manner became commonplace. Many couples were married by a minister at the old Anglican mission in Pangnirtung, built long before the Resettlement Period. One woman, 78, recalls that had her first baby in the fifth year of living with a man: "When we were formally married by a reverend, we had two kids and there was one along the way, but I didn't know it!" Another woman, 82, remembers getting married long after she had three children: "We got married when we moved to the settlement. We had nine more children, but they all died. Two right after each other, a few months apart. Some died in the ocean. I only have three left." Naomi, 63, recalls being married at the mission when she was 19:

> My parents didn't choose for me, but the man asked my parents if he could marry me without asking me first. I didn't even know him. We weren't friends, but he lived in the same camp. I didn't want to marry him, but we all had to obey our mothers and fathers.

According to Stern and Condon, marriages occasionally emerged from mutual attraction, so arrangement of marriage was not a rigid practice that absolutely removed the power of personal choice from women and men:

> While traditional pairbonding was heavily influenced by the availability and economic competence of the potential partners, there was certainly room for infatuation based upon personality and physical appearance. While the amount of "room" for romance was probably small, Inuit society has always been characterized by a high degree of negotiability and flexibility. This flexibility allowed for the expression of individual choice in all domains of Inuit life.[70]

Whether marriage was arranged or followed a period of living together that led to the couple's commitment (or both), it was not always a pleasant experience for the young girl. Like the mythological Sedna, some women abhorred their parents' choice of mate, but older women insist that arranged marriages usually worked out well after a while. People expected couples to make the adjustment for the sake of the community, if not for themselves. Martha explains: "Although they would go through the good and the bad times, they knew they would always be together." She describes how her parents arranged the relationship, not without some pain for a young woman in her teens:

> I was very scared of guys when I was a young teenager. I never wanted to live with a guy, but I had my first child when I started living with my man. I would be in bed with him and he wouldn't do anything because he could see how scared I was. He waited for me.

Did the strangeness and anxiety of being thrown into an intimate relationship with someone who was not yet a friend dissipate with time? Naomi says, "In some cases, we got to know each other and started to love each other and miss each other, more and more. We got along." In other cases, the arrangement led to lifelong unhappiness, as one elder laments:

> A man who was old enough to be my father came to our camp to speak to my parents. They told me to leave the tent and stay in his boat until I was given permission to return. I was in the boat all day and all night, and I knew what was happening. My parents told him that he could have me as his wife, and I was sick with anger and sadness but could say or do nothing.... There were many times when he would go out on the land or to the floe edge to hunt, and in my heart I wished that he would never come back alive, such was my feeling for that man.[71]

Marriage was "scary and painful for some women," Ann Meekitjuk Hanson recalls from her childhood, especially for those who were promised to someone when they were infants:

> ...the young man took the girl, whether she was willing or not. She often struggled and cried. She was very frightened. If they had to travel, she was tied up and held by men. She would struggle and cry until she got used to her new husband. I saw my aunts and their friends crying for help and wrestling with the men they were to spend the rest of their lives with. I am told by my women friends that a kind, considerate man did not force his new wife to have sex with him. He waited until she was tamed! Some women were not so fortunate; they were raped![72]

Linda Pemik writes of her memories of her youth in Rankin Inlet: "Most of my sisters, I remember them getting married and they were crying, they were dragged to the altar, and they were forced to say yes."[73] Qatsuq agreed that arranged marriages were a "bad" custom:

"HIDING IN THE BLANKETS"

I remember one time we were at the church on Blacklead Island, and there was a reverend baptizing the man who was to become my husband. That was before we even met. I was the only one there. That night when I was home in bed with everything on—clothes and blankets and everything—I heard the door open and close. I was hiding in the blankets. I used to have beautiful long hair. There stood a man with long hair, mustache, bearded. I was really scared! He was there to go to bed with me!

I put on my new parka with beads on it. At the back, some pennies made noises like bells. When I moved they made *so* many noises, but my mother never woke up or said anything, which made me hate my mother for ignoring it. I was very unhappy that night.

Anyway, he joined me in my bed. I just lay there because I didn't know what to do. I was scared because my mother always told me not to hang around boys. When we were in bed I tried not to touch the guy, but I think that I touched him when we fell asleep. I thought he was creepy.

We started living together after that night. He stayed with me because my mother thought that I had to learn some more. When I was old enough, we moved to my husband's camp and we stayed with my mother-in-law until I knew how to sew a tent and get ready for the things that my husband needed.

My husband had some very big dogs that looked almost like wolves. They always stayed at the porch of the *qammat* [hut]. Whenever they called me in to eat, I would use a stick to scare the dogs away. I had trouble going in there. I was 16; a year later, my first baby was born. After we became a couple, I was sad because whenever I went out visiting, my husband would go after me—he thought I would be with someone else. He was really jealous.

Qatsuq and her husband formed a new household. Over time, they worked out a balance of power that enabled their family to survive. Women of her generation criticize women who were born during the transitional era, who began to choose their marriage partners. Younger women take it for granted that the choice of mate will be theirs alone. Says Martha, "It was good in that time, but in this new generation I'm seeing that it's not better. The girls aren't scared of the guys anymore." Elders fear that some young girls in the larger settlements may be swept up into prostitution. They lack control and discipline; and their marriages are more likely to end in divorce. One widow in her 60s complains:

The girls get more babies without being married. I didn't really like marrying my husband, but then later I did...I grew to love him. Now, most of the younger ones end up with divorce, like my daughter. She has three kids; she married on

her own without us arranging it. I don't like it. When we were living in Bon
Accord, I never knew about divorce!

Divorce, indeed, was rare after the birth of a child but that may have to do with
the custom of couples living with parents for a year or two.[74] Chances are that
couples that had not discovered irreconcilable differences before striking out on
their own would have little need for divorce later in the relationship: "In many
cases couples who were incompatible did not stay married more than a few days
or weeks."[75]

Respect for Parental Authority
"I was like a slave to them"

Obedience to parental wishes lay beyond the power relationship between
wife and husband. Families brought up children to respect their elders,
male or female: "Whatever they say, it's the law." Even for adults, parental authority held great importance. For example, Jeannie felt unhappy when her husband said they should live with his parents, but she readily agreed because their
parents told them not to talk back to each other: "I was like a slave to them because my husband's mother always had something for me to do." Jeannie would
never argue or shout at her mother-in-law, because her own mother said she
must listen to her in-laws: "Once in a while my mother-in-law would look at me
with a disagreeing face because I would do something that I didn't really know
how to do." What would happen to a woman if she disobeyed her husband?
"Whenever we disagreed about something, either my parents or his parents
would tell us not to do that. They would tell us more about the life that's ahead
of us." Malaya Akulujuk, in her early 50s during the Resettlement Period, explains what that means:

> It isn't too long ago that I was a teenager. We were told to look forward to
> our future and what to expect out of life: "Children, don't forget the real Es-
> kimo way of life, and tell your kids the wonderful Eskimo stories...." Also,
> they used to say that we would be living more like white people, and it's true.
> Our kids will be used to this new life. We have to prepare our kids. I hope
> nobody forgets the things that happened a long time ago. We had a better way
> to live than what we are living now. Life was magnificent.[76]

The "life ahead" of the Inuit during the Resettlement Period presented a
challenge that clearly demonstrated the wisdom of the elders in admonishing
couples to respect each other and balance the power between them. The elders
recall vivid and poignant memories of bad times when animal migrations by-
passed them, or when inexplicable climate changes disrupted ancient patterns of
survival. The elders of the elders, long since dead, could also tell stories about

Inuit persistence through the Little Ice Age (from about 1650 to 1850) and other warming or cooling trends over the course of 3,000 years. Their advice carried the same weight even for twentieth century Inuit, who were about to face an unprecedented combination of challenges: starvation, disease, and resettlement. Now Jeannie tells her own daughters-in-law "to be good to their husbands and not to argue over something that's not important. I'm following in my mother's footsteps." Female power, complex in pre-settlement days, was about to become even more complicated.

Notes

1 Marc G. Stevenson explored this site in the 1980s: *Kekerten: Preliminary Archeology of an Arctic Whaling Station* (Yellowknife: Prince of Wales Northern Heritage Centre, Department of Justice and Public Services, GNWT, 1984).

2 Rachel Attituq Qitsualik, "The Problem with Sedna: Part One," *Nunatsiaq News* (March 5, 1999). One "problem" is that her name was not Sedna (the commonly used but anglicized form) but Sanna, also known as Nuliajuk. Qitsualik explores the many versions of Sedna in a 1999 *Nunatsiaq News* series, Nunani. Others in the series were: "The Problem with Sedna: Part Two—The Father's Rescue," March 12; "The Problem with Sedna: Part Three—The Betrayal," March 19; "The Problem with Sedna: Part Four—The Mythic Being," March 25; "The Problem with Sedna: Part Five—Beautiful Variation," April 8, 1999; "The Problem with Sedna: Part Six—Her Influence," April 15.

3 Qitsualik, "The Problem with Sedna: Part Three—The Betrayal."

4 Asen Balikci, *The Netsilik Eskimo* (Garden City, NY: The Natural History Press, 1970), p. 200. Franz Boas reported yet another version of the Sedna story in "The Eskimo of Baffin Land and Hudson Bay," pp. 163-165.

5 Qitsualik, "The Problem with Sedna: Part Six—Her Influence."

6 Boas, *The Central Eskimo*, pp. 176-181. See also, "Arctic Legend: The Myth of Sedna, Goddess of the Sea Animals" [Excerpted from an 1888 U.S. Bureau of Ethnology report by Franz Boas, published by University of Nebraska Press], *Canadian Geographic* (First Edition, 1998): 86; also, Erik Holtved, "The Eskimo Myth about the Sea-woman," *Folk* 8-9 (1966-67): 145-154.

7 Ernestine Friedl, *Women and Men: An Anthropologist's View* (New York: Holt, Rinehart, and Winston, 1975), p. 40-41.

8 Pauktuutit, *The Inuit Way*. For a full discussion of the distinction between domestic and public spheres, see Michelle Rosaldo, "Women, Culture, and Society: A Theoretical Overview," in *Woman, Culture, and Society*, edited by Michelle Z. Rosaldo and Louise Lamphere (Stanford: Stanford University Press, 1974); and Peggy Reeves Sanday, *Female Power and Male Dominance: On the Origins of Sexual Inequality* (Cambridge: Cambridge University Press, 1981). Rosaldo and Lamphere softened the distinction later in response to a growing literature that documented role-crossover and role reversal. See Rosaldo's "The Use and Abuse of Anthropology: Reflections on Feminism and Cross-

Cultural Understanding," *Signs: Journal of Women in Culture and Society* 5 (1980): 389-417.

9 J. Matthiasson, *Living on the Land*, p. 73.

10 Fossett claims that eighteenth and nineteenth century Inuit societies were "egalitarian within their own confines, but each was convinced of its own superior position relative to all other groups defined as strangers, including Inuit." *In Order to Live Untroubled*, p. 218.

11 Mitchell, *From Talking Chiefs to a Native Corporate Elite*, p. 47.

12 Friedrich Engels made this argument in *The Origin of the Family, Private Property and the State*, but was referring to the advent of patriarchy in agrarian societies: "Patriarchy is all-pervasive; it penetrates class divisions, different societies, historical epochs" (Eleanor Burke Leacock, ed., New York: International Publishers, 1985, pp. 120-121). Since the Inuit did not pass through an agrarian stage, Engels' theory does not exactly apply.

13 Brody, citing Jean Briggs, in *The People's Land*, p. 192. Rowland and Klein define patriarchy as "a system of structures and institutions created by men in order to sustain and recreate male power and female subordination. Such structures include: institutions such as the law, religion, and the family; ideologies which perpetuate the 'naturally' inferior position of women; socialization processes to ensure that women and men develop behaviour and belief systems appropriate to the powerful or less powerful group to which they belong." Robyn Rowland and Renate Duelli Klein, "Radical Feminism: History, Politics, Action," in *Radically Speaking: Feminism Reclaimed*, edited by Diane Bell and Renate Duelli Klein (London: Zed, 1996; Spinifex, 1999), p. 15.

14 John Murdoch, *Ethnological Results of the Point Barrow Expedition*, Ninth Annual Report of the Bureau of Ethnology to the Secretary of the Smithsonian Institution, 1877-88 (Washington, DC: U.S. Government Printing Office, 1892), p. 413.

15 Mitchell, *From Talking Chiefs to a Native Corporate Elite*, p. 4.

16 Mitchell, *From Talking Chiefs to a Native Corporate Elite*, p. 32.

17 Angela Bernal interviewed Hanson in 1988.

18 Aaron Spitzer, "Inuk Scholar Aims to Shake Up Arctic Science," *Nunatsiaq News* (May 4, 2001).

19 Compare Eleanor Burke Peacock's *Myths of Male Dominance: Collected Articles on Women Cross-Culturally* (New York: Monthly Review Press, 1981); and Bernard Saladin d'Anglure, *Man (angut), Son (irniq) and Light (qau): Or the Circle of Masculine Power in the Inuit of the Central Arctic. Anthropologica* 20, 1-2: 101-144, 1978.

20 Boas, *The Central Eskimo*, p. 174.

21 M. Stevenson, *Inuit, Whalers, and Cultural Persistence*, p. 235.

22 Hall, *Life with the Eskimaux*, pp. 523-524. *Angajuqqaq (angakuk or shaman)* also means leader, implying in this case the capacity to give orders to another person. John L. Steckley and Bryan D. Cummins, *Full Circle: Canada's First Nations* (Toronto: Prentice Hall, 2001), p. 44.

23 Fossett, *In Order to Live Untroubled*, p. 208.

24 Uyarasuk, "Rachael Uyarasuk (Inuit)," p. 261.

25 *Inuit, Whalers, and Cultural Persistence*, pp. 137, 169.

26 Briggs, "Expecting the Unexpected," p. 267.

27 Minnie Aodla Freeman, *Life among the Qallunaat* (Edmonton: Hurtig Publishers, 1978), p. 70.

28 J. Matthiasson, *Living on the Land*, p. 85.

29 Jean L. Briggs, "'Why Don't You Kill Your Baby Brother?' The Dynamics of Peace in Canadian Inuit Camps," in *The Anthropology of Peace and Nonviolence*, edited by L. Sponsel and T. Gregor (Boulder: Lynne Rienner, 1994), p. 159.

30 Jenness, *The Life of the Copper Eskimos*, p. 86.

31 Guemple, "Teaching Social Relations to Inuit Children," pp. 132-133.

32 Balikci, *The Netsilik Eskimo*, pp. 109, 116.

33 Maria Alexandra Lepowsky, *Fruits of the Motherland: Gender in an Egalitarian Society* (New York: Columbia University Press, 1993), p. 306.

34 Morrison and Germain, *Inuit*, p. 31.

35 Pudlat, "Boy, Have Things Changed," p. 18.

36 J. Matthiasson, *Living on the Land*, p. 83.

37 See Nelda Swinton, *The Inuit Sea Goddess/La Déesse inuite de la mer*. Exhibition catalogue (Montréal: Montréal Museum of Fine Arts, 1980).

38 Robert G. Williamson, *Eskimo Underground*, p. 55.

39 Giffen, *Men and Women in Eskimo Culture*, p. 6. Another example of women's prominence in spiritual matters appears in DeMallie's review of ethnographic reports on the Lakota. He indicates that gender dictated the division of labor (upheld more by the women than by the men), but that women had considerable power beyond the domestic circle. They were important participants in religious ceremonies. Raymond J. DeMallie, "Male and Female in Traditional Lakota Culture," in *The Hidden Half: Studies of Plains Indian Women*, edited by Patricia Albers and Beatrice Medicine (Lanham, MD: University Press of America, 1983), pp. 237-265.

40 Jenness, *The Life of the Copper Eskimos*, p. 192.

41 Jenness, *The Life of the Copper Eskimos*, p. 193. See also Asen Balikci, "Shamanistic Behaviour among the Netsilik Eskimos," *Southwestern Journal of Anthropology* 19, 4 (1963): 380-396.

42 Hodgson, *Stories from Pangnirtung*, pp. 79-80.

43 National Geographic Society, *The World of the American Indian*, p. 95. For a theoretical analysis of the impact of male absence on female roles, see Janet Mancini Billson and Martha Stapleton, "Accidental Motherhood: Reproductive Control and Access to Opportunity among Women in Canada," *Women's Studies International Forum* 17, 4 (July-August 1994): 357-372.

44 Burch asserts that, in Alaska, the wife equally determined spousal exchange. Ernest S. Burch, Jr., *Eskimo Kinsmen: Changing Family Relations in Northwest Alaska* (New York: West, 1975).

45 Stern and Condon, "A Good Spouse is Hard to Find," pp. 198-199. They conducted their fieldwork among the Kanghiryuarmiut of Prince Albert Sound and the Kanghiryuatjagmiut of Minto Inlet. Because the Copper Inuit are "distinct from other Inuit groups," they point out that generalizations should be made with caution (p. 201).

46 D. L. Guemple, *Inuit Spouse-Exchange* (Chicago: Department of Anthropology, University of Chicago, 1961), p. 1.

47 Guemple, *Inuit Spouse-Exchange*, p. 3.

48 Ernestine Friedl, quoted in Marlene Mackie, *Constructing Women and Men: Gender Socialization* (Toronto: Holt, Rinehart, and Winston, 1987), pp. 40-41; see also Guemple, *Inuit-Spouse Exchange*; Peter Freuchen, *Book of the Eskimos* (New York: Fawcett, 1961); and Clark N. Garber, "Sex and the Eskimo," *Sexology* (March 1962). For other discussions of spouse exchange see Ernest S. Burch, Jr., "Marriage and Divorce among the North Alaskan Eskimos," in Paul Bohannon, ed., *Divorce and After* (Garden City, NY: Doubleday, 1970); Ernest S. Burch, Jr., and T. C. Correl, "Alliance and Conflict: Inter-Regional Relations in North Alaska," in D. L. Guemple, ed., *Alliance in Eskimo Society* (Seattle: University of Washington Press, 1972); David Damas, "The Problem of the Eskimo Family," in K. Ishwaran, ed., *Canadian Family: A Book of Readings* (Toronto: Holt, Rinehart and Winston Canada, 1971); Jenness, *The Life of the Copper Eskimos*; and McElroy, *Alternatives in Modernization*. Spousal exchange also carried the assumption that offspring would be cared for throughout their lives; see Fossett, *In order to Live Untroubled*, p. 212.
49 Stern and Condon, "A Good Spouse is Hard to Find," p. 205.
50 Jenness cites the case of a woman who complied with the spouse exchange requests of a shaman whom she feared (and who had three wives). *The Life of the Copper Eskimos*, p. 86.
51 Jenness, *The Life of the Copper Eskimos*, p. 163.
52 Birket-Smith, *The Eskimos*, p. 140.
53 Dorais, "The Canadian Inuit and Their Language," p. 203.
54 Wachowich, *Saqiyuq*, p. 21.
55 D. L. Guemple, *Inuit Adoption*, Canadian Ethnology Service Mercury Paper No. 47 (Ottawa: National Museums of Canada, 1979), p. 18. John S. Matthiasson stresses that children were valued highly out on the land, and that the practice of infanticide probably occurred only with infants who had not yet been named, mainly with females, and not as frequently as early observers thought: "The Maritime Inuit: Life on the Edge," in *Native Peoples: The Canadian Experience*, edited by R. Bruce Morrison and C. Roderick Wilson (Toronto: McClelland & Stewart, 1995), p. 96.
56 Balikci, *The Netsilik Eskimo*, pp. 147ff; also, Asen Balikci, "Female Infanticide on the Arctic Coast," *Man* 2, 4 (1967): 615-625. See also David Riches, "The Netsilik Eskimo: A Special Case of Selective Female Infanticide," *Ethnology* 13, 4 (1974): 351-362; and Carmel Schrire and William Lee Steiger, "A Matter of Life and Death: An Investigation into the Practice of Female Infanticide in the Arctic," *Man* 9, 2 (1974): 161-184.
57 Balikci, *The Netsilik Eskimo*, p. 149.
58 Balikci, *The Netsilik Eskimo*, p. 152.
59 Burch, *Eskimo Kinsmen*.
60 Clark N. Garber, "Eskimo Infanticide," *The Scientific Monthly* 64, 2 (February 1947): 98-102.
61 Rémie, "Ermalik and Kukigak."
62 Robin McGrath, "Circumventing the Taboos: Inuit Women's Autobiographies," in *Undisciplined Women: Tradition and Culture in Canada*, edited by Pauline Greenhill and Diane Tye (Montréal: McGill-Queen's University Press, 1997), p. 226.
63 Guemple, *Inuit Adoption*, p. 88.
64 Balikci, *The Netsilik Eskimo*, pp. 100, 156.
65 Boas, *The Central Eskimo*, p. 171.

66 J. Matthiasson, "The Maritime Inuit," p. 95.

67 Boas, *The Central Eskimo*, p. 171. Rémie in "Ermalik and Kukigak" said that most residents of Pelly Bay lived with the husband's family after marriage. See also Balikci, "Anthropological Field Work among the Arviligjuarmiut of Pelly Bay, NWT." Patrilocality versus matrilocality undoubtedly varied from camp to camp, region to region, and period to period. See, for example, Balikci's description of flexibility among the Netsilik: Although they tended toward patrilocality, other arrangements could be made on the wife's side (*The Netsilik Eskimo*, pp. 99, 102). Jean L. Briggs, based upon her more contemporary research, documented matrilocality in Pangnirtung: "...the core comprised an old man, some of his married daughters and their families, and his other unmarried children of both sexes." "'Why Don't You Kill Your Baby Brother?,'" p. 158.

68 Stern and Condon, "A Good Spouse is Hard to Find," p. 205.

69 Wachowich, *Saqiyuq*, p. 21.

70 Stern and Condon, "A Good Spouse is Hard to Find," p. 200.

71 Quoted in Hallendy, "Reflections, Shades and Shadows," p. 7.

72 Ann Meekitjut Hanson, "Life in Nunavut Today," pp. 87-90 in *The Nunavut Handbook: Travelling in Canada's Arctic* (*Iqaluit*, NWT: Nortext, 1998).

73 Linda Pemik, "In the Same Year, Far to the South," in *Women's Changing Landscapes: Life Stories from Three Generations*, edited by Greta Hofmann Nemiroff (Toronto: Second Story Press), 1999.

74 Jenness, *The Life of the Copper Eskimos*, p. 163; and Knud Rasmussen, *Intellectual Life of the Copper Eskimos. Report of the Fifth Thule Expedition, 1921-24*, Vol. 9 (Ottawa: n.p., 1932), p. 51.

75 Stern and Condon, "A Good Spouse is Hard to Find," p. 205. In any case, divorce was rare throughout Canada and difficult to obtain until 1968. Margrit Eichler, *Family Shifts: Families, Policies, and Gender Equality* (Toronto: Oxford University Press, 1997), pp. 46-47.

76 Akulujuk was 61 at the time of her interview; from Kikitaet (Kekerten), reported in Hodgson, ed., *Stories from Pangnirtung*, p. 77.

4

Traditional Socialization:
Learning by Doing

My mother taught me everything by showing me how to do things out on the land.
—Meenah

Teachers on Land and Sea

Photo 4.1 A young boy learning how to track and shoot a seal.

The family has risen slowly at dawn, like a flock of birds stirring at first light. Again, Peter and Leah Qappik and their children will be our teachers for a few days. As we gather supplies for the three-hour boat trip to Shark Fiord, the family's traditional camp, we wonder how this scene might have appeared a hundred years ago. We must go out with the tide and come back on the tide, Sheila warns, or Pangnirtung harbor will be too shallow for her father to navigate the boat into its protected place on the beach. The sleepiness that slows all of us down to a dream-like pace tempers the sense of urgency, but eventually we manage to crowd into the small, home-built craft. The bannock has been stowed, and tea is boiling in a dented old pot.

Over the steady hum of the motor, the family quietly chats with us, pointing out landmarks and teaching us a few words of Inuktitut. Susa, eight years old, is the most patient teacher. Her ease in English matches an effortless fluency in her native language. We learn common nouns and how to count to ten. She teaches us the names of the wildlife around us—seals, lemmings, Arctic char, Arctic hares, and various birds.

Suddenly, 10-year-old Paul, who has been riding at the prow in charge of a small rifle, calls out that he has spotted a seal. Hearts begin to pump faster as Peter swings the boat toward a tiny black spot hundreds of feet away. It looks to our untutored eyes like a bit of debris floating along the choppy blue waves. Peter turns down the motor and lets the boat coast toward the seal. Paul takes aim, his young body stretched precariously across the prow. The rifle crack reverberates off the icebergs and rocks, puncturing the deep silence. The single shot has been successful. Peter quickly brings the boat alongside the seal, which now floats slightly below the surface, seeping its rich, red blood into the chilly waters. With one deft stroke, the oldest daughter, Peepeelee, scoops up the seal with a net and Peter secures it with a harpoon; together they pull the treasure onto the stern deck. The seal lies there until we arrive at the camp, its silver fur glistening in the morning sun, still and lifeless. Only its weight keeps the seal from slipping over the side.

Paul seems pleased, but everyone is very matter of fact about this young boy's feat. Peter has been teaching him how to spot, identify, kill, and skin seals since he was a toddler. Now Peter lifts Peepeelee's year-old son onto his knee and lets him help steer the boat until we near the old camp. Teaching again.

As we talk about the day before drifting off to sleep in our tent, we share the strange admixture of emotions the seal hunt evoked: pity for the seal; shock at the ease and simplicity with which one can take a life; the realization that, because this family will use every part of the seal, from food to skin for clothing to innards for their dogs, it is part of the natural and essential flow of their lives.

The scene repeats itself two or three times when we return to Pangnirtung a few days later, since now the family can put the meat into the community freezer as soon as we make shore. By now, *we* are beginning to see the difference between a seal and a wave or a piece of seaweed. We are learning to discern the round-headed ring seal that Inuit prefer to eat versus the hairpin-shaped head and neck of the less desirable harp seal. Inuit also eat square fin seals as well as baby harp seals. For skins, all are useful.

Two days later, an elder woman makes us boots after hammering and chewing dried sealskin from a previous excursion into soft flexibility. The foot is made of bearded seal, the white "spat" is boiled ringed seal, and the leg is plain ringed seal. We have to keep the boots in the freezer, especially during warm weather, but they will protect us on the coldest of days. Out here, on the land and on the sea, the cycle of life seems quite straightforward, after all.

◌

In any culture, gender plays an enormous role in determining a child's self-image, patterns of work and play, and opportunities as an adult. The socialization process tends to reproduce idealized visions of appropriate gender behaviour—what it means to be female or male. Children might resist or reinvent these images, or create new ones for their generation.[1] Nonetheless, the driving visions behind gender identity change slowly, even when lifestyles shift dramatically, as in the case of the Inuit.[2]

Out on the land, both girls and boys learned self-restraint and non-aggressive behaviour, as they were raised without corporal punishment or verbal derision. Teasing and gentle reminders—and ignoring tantrums—were the preferred methods of raising children. This pattern of socialization apparently has changed very little since observations by Diamond Jenness between 1913 and 1918:

> Eskimo children show little respect for their elders in the manner to which we are accustomed. They address them as equals, and join in any conversation that may be taking place, not hesitating to interrupt or even correcting their parents.... Generally speaking, boys and girls grow up like wild plants, without much care or attention from the time they can run about till they approach puberty.[3]

Guemple observed that Inuit view children as "essentially complete social persons" who do not need to be taught so much as they need to be guided. Children represent an opportunity for Inuit parents to invest themselves in for the enrichment of souls and protection of the future. As a father asked when confronted with the prospect of the government removing his children to residential schools: "What use am I, what purpose do I serve, if I cannot bring up my own children? I do not know myself, and I do not know what to do with myself and I have no sense of on-going significance in my life if I cannot bring up my children."[4] Out on the land (and still to some extent today), the child's knowledge was drawn out through direction, experience, and modeling: "From four days after birth a child possesses its entire life potential in capsule form; and the business of socialization becomes one of assisting the new member...to realize the potential of his or her pre-established identity."[5] Thus, much socialization of Inuit children is indirect and very subtle. One direct form of socialization appears in family games that parents create to confront young children with issues that will inevitably challenge them in purposeful games that allow the child to work through the panoply of natural emotional responses—anger, fear, envy, and jealousy. Briggs described one of these minor dramas:

> The games actually enhanced the children's safety even while they elicited their fears. They relieved children of the burden of carrying their painful, dangerous, antisocial feelings alone, and they indirectly suggested solutions for those feelings. The adult who, with no sign of fear, asked a little girl why she did not kill her baby brother instead of carrying him, on the one hand recognized the possibility that the child might want to kill; on the other hand, she was demonstrating that such thoughts were not so terrible that they had to be hidden, and that she trusted the child not to act on them. Most importantly, she was also giving the child an opportunity to realize that she enjoyed nurturing that baby brother and did not entirely want to kill him.[6]

Traditionally, girls and boys each received training in how to carry out the typical male and female roles, sometimes by direct teaching but more often by eye contact, modeling, negotiation, and exhortation. Guemple reported, for example, that Qiqiqtamiut mothers teach their babies to identify aunts and other relatives through eye contact so that by 14 to 18 months old, the child knows the kinship terms and faces for the extended family—up to 35 people in an average camp![7] As the child grows older, games are used to help the child verbalize kinship terms and connections. In turn, these connections spell out for the child how she is expected to interact with various family members, which leads to learning the content of gender roles appropriate for each stage in the life cycle. Other learning about gender roles took place by example rather than by words: "Children expected to learn through observation" how to become a whole person who was capable of fitting into camp life economically and socially.[8] The entire community took part in socializing children about social relations, kinship, roles, and essential survival skills.

Photo 4.2 A boy and his best friends, Iqaluit.

Preference for the Male Child
"He would become a hunter"

Jenness noted seventy years ago that "boys are more apt to be spoiled than girls, probably because they are more errant and come less directly under their parents' influence."[9] Female socialization occurred within the context of favoritism toward males. Oopik insists that when she was a little girl, people valued boy babies and girl babies "just the same," but others claim that when a baby was born, "people seemed happier" when it was a boy. Their own mothers were proud of them if they gave birth to a son. Families revered male babies because they saw them not as babies but as boys who would grow up to be hunters. This tendency to favor male children constituted a critical message that filtered its way into female and male consciousness, self-image, and role blueprints. Indeed, Briggs thought that it was not unusual for a male child to learn how to kill his first animal by four or five years old, albeit with the help of adults.[10] His enjoyment of killing was fostered from infancy so that he might easily assume the mantle of responsibility associated with providing for his family. A family feast would honor the boy's first significant game kill.

The Ideal Woman, the Ideal Man
"All the good things"

Long ago, children wore gender-neutral animal skins that reflected only minor variations between males and females. The direction of decorative lines, for example, was vertical for males, horizontal for females, but babies were dressed similarly in the soft fur of rabbit skins. Beyond that simple differentiation lay complicated expectations for female and male behaviour. Eking out a living out on the land depended on how well boys and girls learned to fulfill crucial roles of provider, protector, and processor of food and skins. Young boys wore amulets that would help them become good hunters. Young girls wore amulets that would ensure their later ability to bear male babies.

Women and men paint the image of a "good Inuk woman" in times past with broad strokes: She was a good seamstress, a good cook, and a good mother. The Inuk woman focused her energies on the home.[11] She took care of the children, preserved the food and cooked it, designed the family's shelter, moved the shelter when seasons or animal movements dictated, and made all the family's clothing. According to Powers, many outsider reports of traditional life among aboriginals fail to adequately document or value women's contributions as processors of food and skins. In the case of Inuit women, her role was absolutely critical.[12] Just as women in agricultural communities helped with the harvest, an Inuk woman occasionally hunted, but she usually stayed close to home.

Elders who remember life in the mid to late nineteenth century and early twentieth century say that a good Inuk woman would not have too many children and would make essential contributions to her family's well-being. Always, a heavy workload loomed on the horizon: "The women used to sew a lot. At that time they were really good workers, but now some are not." If a woman could not do her work properly, she would feel ashamed. Being honest, faithful, and kind—and being a good teacher of the skills necessary to survival—also defined her value as a woman. This vision persists, except that so many of today's Inuit women move beyond the confines of the home in order to help provide for the family's food, clothing, and shelter. Geela explains:

> My mother made clothing and tents from skins and fur. My grandmother showed her how to chew the skins to make them soft. I was part of that, too. They used to come here to the settlement for groceries and things that they needed. Back then, women usually worked on clothing because they didn't wear things bought in a store, only animal fur.

Hunting responsibilities took men on long, arduous journeys far away from the home fires. A clear measure of a man's performance lay in his ability to "take good care of his family," his inner circle of relatives and his neighbors. Muckpah remembers being told that if he did not become a good hunter, he "might as well not think about having a family as they would only starve."[13] When an especially successful hunt yielded a whale or several caribou, this circle extended to the entire community. Precision and acuity in hunting allowed the Inuk male to define his identity and character from boyhood onward.[14] Fathers, brothers, grandfathers, and uncles played a critical role in teaching the young boy the requisite skills. Making dog sleds, harnesses, harpoons, and spears helped him do his job more effectively, as Ben depicts:

> They used to say that you would never become a man until you could manage your own family. You have to be able to hunt polar bears and caribou, and to harpoon seals, without using rifles. You have to make snowhouses and sleds on your own. You have to have a dog team. If the person has this "degree," he's ready to get married. Now it's hard for a young man to prove himself like that.

Qualities of patience and kindness marked the desirable Inuk man. Muckpah recalls being warned as a boy to treat his sister well because "someday she'll give you water to drink."[15] This caution pointed to the need for both male and female skills to ensure survival, each for the other, and each in equal measure.

A Natural Discipline Out on the Land
"My mother told me"

How did these visions of the ideal man or woman come into being? Inuit women believe that the imperatives of survival led to a natural discipline that dictated what it meant to be female or male. The way of life on the land is the best teacher: "You just do it naturally." A story told by Hallendy reveals how the counterbalance between women's cleverness in sewing and man's prowess in hunting defines the gender vision:

> At this point, I asked how she would describe the virtues of her favourite daughter to me so as to entice me to take her as a wife. The room was filled with other women who looked on with amused anticipation. She began by telling me how good her daughter is, how clean she keeps her hair, and, above all, how well she can make things. I replied that was not sufficient to take her as a wife because I didn't know all the things that the girl could *not* do. "Never mind," the mother said, "what she can't do I will show her or do myself. It will be a good match." Then the mother looked at me with a smile spreading over her face and asked, "What kind of boat do you have?" I replied that I didn't have even a small canoe, and she shot back, "Then who needs you for a son-in-law?" The room was filled with gales of laughter.[16]

Although children under five years of age were treated identically by both parents, socialization by the same-sex parent began shortly thereafter and lasted throughout adolescence and into adulthood.[17] Occasionally, Inuit have reportedly raised female infants as boys until puberty—and sometimes vice versa—for pragmatic reasons.[18] "Progress rituals" marked the child's achievements: the first duck egg collected; the first pair of mittens made; or the first rabbit killed.[19] A woman testifies to a natural learning process that helped the Inuit persist through thousands of years in the Arctic: "Me, I'm still learning from the older people. Every time I visit them, I learn more." Parents frequently use the phrases "watch," "listen," and "pay attention" to underscore the practical modeling they give children.[20]

Parents taught their children what they need to know at each age, in line with their level of maturity and readiness to learn. An elder remembers that "the mother would organize the girls and the father would organize the boys." By the age of five or six, girls began to help with childcare and to carry babies on their backs as soon as they were physically able. A mother looked after her family and older daughters assumed responsibility for looking after the little ones, cooking meals, and sewing. Younger girls needed guidance in helping to sew the family's supply of clothing, which had to be replenished every year. Scraping sealskins down to the bare hide and managing the hesitant flame of the *qulliq* added to the growing list of female skills. Even now, it is common to see a young girl walking around with a baby in the hood of her *amautik*, practicing for her own eventual motherhood. By the time a girl emerged from adolescence, she knew what to do and how to do it. This is still very much the case. Qatsuq describes how a mother taught a daughter to be a good Inuk woman:

> I never smoked in all my life...not tobacco or cigarettes or a pipe. My mother always told me not to use that, so I never touched it. When I was with my husband, I would never cheat on him because that's what my mother told me. When I was a teenager, my mother told me not to hang around with boys because she thought it was no good. When I was old enough, my mother made me a *qammat* in Kekerten. Did you see those whale bones? That's where I lived and it's still in the same place.

As in many hunting and gathering cultures, a young girl's first period marked a significant change in her status. Martha, 92, recalls that girls felt very shy about this rite of passage:

> Sometimes we didn't go out because we were scared of people. At that time, long before the reverends started coming here, they would let girls sleep in a little tent when they had their very first period. In wintertime, they would stay in an igloo. If you have your period, you're not allowed to eat raw meat. It has to be cooked. When you had a baby, you had to labour on your own. You had to be out of the main tent. They built you a very small igloo and heated it, or a very small tent in the summertime.

These and other lessons came by example and by word of mouth. Men taught their sons how to hunt and to load *qamutiik* with things they needed for excursions into the wilderness. A young boy latched onto his father because of his physical strength: "If the father said we had to get up at three o'clock in the morning to go hunting, we would get up at three o'clock and bear the hardship." Roposie, born in 1948, grew up on the land with six sisters and five brothers. His father taught him how to hunt by bringing him along when he was young: "I liked it very much. I can't always go hunting now." By ten years old, boys accompanied the men, checking on seal nets or fox lines. They were responsible for tending the dogs during short hunting trips. J. Matthiasson reported that youths who did not meet their father's standard could be subjected to harsh ridicule from the older men.[21]

Names and Naming
"It's a part of the culture that's hard to understand"

Language influences the way an Inuk woman thinks of herself and has important consequences for her relationships with her partner, family, and community. Three practices that affect gender identity and socialization go back for centuries but persist today. First, images of male and female tend to blur as infants are named after a person (or persons) who recently died, regardless of gender. Jenness pointed out that the *nature* of the kin relationship is more important than the *sex* of the individual. For example, rather than referring to nephew or niece, Inuktitut draws the distinction between "a man's and a woman's brother's child, and a man's and a woman's sister's child."[22] This is yet another example of the relative gender neutrality of this language. Second, since Inuktitut has no word for male or female as an identity marker, there is no counterpart to the English pronouns "he" or "she." Third, until recently Inuit women did not take the man's last name upon marriage because Inuit did not have last names until resettlement. This means that historically, at least, women did not necessarily derive their identity from their husband's lineage.

If a grandfather or great-grandfather worked as a whaler or a trader with the Hudson's Bay Company, a family might have an English last name like Ford or Kelly. In 1963, Keith Crowe, then northern service officer in Pangnirtung, launched a process with the Inuit for replacing disc numbers with surnames based on native names. Later, "Project Surname" spread unofficially through the rest of the Canadian Arctic.[23] During the Resettlement Period, Euro-Canadian influence extended to first names. Names from the Bible—the one book translated into the syllabics system that missionaries invented for writing Inuktitut—were "Inuit-fied" by changing the last syllables. For example, Mosesie derives from Moses, Zachiasie from Zachiah or Zachariah, Pauloosie from Paul, Jonasie (or Joanasie) from John or Jonah, and so forth. Some female names appear to spring from older Inuit names: Saila, Meeka, and Peepeelee. Others, such as Leah, Jeannie, or Annie, reflect the Christian tradition.

The first practice, "naming," helps perpetuate Inuit customs, rules, values, and expectations about gender from one generation to the next and provides Inuit children with an identity very early in life. Naming involves passing on the name(s) of recently deceased community members to the next newborn, regardless of gender. It does not matter whether a female child receives a boy's or a girl's name. A boy named after a female might be raised as a female: "People also believed—and some still do—that a male child's sexual parts could split open a few moments after birth, his penis shrinking inside with the boy thus becoming a girl. This phenomenon was called *sipiniq* ('the splitting')."[24] In fact, "a female is commonly named after a male relative, and vice versa. The commemoration—reincarnation—of the important person takes precedence over the gender of namesake...."[25] Dahl found the same tradition among the Saqqarmiut of Greenland: "Thus, when a person dies...social relations are reestablished because the newborn receives the qualities and social position of the deceased person."[26]

A child might be named after *everyone* in a small community who died in the past year, creating a list of five or six names from which people can calculate the year in which she or he was born. Names are imbued with anticipated characteristics (such as independence, humor, or good hunting skills). Because a baby receives names until she is about a year old, relatives have time to allow her to respond to various appellations. If she cries unreasonably, people assume someone (deceased) has yet to be named. Naming helps in the grieving process because those who have passed on "still live." The names evoke memories of former community members, as Nuttall described, and may infuse male attributes into females and vice versa:

> The name is independent and idiosyncratic, a person's life stream through which flows strength and character.... The name contains properties of the deceased which are ineradicable and, to some extent, naming determines a child's developmental path. Once named, a newborn child is both him/herself and the person(s) whose names s/he receives. Acquisition of a dead person's name embellishes, or even creates, a living person's genealogical and social identity. Kin relationships are extended beyond biological kin to encompass a wider network of people related both biologically and socially to the deceased.[27]

The newborn's soul-name ensures continuity and immortality—a place in the living social circle of friends, relatives, and ancestors.[28] For example, Ann remembers a close friend with whom she was planning a trip to England. When the friend died unexpectedly, people gave a child her name almost immediately. She adds: "I recognize that character in this child who is now nine years old. I left my plan to travel with my friend incomplete. Now I have an opportunity to go one day to England with her [through her namesake]. I can complete that action. It is not left unresolved. You don't just drop your emotions when someone passes away. You can complete the circle. It's important to me, and it's part of the culture." Another woman named her daughter after her husband's deceased sister. Her husband asked his father what they should name the child. The husband "had not really resolved the death of his sister, so it was important to him to name her that way." If a baby reminded the family of the namesake in some small way, "you start to love him even more or to spoil him...."[29]

Parents will take a newly named child to visit the family of the child's namesake. One woman told of a baby named after a young man who had committed suicide. When they visited the young man's home, the baby "seemed to be at peace in the father's arms." Naming links the community together in an infinitely complex series of interconnected circles: "The bereaved members are visibly comforted by this young life, whose presence embraces all the hopes that were a part of the life just ended." Naming cements generations and unrelated families into a special bond that is sometimes as strong as blood ties. The practice gives children numerous people to whom they are responsible: "You are not just there with your family; you are a part of everybody, and you have multiple relationships to many different people." Says the Rev. Roy Bowkett, former minister of the Anglican Church in Pangnirtung and director of ATTS: "Naming...binds members of the extended family together. For example, a child named after a past aunt retains the status that the relative enjoyed. Indeed, the child's own siblings will call their sister, 'my aunty.' Of course, the child so named will also be expected to exhibit the qualities of the dead person."[30] A young woman who adopted her baby daughter out to her own mother calls the infant "little sister." In turn, her mother calls a little boy named after her deceased grandmother, "Granny." These traditional naming patterns, which persist today, differ from other cultures, as a teacher clarifies:

> I saw an older person come up to a three-year-old child and shake her hand, and I said to myself that in white culture we would never do that. I went to someone and asked why she did that. It's because that child is named after her husband. Here was a woman of 60 greeting a child as if she were her husband. That part of the culture is hard to understand sometimes.

Women told of a newborn baby who developed a heart murmur; after good medical care, the irregularity disappeared a few days later. Shortly thereafter, the baby's grandfather died of a heart attack. The family took the heart murmur as a "sign of passage...the life was in the name and it was yearning to find a home." As Dorais suggested, naming plays a critical part, along with customary adoption and marriage, in helping to preserve kindreds (closely related family groupings) that characterized life on the land.[31] In other words, naming helps to transport *relatedness* through kinship into communities that are comparatively larger than the camps were. Dorais noted that this survival mechanism can create divisions in the community but also creates "an ecocentric identity" in which "a person's position within the universe cannot be dissociated from his or her active relations with the community, nature, and the material world."[32] The customs surrounding naming contribute to a slowing down of the potential negative impacts of rapid social change. Naming patterns changed somewhat after the influx of missionaries but remain an integral part of Inuit identity formation.

The flexibility of male and female roles, opportunities for role-crossover during childhood socialization, and the gender neutrality of naming patterns all contribute to how girls and boys think of themselves as Inuit children and, later, as Inuit men and women.

Notes

1 McElroy discusses the change process in "The Negotiation of Sex-Role Identity in Eastern Arctic Culture Change," *Western Canadian Journal of Anthropology* 6, 3 (1976): 184-200; and "Canadian Arctic Modernization and Change in Female Inuit Role Identification," *American Ethnologist* 2, 4 (November 1975): 662-686.

2 For a discussion of gender socialization in the Canadian context, see Mackie, *Constructing Women and Men*. Barrie Thorne documents both obvious and subtle transformations of girls' and boys' behaviour into conventional gender roles during the early childhood years in *Gender Play: Girls and Boys in School* (New Brunswick, NJ: Rutgers University Press, 1993).

3 Jenness, *The Life of the Copper Eskimos*, pp. 169-170.

4 Quoted in Robert G. Williamson, *Eskimo Underground*, p. 50.

5 Guemple, "Teaching Social Relations to Inuit Children," pp. 134-135.

6 Briggs, "'Why Don't You Kill Your Baby Brother?'" p. 176. See also her discussion of contradictory values in "Living Dangerously: The Contradictory Foundations of Value in Canadian Inuit Society," pp. 109-131 in *Politics and History in Band Societies*, edited by Eleanor Burke Leacock and Richard Lee (New York: Cambridge University Press, 1982).

7 Guemple, "Teaching Social Relations to Inuit Children," pp. 138-139.

8 Dorais, *Quaqtaq*, p. 95.

9 Jenness, *The Life of the Copper Eskimos*, p. 170.

10 Briggs, "'Why Don't You Kill Your Baby Brother?'" p. 161.

11 Lyn Hancock, "A Good Woman in the North," *North* 22 (September-October): 12-15, 1975.

12 Marla N. Powers, *Oglala Women: Myth, Ritual, and Reality* (Chicago: The University of Chicago Press, 1986).

13 James Muckpah, "Remembered Childhood," *Ajurnarmat, International Year of the Child: Issue on Education* (Eskimo Point, NWT: Inuit Cultural Institute, 1979), p. 40.

14 Markoosie. *Harpoon of the Hunter* (Montréal: McGill-Queen's University Press, 1974); Donald B. Marsh, *Echoes from a Frozen Land* [edited by Winifred Marsh] (Edmonton: Hurtig, 1987).

15 Muckpah, "Remembered Childhood," p. 41.

16 Quoted in Hallendy, "Reflections, Shades and Shadows," p. 8.

17 Balikci, *The Netsilik Eskimo*, p. 104.

18 Jean L. Briggs, "Expecting the Unexpected" and "Lines, Cycles and Transformations: Temporal Perspectives on Inuit Action," in Sandra Wallman, ed., *Contemporary Futures: Perspectives from Social Anthropology,* ASA Monographs 30 (London: Routledge, 1992). The practice of cross-gender socialization has been documented in the Canadian Central Arctic by Bernard Saladin d'Anglure, "Du foetus au Chamane: La Construction d'un 'Troisième Sexe' Inuit," *Études/Inuit/Studies 10* (1986): 25-113; and in East Greenland by J. Robert-Lamblin, "Sex Ratio et Éducation des Enfants d'Ammassalik (Est Gronland): Les Enfant Changes de Sexe a la Naissance" (Deuxième Congrès International sur les Sociétés de Chasseurs-Collecteurs, Québec), 1980.

19 Briggs, "Expecting the Unexpected," p. 269.

20 Briggs, "Lines, Cycles and Transformations."

21 J. Matthiasson, *Living on the Land*, p. 79.

22 Jenness, *The Life of the Copper Eskimos*, p. 84.

23 Valerie Alia, *Names, Numbers, and Northern Policy: Inuit—Project Surname, and the Politics of Identity* (Halifax: Fernwood, 1994), p. 52.

24 Dorais, *Quaqtaq*, p. 64.

25 Alia, in *Names, Numbers, and Northern Policy*, said that only Polar Inuit maintained gender specific names.

26 Jens Dahl, *Saqqaq: An Inuit Hunting Community in the Modern World* (Toronto: University of Toronto Press), 2000, p. 55. An excellent discussion of the kinship and spiritual complexities of naming can be found in Guemple, "Teaching Social Relations to Inuit Children," pp. 134-135.

27 Nuttall, *Protecting the Arctic*, pp. 66-67, 89.

28 For a comprehensive view of Inuit naming practices throughout the Arctic, see Alia, *Names, Numbers, and Northern Policy*.

29 Uyarasuk, "Rachael Uyarasuk (Inuit)," p. 265.

30 Roy Bowkett, "*Keenahvee?* (What's in a Name?)," *Anglican Journal* (May 1996), n.p.

31 Dorais, *Quaqtaq*, p. 103.

32 Dorais, *Quaqtaq*, p. 103.

III

METAMORPHOSIS

When I try to sleep at night, I think to myself, 'how did I pull through all of this?' So many changes in such a short time! Nobody else in the world has seen so many changes in such a short time like Inuit. [1]

—Maata

Photo 5.1 En route to Kekerten Island to visit the old whaling station, 1988.

5

The Bad Times:
Starvation Stalked the Land

We were all confused—even our parents. What are we going to do?
—Qaunak

The River

Photo 5.2 Arctic poppies along the Duval River.

We plod up the Duval River valley, between Mount Duval and Pangnirtung, a determined pair of hikers trying to get a sense of life out on the land. Fed by glaciers and snow banks, the crystal-clear river tumbles crazily down from a pristine lake, rushes along a boggy meadow, and whips past gigantic Tea Rock. The water roars over huge boulders that litter the riverbed just before mingling into the saltwater fiord below. In stark contrast to the river's abandon, we painstakingly make our way up a narrow trail that keeps us precipitously close to the torrent. The rocks edging one side of the path are so large and flat-sided that they perfectly mirror the river's roar, making it sound like there is a second river on the other side. The path gives way to boulders that we must crawl over on hands and knees, risking a fall to the sheer granite below. At one point, the river slips under a frozen ice bridge left behind as the valley snow melted away. The giant white arch defies gravity as it spans the gorge. Banded with a strangely luminescent blue-green, the ice bridge looks as finely sculpted as a snowhouse crafted by an Inuk's knife; but nature carved this remarkable structure.

The river wears its richest garments. In late July, Inuit women gather tiny blueberries from low plants that spread stubbornly after winter's dark yields to summer's light. Flowers skim across the tundra, carpeting the barren land and lining every little creek that gurgles toward the mother river. Arctic poppies nod in a translucent yellow reminiscent of spring sun. Poundnaits boast purple velvet petals that stand out against white Arctic cotton—a royal robe, indeed, for this northern desert. Tiny daisies, white starbursts, and a deep burgundy wheat-grass scatter their colors along the creek banks.

We reach Tea Rock, a favorite resting place for the Inuit, after three hours of hiking along the river. We are famished, thirsty, and ready to sit for a while on the huge boulder's many-colored coat of moss and lichens—ivory, gold, rust, and black. Long ago, it crashed down the mountainside and landed next to the river, teetering precariously on the rocky slope. We make our tea with a one-burner camp stove, munch on trail mix, and stretch our legs. As far as we can see in any direction, no human life, no buildings, no telephone poles or automobiles, no litter or exhaust fumes mar the solitude. The air is as clear and clean as the streams from which we drink. Only a tiny black and white Arctic bunting chirps a few feet above us, as if to announce our presence to her hidden friends. The sense of meditation and of being at one with Mother Earth overwhelms us, and we do not speak. The Inuit call this state of mind *Qiinuituk*:

> This is when you are alone, the lonely living thing far away from earthly things and filled with peace. This sense of peace fills every corner of your mind. It is more satisfying than any joy you have experienced in your conscious life because it runs

deeper than happiness. It can mend broken thoughts and feelings, and having experienced it gives you the knowledge that it can come again when you feel there is nowhere to go.[2]

We make our way back down the gorge reluctantly, using our walking sticks to maintain balance on the uneven trail. We leap across spongy pads of tundra, taking care not to crush the islands of wild flowers in our path. The trip down seems almost as arduous as going uphill. The next day, with aching knees and sore calves, we agree with the older women about the hills—it is hard walking in this place! Two days later, we take a friend up to see the ice-bridge. It has already melted into the river, reminding us that the transformation of the land is constant. Perhaps it is the same for the people.

ଓ

L ife out on the land can easily be idealized in retrospect, but Inuit elders speak openly about waves in the sea of tranquility. For example, shamans had the power to kill in retribution for seemingly minor infractions. Adultery, battering, and fighting occurred on occasion. Nomadic communities left their extremely deviant members to die. Most important, though, were the times when stomachs went empty or mothers watched their children succumb to strange sicknesses. The Inuit died from hunger, accidents, and pneumonia long before the Qallunaat arrived in the North. Elders and babies were always especially vulnerable. The Inuit vividly remember these "bad times."

Hunger and Death
"It's only a story now"

T he turning point came in the mid-twentieth century, when illness and starvation reached proportions that no humanitarian government could ignore. Although the Canadian government's policies toward providing health and social services to the Inuit had been somewhat erratic, and their administration had passed through many agencies, officials felt compelled to bring Inuit families permanently into Pangnirtung (and similar new settlements) during the 1960s. Many Inuit men lost their train dogs to the ravages of canine encephalitis when it swept through Cumberland Sound in 1962. In pragmatic terms, it simply was easier for the government to administer health, social, and economic programs to a centralized population—an argument that appears in many government memos of the period.[3] The decision had enormous implications for the future of the Inuit.

When the deadly combination of highly contagious tuberculosis and canine encephalitis swept through the camps around Cumberland Sound and thirty-mile-long Pangnirtung Fiord, Inuit lives changed forever.[4] Hunger and slow, painful, heart-wrenching starvation faced the tiny camps, recalls Lisah, 47:

> It was especially bad in early spring, when there's deep snow and nobody can go hunting. The whole camp—you get up, nothing to eat. It was bad. My father went to hunt and was gone all day; never got anything. That's why we were hungry. Ran completely out of blubber. No light, no heat.

Lisah recalls that no one died in her camp during that period, although for heat people sometimes burned the wooden frames that supported the *qammat*. They ate old sealskins, originally intended for boots, softened with a little heat from the fire. A carver from Rankin Inlet, elder Mariano Aupilardjuk, remembers eating the boots themselves during times of starvation.[5] During this difficult and sad period, Lisah was relieved that at least they did not have to kill their dogs for food, an ordeal Martha's family faced.

EVERYTHING WAS OUT!

The men used rifles but they ran out of bullets. They also used a harpoon when they went hunting. Whenever we went looking for them, we would see sled tracks, but we never found any dogs. The dogs were dead because the men were eating them—they didn't have anything else to eat.

One day we found a little girl lying beside a rock, covered with a dog skin. She had been walking very slowly, each step right behind the other. She was dead from starvation. Some people at the camp would eat the sealskin on the inside of their tents. We would use bones or the wood to make a fire. Everything was out—everything! The floor, the bed—you name it—it was out!

We used to have two tents, one inside the other, but because everybody was starving and depressed, we would make them into one tent so that we could sleep together. I remember when we were almost starving, whales would come into our camp and everybody would go wild. Good hunting that day!

I remember living in a *qammat* and taking a summer break from the main camp. We would travel to other camps and go to Pangnirtung for supplies. One time we didn't have anything to eat because the men had been gone longer than they planned. We were not starving, but there was hardly anything left. Some people were unhappy about being moved into the settlements. I was happy because they got us just when I thought we would starve to death.

Lucas, 25, proudly mentions that he comes from one of the "special families" who were very good hunters and shared food with starving families. During the peak of the Ethiopian famine in the 1980s, many Inuit families sent money overseas. They understood the agony of hunger.

Many men had to leave their equipment and the remaining dogs behind during resettlement.[6] The invaluable harpoons and sleds were too large to fit into the small planes that ferried Inuit families in from the land. Arnaqo, 40, says his father still remembers the explicit assurances given when he and his family were picked up by an RCMP plane and brought to the settlement in 1964: "We could leave everything behind because special services will look after us. If you talk to those older than me, they will tell you everything was left behind—the equipment, dogs, everything. You find out exactly how the government treated you at that time." An older woman bitterly recalls the forced move to Pangnirtung because of dying dogs. The family lived in tents for several months, and then returned to camp for their equipment. Others were not so lucky in retrieving their belongings. Even today, one discovers rotting *qamutiik* or rusty harpoons on a casual trip out on the land.

In the course of only a few brief hours, then, the men went from being steady hunters and willing providers to being dependent on the government. It was a traumatic moment in both individual and cultural history. Violet Twyee, raised on the land near Baker Lake, remembers being moved to Rankin Inlet so her father could work at the North Rankin Nickel Mine: "We took everything, the dogs and the *komatik*, down to the plane, but they said we had to leave it all behind…we had nothing. No houses, no igloo. We had to sleep in a co-op room with lots of people from many different places…it was too hot and too noisy."[7]

Some elders have recently come forward to accuse the RCMP of shooting dogs in the settlements, early in the relocation process, to control rabies, distemper, and loose dogs: "People were very hurt. We want to put it out in the open, so people in Canada will know what happened in the North." [8] Josie P. Tullaugak remembers "women beginning to cry as if they were losing their own kin. It was a painful experience."[9] Others believe that it was an attempt at genocide, "an attempt to annihilate us." Maata Pudlat eloquently describes the feelings Inuit had for their dogs during the Resettlement Period:

> We never used to tie down the dog-team dogs…they lose their muscles. So we tried that in the settlement [Cape Dorset]…and the RCMP went around and shot all our dogs. Boy, we cried! When you lose your dog, it's like losing one of your family. Dogs don't just mean dogs to us. They're your supporters; they let you live. They were like gold to us—how a white man thinks of gold. Even adults were crying, losing their precious dogs.[10]

The lack of dogs immediately hamstrung hunters in the days before skidoos. As president of the Qikiqtani Inuit Association, Meeka Kilabuk sees the slaughtering of dog teams during the 1950s and 1960s as an act of racism: "Just because it happened many years ago doesn't mean it was forgotten."[11]

Some Inuit remember that a few dogs were flown in, probably from Greenland, but not enough to re-establish normal hunting patterns. Says a carver who vividly remembers the dogs succumbing to illness: "I don't remember many new dogs." Ann McElroy claims that, "after the dog epidemic, according to Euro-Canadian informants, government officials urged the Inuit to remain in Pangnirtung so that famine could be avoided…and the children could benefit from medical and educational services."[12] Only a handful of families ventured back to the land. Others remember the RCMP shooting their dogs (perhaps because they had rabies), which some interpreted as another way to keep them off the land and in the settlements. Geddes writes about Natsiq Kango, a woman who remembers her family's experiences in Iqaluit:

> Her family, along with other Inuit hunting clans scattered around the southeastern tip of Baffin Island, had recently been persuaded by federal authorities to settle at [then] Frobisher Bay. One day, an RCMP truck arrived at the beach not far from their new home, and a Mountie stepped out and shot 25 huskies: "He didn't allow dogs loose and he wanted the families to stay put for their kids to go to school," Kango...recalls bitterly. The slaughter denied her father, Simonie Alainga, the option of taking his family by dogsled back to their traditional winter hunting camp.[13]

The Dislocations of Leaving the Land for Education and Social Services
"We would just say yes"

Officials did not view the informal education in the camps as a valid substitute for the formal, southern-style education available in government or church schools. However, education and social services were contingent upon Inuit willingness to leave the camps and come into the settlements. The government's decision to mandate schooling all over Canada as of 1966 reinforced the resettlement process.[14] Some Inuit resented government agents saying that if they did not comply with the move to Pangnirtung, the authorities would cut off all social services, but they saw no choice because of the hardships they faced during the post-War period. This pattern was repeated in other communities:

> The teacher told us that they would withhold our family allowance checques if we didn't send our children to school. We also thought it was necessary. At that time, our children were taken from their families and put in hostels for ten months at a time. The parents didn't like this so we moved to this place to be with our children. Another reason we moved to this place was...the medical care that was available. (Jacob Oweetaluktuk, Inujjuaq)[15]

Dorais has argued that the government used formal education to make the Inuit into "average citizens." The process, however intended, had assimilationist consequences for the Inuit. Maata's story confirms the coercive nature of school attendance during this period of Inuit relations with the government:[16]

> I had to go school because I was ordered. We were still in the camp when the government came to our parents, and they told us, "Your children have to go to school." My parents had no choice.... I went to school until I was 16. Finally, my dad moved; like most parents, he couldn't be away from his loved ones.... I guess that was the government's idea in the first place, to get the parents to send all children to school.

Once children came to the settlement for education and health care, the families followed. The pain of separation made it easier for government representatives to persuade Inuit parents to live in the settlement so they could be with their children: "Inuit parents had no say in a federal school system that swallowed up innocent unwilling children and spat out bitter, wounded and often badly-educated young adults."[17] Recalls an elder woman in a matter-of-fact tone, "In those days, when the government leaders told us to do something, that's the thing we would do. No excuse or talking back. We would just say yes and wouldn't question the person."

Leah recalls being told that they would not continue to receive the government's baby bonus if they refused to send their children to distant schools: "All kinds of threats I remember. No welfare for us." Asch supports this claim, based on his research during the 1960s with the Dene in the Fort Simpson and Fort Wrigley regions: "Parents who fail to send their children to school without serious reason and notification to the teacher are liable to be fined and jailed. Moreover, family allowance payments may be canceled."[18] In Pond Inlet, a young man reported a similar situation to John Matthiasson: "[He] claimed that the people had been forced to move by governmental pressure. He was convinced that the older people, and camp headmen in particular, had been told that unless they moved to the settlement many economic benefits they enjoyed, such as family allowances and old age pensions, would no longer be available to them." [19] Similar sentiments are expressed by a man who remembers the imposition of culture that affected Cree and Inuit in Northern Québec (Nunavik):

> As far back as the 1940s and 50s, the federal government had a policy that said if we did not send our children to school we would be punished and even put in jail. That's how strongly the government insisted we put the children in school. It is a very powerful imposition...because when our children went to school they lost the importance of hunting, which is why we have lost the old traditional way of our culture. Education, itself, has slowly destroyed our culture.[20]

Tester and Kulchyski document how resettlement policy and the development of Canadian welfare policy coincided with efforts to assimilate Inuit into southern lifestyles and values.[21] The provision of housing may also have been a factor in motivating Inuit to come into the settlements. Whatever the pushes and pulls toward the settlements, Inuit elders "in their lifetime...have experienced *outsiders* taking control of almost every aspect of their lives—including their children's education, their economy, lands, rivers, and the way they can hunt, trap, and use the animals."[22]

Some Inuit came voluntarily to the nursing station for food but were kept there because of illness. An elder recalls: "We came here to get some food from a boat, but a nurse told us to stay here because of red spots on our bodies [probably measles]. Ever since, I've been here." During the resettlement process, the Canadian government required Inuit to wear dog tags with "E numbers" (some say "E" for Eastern Arctic, others for Eskimo—"eaters of raw meat"—a name the people do not now apply to themselves). When Inuit women went to the hospital in Iqaluit, someone might ask for their E number, one elder said. Not until the mid-1960s, when elder Abe Okpik campaigned successfully against the use of dog tags, did the government replace this practice with using names for census and welfare purposes.[23]

Resettlement for health or education brought a dependency that was foreign to the vast majority of Inuit, even those who had worked around the early mission and hospital in the 1920s. Farley Mowat described the anguish of Owliktuk, a Padliermiut who discovered the double-edged sword of dependency on government handouts during the famine in the 1950s:

> Owliktuk and the families who followed him were finding that life at Ennadai was becoming more and more unpalatable. Although they were receiving enough food to keep them living—mainly food and lard—they were being treated with a restraint which made it obvious that the soldiers considered the extra tasks of administering relief and Family Allowance to be a considerable nuisance. The Eskimos were reaping the first fruits from their attachment to the dole, for no matter how sympathetic the giver of charity may be initially, he eventually comes to feel a growing contempt for the recipient...Owliktuk was quick to sense the change in mood and it served only to make him more bitterly aware of his own helplessness. Now it was he and his People, and not the intruding white men, who were the incompetents, unable to survive without assistance. The knowledge burned within him.[24]

Seventy-year-old Leeta contends that to some extent Inuit culture was "spoiled" by the early Anglican missions, the law, and social services:

> For the missions, we have to give up some of our culture just because we have to be religious. That really hurts the old way of life. We start feeding people who don't really need assistance, and that makes people lazy because they don't have to do anything anymore. If they are hungry, all they have to do is go to social services and get their food. They don't have to hike to find a rabbit.

An Inuk social service worker argues the benefits of resettlement: "It was better out on the land, but schooling, education, and opportunities to work [for wages] were in the settlement—it's a good thing if you make it into a good thing." The price paid for alleged economic "progress" was very high for her people, though. She remembers how her parents felt about being brought in from the land so their children could go to school and the family could have a house: "They went along, but Mom still wants to go back to the land." A young sculptor relates: "People from the government told my uncles that they had to come here to go to school or get a job. They wanted to stick with their relatives. They didn't want to be out there when the kids were not with them."

Moving to Pangnirtung for schooling was certainly a major disruption in the lives of many Inuit children who were brought into the settlement for a formal education. Separation from their families contributed to the breakdown of culture and intergenerational communication, as children missed the informal teaching that occurred on a day-to-day basis in the camps. Instead, the emerging public school system exposed them to an all-southern curriculum. As Rhoda Kaukjak Katsak remembers in *Saqiyuq,* "I moved in off the land and went to school when I was eight years old. That is when they started trying to teach me how to become a Qallunaaq."[25] Even children who traveled a few miles to Pangnirtung could not see their families for months at a time. For those who flew to the south for special training, the situation was even more dislocating, often resulting in identity crises.[26] An artist remembers the disruption of being taken from her family so she could attend school in Pangnirtung:

> I was nine years old when I left the camp to go to school in Pang. It was 1964. I was here without my parents for three years. My father came to pick me up in the springtime with the dog teams, before school finished. He had to come in when the ice was still good. I didn't see them at Christmas. My family came here to stay for a few weeks and then they would leave me in the hostel in August or September. It was lonely.

Although she lived in the hostel with other Inuit children from the camps, Geetee missed her family terribly and felt crowded: "There were three bedrooms in each building, and six of us in each bedroom." Maata Pudlat has written in a similar vein about her sister, who was the first to leave home for school:[27]

> When the government officials came to our camp, they approached my dad and said my sister had to go...she was at that age; she was the first child ever to be away from the family. Boy, that was something! We used to cry. My dad would worry, my brothers would worry, [and] we couldn't sleep. We kept thinking, "Oh, she must be crying," because we had never been apart. Most fathers, most parents couldn't face the fact that their little loved ones were away, somewhere, in somebody else's house. Even today, we have never really learned to be apart from our families.

Jooeelee grew up on the land. He and his family were resettled into Pangnirtung in 1962, when he was seven. The next day he went to school, where a white female teacher forbade him to use anything but English: "I was in shock. I felt very emotional about it. This was a totally unknown world to me, so I didn't learn much in school." As happens with any cultural change, what appeared to be a negative experience at the beginning comes to be accepted as a positive force in retrospect, as this Inuit administrator reflects:

> During that time, it was better to be out in the camps. When I was about six, I didn't want to go to school at all, but my parents pushed me. This would have

happened anyway, so I'm glad we have our community, and now I feel that it's better here than in the camps.

Photo 5.3 The runway splits Pangnirtung into two neighborhoods.

The Tuberculosis Epidemic and Other Diseases
"One of every seven Inuit"

Many Inuit claim and government documents of the 1950s reveal that (at least in some cases) the Inuit were relocated as "human flagpoles" that could buttress Canada's claims to the vast uninhabited North. From a government perspective, moving Inuit families from camps into settlements was useful for securing its claims.[28] Scattered, small, nomadic populations of indigenous peoples were not persuasive evidence of Canadian sovereignty in the face of perceived threats from the former Soviet Union, Denmark (Greenland), and the United States. Greenlanders had been hunting on Ellesmere Island in the High Arctic and fishing in the Eastern Arctic waters. The Americans had built DEW line and weather stations, not to mention military bases in the Canadian Arctic (albeit with Canadian cooperation and understanding that such construction was not to constitute any threat to Canadian Arctic sovereignty). The Canadian North's direct proximity to Soviet waters and land posed a possible threat. Jim Bell observes that development took place for the Inuit within the context of larger political issues: "The modern colonization of the eastern Arctic came about because of three world-historical events over which

Inuit had absolutely no control"—World War II, the nuclear arms race, and the Cold War.[29]

Careful documentation of the "sovereignty purpose" of resettlement in the High Arctic can be found in D. Soberman's report to the Canadian Human Rights Commission.[30] The Inuit Committee on National Issues concluded that "Canadian Inuit...have been instrumental in the establishment of Canadian sovereignty" in the Arctic. The relocation of Inuit from Inujjuaq in northern Québec to Resolute and Grise Fiord during the 1950's is an obvious example that "helped Canada's claim to the archipelago."[31] However, the move to Pangnirtung in the early 1960s probably had far more to do with administrative ease in dealing with illness and starvation, and pressure to bring Inuit children into school. In 1996, the Canadian government signed a $10 million "reconciliation" agreement with Inuit "High Arctic exiles." Those who were relocated were disappointed that the government refused to apologize on behalf of public officials who made the relocation decisions in the 1950s.[32]

Although other reasons—such the dogs dying, educating children, or the desire to reinforce Canadian sovereignty in the Arctic—propelled the government to bring Inuit into newly created settlements, the ravages of "white death" formed the last straw. Tuberculosis, polio, and other diseases that directly resulted from contact with white people compromised Inuit ability to support themselves on the land.[33] The Inuit had suffered illness and death caused by the introduction of "white man's" diseases as early as the 1600s. The deadly smallpox and cholera that were still very much a part of European experience in the nineteenth century, and other unwelcome gifts to the New World such as measles and influenza, took a much higher toll on the Inuit than they did on the Qallunaat. When ships moved from harbour to harbour during the whaling period, or when traders fell ill and infected dozens of families who came in from various camps to do business with them, the results were widespread and disastrous for the Inuit. In the 1850s, Margaret Penny wrote several entries in her diary about the Inuit falling ill in close conjunction with a sickness that swept through the sailors on the *Lady Franklin*:[34]

> A sort of influenza has broke out amongst the natives [Nov. 6]. Esquimaux all very ill with some sort of disease like the influenza. The steward is also very ill with a wry-neck and muscular pains in his body [Nov. 13; possibly meningitis].

Brother Warmow recorded that "several of the natives lay dangerously ill of pleurisy and affections of the chest" in the epidemic that raged for two months. Ross recorded that the ship's doctor visited only the Inuit victims, indicating that they took the illness much harder than did the sailors.[35] The ship's log shows zero lost days of work in November, Ross adds: "Indeed, this was the usual pattern when diseases were introduced by Europeans to the native peoples.... Pathogens to which Europeans had long been exposed, and to which they had built up some immunity, often found fertile 'virgin soil' in aboriginal populations."[36] Captain Penny and Brother Warmow both noted in their diaries that the population of Cumberland Sound fell from about 1,000 to 350 during the relatively short (two-decade) whaling period.[37]

Tuberculosis, often thought of as a contemporary public health crisis, hit the Inuit long before the mid-twentieth century. Charles Francis Hall, an explorer, recorded his impression in 1861 that Inuit died from consumption (TB) more than all other diseases put together.[38] In 1889, Turner said that fully half of the Inuit in Kuujjuaq died of "pulmonary troubles" that progressed very quickly.[39] Dr. Wilfred Grenfell, who dedicated his career to Arctic medicine, reported numerous cases of TB in Labrador in 1893.[40] In 1924, RCMP Inspector C. E. Wilcox visited the Kekerten whaling station to help an Inuit woman who had fallen ill with TB.[41] The medical health officer at Coppermine reported in 1929 that "sporadic and isolated" cases of TB had turned into an epidemic that affected 25 percent of the population within eight short months.[42] A memo from Dr. J. A. Bildfell painted a devastating picture in Pangnirtung, which had only a few dozen residents at the time:

> Tuberculosis is so general among Pangnirtung natives that to speculate on any particular percentage is impossible...everything appears to be in favour of the germ, and nothing to the advantage of the native in combating the disease. It is the chief factor in...the high child mortality rate [and] the main cause of death generally.... As far as Pangnirtung is concerned it so eclipses every other diseased condition that it might be said that there prevails but one disease among them. Thus the hospital should be equipped to treat tuberculosis as efficiently as possible.[43]

Interestingly, many other communities had either low rates of TB or no cases at all. By 1945, though, the high death rates among the Inuit were starkly obvious, as a report on the NWT indicated (table 5.1). Severe environmental factors, great distances, and persistent disagreement among government agencies on strategies for coping with the epidemic exacerbated this pattern. It culminated in a crisis a few years later.[44] Duffy states that living in snow houses contributed to the incidence of TB: "For people so poorly dressed, an igloo was always cold and damp. This was a factor in the high rates of tuberculosis and bronchial troubles and one of the main causes of infant mortality."[45] After World War II, TB rates skyrocketed among the Inuit (table 5.2).[46]

The press toward leaving the land became even stronger when tuberculosis reached epidemic proportions in the 1950s. Waldram, Herring, and Young report almost 1,600 cases of TB per 100,000 among the Inuit in the 1961-65 period, compared to only about 280 among the Indian population and a handful in the general Canadian population; the figure dropped to about 1,100 per 100,000 for the Inuit for 1966-70; about 300 in 1971-75; and less than 100 per 100,000 through 1990 (table 5.3).[47] Mass BCG vaccination at birth and, in some areas, mass prophylaxis with the drug isoniazid helped account for the decline in the incidence of TB among the Inuit.

Table 5.1 Inuit Death Rates, 1945, per 100,000

	Inuit	Rest of Canada
Tuberculosis	314	53
Pneumonia	203	52
Diseases of the First Year	166	54
Unknown	740	—
Totals	*1423*	*159*

Source: G. J. Wherrett, "Arctic Survey I, Survey of Health Conditions and Medical and Hospital Services in the North West Territories," *Canadian Journal of Economics and Political Science* 11, 1 (1945).

Table 5.2 Inuit TB Mortality Rates, 1950-1960

	According to Statistics Canada	According to Medical Services Branch
1950	411	718
1951	327	476
1952	569	588
1953	369	386
1954	211	234
1955	169	149
1956	232	231
1957	179	167
1958	126	155
1959	53	79
1960	84	76
Totals	*2,730*	*3,259*

Source: Based on Statistics Canada and Medical Services Program data, Health and Welfare Canada, and adapted from Grygier, *A Long Way from Home*, p. 84.

The epidemic touched countless lives. The total number of deaths from TB among the Inuit (1950-1960) was between 2,730, and 3,259—approximately 25 to 30 percent of the Inuit population (which averaged 10,664 during that decade). Cramped living conditions of the time and poor nutrition during food shortages probably contributed to the epidemic; so did dependence on southern food, which lacked the vitamin intensity of "country food" acquired through hunting, fishing, and gathering.[48] Food supplies often fell when Inuit men left the camps individually to check their trap lines (never a very successful enterprise) or when caribou declined.[49] The RCMP flew to the camps with portable x-ray machines, landing on the ice to determine the extent of TB infection. The Canadian government conducted a large-scale evacuation when it became clear that at least one-third of the Inuit had succumbed to TB, and "by 1956, one out of every seven Inuit was in a southern sanatorium."[50] The average length of hospital stay was two and a half years.

In the Cumberland Sound region, the RCMP brought the very ill by plane or dogsled to the tiny St. Luke's Hospital and Industrial Home founded in Pangnirtung by the Anglican Church in 1930.[51] The Anglican Bishop (Fleming) in the 1930s had wanted to build several hospitals in the Arctic, but government departments refused him permission. Consequently, the Pangnirtung hospital was the only one constructed (and only two others were built by the Catholic Church, in Chesterfield Inlet and Aklavik). The tiny facility in Pangnirtung served all of Baffin Island and Québec's northern coast. By 1941, that amounted to 2,052 people, including 59 whites. St. Luke's was relatively progressive for the period, as it had the luxuries of electricity, an x-ray machine, and an iron lung. Nonetheless, the Eastern Arctic was "medically backward" in comparison to the Western Arctic because of the shortage of hospital beds, poor transportation, poor communications, and an absence of local autonomy.[52]

Figure 5.1 Inuit TB Rates, 1961–1990, Compared to Indian and Canadian Rates

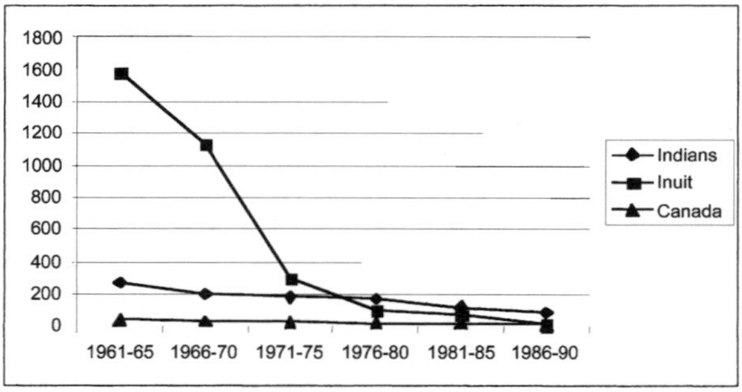

Source: Adapted from Waldram, Herring, and Young, *Aboriginal Health in Canada*, p. 78; based on Medical Services Branch and Statistics Canada data.

Ultimately, small hospitals such as St. Luke's could not handle the complications of such an infectious disease as TB, so patients were sent south for treatment. From Pangnirtung, the hardest-hit patients were flown to sanatoria in Hamilton or Toronto (Ontario), Parc Savard (Québec), Brandon (Manitoba), Edmonton (Alberta), and numerous other southern cities.[53] Whether Inuit should have been treated in (or near) their communities or in the south was the subject of a long debate in the federal agencies responsible for their health and welfare. Sending patients away exposed a large percentage of Inuit to southern culture, the English language, and urban lifestyles for extended periods and, of course, dealt another blow to Inuit family stability.

Before the Eastern Arctic TB patients were concentrated in Mountain Sanitorium in Hamilton or Weston in Toronto, they tended to be scattered across many facilities. This meant that only one or two Inuit would be in the same "san," so language difficulties, loneliness, homesickness, and isolation slowed their recovery.[54] Sometimes the government lost track of where Inuit patients were hospitalized, which frightened families and made some leery of sending their sick members away. Inefficient paperwork sometimes meant that family members were in different wings of the same hospital without knowing it. For these and other reasons, including fear of the unknown, many Inuit avoided the settlements when they knew that a hospital ship was in port. Even the process of transporting the patients south caused considerable anguish. For example, conditions on the hospital ship, C. D. Howe, which transported the Inuit south for treatment each summer, were notably poor.[55] Donald Marsh, Anglican Bishop of the Arctic, among many others, wrote passionately about the situation in a collection of vignettes:

> "CRY THE BELOVED ESKIMO"
> Up the ship's ladder they climbed until they reached the little knot of people standing above. The third person was a woman who, on arriving at the top, tossed back her hood to disclose the small baby in her pouch [*amautik*]. The doctor, a tall white man, spotted it immediately. "Take that baby out and give it to another woman in the tender!" The mother protested, but to no avail. Someone whisked the child from her hood and thrust it into the arms of another woman who was without even a pouch on her parka for the child. The sobbing figure of the mother was hustled below and the unwilling foster mother thrust into a waiting boat. The telegraph rang. The ship sailed.[56]

Minnie Aodla Freeman was a teenager at the Mountain Sanatorium in Hamilton as a patient and later served as an official interpreter for the Welfare Division. Grygier interviewed Freeman about her experiences in 1953, when she interpreted for the first planeload of Inuit to fly from Frobisher Bay (now Iqaluit) to Hamilton:[57]

> The thing that hit me the most was how the women talked, some of them saying, "Where have we gone to? Where are we? Look at all this cement. There's no land here. Where are we going to be put, and what else are we going to ride in? That must be where we are going to" [airport terminal]. Women were crying, really, because they were being separated from the children and the babies they had at their breast. They were saying, "Where is it? Where is it going to be put? Will I see the baby now and then?"

Medically speaking, of course, it made sense to separate the sick from their families, since TB is such a highly contagious disease. The lack of coordination with families or community agencies—and the failure to give the infected people time to settle their affairs before leaving home (by plane or by ship)— drew heavy criticism from both Inuit and southern observers. For those who were taken south by the hospital ship, after being diagnosed positively by X-ray, "The evacuees were not allowed to go ashore to collect belongings, to say goodbye, or to make arrangements for their families or goods."[58] Ruth Banffy and Betty Marwood, two welfare workers who were assigned to the C. D. Howe at different times, eventually resolved the worst of these conditions.

Finally, even for those who were lucky enough to return home cured, the reverse culture shock was sometimes devastating. Younger children had lost their Inuktitut; patients of all ages had lost touch with their families and communities. One report in 1956 reported a disturbing statistic: "Some children had been in the wards for six or seven years without any contact with their parents."[59] They returned home as strangers, marginalized in their own land at a tender age. Some left as children of the land but came back to new homes in settlements that they had never seen.

In the course of discussing their lives, many Pangnirtung women and men mentioned being sent south for TB treatment. Eena remembers having TB and meningitis simultaneously. She went down to Hamilton for treatment. Apea was born in Qimirsurq, out on the land, but she moved to Pangnirtung because her mother had TB. When she and her brothers and sisters succumbed to TB during the 1960s, they were flown to Toronto Children's Hospital for treatment. Apea was nine: "I really liked it and I got to know a lot of friends. I didn't want to come back but I had to because then Pangnirtung was my home. I never went back to the camp." Two of her sisters and one brother died in Toronto. Janie also spent two years in the Hamilton san, from 1957 to 1959; like Apea, eventually she stopped missing her family:

> When I first went down there, my appetite wasn't very good because I wasn't used to their food and TB patients never could walk around. I had to stay in bed for so long. It wasn't too hard for me because I was so young. It was harder for the older patients. I wasn't very homesick. After about a year, I didn't miss home so much. Then I didn't feel like coming back.

Natsiapik Nagliniq, 67, speaking at Iqaluit's Nunatta Sunaqutangit Museum, contrasts the camp life she knew to the "Qallunaat" life she saw as a TB patient in a southern sanatorium:

> I didn't know anything about *Qallunat* cars, their food, clothes hanging to dry…a huge garden and zoo. That was the first time we found out about…French guys, Indians… It was completely different from the things I had known. The wildlife were tame—not afraid of the *Qallunat*. Carriages, cars—they didn't run away… When we went home, it was a very happy time for us. I was homesick a lot—we were down there for many years. We went

home by ship. How everything had changed. Everybody was happy [but] I would miss *Qallunat* food. At home, I used to want to go away a lot—to *Qallunat* land. The things I used to eat were not around here at all. I missed the things I had gotten used to. ...There were a lot of good nurses down there. I used to miss the ones who were good to us.[60]

Natsiapik missed the southern food and cleanliness, which contrasted sharply with the conditions in the sod houses she returned to: "That's why I wanted to go back down South. To see pretty things. There was no sink to wash everything, no water. ...The things I used to find good didn't seem good any more." The high number of Inuit patients in the sanitarium had one advantage, Janie reminisces: "We could talk to each other." A secretary who spent two years in Hamilton recovering from TB says that her family moved to Pangnirtung to be near the small hospital there. Her sister had died of TB in Montreal, so when she became ill her parents brought her to the hospital and remained in the settlement: "They didn't plan on staying here, but they ended up staying." A woman who had come into Pangnirtung briefly because the family's dogs were dying faced another crisis two months later when her daughter was sent south for TB rehabilitation. She was convinced that living in substandard conditions in Pangnirtung was responsible for her daughter contracting TB. Was she angry about the situation? In retrospect, she felt there was no choice.

The extended hospitalizations had a few positive effects for some patients. Serious efforts to educate the Inuit in the sanatoria allowed many children to receive an elementary education in the "hospital schools." Adults developed reading skills in English and other subjects that might help them become employed when they returned home. Some finished Grade 8 and went into teaching or nursing assistant programs before going back to the North. In 1922, McMaster University in Hamilton worked with the Mountain Sanatorium to provide earphones for each bed, which were connected by telephone to the university lectures—the first such attempt in the world to bring education to the bedside of "shut-in" patients. Patients also received instruction in arts and crafts, which helped them pass the time in close quarters. James and Alma Houston (famous for facilitating the Inuit printmaking industry during the 1950s) instructed patients at Parc Savard Sanatorium in carving and knitting.[61]

Far from their families and familiar landscapes, the adult patients helped pass the time by importing their culture to the hospitals. Men carved and women sewed:

Soapstone carving was sometimes frowned upon because it created a fine dust that was bad for the lungs, and the carvers had to wear masks. But it was the preferred medium, and by 1958 the patients at the Mountain Sanatorium were turning out about 200 carvings a month at a retail value of more than $10,000 a year. The sanatorium ordered regular shipments of soapstone from a Québec quarry and peddled the carvings for a 30 percent commission....

The women made *mukluks* [boots], mitts, even parkas, from furs and materials donated to the hospitals. They became very skilled with sewing machines. At the Mountain Sanatorium they made most of the pyjamas and nightgowns, clothing that the hospital had formerly bought. They were paid in lengths of material, with which they made clothes for themselves or their families.[62]

Most of all, the patients missed country food. In Hamilton, some younger men ventured out onto the mountainside overlooking the city and snared rabbits, which they cooked on ward hot plates. In other sanitoria out west, the staff rounded up frozen raw fish and venison or buffalo for the Inuit patients. The patients also hated the soft beds and (to them) over-heated wards. Many slept on the floor when they could get away with it and flung open the windows to counteract the hot radiators. As Minnie Aodla Freeman says, "It was terrible, but it was a war. The people were dying. They had to do something."[63]

By 1970, the number of known Inuit dying from TB dropped to two cases; in 1980, zero cases of mortality were Inuit.[64] The crisis was over. As of 1987-89, Health and Welfare Canada said that Inuit tuberculosis rates had dropped from the highest in the world to less than 1.1 percent of all Canadian cases.

Now, Statistics Canada data show that Inuit rates, though low, are still the highest in Canada (higher than other Native Canadians and Asian Canadians).[65] Moreover, evidence throughout the Circumpolar North indicates that TB might be returning to some areas. Although the number of cases is small, the new strain appears to be more resistant to standard medical treatment. In order to avoid a repetition of the devastating epidemics of the past, the Nunavut government plans to screen students in kindergarten and in the upper elementary grades, and to ask those who have active TB to undergo treatment for a second time, if necessary.[66]

Culture Shock
"I missed the land"

For those who were not hospitalized, or who were lucky enough to return to their settlement alive after years of treatment, adapting to life in a small village was challenging to say the least. When the Inuit came into communities in the 1960s, they suddenly found themselves living in very large groups, by their standards. They were unprepared for what they found. The memories of those who lived in the camps indicate that settlement life seems fraught with conflict, deviance, and confusion, compared to life in the camps. The government moved the Inuit into "hostels," tiny makeshift houses that dotted the Arctic landscape during the Resettlement Period, as Maata recalls:

"MATCHBOXES"
When we moved here, we were put in a very small house. They weren't even matchboxes. We had no toilets, no kitchen, no [bed] rooms, just one little

square room.... There were so many of us then. Inuit had very big families in those times, because there was no birth control or anything....

But we were all confused, even our parents. What were we going to do? There weren't any jobs or well-built houses except for the government employees. They had wonderful houses with bathrooms, bedrooms, kitchens, running water, lights! I remember, the first time I saw those light switches, I didn't know what it was, so I clicked it up and a light went on. Boy, that scared me! ...And as children, we were always scared of white people, like the RCMP. We would hide when they came into our camps. But now, I can walk all over them. That wasn't very long ago, either. I was *so* scared of white people. Maybe because my parents were the same. Not really scared, but just didn't want them around, I guess. But they invited themselves in.

I'm not being prejudiced or anything against the whites. I am just telling the facts...we have learned a great deal in no time at all, and we have coped without having extreme reactions.[67]

Another woman remembers being cold all the time when they came to Pangnirtung, a complaint expressed by many of those who are old enough to recollect the Resettlement Period:

I remember being here in a canvas tent, the only shelter we had in the wintertime. It was very cold. It felt like it was the dead of winter, but my mother says that it was in September. Before we came here, we were living in a *qammat*, and that's a lot warmer than canvas tents.

Many elders had trouble adjusting to a new rhythm of life. When Qatsuq came to the settlement, her work seemed much harder: "I wanted to climb that mountain behind the hamlet—I never did. The mountains are too far. The place we used to live in, it's not far." In the camp, she could go walking; it was flatter, and somehow "smaller," and the mountains were less intimidating. A woman in her 90s recalls that when she first arrived in Pangnirtung, she felt very unhappy. She preferred living out on the land: "In Pangnirtung I usually get tired, maybe because I don't like it here. I miss Bon Accord the most. Long time ago there used to be some white people living there. We used to go whale hunting." Another elder, 78, echoes these sentiments. She likes Pangnirtung but has never adjusted to the lack of activity: "I was very happy in the camps because I was young and could do everything. Now at this age, I get tired easily. I could go by dog team and help with anything because I was younger then. Now, I'm not quite happy because I hardly do anything." Regardless of hardships, life out on the land holds a certain fascination for most Inuit women, compared to life in a settlement, as Maata Pudlat explains:[68]

I think we were happier [in the camps]. Because we lacked food and nice things, we would appreciate things more from inside rather than...from your visual eye.... If I saw that little glass [jar] over there a long time ago, 20 years ago, boy, that would turn me on! I would appreciate things more. We never considered ourselves poor. We were very rich in the heart because we had love and closeness. Now, I see that jar, with so many beautiful things inside...so what? It's just a jar with so many colourful beads. I see it every day; it really doesn't touch me any more. In the olden days, things were just so beautiful. Look at today—we have TV, we have everything.

Even before resettlement, being wrenched away from their loved ones in the name of education or health care hurt the people deeply. So did losing the ability to eke out a living off the land that had been their friend for so many centuries.

Town Growth
"The Switzerland of the North"

After resettlement and the period of major readjustment, it was time to build a new life.[69] People in the North think of Pangnirtung as a forward-looking community—"very materialistic, very politically aware." Earlier, Pang was "a dead, sleepy town." The first small and hastily constructed houses without adequate heating or plumbing seemed hardly more than glorified tents, but during the 1970s and 1980s creation of the hamlet government and construction of more contemporary homes added to the community's sense of permanence. A community center, elementary and secondary schools, the Parks Canada Office, the Angmarlik Cultural Center, a fish processing plant, and other amenities soon followed.

Dubbed the "Switzerland of the North," Pangnirtung lies in an unusually spectacular setting. Mountains embrace the community and a sparkling glacial river links it to the tundra. Auyuittuq National Park—"the land that never melts"—Canada's first national park inside the Arctic Circle, opened in 1974. Because the Park's entrance is twenty miles north of town, local Inuit outfitters take hikers up Pangnirtung Fiord by boat, a much faster journey than trekking up the two-day land trail. This has jump-started the community's aspirations toward becoming a tourism and recreation center, as hikers, scientists, dignitaries, and other visitors spend money on outfitters, in the lodge, billeting with families, or in the handful of stores. Road improvements, a reservoir, a visitor's centre, an arts and crafts center, and other projects have brought more economic activity and hope. The young people play all summer at a baseball diamond, a sign of the town's growth and vision.

Every August the sealift ship arrives with food and supplies. The ship lingers in the fiord for a few days; at high tide, people rush out in smaller craft to bring everything ashore. Barges for the Northern Stores dock along the harbor front; the fuel barge comes in, as well as an occasional Coast Guard icebreaker. The sealift ship also brings prefabricated buildings that are hastily erected before the deep freeze of winter returns: more houses, a school, a day care center. In this way, the industries of contemporary southern Canada supplement what the Inuit produce through their timeworn skills. The landscape takes on a new appearance virtually every time the ship leaves. Ironically, however, it is often the few whites in the settlements who benefit from the sealift. Qallunaat have an economic edge in this case, albeit unintended. The Inuit are not likely to take advantage of the bulk purchasing of food because extended family members would expect an individual or family to share it, and because few can amass the large amounts of money required to secure an order. Whites are able to order bulk food from Montreal in advance, with orders ranging upwards of $1,000. This means that they pay far less for food (and other items) than do the Inuit, who depend on the land and on the expensive local stores for everything they cannot supply themselves.

Race Relations
"Everybody's really nice up here"

Perhaps because of the success of Kekerten whaling station during the late nineteenth and early twentieth centuries, present-day Inuit-white relationships in Pangnirtung tend to be relatively positive. The tension that characterizes race relations in many societies has not dominated social intercourse here. That may be, however, as much a reflection of Inuit tact as of underlying attitudes. Condon, in his study of Holman, concluded that conflicts occurred primarily because of personality differences rather than "ethnic confrontation" and that resident whites who were flexible and had a good sense of humor had the best relationships with Inuit residents.[70]

Although race relations were not a focus of our research, some Inuit commented during formal interviews about contact with Qallunaat resulting in domination, exploitation, or southernization. It is possible that some consultants specifically hoped to make a point that would be published. Our impression, however, after many visits and conversations, was that criticism of whites was balanced and modulated rather than sensationalized or politicized. For instance, an Inuk constable characterizes the relations between whites and Inuit as "good," but adds that notable exceptions exist: "Some Qallunaat teachers do not get along. They just come up here to make money and don't even look at you." Sheila reports that one of her teachers said it was rude for the children to speak Inuktitut in front of him, but she also understood how that might make someone feel left out. Simeonie makes a frank assessment of the absence of the masking that often hides animosity: "If you don't like Inuks, I can tell, even without you saying it. You could tell, too, if I don't like whites, without me saying it to you." These comments emerged in a matter-of-fact way in the spirit of honest reflection and historical analysis rather than in anger, fear, or vengeance.

This public good will might prevail because the earliest Inuit-Qallunaat relationships balanced on the fulcrum of a mutually rewarding exchange. Whalers, as discussed earlier, hired the Inuit to work in their whaling industry. This arrangement brought the Scottish and American whalers cheap labour and brought the Inuit a way to increase their livelihood and to have a few luxuries. The whalers also benefited from aboriginal survival skills, which (from accounts of the time) appeared to build up a wellspring of respect toward the Inuit—and a sense of pride among the Inuit.

White men taking advantage of Inuit women complicated these early relationships, however.[71] (The reverse was virtually never true, as white men did not usually bring their wives or daughters to this region.) Qatsuq, for example, remembers Inuit women, including her mother, visiting the ships in exchange for favors. Matthiasson speculates that Inuit men may have served as brokers (arranging sexual favors in exchange for tobacco, for example) and that some of these liaisons might have resulted in non-consensual, forced sexual encounters, but Inuit elders (male or female) do not speak of the latter case.[72] Other observers have remarked on sexual liaisons between police and Inuit women. Sometimes the women became pregnant. Sometimes the Qallunaat married them, sometimes not, but usually they learned from and helped each other, as a woman leader recollects:

> Predominantly, white men have married Inuit women, rather than vice versa. There is a long history of that in the North, from the early traders back to the early pioneers. They needed women's skills to help them adjust to the community and for survival. It's only recently that it's the other way—that a few white women have married aboriginal men.

From the Qallunaat point of view, most informants who have worked in other settlements in the North believe this community is an exceptionally friendly one. Families take visitors out seal hunting or camping, sometimes for a fee, sometimes out of eagerness to share their culture. A nurse from southern Canada talks about her experience: "The Inuit people are wonderful. You don't get that same feeling of 'us and them' that you can get in other places. They want you to come out on the land with them or visit their house. It's a much warmer community and I really enjoy it." A white RCMP officer agrees: "This place, so far, has been heaven compared to the last place. The people are friendly. You walk down the street and they smile at you. They come up and talk to the wife." A teacher concurs: "They're very gentle people and extremely fun-loving." An RCMP officer's wife says she enjoys the community. She has made a few Inuit friends but finds it hard to get close to them. A white contractor's spouse who has traveled to many Inuit communities feels that the Inuit treat her well but also understands the subtle hostility some feel:

> They respect my rights as an individual, which is a treat when you're white up here, because some Inuit in other communities dismiss you as just another white face that has caused them problems over the years. I don't know if Inuit ever grow to like white people, but they come to tolerate certain ones. I don't think there's ever any great love, and they have no reason to love them, because white people have given them a hard time. Some whites say, "we saved their life, we brought them in off the land"—I don't want to hear that. The settlements are full of "do-gooders"—whites who have been in the North a year or two but have not comprehended the intricacy of the problems. Still, they feel

confident that they have the solutions. The longer you're here, the more you realize how complex the situation is. You're trying to cross 5,000 years. How do you expect them to go to work tomorrow, 9 to 5, and spend a paycheck wisely? It's a completely different world!

In spite of the lack of sensitivity among certain Qallunaat, a white social worker argues that she has found Inuit culture to be relatively accepting of whites. The few times she has felt like a minority—discriminated against or just ignored because she is white—seem normal to her, since "prejudice and discrimination are found everywhere. If you think that this culture 50 years ago knew virtually nothing of the southern, modern world! They have been very accommodating. They have taken things from the southern culture and made them their own...used them in a way that is different. The Inuit have given up things but they have also created something that is unique and new. If you look at television and the Inuit Broadcasting Corporation [IBC], they've made it their own."[73] Resettlement, then, has served up opportunities and crises, advantages and losses. The physical and economic changes in Inuit lives seem dramatic enough, but the transformation of culture dominates their conversations.

Notes

1 Pudlat, "Boy, Have Things Changed," p. 17.
2 Quoted from Hallendy, "Reflections, Shades and Shadows," p. 20.
3 See Pat Sandiford Grygier, *A Long Way from Home: The Tuberculosis Epidemic among the Inuit* (Montréal: McGill-Queen's University Press, 1994) for a discussion of changing bureaucratic models relating to the Inuit during the first six decades of the century; also Richard G. Condon, "Modern Inuit Culture and Society," in *Arctic Life: Challenge to Survive*, edited by Martina Magenau Jacobs and James B. Richardson III (Pittsburgh: Carnegie Institute, 1983); and a government view in Canada, Department of Northern Affairs and Natural Resources, *Northern Education: Ten Years of Progress* (Ottawa: Department of Northern Affairs and Natural Resources, 1961).
4 For an in-depth analysis of the rationale for resettlement, see Janet Mancini Billson, "Opportunity or Tragedy? The Impact of Canadian Resettlement Policy on Canadian Inuit Families," *The American Review of Canadian Studies* 20, 2 (Summer 1990): 187-218; Irwin, "Lords of the Arctic: Wards of the State"; and G. Anders, ed., *The East Coast of Baffin Island: An Area Economic Survey* (Ottawa: Industrial Division, Department of Indian Affairs and Northern Development, 1966). The canine encephalitis epidemic occurred in 1962.
5 Quoted in Kerry McCluskey, "Talking of Shamans and Other Things: Q&A with Salome Awa," *News/North Nunavut* (Monday, March 29, 1999), p. B9.
6 Southerners sometimes refer to the dogs now as CIDs (Canadian Inuit Dogs). Genevieve Montcombroux, *The Canadian Inuit Dog: Canada's Heritage* (Inwood, Manitoba: Whippoorwill Press, 1997). Our consultants said that they continue to call them "huskies."

7 Quoted in McCluskey, "Talking of Shamans and Other Things," p. B9.

8 Jane George, "When They Killed the Sled Dogs in Nunavik," *Nunatsiaq News* (March 25, 1999).

9 George, "When They Killed the Sled Dogs in Nunavik."

10 Pudlat, "Boy, Have Things Changed," p. 19.

11 Denise Rideout, "Racism a Reality in The Arctic, Inuit Say: Conference Calls on Aboriginals to Speak out about Bias and Bigotry," *Nunatsiaq News* (March 30, 2001).

12 McElroy, *Alternatives in Modernization*, p. 91.

13 John Geddes, "Northern Dawn: The Inuit Prepare to Embrace Self-Government with Hope, Fear and Fierce Determination," *Maclean's* (February 15, 1999), p. 26. Natsiq Kango ran for an MLA seat for Iqaluit in the first territorial elections in 1999.

14 Smith, *Inujjuamiut Foraging Strategies*, p. 122.

15 Smith, *Inujjuamiut Foraging Strategies*, p. 123.

16 Pudlat, "Boy, Have Things Changed," p. 18.

17 Jim Bell, "Back Where It Began," *Nunatsiaq News* (March 25, 1999).

18 Michael Asch, "The Dene Economy," in Mel Watkins, ed., *Dene Nation—the Colony Within* (Toronto: University of Toronto Press, 1977), p. 53.

19 J. Matthiasson, *Living on the Land*, p. 141.

20 Gabriel Fireman, Attawapiskat, quoted in Miriam McDonald, Lucassie Arragutainaq, and Zack Novalinga, *Voices from the Bay: Traditional Ecological Knowledge of Inuit and Cree in the Hudson Bay Bioregion* (Ottawa: Canadian Arctic Resources Committee and the Environmental Committee [Sanikiluaq], 1997), p. 51.

21 Frank Tester and Peter Kulchyski, *Tammarniit (Mistakes): Inuit Relocation in the Eastern Arctic, 1939-1963* (Vancouver: University of British Columbia Press, 1994).

22 McDonald, Arragutainaq, and Novalinga, *Voices from the Bay*, p. 63.

23 Olive Patricia Dickason, *Canada's First Nations: A History of Founding Peoples from Earliest Times* (Toronto: McClelland & Stewart, 1992), p. 398.

24 Farley Mowat, *The Desperate People* (Boston: Little, Brown, 1959), p. 171. Tahoe Talbot Washburn writes about her experiences among the Inuit during this period in *Under Polaris: An Arctic Quest* (Montréal: McGill-Queens University Press, 1999). She details the patience with which Inuit women sewed skins for clothing and their generous sharing of scarce resources.

25 Wachowich, *Saqiyuq*, p. 3. The North West Territories Education, Culture and Employment department summarized Inuit perceptions of this superimposed curriculum and future needs in *The Curriculum from the Inuit Perspective,* Yellowknife: North West Territories Education, Culture and Employment, 1996.

26 Robert Davis and Mark Zannis describe airlifting Native children from their homes to alienating, regimented residential schools in the south: *The Genocide Machine in Canada* (Montréal: Black Rose Books, 1973); also, Kenneth Coates, "Best Left as Indians: The Federal Government and the Indians of the Yukon, 1894-1950," in Fisher and Coates, eds., *Out of the Background*, pp. 236-255.

27 Pudlat, "Boy, Have Things Changed," p. 18.

28 Dickason, *Canada's First Nations*, pp. 397-398; Clyde H. Farnsworth, "The Day the Eskimos Were Cast into Darkness," *The New York Times* (April 10, 1992), p. A4; Shelagh D. Grant, *Sovereignty or Security: Government Policy in the Canadian North, 1936-1950* (Vancouver: University of British Columbia Press, 1989); William R. Morrison, *Under the Flag: Canadian Sovereignty and the Native People in Northern*

Canada (Ottawa: Department of Indian and Northern Affairs, 1984), pp. 74-77 and "Canadian Sovereignty and the Inuit of the Central and Eastern Arctic," *Études/Inuit/Studies* 10, 1 (1986): 245-259; Gordon W. Smith, "Sovereignty in the North: The Canadian Aspect of An International Problem," in *The Arctic Frontier*, edited by Ronald St. J. Macdonald (Toronto: University of Toronto Press with the Canadian Institute of International Affairs and the Arctic Institute of North America, 1966), pp. 194-255; Diane Engelstad and John Bird, *Aboriginal Sovereignty and the Future of Canada,* (Toronto: House of Anansi Press, 1992); and Environment Canada, *Environment Canada and the North: The Perceptions, Roles and Policies of the Department of the Environment Regarding Development North of 60, Discussion Paper* (Ottawa: Environment Canada, July 1983), p. 45.

29 Bell, "Back Where It Began."

30 D. Soberman, *Report to the Human Rights Commission on the Complaints of the Inuit People Relocated from Inukjuak and Point Inlet to Grise Fjord and Resolute Bay in 1953 and 1955* (Ottawa: Canadian Human Rights Commission, 1991).

31 Coates and Powell, *The Modern North*, p.13; Hugh Brody, *Some Historical Aspects of the High Arctic Exiles' Experience* (Ottawa: Royal Commission on Aboriginal Peoples, 1993); and several works by Alan R. Marcus: "Canada's Experimental Inuit Relocation to Grise Fjord and Resolute Bay," *Polar Record* 27, 163 (1992): 285-296; *Utopia on Trial: Perceptions of Canadian Government Experiments with Inuit Relocation* (PhD Thesis, University of Cambridge, 1993); *Inuit Relocation Policies in Canada and Other Circumpolar Countries, 1925-60* (Report for the Royal Commission on Aboriginal Peoples, Ottawa, 1994); and *Out in the Cold: The Legacy of Canada's Inuit Relocation Experiment in the High Arctic* (Copenhagen: International Work Group for Indigenous Affairs, Document 71, 1992). Jane George, "Makivik Signs Exiles Deal," *Nunatsiaq News* (April 5, 1996), p.13. For a recent perspective on the sovereignty issue, see Bill Graham, MP, Chair, *Canada and the Circumpolar World: Meeting the Challenges of Cooperation into the Twenty-First Century* (Report of the House of Commons Standing Committee on Foreign Affairs and International Trade. Ottawa: House of Commons, Canada, April 1997), pp. 80-83. The Committee has emphasized circumpolar cooperation and has expressed concern primarily in the context of American submarines passing through the Canadian Arctic Archipelago waters.

32 M. Gunther, *The 1953 Relocations of the Inukjuak Inuit to the High Arctic—A Documentary Analysis and Evaluation* (Ottawa: Department of Indian Affairs and Northern Development, 1992).

33 See Billson, "Social Change, Social Problems, and the Search for Identity"; McElroy, *Alternatives in Modernization*; and L.F.S. Upton, "The Extermination of the Beothucks of Newfoundland," in Fisher and Coates, eds., *Out of the Background*, pp. 45-65.

34 Ross, *This Distant and Unsurveyed Country*, p. 112.

35 Warmow, *Periodical Accounts*, p. 91.

36 Ross, *This Distant and Unsurveyed Country*, p. 112.

37 Clive Holland, "William Penny, 1809-1892: Arctic Whaling Master," *Polar Record* 15, 94 (1970): 40.

38 Cited in S. Grzybowski, K. Styblo, and E. Dorken, "Tuberculosis in Eskimos," *Tubercle* 57, 4 (1976), p. S2.

39 Grzybowski, Styblo, and Dorken, "Tuberculosis in Eskimos," p. S2.

40 Grzybowski, Styblo, and Dorken, "Tuberculosis in Eskimos," p. S2.

41 A. E. Millward, ed., *Southern Baffin Island: An Account of Exploration, Investigation and Settlement during the Past Fifty Years* (Yellowknife: North West Territories and Yukon Branch, Department of the Interior, 1930), p. 44.

42 *National Archives of Canada*, RG85, 1118: 1000/145-1, memo, Martin to Finnie, March 1931.

43 *National Archives of Canada*, RG85, 1872: 552/1-1, memo, A. L. Cumming to R. A. Gibson, 17 May 1937.

44 Grygier, *A Long Way from Home*, passim.

45 Duffy, *The Road to Nunavut*, p. 30.

46 Figure 9 is based on Statistics Canada and Medical Services Program data, Health and Welfare Canada, and adapted from Grygier, *A Long Way from Home*, pp. 84, 141. (Includes both new and reactivated cases.)

47 Waldram, Herring, and Young, *Aboriginal Health in Canada*, p. 78.

48 Grygier, *A Long Way from Home*, p. 31. Grygier, who has done the most extensive study of TB among the Inuit, provides statistics showing that TB peaked during the 1940s and 1950s throughout Canada as a whole (p. 5).

49 Grygier, *A Long Way from Home*, p. 55.

50 Grygier, *A Long Way from Home,* p. xxi.

51 In 1964, the hospital was converted to use as the Arthur Turner Training School (A.T.T.S.), which trains Inuit catechists. All the hospitals were underfunded by the government (which provided medical staff, some construction costs, per diem allowance for indigent patients, medicines, and transportation costs for building materials and annual freight). See Grygier, *A Long Way from Home*, pp. 36-37, 39, 46-47. For an overview of the Anglican Church's Arctic mission, see Donald B. Marsh, "A History of the Work of the Anglican Church in the Area Now Known as the Diocese of the Arctic," in *Anthropological Essays on Tutelage and Ethnicity*, edited by R. Pane (St. John's, Nfld.: Memorial University, 1977); also Hugh M. Sampath, "Protestant Missionaries and Their Role in the Modernisation of the Inuit in the Canadian Arctic," *Sixth Inuit Studies Conference, Copenhagen October 17-20, 1988: Abstracts* (Copenhagen: Institute of Eskimology, University of Copenhagen, 1988).

52 Duffy, *The Road to Nunavut*, pp. 52-53.

53 Grygier, *A Long Way from Home*, p. 77.

54 Grygier, *A Long Way from Home*, pp. 72, 75.

55 Grygier, *A Long Way from Home*, p. 86.

56 This was Marsh's own title. Text cited in Marsh and Marsh, *Echoes into Tomorrow*.

57 Grygier, *A Long Way from Home*, pp. 105-106. Freeman later wrote about her experiences in *Life among the Qallunaat.*

58 Grygier, *A Long Way from Home*, p. 96. Farley Mowat also reports on the separation of families among TB patients from the Keewatin region in *Walking on the Land.* Toronto: Key Porter, 2000, p. 195.

59 Grygier, *A Long Way from Home*, p. 95.

60 Nunatsiaq News, "How Everything Had Changed." *Nunatsiaq News* (March 8, 2002).

61 Grygier, *A Long Way from Home*, p. 111.

62 Grygier, *A Long Way from Home*, p. 113.

63 Grygier, *A Long Way from Home*, p. 116, based on an interview between Grygier and Freeman.

64 Statistics Canada, Canadian Centre for Health Information, *Mortality Deaths (Tuberculosis by Ethnic Origin)*, 1992.

65 Grygier, *A Long Way from Home*, p. 176.

66 Jane George, "Tuberculosis Stages Come-Back around the Circumpolar World," *Nunatsiaq News* (June 9, 2000).

67 Pudlat, "Boy, Have Things Changed," p. 19.

68 Pudlat, "Boy, Have Things Changed," p. 17.

69 McElroy, *Alternatives in Modernization*, p. 90. Frank G. Vallee details some of the status distinctions between those who chose to remain on the land at Baker Lake (*Nunamiut*) and those who came into the settlements "like white people" (*Kabloonamiut*): "Differentiation Among the Eskimos in Some Arctic Settlements," in Valentine and Vallee, eds., *Eskimo of the Canadian Arctic*, pp. 109-126.

70 Condon, *Inuit Behavior and Seasonal Change in the Canadian Arctic*, p. 87.

71 This is in stark contrast to race relations in the United States, for example, where a bitter history of white men accusing African American men of raping their wives during slavery and Reconstruction has left a residue of hostility and suspicion. See Richard Majors and Janet Mancini Billson, *Cool Pose: Dilemmas of Black Manhood in America* (New York: Touchstone [Simon & Schuster, 1993]); and Janet Mancini Billson, *Pathways to Manhood: Young Black Males Struggle for Identity* (Rutgers, NJ: Transaction, 1996).

72 J. Matthiasson, *Living on the Land*, p. 33.

73 Marianne Stenbaek-Lafon describes harnessing mass media for development efforts in "Sustainable Development and Mass Media in the Arctic: The Case of the Inuit Circumpolar Communications Commission," in *Dependency, Autonomy, Sustainability in the Arctic*, edited by Hanne K. Petersen and Birger Poppel (Aldershot, ONT, Brookfield, VT: Ashgate, 1999). Viewing habits are explored in Gail Guthrie Valaskakis and T. C. Wilson, *The Inuit Broadcasting Corporation: A Survey of Viewing Behaviour and Audience Preferences among the Inuit of Ten Communities in the Baffin and Keewatin Regions of the Northwest Territories* (Ottawa: Inuit Broadcasting Corporation, 1984). The IBC was founded in 1981 and has transmitted over CBC since 1982 (Valerie Alia, Un/Covering the North: News, Media, and Aboriginal People [Vancouver: University of British Columbia Press, 1999]), p. 8.

6

Transforming
Traditional Culture

We had everything dumped on us. New beliefs. Traditional ways cut off. They said, "You're going to live like the white man, with white man's laws."
—Pitaloo

Matters of the Spirit

Photo 6.1 Tapestry made by Inuit women, Anglican Church, Pangnirtung.

The Anglican mission, a cluster of wind-worn asbestos shingle buildings dating back to the early part of the twentieth century, sits in the center of the settlement. The chapel bell announces several services a week. The old mission hospital serves as the only Anglican training school in the North (Arthur Turner Training School). Its apartments serve as home for the minister/principal, the ATTS trainees, and other guests. Workers transformed another building into a women's meeting place for sewing, Bible study, prayer, baptismal receptions, and informal gatherings. The small chapel sits nearby.

On this Sunday morning at the end of the twentieth century, we attend the Inuktitut service first. Dozens of parents and children, elders and babies pack into the pews. An elaborate tapestry made by Inuit women adorns the wall behind the altar, depicting the life of the people. The service lasts an hour and a half. A mostly female choir, resplendent in long gowns and choir hats, enthusiastically sings every verse of every hymn. Several "Team Nunavut" sweatshirts and jackets stand out among the congregants, but the Inuit catechists and lay readers wear black choir gowns and surplices during this formal service. Many will return later for Sunday vespers and again Wednesday night for evensong. We remember that Inuit women were instrumental in bringing Christianity into the region, and men into Christianity, with their rejection of shamanism "for worshipping the devil."[1] Inuit women were supportive of such early and influential Anglican missionaries as the Reverend E. J. Peck.

As part of the metamorphosis of this century, an Inuk ministerial student leads the service in Inuktitut. The Inuit have made this service, born hundreds of years ago in England, uniquely theirs. Some Inuit say that adopting Anglicanism was not difficult for them, since Inuit cosmology taught that "the Inuit, the Indians (*allait*), the Europeans (*Qallunaat*) and the mythical *ijiqqat* (invisible beings) are all children of the same mother."[2] The values of mutual aid, honesty, and gratitude characterize both traditional Inuit and traditional Christian world-views, they add.[3] The Inuit creation myth features no men, just one woman who mated with a dog and bore "a litter of dogs and human beings. The latter increased in number and the woman proceeded to plant them out in different places. Some in one place became white men, others in another place Indians, while still others became Eskimos."[4] All had the same mother, though.

Babies sleep in mothers' *amautiit* through the general commotion and singing. Some adults join the service for a while, then leave. Children of all ages ebb and flow through the church, sitting for a few minutes with their parents, and then moving to another pew with a neighbor or aunt. A loose but palpable discipline prevails. Anyone takes responsibility for a toddler who wanders up the aisle toward the altar or starts to cry. This pattern of communal socialization of children, which we have observed many times in other contexts here, expresses a sense of common bonds and mutual support among adults as much as it provides security for children. Adults buttress the child's instinct for exploring and penchant for self-determination, but they also teach the child not to disrupt the service. The sacrosanct hush that typifies southern churches holds no sway here. People talk quietly among themselves and with the children as needed, yet the air remains one of reverence and respect. As the Inuit parishioners leave, we wonder whether a series of concentric circles might be more appropriate for this gathering than the rows of neatly arranged pews.

The English language service begins raggedly at 9:30, with a handful of congregants wondering how to organize to best effect. We sport muddy hiking boots, store-bought parkas, and blue jeans. The Qallunaat minister and ATTS director arrives in denims, a Pangnirtung wool hat, embroidered vest, and graying ponytail. He suggests that we arrange three pews into a more intimate triangle near the front, a circle of sorts. We smile self-consciously as we try to create a semblance of spiritual seriousness.

Winston, who has sailed west to east through the Northwest Passage in a 27-foot steel boat, sits near us. He and his friend John have returned to rescue the boat, which has been ice-bound here since last September. Nine months later, they are still waiting for the ice to clear out of Cumberland Sound so they can head back down the Atlantic coast to the St. Lawrence River and home to Toronto. Many whalers and explorers of other centuries found themselves similarly trapped in the winter ice—and usually owed their lives to sustenance from the Inuit. This time, in an unwelcome twist, Inuit youths have vandalized the boat the previous night. Ironically, the vandals stole John's survival suit, which means an even longer wait until a new one arrives by mail from the south.

Anna Liese, an epidemiologist from Munich, seems hungry for company after hiking alone in the nearby national park for ten days. Ruth and Colin from northern England round out the circle. Ruth has been doing an internship at ATTS to become a full-fledged Anglican minister. Mary, director of the health center, is the only local Qallunaat in our midst. Dwayne, a divinity student in his late 60's from McMaster University, leads our service. Colin and Mary play keyboard and flute. With such a small group, we sing our hymns tentatively, each trying to blend his or her voice into the whole. The hour goes by quickly, followed by a convivial brunch at Colin and Ruth's apartment.

The parable this morning weighs the fruitfulness of casting seeds into fertile soil or among thorns, of planting them at the right depth or too shallow. The minister reflects on this lesson, and although no children sit in our small circle, we realize that in Pangnirtung many are tiny seeds planted too shallow in rocky soil and are expected to grow too soon. That, too, is part of the metamorphosis that has transformed Inuit lives.

T he Inuit have listened to Qallunaat missionaries define their ancient religion as primitive and their shamans as devils. They have watched their language, Inuktitut, slip into disuse generation after generation. Thrust into the value system of a culture that is light years away, many have lost touch with their identity as people of the land. They live in prefabricated mini-ranch houses with indoor plumbing and VCRs. The outside world has impinged on Inuit lifestyle in every conceivable way, from fast food to Nintendo.[5] The Inuit are extremely adept at incorporating southern equipment (such as snowmobiles, which essentially replace train dogs and sleds) and conveniences (such as power sewing machines). These trappings of post-industrial civilization may represent far less impact on Inuit culture, however, than the incursion of Qallunaat perspectives and values through the powerful vehicles of education, religion, and mass media.

A woman who lives in another Baffin community, Pond Inlet, remembers *Qallunaat* telling the Inuit that males should provide for their families (countering the balanced responsibilities of traditional Inuit life): "We were married by the minister because the government told us we should. The government told us that men were supposed to work and support their wives."[6] The sudden shift from a small band to a small town heralded the demise of traditional culture, says a welfare mother of three teenagers, who remembers similar conversations. She is not sure they did the Inuit "a favor" by bringing them in from the land:

> Because the Inuit, us, we lose our culture then. From the beginning of the white people way, we don't have any idea, because it was very different. Our culture is not completely lost, but it has changed in many ways. We still can go fishing and hunting, but we use new equipment. The whalers started it. They had these wonderful, powerful things like rifles, and they started to give them to Inuit.[7]

Many scholars would agree with these women, noting the extent to which the Inuit of Cumberland Sound became integrally connected to external institutions that had broad transformative effects. For example, the Inuit already had a well-developed whaling industry before the American and Scottish commercial whalers penetrated the region during the nineteenth century, altering Inuit life both economically and culturally.[8] Later, in light of the global anti-whaling movement, the contribution of whaling to the Inuit economy declined dramatically. Now, Inuit hunt the great creatures under international management regimes that impose policies that do not necessarily coincide with the subsistence needs of Inuit families.[9]

As whaling began to die out in the early twentieth century, commercialized fox trapping and seal hunting diverted the Inuit from their customary economic patterns. In both cases, fitting into the Qallunaat production system also often led to inadequacies of food and sealskins for clothing and shelter, because of growing dependency on ammunition and gasoline for motorboats. Southern institutions shaped Inuit activities. Moving from the land to the settlement opened the floodgates of "southern" culture from mainstream Canada. For example, "Sometimes the HBC [Hudson's Bay Company] refused to exchange carvings for goods in order to encourage trapping of fox."[10] J. Matthiasson speculates that rifles and ammunition allowed for more plentiful meat. The meat, in turn, allowed the best hunters to feed more dogs and to extend their typical hunting territories. This resulted in a "vicious cycle in which more meat was needed to feed the dogs, and so the dependency on ammunition was reinforced." Culturally, the post-relocation period was a relative vacuum because of the sweeping impacts of Euro-Canadian cultural forces. Religion, schools, and then television served as influential sources of change.

Religion
"Get rid of our practices and our life"

Long before the move into the settlements, missionaries brought Anglicanism and Catholicism to the North. Attirak, 60, has been an Anglican as long as she can remember. Her parents were Anglican: "The missionaries used to come here by ship. They had baptisms at the outhouse down there." Her great-grandmother was a little girl when she was among the first ones baptized in the mid-1800s. Attirak kept her ancestor's papers from this early ceremony. Now, an Inuk man conducts a service in Inuktitut and the Anglican training school in Pangnirtung makes it a point to recruit Inuit trainees from all over Nunavut and Nunavik. In 1991, the first Inuk woman, Loie Mike, entered the three-year program. Will people in the community accept a woman as minister? Iola predicted in the late 1980s that the community would: "We have very good lay leaders in this community. They prove to be really strong and the people respect them." Iola went through this training himself.

Iola realizes that Christianity, through the missionaries, played a critical role in changing the Inuit way of life that has led to "the struggle of the people today." He reminds us that the missionaries considered Inuit beliefs, including shamanism and traditional ways, to be of little value: "They said we have to get rid of our practices and our life." Margaret Penny's diary is instructive in this regard, as she writes about Brother Warmow's efforts to bring Christianity to the Inuit: "The Esquimaux seem to understand very well that they are to respect this day [Sunday], for they go about very quietly and forego their usual occupations."[11] Warmow wrote an impassioned letter to his superiors in the Moravian Church (who did not think that native religion could co-exist with Christianity). He said that because these "natural men" were "not aware of their sin and misery," and therefore did not understand the need for a personal saviour, they would have to be taught the concepts of "sin" and "guilt."[12] Ironically, Brother Warmow believed that the Inuit should not be "cast in a European mould," but that if they adopted Christianity, "true...Christian civilisation will follow...and they will remain what they are, namely Esquimaux."[13]

Iola says that Christianity's dominant values regarding personal conduct and morality transformed the entire culture: "They cannot get rid of their own dignity—this is the major problem for older people. They think they can forget everything they have done before, like shamanism or drum dances. They are missing it, but they may not even realize what they are missing." He believes that the Inuit were seeking truth through shamanism—and agrees that traditional beliefs were remarkably compatible with Christianity. Hantzsch, an ethnographer and explorer who spent two years in the region (Blacklead Island, Nettilling Lake) until his death in 1911, enumerates those values and beliefs: "poverty, freedom from covetousness, contentment with one's daily bread, a widespread community of trifling possessions, and a comprehensive sharing of the fruits of labour and of deprivations [and] meekness."[14] The missionaries dismissed the concept of shamanism, although there were "good shamans and bad shamans"—shamans who saved lives (medicine men and women) and shamans who killed their fellow humans. Against hunger, shamans had no power at all, Iola insists: "Everybody could become hungry, but shamans were not allowed to kill animals. They could show where to go. They could form themselves into animals like walrus. They could be earth. They were very powerful, but they could not kill the animals, even for survival." Other people would bring food to the shamans.

When Christianity came to the North, Iola adds, Inuit "found that truth they had been seeking for a long time. That is the only way they could get rid of shamanism." He means that the Inuit would not have been so ready to embrace Christianity if they had not been searching for a truth that would help them make sense of their lives. Still, since Christianity emanates from Europe rather than from traditional Inuit culture, "We don't have anything that is entirely our own." Dorais remarked that the Christian catechists (*tutsiatitsijiit* or "those who make people pray") may have replaced the shamans, but they performed many of the same functions: communicating with the "suprahuman," "supervising collective rituals, praying for the sick, and advising people."[15]

The church as a social institution may have made the transition into the twentieth century a little easier, but it also brought the Inuit into the twentieth century in the first place. Early missionaries saw the Inuit as heathens, less than human. The oldest woman in town remembers the missionaries telling her that everything about her own religion was "bad." One of the greatest losses was the drum dance, which the missionaries viewed as the embodiment of sin, Iola explains: "Don't touch it! It's bad. You cannot become Christian if you practice drum dances! This was the teaching of the missionaries." The drum dance was not simply the province of shamans, he adds: "Anybody, women too, could do the drum dance for festivals...whenever they gathered together." Today, a few people are trying to revive this ancient tradition and the drum dancer figures prominently in soapstone carvings.[16]

Like other Inuit clergy, Iola believes that "Inuit Christianity" with its own uniqueness could evolve: "We could worship God any way we want. That's what we understand. When we try to worship what we don't understand, we take it for the ritual, just because it's taught that way." The church's physical arrangement offers another arena of possible change, he suggests: "In this community, maybe pews, standing in rows like that, are not the best way to express one's beliefs." Lay ministers could rewrite liturgy and hymns that better reflect Inuit values. Even bringing back the drum dance is a possibility, Iola hints: "It's my objective. If I get my parish, I'll teach my people what we really are and create our own form of practices and worship. We could use the Anglican Common Prayer Book, but why not share what *we* have? We have plenty of good practices that we could do in a circle. There should be what Inuit can understand. That is true worship." The circle of lay leaders has expanded to include Meeka Arnaqaq, Abraham Arnaqaq, Peter Kanayuk, Ooleepeeka Kanayuk, Tommy Evic, Mosesie Qarpik, and Ooleepa Qarpik. Meeka uses the traditional Inuit drum and singing during the services.

As with Native Americans on reserves, Iola argues, it is obvious that whites wanted aboriginal people to learn how to be white. This does not make Iola angry. He simply feels sorry for his people: "When we adopted Christianity, forget our old way of life! Put it aside! Yes, the Bible tells us to have a new life, but we can't put away our dignity and have white man's way of living. The people don't see that." The lay ministers face a special challenge in modernizing the most restrictive elements of Christianity as taught by the early missionaries. Reverend Turner had an enormous impact, says Iola:

> Today, some of the elders don't realize the changes from Christianity of 50 years ago. They think modern religion [clapping hands, speaking in tongues] is all false teaching. It's a big issue. If the older people don't hear what Turner was teaching, they think what you say is false. I'm willing to study the background of our beliefs and our culture. I have to face the people and look to what they can understand. If I just adapt what I learned previously from Turner, they'll be happy, but they're not going to go anywhere.

Iola has "much convincing to do" among the younger people in the settlement but many are more open than the elders: "I can tell by the teenagers who attend church at nine o'clock at night. They clap their hands and they love to sing with actions. That's a good sign. If they go to church with adults in the morning, they stiffen. They follow when they should move." The Arthur Turner Training School has been a "transforming influence," according to a Qallunaat teacher, because it has helped the Inuit adapt to the twentieth century:

> There would have been more friction without the school. When the government took over from the church, all the institutions were in place. The groundwork was already laid. It was not so difficult to build on it. When we were here at first, we didn't realize how deep the spiritual level of the people runs. Their understanding of scripture and spiritual matters is far deeper than we ever realized. They are very perceptive. Because they are Native people, we tend to think that we have to explain things, but often we sit back in awe. When they open up, we realize that we have much to learn from them.

Iola does not work alone. He speaks of an Inuk colleague, the Reverend Ben Arreak,[17] as a dedicated man who goes out of his way to bring the message of Christianity to the people, especially the young: "He has brought many people off the street. Many lives have completely turned around because of his ministry." Until they moved to other settlements, Ben and Iola made regular visits to the people of Pangnirtung, especially on Sundays. Their wives visited with the women, echoing the age-old division of labour. These and other protégés who value mentoring and help with English-language services have thought highly of the Qallunaat directors of the ATTS.

At the dawn of the twenty-first century, the face of religion took on a new look as the Pentecostal movement, which has made significant inroads in other Inuit communities, established itself in Pangnirtung. Although this movement resulted in some inevitable conflict, the existence of a second Christian religion in the hamlet has also rekindled debates and discussions about traditional beliefs versus Christian beliefs. Dorais made the case in his analysis of Nunavik's Quaqtaq (in Northern Quebec) that the struggle for souls does not seem to override basic and mutual concern for the community as a whole.[18]

Education, Southern Style
"Maybe they would give us a spank"

Many of the economic problems that exist in the North stem in part from the educational system the Inuit inherited from government intervention and southern lifestyles. Levels of education among older Inuit are very low. For example, Rosie enjoyed school in the pre-resettlement years when her family lived in Pangnirtung and she attended school at the Anglican mission. The teacher was the Reverend Turner, who taught in Inuktitut. Schooled until age twelve, Rosie was well educated compared to many other women her age. Her friends Meena and Saila, who grew up in the outpost camps, received no formal education. Those who learned their lessons from missionaries out on the land usually received four or five years of tutoring. They never knew what grade they had completed. When Turner died in 1950, formal education ceased temporarily for the local Inuit. What happened later was more disruptive to Inuit culture.

During and after the Resettlement Period, many Inuit fell between the cracks of a southern-dominated educational scheme that did not fit the context of Inuit culture and, even worse, took them away from their families. Many were sent to residential schools that assumed the superiority of southern, European-based culture and education. Parents had to send their children away for the entire year so they could go beyond the lower grades. Residential schools, to which many Inuit were flown for vocational training, were run by whites and taught in English. Confusion in language and values emerges as teachers from the south teach children of the North. Even if the training helps students later in life, the lack of Inuit role models creates a sense of loss. The wrenching separations and the cultural collisions result in loneliness, confusion, and resentment. For their mothers, the issue was not one of leaving the community in order to complete high school or to attend college. It was leaving home in order to receive any formal education whatsoever. Many middle-aged women recall one of the highlights of their life—returning to the camps after being sent away to residential schools.

Minnie remembers how it felt to go home from school to her parents' camp. She attended residential schools for six years during the mid- to late-1960s, learning fluent English. She studied math, science, social studies, English, cooking, home economics, and sewing. The boys took shop instead of the domestic courses: "I don't have very many sad stories, but I had some sad times, being homesick. My parents wouldn't let me go back for the last year, when I was so far away in Churchill for vocational school."

Ida, who was born in a camp and then moved into Pangnirtung, recalls going away to vocational training in Iqaluit for two years. She felt "so alone—that made me sad all the time—with nobody to love or to talk to me." When she returned to Pangnirtung and her family, she felt happy. She never wants to go away again. Theresa finished grade eight in Hamilton, after contracting TB: "I had to go down to the hospital for treatment. I spent almost two years there and one year of school in Frobisher Bay because there was no airstrip here, so I had to wait for the ice floes, for the plane with the skis. I missed my family." She also received some schooling in Pangnirtung when her father came in from the land to study at the mission. Lena completed her education with two years in Churchill for vocationally oriented sixth and seventh graders. Like so many of her generation, she learned some English as a child while recovering from TB in Hamilton but, she acknowledges, "there's not very much for us to do. It's really a sad situation."

Born in Pangnirtung in the early 1950s, hamlet employee Jonah grew up in a camp until the age of eight then lived in the settlement for schooling until age 14. He spent three years in Churchill to complete high school. (Most Inuit who

Photo 6.2 Rebecca Bowkett on the way to camping out on the land.

work in the hamlet administration have finished high school and have gone on to some university courses, but they are the exceptions.) One 50-year-old man recalls: "When I was growing up, the teachers didn't tell me that I could be something." Perhaps the bitterest story comes from Dianne, who disliked residential school for all the right reasons:

"I STARTED TALKING BACK"

The teachers thought I was going against them. I didn't mean to be that way but I always asked "why." They should answer that question just because you want to know. That frustrated me so much that I started talking back to the teacher and they kicked me out of grade nine.

Then I did nothing for a year. I baby-sat a lot—looked after my younger brothers and sisters. We went hunting with my parents. Then I went back to school in Iqaluit. I liked going to school there, but I didn't like the idea of being isolated and living without privacy. I don't know why they made us have four girls in a room, because one story was empty. I stayed on the couch all the time. I had to wait until everyone went to sleep before I could go to sleep. If I try to do anything on my own, it's not allowed.

I lived there for a year. I could have stuck with that, but I'm not supposed to do everything that I like to do. I have to follow rules. When I was going to school, there was no university. For further education, I would have to go down south. I don't know how that operates, so I didn't even bother.

Although Pangnirtung and other settlements eventually built their own schools, the persistence of a southern curriculum and English-language dominance continued to stress Inuit culture (see Chapter 16).

The Lure of Television
"Magic in the sky"

Other changes followed the Inuit into settlement life. Since 1975, television—the "magic in the sky"—has beamed into Inuit homes the foreign and intriguing images of whites living in beautiful houses, eating exotic foods, and driving luxury cars. Glowing relentlessly in Inuit living rooms, TV also reinforces the English language for children. Older Inuit women and men watch Wheel of Fortune, All My Children, or NYPD Blue, even when they cannot comprehend the words.[19] The younger ones, who know English, have full access to the lifestyles portrayed on the sitcoms or soap operas. Exposure to southern culture can indelibly affect them. Children and teens receive a distorted view of southern society and of a woman's life—the splendid kitchen, dazzling clothes, and extravagant cocktail parties that fill the screen day and night. Those images are light years away from the Inuit experience. Videocassettes, always in English, bring an array of violent images.

Because the national Canadian Broadcasting Corporation (CBC) television service was broadcasting over 100 hours per week in English programs, the Inuit petitioned the Canadian Radio, Television and Telecommunications Commission for greater control of TV broadcasting and for Inuktitut programming. In 1975, the Inuit Tapirisat proposed the "Inukshuk Project," which resulted in many indigenous language programs being distributed by satellite to the Inuit communities. That, in turn, led to the Inuit Broadcasting Corporation in 1981. Now, Inuit programming brings the Inuktitut language and traditional culture (as well as contemporary news and features) into Inuit living rooms.

Children seem especially susceptible to the cultural pulls of television. Rosemary, 14, acknowledges that TV is good for some things, bad for others: She learns "good things but about guns and violence, too...it's in between." Another high school student believes that the steady television diet causes "a breakdown of dignity" among Inuit youths. Parents worry that television might be distorting their children's' views of reality. Though it holds a certain fascination for children, not all of them are "glued to the television," because their mothers refuse to allow them unlimited viewing. Apea takes this approach: "Just before their bedtime, I let them watch a little TV. Before school starts, when they try to put the TV on I tell them to turn it off, and they do. I say you can look at that after school. Even if their parents say something, some kids don't listen. They just watch it anyway."

Television also brings graphic portrayals of problems that have become all too familiar now that Inuit live in larger communities, says Leah:

> We have more problems nowadays than before. When I was growing up, I didn't even know about assault or about problems between brothers and sisters [incest], or mothers and fathers [domestic violence]. Since we started having TV or watching movies, the kids maybe learned how to fight. Those days, the women had to make clothes and the husband got the food, maybe that's why they got along. They were proud to do something for each other.

Now, Leah laments, women and men buy clothes when they can afford to, emulating the southern life styles and fashions they see on television every day. Television creates a constant reminder of the duality of Inuit life on the edge of two cultures, neither of which entirely fits any more.

Language
"They didn't allow us to use Inuktitut"

One of the most powerful transformers of Inuit culture was the English language. Conversely, the Inuktitut language was a near casualty of contact with mainstream culture (although today it has a high viability level). Part of the earlier educational experience, especially in residential schools, was teacher insistence on using English as the only acceptable language for academic and even social discourse: "It was all in English when we were in school." Classes were held in this foreign language, and students were discouraged from speaking Inuktitut in the halls or at play. A town employee remembers: "If we say a word in Inuktitut, the teacher would get mad at us for speaking our language. We would get spanked or put in a corner." One woman recalls that she ended up speaking very little in either language:

> The teachers were okay—but they didn't allow us to use our own language. We could use Inuktitut in the bedrooms but not in school. It was very confusing. We had to try to speak English all the time. I didn't have any English then. In the first year, I had a very hard time. After a few months, it didn't bother me anymore.

Louis-Jacques Dorais suggested that "the rate of preservation of Inuktitut as a first language is higher in areas where intensive contacts with the outside world are more recent." Because the Inuit living around Cumberland Sound were in daily contact with English-speaking whalers in the nineteenth century, the infiltration of English and the deterioration of Inuktitut began long before the Resettlement Period (though resettlement certainly hastened the process).[20] In spite of this pattern, scholars define Inuktitut as a "viable language" in terms of having a large enough population base to ensure survival. In Canada, Inuktitut, Cree, and Ojibway are the three most flourishing aboriginal languages. Inuktitut is still spoken in all Inuit communities. Several newspapers and the IBC use the language on a regular basis. According to Norris, over 27,000 people speak Inuktitut as their mother tongue and the language has a relatively high "continuity index" from one generation to the next.[21]

The remoteness of Arctic settlements and recent efforts to bring Inuktitut into the schools are working in favor of preserving the language. Dorais found in the small community of Quaqtaq that language is a complicated matter. For example, he says that Inuit government workers speak Inuktitut all day (except to Anglophones or Francophones) but write reports and memos in English. Inuit children who have learned Inuktitut in school express themselves differently in terms of sentence structure than do their parents and grandparents. Younger Inuit find it easier to express themselves in English when it comes to technical matters and may prefer Anglophone magazines rather than materials that are available in Inuktitut.[22] In 1991, Dorais described the population of Pangnirtung as about 94% Inuit; among the Inuit, virtually 100% spoke Inuktitut. This was the highest percentage among Baffin hamlets. At the time, only about 83% of all Inuit in the Northwest Territories spoke Inuktitut.[23] We have since found that the presence of two or more generations in the vast majority of Pangnirtung households also means the presence of both Inuktitut and English, at varying levels of fluency and for different purposes. The choice of language also depends greatly on the primary language of guests, customers, clients, and observers. As Dorais correctly observed, the Inuit community "now needs more than one language to function adequately" in traditional and modern, domestic and national cultural contexts.[24] He adds that even in communities where Inuit use Inuktitut predominantly and regularly, English is still the "most powerful" language because of the transformation of Inuktitut (with English words being used to describe new technologies and phenomena), the presence of Qallunaat (who have had certain economic and political advantages since contact), and the necessity to communicate with the national government.[25]

Inuktitut oral tradition can be written in two different systems—syllabics or phonetics. Qatsuq remembers learning syllabics and arithmetic at Kekerten. Her mother helped teach the others how to "write in Eskimo," which she practiced every evening at home.[26] Still, the ability to *speak* Inuktitut has slowly dissipated from one generation to the next. According to a nurse, though, almost everyone in town is literate in one language or the other—the legacy of missionary days. This helps in health education and communication about social programs.

The middle-aged, those who grew up on the land and received education during the early waves of resettlement, are fluent in both languages. The younger parents, born after 1960 and educated solely in English-centered schools, struggle to teach their children the little Inuktitut they learned at home.

For the women and men who came to the settlement as small children, and even for some of their children, exposure to traditional culture was haphazard at best. Many find passing on the language to the youngest generation a frustrating and labourious process. Their command of Inuktitut is shaky, and many words and expressions cannot be translated into English (or vice versa). Some women report a comfortable flow from one language to another, and understand the body language, intonations, and signs. Others complain that children do not like to speak their own language:

> They prefer to speak English. If I speak to my daughter in Inuktitut, she answers back in *Qallunaatitut* [English]. They know how to speak Inuktitut, but they always talk in English. They seem to put their language aside.[27]

Wanting to preserve their language and being able to do so are two different things, as Meena explains: "I would like to keep my language. Speak English, sure, but I would keep my language stronger...that's what I want my kids to do. It's really hard for them." The reluctance of young people to try their wings in Inuktitut contributes to the widening generation gap: "Older people and the younger generation do not have good communication." Dramatic differences in language, education, and experience produce misunderstandings, tension, and lapses in discipline, Meena believes:

> There is a breakdown of communication and authority between the elder group, who are so much wiser, and the younger group, who feel they are today's children. They are learning today's knowledge in schools—they know so much more. They dress in today's way. They speak today's language. The teacher who taught us Inuktitut said that even the language has changed. The younger people absorb so many English words.

Young people often do not understand older people because their language seems comparatively archaic. The older ones have to learn the new terms or feel alienated by the conversation. Young Inuit translate and interpret for their parents, in a reversal of dependence that immigrant families also experience. White teachers become the more salient models and leaders, which tends to undermine parental authority. Parents, especially those who grew up on the land, want their children to learn the ways of the land; teachers represent learning the ways of mainstream, southern culture. This split leads to problems of discipline, guidance, and stability, many believe. Children often behave "as if their ears were plugged when their father and mother are speaking," Dorais observed.[28]

This conflict between traditional and modern, parent and child emerges in many of our discussions about language and identity. For example, teenager Sandie thinks people her age may be losing their culture: "I have a hard time pronouncing an Inuktitut word that I've never heard before—or I heard it a long time ago and forgot it. I have to ask what the word means." She is bilingual to a degree that satisfies neither her nor her parents, who speak both English and Inuktitut at home. Like other teens, Sandie wants to preserve her culture and teach her children the ancient language someday, "but I hope I don't forget my English." She expresses the subtle shift toward English as the dominant medium of communication for her generation, although she insists that "my Inuktitut" is most important: "If you can't speak your language, what am I going to call you? You're not Inuk; you're not Qallunaat—what are you? You are nothing if you are not Qallunaat—even though you speak *Qallunaatitut* very well—because you are Inuk. If you don't speak your own language, you're not Inuk."

A few years ago, children started speaking English all the time, especially those with younger parents who went away to residential schools and know English better than Inuktitut. Parents and some teachers wanted children to learn Inuktitut in school but school committee members and other teachers preferred the dominance of English because they believed it would help the Inuit move forward. The battle, only recently won in the late 1990s, frustrates an Inuk woman who teaches the children of her community.

> I am teaching kindergarten in English—and I am fighting the language! This year I asked to teach Inuktitut with the older students, because I really feel I can help the older ones with the language, but they [the white principal and superintendent] haven't decided yet. *Qallunaatitut! Qallunaatitut!* We are losing our language. I don't feel too comfortable teaching *Qallunaatitut* because I am against the language. I don't like the little ones being taught in English, yet I am the one who is teaching them. I would feel more comfortable teaching in Inuktitut because I can speak it and write it. I can *feel* it.

Language reflects cultural identity at a very deep level, according to Dorais, so any attack on Inuktitut "may lead to the destruction, or, at least, the progressive erosion of an original semantic and cognitive structure which, in its integrity, is necessary to the maintenance of the Arctic people's collective identity. [This] would have unfortunate and far-reaching consequences for Inuit individuals and communities."[29] While Inuit, like ethnic groups around the world, perceive a linguistic and a kinship/genealogical dimension to being *Inummarik* (a "genuine Inuk"), being able to speak Inuktitut is a core part of one's Inuit identity.[30] This is why so many of our consultants equated losing their language fluency with losing their culture.

Preserving their culture in the face of other religions, educational models, and linguistic influences presents a formidable task that runs counter to many realities of contemporary Inuit life. The Inuit stress that their culture is not completely lost, but it certainly has changed in dramatic ways. They also agree that they have not been passive victims of cultural and social change. Each step of the way, they have made choices, taken advantage of technology and goods imported from other places, and derived benefits from an adaptive lifestyle. Although social change might have been inevitable for the Inuit, and some changes were imposed, Inuit women and men are quick to point out that their cultural metamorphosis includes both positive and negative elements. They see their future in terms of the challenges presented by change that has permeated every corner of their lives.

Notes

1 Louis McComber, "Anthropologist Unearths Treasure Trove of Inuit Culture," *Nunatsiaq News* (October 16, 1998).
2 Dorais, "The Canadian Inuit and Their Language," p. 187.
3 Dorais, *Quaqtaq*, p. 72.
4 Diamond Jenness, myth no. 72d (1924), cited in Dorais, "The Canadian Inuit and Their Language," p. 201.
5 For a discussion of the impact of rapid social change throughout the Inuit and Dene communities, see Billson, "Social Change, Social Problems, and the Search for Identity." Anthropologist June Helm documents Dene life during the last fifty years in *The People of Denendeh: Ethnohistory of the Indians of Canada's Northwest Territories* (Montréal: McGill-Queen's University Press, Rupert's Land Record Society Series, 2002).
6 Nancy Wachowich with Apphia Agalakti, Rhoda Kaukjak Katsak, and Sandra Pikujak Katsak. *Saqiyuq: Stories from the Lives of Three Inuit Women* (Montréal: McGill-Queens University Press, 1999), p. 112. Pond Inlet lies on the north side of Baffin Island.
7 *Living on the Land*, p. 33.
8 Stevenson, *Inuit, Whalers, and Cultural Persistence*, pp. 84, 98. See also Ross, *This Distant and Unsurveyed Country*, p. 87.
9 Milton M. R. Freeman, Lycrimila Bogosloskaya, Richard A. Caulfield, Ingmar Egede, Igor I. Krupnik, and Marc G. Stevenson, *Inuit, Whaling, and Sustainability* (Sponsored by the Inuit Circumpolar Conference. Walnut Creek, CA: AltaMira Press, 1998).
10 Smith, *Inujjuamiut Foraging Strategies*, p. 122.
11 Ross, *This Distant and Unsurveyed Country*, p. 79.
12 Brother Matthau Warmow's diary, cited in Ross, *This Distant and Unsurveyed Country*, p. 166.
13 Ross, *This Distant and Unsurveyed Country*, p. 109.
14 Hantzsch, *My Life among the Eskimos*, p. 37.
15 Dorais, *Quaqtaq*, p. 72-73.
16 For a description of the cultural significance of the drum dance, see M. L. Asch, *Kinship and the Drum Dance in a Northern Dene Community* (Edmonton: Canadian Circumpolar Institute, 1988); Jarich Gerlof Oosten analyzes shamanistic beliefs and behaviours in "The Structure of the Shamanistic Complex among the Netsilik and Iglulik," *Ètudes/Inuit/Studies* 5, 1 (1981): 83-98.
17 Arreak, who was nominated as Bishop of the Anglican Diocese of the Arctic, lost out in the twentieth round of voting. He worked in another settlement as of 1996.

18 Dorais, *Quaqtaq*, pp. 78-79. See also Cornelius H. W. Rémie, "Culture, Change and Religious Continuity among the Arviligdjuarmiut of Pelly Bay, NWT, 1935-1963," *Études/Inuit/Studies* 7, 2 (1983): 53-77.

19 Dorais documented that television tends to be on "all day long" among the Northern Québec Quaqtamiut; older Quaqtamiut women like to watch *All My Children* and *Bob Newhart*, even (as we noticed) when they do not understand English. Dorais, *Quaqtaq*, p. 83; see also Gary O. Coldevin, "Satellite Television and Cultural Replacement among Canadian Eskimos: Adults and Adolescents Compared," *Communication Research* VI, 5, 2 (1979): 115-133; Nelson H. H. Graburn, "Television and the Canadian Inuit," *Études/Inuit/Studies* 6, 1 (1982): 7-17; and B. L. Green and D. Simailak, "The Inukshuk Project: Use of TV and Satellite by Inuit Communities in the Northwest Territories," paper presented at the American Association for the Advancement of Science Annual Meeting, Toronto, January 1981.

20 Dorais, "The Canadian Inuit and Their Language," p. 193; also Dorais, "Language, Identity and Integration in the Canadian Arctic," *North Atlantic Studies* 3, 1 (1991): 18-24; "The Canadian Inuit and Their Language"; "Inuit Identity in Canada," *Folk* 30 (1988): 23-31; and "Language Revitalisation vs. Language Loss in the Canadian Arctic," *Sixth Inuit Studies Conference, Copenhagen October 17-20, 1988: Abstracts* (Copenhagen: Institute of Eskimology, University of Copenhagen, 1988).

21 Mary Jane Norris, "Canada's Aboriginal Languages," *Canadian Social Trends* (Winter 1998): 8-16. Since the Canadian Government lists 27,000 as the population of Nunavut and only 80 percent are Inuit, and since not all Inuit speak Inuktitut (especially the transitional generation), Norris's figure may be high.

22 Dorais, *Quaqtaq*, p. 82. For a discussion of the generation gap and language, see Martha Borgmann Crago, Betsy Annahatak, and Lizzie Ningiuruvik, "Changing Patterns of Language Socialisation in Inuit Homes," *Anthropology and Education Quarterly* 24, 3 (1993): 205-223.

23 Louis-Jacques Dorais. "La situation linguistique dans l'Arctique." *Etudes/Inuit/Studies* 16, 1-2 (1992): 246-248.

24 Dorais, *Quaqtaq*, p. 83.

25 Dorais, *Quaqtaq*, p. 83.

26 Hodgson, ed., *Stories from Pangnirtung*.

27 Eber and Pitseolak also make this point in *People from Our Side*.

28 Dorais, *Quaqtaq*, p. 96.

29 Dorais, "The Canadian Inuit and Their Language," p. 207.

30 Dorais, *Quaqtaq*, p. 87. Research among Inuit living in Montréal suggests that definitions of Inuit identity may not depend on language, lifestyle, or participation in Inuit culture (all of which have faded among many urban Inuit) as much as on a desire to be included in Inuit political status: "Young men who were raised in Montréal, and Inuit descendants whose spouse or parent was non-Inuit, have begun to regard themselves as indigenous people of Canada, Canadians of Inuit descent, or people of Québec rather than Inuit." Nobuhiro Kishigami, quoted in Jane George, "Inuit Identity: How Do You Know You're an Inuk? Researcher Probes How Urban Inuit Define Themselves," *Nunatsiaq News* (June 15, 2001).

IV

LIVING ON THE EDGE

Today we are in shock from everything going so fast. When I talk to my youngest daughter, she does not know what I am talking about. This depression comes up when we are in between.

—Malaya

Photo 7.1   Walking through the streets of Nunavut's capital, Iqaluit.

7

Culture Shock and Marginality[1]

I remember living in the camp, and I still like to keep my culture. It's hard now because we can't do anything about it. I can move to the camp and try to use it, but it's no use.

—Meeka

The Peninsula

Photo 7.2   Shark Fiord at sunset.

In the cool days of late August we go camping with an Inuit family. The boat has just nosed into a promising place inside the hook of a small bay. We hop across boulders scattered along the beach, and marvel at the perfection of this sheltered spot. A jumble of enormous boulders blocks the view of Cumberland Sound to the west. To the east, a steep, mossy cliff offers a precarious place for children to play above the tundra.

We put up our tent, lay down the sleeping platforms, and cover them with mats and sleeping bags. Seven of us, from 5 years old to 59, will sleep side-by-side across the mats, like sardines packed neatly into a little tin. Tea is on the boil, as always, and fresh Arctic char simmers with carrots and noodles in another kettle. We break off wedges of bannock and sip the hot tea, the perfect antidote to a chilly boat ride.

After supper, we climb a hundred feet above Cumberland Sound to watch the fiery sun descend slowly behind a distant hill. Its reflection sears a scarlet sword into the glacial water below us. As we wander along the ridge, we find the remnants of an ancient campsite, several stone rings that Inuit families used to fasten their tents against the wind, and the weathered wood of old sleeping platforms. In the old days, the distance between these platforms was a good measure of the social solidarity between household and family groupings.[2] We stumble across two wooden coffins that have long since fallen apart; skulls and bones spill onto the tundra, a soft resting place of moss and tiny wild flowers. The rusted bottom of an old *qulliq* lies nearby, confirming that this is a pre-settlement camp of the mid-nineteenth century or earlier.

Whoever these old Inuit were, they had cleverly placed their encampment in a flat, grassy clearing at the crest of what we now realize is a peninsula. Looking down the cliff face to the north, we see our welcoming little beach. Looking down to the south, we see another bay and another beach rimmed with spectacular rocky outcroppings. When we stand in the center of the peninsula, we can see both bays and both beaches. In either direction, we can see ring seals popping up for air and icebergs creeping along the far shores. If we walk toward the north just a few feet, we can see our boat and tent down below, but we lose sight of the beach on the south side. If we walk toward the south a few feet, we lose sight of our boat and tent, but we can easily look down the cliff to the sandy beach on the opposite side.

We walk around the old campsite for a while, keeping an eye on the lingering sunset that illuminates the bay to the north. Then we wander back toward the south to watch the icebergs turning pink and gold with the sun's reflection. Cameras in hand, we feel pulled back and forth across the clearing, trying to get the best shots. Never can we see *all* the beauty of both sides at once.

This place seems to be a metaphor ᴜᶜ Inuit life in recent decades. If the people move closer to the "modern" southern lifestyle, they lose sight of the anchor of their old ways. If they move closer to the "traditional" Inuit lifestyle, they lose sight of the promise of the new ways. Always, they can see part of both sides, both lifestyles, both cultures. Never can they keep one completely in view if they move too far toward the other; never can they completely choose one over the other.

Some facilely say that the Inuit are creating a new lifestyle, unique in its blend of north and south and innovative cultural expressions. That argument holds only so much water, though. We can go down to the south beach and bring up the gold-speckled stones, or descend to the north beach and collect tiny clamshells, but neither exists by itself at the crest of the peninsula. If we try to blend the two, we are still combining elements derived from two separate places. Sometimes the combination stirs the imagination to new creativity; sometimes it jars the soul and confuses the heart.

This conundrum reminds us of an Inuk friend who walks through Pangnirtung in her beautiful flowered cotton *amautik*, a creative blend of new fabrics and old patterns. She wears sealskin boots over toenails painted pink or gold or blue, depending on her mood. She eats Kentucky Fried Chicken from the Northern Store but treasures a piece of dried seal that she tucks safely into her blue jeans pockets. While we are visiting her one evening, the woman slips into the frosty night air to eat raw caribou with a friend on the back steps. She does not want us to see them there, blood on their lips and fingers, "eaters of raw meat," because she assumes we will feel disgusted.[3] When they finish, the woman comes back inside to serve us coffee and croissants, which she also enjoys: The best of both worlds, perhaps, but not without self-consciousness.

The people who lived in this place long ago, with its double perspective and its double attractions, must have realized that they were doubly blessed. Perhaps they too suffered from uncertainty about which way to look and which way to walk from the first moments of contact with missionaries, traders, and explorers.

ᴄ℞

As of 1991, Hugh Brody wrote: "Southern culture has gone beyond merely impinging on the Eskimos' quasi-traditional life; it has now transformed every aspect of Eskimo life."[4] He encapsulated the marginal status of the Inuit who "live in government-built houses with subsidized rents and southern services, who are under the direction of southern political institutions and southern officials." The Inuit, Brody says, are bound to be worried and indignant: "The ground they stand on is forever shifting."[5]

Life no longer depends on a man's hunting prowess but on his ability to buy expensive gasoline for motorized canoes or bullets for rifles.[6] A woman's sewing skills recede into a dimly lit corridor of cultural memories, surpassed by her need to work for wages in a store or a government office. Although many have admired the Inuit for their adaptability, these social earthquakes have produced startling tremors that sometimes knock people off balance. The Inuit are heavily assimilated into southern ways, to the point that Jacques-Louis Dorais, in his study of the Quaqtamiut, distinguished between "assimilated Inuit" and "true Inuit" (*inutuinnait*).[7] Colonialism and paternalism have left far-reaching social implications.

Caught between Two Worlds
"What's going on?"

Inuit women face the same problems that confront other women in Canada, but their marginal status in a nation that is only now coming to grips with the legacy of aboriginal oppression amplifies their daily challenges. As Qaida says, "We ask ourselves, what's going on?" As so many Inuit express eloquently in their own words, they occupy a classically marginal position, straddling two cultures, belonging fully to neither.[8] For Inuit women, individual identity is inextricably tethered to cultural identity. They speak of their marginal status as Native people living between two worlds: traditional Inuit society and mainstream (southern) Canadian society. Rooted in the old culture, the Inuit still must function in a world full of computers, videos, and formal schooling. This excruciatingly stressful situation involves culture shock and aggravates bitterness, depression, and frustration, as Minnie Aodla Freeman describes:

> I keep telling myself that I have been born twice, once to grow and learn my own culture, and again to learn *Qallunaat* culture. Once I was asked which way of life I preferred. I said that I did not really know, and that it would take years to explain my choices and preferences. They both have good and bad, wonderful and sad, easy and hard times.[9]

The social symptoms of marginality signal the pain of economic dislocation and a fractured culture. Although these symptoms manifest themselves in "social problems," the true problems lie deeper in the structural tissue of political, economic, and cultural isolation. Chapter 19 addresses some of these broader issues, including the significance of the creation of Nunavut as a way to achieve Inuit empowerment. In this chapter, we explore the problems that Inuit women face as constant reminders of a complicated past and an uncertain future.

Cultural and Structural Marginality
"No owner of soil"[10]

T he marginal person can be described as "no owner of soil," in the figurative if not the literal sense. One's roots and identity lay split between two cultures. Ownership of a secure place in the social structure becomes compromised. Resettlement succeeded in creating a structurally and culturally marginalized people. Structurally, in relation to wider Canadian society, Inuit are at the economic, political, and geographic fringe. Culturally, Inuit are rapidly losing the traditional life skills that ensured survival for their grandparents; yet, they have not acquired all the skills that post-industrial, techtronic society requires.

Cultural Marginality

This type of marginality refers to the dilemmas of cross-cultural contact and assimilation that the Inuit have encountered during the past century.[11] The clash of cultures produces a measurable psychosocial impact on individual personality, as well as perplexing ambiguities of status and role. As aboriginal people in the North American historical context, Inuit fall prey to cultural marginality, originally described by Everett Stonequist in *The Marginal Man:*

> The marginal man is...poised in psychological uncertainty between two (or more) social worlds; reflecting in his soul the discords and harmonies, repulsions and attractions of these worlds, one of which is often "dominant" over the other; within which membership is implicitly if not explicitly based upon birth or ancestry (race or nationality); and where exclusion removes the individual from a system of group relations.[12]

Structural Marginality

Structural marginality refers to the political, social, and economic powerlessness of disadvantaged groups.[13] It springs from location at the edge of the socioeconomic structure, rather than from cultural or social role dilemmas. Antonovsky suggests that marginality occurs when two cultures—one of them dominant and attractive to the other—experience contact for more than one generation. The marginal group (in this case the Inuit) internalizes the patterns of the dominant culture (the Qallunaat) but cannot completely integrate them with their own values and goals. Attempts to belong to the dominant culture produce discrimination on the one hand and condemnation for betrayal on the other. Antonovsky also stressed the "superior reward potential" of the dominant culture as a factor in its attractiveness for the marginal group.[14]

Stonequist acknowledged that since each of us has as many social selves as we have audiences, we experience at some point in our lives the kind of "dual personality" associated with marginality. Any time a person or group feels caught between two identity-providing orientations but cannot fully embrace the preferred role or either role—because of structural or social limitations—he or she is in a marginal situation.[15]

The Challenges of Marginality
"Two big kids fighting all the time"

Marginality provides the paramount defining characteristic of Inuit women's sense of self. Their strength as keepers of the culture and, increasingly, as breadwinners lies at the heart of their identity. In this case, marginality has affected both gender identity and ethnic identity. A health aide, Ooli, explains:

> I was growing up in two different big groups and they were both strong. One was my traditional race; the other one was school. I was learning southern style—go to school, get a job, plan. Unfortunately, it doesn't work very well for me because I have two big kids fighting inside me all the time! I don't want it to be that way.

Qautuk thinks things have gone too fast for the Inuit: "In 50 years, our people have been changed so fast—for the last 30 years we are lost. I hope it will get better." Ben agrees: "I was like that for a while—which way am I going to have a life? I told myself that I could not go back to where I grew up. I have to accept them both. I was 17." Sometimes Ooli becomes so frustrated that she hikes into the mountains and cries. She says that many of her friends share in those tears: "We take a long walk, talking about it and telling each other, 'You can't give up.'" She tries to control her frustration so that "it's in back of me, not in front of me. I should try to be in front of myself, then there should be someone else in front of me—my Creator."

In this part of the Arctic, mid-twentieth century schools inculcated the patriarchal values of white, Anglo-European society. Parents view education as a key community problem in a time of anxiety and demoralization. After a generation schooled in southern ways and the English language, traditional culture faded rapidly. For decades, Inuit children have spent a significant portion of their waking hours sitting in school, whether away from home or in the community. This experience has opened new worlds, but it has also served to distance children from their parents and their parents' world. Lack of communication undermines many families, Meeka observes: "The kids stay in school all day. When they go home, they want to play outside. They don't live with their parents any more. They live with the teachers—they are raised by them, really." The impact of school was hard to compete with; degradation of ethnic identity was part of the informal curriculum, Sara remembers: "Nine o'clock to four o'clock. We were sitting all day, writing. If I say something in Inuktitut, I go to the office, or I get shit for it, or I get a slap on the wrist, or I stand in a corner. You can't make people learn the hard way. You brainwash them if you do that."

An aide remembers children expressing the anxiety symptoms classically associated with marginal status when they were sent away to boarding school: "They're trembling, they're scared, they can't stop from peeing." As with other women in the transitional generation, her grandmother wanted her "not to forget the Inuit way." She feels caught between two worlds, Maata explains:

"CAUGHT IN BETWEEN"

I try to live balanced, but I'm caught in between! I know how to be Inuk but not fully Inuk like my parents were. I'll never be that...I know the white's way of life but that will never make me a white, so I am in between. I am living both ways. I try to go out on the land as much as possible with my children. When we live down there, we feel free. There is no government out on the land, where my ancestors lived. That's when I have good feelings: "Boy, this is me, I'm an Inuk!" ...Sometimes it hurts me so hard...I don't know the feeling. We go with our kids all the time. We travel long distances, sometimes to Lake Harbour by canoe. The kids enjoy that, but most of my age group are caught in between. They know how to be a bit of white, a bit of Inuk, but they're living both sides.

It would have been far better when white people came up North, a long time ago, if they had listened to us in the first place—learned from us, did things the way we did...and just accepted our culture. If they had learned from us, worked with us, instead of walking all over us, everything would have worked out better today. We would have more of the traditional ways. That wasn't to be, so we have to make the best of things. That's why we try to work hard, to make the best of things. Everything is *so* expensive. There's not very much money or employment. They let us learn...but they have no jobs to offer us in our towns. What's the use of education? I am a kindergarten teacher, but...most Inuit people never really want to get away from home...all the good jobs are down south. The few jobs you see have already been taken. [16]

A marginal person is likely to have higher rates of frustration, identity confusion, depression, anger, anxiety, schizophrenia, and suicidal thoughts. When it comes to violence in intimate relationships, the most marginal generation—people in their 20s, 30s, and 40s—also contains the most perpetrators and victims. The older Inuit, who lived in the camps, remain steeped in the stability of traditional culture, although certainly a few instances of suicide occurred before resettlement. [17] The middle generation suffers the most. An Inuk leader offers her hypothesis: "Children are southernized. The 'in the middle crowd' are confused. They know some of the traditional ways *and* some of the southern ways. They don't know which way to go." [18] This generation forms "the link between life on the land and life in a settlement."

Ooli agrees: "We are caught between two lifestyles—NBA, football, $150 sneakers—and grandparents who still fish out on the land. A frustration comes from being caught in between. Young people feel caught between tradition and the outside world they see on TV. Young people don't know whether to leave tradition behind…or how to blend it if they don't leave it behind."

The youngest generation feels the pulls of marginality, too. A white teacher observes her students: "They're losing the life skills and they haven't yet acquired the skills that technology requires, so they're neither here nor there." Many young people seem disgruntled, she says: "They don't have very happy faces. They don't greet you happily unless you go out of your way and persist in being happy. We are responsible, in their eyes, for bringing all this upon them—in a sense destroying what they've stood for and how they've lived." Even when younger ones do not consciously think or talk that way, teachers, RCMP, and others detect a "subtle resentment" that is perhaps the most elusive, yet most pervasive symptom of rapid social change. This subtle resentment against white domination may be lifting somewhat, the teacher believes. A few years ago, "things were very tense in this community." Now, young women and men are more outgoing; they accept outsiders and talk to them. Teachers see signs of marginal status reflected in the classroom and believe it has a great deal to do with why Inuit teens, especially males, are prone to drop out of school.

Fifteen-year-old Jennie puts it succinctly: "Being an Inuk person is just like being an English-speaking person, but you have to go hunting, and you have a hard time going to the store because you don't have much money." She talks about the poverty in her town and sharing food with those who are poorer than her family. Being an Inuk is different, she says. Sometimes the white teachers yell at the Inuit children, which she resents because she does not want to lose her language: "The Inuit people have a hard time reading English." Jennie clearly feels torn between new and old ways, southern and Inuit ways, as this story of inner conflict reveals:

> I'd like to go back to the old times, but I don't think we ever can because we have all these things, like TV. I am almost stuck to the TV! I don't want to watch TV, but I just can't help it. I like to go hunting instead of watching TV. I want to use the old times, like harpoons and stuff. I don't know why I want to go back to the old times. I think the old way is the best way, because sometimes now Inuit steal things when they don't have any money. In the old times, my grandma always says we would just tell them not to steal things and they would return it. We can't do that anymore because when the RCMP find out who they are, they have to go to court or to jail.
>
> I don't like the new ways. The old people always tell about the old times, but people don't listen. The old times were better because there weren't any drugs or stuff. I don't like it now because taking drugs is serious and you can die from them, and from cigarettes.

Jennie's Aunt Mona knows the pain of being caught between two worlds, and sees her children learning both southern ways and Inuit ways: "I cannot make my child a white person. I can't make her Inuk totally. She is part of both. I *want* her to be part of both, so I have to allow her to do that. That's hard sometimes." Mona feels caught "in between." We don't know this culture that we're trying to get into, and we can't go there because of our culture, our food." She believes things might improve a little for the next generation:

> My daughter is going to know more than I do about the good way from your people and the good way from my culture. She can decide. I know she's going to be Inuk—that's what she wants to be—but she can use your culture to change the way the world is going.

Many women agree that the younger ones seem lost, lacking the skills of either culture. Some feel angry with them, or at least frustrated by their behaviour. In talking about crime and problems with alcohol, Quppa says that she has "very little respect for the younger ones." In the next breath she adds, "It's probably not their fault. They're caught between two civilizations." She would like to see them help themselves more: "You see them around the Northern Store, all day long. There must be twenty people there, scared to death that somebody's going to offer them a job. They are perfectly capable of working. They have lots of smarts...they just don't care." This southern-oriented group does not seem to fit in well. On the other hand, she thinks the Inuit-oriented group that "try to live in the past" may also be chasing a chimera. Udluriak, in her late 30s, expresses this dilemma well:

"I'M SORT OF IN THE MIDDLE"

Today I'm living in a limbo. I'm not working. Taking care of kids? I don't consider that work. I want to work with them and enjoy them, but I found out it's not going to be so right now. They're growing up in front of my eyes, but I'm not enjoying it and I'm not part of it.

I'm the example of most of today's women. I don't know how to do the work that the old people did, yet I haven't found new meaningful work. I know how to make *kamiks*, but I'm not making them every day. I'm not really learning how to make caribou skin parkas. When I was younger, I knew how to make traditional clothing, but I've forgotten how to *start* sewing now. I don't have a career, not even a job. I'm not really up to either one [culture] and I don't know how to move toward either one. I guess I'm sort of in the middle, eh? My mother's life was much harder than my life now. I just do a little teaching. I'm just living today.

Like many other women her age, Udluriak cannot go back to school because she has several children. Her husband is not hunting much, so getting skins for sewing is a problem. She is reluctant to take skins or material away from her mother, whom she sees as a superior seamstress: "She can put good use to sealskin, where I would just break it up and have it in the garbage in no time."

The women of her generation are floating in limbo: "We can't sew traditionally, we can't work, and we can't go to school because of the children," Udluriak explains: "That's why we have a sewing group every week—so we can teach these younger girls." The older women hope the sewing lessons will reduce the impacts of marginality and dislocation that cast a shadow on Inuit lives.

Notes

1 Based in part on Billson, "Opportunity or Tragedy? The Impact of Canadian Resettlement Policy on Canadian Inuit Families." Used with permission.

2 Guemple, "Teaching Social Relations to Inuit Children," p. 133.

3 Nuttall cites George Wenzel's hypothesis that Inuit worry about tourists who witness subsistence activities (such as hunting seals) because they might respond negatively and suppress tourism as a source of income. *Protecting the Arctic*, p.144. It is clear that the Inuit, like all humans, shape their "public performances" according to the audience and whichever reference group is most salient at the moment, points made long ago by Erving Goffman and Robert K. Merton.

4 Brody, *The People's Land*, p. 190.

5 Brody, *The People's Land*, p. 190.

6 Reported also by Irwin, *"Lords of the Arctic: Wards of the State";* and G. Anders, ed., *The East Coast of Baffin Island*. The Nunavut Government views this as such a serious problem that it has decided to offer financial assistance ($300) to "intensive" Inuit hunters and trappers for operating their skidoos, motorized canoes, and naphtha stoves: Aaron Spitzer, "Fund Will Help Nunavut Hunters Fuel Up This Spring: NTI to Offer One-Time Gas Subsidy to Nunavut Harvesters," *Nunatsiaq News* (February 23, 2001).

7 Dorais, *Quaqtaq*.

8 Billson, "No Owner of Soil."

9 Freeman, *Life among the Qallunaat*, p. 71. John D. O'Neil has also linked colonialism to stress reactions among Inuit youths in "Colonial Stress in the Canadian Arctic: An Ethnography of Young Adults Changing," in *Anthropology and Epidemiology*, edited by C. R. Janes, R. Stall, and S. M. Gifford (Dordrecht: Reidel Lancaster, 1986).

10 Georg Simmel used this phrase to describe "the stranger." See Kurt H. Wolff, *The Sociology of Georg Simmel* (Glencoe, IL: The Free Press, 1950).

11 Billson, "No Owner of Soil."

12 Everett C. Stonequist, *The Marginal Man: A Study in Personality and Culture* (New York: Scribners, 1937), p. 8.

13 Billson, "No Owner of Soil."

14 The example of African Americans readily comes to mind. See Majors and Billson, *Cool Pose*. Some observers have referred to "colonization of the Inuit," but we feel this term may be somewhat overstating the case.

15 Billson, "No Owner of Soil."

16 Pudlat, "Boy, Have Things Changed," p. 20.

17 Asen Balikci, "Suicidal Behaviour among the Netsilik Eskimos," in *Canadian Society: Sociological Perspectives*, edited by Bernard Blishen (New York: Free Press of Glencoe, 1961).
18 Hanson, "Inuit Culture," p. 74.

8

The Impacts of Resettlement

What is the biggest challenge facing women? Abuse—physical and emotional.
Alcohol and drugs. So many things.

—Mona

People from the Outpost Camp

Photo 8.1 In the depths of winter at the edge of town.

We want to meet Annie and Lypa Pitsiulak, who live out on the land at an "outpost camp" about four hours from Pangnirtung by boat or six hours by skidoo. Two other families live about one hour outside of the hamlet, but Annie and Lypa live the farthest away. This week they are on holiday in Pangnirtung, camping in a tent at the edge of the fiord. Their presence symbolizes how many Inuit bridge life on the land and life in the settlement. Annie and Lypa build the bridge in reverse, spending most of their time in their camp.

Annie, 46, has high cheekbones and perfect skin. She and Lypa went back to the land when she was only 27. She says modestly, "I knew nothing about living on the land. My husband taught me everything." She was nervous about living without the family and friends she had grown close to after being resettled into Pangnirtung during the 1960s. Lypa insisted they would be fine. They went out with a few families at first, but the others came back into town because of illness. Annie remembers that life on the land was lonely then; now she loves it there. They have a modular home supplied by the government, complete with a generator that runs a TV (for videos only), short-wave radio, and basic appliances. "The one thing I miss is a flush toilet," Annie laughs.

In Pangnirtung, Annie's tent measures about 15 feet across by 12 feet deep. Center posts make it high enough for Annie to stand up inside. Along the side walls, the structure is about four feet high. The permafrost makes it far too hard to pound in stakes, so Annie and Lypa have tied the guy ropes to large rocks; smaller stones weigh down the white canvas perimeter. Annie's sister made the tent as a fortieth birthday present a few years ago. The tent allows Annie and her family to visit the settlement for extended periods in the summer, just as those in the settlement use tents to camp on the land for weeks at a time.

Inside the tent, a sand and pebble floor demarcates the front half of the family's living space. The rear half consists of a wooden platform with mattresses for sleeping and sitting. A neat quilt covers the mattresses, and a baby sleeps there now, oblivious to our conversations. Bags and boxes of clothing, Pampers, and food supplies line the edges of the sleeping platform. On the left of the entry lies the woman's domain of heating and cooking equipment. When men enter, they will sit on the right side, smoking and talking.[1] This layout accommodates up to a dozen family members for sleeping, eating, and entertaining guests. The mixture of old and new elements seems to work well.

A 4-year-old boy bounds through the door and grabs a handful of Ritz crackers from a box, then retreats as quickly to play by the water's edge. A two-burner camp stove keeps a large aluminum kettle simmering for tea. The boy returns a few minutes later, thirsty now. He finds a cup, sets it on the floor, picks up the kettle with both hands, and pours boiling water into the cup. He puts the kettle back on the stove without spilling a drop. He takes the cup to the other side of the tent, where he spoons in sugar from a Kool-Aid container. Annie supervises the spooning in of coffee whitener, but otherwise this youngster handles the operation as though he had managed it on his own many times before. He stirs and drinks the steaming liquid.

We sit on the mattresses to talk with Annie and her adoptive daughter. Annie's niece arrives with her four-year-old son, and then another young mother enters with a year-old daughter in tow, the latter wearing tiny duffel socks and *mukluks*. Toddlers come and go between the tent and the rocky beach, unsupervised, following Inuit custom.

Annie sits thoughtfully for a moment, and then says the hardest times out on the land come with childbirth, illness, and death. Being close to life also means being close to death sometimes: That is when the fragility of life hits home. When the Inuit lived in the camps, Annie says, women prepared the dying and the dead, cleaning them and dressing them in fresh underwear and, in the final moments, closing their mouths and eyes.

In the old days, a few especially wise and experienced women served as midwives. Elder women helped with a woman's first child, but she would typically bear subsequent babies alone.[2] Annie relates a story from the days when Inuit women still practiced midwifery: "The first time my aunt delivered a baby, she was trembling with fear because she had never seen it done before. She was also feeling joy when it was over."[3] On occasion, the woman had to cut a stillborn baby into pieces in order to extract it from the uterus; labour had stopped and the mother, who was in excruciating pain, would surely die. Sometimes the midwife had to turn a breached baby around from outside the womb: "Always, a mother's life came first...another baby could be born but not another mother."

Some men knew how to assist in childbirth if the occasion demanded it. When Annie gave birth to her last child, she could not go to Iqaluit a month in advance, as is customary now for Baffin Island women. She was trapped at home by weather, so a physician went on the air and asked all other radio traffic to remain quiet while he and his nurses walked "midwife" Lypa through the birthing process. People all across Baffin listened attentively to the broadcast of each cliffhanging moment. "Mother and baby are fine," a relieved audience finally heard. The infant's wails, Annie's relieved sighs, and her husband's cries of joy echoed in the background.

❦

Opportunity is a double-edged sword. Like other northern communities, Inuit settlements suffer from a kaleidoscope of debilitating social and mental health problems. Even if the policies of the twentieth century were well-intentioned, their results were less than salutary.[4] Based on her study of the Dene in the Northwest Territories, Lange concludes that if government intervention alters either gender roles or family forms, a community suffers "significant cultural impact."[5] The Inuit have experienced both.

Far-Reaching Social Repercussions
"It was a shock to us"

When Inuit moved into settlements, they came into regular contact with Inuit from other camps and with a growing number of Qallunaat. A few Inuit went south with white people, though few adapted well to a warmer climate and strange lifestyles.[6] In both cases, the structure of Inuit lives was left behind as they entered a new world without a clear plan or a new structure. Duffy observes, "The best efforts of the Eastern Arctic's early administrators, however well intentioned, fell short of the ideal in the results they achieved."[7] Failure to consult with Inuit in creating a new, viable economy eventually caught up with both the Inuit and the government, which then faced the social problems that seem inevitably to accompany loss of livelihood and subsequent dependency:

> Because the Canadian government fixed its attention on the wealth that the Arctic's natural resources could potentially earn, it neglected the troublesome "children of the ice" for whose support it had accepted responsibility.[8]

Between World War I and World War II, when the government might have engaged in a massive planning effort with the Inuit to jumpstart appropriate health, education, and economic development, Duffy claims that little such activity took place. This stands in sharp contrast to Greenland, where the government set up a sheep industry to help Inuit make the transition into towns.[9]

The social repercussions of resettlement reached into every aspect of Inuit life and are only now coming into focus. The use of the age-old language, Inuktitut, declined. Social bonds frayed, as families reeled from the pressures of a larger community. As the population and contact with southern lifestyles grew, the Inuit began to see alcohol and drug abuse, family violence, deviant and criminal acts, divorce, welfare dependency, and unemployment—concepts that were virtually unknown or irrelevant in the camps.[10] As the proportion of Inuit being educated in a southern curriculum rose, "loss of culture"—the one significant challenge mentioned repeatedly by our consultants—escalated. The formal marriage rate dropped as women tried to avoid the violence that comes with frustration and substance abuse.

The Shape of the Population
"We have many young people now"

During the middle part of the twentieth century, the Inuit passed into the second stage of the "demographic transition"—moving from high birth rates and high death rates to high birth rates and low death rates, largely because of better housing and medical care. According to Creery, centralized health care services in the communities and the establishment of "Eskimo Councils" that encouraged participation in local government improved health conditions. The death rate fell between 1941 and 1971 from 25.6 to 6.6 per thousand; and the rate of natural increase (births over deaths) rose from .8 to 30.4. This phenomenon led to rapid population growth, from 2.6 percent annually between 1941 and 1951, to 3.46 percent during the 1950s, to 4.3 percent in the 1960s and 1970s.[11] This very high rate of growth was similar to that "found in the underdeveloped regions of Latin America."[12]

The third stage of the demographic transition—low birth rates and low death rates—depends on acceptance of birth control. It has not yet occurred for the Inuit, and it might not, given the value they place on children and their attitudes toward adoption. During the mid-1900s, Health and Welfare Canada passed the question of birth control to the Education Service of the NWT government, which resisted engaging in birth control education. The Catholic Church, which dominated some Artic communities, "vigorously protested the...attempt to disseminate birth control information through the schools" as an imposition of white values that would threaten Inuit society.[13] At three 1975 conferences in Yellowknife, Inuvik, and Pangnirtung, Inuit women agreed that traditional views of children as a form of wealth should be respected but also that abortion should be legalized and birth control devices should be available upon request. To this day, though, neither abortion nor birth control is popular among Inuit women.[14] However, the rate of population growth slowed somewhat during the 1970s, probably because of the availability of family planning information. Some projections suggest that nearly 100,000 Inuit will live in the Canadian North (including Nunavut, Nunavik, and Labrador) by 2016.[15]

The negative social impacts of resettlement have been cultural and profoundly economic. The impacts stem not only from contact with whites and greater exposure to southern culture but also from the fact that it is extremely challenging for any society to maintain high living standards when it moves through the second stage of the demographic transition *without* strong economic development programs in place: "A growing population requires a matching growth of productive capital, the growth of the population alone being insufficient to produce the supplementary goods needed, the raw materials, houses, schools, teachers, doctors, nurses, and medical facilities."[16] The demographic impacts include changes in fertility rates and infant/maternal mortality rates.

Fertility Rates

Improvements in life expectancy and high birth rates have resulted in Canada's fastest growing and very young population. Statistics Canada predicts that the Inuit population in the North (living primarily in Nunavut) will grow to approximately 84,500 by the year 2016.[17]

- Life expectancy at birth for Inuit in the former NWT doubled to 66 years old between 1941-50 and 1978-82.[18]
- Sixty percent of the Inuit population falls in the "under 25" category (compared to 35 percent in Canada as a whole).
- Thirty-nine percent are under 15 (compared to 21 percent in Canada).[19]
- The proportion of youths in the 10-19 year old age group is very high—47 percent compared to a 27 percent national average.[20]
- The birth rate for the Inuit in general is higher than for Canada as a whole.
- The Nunavut birth rate (for all ages) of 33 births per 1,000 is more than twice that of Canada's (15 per 1,000).[21]
- The Nunavut birth rate is 2.9 percent, compared to 1.2 percent for Canada.
- In Pangnirtung, the birth rate is over 40/1,400 per year.[22]
- In 1994, girls aged 15-19 in the former NWT had a birth rate of 67 per 1,000, compared to the national rate of 27 per 1,000; for girls under age 15, the rate was 2.6 per 1,000, compared to half of that for Canada as a whole.
- The mother's average age at first childbirth in Baffin has dropped from 16-18 to 14-16 years old.[23]

Infant and Maternal Mortality

With a high birth rate and early motherhood, the circumstances of delivery become problematic, especially for younger women and first-time mothers. In the absence of a hospital in the community, women must go south for childbirth (although women can sign a waiver if they wish not to travel out of their community). Because the government has long resisted training traditional midwives in modern birthing techniques, midwifery has all but died out with the elder women.[24] In the absence of local midwives, most mothers-to-be in Pangnirtung opt to go to Iqaluit because they are aware of the high risks involving childbirth for Inuit women. Some communities, such as Rankin Inlet, have southern midwives and Inuit "maternity care workers" who have not received formal training in midwifery (the Nunavut Health Department plans to initiate such training for Inuit women).[25]

- Surgical intervention and transfusions are not typically available in small communities when delivery goes awry.
- Community health centres suffer from chronic under-funding and cuts in much-needed public health education and wellness programs.

- Infant mortality is two or three times the Canadian rate but dropped from 100 per 1,000 in 1970 (just after most Inuit were resettled into hamlets) to 21 per 1,000 in 1978.[26] Creery gives even higher infant mortality rates, saying that the rate dropped from 208.9 per thousand in 1941 to 49.9 per thousand in 1971.[27] Waldram, Herring, and Young showed a drop to less than 25 per thousand in the 1986–90 census period.[28]
- Smoking before, during, and after pregnancy increases health problems of 85 percent of Baffin women during childbearing years.[29]

Most Pressing Issues
"We're going different ways"

Resettlement and rapid social change have left an indelible imprint on Inuit women's lives. They identify their major problems as breakdown of the family structure, alcohol and substance abuse, inadequate economic opportunity, insufficient day care, and violence against women. Although government intervention controlled widespread starvation and tuberculosis, few Inuit now live well by their own or by southern standards. The Inuit have made positive gains since resettlement, but social change has taken a heavy toll. Many Inuit believe that the negative consequences of resettlement substantially offset the gains. Still, they worry about the shocks to their lives: "We're going different ways," Meeka reflects. Interviews with Inuit women and men, social service agencies, the RCMP, town officials, nurses, and teachers generated the list of issues below; data from Statistics Canada and other sources supports the community's view of the most pressing issues that emerged during the twentieth century and continue into this century.

Weakened Culture (see Chapter 8)
The intrusions of law, television, and representatives of Euro-Canadian authority threatened the finely woven intimacy and mutual support of old.
- The use of Inuktitut declined.
- Traditional values, culture, religion diminished.[30]
- Respect for elders declined.
- Hunting and sewing skills dwindled.

Family Relations (see Chapters 9, 11, 14, 15)
- The formal marriage rate declined.
- The divorce rate rose significantly.
- Violence against women ("spousal assault" or "domestic violence"), defined as "any act or threat of an act that causes physical, sexual or psychological harm," became prevalent.[31]
- Child and elder abuse rose slightly.

Other challenges confront Inuit families: inadequate day care, problems in disciplining children, intergenerational conflict, and suicide. The fact that the Inuit constitute a relatively young population compared to other Canadian groups exacerbates each of these problems. Mental health issues dominate conversations with health care workers and members of the Pangnirtung community—the number one challenges reported by Inuit women appear to be depression and violence among intimates—which we view as symptoms of a weak economic system.[32] Alcohol or drug abuse aggravates both physical and emotional illnesses. Domestic violence threatens self-esteem of males and females, family stability, and female empowerment.

Earning a Living (see Chapter 17)

- Per capita income is one half the Canadian average.[33]
- Few full-time, wage-paying jobs exist, even for those who receive training in special programs.
- After resettlement, unemployment rose to almost 40 percent for males aged 20-34; the percentage on government transfer payments escalated to 25 percent; and over 16 percent had no reportable income at all.[34]
- The overall unemployment rate was at least 28 percent in 1999.[35]
- Federal government transfer payments will reach $24,000 per Nunavummiut in the next five years.[36]
- Diminishing wildlife habitat, environmental degradation, and the decline in fur trapping sales and the sealing industry contribute to loss of economic stability.[37]
- The high cost of hunting and fishing equipment discourages many families from relying on traditional methods of providing country food.
- In spite of the high cost of "southern food," the Inuit diet consists mostly of store-bought food, supplemented sporadically by country food provided through hunting and fishing.

Some Inuit men are returning to motorized canoes, rather than the popular Winnipeg boats, because the canoes use less horsepower and are less expensive to purchase and run. In contrast to Dahl's finding among the Inuit of Saqqaq, Greenland, hunting is problematic in Pangnirtung because families lost their dogs in the canine encephalitis epidemic of the 1950s and 1960s. Of the Saqqarmiut, Dahl says: "With the only exception of a few old and retired people living alone, all households own a boat with an outboard motor, and most households have a dog team." [38] The reverse is true in Pangnirtung, a fact that greatly affects both general prosperity and gender relations. Typically, several related families share one boat or canoe, and only one or two families per community manage to retain a dog team. The unemployment and work-related challenges in Pangnirtung are similar to those in other Inuit communities: "The socioeconomic changes taking place in Arctic communities involve a "growing population, crowded housing, and lack of employment opportunities."[39]

Physical and Mental Health (see Chapters 7, 8, 9, 15)

- Widespread starvation and TB had disappeared decades ago but health remains relatively poor and TB has recently flared up again.
- Sixty percent of Inuit in the territory smoke, much higher than the national rate.
- "Lifestyle diseases" such as obesity, trauma injuries, heart disease, and stroke have increased.[40]
- The rate of lung infection and upper respiratory problems—colds, flu, pneumonia, and asthma—is among the highest in the world and is exacerbated by harsh climatic conditions and smoking, especially around babies and young children.[41]
- Recurrent acute otitis media is especially problematic for children.[42]
- The rate of sexually transmitted disease is fifteen times the national average.[43]
- Substance abuse increased (alcohol, drugs, and inhalants), creating physical and mental health problems, and contributing to higher rates of domestic violence and Fetal Alcohol Syndrome (FAS).[44]
- Depression and suicide rose alarmingly (about one death out of every six is a suicide—see Chapter 9: Families Redefined).
- For Pangnirtungmiut, the nearest doctor is in Iqaluit, a one-hour flight away (it is even farther away for most other Baffin communities).
- Women have to go outside of Nunavut to have mammograms.
- Government policy urges Baffin women fly to Iqaluit one month before giving birth; although perhaps medically cautious, this weakens the support system of families and friends.

The nursing staff in Pangnirtung has seen no documented cases of breast cancer among Inuit women (as of this writing). In fact, in all of Nunavut, only five cases of breast cancer were diagnosed in 2000, one in 1999, and only 15 cases between 1992 and 1998. The low rate of breast cancer stems partly from long-term breast-feeding (the length varies, but some women nurse into a child's fourth year). Most young mothers breast-feed unless they have adopted a baby into the family. In addition, the natural Inuit diet contains many fish oils, which may have protective value. Because of the low rates of breast cancer, the government is reluctant to invest in specialized x-ray equipment for the communities. If they do not have one mammogram at least every three years after age 50 during a visit to the south for other reasons, Inuit women are eligible to fly out at government expense for this diagnostic procedure.[45] This means that cancers, once detected, might advance further than if routine mammograms were available in communities.[46] With increasing reliance on southern foods, the rates for this type of cancer could rise for the next generation of Inuit women. Pauktuutit has advocated for a mammogram machine in the territory and the Nunavut Status of Women Council has argued that the incidence of breast cancer among Inuit women is under-reported. The Inuit association stresses that these conditions are "100 percent" preventable.[47]

Housing (see Chapters 1, 6)
- Home ownership is a luxury few can support.
- Good housing is perennially short in Inuit communities, although it has improved considerably in the last decade. The housing shortage has frustrated Inuit families, especially those under age 30.
- Rooms tend to be small and overcrowding is common in the region. In Pangnirtung, the average household consists of four persons, which Statistics Canada no longer defines as overcrowded.
- Plumbing and water supplies are often inadequate. Because of permafrost, pump trucks must deliver water and remove sanitary waste.

Houses built during the initial settlement period were small and lacked plumbing; more recent structures are modern and the older ones have been boarded up, demolished, or refurbished. Now, as the population quickly expands and young couples have children, many single mothers still live with their parents. Most people rent subsidized government houses or housing association houses (if they work and can afford it). Women are fighting what they describe as discrimination in housing distribution. They see housing as an arena for improving their power and independence. Ironically, although rents are relatively low by southern standards, workers have to pay higher rents, a policy that discourages the Inuit from seeking employment. For many residents, being on welfare and paying lower rents could be financially more attractive than holding a wage-earning job. Elders receive free housing and many youths live with them to avoid paying rent—and because they enjoy each other's company.

Crime and Violence (see Chapters 9, 15)
- Homicide and other crimes, especially domestic violence, rose sharply.48
- The "overall rates of criminal code offences in the Baffin Region are much higher than what is found, on average, in Canada...[and the rates have] begun to exceed the rate for the [former] NWT."[49]
- The number of people charged with criminal offenses in Nunavut rose by 17 percent between 1999 and 2000.[50]
- Nunavut is the only jurisdiction in which the number of people charged with violent crimes is greater than the number charged with property crimes.[51]
- Many cases of recidivism occur.[52]
- Northern prisons are overcrowded (43% over capacity).[53]

- Baffin Regional Correctional Centre lacks a permanent alcohol and drug abuse program or sexual offenders' program.[54]

The "Evans Report," produced for the government of the former NWT, concluded that "astronomical rates of alcohol and illegal drug consumption, together with high unemployment rates, poor education and widespread family breakdown, have created an almost perfect breeding ground for violent crime."[55] The dramatic increase around the time of Nunavut's creation may have resulted from differences in reporting methods related to the shift from NWT to Nunavut data. Efforts are underway to create a new, community-based criminal justice system that deals more effectively with the root causes of crime and domestic violence, and the disproportionate effects they have on women and children.

Education (see Chapter 16)

- Until very recently, most teachers in the North were white southern Canadians; in Pangnirtung in 1988, all teachers were Qallunaat; by 2000, Inuit were filling many instructional posts through Grade 6. As more Inuit elementary school teachers become qualified, the training effort will move up to high school and college levels.
- Until recently, the English language and mainstream cultural images dominated the core curriculum; now, Inuktitut is the language of instruction for kindergarten and the first few grades.[56]
- Inuit have the lowest levels of literacy and educational attainment in Canada.57 Education stops at mid-high school for most children, although opportunities for completing high school are increasing.
- In the past, many children had to leave home to complete high school; now, many communities (including Pangnirtung) have 12 years of instruction.
- The majority of Inuit who wish to pursue college must leave home to do so, although the situation is slowly improving.

Education remains problematic for most Inuit in isolated communities but Iqaluit-based Nunavut Arctic College (NAC) has opened branches that offer limited coursework in a few communities, as well as "learning centers" in Pangnirtung and other hamlets. The new University of the Arctic (distance learning) is just getting on its feet. Staffing and funding issues abound.

The Interplay of Issues
"We have to do everything ourselves"

A recent government description of Nunavut stressed the critical role the new territory might play in relieving the negative impacts of resettlement: "Economic development will be key to the success of the new territory, whose people now have the lowest income and life expectancy and the highest unemployment, substance abuse and suicide rates in the country."[58] Statistics tell one story, but we wanted to explore what these issues *mean* in the daily lives of Inuit women. We asked a group of young women attending the Nunavut Arctic College branch in Pangnirtung to talk about the *most* pressing problems for them, how the problems affect their lives, and how they can be solved.

The younger women speak of complex challenges that face Inuit women of all ages (figure 8.1). The problems center on inadequate income and trying to feed and clothe their children within the context of a weak, welfare-centered economic system. Some women feel that Inuit men are not pulling their share of the load. They say that anger simmers under the surface, unreleased and often unrecognized, but found in a complex of self-destructive behavior that promises to numb the pain and blur the mind: drugs, alcohol, gambling, and overdosing.

Figure 8.1 Major Problems Facing Younger Women

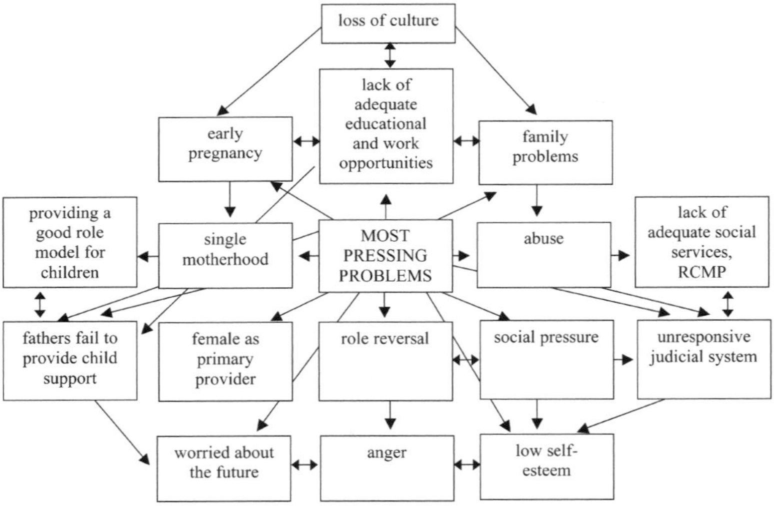

Women admit, too, that uncontrollable anger sometimes results in their own aggressive behaviour toward men, even men who have not hurt them and want to have a healthy relationship. Perhaps most tragically, when a woman does not address the source of anger, her self-esteem erodes. That makes it easier for a woman to accept the role of victim again, thus spawning fresh anger and new reasons to escape from the pain (figure 8.2).

Figure 8.2 The Products of Anger, Worry, and Low Self-Esteem

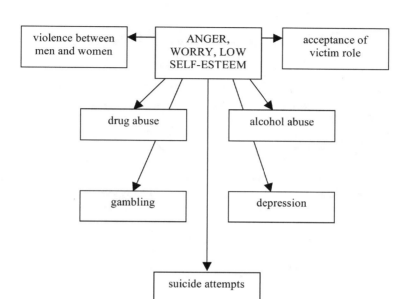

At the root of so many other problems, lack of communication surfaces time and again in our conversations. Women believe that in the camps men were allowed to do whatever they wanted with women's bodies, starting with young girls and continuing with wives and other females in the communities. People either looked the other way or did not talk about it or both. Thus, a covenant of silence enshrouded damage to women. Although family violence may have cropped up less in the camps than in the settlements, it certainly existed. According to elder women, the men behaved as they wished with relative impunity. Women say this attitude of male privilege persists into the settlement, where silence and lack of communication obscure the myriad ways in which males hurt females. That makes it very difficult for healing and understanding to take place.

Younger women feel that the older generation puts too much pressure on them to "live the traditional ways" and play the age-old roles of homemaker and mother. They speak simultaneously of the suffering they have experienced as victims of child molestation and rape during their early years, and of rape and battering in early adulthood. They feel angry with their families and with formal agencies for not supplying appropriate support when things go wrong.

Some women cite the elder men's group as a negative influence in bringing sex offenders and batterers to justice: "Maybe only one of them has *not* committed these acts himself. They try to get the men off." Women criticize a regional judge (ironically, a woman) for serving up "coffee breaks" for men who rape and batter women. The sentences make a "mockery" of the judicial system and infuriate these women, who ask, "But what can we do?" That families, police, and judges fail to take them seriously takes another bite out of their self-esteem. They feel doubly victimized, first by the perpetrators, and then by a system that looks the other way.

Younger women want every age group to face the present realities of their lives, openly communicate about them, and stop trying to cover up the past. They call for leaders (both male and female but especially female) to take a public stand against abuse of women and children, because they see this as devastatingly damaging to one's ability to forge a healthy identity later in life. Men who hurt females lose their self-respect, and the victims suffer in many ways. Women would like to see support groups for men and women together, in which both could learn to communicate more openly about the feelings they bottle up inside. These younger women say that anger and frustration that does not find legitimate expression will eventually come back to haunt families in outbursts of verbal and physical abuse (figures 8.3 and 8.4).

Figure 8.3 An Array of "Family Problems"

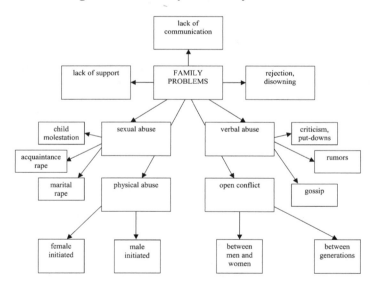

Alongside this rich and closely integrated analysis, young Inuit women simultaneously voice doubt as to whether they can do anything at all to solve their personal challenges, let alone the challenges facing their community. Some worry that people might view them as too outspoken or talkative. For instance, one young woman asked a male friend to make home brew for her at Christmastime. He did, they got drunk, and he ended up raping her at knifepoint for three hours, stabbing her in the thigh, and beating her to the point where people could not recognize her. When she decided to press charges, many people were angry with her for asking for the brew. They blamed her for the incident. Examples such as this one make young women feel overwhelmed, sometimes, and worried about what their future might bring during this era of fast change, turmoil, and new beginnings.

Figure 8.4 The Sources of Anger

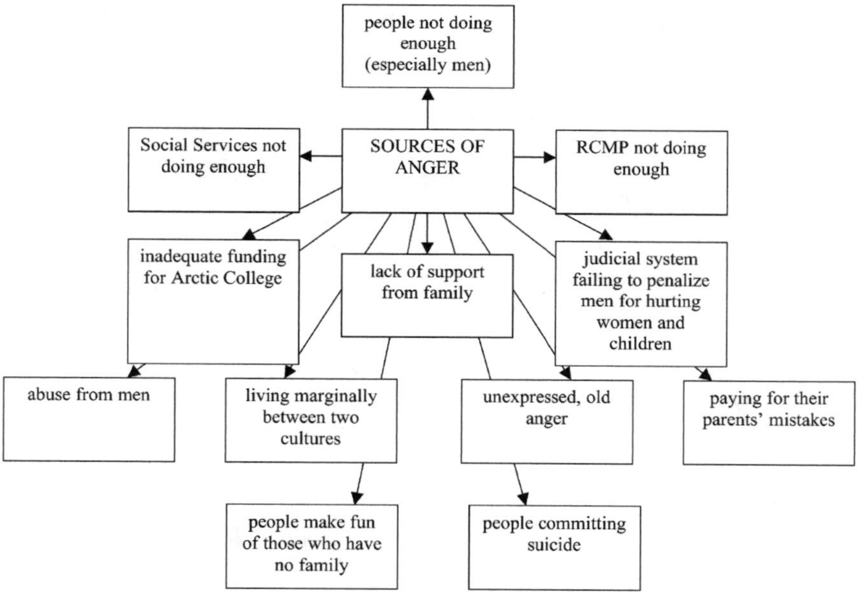

The young women said they want more responsive community agencies that will work with them to create a safer and more supportive environment in which to raise children (figure 8.5). They called for more support of men as well as of women, couples working together, and alleviation of economic pressures.

Interestingly—and in keeping with Inuit folkways—most of their suggestions related to family and community strategies for mutual support, better communication, honesty, and leadership. These women did not turn to government or private sector social service agencies for solutions, although they did express the need for a stronger legal system that takes domestic violence "seriously." Overall, the relationships between women and men, parents and children, are positive and constructive considering the dramatic impact of rapid social change on Inuit life. In the context of shifting gender roles and greater choice for women, some feel that through better communication couples can find ways to make meaningful commitments and have peaceful relationships.

Figure 8.5 Solutions to the Most Pressing Problems

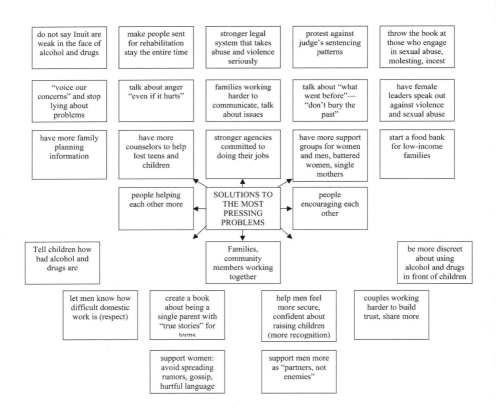

Creating New Mechanisms for New Problems
"They start to share"

Empowerment for women often means connecting the past, the present, and the future in creative problem solving. For example, women have watched as couples and individuals faced their problems together: "That's the only time people start to help themselves—when they start to share their experiences with others." Although the community is relatively strong, people have started to have a better feeling about their family relationships. Women have played pivotal roles on the Mental Health Committee, spousal assault committees, and support groups that help soften the conflictual relationships that trouble many families.

The Spousal Assault Committee

Healing groups and women's groups work (through Pauktuutit and independently) with such issues as spousal assault and sexual abuse. "People are learning," says one woman, although sometimes gossip in a small community defeats confidentiality. The former Government of the Northwest Territories hired a psychologist just to deal with abuse issues: "Some people die with it. They're not healing at all. That's why I looked at other ways outside the community." Another woman says she thinks the spousal assault committee does not work well because people keep going back to the problems that force them to seek help in the first place.

A man criticizes the spousal assault committee and other community-based, self-help groups because he thinks they can actually become havens for abusive men: "One of my friends was in the men's support group. When I inquired as to the group's purpose, his answer was 'to protect us from the women'." Lack of training and reluctance to face perpetrators may weaken the effectiveness of these groups.

On the other hand, women who have sought support and solace in such groups have sometimes found the strength to stop their abusers. Says one: "I'm not afraid to say I was abused as a child. I've learned that there is some value in laying charges. I feel so light. Men are afraid of me now. They know they can't' touch me! My muscles aren't tight any more." Another woman says a lawyer asked why she was bringing charges against an abuser after 20 years. She replied, "I am tired of living with it day after day." The jury found him not guilty on all counts. Undaunted, she insists that support groups and healing groups "have to start talking and doing something instead of being scared to say something to these men."

The Mental Health Committee

The Mental Health Committee in any community can delineate the problems facing its people. A small community reflects the full range of problems that face larger communities. It is simply a matter of difference in scale. Members of the Mental Health Committee in Pangnirtung, established in the mid-1980s, work on a one-to-one basis with those who need help with personal problems. This strategy may be more in keeping with the traditional mechanisms of social control and may be more effective than formal avenues such as the RCMP or social service agencies. The committee receives training from people who come "from down south" and takes its work very seriously. A dozen volunteers, including a few men and many elder women, operate without an office or fees. People can choose whichever member they feel most comfortable with, Osuituk explains: "We meet once a month to discuss pressing issues and make ourselves available to the people whenever they need us. In most of the cases, they come to us individually. Anybody who wants to come to our meeting is welcome. We publicize it on the local radio or in the newspaper."

Women of the Mental Health Committee speak of many problems, but spousal assault and lack of parental ability to discipline their children rank high on the list of complaints. Another problem, which reflects both, is assault by teenage sons against their parents (usually, but not always, the mother). Adamie says this very disturbing problem flies in the face of traditional Inuit values:

"SOMETIMES IT'S VERY HARD"
The worst cases are mothers who come to us to talk because they are afraid of the kids. The kids don't listen to the parents or they get abusive with them. It seems to be happening more and more with the teenagers. Parents come to us because they don't know what to do—they can't control their children. They are upset that the children won't listen. It no longer works to say, "I am your parent and you will do what I tell you," which apparently worked 100 years ago.

Some young people go to the Mental Health Committee because their parents don't care about them. They don't understand or treat their kids seriously. Younger people may avoid the committee, because it consists of so many older people. We see alcohol abuse and depression, marital distress and attempted suicide. Sometimes it's very hard."

On the land, before courts and formal mechanisms of social control, the elders intervened in cases of stubborn children or couples who were in conflict: "Elders would get together with other Elders and try to solve the problem by talking to the youngster. There would be two Elders at first, and if nothing happened, more would join in to talk to them. If the youngsters listened, that was the end."[59]

People agree the Mental Health Committee represents an important step in the right direction for helping solve today's problematic relationships. Says

Meeka Arnakaq, who is one of its leaders: "I'm really happy that we're learning more about how to get advice and where to get help. We learn as we grow up. We learn to talk to solve problems. Sometimes a couple goes to social services and they're told they have to separate. Then they find help to get back together by talking to other people." By the late 1990s, Meeka and her husband, Abraham, have extended their healing talents beyond Pangnirtung. At the invitation of other Baffin Hamlet Councils, they fly into communities and work with individuals and couples to help them vent the anger and confusion that comes from early abuse. The night before they leave each community, they gather all the women and men they have talked with into one large healing group (as many as 40 people). Meeka and Abraham say that they can work with other couples because they worked on their own relationship first, clearing away the debris of childhood pain that too easily translates into discordant and sometimes violent interactions with the opposite sex. They have seen couples grow closer in a relationship renewed by talking away the old hurts. Some need hugs; others just need the example of this gentle, late middle-aged couple who are frank about their own journey from the other side. The young people in the Baffin Correctional Centre in Iqaluit are the hardest to reach, they say, because the pain runs so deep and the consequences for turning it outward and victimizing others costs so much for the community, the perpetrator, and the victims. Meeka and Abraham firmly believe that resettlement lies at the root of the high rates of abuse, violence, and suicide that trouble these isolated communities: "It is like trying to find our way out of a thick fog, like the fog that rolls in from the mountains and the sea, sometimes. It is so hard to find your way in that fog, but you can do it with help."

Another group of citizens helps organize the community's social and recreational life: "It's not really involved in the Mental Health Committee, but it's really helping. Some of the young people have been quitting drugs and helping other people." Parallel to the Mental Health Committee is the team that visits those who have suffered a death in the family. Lay couples and the resident ordained minister and others on the periphery try to help people cope with grief and loss. Each of these mechanisms helps to soften the blows dealt by dislocation and disorientation.

Notes

1 This layout was observed also by J. Matthiasson in *Living on the Land*, p. 63.
2 Uyarasuk, "Rachael Uyarasuk (Inuit)," p. 259.
3 Quoted in Hallendy, "Reflections, Shades and Shadows," p. 9.
4 Douglas Durst, "The Road to Poverty is Paved with Good Intentions: Social Interventions and Indigenous Peoples," *International Social Work* 35, 2 (1992).

5 Lynda Lange, "The Relation between the Situation of Dene Women and the Changing Situation of Elders, in the Context of Colonialism: The Experience of Fort Franklin 1945-1985," paper presented at the Knowing the North Conference, Boreal Institute for Northern Studies, Edmonton, November 1986, p. 4.

6 Kenn Harper tells the tragic story of a young Inuk boy who was taken to New York City with an anthropologist from the American Museum of Natural History in *Give Me My Father's Body: The Life of Minik, the New York Eskimo* (Frobisher Bay [Iqaluit], NWT: Blacklead Books, 1986).

7 Duffy, *The Road to Nunavut*, p. 12.

8 Duffy, *The Road to Nunavut*, p. 12.

9 Duffy, *The Road to Nunavut*, p. 13. We should note, however, that Canadian Government efforts to provide farming and cattle raising opportunities for the Blood Indians of southern Alberta did not necessarily ease their economic redevelopment. Such a strategy would obviously not have been appropriate in the Baffin Region, but some other scheme might have been devised with Inuit input. See Janet Mancini Billson, "Standing Tradition on Its Head: Role Reversal among [Alberta] Blood Indian Couples," *Great Plains Quarterly* 11, 1 (Winter 1991): 3-21; reprinted in *The First Ones: Readings in Indian/Native Studies*, edited by David R. Millwer, Carl Beal, James Dempsey, and R. Wesley Heber (Piapot Reserve #75: Saskatchewan Indian Federated College Press, 1992).

10 For an analysis of the increase in delinquency and crime rates, see Finkler, *North of 60*, pp. 23ff; and McElroy, *Alternatives in Modernization*, p. 71. Matthews distinguishes between "transfer dependency" and "dependency theory," in *The Creation of Regional Dependency* (Toronto: University of Toronto Press, 1983), pp. 69-76. The latter is intended here.

11 Ian Creery, *The Inuit (Eskimo) of Canada*. London: Minority Rights Group, 1993.

12 Duffy, *The Road to Nunavut*, p. 63.

13 Duffy, *The Road to Nunavut*, p. 64.

14 Billson and Stapleton, "Accidental Motherhood."

15 James S. Frideres and Rene R. Gadacz, *Aboriginal Peoples in Canada: Contemporary Conflicts*, 6th ed. (Toronto: Prentice Hall, 2001), p. 265.

16 Duffy, *The Road to Nunavut*, p. 63.

17 Statistics Canada, *Projections of Population with Aboriginal Ancestry: Canada, Provinces/Regions and Territories, 1991-2016* (Ottawa: Statistics Canada, 1995). That figure, of course, would apply to both Nunavut and the residual Northwest Territories.

18 Waldram, Herring, and Young, *Aboriginal Health in Canada*, p. 66.

19 Department of Indian Affairs and Northern Development, *Highlights of Aboriginal Condition, 1991, 1986: Demographic, Economic and Social Characteristics* (Ottawa: Department of Indian Affairs and Northern Development, 1985), p. ix.

20 Griffiths, et al., *Crime, Law and Justice among Inuit; The Canadian Encyclopedia Plus*; and Lilianne E. Krosenbrink-Gelissen, *Sexual Equality as an Aboriginal Right: The Native Women's Association of Canada and the Constitutional Process on Aboriginal Matters, 1982-1987* (Fort Lauderdale, Saarbrucken: Verlag Breitenbach, 1991), p. 31.

21 Http/natsiq.nunanet.com/'nic/A6.8, A6.9.

22 Marion Soublière, ed., *The Nunavut Handbook: 1999 Commemorative Edition* (Iqaluit, NWT: Nortext Multimedia, 1998), p. vi.

23 Jane George, "Babies Having Babies: An Explosion of Infants Born to Teenage Mothers," *Nunatsiaq News* (May 19, 2000).

24 For a discussion of the history and implications of evacuating Inuit women out of their communities for childbirth, see Betty Anne Daviss-Putt, "Rights of Passage in the North: From Evacuation to the Birth of a Culture," in Crnkovich, *Gossip*, pp. 91-114; also, Annie Okalik, "A Good Life" (interview by Angela Bernal, translated by Sadie Hill), in Crnkovich, *Gossip*. We also interviewed the late Annie Okalik (the mother of Nunavut's first Premier, Paul Okalik); her voice echoes throughout this book.

25 Denise Rideout, "Midwives Worry Birthing Centre Is Short-Staffed: Health Officials Say Centre Isn't in Crisis," *Nunatsiaq News* (November 30, 2001). Pauktuutit has called for capacity-building in medically-supported midwifery so more Inuit women can give birth in their own communities, as they did for centuries: "Inuit Women's Health: A Call for Commitment. *The Canadian Women's Health Network*. (Fall/Winter 2001/2002): 1.

26 Condon, *Inuit Behavior and Seasonal Change in the Canadian Arctic*, p. 75. Creery, *The Inuit (Eskimo) of Canada*. See also Charles W. Hobart, "Socio-economic Correlates of Mortality and Morbidity among Inuit Infants," pp. 452-61 in *Proceedings of the Third International Symposium on Circumpolar Health*, edited by R. J. Shephard and S. Itoh (Toronto, Buffalo: University of Toronto Press, 1976).

27 Creery, *The Inuit (Eskimo) of Canada*.

28 Waldram, Herring, and Young, *Aboriginal Health in Canada*, p. 67.

29 George, "Nunavut's Vicious Health Care Cycle."

30 With the creation of the new Nunavut Department of Elders, Culture, and Youth, Jim Bell editorialized: "After years of inattention, well-intentioned floundering, and willful neglect on the part of Inuit organizations who should have known better, millions of dollars that could have been spent on the promotion of Inuit culture and language have gone to waste, ending up in failed projects or dysfunctional organizations." Bell claims that in spite of Canada-NWT language agreements, the GNWT was returning "millions of dollars of unspent aboriginal language money" because no one applied for it. Many Inuit cultural projects "were—and still are—languishing in obscurity and neglect. In many cases, it's Inuit organizations, and no one else, who are accountable for that neglect." Jim Bell, "Who Works for Inuit Culture?" *Nunatsiaq News* (November 6, 1998).

31 This definition was incorporated into the Beijing Platform for Action 1995-2000, as reported in Charlotte Bunch, "Transforming Human Rights from a Feminist Perspective," in *Women's Rights, Human Rights*, edited by Julie Peter and Andrea Wolper (New York: Routledge, 1995), p. 10. The increase of domestic violence is reported by Jim Bell in "The Violating of Kitty Nowdluk," *Arctic Circle* (July/August 1991): 32-28 and in Billson, "Violence toward Inuit Women and Children." The terms spousal assault, domestic violence, and violence between intimates are used interchangeably here. Lori L. Heise, Jacqueline Pitanguy, and Adrienne Germain provide a more inclusive term, "gender-based violence," to include "rape, domestic violence, mutilation, murder, and sexual abuse." They cite World Bank data that estimates that "gender-based victimization is responsible for one out of every five healthy days of life lost to women of reproductive age...female-focused violence also represents a hidden obstacle to economic and social development." *Violence against Women: The Hidden Health Burden*, Discussion Paper #255 (Washington, DC: The World Bank, 1994), p. ix.

32 Laurence J. Kirmayer, Chris Fletcher, Ellen Corin, and L. Boothroyd explore these definitions in *Inuit Concepts of Mental Health and Illness: An Ethnographic Study* (Montréal: Sir Mortimer B. Davis-Jewish General Hospital, Institute of Community and Family Psychiatry, 1994).

33 This is similar to First Nations figures: "The average total annual income for all Canadian males (aged 15+), at $30,200, is more than double the $15,000 of their First Nation counterparts. The disparity among females is less ($17,000 vs. $11,000), but very pronounced, nevertheless." Based on data from the Royal Commission on Aboriginal Peoples, in J. Rick Ponting, *First Nations in Canada: Perspectives on Opportunity, Empowerment, and Self-Determination* (Toronto: McGraw-Hill Ryerson, 1997), p. 102.

34 Department of Indian Affairs and Northern Development, *Highlights of Aboriginal Condition*, p. xix; also, Jim Bell, "Canada's Crime Capital (Part One)," *Nunatsiaq News* (October 9, 1998).

35 Geddes, "Northern Son," p. 20.

36 Jim Bell, "Human Development Key to Nunavut's Economy. Think-Tank: Health, Education in 'Desperate' Need of Attention," *Nunatsiaq News* (June 22, 2001).

37 Hedican, *Applied Anthropology in Canada*, p. 115; and Inuit Circumpolar Conference, *The Arctic Sealing Industry: A Retrospective Analysis of its Collapse and Options for Sustainable Development*, Inuit Circumpolar Conference, Nuuk, 1996.

38 Dahl, *Saqqaq*, p. 190.

39 Myers and Forrest, "While Nero Fiddles."

40 Jane George, "Nunavut's Vicious Health Care Cycle: Less Money, More Sick People," *Nunatsiaq News* (September 24, 1999).

41 Jane George, "Study: Smoking Sickens Baffin Babies," *Nunatsiaq News* (June 29, 2001). Dr. Anna Banerji, a Vancouver pediatrician and infectious disease specialist, conducted the study at Baffin Regional Hospital in Iqaluit. She found that "adopted infants stayed in hospital for 12.6 days on average, compared with 5.7 days for non-adopted infants. Breast-fed infants stayed in hospital for a mean of 6.5 days versus 10.4 in non-breast-fed infants." Because of the high adoption rates, the rate of breast-feeding is relatively low among Inuit women. The researcher suggested that the risks of smoking to infants are "magnified in the Arctic by increased time spent indoors in relatively airtight housing."

42 Nurses at Pangnirtung Nursing Station made the point that frequent ear infections interfere with school attendance for many children. See also Neil J. DiSarno and Craig Barringer, "Otitis Media and Academic Achievement in Eskimo High School Students," *Folia Phoniatrica*, 39, 5 (1987); and L. Duval, S. MacDonalds, L. Lugtig, et al. "Otitis Media as Stigma or Process: Conflicting Understandings from Inuit Culture and Biomedicine," pp. 676-679 in *Circumpolar Health 93, Proceedings of the Ninth International Congress on Circumpolar Health*, edited by G. Pétrusdottir, S. B. Sigurdsson, M. M. Karlsson, and J. Axelsson, *Arctic Medical Research* 53, 2 (1994).

43 Geddes, "Northern Son," p. 20.

44 Valerie G. Connell, "Pauktuutit to Make Video on FAS [Fetal Alcohol Syndrome]," *Nunatsiaq News* (July 21, 2000).

45 Michaela Rodriguez, "Nunavut Women Must Travel South for Mammograms," *Nunatsiaq News* (October 29, 1999).

46 Miriam Hill, "Breast Cancer Strikes Inuit, Too: Nunavut Women Can't Get Mammograms in the Territory, So Cancer Often Goes Undetected Until It's Too Late," *Nunatsiaq News* (September 28, 2001).

47 Connell, "Pauktuutit to Make Video on FAS."

48 Griffiths, et al., *Crime, Law, and Justice among Inuit.*

49 Griffiths, et al., *Crime, Law, and Justice among Inuit*, p. 35.

50 Jim Bell, "Is Violent Crime on the Rise in Nunavut? Violent Crime Exceeds Property Crime in Nunavut," *Nunatsiaq News* (July 27, 2001).

51 Bell, "Is Violent Crime on the Rise in Nunavut?"

52 Jim Bell, "Canada's Crime Capital (Part Two)," *Nunatsiaq News* (October 16, 1998). Bell cites "Crime and Corrections in the Northwest Territories," produced for GNWT by a Vancouver consulting firm, James Evans, Management and Policy International. The Evans Report based its conclusions on statistics from the entire (former) NWT.

53 Bell, "Canada's Crime Capital (Part One)."

54 Bell, "Canada's Crime Capital (Part Two)."

55 Bell, "Canada's Crime Capital (Part Two)."

56 See Harry Goldfarb, "Ottawa Wants Education to Aid Eskimo Integration," *The Toronto Daily Star* (June 22, 1970), for a description of government intentions regarding Native education in the not-too-distant past.

57 Bell, "Canada's Crime Capital (Part One)."

58 Canadian Embassy, "Nunavut Joins Canadian Federation on April 1," p. 2.

59 Uyarasuk, "Rachael Uyarasuk (Inuit)," p. 271.

9

Families Redefined

As I look back, I miss the whole families.

—Ooleepeeka

Suicide and the Cry for Help

Photo 9.1   Children running toward the future.

As we walk through the settlement one evening, a young man asks for $25, exactly the price, we have learned, of a small packet of marijuana. We refuse and tell him why. He readily admits the connection and talks about what the habit means to him. In a surprising eruption of frankness, he launches into a heartbreaking saga of being a victim of sexual abuse as a child, dropping out of school, getting involved in drugs and solvent sniffing—hating himself and trying to straighten out—but always slipping back into the dreaded cycle of despair. Even his family has grown tired of his constant troubles, he says. Now he is the perpetrator, taken into custody more than once on charges of sexual assault against a young cousin: "No one likes me, I think."

He speaks of friends who have succumbed to the same cycle of abuse, dependency, pain, and loneliness. Unfortunately, this pattern touches many in his generation. He describes a friend who has tried to commit suicide several times by swallowing razor blades and shooting himself in the abdomen. Every time, someone has managed to save his fragile life. Another friend has overdosed on drugs and alcohol mixtures over "girl troubles." A third has spent long stints in jail for armed robbery and in a regional psychiatric center, but neither incarceration nor therapy created a positive sense of self.

The young man recounts the major events of these young lives, as though drafting the skeleton of a bad soap opera, because he wants us to understand. We ask if going out on the land and learning how to survive in the old way might be an antidote to the gnawing suffering that haunts these young men. He replies that they all "do hashish," some have "blown their minds" on solvents and glue sniffing, and some do drugs even when they are out on the land: "Sometimes a guy will kill himself out there. I don't know why."

Later that evening, a woman in her 50s comes to visit. As the conversation turns to the impacts of resettlement, she says quietly that her son committed suicide two years ago. Just before he died, she was standing on the porch and saw a rainbow. A friend told her later that the rainbow symbolized her son dying and entering heaven. The next year another son shot himself in the heart. He was unmarried, unemployed, hated school, and had dropped out of the 9th grade. The woman adds that when her husband went to identify their son at the nursing station, "He held our son's hand up to God and said, 'Here, take him.'" The woman cried so much at this exceedingly cruel second loss that she saw a white cloud and a flat rock on her chest: "It was very hard for me, but my faith keeps me going. It was God's will."

Whatever the explanation, the method, or the cause, news of a suicide travels fast through a special crisis management group that personally visits family members and neighbors who must hear words that hurt more deeply than words can say. Our consultants offered the cases in this section in the context of trying to understand the ultimate pain of modern life. They, too, want to know why the rates of suicide are so high in their community and what they can do to stop the loss of fragile lives.

ॐ

F amily life easily falls prey to the ravages of rapid social change in any society. For example, when the former Union of Soviet Socialist Republics (USSR) resettled aboriginal peoples in its north, dislocations and social problems emerged: "The displaced population...was removed with the use of militia, peoples' courts [and] prosecutors...[they were] moved out and resettled in industrial cities, seaports and administrative centres...a terrible unemployment began, and from there followed the social consequences. Men and women were destitute...they turned to drink, and the wives and daughters of former hunters and fishermen became prostitutes."[1] The assimilationist, Russification approach was officially abandoned during the Gorbachev administration.

Nor are Canadian Inuit alone among aboriginal people who have problems with severe substance abuse. Among the Innu (Indian) of Sheshatshiu, Labrador, gas sniffing reached such drastic levels in 2001 that parents asked the Canadian government to remove their children for detoxification and treatment. The Innu "trace their problems with poverty and substance abuse to government relocations that forced them to give up their nomadic way of life." They also draw connections between substance abuse and chronic physical and sexual abuse suffered in Christian residential schools in mid-twentieth century. Over half of Sheshatshiu's 300 children between five and fourteen have sniffed gasoline: "Half of the adults are addicted to alcohol, 42 percent have thought actively about killing themselves and 28 percent have attempted suicide."[2]

Not surprisingly, many Inuit believe that "family breakdown" is the biggest problem facing them today. Suicide, violence, substance abuse, and other problems may be "a function of increasing discordance between men's and women's roles," but many other factors conspire to create enormous challenges to Inuit families.[3] Meeka explains: "Relatives used to be very close. Right now they hardly talk to each other."

Some Inuit women think that families may draw even closer than before because they can easily visit each other in the settlements. Extended families used to coalesce in separate camps. If a woman married a man from another community, she would have to separate from her parents. Now, most members of an extended family live within the same hamlet and it is easier to travel to those living in other communities. While proximity to family members may not present much logistical difficulty under normal circumstances today, the Inuit family has suffered several historical blows. As discussed earlier, when tuberculosis was a plague upon the land, Inuit women would have a husband in the camp, a son being treated in Montreal, two children in residential schools, and relatives in the new hamlet: "Some families never got back together again. That's reason enough to hate white people, right there" (see Chapter 3). The long-term impacts of such blows help shape the way Inuit women define their lives.

The availability of time and how people spend it reflects other concerns about family breakdown. Working women may find it difficult to spend sufficient quality time with their families. A nursing assistant in her 30s laments the situation she and many friends confront: "I'm always busy. After work, I have to go to meetings or sew something or clean up. That's what I really don't like...not having enough time with my family." An assistant minister sees gambling, bingo, cribbage, and card games as contributing to family breakdown among the middle aged and elderly: "Maybe they play 'patii' or Crazy 8's, but instead of putting it on paper, they play with money." Stakes can run as high as $50 a game. He defines this as a problem, especially for men, because when older women gamble too much, they cannot look after their homes and families: "The husband usually spends quite a long time alone. The wife may leave around six o'clock and not come back until two o'clock in the morning—or all night! I couldn't take that!"

Daycare
"They have a hard time finding a baby-sitter"

Just before the daycare center arrived on the 1988 sealift ship, many women agreed that the most serious problem facing them (besides the scarcity of jobs) was "no baby-sitter." As we were leaving Pangnirtung that summer, an Inuk father mentioned that a ship would be coming up Cumberland Sound toward the end of August to deliver a new modular daycare center. We said, "Oh, the women must be happy about that!" He replied, "What do you mean the women? It's the men who will be happy!" Indeed, many men have put in more childcare time than they find comfortable, although they love children and carry the little ones all over the settlement.

Even since the center opened, women continue to complain that the facility is too small (it was expanded slightly in 1996). A recent study shows that daycare facilities throughout Nunavut are woefully under-funded and under-staffed.[4] The new government has vowed to resolve these problems. Particularly for those without relatives who can help, inadequate community-based daycare presents perplexing dilemmas. A weak link between childcare and working outside the home discriminates against women and keeps them dependent. If her partner helps with childcare, a working woman may still confront problems when he goes hunting: "They have to hire a baby-sitter or they send the parents to look after them. That might also cause a problem for the growing children."

Lena and others believe that improvement of childcare services will increase the choices available to women:

> Many women here have a baby and want to work; or teenagers keep their kid and want to go to high school—they have a problem because the baby-sitting house is too small. Women are supporting husbands, but the husbands don't think childcare is their job. They don't want to do it all day. That was my biggest problem, too.

In spite of their frequent role as major provider, most Inuit women voice a preference for staying home with their newborn children rather than relinquishing them to daycare. Those who distrust daycare rely on their mothers or other close family members. Lisa, 26, worries that a baby-sitter would "do bad things in the house or neglect the children."[5] She wants to stay home with her children until they are old enough to go to school. In a small community where kinship bonds weave a complicated social network, women do not pay each other for baby-sitting. A woman finds someone who will look after her child—at another point in her life she may take their child: "It's the extended family system more than anything else, not a paid baby-sitter service."

Women also express concern about the cost of daycare. Lisa asks, "If you are single and hardly have enough money to pay for food or electricity, how can you pay for daycare?" Naiomi says that if she were married with children and wanted to work full time, she and her husband "would have to talk about baby-sitting money and whether we could trust the baby-sitter. If my kids didn't know the person, then they would always be bad for the baby-sitter." She thinks she would wait until they were in school before going to work, and reflects the concerns many other mothers have about both the cost and quality of professionalized daycare: "At the daycare center, women should be educated about taking care of children, and must like children. They would have to pay them."

Photo 9.2   Father and child at a community gathering.

Because they often end up raising wave after wave of children (their own at various ages, then their daughters' children), many older women approve of and, indeed, welcome daycare. Saila, 33, likes the daycare center: "It is better for women who have jobs to leave their children there. That way, more women can have jobs—before, some women quit because of lack of baby-sitting." The daycare center seems to fit into a culture that so greatly values shared responsibility toward children, and seems to work as a preferable solution to paid baby-sitting. It is a communal response to a felt need.

At the tapestry studio, women may bring their children when they cannot make other arrangements. Says a supervisor, "When there are too many children in the studio, at the next meeting we'll say that children are allowed only in emergencies. We'll allow a small infant for a morning if there's no baby-sitter; we'll let the child sleep on the floor for a couple of hours. If the child has to go to the nursing station with the mother in the morning and she doesn't want to go back home to pick up the child, she brings it to work."

Childcare concerns point to consequences of fundamental changes in family structure. Out on the land, the community cared for children and mothers worked close to home. With the new economic base of settlement life, the family no longer functions the way it once did to protect and socialize the next generation.

Guiding Their Children
"Not enough discipline"

The childcare issue becomes entangled with views on how to raise children. Older women cite lack of discipline toward children as a serious problem. Major cultural transitions and changing family structure doubly complicate the normal challenges of parenting. Since Inuit have moved into settlements, adolescence has become a more pronounced stage of life with less purpose, more leisure time, and less parental guidance in practical matters.[6] Thirteen-year-old Kara says her mother dislikes it when she resists her requests for help: "She won't like me when she asks me to do the dishes and I make the wrong face." When her mother tells her to do something, Kara says she hesitates for fear of making a mistake: "When we go camping out on the land, I always am good to help my mother, but in Pang I don't help her." Another teenager, though, craves the discipline and order that she hopes would come from greater parental guidance: "I'd like to see the town cleaned up, especially when I hear in school about environmental problems and litter. I don't like kids who just throw things away and make a mess. I like living in the settlement but not the men and women who are always getting drunk." Police searches, arrests, trouble, and noise upset the calm she would prefer in her young life. Parents should exert more control over their children, she suggests.

The RCMP report that a small group of young males accounts for the majority of crime and "trouble" incidents in each hamlet. Why should this happen at all? One Inuk constable speculates that now families can get anything they want at the stores. This separates them from the land and their culture. Sometimes the incidents seem amazingly careless, as though life held little value, a police constable reflects: "A few years ago, three teenaged boys were in a nylon tent, sniffing propane. The fourth guy showed up with a lit cigarette in his mouth and blew them up. They were burnt but they all recovered." Residents, too, complain about the "tyranny" and "terror" created by the few. The most recalcitrant cases take themselves and their community through a whirlwind of crises and a revolving door of agencies that often seem miserably uncoordinated, with under-trained and overworked staff. Burnout runs high all around. The police, social workers, parents, nursing staff, clergy, teachers, and the youths themselves simply grow weary of trying to deal with seemingly insoluble problems.

Iola sees a lack of love and discipline as the "problem in our life." Children do not listen to their parents and parents do not know how to communicate with children.[7] The generation gap can become so poignant that it leads to suicide attempts on the part of both teens and parents: "They put out a false love to their children as they grow up. Not enough discipline. If my boy breaks a window, and I defend my son when other parents say something to him, that's spoiling him. That's a big problem. When they are 17 or 18, their parents cannot talk to them. They're afraid of their own children, who control everything!" The generation gap is even worse than usual because of the language barrier. Years ago the children had to sit still in church; now they run around. When Iola grew up, his mother taught him that "in church, only your eyes were supposed to move around, not your body. If it's boring, we have to sit still, even if we have to cough. It's a different world today."

An Inuk RCMP officer reports that children become used to being alone in the house. When children come home, their mothers encourage them to go outside to play:

> The mother will say, "I'll give you $5. Why don't you go to the store, buy some candy or something. Stay out." That is sad for me because I grew up very close to my family. I learned from the way they looked after me. They were the only ones who cared about me. I know if I don't have parents, I don't live. Children are running around out there day and night...all ages. They're always well clothed, the hair is cut, but you never see parents with them. At seven a.m., you'll see 18-month-old kids out, all by themselves, but not in winter.

Lack of supervision and guidance contribute to parent-child conflict, which in turn can become a serious problem: "We'll go into a house at night and there will be a 30-year-old man in good physical shape sitting in the corner howling and trembling. His 15-year-old brat is sitting at the kitchen table, drunk, and the father doesn't know what to do with him. He has no control there." A constable agrees: "Parents will say, I have no control over him—I don't know what to do. The teen is drunk or stoned. I've had very capable 30- or 40-year-old men call and ask that we remove the teen because he was terrorizing his mother or father. The father is scared of the kids."[8]

Giving their children guidance and instruction is important but not always easy or effective: "When they can't control their kids, sometimes ladies fall into depression. That's the main thing I've seen," a counselor concludes. Lorie, mother of two young girls, explains the dilemmas inherent in trying to raise children by the old values: "Our mothers say that we have to tell our kids not to do this and that—from the time they are born until they're 18 or older." Inuit women take this admonition from their mothers very seriously. Although they realize that mothers in the south also have problems controlling their children, Inuit women feel that somehow they are to blame or out of control. A middle-aged woman who helps run a support group for parents reassures them: "We always tell them that it's not their fault. The kids are doing things they're not supposed to do. They try to understand that it's a different generation and all kinds of things are coming. It has changed from the time we were kids. We can't go back."

At 19, Adeena juggles the dual roles of young mother and part-time student at the local branch of Nunavut Arctic College. She compares her generation to her mother's: "Back then it was old ways. You had to do whatever your mom told you to do. You had to listen to whatever she said. You couldn't disagree with her; but now it's not like that." Adeena's mother was the eldest in her family. Since her mother was excessively strict, she vowed never to be that way: "She knows how it feels."

Traditionally, the mother had more control over females than males. Reepa believes that "they had it really easy as far as knowing where their children were or what they were doing. There was not much to worry about, except for surviving. They had a peaceful, worry-free life, compared to today, with the drugs and alcohol." With her own children, Reepa says that before they "do anything bad I would tell them right and wrong. That's the only way it works—tell them that they're not supposed to do any bad things."

In the summer daylight season, the sun never really sets, so the days blend into a dusky night that invites outdoor play and roaming through the streets of the settlement. Several women grumble about children who stay up all night, then sleep in late the next day, a custom that started in the settlements. They make too much noise for those who are trying to sleep. Older Inuit claim that their parents would not allow them to do this when they were children. Arnaqo, a middle-aged man, reminisces about his early years: "When my father woke up, he would wake me up. If we were going hunting, he would say, 'Son, you get ready my dogs and my *qamutik.*' Even if I don't want to get up, I have to obey. They don't do that anymore. That's why kids think they can stay out or sleep in as much as they want."

Ironically, loss of parental control can be a bigger problem with girls than with boys, because of rumors of prostitution or the danger of early pregnancy. Qatsuq worried about her children regardless of their ages: "I love my children as if they were small, even if I cannot give my love away very deeply. I lost a child and was in a shock for a while. I went into another shock when my daughter...went from one man to another. I didn't want her to do this."[9] Older children land on the wrong side of the law, especially with breaking and entering during the darkest months. Boys break into warehouses and other facilities, exasperating both their victims and their mothers, who have to deal with the police and the court system.

With less of the natural closeness that stems from working together for survival, some mothers seem to have lost touch with their children. This worries the older generation, says a librarian: "They want them to keep the traditional life, but some younger women don't feel there's a real need for it. Children rebel against the close control. The elders say, 'We never used to do that when we were your age.' They still don't want to accept that things have changed."

This parent-child standoff worries young women who anticipate how they might approach the problem with their own children someday. Apea feels that parents should take more control of the children—sending them to court and to jail is not going to solve their problems. Even some teenagers feel the dangers of too little discipline and guidance, as this 16-year-old relates:

> Kids shouldn't stay out all night! I don't stay out all night because my mom tells me I shouldn't. When I look outside, I see my friends playing—some of them don't help their parents at all. My mom tells me to help her. Kids who are only nine or twelve years old smoke because they stay out all night. The person who stays out learns how to smoke, that's what my mom tells me. They have to learn how to say no. I tell them to quit because they're going to get lung cancer. When I have children, I'll make them stay in at night. I'll tell them to help more because that's what they should do.

Another aspect of the generation gap comes when older Inuit believe they have no right to speak about their problems. They feel unqualified to tell younger people how they feel, says a counselor, "because they don't have a certificate or something." This gives people the wrong idea—they fail to consider their true abilities. Younger people, on the other hand, may feel they are superior because they have gone through high school and have the certificates. They adopt an arrogant attitude: "You have no right to tell me what to do."

Not all parents abdicate responsibility for disciplining their children. Pitaloosie speaks of her son, who broke into a store when he was 15: "One time he was in trouble, but he hasn't had trouble since. We talk to him. We try to make him understand that he's not to do this: 'You'll make everybody unhappy in the whole family.' He understands." In families that work hard on keeping the lines of communication open, discipline appears to be easier and more effective.

The Seductions of Alcohol and Drugs
"We never want to refuse"

It is clear that the magic potions of modern times that have proved to be so seductive for other communities in the world have been no less so for the Inuit. In a way, the problems caused by substance abuse are even more devastating because the Inuit are geographically isolated and especially vulnerable during this period of exceedingly rapid social change. The rate of heavy drinking in Nunavut is three times that of Canada as a whole; solvent sniffing is twenty-six times more prevalent than the national pattern.[10] The residual effects of resettlement, unemployment, and cultural dislocations contribute to these high rates. Despite being an officially dry community, experimentation and serious problems with intoxicating substances form part of the Pangnirtung experience.

Alcohol

As in other communities, alcohol and drugs help to drive a wedge between the elders and the younger generation. Tempers flare and words spoken from caring feel more like accusations or criticisms than expressions of love:

> Things are different because of the alcohol. The elders today are just as knowledgeable as before, but we don't talk or instruct the young people as much anymore…when that person gets drunk he might get mad at the elder for having said those things. He might go over to the elder's house and start yelling. He might scream at the elder when he is drunk, and say things like, "I won't take it anymore!" The alcohol—that is why the elders don't want to talk anymore. It is because when young people get drunk, they get abusive towards the elders.[11]

Inuit women speak freely about the intrusion of alcohol into their lives. The source of the problem goes back to the whaling period, according to elder Qatsuq: "The Qallunaat sailors used to bring it here, but one day an Inuk got drunk and died. We told them not to bring alcohol here again, but they never listened to us." She never saw a drunken Inuk, but remembers that her mother did, which confirms the notion that the problem emerged in the mid-nineteenth century. Similarly, Margaret Penny's diary from 1857-58 laments the scourge of alcohol abuse: "They are so kind if left to themselves but I am sorry to say they have been taught much evil [by the whalers and other whites]."[12] A Moravian newspaper in 1871, in reviewing missionary activities among the Inuit, noted that the influence of British and American whalers "especially in the introduction of spirituous liquor" was "proving very injurious, and evidently leading to their rapid extermination."[13]

The Inuit are surprisingly willing to take equal responsibility for the human wreckage produced by the misuse of alcohol. Ottokie says: "When white people came up here with all the booze, we used it. I don't blame only whites for it." Obviously, however, the Inuit had no alcohol until they interacted with Scottish and American whalers. Although Reepa's mother always insisted "they never did [drugs and alcohol] out there," Reepa has heard that people fell prey to the seductions of whiskey long ago.

> My grandfather was living in Kekerten as a boy. He saw people drunk back then. They got whiskey from the whalers." They were doing it, I've heard. Not a lot...maybe a few times. I was so surprised to hear it, because I was told it was never done! My grandfather saw people drunk even back then. They got the whiskey from the traders and whalers, but it was nothing compared to today.

Now Qatsuq says the biggest problem facing her community is that some people, both male and female, drink too much: "Alcohol is ruining the families. That's the only thing they can do to be happy...drink. It might be better if women went back to sewing." Elder Pitaloosie feels that Inuit politeness amplified the temptations of alcohol in times past. Maata also points to a combination of pressure from whites and Inuit cultural traits:

> Booze started coming in and most tried it. We are a very sharing people. When someone—even a white man—offers something, in our tradition it is very impolite to refuse. It's very unkind; it hurts the one who's offering. We're so used to sharing and doing things together. That's what happens with booze and drugs. We have more common sense now, but that is how it started. [14]

A woman in her late 40s has a slightly different analysis of how the Inuit ran into trouble with alcohol and, to a lesser extent, drugs: "Living in one place too much" has damaged her people. Alcohol offers a door out of anxiety and lost dignity. Indeed, alcohol spread rapidly throughout the Canadian Arctic in the early twentieth century and became even more readily available during the Resettlement Period.[15] "Sometimes I think life would be solved if we moved out into little communities again and everyone could take care of one another," she adds. "That won't be happening now."

How do the Inuit obtain alcohol in ostensibly dry Pangnirtung? A nurse says that controlled communities like Iqaluit have an alcohol board: "You can order alcohol through the warehouse there, but if you live in Iqaluit or stop there on your way North, you can't just walk in and ask for it." She believes that there must be a bootlegger in Iqaluit, that locals buy alcohol in Montreal or Ottawa, or that they have people send it on the planes to Pangnirtung. It is very easy to obtain alcohol, says a young man: "People want cash so bad, they'll do anything for it." People pay others to bring alcohol in from Iqaluit by skidoo or plane.[16]

The RCMP cannot open boxes as they come off the planes unless they have "reasonable and probable grounds" to suspect smuggling. (Canada Post has recently agreed under certain circumstances to open "suspicious packages" sent by mail.) Some Inuit apparently make their own alcohol, which is why the local stores restrict the sale of yeast and brown sugar. Kara reflects: "Some people drink. Those of us who don't drink think it's bad because you're not supposed to take it. When my father is away he drinks a lot, but we don't mind because he's not at home." Her father drinks occasionally when he takes whites out fishing: "Some of them bring alcohol and give him some. I've seen him drunk twice." Whatever the source, the nurse observes "there are people who always have liquor. I guess the RCMP know who they are. They confiscate it and fine people. We know they have it because we see the results of alcohol-induced assaults here in the nursing station."

Some professionals believe that Pangnirtung has far fewer problems with alcohol than Iqaluit and other northern communities. The percentage of residents who feel alcohol abuse is a problem in their own community varies from a high of 72 percent in Iqaluit (the largest community) to a low of 20 percent in Lake Harbour. Just over 50 percent of Pangnirtung's residents see alcohol as a problem, but that figure may be more significant than appears on the surface since this is a dry town.[17] Sam, a white RCMP officer who previously served in a predominantly white and Indian community in the Western Arctic, draws a comparison: "This place of 1,400 people averages about 65 prisoners a year. The other place is 900 and we averaged between 500 and 600 prisoners a year—90 percent of all the crime was liquor related. In Pangnirtung, people don't go in for drinking. If you have 65 prisoners a year, that's a drop in the bucket. On my last shift in the other community, we put 15 in jail!" Another officer has worked in Iqaluit for one month, and reports that they averaged 25 alcohol-related jailings per night. In the first six months of 1996, 41 people were jailed in Pangnirtung: 16 were alcohol-related, five drug-related, six assaults, five spousal assaults, and the rest for a variety of offenses. Sometimes the offender is jailed "until sober": "We confiscate the alcohol and send him on his way...but he'll probably do it again next week." For those whose lives are damaged by alcoholic excess, the results are devastating: "Pang people used to say, 'Frobisher [Iqaluit] is a really bad place. Lot of people drinking, lot of problems down there.' They forget their own problems here."[18] The tiny minority who consistently find themselves in alcohol-related trouble wreak havoc with their families.

Drugs and Solvents

With alcohol, the modern scourge of drugs presents exceptional challenges to the contemporary Inuit family. In the absence of alcohol, other substances may become more attractive, but "people never want to talk about it." Nunavut has the highest drug use rate in Canada (Figure 9.1).[19]

Pangnirtung, like many other communities, has banned hair spray because both men and women drink it for a cheap high. Drugs "drain the economy of our community," observes a 22-year-old woman. She and her two girlfriends have tried "hash and booze." They say they succumbed to the influence of peers: "Acid is available, too," but LSD and cocaine are rare. Meeka worries about the children: "My biggest concern is that drugs are coming up North so much. I was taking drugs now and then when I was growing up. I know it's very hard to resist when you are young; when you get older, you can kick them off."

Figure 9.1 Drug Use in Nunavut, Western NWT, and Canada

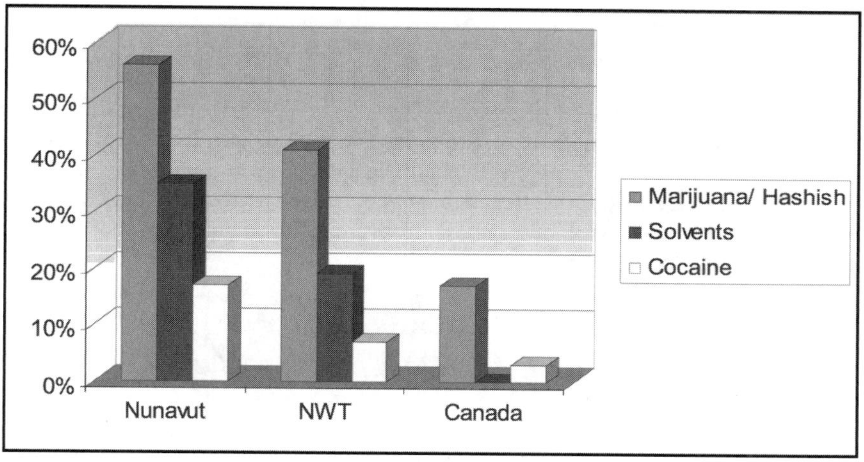

Source: Bell, "Canada's Crime Capital (Part One).

Reepa remembers that as she was growing up she was not involved in drugs or alcohol at all, but her friends were sniffing glue or solvents. She tried it and her mother found out: "I don't do that anymore. I've done it maybe twice in my life with friends." A nurse corroborates the incidence of solvent sniffing, especially among teenagers. Their parents bring them to the nursing station with complaints of headaches or feeling dizzy and sick: "You know you can't really pinpoint it; you ask them and they deny it." Inuit may be reluctant to admit drug or alcohol abuse, she adds, because they are afraid that the nurses will report them to the RCMP. Females are far from exempt, a constable insists:

We had four young girls between the ages of 13 and 16 behind the lodge in the wintertime, each of them hanging over a 100-pound bottle of propane. There were 30 or 40 bottles and they had them open. One stepped back to light a cigarette. The flames just fired from one bottle to another, and burned their faces up really good. The only thing that saved them was that the propane, because it was heavy, ran downhill and off to the ocean.

Ben has counseled local Inuit who have become dependent on drugs, which can be a more serious problem than alcohol because of the hidden market. Some users become desperately drug dependent: "People never say, 'This guy has it.' It's underground." When users run out of drugs, they start breaking and entering to support their habit. Drugs create anger and marital problems such as spousal assault, he adds, because the user becomes "restless." Ben adds that drugs cause "problems with support of families—they go into debt on their rent and can't pay their account at the Northern Stores or the Co-op. Some of the young people shoplift to get drug money."

The community started a Drug Addicts Anonymous support group to try to deal with this modern epidemic: "They started well, but in the springtime the leaders went out camping and it was discontinued." Why do Inuit turn to drugs? A teenager finds it difficult to explain: "They might have friends who introduced them to drugs or they might have problems with their families. It starts in the teens, but some still use drugs in their 30s because they started early." A nurse sees drug and alcohol abuse as a coping mechanism that often backfires. An Inuk constable maintains that drugs are "prevalent in Pangnirtung, just like any community in North America."

Suicide
"They may have a problem with self-esteem"

Unfortunately, Inuit communities have had all too much experience in dealing with suicide. Living between two competing cultures both produces problems and intensifies them. That so many men, and too many women, have succumbed to the numbing escape of alcohol and drugs or the final flight of suicide reveals both a cause and a symptom of their marginality.

Rates

A Royal Commission study in Canada, which has the third worst teenage suicide problem in the world, found that the rate among aboriginal teenage boys is five times the non-Native rate. The rate in Nunavut is more than six times the Canadian rate and is three times the rate for the western part of the former Northwest Territories.[20] For *young* Nunavummiut, the rate of 1 suicide per 1,000 (or 100 per 100,000) contrasts with the Canadian youth rate of 78 per 100,000.[21] In the Baffin region, suicides occur at nearly double the rate for all aboriginal people in Canada and nearly five times the overall Canadian rate.[22] Figure 9.2 shows the comparison across age groups between Inuit, Indians, and the Canadian population as a whole (as of the early 1990s).

The mean annual suicide rate per 100,000 people for the 1981-1990 period was 60 in Pangnirtung, compared to a high of 205 in Broughton Island and a low of 23 in Igloolik.[23] (It dropped in Pangnirtung in recent years.) For the former Northwest Territories as a whole:[24]

- Most victims have been between 16 and 30 years old.
- Most (over 75 percent) have been Inuit youths.
- Nearly 50 percent have occurred in the Baffin region.
- Nearly 50 percent have occurred between May and August (coincidentally, when the light lasts virtually 24 hours a day).
- Males account for three-quarters of these suicides.
- Suicide hits the young hardest—most victims are unemployed youths or in school.
- In the last ten years, only two suicide victims from Pangnirtung were *not* between 15 and 19 years old.

The problem has become so epidemic that people now use "suicide" as a verb, as in, "She tried to suicide" or "He suicided last night."

Figure 9.2 Suicide Rates per 100,000 for Inuit, Indians, and Canada

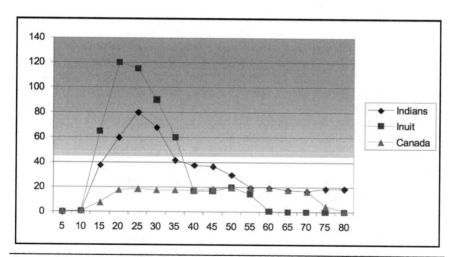

Source: Adapted from Waldram, Herring, and Young, *Aboriginal Health in Canada*, p. 91; based on Medical Services Branch and Statistics Canada data.

Struggling to Understand "Why?"

An elder notes that taking one's life is far from a modern phenomenon. Out on the land, the elders say, a person who had become too frail or infirm to contribute to the band's survival would simply offer to stay behind when the group moved on to new hunting grounds. They preferred to die a slow death of starvation and freezing rather than become a burden on their families. Balikci uncovered several reasons for suicide attempts in earlier times: grief (following the death of a close relative), personal disasters or illness, marital dissatisfaction, or old age.[25] When a person felt useless and incompetent from age or illness, her self-esteem would plummet to unbearable depths: "One's identity stemmed from one's usefulness. The awareness that one was not useful was one's worst nightmare. Without utility, there could be no sense of self.

In a society that firmly believed in the transmigration of the soul to a better world—suicide or not—escape from such an existence seemed preferable to life."[26] In pre-Christian times, suicide was not a sin but almost a duty toward one's community. A few early explorers and anthropologists noted that it was not only the old who took their own lives—often it was young males or females: "And all such Inuit killed themselves in terribly inventive ways. It seemed, upon closer inspection, that whoever felt isolated or derided by the group, sick or otherwise handicapped, was quick to die."[27] Margaret Penny writes in 1858: "While sitting below [deck] a native came...two females having found a woman dead on the hill. Poor creature, she had hung herself, for what cause we cannot tell, but there appears to be some mystery about it."[28]

An older person speculates that suicides happen today because the younger people are not used to "being in hardship." They have not had time to think for themselves, so they try to kill themselves when faced with a problem: "In our ancestors' days, when there was extreme hardship, suicide was totally nonexistent because when problems arose, they immediately tried to solve it and overcome it. In the last 30 years, we have been spoiled. We have been in a period where we didn't have to try at all."[29] In any case, the pattern of suicide has persisted into modern life, devastating families and communities as they watch their loved ones, especially the young, die by their own hand: "Why? The answer is quite simple: The need to belong, to feel useful still remains as strongly as ever. Inuit have retained this need, while having been herded into a modern system of living where the individual is marginalised or altogether disregarded."[30]

The reasons for suicide are complicated by drug and alcohol use, to be sure, but marginality and the sense of uselessness may be the strongest explanations of all: "Caught between life on the land, about which they do not know enough, and the modern labour market, whose doors seem reluctant to open up to them, many young people have developed a feeling of being totally useless."[31] The Inuit explain uselessness in terms of lack of education and meaningful, steady work, which contributes to the hopelessness that many young people feel. Uncertainty about their ability to support themselves and a family, coupled with high rates of alcohol and drug abuse, creates disequilibrium for both individual and community.[32] In a few cases, the family's ability to hold itself together seems all too fragile and one member, usually a young male but sometimes a female, slips away.

Other Inuit blame "boredom, lack of opportunity, and an inability to cope with personal and family conflicts"—and being "caught in the middle" between two lifestyles.[33] For young people, suicide may be a cry for help but, as a nurse speculates, it also can serve as a way of coping with deep-rooted problems that must be hidden in a small village. It is a way out of the trials of a broken life. "Kids hang themselves in closets," says a teacher. "When the parents come home, there is Johnny, dangling from an electrical cord. Or they shoot themselves."

Beneath suicide lies the fundamental cohesion of the community. As Durkheim found a century ago in his classic study of the causes of suicide in France, those who were the most integrated into society (for example, married Catholics with children) were the least likely to take their own life. In contrast, those who were least integrated (for example, single Protestant or non-religious people without children) were most likely to commit suicide. Following Durkheim, Balikci observed that among the Netsilik Eskimo "two opposing forces—cohesive factors and disintegrative factors—were in constant conflict with one another."[34] Lack of social integration in a tight community, combined with marginality, substance abuse, or personal tragedy, might account for the majority of contemporary suicides.

Michael, in his early 20s, supports the social integration hypothesis. His uncle "suicided" when Michael was 12: "It was very hard to see." He believes that most suicides result from failed male-female relationships that end in break-ups or affairs: "Love is the cause." Often, he says, the male is trying to punish the female by committing suicide (an "I'll show you and make you feel guilty— you'll be sorry" attitude). This happened to Michael when he thought he and his girlfriend were breaking up. He was devastated and threatened suicide. They stayed together until he was over his despair. Now, they continue to be "best friends," but they no longer live together. From this liaison, Michael has a three-year-old son whom he does not see very often. He thinks he and his girlfriend might get married at some point, but Michael must finish high school first: "Most couples fall in love once and expect that person to be 'the one' for life. Inuit do not do much dating or have relationships right after the other. If we broke up for good, I would feel like suiciding, but I'd work my way out of it."

Many Inuit and outside observers have suggested that if young people only knew more about their traditional culture and spent more time on the land, they would not contemplate suicide. Yet, being close to the land does not necessarily insulate young people from the feelings of despair. One couple who taught their children the traditional ways could not fathom why their oldest son—who seemed to have everything to live for—committed suicide out on the land. A friend of the family tries to explain: "He knew how to live on the land, having spent much of his young life out there. He still succumbed. It was probably drugs. They lose hope." In a parallel case, an Inuk mother born in a camp and raised with traditional values, which she tried to pass along to her children, was devastated when her teenage son killed himself. An Inuk minister believes that it has to do with a sense of worthlessness and lack of communication in families:

"YOU'RE WORTHLESS!"

It doesn't really have one definite answer. It depends on the individual person. They may have problems when they're growing up, feeling unloved or unwanted. They may be involved with drugs or with the girlfriend or boyfriend. Sometimes they may have a problem with self-esteem. They feel, "I'm stupid, I don't know how to do anything, I don't know anything."

Many teens aren't interested in going hunting or fishing with Dad, who then says, "You're worthless!" The kids would rather stay home than spend two weeks in a stinky old tent on the land. The parents say, "You'd rather stay home and watch TV, smoke some hash, do nothing." The parents may reject and criticize them. It's a generational thing.

Adoption may have an effect down the road somewhere—giving children away so easily. Freedom may feel more like benign neglect. In Arctic Bay, one in six suicide victims had been adopted and had had major problems along the way: "Why did they give me away?" They grow up across the street from their natural parents and may feel rejection and resentment, especially in a family where there were lots of kids: "Why me?"

The majority of those who attempt suicide usually have the same problem—lack of communication in the family, the minister continues: "They don't know where to go. They don't think that people care. They don't have a person to share their problems with, and they have really isolated themselves." Communication seems key to those who work with struggling families. Talking with parents helps young people feel more accepted and brings them closer to the adults. Youths who have been to the brink of suicide and returned (as nearly all do in Pangnirtung) help by talking to others who are depressed. A man who has seen many changes in his 70 years, Ottokie hypothesizes that modern day living makes everything too easy—the young do not have to work hard for anything:

Maybe it's like computers or calculators. You don't even have to use your own mind anymore. When you have a problem and have to add numbers, all you do is go to a calculator and dink-dink-dink, the answer is right there. If you go on a computer, you don't have to work hard...all you have to do is press some buttons and it just comes out. They don't realize that life is not like that. Life is always going to be hard work. If you want to be a strong person, you have to work hard. You have to do many things before you are able to help other people or feel good about yourself.

When the young person realizes that life is difficult, he or she may conclude that life is *too* hard. The only alternative is death, the ultimate escape from seemingly overwhelming problems.

In a community of 1,400, four or five attempted suicides come to the attention of the nurses every year. The social services department has only one social worker and one Inuk counselor for three communities, so families often telephone the health service during a suicide crisis. Many come through the health services if they have taken pills, overdosed on drugs or alcohol, or tried to shoot themselves, creating a medical emergency. Someone commits suicide one way in a particular community and others copy it. Males choose hanging and shooting more often than females, who typically prefer overdosing on pills. In Pangnirtung, the preferred method of suicide has been hanging or gunshot wounds. At one time, overdosing on Tylenol or Anacin appeared to be the most popular method, as a nurse relates: "Anacin was a big one because you can buy it at the local store." In other communities such as Cape Dorset, suicide victims tend to shoot themselves in the stomach.

Female Attempts

Being young and female does not provide immunity against suicide attempts. More females than males attempt suicide in Pangnirtung, as is true also in the south, but males usually make more serious attempts: "We see a lot of younger women who take fifteen or twenty pills and some antibiotics, and then they throw up. It's usually because they've had a fight with their boyfriend. They come to us right away. They're sorry." Young women offered these contrasts between male and female attempts: "Men are gutsier when it comes to dying. Women call for help with pills. Men don't look at the future and who it will affect. Women do look at the affect on others." Why do more females attempt suicide? A nurse speculates that girls start intimate involvements early, as they do in other communities. Young teens encounter relationship problems but do not know how to deal with them. She also acknowledges that females may be more willing to come forward for help than males. This is true for regular medical visits to the clinic: "We see far, far more women than we do men. The men just don't come unless they're really sick."

However, the RCMP say that suicide *threats* abound: "Women in jail say, 'I'll take my baby and kill myself.' They are drunk. Or they have a fight with a boyfriend and say, 'If he doesn't stop calling me on the phone, I'm going to suicide.'" The threats come from young people of both sexes. A nurse says that those who make repeated suicide *attempts* tend to be "manipulative," while those who succeed usually have never presented themselves for help in the past.

Because of the trend toward role reversal, females between 12 and 25 fear that, even if they finish high school, no meaningful work will be waiting. They wonder what kind of life they can possibly have in a community where between

60 and 80 percent of the population exists on welfare. One woman in the sexual assault survivor's support group said that she does not know any female who committed suicide who had *not* been the victim of sexual assault.

Three young women in their 20s sit around a kitchen table, quietly discussing why people might choose to take their own life. Slowly, they tell the stories of suicides that have touched too close to home, and then the conversation turns to their own suicidal thoughts:

"I REALLY DID WANT TO DIE"

A: I have two cousins and two friends who committed suicide, and one friend who was assaulted by several guys. She got depressed, but I thought she was over it. She made one [suicide] attempt before hanging herself in a closet at age 15. She felt her family didn't love her. That was last year. I felt like I should have talked to her more. She didn't want to talk to her mother, which I suggested. I even offered to talk to her mother with her, but she wouldn't do it.

B: My sister, when she was 14 or 15, tried to commit suicide. When my grandfather died, she missed him and felt unloved. She was adopted to my grandmother. She swallowed pills a second time, but she's OK now. My cousin suicided—a guy, 15 years old.

C: My uncle.

B: My relatives in Broughton Island. Too many to count. Mostly males. Most hang themselves, both male and female, 15 to 20 years old.

A: I thought about suiciding at age 16, but I didn't attempt it. I blamed my [disability] on my parents. Did God not love me? Did you do drugs or alcohol when you were pregnant with me? Now I think my life is worthwhile. I can do a lot that other people can't. I'm worth it. But at that point, I really wanted to die. I imagined myself hanging in my closet. Now I'm building confidence.

B: It scares me. When you kill yourself, where do you go? I thought about it at 12 or 13. I didn't accept how I look. My friends said I was okay. My mother made me feel special. I told both my parents how I felt. Now I feel I can do anything I want to do. I am proud that I have achieved a high school diploma and now I'm getting a college education.

C: I thought of it. I was 20 and in a relationship before the baby was born. My uncle and my boyfriend sexually abused me. Then I found out I was pregnant. I wanted to see my baby grow up, so I put aside thoughts of suicide.

A nurse argues that women are more vulnerable because "there are still females out there who feel very afraid of the man, and they don't get much support from their relatives. Some people seem to want to shut off what's happening." Violence in the relationship, or non-violent conflict, may result in the woman trying to kill herself: "I see people who don't want to do anything about it. They just want to close their eyes to the violence. The women seem to get more depressed about that here." Others think that males may be more "self-satisfied" and the females more frustrated.

When Suicide Hits Home

The Pangnirtung Inuit realize that many young people in other Native communities try to take their own lives, but the grief comes crashing down when suicide hits home. Naturally, as in other hamlets, a cloak of confusion and despair descends in Pangnirtung every time a young person attempts to commit suicide or, most tragically, when he or she succeeds. One man grimly describes the fact that his teenage son, step-son, and two step-brothers have committed suicide, all young men who have succumbed while their families stood helplessly by: "We have a thing called drugs here," he comments dryly. The burden of emotional pain resides on the shoulders of the young, who feel so desperate and hopeless, and on the shoulders of their mothers and fathers. Osuituk, in her 60s, describes her situation as a typical case:

> I had ten children. Three girls are dead and one boy killed himself. One newborn girl got a cold and died. The other girl was three when so many of the children were dying...she died of TB. Then the twin died. The boy killed himself when he was 18. He got into trouble with the RCMP and he felt bad. Maybe he didn't really know who he was—he wasn't a very strong person. Maybe he lost his dignity. I don't really know why. I miss them all.

A female RCMP officer outlines the trauma and agony that surrounds suicide in a small community:

> "THE CHAIR SLIPPED AWAY"
> It happened the night I arrived here. The other officer went first, and then he called me on the radio. A female hanged herself on a metal bar with a belt and a choke chain you use on a dog. She wrapped it around her neck, knelt on a chair, and then let herself go. When she passed out, the chair slipped away. She'd been dead for a few hours. Her family was out on the land; her twin sister was in Iqaluit having a baby. She was 16.
> Her friends and neighbors were there. There was so much wailing and crying, the officer couldn't hear me calling him. Guys in their late teens and early 20s were wailing. Her friend came looking for her, banged on the door. A neighbor came out and said, "She's in there; we saw her earlier." She wasn't answering the door or telephone, so they went in through a common crawl space and found her. They cut her down and called for help to see if she was still alive, but no. The local elders came. The head of the men's support group and the women's support group arrived to deal with the upset and to advise the family. Her best friend had done it the week before in Iqaluit. She hanged herself, too.

The police and the Mental Health Committee (a "tundra roots" movement comprised primarily of elder women) worried about the contagion effect that could ensue, but no other suicides followed in the few months after that horrible night. Each suicide hurts as much as the last one. The pain does not fade because the community has endured similar losses in the past. When the daughter of then Nunavut Territory Commissioner, Peter Irniq, took her own life in Hamilton, her father wrote these words:

> Teresa grew up away from the North and she did not understand or accept the part that her Inuit heritage played in her life. My daughter searched for her place on this earth and I could do little to help her find it.... In my daughter's memory I am determined to carry on the work to preserve, protect and promote Inuit culture and language through Inuit Qaujimajatuqangit [Inuit Traditional Knowledge] so that our youth—our future—will have a better understanding of where they came from and therefore know better where they want to go. I invite all Inuit leaders to join me in this important cause! There is so much meaning about where we Inuit came from and why it was so important to allow all of us together, Elders and Youth, to create a Nunavut where we all can live to our fullest.[35]

In that spirit, a woman relates the story of an Inuk friend, whom she visited a month after she found her son hanging: "She first went into a deep depression. When I returned a year later, she and her husband were raising a beautiful three-month-old adopted son given to them by his brother and sister-in-law. They named him after the dead teenager. Their lives and spirits were renewed. Their family, community, and in effect their culture had reached out to them with a generosity unparalleled in our culture."[36]

Some Inuit become trapped in the cycle of violence that they are trying to help others break. As a tragic example, Geela Giroux Patterson, a respected Pangnirtung woman who had served many others as a suicide prevention counselor, took her own life in the early summer of 2000. She had gone to Iqaluit to serve as the senior advisor on women's issues to the new Nunavut government's Department of Culture, Language, Elders and Youth, linking it to the Inuit women's associations.[37] People said that her death was a tragic symbol of the struggle so many Inuit women and men face in coping with personal pain and the problems of cultural transition. A few days later, Geela's young daughter, Linda, a new mother in her early 20s, died suddenly of a brain aneurysm. The people of Pangnirtung were united in their explanation: Grief and shock overcame Geela's daughter, as it did the entire community.

At the same time, people were angry and disappointed in this woman, whom *Nunatsiaq News* had featured just the week before her death in an article on the significance of her work and her appointment as government liaison. Ironically, on the following page of that issue, was an eloquent editorial by Rachel Attituq Qitsualik on the terrible impact suicide has on the social network: "But the real horror of suicide cannot be conveyed by a story, nor can the devastating impact upon the loved ones left behind in the wake of a true suicide.... Most of those who commit suicide have no clue as to what effect it will have upon those who survive them. The survivors are themselves deprived of their own reason to live —love itself."[38] Qitsualik's words rang true, especially for Geela's daughter.

The Nunavut communities not only lost a counselor and an advocate but also the promise of a true role model—an effective, compassionate woman who seemingly had found a way to balance her life and give back to her community. Marginality—living between two worlds—creates unspeakable strains. A new rash of suicides followed Geela's death.

After Geela took her life, Peter Irniq wrote again about marginality, recalling that his father used to say to him, "Annakturniaqmijugut—we shall survive." Young people seem to have lost that strength, he says:

> I think the time has come for us to realize that we have to take the better of two worlds; we must carry into our hearts the values of our ancestors and marry them with today's way of living. Technology is valuable but does not necessarily bring the strength and happiness we need. Our youth are caught between two sets of values and it makes it difficult for them to choose which way to go. When I was a young boy, my father told me that there were hardly any suicides, except for a few very old people. They only committed suicide when they felt useless to the family members, not being able provide food. And they committed suicide so that the youth could have more than they had. The suicides were infrequent. These last couple of week's sad occurrences may have brought more confusion to these young minds. We must…try to pass on to our children the very same values our elders held close to their hearts….[39]

The Assembly of First Nations and the Royal Commission on Aboriginal Peoples held a special consultation on suicide prevention in 1993. They recommended several strategies, including improved education, traditional and contemporary healing models, strengthening family units, and community-based justice systems based on traditional values.[40] In mid-2001, the Nunavut Department of Health launched an aggressive anti-suicide campaign, including posters, radio announcements, television commercials, and newspaper advertisements designed to "break the silence" and command the attention of young people at risk, as well as their families and friends. Inuit families whose lives have been directly touched by suicide offered the messages: "Everyone matters," "Everyone is important," and "Inuit values and beliefs are the key to survival."[41] Community-based support, a manual for professionals, and training in trauma, stress, sexual abuse, and grief signify a multi-pronged effort to reduce the highest suicide rate in Canada. Resourcefulness, perseverance, reaching out to others, and strength are being promoted as "the Inuit way," rather than suicide, isolation, and silence. Television commercials underscore the importance of elders and of reducing the generation gap: in each of them, "the aged hand of an elder reaches down from a corner of the screen to grasp the hand of a child."[42]

Notes

1 Vladimir Sang, founder of the Association for the Small Peoples of the Soviet North, quoted in Valerie Alia, "Aboriginal Perestroika," *Arctic Circle* (November/December 1991), pp. 3-29.

2 Mary Rogan, "An Epidemic of Gas Sniffing Decimates Arctic Indian Tribe," *The New York Times* (March 18, 2001).

3 Marc G. Stevenson, cited in Nunavut Implementation Commission, *Footprints 2: A Second Comprehensive Report from the Nunavut Implementation Commission to the Department of Indian Affairs and Northern Development, Government of the Northwest Territories and Nunavut Ungava Incorporated Concerning the Establishment of the Nunavut Government* (Iqaluit, NWT: Nunavut Implementation Commission, October 21, 1996). See also Marc G. Stevenson, *Inuit, Nunavut, and Government* (Ottawa: Report Prepared for the Royal Commission on Aboriginal Peoples, 1994).

4 Sean McCabe, Report: "GN Doesn't Know Why Daycares Going Broke," *Nunatsiaq News* (July 7, 2000).

5 Gwen Reimer also heard this same fear about harm coming to children, "in terms of possible child abuse, [a] chronic problem in many Arctic communities [that] demonstrates the current ill health of the *ilagiit*." "Female Consciousness," p. 87.

6 Condon, *Inuit Youth*.

7 Richard G. Condon also documents this effect in "Adolescence and Changing Family Relations in the Central Canadian Arctic," *Arctic Medical Research* 49 (1990): 81-92.

8 Increasing adolescent aggression is discussed by Richard G. Condon in "Changing Patterns of Conflict Management and Aggression among Inuit Youth in the Canadian Arctic," *Native Studies Review* 8, 2 (1992).

9 Quoted in Hodgson, ed., *Stories from Pangnirtung*, p. 85.

10 Geddes, "Northern Dawn," p. 27.

11 Wachowich, *Saqiyuq*, p. 136.

12 Ross, *This Distant and Unsurveyed Country*, p. 169.

13 [Moravians], *Periodical Accounts Relating to the Missions of the Church of the United Brethren Established among the Heathen,* 28 (1871): 66. The reference to "extermination" was probably more accurate concerning diseases that swept through the whaling stations.

14 Pudlat, "Boy, Have Things Changed," p. 19.

15 See Don Claremont, *Notes on the Drinking Behaviours of the Eskimos and Indians in the Aklavik Area, Report 62-4* (Ottawa: The Northern Co-ordination and Research Centre, Department of Northern Affairs and National Resources, 1962).

16 The RCMP has tried to arrange for drug-sniffing dogs in Iqaluit airport, which could virtually shut off the drug traffic in Baffin. A few years ago, Judge Brown said she did not want a dog used at the airport because once she has ruled, that establishes case law and she must rule in the same way in other cases.

17 Griffiths, et al., *Crime, Law and Justice among Inuit*, p. 41.

18 Iqaluit's higher crime rate has plagued local authorities for decades. The town has made a valiant effort to reduce crime, especially now that it serves as capital of Nunavut. See Harold W. Finkler and A. Parizeau, *Deviance and Social Control: Manifestations,*

Tensions and Conflict in Frobisher Bay (Montréal: Universitet de Montréal, Centre International de Criminology Compare, 1973).
19 Bell, "Canada's Crime Capital (Part One)."
20 Geddes, "Northern Dawn," p. 27.
21 K. L. Capos, "Canadian Territory of Nunavut Pushes to Expand College Offerings," *The Chronicle of Higher Education* (July 27, 2001), p. A38. Suicide rates are measured in various ways, which produces some seemingly inconsistent figures.
22 L. J. Kirmayer, "Suicide among Canadian Aboriginal Peoples," *Tran cultural Psychiatric Research Review* 31 (1994): 3-58; S. Malcolm son and E. Hood, "A Study of Suicide in Baffin Zone, NWT, East Canadian Arctic," *Arctic Medical Research* 27 (1980).
23 Griffiths, et al., *Crime, Law and Justice among Inuit,* p. 48.
24 P. J. Garston, "Igloolik Mourns Again," *News/North* (Monday, July 15, 1996), p. A14. Igloolik, which had few suicides in the past, has experienced a disturbing wave, including the suicide of a 16-year-old boy after he had a fight with a former girlfriend. Counselors in the community reported that they were not trained to deal with suicide.
25 Balikci, *The Netsilik Eskimo,* p. 166.
26 Rachel Attituq Qitsualik, "Suicide," *Nunatsiaq News* (June 30, 2000).
27 Qitsualik, "Suicide."
28 Ross, *This Distant and Unsurveyed Country,* p. 171.
29 Reported in Griffiths, et al., *Crime, Law and Justice among Inuit,* p. 46. See also D. Bray, "A Study of Youth Suicide in the Canadian Urban Arctic," paper presented at the Fourth Annual Inuit Studies Conference, Hamilton, November 1984.
30 Qitsualik, "Suicide."
31 Dorais, *Quaqtaq,* p. 69.
32 See, for example, Geddes, "Northern Dawn," p. 27.
33 Griffiths, et al., *Crime, Law and Justice among Inuit,* p. 4.
34 Balikci, *The Netsilik Eskimo,* p. 171.
35 Peter Irniq, "[On Suicide] Place Faith in Inuit Culture," *Nunatsiaq News* (April 28, 2000).
36 Personal communication from Deborah Hickman of Nova Scotia, regarding an Inuit family in Labrador.
37 Nunatsiaq News, "GN Women's Advisor Takes Own Life," *Nunatsiaq News* (July 7, 1999).
38 Qitsualik, "Suicide"; see also Lawrence J. Kirmayer, M. Malus, and L. Boothroyd, "Suicide Attempts among Inuit Youth: A Community Survey of Prevalence and Risk Factors," *Acta Psychiatrica Scandinavia* 94 (1996): 8-17; Hugh M. Sampath, "The Changing Pattern of Inuit Suicide and Attempted Suicide," pp. 141-149 in *Looking to the Future: Papers from the Seventh Inuit Studies Conference,* edited by M-J. Dufour and F. Thérien (Ste. Foy, Québec: Université Laval, 1992) and "Inuit Depression in Cross Cultural Perspective," in the *Sixth International Symposium on Circumpolar Health, Proceedings,* edited by B. Harvald and J. P. Hart Hansen, 1981; and Jørgen Thorslund, "Why Do They Do It? Proposal for a Theory of Inuit Suicide," Seventh Inuit Studies Conference, University of Alaska Fairbanks, 1990.
39 Peter Irniq, "Let Us Care for One Another," *Nunatsiaq News* (July 14, 2000).

40 The Royal Commission on Aboriginal Peoples, *Choosing Life: Special Report on Suicide among Aboriginal People* (Hull, Québec: Canada Communication Group, 1995).
41 Jim Bell, "Anti-Suicide Campaign," *Nunatsiaq News* (February 23, 2001).
42 Bell, "Anti-Suicide Campaign."

V

LIFE IN TOWN:
THE CHANGING BALANCE
OF POWER

Before, men had more control over the boys and women had more control over the girls. Right now, they can work together to support their children. The woman's voice is heard as much as the man's voice.

—Geetee

Photo 10.1 Girls dancing in caribou skins, Iqualuit.

10

Contemporary Roles:
The Female Advantage

We're no longer married to hunters, most of us, but we're still following the pattern of our grandmothers who went before us to prepare us for the future, for making decisions. They have always passed that on. It's not written...it's not a law...it's just here.

—Geetee

Visiting

Photo 10.2 Rosie and Pauloosie Veevee scraping and cleaning a seal.

Many townspeople recognize us as we walk around, greeting us with smiles and hellos. We are making new contacts and checking on old friends. We drop in at the home of Rosie and Pauloosie Veevee, who helped us so much during earlier visits. They remember us immediately, and seem pleased to receive a copy of *Keepers of the Culture*, which includes a chapter on Inuit women of Pangnirtung.[1] Naiomi, who was just a young teen when we visited them the first time, is now a 20-year-old mother of two babies; she lives in her own house. Her older brother, William, still lives at home. Rosie hugs us, and then gestures to a picture of us that stands on the living room bookcase; it sits next to one of Jean Briggs, author of *Never in Anger*, who also had stayed with the Veevees. This older couple lived the more traditional life out on the land; after resettlement Pauloosie worked as a wage earner, driving a hamlet water truck, and Rosie worked as a homemaker. Now, Rosie works in the day care center and Pauloosie does commercial fishing. They recently adopted in a boy of six, and gather their children and grandchildren around them as they enter their later years.

We leave the warmth of this home and go to the other side of town where Peeona Shukulaq, who served as our interpreter on another visit, lives with her common-law husband, Jolly Atagoyuk: "We've lived together for thirteen years," he says proudly. We bring Peeona a copy of *Keepers* and a T-shirt. Seeing her name in the acknowledgments thrills Peeona. Jolly, an artist and printmaker, is more interested in the moon and sun designs on the front of the shirt. He studied woodcutting in Pangnirtung, then printmaking at Nunavut Arctic College. Jolly's art dominates the walls, interspersed with Peeona's crafts and hanging plants. Jolly's father is a CBC reporter, his brother an IBC reporter, and his mother a sewing teacher at the elementary school in Iqaluit.

Although someone turned the volume down as we entered, the television remains on day and night, as in so many other Inuit homes. But here, as though trying to mediate the effects of the color TV's endless round of American police stories, the parents tune the old black and white set to the Inuit Broadcasting Corporation station. The image of an Inuk man in a small rubber raft moves slowly across the screen. No one pays much attention to either set, though, for on the other side of the room is a third screen: a new Compaq computer from the Northern Store. "I'm still paying for it," Peeona laughs. The children gather around the computer monitor, taking turns at the joystick for a game whose name in English they do not understand. Nonetheless, the skills and excitement magnetize them. Even little Janis, 4, knows how to play this computer game.

This younger couple typifies some of the shifts in female and male roles in Inuit communities. He works at the Uqqurmiut Centre for Arts and Crafts; she works at the Northern Store. He has prepared a dinner of Arctic char baked with onions, salt, butter, and pepper. Although they have finished, he offers us some fish, tea, and bannock—a perfect Inuit meal. She offers her recipe for bannock. Their daughter, Nancy, 9, tries to teach us how to read Inuktitut syllabics. We suggest that Nancy would make a good teacher—she listens carefully to our questions and explains patiently. Peeona replies that Nancy does well in school.

We talk about how the roles of men and women have changed so much in the last few years, often toward blurring of roles or outright role reversal, with women taking on a larger share of providing for their families. Jolly says this is true for many of the young couples they know. He stresses the importance of keeping the old roles intact while branching into new ways of surviving. He is teaching his 7-year-old son, Joanasie, to hunt, as his father taught him at a tender age. He remembers shaking when his father gave him the rifle and told him to keep the crosshairs on the seal's head. At eight years old, Jolly got his first ring seal with the first shot. As if to underscore his point, Jolly takes us outside to pose for photographs, proudly but a bit self-consciously, with the harpoon his father gave him when he was only five.

Peeona says their lives seem very busy with both of them working, but she finds time to show Nancy how to make crafts out of quilted cotton, ribbon, and braid: "I watched Mom, and my daughter watches me. Occasionally, I will explain something. I taught myself how to crochet out of a book." Her handiwork adorns the sofa and chair backs. She also makes miniature "Pang hats," which we admire. The next day Peeona presents each of us with a tiny crocheted helmet with earflaps and pompoms.

In the kitchen, an automatic coffeepot and modern appliances stand next to an old tea kettle. A battery-powered ballerina doll sits in Janis' lap. In the dining area, Peeona's new sewing machine awaits her spare moments after work. Resettlement has meant a dramatic transition for this family.

ℭ

When the Inuit moved from a hunting economy based on sharing and cooperation into the settlements, the man's role was transformed. Inevitably, in a society marked by such uncommonly balanced gender roles, the woman's role changed as well. Not only resettlement but also the "destruction of our fur-based economy as a result of the anti-fur movement" forced changes in male and female roles, as Ambassador Simon pointed out in discussing the future of a comprehensive Arctic policy for Inuit:

In terms of family responsibilities, reference is gradually being made to "parental" functions where once they were viewed as purely "maternal." Both men and women are slowly beginning to acknowledge the need to share family tasks rather than emphasize separation of roles.... The additional income in some families earned by women working outside the home has helped families to meet harsh economic realities and improve the standard of living.[2]

After resettlement, the Inuit were no longer dependent on what a man could bring home from the hunt but on wage labour, store-bought food, and welfare. Because other ways emerged to meet the family's food needs, the man's role became circumscribed. He watched his well-worn role break down as he came to rely on twentieth century means of earning a livelihood. If he finds a job, it may be seasonal or temporary. An Inuk counselor puts the male dilemma in a nutshell: "Survival doesn't depend on brute strength anymore. The man has to depend on a woman to bring in the dough." Without cash, the contemporary male cannot hunt to supplement the family's food. Some men take construction or other seasonal jobs in order to bring cash into the household, but regular "9 to 5" jobs interfere with hunting.[3]

Many observers have noted that women seem to adjust more readily to the impacts of change and development. Bodenhorn, for example, theorizes that Inupiaq men "have had a harder time with the recent changes" because women have greater control over their own labour and therefore move more easily than men do into the wage-labour sphere.[4] As Reimer notes, "The female labour force participation rate in Pangnirtung has grown in direct proportion to the growth of the wage economy."[5] Males gain personal and community esteem from hunting, and females gain esteem from holding a wage-earning job. Often young Inuit women find decent jobs while their brothers drop out of school and seek satisfaction in occasional hunting. Now the roles in a wage employment, consumer economy are reversing.

Role Expansion and Role Reversal
"Goodness, we're very busy people"

For women and to some extent for men, role reversal actually involves an *expansion* of role repertoires and *role crossover* into activities formerly defined as the purview of the opposite sex. For example, many men continue to hunt on a part-time basis while adding the responsibilities of home and childcare: some men are "happy that their women have jobs and make money." Many women continue to sew and prepare traditional food while fishing, hunting with their mates, and holding down a full-time wage-earning job. The strengths engendered by generations out on the land surface in a different arena today. This story suggests the radical redefinitions of men's and women's work:

"THEY DO MANY, MANY THINGS"
My aunt hunts, she fishes, she traps in the winter to catch foxes—that's to help her husband have more money, so they can have more food, clothing, and

hunting equipment. She's not the only one. Many women try to help their husbands so they can live more comfortably. They do many, many things. They're involved. Some of them have jobs in the community, working for the government or the school. At the same time, they take care of their children.

When they have a spare moment they sew *kamiks* and seal skin boots or *amautiit*—they have so many things to do! They volunteer for community work or in the Anglican Church. They help women deliver babies. When people are sick, they stay with the sick person and cook for their families. That's what most of the women I know are doing right now.

My husband has a stronger role with the children than my brothers do with theirs. He is not interested in helping with dishes or around the house, but he helps me with the big tasks. Men and women have different jobs, though. Take hunting. Once the men bring the game home, it becomes the woman's responsibility. When we were first together, my husband caught an animal and brought it home. I just left it on the counter. He got quite upset with me and I didn't understand why: it was my responsibility, and I didn't understand that.

Alicee, in her 30s, works outside the home at a full-time job. In her absence, Alicee's husband does the cooking for the large noon meal. The same situation holds for Hannah. More and more men, they say, are taking over the traditional domestic role of women. Most like it, they believe, but sometimes the men grow tired of doing the cooking: "They say, 'I have to do this all the time, it's your turn.'" When their husbands are away hunting, modern Inuit women return to their traditional cooking duties. The interchangeability of male and female roles, reflected in so many facets of Inuit culture, means that a woman can do some of the things designated as a man's job. In turn, he can do some of the things traditionally considered a woman's responsibility.

According to Williamson, both persistence and adaptation characterize the Inuit woman's response to change.[6] Her role as homemaker has diminished less dramatically than has the man's role as hunter. We believe, first, that in spite of her growing presence as a worker in the public sphere, the woman's long-standing domestic role remains largely intact. This may help insulate her from the ravages of rapid social change. She still cooks, cleans, looks after the children, makes the clothes, and does the shopping. She still plays the principal role of domestic organizer, planner, processor of food and skins (when available), teacher of children, and helpmate. Second, in many cases, she brings her management skills, ingenuity, and persistence into the world of work beyond her front door. This duality—as exhausting as it often may be—probably serves as a buffer for women against the negative impacts of rapid social change and marginality discussed in Chapters 7 and 8.[7]

In a similar vein, Reimer concluded that "female consciousness...tied to the deep-rooted, age-old experience of women in giving and preserving life, nurturing and sustaining the family" characterized their contemporary role.[8] Female consciousness refers, specifically, to the fact that Inuit women are still "motivated by the rights and responsibilities" that *always* marked their role as females; this motivation provides a "recognizable continuity of the female role of keeper of the camp from past to present" in protecting the "social well-being of the contemporary 'camp' in which families now reside."[9] Reimer found that "Inuit women experience reciprocity among themselves and believe in their competence to preserve life. [They have a] sense of their collective right to supervise everyday life in the community, even if they have to confront authority to do so."[10] This expression of female consciousness depends on each woman's generation: those who grew up on the land versus the transitional generation versus those who were born and raised in the settlements have different ways of living the "Inuit way," but all express female consciousness that helps them cope with new lifestyles.

Role expansion means that women add new responsibilities to their traditional roles. As Dahl learned regarding Greenland Inuit, men continue to engage in whatever subsistence activities occur (hunting and fishing).[11] If men were to discontinue those activities in order to take a wage-earning job, women would find it difficult to take over the male's traditional subsistence activities. Therefore, it seems more logical for most couples that women should take the wage-earning positions and free the men to pursue subsistence activities whenever they can afford to do so. To the extent that her male partner no longer brings home skins, the woman's traditional role as processor is equally diminished but not necessarily eliminated, as other males in the community may hunt successfully and continue to share their bounty. Thus, the contemporary Inuit woman redefines her work to encompass two roles—the traditional (according to availability of skins and her own skills) and the contemporary (typically in wage-earning jobs). While the man finds his role as provider and hunter problematic within the settlement context, the woman holds on tightly to both roles. Because women hold the majority of wage-earning positions, a female often becomes the primary provider for the family's basic needs. For example, Dahl found in Saqqaq that women hold three out of four wage-earning jobs.[12] Exact figures are not available for Pangnirtung, but the pattern is similar.

Moving to the settlements resulted in erosion of male self-esteem and mounting rates of alcohol and drug abuse. As they left their dogs and equipment behind in the camps, many men lost the means to economic livelihood.[13] Fortunately for women, they were able to squeeze their sewing supplies, *ulus*, and other small tools into the crowded planes. Role complementarity and persistence keeps women at the center of settlement life, as she was the center of camp life, but at the same time, role reversal brings her more squarely into the public sphere than was true of earlier times. Brody explains the shift from the distinction between "the home and the hunt" toward a reduction of hunting and an expansion of home: "The charge of a permanent house and large numbers of children has consolidated the position of women; the shift to sporadic hunting and occasional wage-labour has undermined the position of most men."[14]

This means that now a man cannot depend on his partner to take the traditional female role: "He is apt to feel uneasy and suspicious...when drunk, may attack his wife with considerable ferocity." Some men find it difficult to see women fitting so readily into the employment picture and mourn the loss of their historical place as main provider. Wenzel found that even the most experienced harvesters find themselves unable to provide the spoils of hunting and fishing with the same regularity that they enjoyed before resettlement. This trend toward transposition of gender roles generates positive and negative consequences.

The Impacts of Role Reversal
"Things have changed over the years"

The reversal of roles frustrates many Inuit men. Because historically men were in the forefront, role reversal takes on added poignancy when the *only* work men can do is in the domestic sphere. Some men embrace the activities previously located solely in the woman's domain, but others feel somehow diminished by housekeeping, cooking, and childcare. Some wrestle internally with their resentment and become depressed or turn to alcohol. A few engage in verbal or physical abuse to regain some semblance of power in the couple relationship. Many Inuit tie the higher rates of substance abuse, depression, and violence among males directly to role reversal and male loss of the provider role. The Inuit paint this picture with broad strokes, but no one doubts that men feel more stress and pressure that can lead to an identity crisis: What am I going to do now, if I can't grow up to be a hunter? Jolly explains:

> There have been some changes for the men. They will still do the traditional things, but getting a job—that's where the crush comes. Right now, I am working. I'm earning some money to feed my kids. When it comes to hunting, I still feed my kids and my wife that way, too. If I get a broken button or something, I expect my wife to do it. For better shopping, I expect her to do that—I am a very bad shopper.
>
> When something needs fixing in the house, women ask the men to do it. It seems that the role of the men is to fix things...so they can say, "We can still look after things, overall." Things have changed over the years. Look at Margaret Thatcher. Not too many years ago, we never see a female world leader. I ask, "How could a woman do this?" Things are changing!

A man in his 30's believes that role reversal may hurt the self-esteem of Inuit men whose wives support the family: "Maybe he feels that he's not a whole man because he's not able to provide for them." He adds that when the woman is working and her husband is not, some people may think, "This is not part of our culture. The man should be looking after the families, not the woman. Her job is to look after the children and to help them grow." A clerk, 45, underscores the importance of the mother role in Inuit families: "If the mother is not looking after the children well, the kids have a different attitude about life. Even though it's also important for women to have a job, in our culture it's really different."

When Margaret Brooks Terry compared women who work for pay outside the home versus women who work only within the home, she found that women who worked outside the home had attitudes that are more "modern".[15] This appears to be true for the women of Pangnirtung, as well. Although there are "some very progressive families in this town" and couples with a good education and jobs, women say that chauvinism abounds: "If they've got kids at home, men wouldn't baby-sit. They wouldn't change a diaper—that's women's work. Do the dishes? You have to be kidding! The woman cooks, does the dishes. He doesn't care if there are ten kids and one on the way. That's her job." This creates a tension for both men and women, as a teacher observes: "Women are supporting their husbands—and the men like it when we find good jobs—but they don't think child care is their job. The '90s man' will take care of the kids, though, if we explain how important it is to the family." This situation leaves Inuit women with a "double burden" experienced by many women worldwide.[16]

Women as Hunters
"I had my chance to shoot the polar bear and I got it!"

Perhaps the most symbolic shift in traditional gender roles is women's expansion into hunting. Hunting is an integral part of traveling around Cumberland Sound and Pangnirtung Fiord. When Inuit families take their boats out to visit an historical site, search for whales, or go camping, they inevitably have a rifle on the bow of the deck, ready for seal hunting. Significantly, females can use the rifles if they show an interest in it. For example, Alicee and Hannah discuss the most important events in their lives. Their comments reflect the two worlds they inhabit on a daily basis— traditional and modern—and how the role of a competent woman has brought them further into formerly male domains. Today, when Inuit families go out on the land, women and men both engage in hunting and fishing, says one woman.[17] Hannah claims that she enjoys going out seal hunting with her husband. She has learned how to use the rifle. For cleaning the seals, her husband made her an *ulu*, the woman's traditional curved blade knife, out of an old saw.

When asked, "What have been the happiest times of your life?" many women point to boating, going inland for caribou hunting, camping, and fishing. Although Leah and others admit that the bitter cold presents formidable challenges, the joy of being out on the land shines through in their stories. "At the outpost camps, the men catch the seals. The women dry the meat and clean the skins. Sometimes they go fishing with the men. In wintertime, only the ladies go fishing by themselves, but I haven't seen women going on a boat or hunting by themselves…only by skidoo."

"One caribou, one seal, and lots of fish" are Geela's hunting prizes. Lena has killed caribou and seal, but she has never been polar bear hunting: "I almost killed one but we weren't allowed. Last year when we were out caribou hunting, there was a polar bear. We didn't kill him…we just chased him." Rosie goes out hunting with her husband. She has felled caribou by herself. Her neighbor Meeka tells about fishing expeditions and her hunting prowess:

"I SHOT ONE!"

I've hunted for seal, caribou, and polar bear. We can't just go out and hunt for polar bear. We have to have a license from Fish and Wildlife. We draw names, because there are only so many polar bears we can catch in this community. They picked my name one time, and my husband's, too. We were lucky. We went out and I shot one! It was very cold that year. It was minus fifty degrees. I was more afraid of the cold than I was of the bears! We went about 100 miles away, southwest, across the Cumberland Sound. We had to look hard for the right area; we used binoculars. My husband spotted one and we went after it. It was sleeping by a big iceberg. When he stopped for a rest, I had my chance to shoot the polar bear and I got it! I sold it. I needed the money. We had to bring the meat back so we could give it to anyone who needed it. I am still proud of myself. Out of five of us in the group, only my husband and another guy didn't get one. I haven't hunted for wolf. We hunt for the fur and the meat for our own use whenever we have a chance. We can't use the meat from the Bay. It's too expensive. I can buy some, but not for the whole year. It's cheaper to hunt.

Not all the younger women feel as attracted to hunting, although they love being out on the land. Reepa explains: "I'm going out on the land tonight. I always go out on the land. My Mom and Dad taught me to be out there, and I love it. I can't bring myself to shoot an animal, though." Reepa fishes a little but not in the traditional way. She learned how to scrape a seal and cooks country food at home. Jeannie describes herself as "a hunter who loves hunting." She goes out whenever she can with her father or brother. She has "caught ring seals, harp seals, and the ones that are bigger than the harp seals. Not walrus. Caribou. I went polar bear hunting, but I wasn't lucky." Meeka does not like to go seal hunting but she likes to hunt for caribou: "Hunting seal, you have to wait for a long time. In the wintertime, I don't like that." Meeka's young neighbor, Rosemary, goes hunting with her family and enjoys every minute of it. She enjoys watching the caribou run in herds: "When they stand still, they always look at you." She dislikes seeing the animals killed but tolerates it because she likes "Inuit food." Rosemary has been whale hunting and joined in a polar bear hunting party; she was not fortunate enough to see a bear: "I hope I'll see one alive—so far I have only seen photographs and videos."

Males in the family support a girl's involvement in hunting from a very early age. For example, Ann's 1-year-old daughter was visiting her grandfather out on the land when her older brother brought a small bird so she could kill her first animal: "Everyone was very proud that this little bird was her first kill." The toddler had gained some identity as a hunter, as a person who has taken the spirit of an animal. Similar rituals exist when a boy kills his first seal or caribou.

Jonah and his wife are in their 30s. Like other couples their age, they enjoy "doing things together, especially hunting and fishing." His father took Jonah out in the old days, but he would not take his wife "because she's the woman." Jonah observed that pattern when he was growing up but prefers a different lifestyle: "I take the whole family." Jooeelee captures the emotional as well as the practical side of hunting in reminiscing about times he hunted with his father: "I don't have a favorite memory but every time we go, there's pride and openness and enjoyment. The weather is not always pleasant, but it's a release." They store the beloved Arctic char, seal, and caribou in the community's free deep freeze "so we can use it as we want."

Photo 10.3 Scraping a seal skin with the woman's ulu (knife).

Notes

1 Our fieldwork resulted in an earlier description of traditional Inuit life and roles: Janet Mancini Billson, "Daughters of Sedna," in *Keepers of the Culture: The Power of Tradition in Women's Lives* (Lexington Books, 1995/Ottawa: Penumbra Press, 1999/Rowman & Littlefield, 2006).

2 Ambassador Mary May Simon, *Inuit: One Future—One Arctic* (Peterborough, ONT: The Cider Press, 1996), p. 41.

3 See George W. Wenzel's discussion of the mixed wage-earning and hunting Inuit economy in *Subsistence, Cash and the Mixed Economy: Adaptation among Baffin Inuit,* Unpublished Report SC 257400 (Iqaluit, NWT: Department of Economic Development and Tourism, Government of the Northwest Territories, 1985).

4 In addition, the Inupiaq have defined knowledge and skills as gender neutral. Therefore, women with knowledge and skills are not necessarily excluded from public sphere (political and economic) leadership positions. Bodenhorn, "'I Am Not a Great Hunter, My Wife Is,'" p. 67.

5 Reimer, "Female Consciousness," p. 89. This finding was also recorded by Robert G. Mayes, *The Creation of a Dependent People: The Inuit of Cumberland Sound, NWT* (PhD Thesis, Department of Geography, McGill University, Montréal, 1978).

6 Robert G. Williamson, "Value and Functional Change and Persistence in Female Role: Inuit Women in Modern Arctic Society," *Sixth Inuit Studies Conference, Copenhagen October 17-20, 1988: Abstracts* (Copenhagen: Institute of Eskimology, University of Copenhagen, 1988).

7 For a discussion of the insulating function of women's dual role, see Billson, "Standing Tradition on Its Head."

8 Reimer, "Female Consciousness," p. 78.

9 Reimer, "Female Consciousness," p. 77.

10 Reimer, "Female Consciousness," p. 79.

11 Dahl, *Saqqaq*, p. 186.

12 Dahl, *Saqqaq*.

13 Montcombroux portrayed the economic functions of the sled dog for Inuit well being in *The Canadian Inuit Dog*.

14 Brody, *The People's Land*, p. 196.

15 Personal communication. Brooks Terry based her definition of "modern attitudes" in Alex Inkeles' work on Overall Modernity versus Individual Modernity.

16 Janet Mancini Billson, "Double Burdens, Double Roles: Jamaican Women in Toronto" (paper presented at the Annual Meeting of the Western Social Sciences Association, Portland, OR, April 1990).

17 Mary Crnkovich, "Women of the Kitaq," pp. 35-36 in Crnkovich, ed., *Gossip*. Angela Bernal conducted the interview and Kyra Mancini transcribed it for *Gossip*; the authors are grateful for editor Crnkovich's permission to use this interview.

11

Contemporary Power:
A Reversal of Position

We've heard many times that in the past the woman was the slave of the man. The man was the boss, but women always have their own power.

—Iola

In the Wilderness¹

Photo 11.1 Pangnirtung Pass in the summer, with Base Camp Overlord on the far shore.

We decide to hike into Auyuittuq National Park, just twenty miles north of Pangnirtung. We cover ten miles a day for four days in total, undeveloped, uninhabited wilderness. Everything we need for survival is on our backs in thirty-five–pound packs. Inuit wardens hike the pass, covering an astonishing twenty miles a day along the treacherous Weasel River Valley, keeping an eye on the 380 or so hikers who attempt the park each summer. Every eight miles a tiny hut awaits the weary hiker—not to sleep in (except in dire emergency) but to record names, weather conditions, and wildlife sightings in the log book.

The river snakes through the Arctic desert, embraced by craggy mountains on either side that thrust sparkling white glacial tongues into the valley. We camp near huge rocks to break the wind that seems an almost constant companion. It is August and the temperature hovers around forty degrees while an unbearable heat wave flattens southern Canada and the northeastern United States. The sun shines all but two or three hours a day. One night at Windy Lake our tent is the only one left standing. Kyra and a few other campers huddle in the safety hut while the wind grabs and twists our small dome tent in a thousand directions.

Morning comes and we begin the long trek back to base camp Overlord, where we will sleep overnight prior to being picked up by an Inuk outfitter. The journey proves to be a near disaster. The last two sunny days have begun to melt the glaciers. What had been a half dozen minor streams to ford on our way out have now multiplied to forty or fifty major streams, each fed by a wide mother stream that cuts down the mountainside into the Weasel River. We must ford the streams, taking our boots off and putting them back on after each crossing so that our sneakers, not our boots, get soaked. We pick our way gingerly through rocks and sand and gravel and more rocks, slipping and leaping, trying to stay dry enough to survive. Suddenly, it hits all of us that we could die here, now, in this unforgivingly harsh and isolated landscape whose beauty lets you forget how delicate the balance is between humans and nature. Suddenly, I realize what the Inuit women and men were talking about when they insisted that each one's role is crucial to survival.

We plod on and on, hours past our expected arrival time at the base camp, which is nothing more than a collection of three tents, a campfire, and a small warden's cabin. Norm is imagining the pebbles to be rubies and emeralds and sapphires. We no longer speak. I am using two walking sticks, mine and Kyra's. I am past exhaustion. Miraculously, two figures emerge from the gloom to greet us. These other hikers, who have watched through binoculars how our pace has dangerously slowed, carry our packs across the last, painful mile to Overlord, where other hikers sit around a campfire sharing stories of their journeys. The soup they have saved for us seems more like filet mignon.

At 11 o'clock, fourteen hours after we started walking, we climb into our sleeping bags. I keep my sweater and jogging suit on because I can't seem to warm up. Within two hours, having defeated the reflective nature of the sleeping bag's inner lining, I wake up shaking violently. My head feels like ice; my legs are numb. I slip in and out of sleep for a few minutes, each time dreaming of the Inuit families who froze to death in Farley Mowat's novel, *People of the Deer*. I must call for help or die, but, as in a bad dream, my voice will not work. At last, in an effort that feels like heaving a giant rock from my chest, I call Norm's name. Another hiker wakes up and shouts, "She has hypothermia!"

Suddenly, I am under the stars with Kyra and Norm on either side me, stumbling around the dimly-lit tundra. It is too late. My speech is slurred. My legs are like jelly. I cannot think. Some instinct takes over and I blurt out, "Take me to the warden's cabin." They drag me a few yards up the slope and pound on the door. It is after 1 o'clock in the morning, but the two Inuit wardens are playing cards. They take one look at my white face and swing into action. They sit me on the edge of a bed, throw an old Army blanket over me like a tent, place warm plastic gel packs under my arms and on my stomach, and draw the camp stove near. After a few minutes, they make me sip hot Tang. Slowly, color starts to come back into my face, so they let me go to sleep in their bed. One turns to Norm and asks, "You her man?" He nods. The wardens order him to get into bed next to me and motion Kyra to lie on my other side. This is the best antidote to hypothermia: the warmth of other humans. The wardens play cards all night, waking me every hour to count to ten and say my name.

The next day I am medivacked back to Pangnirtung, where a van waits at the harbor to take me to the Nurse's Station. My vital signs are fine, but I suffer from chest pains for several days. The wardens say I was lucky to have made it through the night without a heart attack. I say I am lucky that they know the arts of survival.

∞

Traditionally, a woman had substantial control over her house and her children, and people understood the importance of her role. As we have seen, a man was powerful because of his strength and fine hunting. A woman grew accustomed to running things by herself when her husband left for extended trips, but the male claimed the title of major provider and boss. Power in intimate relationships followed the complementarity and mutual respect involved in traditional roles. Although women agree that in their mother's and grandmother's generation men had more say because of their knowledge, men and women were equal in some elusive way. Now, though, women think that females often have *more* say. The picture is a complicated one.

Many Inuit men feel threatened by their loss of status and identity, and by women's elevated place. In the camps, from the male point of view, men and women had equal power, and if either partner was "superior," it was the man. In the settlements, women have tended to learn English more readily, to complete available schooling more frequently, and to hold onto a steady, wage-paying job more easily than men do. For many couples, this means that the woman is bringing home cash (over which she feels she should have some control). The man has to depend on her success—the woman no longer depends entirely on her male partner for sustenance and security.

Balancing Act
"Nobody should be more powerful"

Contemporary Inuit women find themselves trapped between old expectations of ultimate male supremacy and new pressures toward equality that stem from role reversal and the creeping influence of the mainstream women's movement. Ironically, as much as Inuit women agree that preserving or reinventing traditional culture must become a high priority for community survival, they realize that the old ways accord women respect but sometimes less power than men have. The tug of war between past and present creates a formidable challenge for women and men alike.

Analysis of contemporary gender relations must proceed with caution, because the attitudes of Inuit and other aboriginal women have been touched not only by traditional values and practices but also by the dialogue between Native and mainstream culture, between North and South, and between feminists and those who treasure independence but do not define themselves as feminists. For example, Inuit women observe that essential equality between men and women derives from fundamental aboriginal rights and traditions, not just from a legal document such as the Canadian constitution.[2] Like many other Native women in North America, they find mainstream feminist notions, such as the inevitably and universality of male subordination of women, irrelevant and lacking explanatory power for gender relations in their culture. Inuit women have not applied feminist strategies to gain influence in Canada, in Nunavut, or even locally. Rather than aligning themselves with the feminist movement and the network of southern Canadian women's organizations, they have tended to distance themselves in order to focus on ethnic solidarity. As with other Native people, it is more important to establish themselves fully as Inuit in the Canadian family, rather than as women. This has changed somewhat with the establishment and influence of Pauktuutit. Yet, when the International Women's March came to Iqaluit in July 2000, only twenty Inuit women attended the gathering, even though its purpose was to help diminish poverty and violence against women—two causes with which Inuit women can sympathize.[3]

It is important to stress the differences in how Inuit and many other aboriginal women define power and equality. Rather than equalist visions in which males and females achieve sameness, some Native women think more in terms of a communitarian ideal in which women played and continue to play a central if not dominant role. Osennontion, a Mohawk woman, explains that when feminists speak of equality, they mean "sameness" but that aboriginal women do not want to be "the same as a man" or treated the same as a man: "Aboriginal women are *different*...I certainly do not want to be a "man"!⁴ Similarly, Turpel-Lafond, a Cree woman, insisted that equality is not the central organizing political principle in Native communities. In fact, people might construe equality as a selfish, individualist notion that would alienate members of the community from each other:

> We are committed to what would be termed a "communitarian" notion of responsibilities to our peoples, as learned through traditional teachings and our life experiences. I do not see this communitarian notion as translating into equality as it is conventionally understood.... Presuming equality is the prime feminist objective, why would First Nations women want to be like [white women]? Women are at the centre. We are the keepers of the culture, the educators, the ones who must instruct the children to respect the Earth, and the ones who ensure that our leaders are remembering and "walking" with their responsibilities demonstrably in mind.⁵

To the extent that some Inuit men oppress women, Turpel-Lafond and others stress that Native men are not fully to blame for embracing the attractions of "learned patriarchy." Finally, Inuit and other Native women may see equality more in terms of achieving equal legitimacy with mainstream society—as a cultural and political system—rather than between women and men:

> Gender as an isolated category is useful, primarily, to women who do not encounter racial, cultural, or class-based discrimination when they participate in Canadian society. Moreover, to look only to an objective of equality with men is clearly insufficient for First Nations women's struggles and continued identities because it cannot encompass our aspirations to continue as distinct, albeit dynamic, cultures. I cannot separate my gender from my culture.⁶

With these perspectives in mind, our interviews showed that some Inuit women in their 40s and 50s—women of the transitional period—still tend to accept ultimate male authority. Younger women, who grew up in the settlement, crave equality. They resist defining the man as boss, partly because so many men have lost their economic role while women have an increasingly strong role to play. Especially for the women of Pangnirtung, the early presence of a hospital exposed them to the "no-nonsense British midwife types" who offered a positive model of strong, respected women working outside the home for pay.

They want and fight for respect, position, and recognition as central players in community life. Winning that fight is not always easy, however.

The old power differential becomes apparent in self-perception. Because women of old had to flow with the male-driven tide of daily affairs in order to survive, in some ways Inuit women see themselves as less powerful than men. Younger girls are becoming more modernized, but older women whose husbands still hunt feel that men remain boss of the household. The wife is powerful; she is simply lower on the list.[7] Women who were born and raised on the land told Gwen Reimer that they "felt more productive and useful when they still lived in the camps...these older women tend to view themselves as more subordinate to men now than they were in the past."[8] In many Inuit families, women say that children may come before the wife. Women agree that even today a husband might make the decision about adopting a child in or out of the family, as was common historically. Even if his wife disagrees, he would expect her to give up a newborn baby to equalize the sex ratio in the family of a close friend or relative. A woman might protest more today, but the practice is still common, according to our consultants.

Victor, 29, believes that the man is the boss "everywhere in the world," except in the home, again underscoring the crucial respect for differing roles: "About the woman's work, I cannot be boss. I can't really argue with my wife when she's making *kamiks*. I have to agree with what she has to say because she knows. She has to agree with what I have done for house building. I think it's equal; it's always like that."

The servant image of women is diminishing. In the old days, argues a seamstress in her 40s, things were different: "Men controlled almost everything. It's the other way around now. Women have more control over things." Out on the land, the woman cooked, but now "even a man" can cook for the family. This is a better situation, she adds, although sometimes it is tempting to romanticize the old ways. For the new generation, "everything seems to be going pretty well. At that time, parents used to struggle to keep their families alive."

Now couples in their 30s and 40s agree on joint control over money before marriage: "My wife and I have one account. We are equal in that respect." They both can write checks and they would discuss any major purchase. Meeka agrees that men and women in their 50s are more likely to share power as a couple. If they have good personalities, communicate well, look after their family, and are trustworthy, they should be able to construct a relationship of equality. Most women of her generation do not accept male domination: "They have to communicate and look after the family well. I don't believe that just one side of the couple should be the boss for the whole family." Though their mothers may have accepted a slightly subordinate role, younger Inuit women assert their right to share power. Quppa, a woman in her late 50s who grew up on the land, relates: "When I was growing up, I didn't always agree with my father's side. He sent me here when I didn't want to leave my parents. I felt hurt. I never forgot. I don't want to control my family just from one side. I like to control my family from both sides, to talk about it and deal with it. My husband likes that."

Power Differentials
"I expect my wife to be the boss"

Since Inuit women are reliable, dependable, and persistent workers, they typically hold a job longer than men do, build enough seniority to enhance security, and may earn higher wages.[9] This pattern undergirds a shift in power between males and females. Lucas, in his 20s, states that it is acceptable "for a younger man to share power equally with his wife." A man in his 40s agrees that now things are reversing—but not always happily. He was only 17 when he married a woman who was older and "already powerful." She stayed that way as he grew into maturity and they had some problems, but eventually they "worked it out." He suggests that insecure men use spousal assault as way of rebalancing power.

An Inuk woman who works in a social service agency adds that now women who support their families also define themselves as "head of the family." If they have a problem with their husband, they go to the social worker or bring charges against him with the RCMP: "The women seem to go too fast, they reverse it" (the traditional power relationship). Wenzel claims that in Clyde River, an Inuit community about half the size of Pangnirtung, Inuit "no longer share secure access to money...which has now become as critical a resource to modern subsistence as time and energy...[therefore] production is increasingly becoming the province of those men who can successfully participate in the wage economy.[9] The shift in roles creates complexities. In fact, some men have money to hunt *because* their female partners successfully participate in wage labour, which gives women ready access to cash and irrevocably changes the power balance between the sexes, as Reimer also found:

> Settlement life has turned gender roles upside down...women seem to be taking a "superior' position over men in terms of wage employment... Many Pangnirtung women who hold full-time wage employment provide the cash resources necessary to allow [men] to provide country food resources.[10]

Wenzel calculated that less than 10 percent of the population working full-time supplies at least 60 percent of the cash in circulation among Inuit residents.[11] Income gives the Inuk woman more power and authority, or so she believes. Yet, because traditionally the people shared whatever resources fell to bands or families, the ethos works against unequal power based on mere earnings: "Before, if one man in the camp brought many seals, the whole camp shared it. If a woman brings the money, it still belongs to the whole house." Pressure can be extremely high on the minority who work full-time for wages to provide funding to family members for various purposes. As Wenzel discovered with the Clyde Inuit, *ningiqtuq* (sharing) is a well-organized system of resource distribution that often involves non-monetary items such as food. Sharing is based on a norm of reciprocity that is tied to kinship, residence in the same village, and values surrounding cultural solidarity.[12] This communal relationship to wages is harder to establish than it was to food, though: People say they feel less inclined to share something that money can buy, which tends, ironically, to soften the power that women might have derived from role reversal. It also risks alienating family members and ultimately frays the community fabric of interdependence.

Even though many women bring in the money every month, many men still view women as slightly lower in status than men. This attitude, which hearkens back to an older set of assumptions about male-female power, causes friction. Men feel frustrated, says 36-year-old Pauta, who has been hoping for a job with the local government: "We grew up seeing our mothers being treated like servants by our fathers." In "the time before," the woman was there to nurture; now she secures a paycheck while he nurtures home and children.

Role reversal leads to subtle "bargains" in balancing power between the sexes, as a hamlet employee relates: "I expect my wife to be the boss in the house. There's nothing wrong with that, but I don't expect her to be the boss when I'm out on the land. We understand each other and it works." Indeed, while some express concern that a woman who earns money may act as though she is now head of the family, many women speak of the deep respect they accord men when they are out on the land. This young woman's story highlights the high degree of flexibility in role and authority for both women and men:

"HIS WIFE IS HIS SERVANT"

The male role depends on the kind of man you married. For example, my stepfather is a very traditional Inuk. We were camping one week without the children. He doesn't speak any English. He's a very strong person who comes from a very strong family with many leaders. When we returned, my husband said, "What a difference! In town, your stepfather is very soft. He'll do anything for his wife around the house. He'll do the dishes, he'll clean, he'll do the washing—he's always doing whatever his wife wants him to do. Out on the land, though, he's the boss, and his wife will say, "Yes, sir!" He knows what he's doing, so his wife is his servant. I had never noticed that before until my husband pointed it out to me. I said, "You're right, they are like that." I have observed that it's true, because the men know the weather, the tides, all the islands, and the water. In town, though, sometimes he's like your servant. If he's a very good person, he'll help you with the children. Sometimes you marry a real s.o.b. who will not pay attention to you. I would *rather* have a man who knows what he's doing on the land, because I wouldn't know how to survive. Out of respect for the man, even those who know how to survive out there will do what he wants them to do.

Although they share in money management, Jessie's husband would make the decision to move to another community if he found a better job. Eeva, 33, who worked in Iqaluit as a correctional officer, had to resign when her husband accepted a position in Pangnirtung. He would like her to find another job, but his work came first. Sheila, 19, believes that people view the man as boss now, particularly when it comes to handling money and the house: "Maybe they would agree on some things but, from my point of view, some men are very strict. They might say, 'We're moving to this house,' but some would talk about it first." Sheila believes that she and her boyfriend would easily agree on things.

Eeva's brother, who is 39, says he tries to accept female equality. As he talks about his very bright and articulate teenage daughter, he expresses ambivalence about how she will "make out" in life: "She's different from my other daughter. She talks back. She never settles just to say yes. She always has something to say." Her style stands in contrast to the traditional Inuk woman, who would comply with her husband's wishes even if she disagreed with him. Since "parents educate the guys like that, they expect the woman to conform," he remarks: "My father was the boss. We didn't argue about it. We respected him more than anyone when it came to running the family. It's not like that now."

The Generational Lag
"There are many things that women know"

Some middle-generation women believe that men still assume the right to be head of household but will discuss an issue and compromise before they make a big decision. Others want consultative dialoguing but insist that it does not occur often. Most Inuit women believe that men are stronger, more powerful, and more likely to run their community than are women. Briggs found that Inuit women she lived with exhibited passivity "beyond belief": "Utku women, as far as I could tell, did not feel beleaguered by the demands of their men. A woman did not resent it when her husband took the best of the lighting and cooking equipment with him on his trips...leaving her to suffer from the cold."[13] When confronted with the question of *why* women accepted men bossing them around, one woman replied: "It's just because the Bible says women should obey men; that's the only reason."[14] This response demonstrates the powerful influence of the missionaries but may also reflect a more traditional deference based on women's belief that it does not hurt women to go along with the men because the men "have the hardest work to do." In fact, what appears on the surface as passivity or deference may be a deeper understanding that men would need better equipment out on the land than women would need in the camp (or in town). Many apparent inconsistencies may boil down to generational differences.

Eena and her mother illustrate the generational change in attitudes toward male domination. Eena's mother, in her 50s, says that for older women the "men are a little higher." She is not sure why it worked out that way. For their daughters, though, equality is the byword, Eena insists: "If it weren't equal for me, I don't know if I would still be with my man now. I believe that men and women must have equal rights." Her mother defines women's power as "not having to agree." That is difficult for women because "men have always been higher, but there are many things that women know, too." For example, sometimes women seem more intelligent than men do. Eena argues that men do not have to be more powerful but try to be. She has no idea what engendered the difference between her mother's generation and her own. At school, the boys see girls as "more or less" their equals, except when it comes to sports: "Automatically the boys take over and the girls are left to last." This dominant mode is most obvious as adolescence progresses. Boys and girls are equal in the junior classes "until the boys grow big and strong and tough and rough."

Adolescent girls prefer equal power in their relationships, although they admit that boys their age still want to be the boss. How could they negotiate this discrepancy? Rosemary suggests talking it out: "If we had kids, the father would want to be the boss, but making it equal would be better for the children. They wouldn't have to figure out which parent is making the right decision."

The gap is closing a little in the community's political life as well: "Some have ladies on their committees. It's getting closer together." What propels this general shift in male-female power? A teacher's aide reflects on the traditional ways: "Maybe the previous role that the man played is breaking down. Remember, out there at the camp the man calls the tune...what time you get up, when you go hunting, who brings the food. Now, women want *their* say."

Whatever its source, the power differential emerges early. According to a white teacher, Inuit high school children listen more readily to a male authority figure: "You're listened to...you're heard...you're given attention. Even if you're a principal and you're a woman, the boys just ignore you. No response! The boys will do something when you tell them to, but it's because *they* want to, not because of your authority. If they come to a male teacher for help and you walk in, the atmosphere changes." Of course, generational differences in perceptions of power become more obvious among younger families in which the woman works outside the home.

Communication and Emotions
"That feeling comes out"

Throughout Nunavut, as we have seen, males more than females tend to commit suicide, succumb to drug and alcohol abuse, die in car accidents, and engage in law-breaking behaviour. Furthermore, "the majority of violence in the Baffin Region [is]...by Inuit men against Inuit women."[15] Men batter women at alarming rates that neither men nor women condone. Communication between males and females can make for either rough sailing or smooth seas.[16]

For older couples, having clearly defined gender roles means that they need to engage less in the small talk that comes with negotiating and redefining tasks. Leah admits to having serious disagreements with her husband, "but we say it out loud...we don't get into a fight." Others echo the complaint of millions of North American women that the men in their lives do not communicate openly: "Couples don't even talk to each other or say what they want to say. Even if they talk privately, men have so many secrets."

Gender differences characterize the ability to communicate. Failure to communicate leads to the explosive or inappropriate release of pent-up feelings when the pressure builds too high. As Mary indicates: "Couples don't say what a woman and husband should say to each other. They're not open. Then, when they're really up to here, they burn themselves out and say it. People are...keeping so many things to themselves. They could have said it in the first place. Sometimes they will talk in bed...maybe it's better!" This syndrome exists occasionally between parents and children as well: "They just build it up, then when the kid does something wrong, they finally say it and it's too late."

Inuit women say they can see that from a very early age their sons communicate less than their daughters do. Lena says her 12-year-old son "seems not interested at this time to talk about life." The women agree that perhaps they are closer to their daughters when they are young, a difference that may result in a communication gap for the males as they mature. Another woman says that she spent more time with her son when he was young, because her daughter liked to visit her grandmother. Her son "maybe will grow up to be one of those men who talks, because I can easily talk with him." However, she is closer to all of her children, regardless of gender, than is her husband. She guesses that males learned to be this way long ago. Traditionally, when a son spent countless hours learning about being a man from his father and grandfather—who did not talk very openly about personal or emotional matters—he also learned to be less forthcoming: "A man doesn't communicate with his son as a woman communicates with a daughter. My husband doesn't communicate with our kids as much as I do. I've tried to talk to him about it, but he says that's how he was raised."

Lena, a social work aide, believes that such patterns link directly to men's reluctance to discuss things: "When men have problems or are going through stress, they don't talk to a person the way we women do. They don't solve their problem. When they get really mad, that feeling comes out of hiding."

As is true in Canadian and American societies generally, when Inuit women face a problem, they seek professional help more often than men do and they talk to each other about their feelings. Many more women than men approach social service agencies in Pangnirtung. Their male partners hold their emotions and guilt inside. Not surprisingly, most of the people who come to the Mental Health Committee for counseling are women. Perhaps more women than men have emotional problems and therefore seek help more often, but all accounts from both sexes point to the opposite direction. They say that men have more emotional, life style, or addictive problems, yet solicit help far less often: "When Inuit men have a problem, they don't admit it." Many studies of males in different cultures have found the same pattern: Male gender role expectations suggest that they should strive for power and control, while counseling may feel like the opposite: "Stereotypical masculine beliefs negatively relate to willingness to seek [counseling] help."[17]

The ability to express feelings openly works to the advantage of women and the disadvantage of men when it comes to spousal assault. Women feel freer to share their experiences with other women, "Just to let them know that they're not the only ones." Says a social service aide, Reepa, women are more open about their problems: "It's what I went through and have heard so many times. The boyfriend or the husband doesn't want to say anything to anyone. When she can't take it anymore, she opens up to someone against his wishes. We're caught much of the time." A male social service worker suggests that perhaps women simply like to talk more than men do, and that perhaps men need an association, which women already have.

The Inuit assume that younger couples can seek their parents' advice for sorting out their conflicts. Women have an edge based on their more open communication style. Peah explains about her mother-in-law: "If her son and I are having problems and we go to them for help, she'll be the only one who is advising us or talking, even though her husband seems to have more power. Where does the husband's power go when it is really needed? He seems to listen and observe more." Mothers try to help the couple communicate and say something to keep the couple together, "Life can get better. Men—they're men. They don't say anything. Are white husbands like that, too?"

Intimacy, Affection, and Sexuality
"Now it's different"

As with open communication, free expression of affection and concern for a woman's sexuality might lead to firmer commitments. There is little open display of affection in this culture between couples, especially in comparison to the warmth expressed toward children through kissing, hugging, holding, and playing. A white woman describes what she has noticed over the years: "Inuit people just love kids. It's kind of depressing when you see a 15- or 16-year-old with a baby, but everybody loves them. A kid will be playing in the street and an adult will give him a kiss and a hug, and then keep on walking."

Some women observe more expressiveness between younger couples than exists for the older generation. Couples show affection as they get to know each other better, "then a year later they know each other too well, and they might not want to do that in front of other people." As in most cultures, the man's pleasure historically defined the nature of sex. That is changing for Inuit couples in their 20s and 30s. Geela says she heard that, in earlier times, men "would have sex with a girl even if she didn't want to. Now it's different because usually they would agree before—if you don't want to do it, they won't."

Naturally, reluctance or inability to express emotions creates a barrier in the intimacy men and women can establish with each other. As Arlie Russell Hochschild explained in her sociology of emotions theory, refusing to communicate can also serve to perpetuate male power and control by forcing women to do more "emotional labour" in relationships, families, organizations, the workplace, and the community. This places another burden on women, makes them anxious, and leaves them in doubt about male intentions or feelings.[18] It also contributes to generally higher rates of depression among women and to the fact that, compared to its impact on men, marriage is detrimental to women's emotional and mental health.[19] (We could not document the second part of that finding in Pangnirtung.) Perhaps most critically, when men hold their true feelings inside, or cannot uncover them, chances are much greater that they will lash out at women and children when angry or frustrated.[20]

Inuit women's greater openness generates strength, not weakness. In very practical ways, that openness contributes to solidarity among women. A woman in her late 30s, who established a support group for assault victims, believes that women dominate emotionally: "I talk to many, many women my age, and we are very strong. If we go through something really bad, we'll talk to somebody. Men just keep it to themselves." The few token men on the Mental Health Committee, she adds, "don't usually have a lot to offer, although they are more likely to go to the larger communities for regional board meetings."

That women seem to adapt to settlement life more readily than men do complicates the balance of power. Beyond the power emanating from wage production and emotional strength, in many Inuit communities some women gain power as they take on major political responsibilities. Now, Inuit women attend meetings of the National Council of Women or the Inuit Council, or become involved in hamlet administration. Women hold many "high places" in both local and territorial governments (see chapters 18 and 19). With the advent of Nunavut in 1999, opportunities abound for women to broaden the scope of their powers and for men to help balance power equitably.

Notes

1 An earlier version of this story appears in Billson, *Keepers of the Culture*, pp. 134-136.

2 Krosenbrink-Gelissen, *Sexual Equality as an Aboriginal Right*.

3 Valerie G. Connell, "Women's March Organizer Takes Message to Nunavut," *Nunatsiaq News* (July 28, 2000).

4 Cited in Mary Ellen Turpel-Lafond, "Patriarchy and Paternalism: The Legacy of the Canadian State for First Nations Women," in Caroline Andrew and Sandra Rodgers, eds.,

Women and the Canadian State (Montréal: McGill-Queen's University Press, 1997), p. 68.

5 Turpel-Lafond, "Patriarchy and Paternalism," pp. 68-69. Billson documents the role of women as "keepers of the culture" for Mohawk, Blood, Inuit, Jamaican, Mennonite, Chinese, and Ukrainian women in *Keepers of the Culture.*

6 Turpel-Lafond, "Patriarchy and Paternalism," p. 72.

7 The power balance between Mennonite men and women parallels this pattern: the wife is revered and respected for the value of her contributions, but the husband has ultimate authority in the home. See Janet Mancini Billson, "Keepers of the Culture: Attitudes toward Women's Liberation and the Women's Movement in Canada," *Women and Politics* 14, 1 (1994): 1-34.

8 Reimer, "Female Consciousness," p. 83.

9 Wenzel, *Animal Rights, Human Rights Ecology, Economy and Ideology in the Canadian Arctic*, p. 176.

10 Reimer, "Female Consciousness," p. 83.

11 Wenzel, *Animal Rights, Human Rights Ecology, Economy and Ideology in the Canadian Arctic*, p. 177.

12 Wenzel, *Animal Rights, Human Rights Ecology, Economy and Ideology in the Canadian Arctic*, p. 99. Franz Boas was somewhat skeptical about sharing as a universal imperative among Baffin Inuit. He observed hunters sharing their catch, but also pointed out that some received more than others: "Beyond the hunting partnerships, meat and blubber were shared within extended family groups, but only when food was scarce," according to Fossett. However, the extended families were broadly defined (especially because of customary adoption practices) and scarcity occurred on a regular basis. Fossett, *In Order to Live Untroubled*, p. 205.

13 Briggs, *Never in Anger*, p. 107.

14 Briggs, *Never in Anger*, p. 107.

15 Interviews with consultants and with RCMP officers. Also, see Griffiths, et al., *Crime, Law, and Justice among Inuit*, p. 53.

16 See, for example, Deborah Tannen, *You Just Don't Understand: Women and Men in Conversation* (New York: William Morrow, 1990).

17 Linda Brannon, *Gender: Psychological Perspectives* (Needham Heights, MA: Allyn & Bacon, 1996), p. 432.

18 Arlie Russell Hochschild, *The Managed Heart: Commercialization of Human Feeling* (Berkeley: University of California Press, 1989).

19 According to several researchers, "married women suffer more mental health problems than married men" and marriage appears to improve men's mental and physical health. Linda L. Lindsey, *Gender Roles: A Sociological Perspective* (Englewood Cliffs, NJ: Prentice Hall, 1994), p. 33.

20 Scholars and practitioners alike have questioned Freudian and later theories that postulate an *inevitable* link between frustration and aggression. Many psychologists believe that frustration *can* lead to aggression, however, toward an inappropriate person ("displacement"), especially if the person suppresses feelings of anger. Brannon, *Gender*, pp. 209-210.

12

Contemporary Socialization:
Passing on the Culture

Young people have children before they even know how to sew or make seal skins, or how to look after their houses. That might cause a bit of a problem.
—Martha

Needles and Dreams

Photo 12.1 Annie Shoapik Bowkett with baby Rebecca in her amoutik.

The older women often say that the younger ones should sew in order to find solace, help their families, and stay centered. For Annie Shoapik Bowkett, this bit of wisdom has become the fulcrum of her life. Her sewing shop, "Miqqut" (needles), opened in 1996 to become the first private, woman-owned business in Pangnirtung. She receives support in her work and her dreams from her husband, the Reverend Roy Bowkett, and from family and friends. (Joave Aviluktuk opened the first Inuit-owned business in Pang, an outfitting company.)

We talk to Annie and Roy over several days and endless cups of tea. They prove to be strong teachers, and we value every moment with them. It happens that Annie is one of Qatsuq's granddaughters. Our visit comes just as the sewing shop is opening, but it seems as though a dream about to come true is almost too fragile to view, lest it suddenly burst and float away. Annie has been working feverishly to build up her stock and prepare for the grand opening. Roy has been putting the finishing touches on the hut's exterior, varnishing and painting. Finally, after many conversations about the meaning of sewing to Annie, she takes us on a tour of her life's work.

First, we must see the makeshift sewing room she has been working in for the last few years, down in a shallow cellar beneath their apartment—windowless, chilly, dimly lit, cramped. Bits of old carpeting cover the damp floor. Bags and boxes filled with the debris of fervent productivity lie scattered everywhere.

Next, Annie leads us back upstairs and down the hall into a locked room. She opens the door, baby Rebecca in her arms and son Simeonie at her side, and switches on a light. Stacks of mittens, gloves, boot socks, tapestries, and slippers, all made of wool duffel and rimmed with fur, bury the long wooden table. The colors—purple, bright blue, fuchsia, and charcoal black—reflect the jewel tones of an Arctic sunset or the depth of a mid-winter sky. Annie's impeccable embroidery graces each piece. Each displays its own unique character. Poppies and poundnaits and other Arctic flowers march across the pieces in a unique blend of flair and precision.

As though turning the page of a book, Annie says it is time to visit her new sewing shop, down by the harbor and across from the visitors' center. The tiny two-room cabin boasts plenty of windows and light, a polished wooden floor, ample shelves for the warm and beautiful handicrafts, deep storage cupboards, and a cutting table Annie designed herself. "Long term" she plans to have a water tank installed and plumbing for a lavatory: "Until then, I will use a honey bucket."

When she had a heart problem at age six, Annie was sent to Toronto Children's Hospital, then to Moose Factory, Ontario: "I forgot here...I forgot my family, my parents." For two years, she was "hurting inside," so she learned to sew and do bead work. After trying both, she chose Inuit sewing. It soothed her sense of loss and emptiness: "It helped me get through a bad time, then and later."

Annie plans to open half days for retail sale and sew the rest of the time in the shop. She repeats the phrase "long term" in speaking of her business, with no apparent sense of urgency or detailed development plan. Rather, for now she simply savors the bliss of having her dream materialize. "I sit here in the chair and think, 'this is mine. No one will tell me what to do.' I can't believe it! I don't know where to start!"

Annie hopes to get orders from friends, neighbors, and visitors from afar. She has thought about the ethics of her business: "I will make orders in the order I receive them; I'll be fair, honest, and hire only women who do quality piece work." She makes one of us a "strap amautik," which can be worn front or back: "When you put the baby in, you say, 'ama' and the baby will learn that means comfort."

On return visits, we discover that Annie's dream had come true. Within eighteen months, the business had paid off the mortgage on the little building. By 2000, her shop was filled with the creativity of a half dozen Pangnirtung women. The business was doing so well that Annie could quit her part-time job as school janitor, and she was planning to add another room to the building. Annie speaks about how she, like so many others, suffered abuse as a girl, and how having her own shop amazes her. She reflects, "Pangnirtung is really my home, now...this is healing the wounds inside me."

ൠ

The lack of rigidity that marked traditional Inuit culture seems somewhat compromised by contemporary socialization practices and attitudes toward gender identity. People living in an economically fragile situation feel most keenly the impacts of influences external to the family. Today, the Inuit face equally critical challenges in teaching their children how to be resourceful in a changing world. The traditional teachers, parents and grandparents, long respected for their invaluable survival experience, have lost some skills and knowledge with each passing generation. The new socializing agents—schools, television, videos, magazines, and southerners—bring strange and sometimes clashing values into young people's lives. Contradictions of old and new fuel conflict across the generations. Socializing their daughters and sons into skills and knowledge that will keep them appropriately tethered to the past and draw them into an unknown future is difficult for Inuit women and men alike.

Today, children spend hours every day in school, still taught primarily by Qallunaat teachers. Children are raised by a much wider circle of relatives, neighbors, and other residents than was true in the smaller enclaves out on the land. Nonetheless, security, attention, and stimulation characterize the socialization of children now as they did in traditional times. This prepares them to enter a tightly-knit community, Condon observes: "The intense interaction that occurs between infants and numerous caretakers helps prepare the infant for the cultural emphasis placed upon close interpersonal relations and interdependence that will become an integral part of his life as he grows older."[1] He adds that, by southern standards, Inuit children "have a great deal of freedom to go where they want and do what they please."[2] This picture fits in with our observation of Inuit families: parents and other relatives treat children with great affection and give them relatively broad scope in exploring their social and physical worlds.

Others have written of the fact that Inuit "children are generally free to learn by exploration, play, and the encouragement of adults."[3] Nuttall observed that Inuit see the naming process as leaving a child with intelligence, consciousness, and reason far beyond its years. Birket-Smith agrees: "The children grow up in a free and unrestrained life. They almost always get their own way and are never punished, which perhaps has some connexion [sic] with the fact that through their names they are often in close association with dead relations."[4] In the settlements, toddlers and small children play outside at all hours of the day and night, especially in the midnight sun of summer but also during the coldest, darkest months: "Children eat in whatever house they wish, and since mealtimes or bedtimes are irregular, it is unusual to hear a parent express unease about the whereabouts of a child."[5] Other than attending school, the child chooses how to spend its day. Brody, too, "could not find evidence of socialization in any careful and self-conscious provision of what parents hold to be the child's real needs."[6] In fact, the Inuit appear to avoid controlling, manipulative, or authoritarian treatment of young children. Nonetheless, women report that important gender differences exist in socialization. Boys play road hockey in the winter and girls play with Barbie dolls, reflecting both past traditions and the impact of gender stereotyping in the media.

A Preference for the Male Child
"Today it's the same thing"

The historical preference for having a male child to some extent continues today, affecting female self-image and sense of worth. It also alters the extent to which a community will offer women equal opportunities in education, economics, and politics (see Chapters 16–18). One woman admits to us that she loves her first son more than she loves her daughters, echoing the old patterns. Condon commented in 1981 that, although "all newborns are a source of pride to the mother, the traditional preference for male infants persists in the society."[7] When asked why this pattern cuts across so many cultures, one Inuk woman in her 30s ventured, "It was meant to be. That's why the other cultures are the same." Others insist that girls make better children but "the guys are stronger."

Contemporary socialization of children reflects the shift in male and female roles. Favoritism toward boys may be diminishing, but it also takes a different form. As was true historically, elder Elisapee thinks that girls should do more in the house and boys should do more outside the house: "The boys, they expect everything to be done for them" at home. This favoritism and "catering to boys" rankles the teenage girls.

In an earlier time, gender segregation of skills existed but it was not rigid or linked with inequality of the sexes. Gender differences in the socialization of children persist—"if it's a little girl she learns sewing; if it's a boy the father teaches him how to fix things." Younger women insist they treat children as equals, however, regardless of sex. Geela lets her sons and daughters help both inside and outside the house: "I treat them equally." Although younger mothers may teach their sons how to cook and wash dishes, the *primary* responsibility for such domestic activities still rests with daughters. In fact, some women feel that the sexes are more rigidly separated now than they were in the past.

Through all of these complexities, one pattern stands out: Gender socialization tends to follow the familiar male and female roles, but the boundaries around these roles remain surprisingly flexible. Moving closer into the sphere of influence of mainstream culture makes a difference. Now, southern assumptions of male superiority and female weakness define Inuit roles as well. A white teacher explains: "You don't see many girls going out to become carpenters and mechanics. The culture that they're coming into is a sexist culture—and the schools are training them to be part of that." Boys and girls are segregated in school. Sometimes that results from Inuit attempts to hold tightly to the past division of labour that served them so well:

> We've tried in the past to have girls do shop. As long as there is a southern teacher, it's possible, but if you have an Inuk teacher, they won't have it. Some of the girls in my class have asked why they can't learn shop. I'll speak to the teacher and see what he says—point blank, "No!" So the girls do sewing and things like that...traditional crafts.

Why would contemporary Inuit insist on role separation in learning skills? The answer lies not so much in any effort to devalue female work or restrict female opportunities, but out of concern for preserving traditional Inuit culture. Many of the old skills persist in the face of considerable adversity, but more have been lost or weakened: "The new generation has a lack of learning," middle-aged Ovilu says. They miss wisdom that women of her generation took for granted as central to their role: working with skins, sewing, and preparing food the traditional way. Furthermore, confusion reigns as to which skills from traditional life are worth maintaining in modern Inuit life. Since people may not value the skills and knowledge associated with the young girls' world, they do not pass them along. Even when the skills retain value, daughters may resist learning because southernized culture distracts them and mothers may feel reluctant to teach their daughters for fear of wasting materials.

The reasons for extending special privileges to sons become even more complex in the settlements because males seem to have more problems adjusting to contemporary realities than females do. Meeka admits: "I've always worried more about my son. I don't know why. When they get to be teenagers, boys break in more than girls do." They also tend to succumb more often to alcohol, drug involvement, and suicide compared to females. Because they feel anxious about their sons, women often spoil them, says Geela: "Maybe we've given the boys more freedom than the girls. Sometimes we don't expect them to do as much around the house." Women wonder with exasperation why the males become more violent than females and seem to have less confidence or drive in planning for a productive future.

Biological differences also play a role in how Inuit women raise their daughters. They try to curtail their freedom because "girls can get pregnant when they go into their teens." Condon reported that "sexual intercourse is fairly common" among Inuit teenagers, despite the tendency toward same-sex activities: "Young people do not have the same problem finding a meeting place as do young adults in the south. They may go to a married brother's or sister's house or even to their own parent's house to engage in sexual activity. Due to the extreme openness of parental attitudes toward sex, there is little or no worry about being 'caught'."[8] Girls receive somewhat more supervision. Says a middle-aged woman: "When I started going out to movies or staying out late at night, Mom would always be on top of me, and yet she would let the boys be more free. I think I'm going to be quite the same! I get so worried when my daughter's not home by the time she is supposed to be. A guy might pick her up. I'm beginning to understand where Mom was coming from!"

Like other mothers, this woman worries less about her son in this regard. One Inuk woman notes that disciplining boys might be more intimidating for women: "Boys, they're harder to talk to, telling them...but I wouldn't let my girl play out all night." When families travel out of the settlement, they worry about leaving either male or female children alone.

The Ideal Woman, the Ideal Man
"Pink is for girls"

In contrast to the relatively gender-neutral clothing of earlier times, now Inuit gender differentiation begins early in the child's life by dressing girl babies in pink and male infants in light blue. Either sex can wear white and pale yellow. Would Inuit women dress a little boy in a pink sweater? "No way! Not my boys. Pink is usually for girls." A girl can wear a blue sweater, however. Meeka characterizes the changes in raising children that have occurred in just two decades:

> Here I am working, being a mother, but I am a mother in a very different way than my mother was. When I was a child, just over 20 years ago, I was a child

in a real Inuit way, an old traditional way. I was clothed in skins when I was a baby. We had no materials or fabrics. So, in a very short time, my kids had no way of seeing what I went through.

Resettlement has thrown the Inuit into a dual economy—the modern wage-labour sector that exploits nonrenewable resources and depends on southern-style technical skills versus the traditional sector that exploits renewable resources and depends on aboriginal technical skills.[9] This juxtaposition of economies has had a major impact on the definition of both female and male identities. Contemporary Inuit women take knowledge of traditional skills very seriously, although the middle-aged and younger women have not had enough opportunities to learn them well. This lapse in socialization means that the ideal Inuk woman may no longer be defined in terms of her sewing and cooking skills. Instead, female identity resides in acquiring a good education, finding a wage-earning job, and supporting children and a live-in partner if necessary.

The thrust toward wage-labour means that the Inuk woman who fails to learn traditional skills may be defined by herself and by others (male and female) as less than adequate as a provider for her family. One woman in her 40s explains about her recent experience with trying to be a good wife: "When we first married, I wasn't able to sew the sealskins properly or take the right amount of fat off the skins. I felt that somehow I was letting my man down. I've tried to learn many things. I'm not very good at them, but my husband is a very good teacher." She wants to fill this gap in her ability to support her family, even though she contributes cash from her job with the hamlet.

Similarly, some Inuit women refuse to characterize young men today as "good" because they are *not* good hunters. Their reluctance underscores the centrality of the hunting role in the past and its enduring utility. Elder women describe their sons as "good" because they share the spoils of their hunting. Younger women counsel their daughters to look for "a man who has a good job and who can look after her...or a good hunter who cares about her." He must not use drugs or alcohol, and he should be faithful to her. He knows how to bring her country food, but the good hunter formula no longer suffices. A good Inuk man should also be affectionate, gentle, and kind. Eena expresses for many others the depth of her feeling in this regard: "If my daughter lived with a guy who gets mad and outrageous, I would get mad and start hitting him. I don't go for that stuff." By the 1990s, the Inuit were living in "a mixed economy consisting of traditional land-based, wage labour, and market sectors."[10] The good man must find his place in one or both sectors of this mixed economy in order to provide for his family.

While she is aware of the dichotomy that tests male identity, Geela believes that defining the good man may be irrelevant now. Even though mothers had a major role in selecting a daughter's partner in the past, now they prefer that young women use their own judgment: "If my daughter likes him, then I guess that's the way it is." Women say they also look for a man with a good personality, a "good attitude," and some education ("training to be a professional mechanic or something"). For example, Maria, 19, reflects on her boyfriend and father of her baby. Friends and family in Iqaluit, an hour away by plane, told her about a young man they felt would be a good match for her. She agreed:

> I liked him a lot. We had never met, but I knew from what I had heard that he was a very good person, kind and open; he knows what he is doing. He wants the training he's in right now, and nothing is more important than that. When I met him—because I really wanted to—I think that was my happiest day.

As with women, some men find the traditional mandate relatively unappealing, which leaves them in a cultural vacuum. A woman in her 60s relates this story:

> One son likes to go hunting. Sometimes he goes by himself for ptarmigan. One time he got a caribou by himself. He goes fishing—he really enjoys it. Yet, my older son does not like hunting. We used to take him out every week, but he started to stay home when he was 15. We liked to take him, but he did not like going. My mom is home, so I guess he wants to be home with her, in town. He likes fishing, but hunting bores him.

Although his family might show tolerance toward his unusual behaviour, most women would not describe him as the "ideal Inuk man."

Ulus and Harpoons
"We help when we go camping"

Inuit women lament that youths, both male and female, seem "too lazy" to help family or community. Naiomi, 12, acknowledges that she has not yet learned how to clean a seal with an *ulu* as her mother so skillfully models: "We go to school all the time. We watch TV, do homework. That's why we don't help a lot." Naiomi knows how to sew *kamiks*, mittens, and duffel socks—but she did not learn at her mother's knee, as her mother learned from her mother. Rather, Naiomi learned these traditional skills in school from one of the most respected seamstresses in the settlement. Her brothers have learned how to hunt by going out on the land with their father. Naiomi helps her mother with domestic work because she asks her to, yet she feels free to learn male skills as well: "Sometimes I have problems making supper. I make soup, hot dogs, hamburgers, or steak. I don't know how to stuff fish and put it in the oven, so I watch my Mom. I want to learn how to cook. Sometimes I like to help my father when he goes hunting. A man needs help with the boat."

Teenager Rebekah knows how to fish the traditional way, "jagging" with hockey sticks turned into makeshift harpoons. She may be learning more about the boy's kitbag of skills because her little brother is so young: "Usually the boys my age help their Dad. The girl doesn't get to do it, but when the brother is doing something else, the girl has to help." Rebekah tries to help her grandmother because her male cousins "sit down and don't help at all; and she always has sore bones and has a hard time walking. I like to go hunting and to help my grandpa. Some kids don't help their fathers and mothers—I learn by helping."

As an antidote to modern life, most Inuit families take off six to eight weeks during the summer to go camping. Living on the land, even temporarily, brings children into the whole world of knowledge and skills that allows them to survive and enjoy their dramatically beautiful but ever-threatening natural environment. Children may not be aware of the vast knowledge they glean from only a few weeks out on the land until someday nature's trials test their survival skills. Braving a blizzard, getting lost on the open tundra, running out of food in the unforgiving winter cold, or being caught on an ice floe in the spring break-up could happen to anyone. Knowing how to find their way in all kinds of conditions and terrain could save them from wandering too far from home. Having learned to catch and dry Arctic char or to hunt and freeze caribou could easily save them from starvation. Being able to tell the difference between edible plants and poisonous plants offers further protection.

Cultural Inclusion
"They teach the children skills"

What will life be like in Inuit communities twenty years from now? Meeka responds: "It's hard to say, but I think my culture will die mostly." However real that risk might seem, she acknowledges, it could be the other way around. If her age group works hard to teach children their culture, it will not disappear. Women say they need to embark on a deliberate campaign to protect, preserve, and pass on Inuit culture. Men are also fighting to keep the culture alive, Lena believes: "They still go hunting. They don't want to lose their hunt or their tradition. They're concerned." Once, survival meant depending on one's family, communicating well with them, and helping each other. Now, Loie says, "It's really different. It's not even funny. I feel sad. We're going to keep losing our culture if we don't do anything about it." A woman in her early 30s laments this loss of culture: "We live like Qallunaat today. We can't live the traditional way. We don't know how to live on the land anymore—that takes many supplies. It's really sad, especially for our children. Nobody is teaching them anymore. We don't have the skills or interest in living on the land, but we also don't have skills for this world."

Learning traditional and contemporary skills, noticing the preference for male children, and experiencing the sometimes-contradictory messages of school and television all leave an indelible print on the emerging identity of Inuit women. Those we interviewed quickly add that the problems they face are not especially unique; other Inuit communities share in these same dilemmas. Teaching children Inuit ways in "cultural inclusion" classes in the hamlet school helps bridge the gap between old and new.[11] Pangnirtung's Alookie School teaches kindergarten through sixth grade in Inuktitut. In this way, children receive a basic education in their language and culture. Parents assume that English will be part of their lives outside school and in the later grades—a sense of urgency prevails toward children learning both languages. A white teacher who strongly advocates cultural inclusion sees Inuit culture gradually diminishing:

> That's the minus side. On the plus side, the government is doing all it can to make sure that the culture is not lost. With cultural inclusion, older members of the community come in and give lectures and demonstrations about the old ways of life. In early spring, elders take the children out on the land by dog team to spend a day. The young ones go for a picnic or a hike; the seniors, from grade seven and up, go for a week and leave the trappings of the twentieth century behind. They go by snow mobile and by dog team. They learn how to build igloos and live in them...have fun, fish. In school, they have shop, where they learn how to make traditional *qamutiik.*

Elders and middle-aged Inuit who grew up on the land visit the elementary and high schools to share their knowledge and skills. They teach children how to make Inuit drums or headbands, and sing traditional chants and songs. Leah explains: "My mother taught me to do skins this way, so I teach the children to do it this way. The boys learn how to make an igloo." Inuit men from town take the children out caribou or seal hunting. The local school board pays the elders: "The teacher calls them and they're very willing."

Even picnicking along the fiord for a few hours teaches children the old ways, says Martha: "The children come with us and help out—that's the only way they learn." A woman in her 40s, who has known both camp and settlement life, adds: "In my generation we were *so* interested in the southern lifestyle, the Qallunaat culture. That's mainly why we didn't learn at that time. When our mothers were young, they would sit right beside their mom, watching her sewing all day long. We didn't want to do that. We had other things to do."

Says a teacher's aid, "With cultural inclusion, students have a chance to learn to sew the traditional way. The kids really enjoy it. They think it's great." It is not too late, she hopes, for young girls to learn the old skills that so critically defined the woman's role. Children of younger parents who avoid school concern some Inuit women. They have no other way to learn critical protective skills: "This is a cold country and they have to survive in the wintertime."

Cooking and Country Food
"I don't know how people cope"

Food forms an essential element of any culture. On the land, where scarcity often dictated the menu, food belonged to everyone in the social network. Today, too, Inuit share the precious fruits of berry picking and the spoils of hunting and fishing within a broadly defined extended family that often includes neighbors and close friends. Men skin and butcher the caribou and carefully cache the meat in the Hunter's and Trapper's Association community freezer, or underground, just above the surface of the deep permafrost, where it will keep safely from one year to the next. Seals are left inside their skins for freezing. Using these treasures, all but the youngest Inuit women cook traditional country food. Kitchens are redolent with the aromas of boiled seal meat, fried caribou steaks, broiled Arctic char, and occasional delicacies such as walrus meat or whale blubber.

Some women continue to make hearty stews laced with the blood of seals. Women say that out on the land a "good Inuit mother" would give each of her young children a cup of seal blood every day. Always the staple of Inuit diet, the magnificently endowed seals provide a virtually complete source of nutrients— fat, protein, vitamins A, C, and D, calcium, and other essential minerals.[12] Lunch, the day's main meal, might consist of boiled caribou meat with salad, Arctic char, or seal meat. In the evening, the family might munch on a bit of boiled or raw *mattaq* (or *metuq*)—the black skin of the Beluga whale: "Eat caribou meat raw or seal meat raw, fish raw, anything raw. That is traditional food! Eat it in the evening, like a snack. Dried caribou meat, dried seal meat, dried fish." Younger women keeping their own households find it difficult to cook the way their mothers did, however. With the decline of hunting, they simply do not have enough country food to form the centerpiece of daily meals.

The typical contemporary Inuk woman, young or old, does retain the custom of making bannock every day, cooking the tender bread on top of the stove in a frying pan. Virtually every Inuk woman we visited proudly served her version of this straightforward staple of Inuit life, a legacy of the nineteenth century contact with whalers. Bannock bakes slowly on the back burner, providing the warmth and calories essential for survival. The people carry bannock on excursions out on the land or in the boats, and consume it in great quantities at home as well. The ingredients of bannock vary slightly in proportion from hearth to hearth, but many women offered this basic recipe:

Bannock

2 cups flour	*1/2 teaspoon salt*
2 tablespoons milk	*2 to 4 tablespoons shortening*
2 teaspoons baking powder	*1 cup water*

1. Mix dry ingredients, cut in shortening, add liquid; shape into a flat, thick disk.
2. Cook over very low heat on stovetop in an ungreased, heavy iron frying pan for one hour, turning over after 30 minutes to cook both sides evenly through to the middle.

An alternate recipe uses 3 cups flour, 2 tablespoons baking powder, 1/2 cup shortening, and 2 cups warm water.

In times past, Inuit women made bannock with seal oil so it would not freeze.[13] Today, some use vegetable oil "because it is closer to the old way." Some women add a bit of sugar, and others add raisins, if they are lucky enough to have these extra ingredients. This persistence of culture occurs not out of a nostalgic longing for the old way of life, although it may serve that purpose, too. Rather, it persists because prices are exorbitant for the only available non-country food, flown hundreds of miles up to the Northern, High Arctic, or Inuit Co-op stores. When Inuit families shopped at these stores in the past, they concentrated on staples such as flour, dried milk, salt, sugar, and cigarettes. Although some of the stores carry such country food as caribou meat and scallops and Inuit community health workers have stressed country food as still being the healthiest for their people, everything from frozen chocolate éclairs to cookies claims local dollars today.

Sewing, Embroidering, and Weaving
"Women were always sewing"

S ewing with skins and furs forms a pivotal part of Inuit women's culture "as far back as you can go." In the absence of grass, basketry did not emerge as a woman's craft. However, in pre-settlement days, sewing and embroidery brought both pride and functional value to the Inuit woman's role.

Sewing

When she was growing up, a child learned the skills most appropriate for her gender through play and games, an elder woman recalls: "We had homemade toys made out of seal flipper bones. We cooked them first and played 'pretend house' with them. Our uncles, fathers, and brothers made wooden dolls for us—that's how we learned to sew and how to talk at the same time. We made clothing for the dolls...parkas. We didn't know we were learning with all these homemade toys." The dolls disappeared—"most of them are museum pieces now"—and the skills almost disappeared too in the transition from the older generation to the younger.

Meeka believes that one of the primary markers of dramatic cultural change has been the decline in women's sewing. Many Inuit women still sew, but they use electric sewing machines and thread, pre-made trims, and lace instead of thimbles, needles, and sinew. It is a matter of deep pride for a woman to be able to cut her own patterns for boots, mittens, parkas, and leggings, but young women have lost the ability to make patterns and have had little opportunity to work with skins: "We don't know how to sew traditional clothes," laments Lena. "If somebody cuts the pattern, we could sew, but we can't even make *kamiks*. We didn't learn...nobody showed us how." Dahl also found this phenomenon among young Inuit women in Greenland, especially during the 1980s. He found more skills development among this group in the mid-1990s, which we, too, have noted in Pangnirtung, although the number of young women learning traditional sewing skills is still very small.[14]

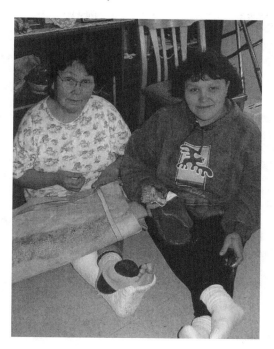

Photo 12.2 Mother and daughter sewing sealskin boots and mittens.

"In the old days, women were always sewing clothes for the family," Apea adds. "Now we can buy our clothes in the stores, but I still sew caribou parkas and *kamiks*. I like to keep my culture." For her generation, though, the learning has not been so easy: "Even when we wanted to learn, sometimes our mothers would refuse. They would say, 'You're going to waste that material!' Maybe if they had taught us, we could do some traditional sewing. We know how to do duffel socks and parkas but not the traditional clothing." Her friend, Eena, agrees: "We're the generation that missed out. We can't make *kamiks*, either. We didn't learn how to do it."

Some younger women give caribou skins to their mothers or mothers-in-law because they are not trusted to work in skins. Especially when there is a shortage, as occurred when prices were artificially inflated because of a southern craving for sealskin trimmed clothing and boots during the 1960s (before the baby seal controversy peaked), the possibility of damaging or wasting skins creates an unacceptable risk.[15]

For women with small children, learning to sew is problematic and often undermines the intention to develop new skills: "You work all day, so there is no time. I just want to stay home," explains one woman.[16] She adds that when younger women feel overwhelmed, their mothers make traditional clothing for them: "That's the bad part, I guess. She just provides us with what we need. I like traditional clothes...they're cheaper and warmer."

Some women in their 30s admit they may not have pressed their mothers for information, but they also feel that many mothers resisted teaching their daughters sewing. The older women know how to sew, of course, and are increasingly becoming aware that they must find ways to pass skills on to their daughters. For example, the women of the Pangnirtung *kitaq* have a sewing group every Thursday and Saturday, for "anybody who wants to sew.... The women try to welcome as many young people as want to come."[17] Sarah Tokolik of Spence Bay talks about a women's sewing group that meets in another Inuit community every week.[18] They stitch and talk about anything on their minds—childbirth and midwives, teenagers having babies or not learning Inuktitut. Weekly classes to teach younger girls to work on skins are sprinkled liberally with gossip and commiseration. Some go to learn and others go just to buy homemade clothing from other women. Sarah describes how she tries to pass on the ancient secrets to the younger generation:

> They start by learning to soften the caribou and sealskins. We can do the stretching outside, freeze the skins outside in the wintertime, and show them which way to cut the [caribou] legs.... In the North, you need those clothes. You'll freeze if you don't wear them. In December and January, people wear them. I know many young girls are not learning anything at all about their culture, such as cleaning skins or making clothes...We've been doing this and it's helping, I know it's helping.[19]

Jeannie's mother taught her how to sew, and then she honed her skills by practicing. Jeannie's daughter, 25, does not sew: "I am interested; when I have the time I will learn." Lena, 32, sews modern clothes as well as traditional boots, duffel socks, and mittens. She learned from what her mother told her, but "I learned from myself, too, by watching." Saila's mother died when she was young, so no one taught her how to sew. When she was a teenager, she used to look at clothing and admire the handiwork of other women. Through trial and error, she taught herself.

Older women fear that the younger ones are growing up without a culture. Sewing, they believe, is essential to female identity.[20] What can women do to alleviate some of the social problems facing the Inuit now? Qatsuq unhesitatingly replies, "Make *kamiks*—sew!" The pride of conquering nature through time-honored skills shows through in Sarah's account:

> I made a caribou parka for my son. That's the first time. I couldn't believe myself. I should have done it years before but I didn't! I just started making

waterproof *kamiks* not long ago. My mom wanted to do it [for me]; she thought I wouldn't do it as quickly, but I did. The ladies were really proud of me! My mom, who has been sewing for a long time, wouldn't let me do it because she thought I was going to spoil it. I wasn't trying hard enough I guess, because she kept telling me, "You're going to spoil it...you won't do it right." I was eager and I did it very well.

We shouldn't just leave it up to our mothers. We should do it ourselves, and teach our kids. If I show my daughter how to make *kamiks* and she spoils them, it's okay...she keeps trying...that's the only way she's going to learn.

You take the fur off the sealskin first. You have to dry it, and then you have to chew it with your teeth, to make it really soft.... You have to keep the skin frozen so it won't spoil.[21]

Lena talks about the Sewing Centre funded by the federal government that used to supply work, income, and pride for the women. A few years ago it was closed because, women speculate, it "went bankrupt": "We had a sewing centre that the women looked after. When that building closed down, we lost everything. We didn't lose material or anything, but it was helping the ladies to get an income, even if it was a low income. They closed it because it cost too much to run. The government gave us a grant; I guess they wouldn't give more funding because it didn't make enough money." Like trapping, seal hunting, and jobs at the DEW line sites built throughout the NWT in the 1950s, the sewing centers also disappeared as sources of steady income.[22] The closing was a hard blow to a community with a fragile economy. Women, who had given men gas money for hunting, in the time-honored pattern of reciprocal responsibility and support, could no longer do so. This further compromised hunting, which supplied materials for sewing.[23]

A woman who worked as a seamstress until the old shop faltered found herself struggling for seasonal employment at the fish plant. Occasionally, she works part time for her brother, fishing for scallops.[24] She tried, with other women, to start her own sewing business but closed it because "it was always too cold and it cost too much to keep the shop going." Nonetheless, many women continued to sew in their own homes, selling occasional items to tourists and those who never learned how to sew.

Pride and satisfaction transform into economic advantage as well. If there were some seed money to support the fledgling but high-quality sewing business in Pangnirtung, more women could work at producing the *amautiit*, *kamiks*, mittens, scarves, slippers, and hats. They could easily compete with the garments sold through northern suppliers. A privately-funded sewing shop that sprung up in the mid-1990s marks a significant shift in the way Inuit women contribute to economic growth, to the preservation of arts and crafts, and to the revitalization of Inuit culture[25] (see "Needles and Dreams," Chapter 17.)

The former NWT government began buying sealskins from Inuit hunters in 1995 in order to supply a rekindled fur trade in the south; the current Nunavut government retained this program. Although many sealskins are auctioned off for use by commercial furriers, since 1997 a Montrealer, Ingo Moslener, has been teaching Inuit women modern methods of sewing sealskins for export. In 2000, the territorial government sent a Nunavut Inuit fashion collection to Montreal's North American Fur and Fashion Exposition, "complete with Inuit models." Although this opportunity involves very few Inuit women, it is another way to express their talents in a way that is compatible with time-honoured skills.[26] Pauktuutit has worked to protect the intellectual property rights of Inuit women regarding the *amauti* design as a "collective cultural property," [27] which further underscores their talent and cultural contributions.

Embroidery

One of the most popular expressions of women's creativity, embroidery was taught to Inuit women in the late nineteenth and early twentieth century by white women who occasionally came to the Arctic. For example, Qatsuq remembers a "Qallunaat lady who came to be a teacher." She asked Qatsuq to make a parka for her. After she finished, the woman asked her to embroider a dog team on the parka. Qatsuq had never seen embroidery. The woman said, "Just try it," and gave her a few tips. Qatsuq says she embroidered the dog team but not very well. Still, she thinks she was the very first one to do embroidery in her area: "All the women started embroidering when they saw it."

Now, Inuit women's embroidered tapestries grace the walls of homes in the North and throughout Canada and abroad. Embroidery identifies women's contributions to the budding sewing industry as igloos, seals, polar bears, train dogs, birds, harpoons, and other symbols of Inuit culture come to life on soft wool duffel hangings, mittens, coats, and duffel socks. Along with miniature people in *amautiit*, figures tell stories of ancient myths and modern dreams in tiny stitches and glorious colors.[28] At night in the settlements, children knock on the doors of homes where visitors from the south are staying to sell these unique offerings from the Inuk woman's world.

Drawing, Printmaking, and Carving
"An important identity"

Today, the Uqqurmiut Arts and Crafts Centre encompasses the Pangnirtung Tapestry Studio or "weave shop" (which employs several women full-time in the art of tapestry weaving) and the Pangnirtung Print Shop (dominated by male artists but increasingly embracing of women's drawings). The Nunavut Territory Arts and Crafts Association helps 1,000 to 2,000 Inuit artists and artisans market their work more effectively to southern buyers.[29]

The art of Inuit women opens a window on a remote and fascinating world that most will never see. As Odette Leroux notes, their art "leads the viewer into a world torn between the traditional and the modern, the mystical and the rational." Drawing, printmaking, and carving show us the enduring customs and the nagging conflicts through the lens of a woman's everyday life-world— children, relationships, colors, chores, landscapes, and wildlife.[30] Pangnirtung's exceptional artistic output affects virtually everyone in one way or another. Artists find self-expression and financial reward; the community benefits economically from tourists who come to enjoy the magnificent views and to buy art; old and young alike have the chance on a daily basis to see both their history and their contemporary life documented in prints or stone, tapestries or weavings, sealskin and duffel fashions, Western Arctic braiding and embroidering. Weissling characterizes the Co-op, established in 1968 as an outlet for Inuit carving and handicrafts, as the first formal source of cash income source for women in the region.[31] It and the sewing centers created in Pangnirtung and Broughton Island have helped Inuit women make the transition from old to new lifestyles.

Minnie Aodla Freeman sees art as a prime way for Inuit women and men to develop both culturally and economically. What emerged in mid-twentieth century as a minor occupation now produces artwork that commands respect and serious commissions from galleries, museums, collectors, and corporations. Jose Kusugak, President of Inuit Tapirisat of Canada, encapsulates the maturation process of Inuit art: "In art, as in politics, Inuit values are entering a new phase of expression, reaching out as equals to non-Inuit."[32] As of 1998, approximately 3,000 Nunavummiut (about 20 percent of the adult population) engaged either part-time or full-time in art; they contribute an estimated $40 million annually to the economy of the territory.[33]

Within the context of a rapidly changing culture, art stands out as a profession that some young people might overlook: "While the children of these famous artists are studying for their future professions at school, the artists are holding together the very foundations of their culture through their art. Although some young Inuit may not realize it, the answer to their need to have an important identity is right under their noses in their parents' art. How many will take up art is not known."[34]

Carving is not the sole domain of men, though it was more so in the past. Women occasionally carve and many women supply drawings and serve as printmakers. Kenojuak, a Cape Dorset artist, says in her autobiography that she was reluctant to offer her artwork to the print shop during the 1960s because "men made drawings." Her artistic talents and recognition eventually opened the door for other Inuit women.[35] Now, the Pangnirtung printmaking shop brings male and female talents together in creating world famous prints. Peepeelee Qappik, for example, served as printmaker in the late 1980s and early 1990s, translating the drawings brought to the Pangnirtung studio into beautiful prints.

Rosie Okpik was the chairperson of the Uqqurmiut Inuit Artists Association board from its inception in 1987 until her death in 1997. Her drawings came to life in both prints and Pangnirtung tapestries. In the 1990s, several women joined the legions of the hamlet's famous male artists: Elisapee Ishulutak, Annie Kilabuk, Ida Karpik, Mary Kewkingak, and Geela Sowdluapik, among others, have supplied master drawings for the printmakers. Jessie Oonark of Baker Lake is considered one of the most sophisticated Inuit artists whose drawings were made into prints and tapestries. As with other Inuit women, she incorporated the ulu and other symbols of the woman's role into her visual renderings.[36]

Pangnirtung Tapestry Studio
"They're very experienced now"

In the absence of equipment or grazing land for wool-producing animals, weaving with looms was not part of Inuit art life prior to contact with Euro-Canadian culture. Missionaries introduced finger weaving in the late 1930s and 40s, a very sophisticated braiding technique that women use to produce sashes and bands, without equipment: "You just strap the material on your foot or something that is firm, and then weave." A government-funded project designed to help employ Inuit women introduced loom weaving after resettlement. Large-scale looms made in Québec now mark the enterprise. A southern Canadian, Don Stuart, taught the women how to use the looms. An Inuk woman manages the tapestry studio now. Lena explains how the weaving shop operates:

"YOU MAKE THINGS THAT YOU SELL"
This is where the government comes in: It takes a lot of money to initiate a weaving project like this. There was a need for these women to find employment. If they didn't work here, these women would most likely be on social assistance. They wouldn't work at all because they don't have the qualifications to be an office worker or a teacher. They haven't learned a trade. Traditionally, you would go hunting and take care of your children, but that wasn't enough to feed your family after we moved into the settlements. So you either live on social assistance, you make things that you sell, or you learn a trade. The weaving shop is an alternative way to maintain some of our lifestyle but still earn money.
    I make Western Delta braid for trimming dresses and parkas. That originated in the Mackenzie Delta region of the Northwest Territories. I make it on the sewing machine. When I went to a World Crafts Council in Japan, I first saw Delta braid. A lady from Fort McPherson had trimmed a parka this way, so when I got home I learned it.

The Council provided workshops for women to learn a variety of crafts, but Lena learned weaving and material dyeing "without the equipment they use." According to former managers, "This is a unique set up. There's no other shop like ours across the whole territory." The studio was designed to give unilingual local women a chance to learn, gain experience, and make extra money without investing in extended schooling. It started in the late 1960s with three women in a "weave shop," and then grew to over a dozen. Subsidized by the federal government, the studio grew from small projects such as scarves, sashes, and placemats to ambitious projects such as large tapestries and rugs.[37]

Photo 12.3 A skilled tapestry worker at "the weave shop."

Women have participated in training programs, learned weaving techniques, and developed their talents over the years. They sell their exquisite tapestries, many of which cost thousands of dollars, in Pangnirtung's Uqqurmiut Center to tourists and in the south through a gallery system. Regardless of which local artist or printmaker drew the "cartoon" for the tapestry, the weaver signs each piece. Galleries in places such as Vancouver, Ottawa, and Toronto represent the shop and contract for a show every two years, as the director explains: "We send them between twelve and twenty hangings for a month-long show. They send back whatever has not sold. They pay only for what they sell." Says a weaver:

"YOU COULD LIVE ON IT"

The cooperative weave shop was created through Economic Development and Tourism. We are an enterprise of the government. The weave shop trains all the women it employs. There's no school, so you find training here.

Before, the only type of yarn that we could spin was from muskox, but we have no muskox in this community. This geographical location doesn't have any yarns or fiber, so we bring all of our material up from Canadian wool manufacturers.

We have a shop assistant, a sewer, and a finisher who work on an hourly pay rate. All the other full-time weavers earn a combination of set rates, regular benefits, holiday pay, and royalties. We also receive a piecework rate. It depends on how difficult a wall hanging is—more difficulty means more pay. Hunting season starts soon, so some of the weavers will go camping. Sometimes we want to go out on the land early, or we have to take care of a child, so we like to have the checks early. They are very flexible. How much you make is up to you. If you come in every day, and you don't take long coffee breaks, you can make more money. If you have a lazy week, your paycheck will be smaller the next week. If you're very productive, you can make a living from it. You will never be rich. A teacher earns more than a weaver does every year...but it's more than you would get on social assistance.

Aipilik, in her 50s, characterizes the women as "a group that works closely together." Because they are mature women, "it is an unwritten rule that they like to speak only Inuktitut with each other, even though they can speak a few words of English." As some of the older weavers retire, the studio tries to hire younger, more educated women with stronger English. This creates a mixed group that challenges the shop manager's skills. Aipilik says the younger ones do not want to offend the older ones, and the older ones stand very firm in their beliefs: "We have a meeting and vote. We would not vote a young girl—very talented, with some weaving knowledge—into the group because we want to keep the group mature. In a way you could call this the 'old ladies' club'...it's an unwritten rule, amongst ourselves. We have only so many spots."

The weave shop women do not advertise. Fortunately, they have a one-year waiting list for some hangings, which pleases the director greatly: "We can't handle more publicity because we wouldn't be able to supply more people. We have more orders than we can satisfactorily handle. If we marketed our stuff, we would suddenly have production problems. We couldn't produce it as fast as the orders came in." Recently, a new shop was built, expanding both productive and marketing capacities. Jeannie, a "weaver among weavers," explains the system:

"WE ALWAYS EXCHANGE"

When one of our tapestries sells, we get a certain percentage. I learned to weave here. The other women taught me. I like it. You're working with mature women, but the mentality is very playful at times; there is also teasing—let's see how far we can go with the coffee break! We expect the lead woman to go in and chase us back to work, because that's her job. It's silly, because we're paid by piecework. We have staff meetings once a month, and when things start getting out of hand, they expect us to talk about it. Then for a couple of weeks it's good again. There's no gum chewing, no sticking gum on the looms, and no smoking. It's not just one person staying on their equipment, working on their piece. There's talking going on across the room, and the radio is on. If somebody needs help, she'll ask a neighbor. We always exchange, even when we're working on a wall hanging. We just look at who did the one before that was like it, rather than figuring it out by ourselves.

Experience and practice produce speed. It is important to have harmony within the group because the women help each other. According to M'Closkey, the Pangnirtung weaveshop stands out among others in the world because people regard (and promote) women's productivity as art rather than craft.[38] As one of the most successful workshops in the Arctic, the weaving shop has been in continuous operation longer than others have; it has helped bridge the gap between living on the land and living in settlements. The women's visual representation of Inuit culture since the weave shop's inception in 1970 is detailed in *Nuvisavik: The Place Where We Weave*, a collection of interviews with artists and weavers edited by Maria von Finckenstein.[39]

Dancing and Singing
"Reels and jigs and fiddle music"

The only musical expressions that elders recall before contact were drum dancing and throat singing, but even in the late nineteenth century these ancient Inuit expressions were vanishing. However, with a renewed sense of urgency in preserving Inuit culture, such groups as Sikumiut Inuit Dancers and Drummers and Aqsarniit Drum Dancers and Throat Singers have consulted with their elders in the last decade to revive these cultural forms. Drums were originally made of driftwood and caribou hides; the accompanying *ajaaja* (song) emanated from personal experiences and relationships. Individuals or groups, women or men, can engage in drum dancing. Throat singing, however, is a female artistic form that originated a long time ago as women went through their daily activities:

> Mothers sang to their children, little girls sang to their puppies, and women attracted geese. Women also sang for entertainment in friendly competition, imitating sounds of animals such as geese, seagulls, dog teams, walrus, and other sounds like the saw...(sled) runners, the wind, boiling seal meat, and small waves.[40]

Before the revival of drum dancing, when contemporary Inuit referred to "traditional music and dancing," they were most likely speaking of the legacy of nineteenth century contact with whalers. At Kekerten whaling station, where many Pangnirtungmiut labored, Scottish jigs and reels echoed through the still Arctic air. Whalers taught Inuit men and women how to play these lively tunes on accordions they brought from across the sea. These dances have become a favorite Inuit pastime, especially on holidays or special events: "If you were to come at Christmastime, we have a week's celebration. Twenty-four hours, non-stop." At night the people dance and hold Inuit games at the cultural center, the school gym, or on the frozen fiord, Jolly relates: "You find fat old men and scrawny old women, and all sorts of shapes and sizes. They jump and dance and sing with no inhibitions at all. The dancing comes through the Scottish people. Whenever we have occasion for celebration, we bring out our old instruments and dance."

While many Inuit women mentioned the "dying" or loss of culture as one of the most important issues facing them, at the same time they do not make these comments to express a sense of defeatism. Not to recognize it would, indeed, be a tragedy. Significantly, more women mentioned loss of culture in our earliest interviews (1988) compared to our latest interviews (2001), when many looked to Nunavut as a vehicle for preserving and rekindling the best of traditional ways. It is not too late, they say, to turn the processes of assimilation and acculturation around so communities such as Pangnirtung can intentionally craft a vital culture that blends the old and the new in creative ways. As "keepers of the culture," Inuit women feel increasingly empowered to face this major challenge of the new century.

Notes

1 Condon, *Inuit Behavior and Seasonal Change in the Canadian Arctic*, p. 77.

2 Condon, *Inuit Behavior and Seasonal Change in the Canadian Arctic*, p. 77.

3 Nuttall, *Arctic Homeland*, pp. 69-70.

4 Birket-Smith, *The Eskimos*, p. 154. See also Robert G. Williamson, "Some Aspects of the History of the Eskimo Naming System," *Folk* 30 (1988): 45-263.

5 Brody, *The People's Land*, p. 194.

6 Brody, *The People's Land*, p. 194.

7 Condon, *Inuit Behavior and Seasonal Change in the Canadian Arctic*, p. 75.

8 Condon, *Inuit Behavior and Seasonal Change in the Canadian Arctic*, p. 83. We observed that caution along these lines varied from family to family and among communities. Arviat apparently has Nunavut's highest rates of both teenage pregnancy and sexually transmitted diseases, both probably a result of parental resistance toward teaching about contraception at the high school level: "Every year at Arviat's Qititliq High School, between 10 and 15 students from age 13 and up become pregnant.... When the high rates for STD's in Arviat were posted around town, showing Arviat's top position, many were reportedly impressed rather than worried. 'We're winning!'" Jane George, "Nunavut's Teen Mothers Face Difficult Adjustments," *Nunatsiaq News* (May 19, 2000).

9 Hedican, *Applied Anthropology in Canada*, p. 118.

10 McDonald, Arragutainaq, and Novalinga, *Voices from the Bay*, p. 51.

11 Cultural inclusion has been a common practice in the former Soviet Union since the 1940s. Terence Armstrong, "The Administration of Northern Peoples: The USSR," in MacDonald, ed., *The Arctic Frontier*, pp. 57-88.

12 Kirsten Borre, *Dietary and Nutritional Significance of Seal and Other Country Foods in the Diet of the Inuit of Clyde River, NWT*. Technical Paper 11 (Montréal: Royal Commission on Seals and the Sealing Industry in Canada, 1986) and "Seal Blood, Inuit Blood, and Diet: A Bio-cultural Model of Physiology and Cultural Identity," *Medical Anthropology Quarterly* 5, 1 (1991): 48-61.

13 J. Matthiasson, *Living on the Land*, p. 76.

14 Dahl, *Saqqaq*. Inuit women's highly developed sewing skills are legendary around the Circumpolar North. See, for example, Valérie Chaussonnet, "Needles and Animals: Women's Magic," pp. 209-226 in *Crossroads of Continents: Cultures of Siberia and Alaska*, edited by William Fitzhugh and A. Crowell (Washington DC: Smithsonian Institution Press, 1988).

15 J. Matthiasson, *Living on the Land*, p. 64. Brian and Cherry Alexander quote sealskin prices in the $60 range during the 1970s, but dropping to an average of under $6 by 1995: "Out on the Land," p. 143.

16 Crnkovich, "Women of the Kitaq," p. 35.

17 Crnkovich, "Women of the Kitaq," p. 35.

18 From Sarah Tokolik, "The Spence Bay Women," in *Gossip*, pp. 265-267. Angela Bernal conducted the interview and Kyra Mancini transcribed it for *Gossip*; the authors are grateful for editor Crnkovich's permission to use this interview.

19 Tokolik, "The Spence Bay Women," pp. 266-267.

20 Judy Hall, Jill Oakes, and Sally Qimmiu'naaq Webster document the critical role of sewing in the lives of Inuit women in *Sanatujut—Pride in Women's Work: Copper and Caribou Inuit Clothing Traditions* (Hull, Québec: Canadian Museum of Civilization, 1994); see also Marie Meade, "Sewing to Maintain the Past, Present and Future," *Études/Inuit/Studies* 14, 1-2 (1990): 229-239.

21 Tokolik, "The Spence Bay Women," pp. 266-267.

22 L. Weissling, "Inuit Redistribution and Development: Processes of Change in the Eastern Canadian Arctic, 1922-1968," PhD thesis, Department of Geography, University of Alberta, Edmonton, 1991.

23 Jill Oakes, "Climate and Cultural Barriers to Northern Economic Development: A Case Study from Broughton Island, NWT, Canada," *Climate Research* 5 (February 23, 1995): 93; see also Jill Oakes and Rick Riewe, "Factors Influencing Decisions Made by Inuit Seamstresses in the Circumpolar Region," pp. 89-104 in *Braving the Cold, Continuity and Change in Arctic Clothing*, edited by C. Buijs and Jarich G. Oosten (Leiden: Centre of Non-Western Studies, 1996).

24 Many Inuit women fish for enjoyment and to help supply their family's food. See Constance Hunt, "Fishing Rights for Inuit Women," *Branching Out* 4 (March-April 1997): 6-7.

25 The Minnguq Sewing Group in Broughton Island has achieved some success with training support from the Department of Economic Development and Tourism, University of Alberta, and Inuit Tapirisat of Canada. With the help of space provided by the hamlet, freezers from the Hunting and Trapping Association, access to Xerox machines from the Housing Corporation, and computer access from the schools, they have been able to create a "community-based sustainable development project with socially significant returns. Seamstresses used the by-products of seals, providing hunters with one small outlet for seal skin sales." They receive training and chances to develop entrepreneurial skills. Oakes, "Climate and Cultural Barriers to Northern Economic Development," p. 94; and B. Issenman and C. Rankin, *Ivalu: Traditions of Inuit Clothing* (Montréal: McCord Museum of Canadian History, 1988).

26 Maclean's, "Fashion, Inuit-Style," *Maclean's* (April 23, 2001), p. 20.

27 Alison Blackduck, "Pauktuutit to Continue Work on *Amauti* Protection: Rankin Workshop Impresses Federal Officials," *Nunatsiaq News* (June 1, 2001).

28 Leena Evic-Twerdin documented some of these stories in *Traditional Inuit Beliefs in Stories and Legends* (Iqaluit, NWT: Baffin Divisional Board of Education, 1991).

29 Geddes, "Northern Dawn," p. 28.

30 Odette Leroux, "*Isumavut:* Artistic Expression of Nine Cape Dorset Women," in *Inuit Women Artists*, edited by Leroux, et al., p. 18.

31 For a discussion of the role of the cooperatives in Inuit art, see Arctic Co-operatives Limited & NWT Co-operative Business Development Fund, *The Co-operative Movement in the North West Territories: An Overview 1959-1989* (Arctic Co-operatives Limited & NWT Co-operative Business Development Fund, 1990); and Frank G. Vallee, "The Co-

operative Movement in the North," pp. 43-48 in *People of Light and Dark*, edited by Maja Van Steensel (Ottawa: Department of Indian and Northern Affairs, 1966).
32 Jose Kusugak, "Inuit Art, History, and Culture, and Today's Politics in Inuit Canada," in St. Lawrence University, *From "Nanook" to Nunavut: The Art and Politics of Representing Inuit Culture* (Exhibition Program, St. Lawrence University Festival of the Arts, Canton, New York, February 21-March 7, 2001), p. 12.
33 Alison Blackduck, "Commentary: Exploitation of Inuit Children Must Stop," *Nunatsiaq News* (July 13, 2001). She pointed out that children have become the purveyors of Inuit art in the informal economy, because most artists (like most Inuit) live in public housing, where it is illegal to show or sell their art. Children go door-to-door and approach tourists in order to sell art made by their family members and friends. Blackduck calls for an end to this "child labour" and for more support for Inuit artists.
34 Minnie Aodla Freeman, "Introduction," in *Inuit Women Artists: Voices from Cape Dorset*, edited by Odette Leroux, Marion E. Jackson, and Minnie Aodla Freeman (Vancouver: Douglas & McIntyre/Canadian Museum of Civilization and University of Washington Press), 1994.
35 McGrath, "Circumventing the Taboos," p. 225. She concluded that Inuit women have favored autobiographical accounts of their early years rather than essays regarding their adult lives.
36 Bouchard, "Power of Thought: The Prints of Jessie Oonark," p. 7.
37 The federal and the territorial governments have contributed to the cost of the spacious new centre, opened in 1996, but public fundraising and private donors also expressed the high value placed on supporting the work of both female and male artists. Karen Albu, "Pang Print Makers Celebrate the Realization of Their Dream," *Nunatsiaq News* (June 14, 1996), p. 15.
38 Kathy M'Closkey, "Art or Craft: The Paradox of the Pangnirtung Weave Shop," in Christine Miller and Patricia Chuchryk, eds., *Women of the First Nations: Power, Wisdom, and Strength* (Winnipeg: University of Manitoba Press, 1997), pp. 121. See also Marybelle Myers, "Inuit Arts and Crafts Co-operatives in the Canadian Arctic," *Canadian Ethnic Studies* 16, 3 (1984): 132-53; and Donald Stuart, "Weaving at Pangnirtung, NWT," *Craftsmanslash: L'Artisan* 5 (1972): 16-17.
39 Maria Von Finckenstein, ed., *Nuvisavik: The Place Where We Weave* (Montréal: McGill-Queen's University Press and the Canadian Museum of Civilization, 2002).
40 St. Lawrence University, "Performance by Aqsarniit Drum Dancers and Throat Singers," in St. Lawrence University, *From "Nanook" to Nunavut*, p. 20; see also Franz Boas and H. J. Rink, "Eskimo Tales and Songs," *Journal of American Folklore* 2 (1889): 123-131; and Beverly Anne Cavanagh, *Music of the Netsilik Eskimo: A Study of Stability and Change*, Ph.D. dissertation, University of Toronto, 1979 (Mercury Series, National Museum of Man, Canadian Ethnology Service 82), abstract in *Études/Inuit/Studies* 6, 2 (1979): 161-162.

VI

THE BONDS OF INTIMACY

There's no starting or stopping of childbearing age—children are totally part of your life from birth to death.

—Leah

Photo 13.1 Three generations of the Qappik Family.

13

Love and Living Together

Being a pregnant teenager here is accepted more easily than it is in the south. We don't have the social stigma attached to adoption that you find in most of Canadian society.

—Saila

Qatsuq's Daughter

Photo 13.2 Waving the new Nunavut flag, April 1, 1999.

We meet Sheila Kunilusie, 31, and she learns that we had interviewed her adoptive mother, Qatsuq, a few years ago when the elder was close to 100.[1] This simple fact warrants an invitation to visit in the evening. Sheila, her husband, Billy, and their two young children, Charlie and Marina, live in this newer two-story townhouse with a view across the fiord. The walls of this spotless home are covered with homemade country crafts—hearts, pillows, frames, hats—all made with quilted floral prints. Sheila makes these herself (as do many women in the hamlet) and says she will teach Marina someday. Aptly, her mother has given Marina the middle name of Qatsuq. Qatsuq adopted Sheila as a newborn baby when she was in her 75th year. Sheila took care of Qatsuq when she "got old." During the woman's last few years, she would bathe Qatsuq and make sure her house was clean.

We tell Sheila the story of the fourth day of interviewing Qatsuq, when we asked if we could bring her anything before we left. She said some water was chilling in the refrigerator. When we opened the door, only two items sat on the otherwise bare shelves: a huge pot of boiled seal meat, supplied by a grandson, and a pitcher of water. Sheila laughs and acknowledges that seal was virtually all Qatsuq consumed, except for an occasional bit of whale blubber or frozen fish. She confirms that until 1992, when she died at 102, Qatsuq sat outside for an hour every day, regardless of the weather. Her birth year was 1890; when she described the whaling period with memories from her sixth year, she was painting a picture of life exactly a century before our conversation. Now, Sheila's daughter is going on six; her son, Charlie, is five years old.

Sheila was happy that her wedding took place before Qatsuq died. Her photos show Sheila and Billy on either side of the centenarian, Sheila's white gown and veil flowing like a bridal glacier. "She was coughing then," Sheila observes. "That was less than a year before she died."

After some small talk, Sheila almost reverently begins to show us the contents of an old box of papers, photos, and jewelry that Qatsuq left her. Old church cards show the dates and times of services. The photos record the significant events in Qatsuq's life. One crumpled black and white picture was captured in the early twentieth century, as the whaling period was ending. Later black and white photos from the 1940s and 1950s feature Qallunaat, and gifts from Qallunaat, including a double strand of pearls.

A pair of red button earrings with screw backs (probably from the 1940s) sparks a grin from Sheila: Qatsuq never wore them. Sheila pauses, and then offers them to us. Deeply touched, we thank her and politely refuse, suggesting that someday Marina might appreciate them. Next, she produces a silver ring, one more treasure from her mother's long life. Sakiasie Sowdlooapik, Qatsuq's great-grandson, has the diary she kept.

Qatsuq knew syllabics, probably because her father and mother worked at the hospital built in Pangnirtung by the Anglican Church long before the Resettlement Period. At 95 years of age, Qatsuq made a list in syllabics of all her children, grandchildren, and great-grandchildren, including those whom she adopted in or out, and those who had died. It was a very long list.

❧

Love and marriage have shifted onto the quicksand that often characterizes cultures in transition. Since resettlement, marriage rates have declined and time has substantially rewoven the warp and woof of Inuit family life. As centrally important as the family may be, younger Inuit women feel less inclined to embrace the legal and religious overlay of marriage. Family closeness exists without a formal ceremony. Quite simply, marriage holds few economic advantages for women, who have steadily gained in independence. Ironically, this "new" pattern of common law marriage parallels traditional custom, in which the community recognized a man and woman as a couple when they lived together and had their first child.[2]

The Reluctant Brides
"I would refuse and go my way"

In any culture, religious beliefs influence the decision of whether, when, and how to marry. After the missionaries began to preach the Bible in the late nineteenth century, Inuit women redefined the significance of commitment to their partner. No longer did family loyalty and sheer survival cement their relationship. Gradually, marriage took on a moral imperative: "In the religion days, it's better to be married under God."

The institution of arranged marriage persisted well into the 1970s, but women who were in their 20s and 30s could exert choice in marriage partners. Although the romantic imagery of a wedding, social pressures, and religious influences push Inuit women toward marriage, Inuit women are reluctant brides. An artist offers her blunt opinion: "We have a say in it now. If we don't want to marry, we don't have to. I never have been asked the question, but I know I would refuse and go my way."

People ask an unmarried couple, "When will you get married? There *is* a minister." As one young woman says, she is in no rush to enter contractual marriage: "For my kids' future, I don't want them to have to settle down at an early age like me." Jukeepa, who met her husband at a community dance 27 years ago, was 17 on her wedding day and 18 when she gave birth to her first child.

She feels sympathetic toward the women a generation behind her, for although she has not experienced these problems in her own marriage, she thinks fear of assault and alcohol abuse might be one reason the younger women hesitate to marry.[3]

Some women may avoid a trip to the altar because they fear marriage could break up the relationship. A 30-year-old salesperson echoes the trend toward remaining single: "I'm not married. I guess I don't believe in marriage. No, I do, but it just never comes by. I've been with my man for 11 years. No marriage yet, although we have talked about it." A lay minister observes: "Couples may want to have the perfect relationship before they get married. That's another problem, because a marriage is never going to be perfect. Two different people living together and working together and sharing together—it's never finished!"

Jukeepa reflects the pervasiveness of changing attitudes toward marriage: "There's hardly any marriage going on these days...once every year or two." A minister usually performs weddings. Expenses do not amount to much, Inuit women say, and do not present a deterrent to formal marriage: "You get married at church so anybody goes there. After the wedding, they usually have people over to the parish hall to have tea and baked stuff. Anybody goes there, too, so you don't have invited guests like you have down south." These new traditions were established after resettlement, in the late 1960s and early 1970s.[4] Apea emphasizes the factor of free choice in explaining why women are not marrying so readily now: "It just seems to be that way. They had to get married before, right away. The woman and man didn't even agree about it. The husband would ask for the lady and if the parents agreed, even if the woman didn't want it, they would get married. Now it works out better as a boyfriend." The decision to stay single stems at least in part from the fear of having to announce a divorce to a small community and in part from the threats of alcohol abuse, spousal assault, and infidelity that might place a woman in jeopardy, trapping her in a marriage she no longer desires. A failed marriage would result in feelings of guilt.

The reluctance to marry stems from a deeper logic. A woman from the south conjectures that "some girls would love to look at wedding dresses and to put them on because they're so pretty, but they worry that marriage will spoil everything." Beyond fear, economic instability discourages many couples from marrying. When asked directly whether finances might be a factor in declining marriage rates, women agreed. Jobs are scarce. If a 23-year-old male gets a woman pregnant, both of their choices instantly become limited: "Some people just live together and help each other, because they love each other and their children. They start to have problems and split up for a while." When economic uncertainty takes its toll, the door stays open. This pattern, in fact, seems to prevail in most Inuit post-resettlement communities and has more to do with lack of housing, lack of wage-earning jobs, poor hunting conditions, and the rise of domestic violence than with changing morality.[5]

Also reflective of the caution toward marriage, a teenager says that her mother took her father's last name when they married. After an unhappy relationship, she urged her daughter not to give up her own last name if she decides to marry someday. Lisa treads the same fine line between security and independence that women in many other cultures do: "I think I would keep my last name in the middle and then put my husband's last." Rhoda worries about how her adopted sons will find wives in the amorphous social context of free choice. Her natural sons "found wives when the booze wasn't up here too much." The younger generation concerns her: "I don't know what kind of woman they will take. I just can't imagine how it will be when they have to get wives; that puzzles me."

Women may have difficulty finding a man who is their educational and professional equal, as a young college student suggests: "I would get married in a year or two if I found a guy who will be an equal partner to me." Another adds: "Only if he is well educated, is more a mother than me, and has a job."

One single mother confides that she would marry if she could find a man she could trust: "I want a man who is handsome, educated, cooks, and loves me, *but* I'm afraid of a relationship that might be abusive to my son. I was abused." It is not uncommon for the man to "walk out" at some point. For example, Molly, 22, is unemployed and on welfare; she lives with her parents. She has two young babies, a year apart, each with a different father. Marriage was out of the picture: "They didn't want to have any kids. They didn't want to have anything to do with us." She is angry that neither man wanted to take any responsibility for their children or for her well-being. She did not plan on her life turning out this way: "Not the first guy, because we were planning to get married—he left us. The other guy I met in another hamlet. I didn't find out that I was pregnant until I was back here. By then he had already found a girlfriend and married her."

Her parents have been supportive by adopting one son and allowing Molly and the other son to live with them. Her current boyfriend "doesn't mind" that she already has two children. If they marry, she would take only the youngest son with her. Somehow it seems premature to worry about marriage, Molly says, since they have been going together only for a few months. Perhaps "someday."

Living in Common Law
"We're protected in a way"

Many women speak of common-law unions as a viable alternative to formal marriage. For example, Gloria, who works full time and describes herself as a regular churchgoer, describes her situation: "We thought about it and we're still thinking about it. Seems like we're waiting for the right time to get married; we've been living together more than eight years. When we finally have a quiet time in the evening, we try to talk about it. It seems hard when the kids are around. Marriage doesn't make any difference. It just changes your last name, that's it." Maggie, 24, agrees: "My boyfriend wanted to get married when we had our first child, but I don't know what happened. We agreed and we never got married!" After five years of living together, she can now claim to be married under common law, which takes some of the pressure off the decision to marry in the church. She could inherit his estate, and vice versa, if they were to draw up a will: "Or, if you're a working couple, you can fill out a form that says who would get what if something happened to you. You usually put your common-law spouse—just like a husband and wife. We're protected, in a way. We could get each other's pension."

For Sheila, living with her boyfriend feels comfortable: "I've never really thought of marriage." She is not sure she would like marriage; although her boyfriend has mentioned it, "We never really talk about it." After two years of living together, she continues to use her own last name; her first child also carries her last name but the second has his father's last name. The children of common law unions have the same legitimacy as do children of formal marriages. Their situation contrasts with that of children born to women who have no live-in mate.[6] Although early missionaries tried to define births to unwed mothers as "illegitimate," for the Inuit they represent an economic advantage rather than a social burden. This helps explain why grandparents often adopt such children in order to provide for them.[7]

Many women feel that a formal marriage would not have protected them anyway. Alimony and child support are mythical benefits in the case of underemployed or unemployed men. Instead, the extended family provides the cushion, as a 32-year-old health care worker explains: "If we run into that situation, we have support from our brothers or sisters or parents." A woman who lives with her common-law husband and two children believes that even without a formal marriage, "you can have the social workers help you get child support from the father. If you want to go through the court, you can find legal aid and call them up—there's one here in town." The message is clear: if a woman does not lose her protective rights by avoiding formal marriage, she has less incentive to take the vows. If the relationship fails, she does not have to face the humiliation of divorce.

The Stigma of Remaining Single
"A subtle class distinction exists"

Acceptance of living together depends in part on a woman's generation. Women over 70 understand that choice because they remember the time before missionaries insisted on the morality of a church marriage. Even in the old days, many Inuit women had relations with their future husbands long before a marriage took place. Many had their first child by someone other than the man they eventually married; usually the husband would adopt that baby into the family. Elder Sudloo paints a not uncommon scenario: "I was just with my mother. I didn't have a father. That's what I remember most, not having a father. I have brothers and sisters from when my mother got a husband. I was in my teens then."

Middle-aged women have difficulty understanding the modern propensity toward "just living together," as Loie notes: "In my time, I catch most of the culture that my parents had. We had to marry in the church when I was 17, not long after we got together." A 50-year-old single parent, Anna neither married nor lived with the man with whom she had her first and only child at 16. She raised the baby by herself, without much help from her family: "It wasn't too hard." Yet, according to an adult education specialist, even women who are upwardly mobile and achievement oriented dream of marriage and the status it entails: "I asked the young women in my class to write in confidence about their deepest heart's desire. Some who were 'living together' wanted to get married. A subtle class distinction exists in spite of everyone saying that it is all right to live together. Many young people who used to live together are getting married now."

Some elder women think that the younger generation does not try as hard in a relationship as the older married couples did. An 86-year-old great-grandmother disapproves of the resistance to marriage and the high incidence of breaking up: "Up here, the younger kids say, 'my boyfriend lives with me sometimes. Then I kick him out and he comes back after a week...we have an argument and he leaves again.' It's just up and down all the time. Most of them get along pretty well." Adds a woman in her 40s: "There's a lot of bed-hopping going on in town."

Typically, the consequence for choosing to live separately is also to raise one's children alone. In fact, Inuit lone parent families have increased from 12 percent in 1981 to 17 percent in 1996 (most of them women), compared to an increase from 9 percent to 12 percent among "other Canadians" during the same time period.[8] Older Inuit women are more likely to be single parents than any other older group of women in Canada, probably because of customary adoption. Usually the woman takes custody and care of the children after divorce, separation, or desertion. Women's wage earnings often support their families, particularly in the case of single mothers. Although their jobs tend to be lower in status and income than men's jobs, women seem to work more steadily. Peepeelee draws the connections clearly: "Lack of jobs...it's becoming a trend. More women are having babies and they should support them, but they can't do that all the time when there are no jobs. They have to depend on their parents and the rest of the family to look after the baby with them. Men, who are making them have babies, should find a way to help the women, but too many don't." Another woman in her 20s takes exception to this view:

> This does not sit well with me, because we as women also are responsible for our own contraceptives. It seems like everybody is blaming the fathers, but we mothers should have thought about it, too. I've had three kids with three different fathers, and I alone am responsible for bearing them because I didn't use any protection. Lack of self-esteem and self-worth make us forget to take care of ourselves. We had no education on the responsibilities of raising a

child alone—we were not prepared. It all comes down to whether you love yourself enough to discipline yourself and wait until you're ready.

Many Inuit women have adapted to single parenting, often at an early age. Rebecca, now 30, had her first baby at 20, never marrying. Lizzie, 20, has two toddlers, the first one born when she was 16. Her mother had her first child at age 17; neither married. Val, who has two young sons, has a "live-in boy friend." She had her first baby at 17, as her mother did before her. Their situations are not at all uncommon. Since leaving her husband, 33-year-old Rachel has raised three children herself. The first was born when she was 16: "It's hard, I can tell you that, but rewarding as well. I'm finding that I didn't really know myself then, but I'm climbing up the ladder. It's much easier for me raising my children alone, than staying in a bad marriage."[9] Rhoda, 45, echoes the belief that it might be better to stay single. Raising her children after divorce is easier than it was during a tempestuous marriage: "I didn't want my children around when we were fighting. I didn't want them to go through what we were going through. That was the reason we divorced."

Although Inuit women discern the economic fragility of the male role and understand that they may very well become the main providers for their children, they do not use contraception often or consistently.[10] Inuit women place a high value on their children. Customary adoption provides an alternative to contraception or abortion (see section below). Extended family childcare and the common perception of children as a necessary support in one's old age also influence the decision not to use contraception. Other factors include a lingering sense that children are an economic asset; that many babies ensure survivors; and that children signal male virility and female fecundity. Thus, Inuit view a child as a multifaceted blessing rather than as a liability.

Approximately 20 percent of Inuit women living in Pangnirtung bore a child during 1988, a relatively high birth rate compared to the south but typical of Inuit communities.[11] Observes a nurse, "As soon as a girl gets her period, she is viewed as being able to have children and that's okay—it's a natural part of life, not a concern here." As Jukeepa says, "Inuit like to have large families." Contraceptive use is very low among Inuit teenagers. For all females of childbearing age, about one in five uses birth control.[12] A health care worker confirms that "many teenage girls don't use contraception, although they worry about getting pregnant." Minors must obtain parental consent to obtain birth control. A nurse guesses that most women who *want* to use contraception feel free to do so now, although many deny the need for it: "They can easily become pregnant, especially when changing partners."

Inaccessibility of services and opposition from older women makes it hard to have an abortion. Ulayok, a 26-year-old health care worker, states that "abortion isn't very popular here." A nurse explains the procedure for abortion services and the dilemma that often accompanies the decision to have an abortion:

We can't perform abortions here, but we refer women to Montreal two or three times a year. The young women find it difficult. They're pregnant and they're in turmoil. The older society frowned upon women having an abortion. In addition, they have to go to Montreal, where they've never been. Then it could be $50 to $100, which doesn't sound like much, but to people here it is. Sometimes the woman gets down there and changes her mind. Probably about half do that.

Teenagers must have parental consent for an abortion, as in the case of contraceptive use, which presents another deterrent. Rose, a young mother, recounts her story: "I wanted an abortion because I felt I was too young to have a baby. My parents said I got into it and I would have to stick with it." Another woman agrees that pregnancies among young women can create problems:

We've been having abortions, the ladies here in town, and we have had a couple of very young girls having babies—12, 13. We talked about that in the women's group and agreed that the group would talk to the girls to explain things—tell them that we shouldn't have babies while we are so young. I just told my 11-year-old daughter about having her period. She hasn't had it yet. Later, I'll explain that you can't start going with boys until you are ready to have a child.

Elders frown on abortion. In their view, a young woman who is not ready to be a mother can adopt out the baby to her own mother, another relative, or an approved family. An informal "counselor" trusted by teens, Leena reports: "Girls are pregnant and their kids go into adoption. There are some short term relationships going on, but they end quickly." By far, the Inuit female's preference is for adoption over abortion. Teachers confirm that high school girls are more likely to have and adopt out their babies than to turn to abortion: "A couple of girls had babies and gave them up for adoption." One girl, who was only 16, said, "I don't want to become a bum like my sister." Her sister's boyfriend was tyrannizing her. Because she saw no way to extract herself from the situation, she gave her daughter up for adoption to her parents and came back to school "all gung-ho to get ahead."

Customary Adoption
"Usually her mother would take it"

Although customary adoption has its roots in ancient Inuit tradition, the practice is still important for contemporary Inuit families. Adoption is "a culturally sanctioned means of transferring membership from one family to another such that the adoptee's status in the second family is approximately equal to that formerly enjoyed in the first."[13] The Inuit refer to an adopted person as holding the status of *tiguaq*, which has its roots in the verb base *tigu*—literally to take or to hold. Thus, Inuit women speak of a child who was "adopted in" to the family or "adopted out" of the family into another home, weaving a "continuous web of kin and relatives."[14]

Historically, the practice of customary adoption was critical to survival: "The more people you have, the more you know you are going to survive." With tiny numbers and extreme hardship, there was no such thing as an unwanted pregnancy or an unloved child. For one thing, out on the land, a pregnancy that resulted in a live birth might not necessarily result in a thriving baby who lived past the first few days or months. Inuit mothers told Briggs "they don't love their babies until they are fat, or until they smile—that is, until the baby has a good chance of living."[15] Thus, the people learned not to take the birth and health of an infant for granted. Even before the days of bottles, Inuit women adopted each other's infants: "When babies got hungry, we would feed them meat, broken up like banana, broth, and water."[16]

In pre-settlement days, an Inuk woman did not have to feel embarrassed that she was having a child outside marriage, but out on the land it put her at greater risk in terms of survivability. Ulayok recalls the dilemma faced by her mother long ago:

> My mother was widowed when she was pregnant. Because she had no more man to look after her in hunting, she adopted her baby out as soon as it was born. Not long after, a man—my stepfather—wanted to marry her. She said yes right away, for survival. Otherwise, you're not very independent. So many families would look after you, bringing food and hunting for you. That's not a very good life for somebody who wants to be independent.

The practice of "customary adoption" persists into this century, and without the expense, psychological trauma, or isolation of children from their natural parents that typifies other contemporary cultures. According to a nurse, between a quarter and a third of all children in the community are adopted into a different family and some adoptions occur between Pangnirtung and Iqaluit or other Baffin towns.[17] Guemple estimates that, as opposed to the Canadian adoption rate of about one percent, contemporary Inuit adoption rates range from about 15 to 36 percent, depending upon the community. The rate has been higher in earlier decades (e.g., as much as 44 percent in Repulse Bay of the early 1920s and 70 percent at Coral Harbor during the 1950s), dropped after resettlement, and has been increasing again. As with the trend toward common law rather than formal marriage, this may be another return to more traditional modes of family structuring.

One couple adopted out a daughter who now lives in another settlement; the baby was born when the first child was only one year old. The mother reflects: "Maybe I was too young, but I didn't think I could handle it...two kids so close together." She is still in contact with her daughter by telephone and sees her occasionally. Kelly, 24, has a son who is adopted to her parents. She helps takes care of him; he knows his natural father:

He has two mothers. I regretted it a bit, but he has good life. I am really bad with money, and I couldn't consider abortion. Mom made the decision not to have an abortion; she said right away that she would adopt my baby. I was very depressed at being pregnant because it meant that I had to give up college. At first, we denied the baby; now I'm grateful to have him.

Guemple estimates that approximately one half of all adoptions occur when the child is under one year of age and most are by kin (especially grandparents). Often, the adoption takes effect right from birth and, indeed, frequently is arranged by the parents before the infant's birth:

The adoption of a child "on the spot"—i.e., without prearrangement—is [also] consistent with Inuit emphasis on spontaneity...and occurs with some regularity. Often if the parents of a newborn child decide that a child is not wanted, someone will express a desire to have it and the child will be given to them. In Repulse Bay...a mother took one look at her child and decided that she would not keep it. She took it home and laid it on the floor and said that anyone who would pick it up might have it. The child was eventually adopted by its grandmother.[18]

Often, a girl's parents or grandparents offer to adopt the infant, says Andria, 17: "If a girl my age got pregnant, and she didn't want to keep it, usually her mother would take it." Middle-aged parents find themselves raising infants and toddlers to assist their daughters, or to ensure a helping hand as they approach their senior years. Rita was only 16 when she had her first baby out of wedlock. She kept the baby and, when she married another man the following year, he adopted the baby. In turn, Rita adopted in her youngest son, now 18: "I really like him. He can help. He does what I ask him to do." Women who know that their baby will be given up at birth may try to maintain an emotional distance from the fetus that will facilitate separation. For example, Guemple reported a saying among the Aivilingmiut: "When a mother knows her child is to be given away, she won't let her love for it grow."[19]

Historically, conceiving a child before marriage made a woman an even more desirable mate because her pregnancy *proved* her fertility.[20] Community norms supporting adoption by family and friends continue to reduce the shame of conceiving out of wedlock, the necessity of entering marriage prematurely, or the tendency to slip into poverty just because of pregnancy. These cultural patterns also contribute to the highest rates of teenage pregnancy and childbirth in Canada. Instead of aborting a child, a woman explains, "we would rather adopt out, usually to our relatives." Pregnancy does not necessarily lead to a wedding because adoption offers an alternative way to ensure that children receive proper care.

Apart from the primary reasons of solving problems of infertility and ensuring that children are properly cared for, Inuit-style adoption helps keep extended families together and balances the sex ratio within each family unit.[21] The practice enables couples with infertility issues to adopt from a relative, friend, or neighbor. Adoption can also tie unrelated families together, create alliances, repay debts, keep families small enough to support under conditions of scarce resources, provide a home in the event of a parent's death or illness, or replace a child who died.[22] An older child can request adoption. Sometimes a difficult childbirth may influence the mother to give her newborn away in order to avoid "soul incompatibility." Older Inuit couples like to adopt babies in order to have a young person in the house as they age, and to ensure practical assistance in their declining years. Significantly, older women (including widows) adopt young children not only for companionship and help but also for "social renewal" and to continue a life of usefulness to the community.[23] For example, in the Belcher Islands, women say that "when babies are in the household an old woman feels young again... [but] when there are no young children about, a woman feels old and close to death."[24]

Adoption helps balance the sex ratio, as mentioned above. If a couple already has two daughters, they might adopt out a third female newborn if another couple close to them wants a baby—or needs a girl. This is not an expression of sexism, since the same situation would occur if the first two babies were boys:[25]

"WE'D LIKE TO HAVE YOUR BABY"

If you are pregnant, friends will come to you and say, "we'd like to have your baby, if you don't mind." It's planned ahead of time. The parents know they will let the baby go. The mother might be willing to make this decision if her other children are small. She'll be too tired to have another one...she'll be sick. So, to unload the burden off the mother, who's had all these children, they'll ask for the baby, regardless of sex.

In the North, not many people have abortions, because we have more opportunities to adopt—it's not that big a deal up here. It's not a shame or a disgrace for a woman to have a baby without being married. Inuit love their children so much that if they do get pregnant, they're more likely to have the child and adopt it out.

Guemple underscores the lack of stigma. The Inuit see no reason to arrange adoption of the child of an unmarried mother *unless she so desires*: "There is no need to punish her, no need for societal supervision of her or the child, and no need to 'protect' society, the mother or the child."[26] Families and friends handle adoption privately, without any fee or investigation. They know each other well and usually live in the same community. Registration of the transaction with social services is, in most cases, informational rather than a matter of government intervention. The Inuit view the process of adoption as a natural, logical, and efficient means of ensuring that families who want children can find them. Mothers who cannot give a child a good future feel comforted by knowing he or she lives in a secure, welcoming home. Even children with physical, mental, or emotional problems readily find a home. At least in the past, if the adoptive relatives died, a child had the right to return to his or her birth parents if no other arrangements had been made in advance.[27]

Julie, 35 and a health care worker, has four children at home and one adopted out: "I have two boys and two girls with me. When I was 18, I gave birth to a premature baby. I wasn't ready to take care of it, so I adopted it out." Sophie, in her early 30s and married since age 18, comes from a typical family—six males, six females, and one male adopted out to a family short on males. She herself has eight children—two adopted out, five at home, and one more she adopted in last year. She had a daughter first, then a son. The third-born child, a girl, was adopted out at her husband's request. After three more boys were born, the last male was adopted out, at her request: "The one I adopted in is from my sister. I didn't want anybody to adopt her from outside the family. The first one I adopted out was my husband's idea and the second was mine. It was a boy and I had too many boys."

As in times past, the male may have more power in deciding on adoption. For example, adopting her children out made Sophie "feel awful," but she accepted her husband's decision because "he's my husband and he's the boss." Similarly, Amy's friends wanted to adopt. When her mother was pregnant with a fourth child, they asked if she would be willing to adopt the newborn out to them. When Amy's mother refused, the friends asked her father, who concurred: "Mom never really agreed with the adoption but my father did." Two children had already died, so that left her mother with only one child at home. That was thirty years ago, when Inuit families still lived out on the land. Women feel that now the mother has more say in whether a child should be adopted in or out. Says one young woman, "if I didn't want to adopt a child out, I wouldn't. I don't know how I will feel later on—maybe I would agree—but not right now."

Women can use adoption in the case of failed birth control. One woman in her 30s, who has a stable marriage and works part time as a clerk for the hamlet government, has three children with her and one adopted out. Her first two children were born before her marriage. The second child was adopted out: "I was taking birth control pills and somehow I got pregnant. I didn't want to keep it." Her sister adopted the baby. When the sister died, her brother-in-law raised the child.

This pattern underscores the desirability and utility of children. A seamstress in her 40s has two natural sons, the first one born when she was 23. In addition, she has four adopted children, again balanced by sex: two boys, two girls. The younger ones still live at home, insurance against old age. Darleen, 19, has four brothers, "originally five, but one is adopted by our uncle on my father's side. And I have four sisters." The children range in age from 32 to nine years old. Their mother is 48, meaning that as she ages she has a child to look after her who is younger than if physiology alone had dictated the acquisition of children.

Perhaps the most fascinating aspect of Inuit customary adoption is that many children continue to have routine contact with their natural parents. In striking contrast to the shroud of secrecy that usually surrounds adoption in the south, Inuit children not only have contact with their natural parents but also sometimes very close relationships with them The adopted child knows the identities of the biological parents from the start—"there's no hiding" and no guilt or shame. In small settlements or out on the land, that information would be especially hard to keep secret. Primary loyalty usually rests with the adoptive parents, but both child and natural parents typically know and recognize each other; they value their special relationship.[28]

In one unusual case, two sets of twins were born to a couple within a year of each other—the second set (girls) was adopted out to the mother's sisters. Now adults, the twins agree that they never felt rejected by their mother. Says Helena, 48, "I quite understand why it was. My mother told me all about it when I got older, maybe in my 20s. I knew about it before that, because when I was 11 years old I had TB. On my way to the hospital down south, I landed in Iqaluit and had to stay overnight. That's when I met my real parents. They lived in an outpost camp when I was born and moved to Iqaluit later." Their relationship is friendly and they visit each other regularly: "I'm very close to them." Helena has adopted one of her own children out: "My daughter stayed with me and with her sister last night. We see her often, so I don't really feel like I lost her. I'm not as close to her as my daughter at home...maybe when she gets older...but I didn't care whether I see her or not."

The following story told by Quppa, 59, who grew up in a camp, illustrates beautifully the intricate bonds of family loyalty and responsibility:

"WE HAVE ADOPTED HER BY CUSTOM"

Adoption is very much part of this culture. Inuit think of children as always being part of one's life. People adopt for many reasons. For example, in my husband's family, there are five or six natural children, followed by five adopted children. I adopted my oldest child. She became part of our family in a strange kind of way. She is the natural child of my husband's sister. The traditional belief is that if you have three children of the same sex and you give the third child away, then you will get a child of the opposite sex. My husband's sister had two girls. When the third girl was born, she was given for adoption to my husband's parents. They live on the land year round, about 60 to 70 miles from here.

When the child was born, someone notified them to pick her up. The hospital would not keep the child and the mother was afraid that if she took the child home, she would be unable to give her away. She called me from the hospital and asked if I would keep this child until her parents arrived. I took her home from the hospital when she was two days old and I gave her away to my husband's parents when she was five days old.

When she was three months old, my husband's mother became ill with cancer. She was too ill to look after the baby, so we kept her. They had no place to stay. They were living in a tent. When the baby was months old, the adopting mother died. It was December and too cold to take a little baby on the land at 60 degrees below zero. They had to leave the child here for the winter. The original understanding was that when summer came, they would take the child back. Then they realized there wasn't a woman at the camp who could look after that child. My father-in-law asked if we would like to keep the baby.

We loved her very much by this time. We were attached to her and she was attached to us. We didn't want to deny his rights yet, so we told him that we would let him think about it for a while longer. We thought that perhaps when she was walking he would take her back. We waited and asked him again if he wanted to take her. He said that we could keep her. We have adopted her by custom, really, by the tradition that whoever in the family is able to look after the child would do so.

Traditionally, if the adopting mother died shortly afterwards, the baby would have gone back to the natural parents. By this time, though, the natural mother was pregnant again and she couldn't take care of two small babies. The next person in the family who was able to care for her would have the responsibility for doing that. The baby still calls my father-in-law "father." Her brothers are still her "brothers." She calls my husband not "dad" but "brother"! She calls me "daughter-in-law"! She is used to these terms—the relation of the person she is named after, not her birth relation. She is also named after the mother who passed away, so her natural mother calls her own daughter "mother."

Inuit women speak glowingly of customary adoption, but sometimes it presents problems. Adoptions of older children may not result in happy family relations and children sometimes experience a sense of uncertainty or lack of belonging.[29] In spite of the safety valve of customary adoption, "getting babies without any husbands" presents difficulties, especially for young girls who experience physical and emotional trauma during delivery. Occasionally, a woman changes her mind about losing the immediacy of the mother-child bond. In the case of Carolee, a young mother whose parents adopted her baby, she would like to take her son back if she marries her boyfriend (not the child's father). Since her mother is now her *son's* mother, her wish would probably not be granted. Carolee says she would not mind too much, because she can see him whenever she wants. Other mothers may not be as accepting.

Although in some cases Inuit children have not been fully informed of their status, or they have hard feelings about being adopted out, these cases seem the exception rather than the rule. The adoptive child is a "real child," and may not marry a biological child of the adoptive parents.[30] When birth parents observe that the adoptive parents are mistreating or neglecting the child, they will either pressure the parents to provide better care or, in extreme circumstances, attempt to reclaim the adoptee.[31] Some questions arise about whether children adopted into a family have the same status as adoptive grandchildren or a couple's own natural children. (People would introduce a child to us as "that's the fifth child—she's adopted in.") A teacher notes that parents seem to treat adoptive children equally. The children usually seem devoted to them in return: "One woman's adoptive parents' house caught fire, and she has given up her house for them. The daughter's living in a tent now."

Inuit women are no different from women in any culture who find it excruciatingly difficult to give up a newborn child, as Salome Awa describes:

I have three [children], but the first one was adopted by my brother. I had him when I was 19. He wanted a baby for a Christmas present so I gave him that. I wanted to keep the baby, but my dad said no, so we gave him away, which was very hard. I had him for three days before I went back to Pond Inlet. When you have your first child, it's a son, and healthy and cute, you just want him. ... [it still hurts]. When you give that child, you know he's not yours anymore. Right away, you start thinking "my brother's son." In Inuit history, obviously, adoption is very clear and traditionally, they didn't try to make it difficult...because you gave your child to your uncle or your brother so...you would see that child on a regular basis. I think that's better because you know he's OK and you see him regularly.[32]

Will customary adoption work for the next generation of women who have other interests and pressing responsibilities outside as well as inside the home? Modern-minded Leeta resists the idea that her generation should take care of *their* daughters' babies: "I never would! I'm a modern grandmother. I want my independence! It happens very often, though. I told my friend, don't look after your grandchildren—go fishing or go out on the land—you don't have to baby-sit anymore!" Leeta agrees that customary adoption is "very wonderful" because every child has a mother and a father.

Photo 13.3 Bundled up against the Arctic cold.

Notes

1 Her husband, Eevic, used only "Eevic." By that time, a woman took on her husband's name, so she was known as Qatsuq Eevic. Some families use "Evic."

2 See Guemple's description of the patterns of common law marriage, *passim, Inuit Adoption*, p. 80. Sylvia Van Kirk discusses the development of common law marriage ("*a la facon du pays*") between Native (Indian) women and whites during the fur trading era: "The Role of Native Women in the Fur Trade Society of Western Canada, 1670-1830," in *Rethinking Canada: The Promise of Women's History*, 3rd ed., edited by Veronica Strong-Boag and Anita Clair Fellman (Toronto: Oxford University Press, 1997). The length of cohabitation required for legal recognition of spousal privileges in inheritance, employment benefits, or support after dissolution of the union varies among the provinces and territories. As of 1991, 10 percent of all married couples in Canada were common law couples, according to the official census. Eichler, *Family Shifts*, pp. 44-45.

3 No one raised the possibility of women living together as loving couples. When asked directly about lesbianism, women insisted that this practice has never been accepted among the Inuit. Responses included: "I heard about two girls and it really grossed me." "They are white southerners and I know them. They are my friends." "People disapprove of it." "Unusual here."

4 Similarly in Holman, the first formal wedding with a "southern-style ceremony complete with white wedding gown and tiered cake" occurred in 1972—after resettlement. Stern and Condon, "A Good Spouse is Hard to Find," p. 211.

5 As marriage became less of an economic necessity in Holman, a decline in the marriage rate occurred that was similar to the trend we found in Pangnirtung. Stern and Condon, "A Good Spouse is Hard to Find," p. 213.

6 Guemple, *Inuit Adoption*, p. 80.

7 Guemple, *Inuit Adoption*, p. 81.

8 Jeremy Hull, *Aboriginal Single Mothers in Canada 1996: A Statistical Profile* (Ottawa: Research and Analysis Directorate, Department of Indian Affairs and Northern Development, 2001), p. 15

9 Department of Indian Affairs and Northern Development, *Highlights of Aboriginal Condition*, pp. x, 68. Inuit have the highest percentage of married couple families of all Aboriginal groups in the Canadian census (81% in 1991). The percent of single-parent families that were headed by women increased from 73.4% in the 1986 census to 79.9% in 1991.

10 Billson and Stapleton, "Accidental Motherhood." For comparative data on general perceptions and practices in Canadian families, see Angus McLaren and Arlene Tigar McLaren, *The Bedroom and the State: The Changing Practices and Politics of Contraception and Abortion in Canada, 1880-1980* (Toronto: McClelland and Stewart, 1980).

11 Statistics provided by the Pangnirtung Nursing Station. According to a study conducted in Alberta, "Indian/Eskimo women are considerably more fertile than the women of any other ethnic group, at all ages." Northern Development Branch, Alberta Department of Business Development, and Alberta Department of Social Services and Commu-

nity Health, *Alberta Family Planning Project No. 55-35070* (Edmonton: University of Alberta Press, 1970), p. 13.

12 Based on data provided by the Nursing Station at Pangnirtung.

13 Guemple, *Inuit Adoption*, p. 3, argued that the Inuit do not really practice "adoption" at all, but a form of child exchange that only loosely resembles what most people in the United States or Canada as a whole would consider adoption (a legal arrangement that historically resulted in anonymity of the birth parents). We would suggest, however, that the recent movement among adoptive children to find and/or learn about their birth parents brings the mainstream practice closer to the Inuit practice. Guemple pointed out that "the term for son, *irniq*, may be applied equally to a natural child and an adopted child... [implying] complete absorption into the family" (p. 5). The same would be true for a daughter.

14 Dorais, *Quaqtaq*, p. 66.

15 Briggs, "Lines, Cycles and Transformations." Guemple (in *Inuit Adoption*, p. 89) cited an older study by Dunning, who thought that Inuit adoption could be understood in terms of "the demographic hypothesis"—adoption is "an efficient means of coordinating population with production." Others have argued that the institution helps support the adopters more than the adoptees. Probably both views have merit in an economy characterized by fluctuations between scarcity and surplus.

16 Uyarasuk, "Rachael Uyarasuk (Inuit)," p. 262.

17 Guemple, *Inuit Adoption*, pp. 8, 85. Dorais places the adoption rate at about 32 percent, in *Quaqtaq*, p. 66.

18 Guemple, *Inuit Adoption*, pp. 9-10.

19 Guemple, *Inuit Adoption*, p. 11.

20 Guemple, *Inuit Adoption*, p. 31.

21 Guemple, *Inuit Adoption*, p. 2.

22 See Briggs, "Lines, Cycles and Transformations"; and Guemple, *Inuit Adoption*, pp. 28-29 and pp. 25-30.

23 Guemple, *Inuit Adoption*, p. 33.

24 Guemple, *Inuit Adoption*, p. 33.

25 Guemple reported limited data indicating that adoptions might historically have followed the preference for male children, but that contemporary trends might favor adoption of female children. Social service records, which would shed light on current patterns, were not available to us for Pangnirtung. *Inuit Adoption*, pp. 14-15.

26 Guemple, *Inuit Adoption*, p. 79.

27 Guemple, *Inuit Adoption*, p. 21.

28 Balikci, in *The Netsilik Eskimo*, also noted this phenomenon (p. 108).

29 Briggs, "Expecting the Unexpected," p. 261.

30 Jenness, *The Life of the Copper Eskimos*, p. 84. The same rule applied historically when children resulted from spouse exchange.

31 Guemple, *Inuit Adoption*, p. 23.

32 Quoted in McCluskey, "Talking of Shamans and Other Things," p. A23.

14

Marriage and Divorce

Fear and guilt run people's lives, then they finally realize what is happening.
They're in a vicious circle. It's good to see them breaking the patterns.

—Loie

Like Moths to a Candle

Photo 14.1 A modern day shaman does the drum dance in Iqaluit.

They say the shamans of old could fly over the land to see what dangers lay ahead. Wise beyond human bounds, capable of visioning past, present, and future, the shamans, both women and men, could help the people resolve conflicts and solve problems. They had no church, no wine or sacramental trappings, but the "good shamans" saw into the hearts and spirits of the people, the animals, the plants...of all living creatures. The "bad shamans often fought other people," a young woman believes.

Today, shamans appear in other forms. One woman sees through the terrors of domestic violence into the hearts of men who hate what they do. She helps them find their lost spirit so they can stop hurting women and children. She helps women find the spirit to resist and protest the abuse that floats like a rough wool blanket over the settlements. She tries to vision the future, using images of the past and reaffirmations of self-worth in the present. She listens as they try to reconnect broken hearts of today with the whole selves of yesterday. She weaves women together into support groups where they can tell the terrible secrets of abuse and assault. She helps them admit their own hurtful actions.

Like moths to a candle, seeking light and a vision to lead them over the land, they gather to her. Like the shamans of old, she has fought her own demons. She, too, has seen the white lights of agony and anger and guilt, blaming herself and hating men. She has also seen the light of healing and rebirth. She and her husband have found peace and healing in their own relationship.

She flies over the land, using the gift of modern technology rather than a trance, to live in Iqaluit, where the only shelter awaits the abused women and children of Baffin Island. She knows that when "man was the hunter, and woman was the bearer of children and made sure the hunter was clothed," abuse was less commonplace. "The roles have become very blurred in this time," she observes. "Often women have the 9 to 5 jobs to bring in money to let the man go out hunting. This works for some, but not for others."

Uncles, fathers, stepfathers make victims out of women and girls. She asks why the victims must leave their homes behind while the men walk free, but insists that the whole community must work together on healing, even those who do not face these special problems. Because she sees the dangers of flying ahead into a new time without bringing the tools of the past, she helps her people forge new tools out of the old culture and the realities of a turbulent time. So they will know her as a healer and teacher, the Reverend Loie Mike wears the collar of an Anglican minister, the first Inuk woman to be so named.

◌

T he causes of divorce are always complex. For older Inuit women, contact with white men drastically altered traditional attitudes toward marriage, divorce, and separation. For younger Inuit women, raised in settlements and with greater educational and economic opportunities, divorce still occurs infrequently because many have chosen not to marry in the first place. According to a Task Force on Spousal Assault report, women endure extreme pressure to stay with a man who hurts them or their children: "The concern to keep families and communities together appears to keep many victims from making complaints, from seeking help, or from leaving. Parents and grandparents encourage victims to return to their spouses for the sake of the children and extended family."[1]

The powerful aversion to divorce may be creating a community of victimized women who have nowhere to turn. Reimer described the priority given to family: "Cultural values give priority to the *ilagiit* [the] abused woman will garner support only so long as her reaction does not disrupt the family unit."[2] Otherwise, she will encounter criticism, gossip, and withdrawal of family support if she presses charges against a perpetrator. The pressure toward family loyalty cover up abuse: There is a "tension inherent in the dual obligation felt by Inuit women to support both the family unit and each other as individuals."[3] One woman paints a picture of pressure and blaming the victim:

> I was black and blue in the face and I had my kids with me. So I went to my grandmother's...when she saw me, she says, "Get out of my house." I said, "Why?" "Because you deserved everything you got..." She told me that it was my husband's way of disciplining me. The elders are still holding onto that, so that makes it harder for the younger generation to fight for their rights.[4]

Inuit women's groups have complained that the right voices may not be heard regarding abuse and assault. People listen to male but not female elders, or elders rather than younger women. To complicate matters, community justice initiatives may not be protecting women—sanctions are inadequate, there is too much probation, and sentences are too short. One woman asks rhetorically: "Where is the community support for separating or divorcing when the overwhelming message is, 'It's okay for men to do as they please with their women...and women, you should put up with it.'"

Women say that the community lacks trained counselors or therapists who could help them work on self-esteem issues. In reading a draft of this chapter, one young woman wrote in the margins: "There is no such thing as an educated counselor. They come once a month, so they don't know what is going on. We need a real counselor who will stay in town—who knows what is going on and is not hearing just one side of the story." Another complained that the nurses, who treat the physical results of abuse, cannot offer counseling help: "All they do is write what you say on the paper—but what is the point of writing on the paper when it's not going to heal that person? When another new nurse comes and reads it, she [labels] this person." In a small settlement in which everyone knows everyone else, finding a neutral, supportive and therapeutic relationship is extremely difficult: "Ever since I can remember, the social service office has been there for pay checks and not for dealing with people's problems. When you do talk to them about a relationship problem, if the person is their relative, they take that person's side. They don't follow the rules of their work."

Women who choose to stay in a conflictual relationship find themselves caught in a cycle of violence that only seems to get worse. The violence spills over to women's behaviour as well, as Leena points out: "Not only men do these things. It could be women doing this to a guy or their children." In any case, women become prisoners in the relationship because leaving may cost them the one thing they want the most—love and support of their family. A nurse completes our conversation: "If she leaves, she walks away from her whole life."

Divorce
"If you break this, God will condemn you"

Leena has seen both the avoidance of marriage and painful divorce: "The biggest problems are violence in families, sexual abuse, and partner abuse." Younger women rail against how some older ones seem to accept this from men: "My sister, my aunt—they don't deserve to be treated that way." The younger ones have a hard time understanding why the older women resist divorce.

The Legacy of Guilt

Among older women, whose marriages were arranged and for whom divorce meant severe social and religious repercussions, divorce is almost non-existent: "We were taught not to get a divorce when we get married. It's against the law or traditional Inuit belief." A social work aide observes that marriage can be hell, but divorce can be hell, too. "The old family members will say, 'My God, I thought you were a Christian—Christians don't break up their family!'" Many women delay or avoid a legal commitment when abuse mars their relationship or when they fear that it might. The social worker describes the vicious circle that ensnares some couples: "They take drugs and alcohol, they start to fight, they separate, and then they get back together again. That's the biggest reason they don't want to get married." Divorce for an Inuk woman is fraught with an overlay of sin and guilt, the legacy of nineteenth century missionary zeal.

Ovilu, who sees herself as a religious woman, feels perplexed: "I don't go out without putting my God in front of me. When I look in the Bible, it's not written that way about divorce. If I try to explain that to my parents, they say I'm false. Why? Because the Bible was translated by a Qallunaat preacher." According to an Inuk ministerial student, communication was difficult during the early contact period and missionaries overstated the Anglican position against divorce to impress upon Inuit couples the sanctity of marriage and the importance of commitment. The missionaries did not know how to explain the subtleties in Inuktitut, so confusion arose. The fact that Inuit are translating the Bible again and more accurately into Inuktitut comes too late for the transitional generation. In retrospect, the student guesses that "the impression was the wrong way—you shall not divorce your wife—if you do, you break God's law." The missionary phrased it that way to protect the institution of marriage, he says, but it backfired: "That just urges people the other way around. There's no love in it. There is condemnation in the promises they make. 'If you break this, God will condemn you.' They're afraid of that." In contrast, he believes that in pre-missionary times, when a couple was "really committed to each other, they thought they should get married." Stern and Condon theorize that the missionary zeal for marriage, and their preachings against spouse exchange and divorce, changed mating patterns in ways they might not have appreciated:

> Oddly enough, in their attempt to guide the Inuit from a "heathen" existence to a Christian life, the missionaries may have inadvertently contributed to an increase in illicit sexual activity by eliminating a culturally approved and open system of spouse exchange.[5]

Guilt forced many women to stay with their husbands even in abusive situations. "I'm not criticizing our religion at all," remarks Theresa. "I'm an Anglican. Mom and Dad are both very active Anglicans. At one time older people didn't agree with any separation or divorce, because of the church.[6] Mom had that on me for so many years, and I felt so guilty that I couldn't leave a bad marriage—back then but not today."

Confirming Theresa's perceptions, many older women say they are apprehensive about the high divorce rate among young Inuit families. Kudloo says: "I don't like all this divorce now. I believe in God, in that book—the Bible—that they shouldn't separate. It's both the man's fault and the woman's fault. When they get angry at each other, they go for a divorce or separation." She thinks they should try harder to solve their problems. In part, the greater instability of contemporary unions stems from the changing economic context of marriage and the changing definitions of a "good Inuk woman" and a "good Inuk man."

Infidelity, Jealousy, and Divorce

Estimations of attractiveness and personality characteristics weigh in heavily. Premarital sex and "fooling around" centers on these contemporary attributes rather than on whether a liaison will lead to a stable economic union.[7] Infidelity, and the jealousy that surrounds it, sometimes leads to divorce: "Many married couples get their problems by cheating one another." As with attitudes toward marriage, we have to return to mid to late nineteenth century to find the sources of change. Those who remember that period say that whalers treated Inuit women well, especially if they slept with them. For example, American whalers left a deep impression on the area when their boats bogged down in the ice, forcing them to winter over.[8] Qatsuq's grandmother became pregnant after a liaison with one of these men: "Even though Inuit women had Inuit husbands, they would 'see' a Qallunaat. If women went to bed with them, the whalers would be very good to them and their whole family. The husbands didn't really mind. Maybe some were angry, but everybody is different. We'll never really know what happened. The book is finished."

From earliest contact, some RCMP reportedly had affairs with Inuit women. There were complaints, according to an Inuk constable: "It did happen and does happen. I don't think the RCMP cleaned up its act. The RCMP decided to accept married men around 1975. Now most of the guys on the force are married and have kids. Back then you had to be single and stay single for up to twelve years before you could get married. If a single guy in a community cannot marry, of course he's going to have affairs. It has nothing to do with being a policeman. I'm sure there will still be some more blond-haired, blue-eyed Inuit." In some northern circles, he continues, "it was the accepted thing to have an Inuk or a Dene [Indian] girlfriend, because there is nobody else around." Another officer says he has not heard of that happening in this particular community.

Out on the land, men had more liberty when it came to having affairs than did women. People were punished severely for breaking rules that bound people together, but women were punished more severely for adultery. Says an elder of the twin fires of jealousy and gossip: "The two worst things that could happen to a woman in the camp was for other people to say that she was a gossip or that she was a woman that could be had by any man. Gossips cannot be trusted, and loose women not only are resented but also can be the cause of serious trouble between men."[9] A woman could do very little if her husband slept with another woman, though her heart was breaking and her temper fanned. An elder recalls:

> I remember being so hurt one time that I was determined to smash my husband's rifle in half, then go over to his girlfriend's tent at night and slash it to ribbons. My friend's husband decided to take a young woman along on a hunting trip. She was so angry that she attempted to turn over the canoe and didn't care if she drowned along with the younger woman.
>   I remember the time that my husband crawled into bed and wanted to get on top of me. I told the old fool...politely...to go and undo his pants in his girlfriend's tent. I guess I was a pretty independent woman.[10]

Some say that problems like infidelity typically occurred only during "good times," when there was a surplus of food and "they would start to go after another man's wife or another woman's husband." When they were working hard, fighting the specter of starvation, "that kind of fooling around" was uncommon. (Female infanticide may have led to imbalanced sex ratios, which could also have triggered fierce competition for women and resulting jealousies).[11] Poor communication can also contribute to marital instability (see Chapter 5).

A ministerial student offers three weeks of premarital counseling. The sessions focus on open communication and the meaning of marriage: "I usually show one filmstrip that talks about the Common Prayer Book, and what we really mean. I talk to them about my own marriage, what I thought when I was younger, and my experience with helping couples solve their problems. It seems to help." He wants to reword the ceremony "sometime in my future" to emphasize the love and sharing that characterized earlier generations. Rewriting the service would help clarify the commitment in terms that Inuit couples could embrace more easily: "We need a better way to word the matrimony."

The Stigma of Divorce
"It must be your fault"

Even if the decision is in response to persistent abuse, a woman who seeks divorce elicits scorn and rejection from her community. She feels stymied and risks severe stigmatization. Contemporary Inuit women can decide whether to marry, can choose their own mate, and can opt for divorce if the relationship fails. Still, the freedom to make choices carries heavy costs and the incidence of divorce remains low among Inuit women. Inuit women suffer as all women do from the social stigma associated with divorce, not to mention the usual legal and economic difficulties.

People perceive the woman as the one who should "keep everything together...it must be *your* fault that you're getting a divorce." The assumption, especially among older Inuit, is that the man can do no wrong: "He can be very hard on his wife and she has nothing to say. She must continue to serve him. If he complains to her parents that she is lazy or not good to him, they are angry with her and will even beat her."[12] Are parents more likely to be critical of a woman who chooses divorce? Says elder, Martha: "Whenever I hear about somebody who just separated or divorced, I always feel unhappy. I also love them, and I would not show my sadness because they're from the same community, but it's as if they're strangers. It's difficult to let your love show if you don't even talk to them." Lena says her parents dislike her separation:

> It's not my friends. It's my family. Mom, especially, doesn't believe in divorce or separation. The woman is supposed to keep it all together. The woman has to make up after a fight. It's always the woman!
> I'm in a support group. I talk to people whenever I need to, or they call and ask me to come over. I'm not alone. I have a friend whose boyfriend very badly abused her, mentally and physically. The boyfriend's mother came to her and cried right in front of her, "Don't leave him—go back to him! I'll pay your airfare, so you can be near him." He's in jail right now. They don't have any

idea what the woman goes through. Mentally, especially...they don't see what's there. They can see the bruises from battering, but they don't see what's inside.

This comment underscores a common understanding: The mentally abused woman may suffer as much as the physically abused victim does. A man can destroy her self-esteem and faith in commitment.[13]

Traditional Ways to Resolve Conflict

If divorce is not the answer, some feel that returning to the traditional mechanisms of conflict resolution and problem solving might be more fruitful. In the past, when the community became aware of disruptive marital problems, a delegate would give the partners a "tongue-lashing" at a public feast: "The couple who had disturbed the peace would be humiliated, and at the end would be 'told to keep a harmonious relationship.'"[14] More recently, a thinly veiled rebuke might be incorporated into an Inuk lay minister's sermon on Sunday morning. One elder believes that "it would help the couples now if the parents sat down with them and told them about the long life ahead of them," as they did traditionally: "As long as they don't shout at each other, sitting down and talking is the best way."

For Sara, 39, whose husband battered her for years, the traditional mechanisms may not work in a contemporary setting. Rather than proceed with a divorce, Sara decided to tell family and friends that her husband was hitting her—in keeping with the traditional method of turning to the extended family for help. He stopped the hitting, only to replace it with mounting verbal abuse. She cannot understand why her husband seems so unable to communicate positively, especially when he claims that he still loves her and wants their marriage to work: "From what I've been through—and from talking to the other girls and the men about family violence—it's the way they were raised that's not working in today's pace."

Yet, as a homemaker, Sara immerses herself in traditional hunting, camping, and cooking. She respects the idea of the old mechanisms and she reserves her right to take the elements of tradition that truly work for her. Her parents raised her to accept any kind of treatment, "because love and sharing and forgiveness will cure it all" in time. Now, Sara is ready to tell her parents that what they taught her is not working: "Look, I'll use what you taught me but to a point where I don't have to take it anymore. I'll use their way because it's how *I* understand things, not because they told me to do it." Sara says her family cannot understand why she would not keep trying to make her marriage work.

Notes

1 J. U. Bayley, *Task Force on Spousal Assault* (Yellowknife, NWT: Government of the Northwest Territories, 1985), p. 10.

2 Reimer, "Female Consciousness," p. 87.

3 Reimer, "Female Consciousness," p. 87.

4 Quoted in Griffiths, et al., *Crime, Law, and Justice among Inuit*, p. 203.

5 Stern and Condon, "A Good Spouse is Hard to Find," p. 202.

6 Stern and Condon also found only two "divorces" among the Copper Inuit of Holman, NWT, between the 1940s and their 1982-83 research. By 1988, however, they discovered many divorces and separations as they updated their household census records. As with our findings in the 1990s, that pattern shifted toward later pair bonding, fewer marriages, more common law relationships, and more separations. "A Good Spouse is Hard to Find," p. 202.

7 Stern and Condon found the same pattern in Holman: "Most of the teens we interviewed in 1983, both boys and girls, cited personality rather than physical characteristics as desirable qualities in a potential spouse, even though physical attraction was clearly important for sexual partners." ("A Good Spouse is Hard to Find," p. 213).

8 Later, they chose to winter over when they realized they could safely do so.

9 Quoted in Hallendy, "Reflections, Shades and Shadows," p. 7.

10 Quoted in Hallendy, "Reflections, Shades and Shadows," p. 9.

11 Balikci, *The Netsilik Eskimo*, p. 175.

12 Quoted in Hallendy, "Reflections, Shades and Shadows," p. 7.

13 For research confirming the impact of sexual abuse on self-esteem, see Mark F. Yama, Stephanie L. Tovey, and Bruce S. Fogas, "Childhood Family Environment and Sexual Abuse as Predictors of Anxiety and Depression in Adult Women," *American Journal of Orthopsychiatry* 63 (1993): 136-141.

14 Muckpah, "Remembered Childhood," p. 41. Briggs observed this custom once among the Baffin Inuit in mid-twentieth century. "'Why Don't You Kill Your Baby Brother?'" p. 163.

VII

THE CHALLENGES OF CHANGE

Back then they didn't have alcohol, they didn't have drugs, and they didn't have planes so the man could just take off.

—Ovilu

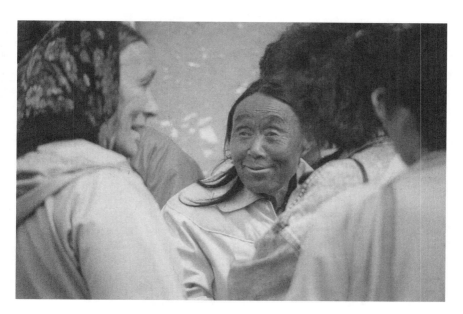

Photo 15.1 Elders at the opening of the Angmarlik Center.

Violence against Women and Children: The Complexities of Power[1]

We hear about it a lot in this generation. Then, and now, we talk about the weather, about food, about hunting—about anything but what is hurting us.

—Leah

Coming of Age in the Midnight Sun

Photo 15.2 Two girls run through the hamlet in summer light.

The doleful wails of a child outside our window wake us out of a deep slumber. Curiosity wins over the need to sleep, so we peek through the flowered curtains to see what small creature could be making such a huge racket at one o'clock in the morning. A two-year-old boy is screaming at his mother, who calmly walks thirty feet ahead, her five-year-old daughter in tow. The boy winds his tantrum up to a frantic pitch, but the woman deliberately plods on, throwing a few words of comfort over her shoulder. By the end of the block, he has closed the gap between them, dried his eyes on his denim jacket sleeve, and decided that companionship beats isolation. She talks to him now as if nothing had transpired but a quiet walk through almost deserted streets in the midnight sun. Not once has the little girl let go of her mother's hand, though she has thrown a few inquisitive glances back toward her wayward brother.

Less than an hour later, peals of laughter and the exuberant "varooms" of two eight-year-old girls riding bikes pierce our dreams. They careen along the gravel street, energetic and unencumbered, making circles and leaping ditches on their mechanical steeds. We watch as they slip off the bikes, laughing and kidding each other about their daring maneuvers. Free as the birds that play along the cliff face above town, the girls develop an unusual strength and autonomy nourished by almost total liberty. Nevertheless, a basic contradiction appears in this scene. It seems safe here, outside, in the summer night. For some girls, it may even be safer than inside their homes, where they fall prey to incest and molesting by uncles, stepfathers, fathers, and other men "because we live so close."

Children need more protection than they now receive from their loved ones. Yet, closer supervision might contradict the positive effects of the unusual lack of restrictions. Partly because of the smallness of the community, partly because of the lack of vehicular traffic, little girls also grow up with many opportunities for developing independence, autonomy, self-assurance, and creativity. Liberty engenders confidence and empowerment as girls mature toward womanhood.

One woman says she would not let her daughter, 6, play outside in the subdued light of a summer night, although she grew up with that freedom. She paid the penalty as a young teen of too little supervision. A man, who believed that it was his culturally approved right to use any female as his private possession, molested her. It was a lesson about being a woman, taught to a girl, that she has never forgotten. When, as an adult, she confronted her abuser in a public manner, people condemned her as a troublemaker. The age-old prerogative of sexual domination that men assume over girls in so many cultures undergirds the economic and political inequities that emerge later in life.

CR

ince the inception of Nunavut, "day-to-day life in the settlements hasn't improved all that much... [the settlements] may become Arctic ghettos plagued by increasing rates of crime."[2] Clairmont explains the comparatively high rates of crime in Nunavut in terms of three major causes: "Colonialism, patterns and policies of concentrated settlement, and alcohol and substance abuse...the major, ultimate explanatory factor is colonialism which set in train other destabilizing causes and interacts in complex ways with alcohol and drug abuse...."[3] Clairmont emphasizes, as did our consultants, the disproportionate contributions of young males to criminal and deviant acts, incarceration, and suicide. For example, Nunavut males were charged with 676 crimes of violence in 2000 (up from 484 in 1999). In contrast, female rates were far lower than male rates and dropped slightly: they were charged with 119 crimes of violence in 1999 (compared with 98 in 2000).[4] Clairmont echoes the words of our consultants in trying to make sense of the male-female differential:

> Males are, in very significant numbers, reportedly angry, confused, ill educated, and underemployed compared to their female Inuit peers, striking out at themselves and others, and locked in anti-social alcohol and drug abuse adaptations. There appears to be no effective justice system response to their behaviour and very few therapeutic resources have been targeted at this status group...that makes it the lightening rod for the negatives of colonialism, decline of family and community controls and ineffective justice system response.[5]

Of all violent crimes, Inuit women identify spousal assault as the most serious. Spousal assault (the term most Inuit women use in conversation) describes violence between couples (including female assault of males, which occurs less frequently), regardless of formal marriage status or living arrangements. Every year in Canada, an estimated one million women are beaten by their husbands.[6] Acts of violence against women deeply affect Inuit communities and sound the alarm that gender relations are far from balanced in a time of rapid change. A woman may face the double challenge of maintaining a family under pressure while taking care of her own safety and that of her children. Spousal assault suggests unresolved problems with economic dependency and assumptions about male dominance. It also raises questions about how to resolve such conflicts in a way that is compatible with Inuit culture, traditional and emergent.

Rebecca Kudloo, who served as Eastern Arctic Vice-President of the Status of Women Council of the former NWT, has called for a more realistic view of domestic violence, because she believes people tend to ignore the devastating statistics for the Inuit: "Shelters don't cause the breakup of families or suicide; violence does.... We are living in an epidemic of violence," which causes suffering but also, in our estimation, serves as a symptom of deeper structural problems in Inuit society.[7]

Hicks suggests that southern Canadians might be shocked by learning that "living conditions in a region comprising a fifth of the country resemble those of

Third World countries."[8] As an RCMP officer noted, "There's more assault here than in the south of Canada, who are becoming more educated into realizing that they don't have to take it...women up here still think they have to take it."

Whatever the causes, and they are complicated and many, community members, government agencies, the RCMP, and researchers leave no doubt that the rates of crime and violence in Nunavut, especially violence against women and children, are unacceptably high and must be lowered with all due speed.

The Traditional Patterns
"Everybody got along"

Although anthropologists have reported "repeated wife beatings and jealousies and hatreds" prior to resettlement, it is significant that older women perceive a substantial increase in the rate of spousal assault since resettlement.[9] Rape was uncommon out on the land and rare in established camps, where people had to face each other day after day. When Major L. T. Burwash, an engineer-explorer who worked for the Canadian Department of the Interior, conducted an economic survey of the southern Baffin Inuit in 1923, he wrote of Pangnirtung: "Crime is practically unknown among these people...."[10] Simatuk, who is 79, recalls that rape and affairs were unusual:

> Only once in a long while the wife cheated on the husband. There never used to be those kinds of problems. Everybody got along, working with each other. Nowadays, it's happening more and more. For some, the problem is alcohol or drugs, but when they get too much on their minds because their kids are up to something bad, they start worrying and fighting.
>
> When I was young, when men tried to come on to me, I said no and they would just go away. It didn't bother me; but now if someone tries to rape a woman, even if it doesn't happen, we worry about it for a long time. I don't understand that, why women worry about it so long afterwards. It didn't bother me, I was just happy that it didn't happen.

The elder women agree that for many reasons violence between intimates was also rare in an earlier era: "We were told not to do things like that." Leah insists that she never saw violence in families when she was a child: "It all seemed like happy families." Most of the women old enough to remember life in the camps say that people considered family violence despicable. An elder remembers only one case of "a lady being hit." The incidence of such events is much more alarming now, she adds. Still, violence between intimates existed in the camps, as one woman insists:

> Men could do anything to women and girls sexually and no one talked about it. There might have been less domestic violence in the camps, but women certainly suffered. Rape and incest happened. It damages everyone, including the men, because they lose self-respect. I went right up to the man who raped me when I was 14 and said, "Remember what you did?" It was right in front of

other people, so that made them angry, but it helped me heal. He is weak now, but he was stronger than I was then.

While domestic violence was undoubtedly easier to deal with in the immediacy of camp life, in many camps rivalry over women occasionally led to wife stealing, fighting, and even killing.[11] Women and men concur that few problems existed between married couples. Two hundred years ago, if husband and wife did not get along, they could break up. The man could take another wife—even more than one in certain circumstances. The unhappy wife could simply announce that she was finished with her husband, even a hundred years ago, but for her the penalty was high, as Ovilu points out: "She could say that, but she would be left alone. Not shunned or abandoned, but it would be very hard for her to get another husband. If she was on her own, she wouldn't survive because she wouldn't know how to hunt." Thus, the importance of the male's provider role cemented the wife into her marriage, happy or not. Informal social control operated against the man as well. Kuluk, a counselor in her 40s, details the old ways:

"TAKE A HIKE!"

If other people heard that a woman's husband was hurting her, they would protect her. The elders or others who felt concerned would go to the husband right away. They would tell him, "If you don't stop that—if you don't wake up and realize what kind of mistake you're making—then take a hike!" It was never shunning or rejection, but if he kept doing that, they would tell him, "It's not nice to hit your wife. She's your *wife*! You're not allowed to do that. It's not our nature. If you can't control yourself, let us help. If you don't want help, forget it and take a hike." He would have to change or leave.

If the woman *was* doing something wrong, the elders would come to the woman and say, "You're not being a good wife." If her husband was beating or neglecting the woman, the elders would come forward and help her.

Although some men argue that it was acceptable for a man to hit his wife, and maintain that they can still do so if she fails to obey, Quppa counters that argument: "We say traditional, but was it traditional? If you look back at our culture, assault wasn't traditional. There wasn't a lot of wife beating out on the land, because there weren't all the social pressures. Maybe the wife beatings became more prevalent as the social pressures increased. Then we accepted it. I can beat on her...she's my property and she's supposed to obey."

Martha compares life in the camps to life in the settlements: "I don't really know why men beat up their wives now, but in the old days men used to go hunting every day if it was good weather. If the weather was bad and the men had to stay home, they became irritable and angry. More men are staying home nowadays, and some even baby-sit—maybe it makes them feel weak. Maybe they get angry." She was raised to know that if a man becomes angry or hits his wife, "you don't have to hit back or talk back because you know the man is stronger than you."

The Contemporary Patterns
"I hear rumors"

Violence between intimates certainly presents a problem for contemporary Inuit women. The RCMP reported ninety sexual assault cases in 1999 and eighty in 1998, in Nunavut as a whole, but those figures represent only those cases in which a victim or the police brought the assault into the light, and they do not include the far greater numbers of non-sexual physical assaults.[12] Because of the devastating consequences in tiny communities, Inuit women consider interpersonal violence to be a major issue.

Rates of Spousal Assault

The rates of domestic violence vary from community to community, depending on size, relative economic prosperity, and, perhaps, the availability of alcohol. Smaller, tighter communities, especially those that prohibit the sale and/or consumption of alcohol, are less likely to have severe problems in this area. Generally, larger communities tend to have higher rates of domestic violence. Social control depends more on formal rather than informal strategies and deviant behaviour is easier to hide from extended family and friends in larger hamlets.[13] Poorer communities show higher rates of violence because economic stress magnifies other problems. Employment is not an antidote to spousal assault, however; many cases involve employed males.

The percentage of Inuit adults who feel that family violence presents a problem in their community ranges from a low of 20 percent in Lake Harbour to a high of 65 percent in Cape Dorset. Responses in Pangnirtung weigh in just above the regional average of 50 percent.[14] Wood's study of twelve Baffin communities documents the uneven rates of violent crime, even though the communities share small size, remoteness, and homogeneity of population. Many couples seem to remain untouched by violence between males and females. As one young woman says, "Not all the men are like that. My husband and I work together very well." An Inuk minister has seen spousal assault in other northern communities: "It's just about the same. It's all over." He was based in Northern Québec for several years, traveling to a different community every two weeks. This experience gave him a wide-angle lens on the issue: the same kinds of problems appear in a slightly different form or communities handle them differently, but domestic violence is pervasive. The major problems come from "other than our culture," he believes. Problems between couples are universal and persistent, "because that's a never finishing job."

Often, spousal assault surfaces only in the occasional call for police, nursing, or counseling help, or in the unexplained bruises. Even in towns where people suspect that spousal assault rates are high, they seldom hear anyone talk about it. As Udluriak, in her 50s, comments: "It's something that is very private. It happened to a couple friends of mine, but it's something that they just don't want to discuss. I hear rumors, and I see the black eyes and the bruises." Differing views on the incidence of spousal assault stem in part from the frequent "invisibility" of violence between intimates: "Women will not discuss it even with their families or friends," says Reepa: "We hear about it once in a while. My sister has been beaten up by her husband...I've heard about other people." In the past, Inuit women would keep violence and abuse to themselves, perhaps feeling ashamed of it. Now they dare to come forth more often, but too many prefer to keep their tribulations quiet. A woman risks being forced to "leave the camp," symbolically at least, if she seeks divorce in order to stop the offending behaviour. Stigma, shunning, and criticism may haunt her for years. Nonetheless, posters against domestic violence line the walls of the women's hut, the *kitaq*, bravely protesting the troubling presence of battering among an ordinarily peaceful, cooperative people.

A male RCMP officer says that in Iqaluit, which is far more diverse than Pangnirtung (and four times as large), the police receive a far greater number of family violence calls. In Pangnirtung, few calls come in to the RCMP; most involve younger families: "We used to get more. It seems to be getting better, or maybe somebody else is hearing about it other than us. The Mental Health Committee is becoming involved in spousal assault." He characterizes this community as relatively quiet: "Break-ins and drunks. Disturbing the peace. Those are the main calls. Very few family problems."

Another male officer claims, "The women don't really have a problem here. Maybe a few get beat up by their husbands." He bases his conclusions on the fact that he does not see the bruises or black eyes that typically suggest unreported assaults: "We're lucky here that we don't really have that problem." This comment supports the complaint by many Inuit women that police often fail to define domestic violence as a serious offense and as a criminal act. A female member of the RCMP force offers another view:

"THERE'S A FEAR IN THERE"
Man *is* the head of household. Not a lot of Inuit men pitch in with cooking and cleaning or taking care of kids. They come and go as they please. Many of the women are working, and their men don't—they go out hunting and fishing. When you are there with both, he does most of the talking. It's very difficult to get her to say anything; what he says goes. Much of the spousal assault and abuse goes unreported. Not one tenth is reported to this office. The women think this is their lot in life. They make excuses for the men: "He was tired. I should have had supper ready. I made him mad. He was sleeping and the kids woke him up, so he beat me." They don't understand that they don't have to accept that. You see women around town with visible signs of beating...bruises. You hear it through the grapevine. They think telling us will make it worse. This policy of zero tolerance may drive reporting underground.

A nurse agrees with our consultants: she estimates that professionals see "only a quarter of what is actually happening." Although most cases do not require medical treatment, she believes spousal assault represents a serious problem: "It's something that the whole community must address. Women want help at the moment, but it's a cycle—they just go back. The community should have a support group—and they're trying." Many younger women state clearly that they do not have to tolerate spousal assault anymore. With optimistic views of the future as male and female roles begin to rebalance, these women characterize couples in the new generation (under 25) as "happy." In the late teen group, assault seems not as prevalent, women observe.

Causes of Spousal Assault
"I don't want it to happen"

Explanations for family violence abound, as do the difficulties in coping with its impacts on both families and communities. Women and children have suffered from these modern ills, all too often victims of the men who are themselves victims of violence and abuse in their own upbringing, and of the disruptions brought by resettlement. Wood found "little support" for a clear link between crime and economic underdevelopment or low incomes caused by a declining seal industry. However, he found that being resettled off the land into hamlets seemed to correlate with unusually high rates of violent crime. In other words, economic underdevelopment in itself may be a less powerful predictor of violent crime in Inuit communities than the social, political, and economic earthquakes caused by relocation and resettlement (which is exactly what our Inuit consultants report). Resettlement creates upheavals throughout the social system and shakes traditional values and lifestyles. As it happened in Pangnirtung and other Baffin communities, resettlement also caused economic dislocation and underdevelopment. We believe that, in practical terms, the two phenomena cannot be separated—both laid the groundwork for domestic violence and other forms of deviant and criminal behaviour.[15]

Inuit women cite the social tremors and loss of balance caused by moving into hamlets, superior male physical strength, alcohol and drug abuse, male jealousy, and failures in interpersonal communication as the crucibles of violence between intimates.

Loss of Balance in the Settlements

Role reversal and women's successful adaptation to settlement life may constitute the key underlying reason for alarming spousal assault rates that beleaguer northern communities like Pangnirtung. Kuluk, who is trying to reconstruct traditional mechanisms for coping with domestic violence, observes that Inuit men "do not want to work because they know that they can get welfare, which is wrong." She adds that ever since resettlement, dependency on government assistance has hurt relationships between men and women: "The government totally makes you a wimp. You can't do anything—you might as well dry out. That's the image we were given. We didn't ask for it, but that's what the men say—

'I've been hanging on a clothesline too long.'" One way men feel they can restore the balance of power, she guesses, is to hit the women.

A man might exert abusive power when he perceives his woman as the dominant force in the relationship. Rachel, a housing officer who separated from her husband, explains: "In my case, I was working and he was not, so the relationship didn't work out. It seemed like he was threatened about anything." Brody also documents recent changes toward female dominance, citing a sharp and inevitable shift in the traditional balance between men and women:

> The wife in many settlement families is now clearly the dominant partner. Such women send their husbands on errands, do not hesitate to serve themselves first with the best pieces of meat, and feel quite entitled to enter extramarital sexual liaisons without regard to their husbands' views of the matter.[16]

A high school teacher concurs with this characterization of women's dominance: "This idea of women having a right to speak, or young people questioning adults, is not an indigenous idea, but it is important." Women learn through the media and school that many types of power lie within their reach. They test it out, which triggers disruptions in the home. The Canadian Panel on Violence against Women stressed the impact on family violence of "a fundamental imbalance of power between men and women."[17] For aboriginal people, the imbalance nests inside the inequality that exists between aboriginal and non-aboriginal society. The resulting humiliation and frustration can provoke violence in some people. One person interviewed for the panel explained:

> The oppressed begin to develop what they call 'cultural self-shame' and 'cultural self-hate,' which results in a lot of frustration and anger. At the same time...we begin to adopt our oppressors' values, and in a way, we become oppressors ourselves.... We begin hurting our own people. When you talk about things like addiction and family abuse, elder abuse, sexual abuse, jealousy, gossip, suicide and all the different forms of abuse we seem to be experiencing, it's all based on [oppression].[18]

The Male Physical Advantage

Sheer strength creates an indisputable source of power for men. In combination with suppressed emotions, alcohol, and anger, it creates an ominous force. Aili, 54, describes this male-female differential: "When a guy gets mad, if he thinks he is stronger, he easily hurts the woman. When the man thinks that he is the boss of the house, he might be mean to his people. When the married couples don't understand each other or talk about their feelings, they end up fighting." Adds a teacher's aide, women stand to lose in a physical confrontation, "but they aren't taking that lying down."

On rare occasions, the woman delivers the first blow. Women are apprehensive about being the aggressor, but it happens. Johnniebo, an RCMP constable, reports: "I can think of a couple of cases in which a man was charged with beating his wife. After he was convicted, he would say, 'She started it, she hit me first,' and his wife would agree." This may be an under-reported phenomenon because men feel reluctant to admit that a woman hit them first. Even when women initiate a violent encounter, though, they are likely to suffer greater injury and to experience greater fear. On average, the male's superior upper body strength tips the equation in his favor, an RCMP officer supposes: "Women are apprehensive about male power. That may hold them back from being the aggressor. Wives are 'possessions' here."

Alcohol and Drug Abuse

Although it was not a widespread "traditional" practice, drinking liquor has been a part of Inuit lifestyles for at least 140 years. Kuluk hypothesizes that alcohol takes a terrible toll because drinking was not a part of ordinary Inuit life on the land: "Inuit people never invented alcohol, so when an Inuk man drinks, he easily drinks his senses away. When he doesn't know what he's doing, he can beat up his wife."

A study of twelve Baffin Island communities concluded that the presence of alcohol alone or a community's stand on alcohol (wet or dry) do *not* necessarily correlate with the level of crime. This is a complicated issue, because if domestic violence crimes were separated out from all other crime statistics, the correlation between alcohol *abuse* and spousal assault might become even more evident.[19] Some Inuit women say they think alcohol is the major culprit behind violence against women. "The increase in alcohol and drug abuse through the Canadian Arctic," according to Stern and Condon, "has unfortunately contributed to a growing tide of spousal assault."[20] All too often, alcohol or drug abuse aggravates the power imbalance and spurs the violence.

Local RCMP officers estimate that "probably about 80 percent" of spousal assault cases involve alcohol abuse. For example, larger, wet communities with high levels of unemployment often suffer from higher rates of spousal assault and of *all* types of violence because alcohol is easier to find. However, being an officially dry town does not protect a community from domestic violence as much as the amount of alcohol available at any given time. A nurse explains: "The rates of spousal assault go in spurts, related to how much alcohol is in town. If someone gets a shipment in, we may see two or three people in a weekend, and then nothing for another month." In wet towns, women and men are much more likely to cite drinking as the major cause of spousal assault. Johnniebo says that most cases of spousal assault have involved intoxication, and not necessarily only on the part of the accused male: "The victim arrives home after having been drinking, the spouse becomes angry. Or both have been drinking."

Another Inuk constable acknowledges the linkage between alcohol abuse and violence against women. Some people use alcohol to justify violence: "Hitting your woman is a criminal act that is not acceptable to the community. Supposedly, you will be punished. Meanwhile, people say, 'Maybe she deserved it.

A guy has the right to knock his wife around a little bit.'" The woman may buy into that rationalization, thinking, "You were drunk. I understand, honey, and I know you won't do it again." These reactions fail the woman and subtly encourage men to continue violent behaviour.

Geela, who leads a relatively traditional life style, names spousal assault as the most pressing problem facing her community: "I would list that as a first priority, because I don't want it to happen." She blames drugs and alcohol for the loss of control, and believes that all too often both partners are drinking when violence occurs. The loss of judgment, the hypersensitivity to any cue, the depression and haziness affect both partners and throttle reasonable discussion of their differences.

Disagreement and Jealousy

Disagreement lies at the core of assault for both married and unmarried women. A normally compliant woman may find herself the victim of spousal assault if she speaks up or disagrees, says Julie: "If I married this guy, and all the time I said yes to him even if I didn't want to obey him, then I got tired of it and started saying no, he would beat me. That's what happens." Some women argue that even if they "obey" their men consistently, they may still become victims of assault. This explanation suggests that the old model of "man as boss" may be firmly entrenched in spite of other signs of reversals in role and power.

Inuit women frequently mention jealousy and suspicion as contributing factors to intimate violence. A man might become obsessed with the idea that "his woman is having an affair." As in other cultures, the notion of a man's right to possess "*his* woman" creeps into the bond of trust. Aili cannot say why men hit women, but she knows first hand how it feels: "It happened to me. The thing that used to make him abuse me was that he thought I was with somebody else. Jealousy! He wasn't drinking when he hit me—he has never touched a drop." Rosie concurs: "Men hit their wives for different reasons. Maybe he's jealous or the woman cheated on him. If he had a problem and didn't talk to anyone, it's all bottled up inside. He gets angry and takes it out on the wife." Minnie, who works for a store, laments her former husband's jealousy. He felt threatened whenever she visited friends or relatives: "He would question my visits...to anywhere! Whatever I did seemed to threaten him. Very jealous!"

The double standard common in western culture obtains for the Inuit as well. It is far more acceptable for a man to have an affair and to expect a woman to accept it than the reverse. Often, the man is the first to cheat. The woman feels angry and wronged. If she confronts her partner, she may receive blows instead of an apology. Molly expresses her fear of commitment: "That was one reason I never want to get married too soon in my life. That could be a problem when you're young and growing up together. You get depressed with each other for a while." She will wait for someone who will not for any reason "be mean" to her.

Lack of Communication

Many Inuit women believe that assault comes when the man holds in his feelings and gets angry or jealous. Poor communication makes it more difficult to develop the intimacy and trust required for a strong relationship during rapidly changing times. When anger, self-doubt, fear, and guilt cannot find direct expression verbally, they come out all too often in physical abuse of women and, less often, of children. Instead of communicating openly about their feelings with the women in their lives, men strike out in a release of frustration and tension. Stifled emotions fester until they blow up in the woman's face, says a counselor: "Release! Maybe that is the purpose their wives or women serve."

Young Lucie's boyfriend "doesn't hide anything," but she characterizes him as an exception: "He's really open. Guys who hide their feelings usually beat up their girlfriends. If a guy is too shy to express his feelings and something happens, he starts beating her and goes to jail. People start blaming the girl, which I don't like." The feelings come out in one form or another, hurting loved ones.

What should a woman do if her partner starts drinking and beating her? Characteristically, Lucie recommends trying to talk to him, but the process of confronting a man who feels more comfortable masking deep emotions would have to be slow and gentle: "Show him that you really love him. Tell him step by step your feelings for him and the change that you're seeing. Talk to him one day at a time, or whatever it takes, if you want to keep that love." A straightforward approach would not work well. If Lucie had to tell her partner the changes she observes, she would not know what to do: "I've never been hit before."

Children as Victims
"They're not all being reported to us"

For both traditionally and in modern times, Inuit characterize intentional physical assault against children as a rare occurrence. They agree that children are unlikely to be on the receiving end of parental blows. If an Inuk flies out of control, he is more likely to hit his wife than to hit his children. A woman who has worked with victims and has been a victim herself says the rates of sexual abuse are much higher:

> Out of ten houses in a row, every one would have had some history of sexual abuse. People are non-responsive, even sullen, because they have too much pain in their hearts and either don't know what to say or don't trust anyone or both. Too much pain. Incest and sexual abuse are the big family secrets—it goes round and round in families, through the extended family, from generation to generation.

Incest and sexual assault exist in Inuit communities, as they do everywhere. According to Adamie, "Complaints surface on occasion. I don't think we'll go a whole year without one surfacing again; they're not all being reported to us, especially father-daughter." RCMP and nurses report little child abuse in the files but say that a great deal goes unreported in this community. "A fair amount of child abuse is by stepparents—hitting and verbal abuse ('You're stupid, you're not even mine')—putting them out in the garbage box." Cases abound involving foster parents, uncles, and stepfathers molesting young girls. "We don't hear about much of this in our official capacity," says a nurse, "but among these people who are known for cherishing their children, as everywhere, some abuse exists." Says Johnniebo, "I'm sure that the nursing station sees these kids day in and day out. They would notify us if there was any evidence of child abuse, and we would notify them."[21]

The tradition of customary adoption makes it difficult to define incest in this culture: "You go into any family unit and the people that kids are calling 'mommy' and 'daddy' aren't mommy and daddy at all." They are aunts and uncles or other adoptive parents within the household. Some women remember being afraid of sexual assault when they went away to residential schools in Iqaluit.[22]

Most documented cases of incest involve the father figure and younger female between eight and twelve years old. Two points of view prevail. Some Inuit argue that incest, especially involving adopted children, was accepted traditionally. For example, a recent case involved a man of 66 and a girl of 14 whom he violated a few years earlier. The courthouse was "just stuffed with people and there were many who really couldn't understand why the court was taking the attitude that it's unacceptable," Adamie recalls. Others vehemently deny that viewpoint. The truth probably lies somewhere in between, Simatuk offers: "People did it and got away with it because there was no law to face. We knew it was going on, but it wasn't accepted."

Emotional abuse creates an all too frequent companion for some children. The victimizers are not always men. One young woman tells us that her aunt abuses her children both emotionally and physically: "She calls her little boy 'Satan' and hits him." She adds, "We need programs for parents." Though only a small number of families engage in sexual, emotional, or physical abusiveness, and "they get it from their parents," the wounds run as deep as the code of silence that protects the perpetrators. Many Inuit women say that childhood sexual abuse is the "most serious" of problems, because long-term scars make it hard to trust an intimate partner when the child becomes an adult. Elders who experienced abuse a long time ago held the secret inside, which negatively affected family life. "Baffin Island seems to be the worst," says a nurse who knows the territorial statistics.

Even women who have not been victims as children offer examples of abuse against other girls or their own experiences with rape and battering. They wanted to talk about it as part of our discussions of socialization and women's power. Not to do so (or for us not to report their words) would be to support that code of silence and to negate a painful and shame-making experience that deeply affects female identity.[23] In the late 1980s, Graburn documented the existence and nature of child abuse among the Inuit.[24] Now, women condemn this ancient crime against girls as completely off limits under any circumstances. Children who grow up in a violent home become victims in another sense, though, even when they are not the direct targets of physical assault. Geela reflects the feelings of many women about the impact of family violence:

> It really hurts me when children see fights. It is one of the most serious concerns with couples that have children. The kids are exposed to violence. It happened to my kids when they were young, and it has had some influence, especially on my boy. The girls don't seem to have been bothered that much, but my boy...I don't know what it is. I try to understand him. I think he has anger. When someone bothers him, he lets his anger out easily. I see it in other kids, where the parents just keep fighting. That's where it hurts the most...the children are caught. When they see anger between their parents, they get afraid and confused.

Children hold fear and anger inside until it comes out later, Geela adds, perhaps in school where an inappropriate outburst can land them in trouble. Even for those who were young when their parents separated, the trauma leaves an indelible impression. Of course, research indicates that growing up in violent homes deeply affects girls, too. Later in life, they may tend (albeit unconsciously) to seek mates who will perpetuate abuse in their lives.[25] These long-term consequences help explain why one woman vows, "I would *kill* anyone who touches my daughters."

An Inuk minister observes that even when children are not physically or sexually abused, they may suffer from emotional or spiritual neglect, lack of communication, and lack of discipline. Occasionally, Inuit children assault their parents—again, an expression of the breakdown between generations experienced in many cultures.

The Complexities of Reporting and Intervention
"The women are scared"

In the old days, Udluriak remarks, if a mother saw her daughter with a man who was not treating her well, she and her husband would talk to the man. Some women try to use traditional methods, as Apea suggests: "If a man started treating my daughter like dirt, I would talk to him. I wouldn't see him hitting my kids. I don't like that situation and I don't get treated that way." Other families wish it were that simple in an era of legalities, rights, and police involvement in the most emotionally charged—and dangerous—moments of family life.

Now, a woman who turns to the police risks becoming entangled in a host of legal problems because of the policy on pressing charges. Taking complaints forward means, "We're going to disrupt this whole family." Teressa Nahannee's study of sentencing disparities in major sexual assault cases in the Northwest

Territories found that, when both the perpetrator and the victim are Inuit, sentences tend to be relatively short for reasons of "cultural sensitivity" and reluctance to send Inuit men to federal penitentiaries in the south, the only option for terms over two years.[26] The pattern of relaxed policing, failure to charge and prosecute vigorously, and lenient sentences in family violence cases draws fire from the Inuit Women's Association, Pauktuutit, which takes a dim view of officers, judges, and community members who diminish the importance of assault against women and children:

> When the northern judiciary consistently gives lenient sentences in cases of major sexual assault based on cultural and sexist mitigating factors that discriminate against Inuit women, the constitutional right of Inuit females to security of the person and to equal protection and benefit of the law is infringed.[27]

In a positive vein, though, our consultants knew that Canadian law protects them against gender discrimination, assault, and economic exploitation: "We know we have our rights now. We don't have to have a male leader like before," Attirak proudly states. Women's rights might be protected on paper, but reporting and laying charges gives rise to one of the most paradoxical issues surrounding spousal assault. Many women feel disinclined to report assaults because of the national RCMP policy, which mandates that if either the victim or independent witnesses provide initial evidence, police *must* lay charges. Johnniebo describes the policy: "If we are presented with any evidence of assault, we have to lay charges, and that's it." The policy reflects the fact that, in Canada, all offenses are against the person *and* against the Crown (the common good). The court will subpoena the woman, who might be reluctant to testify against her partner. If subpoenaed, she must take the stand, although she might choose to remain mute. If she has given a written statement before her appearance, the Crown must decide whether to deal with her for not giving evidence or to let the case die.

This situation proves uncomfortable for women who would have preferred to forget a violent incident. The policy often deters women from calling for help, says the officer: "Spousal assault is prevalent, but it's becoming hidden. In this community, it's going underground. I don't think there's anything we can do about it as law enforcement officers, because the women are scared." Recently, videotaped testimonies have been recorded in order to strengthen the Crown's case against the perpetrator:

> It's like a "KGB" witness statement. The victim has to swear on a Bible and make her statement. It's very emotional. You can see the evidence on her face and body. The tape can be introduced as evidence without her presence if she refuses to appear in court. This technique brings in many more guilty pleas. Injuries are the critical evidence. Men tend to deny hitting a woman hard enough to hurt her. The videotape shows how hard he did hit her.

This practice emanated from the inability of police to charge (and the Crown to prosecute) on behalf of women and all citizens. In an earlier era, women turned more often to the RCMP for help. The police would try to defuse the situation in the home and "could show discretion on the scene." If the woman preferred not to lay charges, the police would withdraw from the case until the next call for help. "That wasn't solving anything either," an Inuk officer explains. "The husband would see us walk in and defuse the situation; we'd walk out; he wouldn't be charged; he wouldn't have to pay any kind of penalty for it. It was just as easy to beat her up the next time." This was frustrating both to police and to women's groups nationally, who realized that threats against women by their partners were discouraging them from pressing charges. Johnniebo thinks the new policy is useful, though it has some negative consequences:

"I DIDN'T THINK I HIT HER THAT HARD"

In my last spousal assault case, I got a call from the health center—fractured skull under the eye. He told her if she went to the police, *she* would have a police record, not him. The officer videotaped the wounds and asked her to swear that this is how she got the injuries. The truth. Very dramatic. They cry. You can see the injuries. They have to tell the truth or they can be charged with public mischief. She reconciled with her common-law husband—she *swore* she never would! I can use the videotape as her testimony, in order to convict him.

A woman would come in at three o'clock in the morning and say her husband had beaten her up. You take the statement, you make up the file, you lay the charges, and you've done a fair amount of work. Then two days later she comes in and says, "Oh, we're in love again—I want to drop the charges." That was happening constantly. The police were getting so used to it, they would say, "Come back in three or four days and if you still want to lay charges, we'll do it. Or come in two days, but you have to swear the information and lay the charges yourself." That's where the bad reputation started—"The police won't do anything about it."

Recent case law decision supports the "common good." The man should be punished for what he did to her. He would be gone away at least for a few months. That's what we're finally doing, and it's working. This may result in more guilty pleas because defense lawyers don't want a jury to see those videotapes: "I didn't think I hit her that hard" won't work anymore.

Once the evidence is before us, everyone realizes that charges will be laid. The wife can go home and say, "What can I do? They won't listen to me...they won't drop the charges." Maybe it takes the heat off her. Still, we don't get as many calls about spousal assault. A woman realizes that if she goes to the police to report a beating, three months from now she will have to face a judge. If by then she has reconciled with hubby, she will tell the judge that she doesn't want to say anything. The judge will say, "Too bad, you *have* to tell me what happened."

Like many Inuit women, the constable is of two minds about this dilemma. The policy is a bit too strict, with little leniency in applying it. On the other hand, he understands the rationale behind it and agrees with the basic concept: "There should be an out, though, and right now the force is very firm with it. That *is* the policy and you will stick to it."

Because of this complicated situation, now women are as likely to take their complaints to social services or the Mental Health Committee as they are to go to the RCMP (see Chapter 15). Elder Higilak explains: "Some members in the Mental Health Committee don't agree with the law. I believe it to a certain point, if it can't be stopped by the parents or the people in the community." Worse, yet, many do not appeal for help at all. For example, a woman trying to complete an advanced degree in the south at a highly prestigious university "is in the middle of a situation right now." A year ago the RCMP were going to charge her husband with spousal assault, but she begged them to desist since they were going to move south for her schooling. She wanted a chance to "get her life straightened out" and believed that all it would take to get them back on track was to leave their environment. The RCMP agreed: "If we charge him, everything would be disrupted. She's going to be down in nursing school and he's going to be up here. We're going to have to drag her up here for the trial, so we backed off. Within four weeks he was charged again." The couple has since returned to the North and she has asked the police for a peace bond to protect her from her abusive husband.

Shelters and Safe Houses

Many societies utilize community-based shelters as a mechanism for providing support and protection to battered women. In large urban areas in southern Canada, shelters make sense and serve a limited purpose. Almost half of the 324 women who used the Native Women's Shelter of Montreal in 2000 were Inuit, signaling the "horrific pasts" that drive them to seek a haven from destructive relationships. The shelter offers a warm, secure place to stay in a cold, lonely city: "We are safe, we are confidential, and people know where we are."[28]

In small northern communities, though, shelters may not be an ideal answer to the problem of spousal assault. A social worker suggests that in a settlement of 250 or 1,000 people, the hamlet would have to build "more than a couple of shelters because it wouldn't take long for a man to find out where his wife is staying." Flying a victim to a larger community, such as Iqaluit or Montreal, also removes the woman from her usual support network of family and friends, interferes with her children's schooling, and jeopardizes her ability to earn a livelihood if she is working outside the home. Removing the woman also makes it even more difficult to effect reconciliation with her partner, if she chooses to attempt that course of action. Otherwise, men still have the defining power in cases of domestic violence. Adamie relates an episode:

> Younger women know they have rights...even for little stuff they come! A girl came crying, "My husband told me to get out. He doesn't have a right to tell me to get out, because it's my house, too." I went back there with her. I said, "Maybe your husband doesn't want you in here for a while because he's mad. He cannot stay mad forever and he's going to let you in again. Why don't you go to a friend's house? She said, "I don't want to go there. I belong in my

home." These are difficult things. Younger women are more stubborn. For divorce they say, "I have a right to do what I want." We support her when she says that, because she does have rights.

It's hard for me to do the job. I feel strongly about my culture, but I have to do these things, even if I know it's not our culture. It's not a big, big problem. It's a subtle thing. It will be a little better maybe for the next generation.

This case echoes the underlying concern that Inuit women express over the double victimization of assault when they are hurt, then also have to leave their homes for a shelter or safe house. Women put up with assault from those who supposedly love them because socialization impresses upon them that conformity and pliability will be rewarded, if not today, then ultimately. When women apply their stereotypically strong qualities—being patient, loving, and understanding—to men who are in trouble, it sometimes comes back to hurt them in the form of verbal or physical abuse. Inuit women, like their sisters in other cultures, are trying in constructive ways to solve this frustrating paradox. According to Minnie, whose best friend has been victimized by a former partner, "We have to get a shelter here in Pangnirtung. Some people say they think it won't help, but I say it will. When couples have these problems, both need a place to talk privately. That's one of the goals of our Mental Health Committee."

Shelters can be effective in cases involving alcohol: "Most of these guys are drunk when assault occurs. You can't talk any common sense to them. They're stubborn...there's tunnel vision." A protected cooling off period can sometimes work to a couple's mutual advantage. The RCMP has no authority to remove an offender from his own home in many cases, so removing the victim might be the only choice. An officer notes that there is substantial pressure from extended families not to use shelters: "It is not the Christian thing to do to break up the family."

Internal RCMP policy does not readily mesh with the use of shelters. The police fear that shelters can be misused to subvert tough enforcement of the law. This is ironic, since both women's groups and the RCMP are trying to protect women from recurring harm. Adamie, an Inuk special constable, outlines the problems of charging perpetrators and of using safe houses that are not safe:

"SPOUSAL ASSAULT IS A CRIME!"

Let's say you're running a safe house and you notify me that Mary is down there—she just got a severe beating—so if the husband shows up, we can come for him. At that instant, I'm obligated to talk to her and to pick him up. Spousal assault is a crime! If you notify me only when the husband is acting belligerently or trying to break the door down, it might be too late.

Even "safe houses" [existing homes in an underground, informal network] present problems. People try to defuse the situation and get the woman out without police involvement. Often they haven't solved the woman's problem at all—they're trying to keep the guy's butt out of court. If that's the case, we're not going to support them at all. We're getting a shelter—renovating the old church house. It will never be a secret that the victim is staying there. We'll have to employ a by-law officer or something for security. A shelter will get women and children out of a volatile situation at least for a short time until we can complete our investigation. We don't have authority to remove a suspected batterer from his own home until he goes to court. I hope that there would be counseling in place and a way to get some guidance.

RCMP will support the shelter system if it keeps the woman's interest at heart: "Get her out of that house so he can't beat on her; give her a safe place where she can get her head straight and decide she's not going to put up with that anymore; then call the police in and charge the offender." However, if shelters mean simply removing a victim long enough to defuse the situation and avoid police involvement, she will return to a potentially hazardous environment.

One solution to the shelter problem in small communities may be to reveal the shelter's location, inform the husband that his wife is there (with her permission), and set a time when he can come to visit her. Some Canadian provinces use this method. Rules of visitation state that the man must be sober and understands that staff will call the police immediately if he makes any disturbance. This provides a cooling-off period, ensures sobriety of both parties, and offers a controlled environment for discussion and decision-making. Locks on the doors and peepholes provide control over access. In cases of severe assault or use of weapons, the police can be involved.

Kahina is a 28-year-old woman with two young children. Her story, which she says is a typical one, illustrates the dilemmas of seeking help under traditional methods for addressing domestic violence:

"I WAS BEATEN"

After I lived in another settlement when I was younger, I came back, found a little job, fell in love, made a mistake. Now I'm getting shit for it. I hate to admit it, but I have to get it out. It was so difficult in the beginning, but I can talk about it now. I don't have to be hiding in a closet anymore. I was beaten. He was an alcoholic, in a place where there's no help for alcoholics or people that are beaten. It's very difficult here. I put up with it until I was ready to die and then I told him, "Okay, before you kill me, let me tell you this," and that's when he woke up.

I asked him, "Is this the kind of love you show your people? In case I die after you beat me up, give me a pen and paper now that would allow me to give my kids to someone else, not to you." All the while, the fist was right up there, but I had to grab that moment. It was a moment that saved my life. You never know. One little blow can damage your brain and a hemorrhage can happen.

You don't need to use force to get my attention. I guess he was raised that way by his mother. Violent. I didn't know about it until he started telling me. His mother was verbally abused. I don't blame her. I liked her a lot. She used to tell me why she went through it with her husband and why I'm going through it now. She hated me afterward because she thought it was my fault that we were thinking of divorce.

I wanted desperately to leave my husband, but nobody wanted me, not even my parents. Divorcing here is like going to hell, especially for my parents' generation. Since you're going to hell, we might as well have nothing to do with you. That's how it is up here. Mom used to tell me that I just had to hang in there—that we would eventually solve our problems—but she didn't know what I was going through. My ex used to see his friends and stay away for days or nights. He didn't bother to call me. They couldn't do that back then because they didn't have all these other outside influences. It was much easier to correct the problem than it is today. Now it's so hard.

Kahina hid her situation for a long time. Since she had grown up in an environment full of love and sharing, she became perplexed when her husband said that hitting her was the only way he could achieve discipline. Expressing feelings violently did not make sense to this woman. As far as using the traditional method of talking with parents and other relatives, Kahina was willing to do so until she concluded that it was not working. The violence continued and she grew despondent. Finally, she declared that she would use the most despicable method to stop the beatings: "Divorce. If you don't like it, tough." That caused more blows, "even harder." The choice came down, for her as for many others, to divorce and survive or to remain at risk in the marriage. In Kahina's darkest moments, she wondered if her parents would rather have her die or go to a mental institution. That might save her marriage and prevent her from "going to hell," but she finally appealed to them: "What do you value more—a piece of paper saying that I'm married or me, a human being created by God?"

To her parents, whom she loves and trusts, Kahina tries to show only behaviours and values they will approve: "Whatever I do at home, I make sure they agree. If they don't like it, I hide it from them, because I don't want to be criticized. I don't deserve it. If it's something that I like to do, I'll do it in private. What they don't know won't hurt them. But sometimes I want to talk with them, and they ask me if I'm sure I know what I'm doing...that kind of attitude." Kahina finally filed for divorce because she simply could not take it anymore: "I didn't really know who I was. I had to say "no more" for my own mental health."

Women like Kahina do not have to face violence alone. Inuit women's groups are taking a strong position against sexual abuse, sexual assault, and spousal assault. For example, in a highly visible case in Resolute Bay, in which a coroner's inquest concluded that being a victim of childhood sexual abuse had led a young mother to commit suicide, Pauktuutit and other organizations closed ranks effectively. They called for increasing the number and training of sexual abuse workers, for studies of sexual assaults and child sexual abuse, for early intervention and treatment of victims, and for programs to help sexual offenders come forward to take responsibility and foster reconciliation.[29] In response to other cases tried in Iqaluit, then Pauktuutit leader, Veronica Dewar, called for a tougher stance on sexual abuse and assault, and more support for both victims and perpetrators: "In discussions with Inuit women over many years, it is clear that they also want sentencing to act as a deterrent and to send a message that acts such as these are criminal offences. There has to be some sort relevant programming in jail."

Formal systems of criminal justice, including rehabilitation, have not worked especially well, however. As many elders state very simply, if contemporary Inuit were to follow traditional Inuit law, the need for courts, prisons, and shelters system would not exist in the first place: "If our laws were written I think some people would follow our laws...If people followed the Inuit laws people would not be sent out to prison at all. The people would be brought together to talk and advise, not lecture, and bring everything out in the open. After discussions, forgiving would be a major role."[30]

The Criminal Justice System
"Look at it!"

Of course, Inuit commit (and suffer from) the full range of crimes that occur elsewhere in Canada, but the crimes of violence within the context of intimate relationships hurt the most and seem to be the hardest to deal with sensitively and justly. Anger overwhelms the victims and shames the perpetrators, but small, isolated communities seem hard-pressed to find adequate justice or counseling for either person. Convicted offenders in the Baffin Region are "often given community-based sentences by the circuit court, creating the possibility of re-offending and additional victimization."[31] Stealing to obtain money or bartering power for drugs and alcohol unsettles the community. An RCMP officer claims that the justice system is "starting to get smarter. We don't go to court as much as we used to. We talk to the kid and to the storeowner. We ask the kid to give back whatever he took, to work things out. Maybe he could wash the floor or help in some way. We assume the kid feels sorry. Court is not the answer. We are using more diversion, restitution, and alternative measures." An adult juridical committee and a youth justice committee help find the right balance of community-based and external, formal justice.

Inuit women feel frustrated and angry when the system fails to convict even when confessions and evidence converge to paint an unquestionable picture of guilt. Convictions won after hard police work and willingness of victims to come forward usually meet with probation or pathetically short sentences.[32] Protecting the family is all too often done at the expense of women and children, a resource worker laments: "Sometimes I want to bring the judge up here and say, 'Look at this!' It's sad that little girls, like two-year-olds who have been raped, have VD and the offender gets a year in jail, at most. That little girl is scarred for life, but the judge doesn't see it that way. The guy just gets out of jail and goes and does it again."[33] Light sentencing is often true for crimes against property and so-called "victimless" crimes such as drug dealing.

When society fails to prosecute and punish men who harm women and children, it damages the social fabric of trust. Pauktuutit has fought for fair enforcement of the *Criminal Code*, victim participation in sentencing, and protection of Inuit women in their communities. It has also demanded that the "judiciary recognize that rape is a crime deserving of deterrence and denunciation regardless of the race or culture of the victim."[34] Women in Pangnirtung are well aware of Pauktuutit's work in this area, and are quick to describe the violence that afflicts them. They are equally quick to emphasize that the causes of violence are complicated, and that not all couples fall into the downward spiral of abuse and alienation.

The problem lies in a criminal justice system that was superimposed from southern Canada without regard to Inuit cultural differences. The system is a reflection of southern practices and values, administered by federally funded and trained RCMP, oriented toward incarceration, and prone to devalue domestic violence complaints. The Nunavut Justice Research Program (NJRP), sponsored by the Canadian Department of Justice, has built a research base to help Nunavut design a new, more appropriate justice system than the one put in place under the aegis of the former Northwest Territories. Creating the new territory was intended, in part, to bring control over such matters as crime and domestic violence back to Inuit and other Nunavut residents.

A new system should stress "community control of justice, dependent upon community mobilization and civic culture, and [be] rooted in a restorative justice philosophy."[35] The RCMP is playing a role in NJRP by reviewing crime statistics by community and attempting to correlate the data with other community characteristics (for example, substance abuse). Some Inuit and government agencies have called for a system based on "restorative justice," which builds upon "family conferencing, circle sentencing, and victim-offender mediation."[36] This approach fits well with the healing circles that many Inuit women have advocated, but others warn that restorative justice can help the *offender* avoid incarceration and receive treatment at the expense of ignoring the *victims* of crime (especially domestic violence and child or elder abuse crimes). Mary Crnkovich and Lisa Addario, also involved with NJRP, argue that the "impact of this very high crime rate falls disproportionately on women and children."[37] They call for a system that is "more responsive to, and representative of the men, women and children it serves," and for more training, improved supports and services for victims, and ongoing evaluation to make the criminal justice system accountable to the community.[38] Solutions must be found if Inuit women and children are to be protected under any revised justice system.

Inuit women are certainly not alone in confronting the challenges of violence in their relationships. And, like women in many parts of the world, they look to education as a way out of the problems that rapid social change has generated.

Photo 15.3 Elder male wearing a prized "Pang hat" from the weaving center.

Notes

1 Segments of this chapter appeared in an earlier form in Billson, "Violence toward Women and Children."

2 Hicks, "The Nunavut Land Claim and the Nunavut Government," p. 45.

3 Don Clairmont, "Review of Justice System Issues Relevant to Nunavut," in *The Nunavut Justice Research Program: Project Summaries*, prepared by Albert Currie, Tina Hattem, and John Clement (Ottawa: Department of Justice Canada, Research and Statistics Division, Policy Sector, October 1999), p. 5.

4 Bell, "Is Violent Crime on the Rise in Nunavut?" The overall number of criminal offenses charged against *Nunavummiut*, as compiled by Statistics Canada, rose from 5,085 in 1999 to 6,130 in 2000. Cited in Jim Bell, "Coping with Crime in Nunavut: High Violent-Crime Rate Doesn't Surprise Justice Officials," *Nunatsiaq News* (August 3, 2001).

5 Clairmont, "Review of Justice System Issues Relevant to Nunavut," p. 5.

6 S. J. Wilson, *Women, Families, and Work*, 3rd ed. (Toronto: McGraw-Hill Ryerson, 1991), p. 131.

7 Rebecca Kudloo, letter to *Nunatsiaq News* (February 11, 1994).

8 Hicks, "The Nunavut Land Claim and the Nunavut Government," p. 42.

9 See, for example, Balikci, *The Netsilik Eskimo*, p. 170. As with other social processes, domestic violence also varied from camp to camp and region to region.

10 Millward, *Southern Baffin Island*, p. 66.

11 See Janet Mancini Billson, "Violence toward Inuit Women and Children," pp. 151-162 in Crnkovich, ed., *Gossip*.

12 Sean McKibbon, "Nunavut's Shocking Sexual Assault Rates," *Nunatsiaq News* (June 30, 2000).

13 W. Rasing, *"Too Many People": Order and Nonconformity in Iglulingmiut Social Process* (Nijmegen: Recht and Samenleving, 1994).

14 Griffiths, et al., *Crime, Law, and Justice among Inuit*, p. 40.

15 In *Violent Crime and Characteristics of Twelve Inuit Communities in the Baffin Region, NWT*, Wood questioned whether alcohol consumption is higher among the Inuit in these communities than in the Canadian population as a whole and concluded that it is possibly even lower when *percentage* of drinkers is considered. He also found no relationship between per capita consumption of alcohol and amount of violent crime, but that measure does not take into account the fact that alcohol use does not indicate alcohol *abuse*. Our consultants have stressed the abuse of alcohol that leads to violence between intimates.

16 Brody, *The People's Land*, p. 195.

17 Canadian Government, *Inuit Women: From the Final Report on the Canadian Panel on Violence against Women* (Ottawa: Government Printing Office, 1993).

18 The Royal Commission on Aboriginal Peoples. *Final Report (Five Volumes):* "Looking Forward, Looking Back"; "Restructuring the Relationship"; "Gathering Strength"; "Perspectives and Realities"; "Renewal: A Twenty-Year Commitment" (Hull, Québec: Canada Communication Group, 1996-97) (website).

19 Wood, *Violent Crime and Characteristics of Twelve Inuit Communities in the Baffin Region, NWT*.

20 Stern and Condon, "A Good Spouse is Hard to Find," p. 215.

21 One reason for this perception may be under-reporting. Canadian law does not require someone who witnesses child abuse to report it: "The law doesn't read that way. In the States, if a doctor sees a victim of a gunshot wound or a knife attack, he or she is obliged to report it. Not in Canada. But aside from the law, these professions have certain ethics that oblige them to report things like child abuse."

22 "Girls have told how they lay awake at night, their doors locked, fearing assault." Quoted in Brody, *The People's Land*, p. 190.

23 Several major studies in the United States have consistently shown that about twice as many girls than boys fall prey to molestation during childhood (24 percent versus 11 percent). Brannon, *Gender*, pp. 268. Discussions with Inuit women and men indicate at least the same proportion, if not more heavily weighted toward girls.

24 Nelson H. H. Graburn, "Severe Child Abuse among the Canadian Inuit," in *Anthropological Perspectives on the Treatment and Maltreatment of Children*, edited by Nancy Scheper-Hughes (Dordrecht, Holland: D. Reidel, 1987).

25 Robin Norwood documented this in *Women Who Love Too Much* (New York: St. Martin's Press, 1985).

26 Cited in Martha Flaherty, "Inuit Women and Violence," in Caroline Andrew and Sandra Rodgers, eds., *Women and the Canadian State* (Montréal: McGill-Queen's University Press, 1997), p. 182.

27 Martha Flaherty, "Inuit Women and Violence," p. 181.

28 Jane George, "A Secure Place for Inuit Women in Distress," *Nunatsiaq News* (January 21, 2000) and "Homeless Inuk Woman in Ottawa Dying Alone of AIDS," *Nunatsiaq News* (October 8, 1999).

29 Jim Bell, "Group Will Fight Sex Abuse against NWT Children," *Nunatsiaq News,* August 16, 1996, pp. 2, 18.
30 Pauloosie Angmarlik, "Pauloosie Angmarlik (Inuit)," in *In the Words of Elders: Aboriginal Cultures in Transition,* edited by Peter Kulchyski, Don McCaskill, and David Newhouse (Toronto: University of Toronto Press, 1999), p. 285.
31 Griffiths, et al., *Crime, Law, and Justice among Inuit,* p. 12.
32 Griffiths, et al., *Crime, Law, and Justice among Inuit,* pp. 144ff.
33 Griffiths, et al., *Crime, Law, and Justice among Inuit,* p. 144. For an analysis of the programs and facilities available in the Baffin region, see Harold W. Finkler, *The Baffin Correctional Centre: A Review of Current Programs and Alternatives* (Ottawa: Department of Indian and Northern Affairs, 1981); "Inuit and the Criminal Justice System: Future Strategies for Social-Legal Control and Prevention," *Études/Inuit/Studies* 9, 2 (1985): 141-152; and "Violence and the Administration of Criminal Justice in Northern Canada," in *Insights and Strategies for Confronting Violence,* edited by K. Johnston (Anchorage: School of Justice, University of Alaska, 1983).
34 Martha Flaherty, "Inuit Women and Violence," p. 184.
35 Clairmont, "Review of Justice System Issues Relevant to Nunavut," p. 4. Willem C. E. Rasing analyzes a case in Igloolik that illustrates the discontinuities between Inuit culture and southern-style justice in "The Case of Kolitalik: On the Encounter of Iglulingmiut Culture and Canadian Justice," pp. 91-107 in *Continuity and Discontinuity in Arctic Cultures,* edited by C. Buijs (Leiden: Universiteit Leiden, Centre of Non-Western Studies, 1993).
36 Clairmont, "Review of Justice System Issues Relevant to Nunavut," p. 7.
37 Mary Crnkovich and Lisa Addario with Linda Archibald, "From Hips to Hope: Inuit Women and the Nunavut Justice System," in *The Nunavut Justice Research Program: Project Summaries,* prepared by Albert Currie, Tina Hattem, and John Clement (Ottawa: Department of Justice Canada, Research and Statistics Division, Policy Sector), October 1999, p. 10.
38 Crnkovich and Addario, "From Hips to Hope," p. 10.

VIII

A NEW CENTURY EMERGES

There are strong and weak families everywhere in the world, but here in the North you have to be very strong. It's totally different.

—Sheila

Photo 16.1 New housing and a hamlet maintenance truck in late spring.

16

The Promise and Price
of Education

To be well educated, you have to be away for so much time. Even today, we don't like to be away from our settlement too long. That's one reason kids don't always graduate from school. It's very hard for most Inuit to be apart.

—Ooleepeeka

The Carvers: A Certain State of Mind

Photo 16.2 Jaco Ishulutaq and his carving of Sedna.

315

An elder remarks that schools often do not enable students to achieve a state of mind conducive to real learning or fine achievement. Take, for example, the carvers. Many of the best, both older and younger, have received little formal education. Yet, their art rivals that of graduates of the best art colleges in the world. Their ability to communicate in the language of a three dimensional world seems almost uncanny.

One state of mind is *Angutiisiaq*, another elder explains: "There are certain people who are known by all others as special people because they do everything well. They make the best things. They are the best hunters...they have a state of mind that does not allow them to do things in an ordinary way. They are compelled to do the simplest things as perfectly as can be done by a human being.... It is a way of living."[1]

Almost every night someone knocks on our apartment door at the mission. News spreads fast about visitors who might be interested in seeing local art. Tapestries, prints, and carvings parade past the threshold in surprising volume. Tonight, we open the door to find a young man whose face is badly bruised and swollen. He apologizes for his appearance, says he has been in a fight, and quickly adds that his cousin told him we might like to see his carvings.

We invite him into the warm living room. He unwraps four small carvings that he had painstakingly chiseled out of caribou antler or whalebone. A harpoonist, sitting in his *qajaq*, cleverly swivels in place to aim at his prey. Slim bands of sinew tether the harpoon firmly to its tiny toggle point. On another perfectly honed *qajaq*, a hunter looks dreamily past a seal that rests across the bow. The seal is made of the rough, almost furry part of an antler. The third piece, a shaman urging the hunters on to success, stands on an island of green soapstone. The fourth, a seal carved larger than the others in this Lilliputian hunting party, seems out of proportion by artistic scale but not by the critical role he plays in Inuit life. He lies prone, his head hanging lower than his body, slightly turned, as one sees on the boat trip home after the hunt.

This young man, who dropped out of school in his early teens and has never studied art, has begun to achieve *Angutiisiaq*—perfection. He refers us to his idol, though, a master carver in his early 50s, who might have a large carving for us to take home as a special gift. As he leads us across the runway to the other side of town, he admits that the fight was over a drug deal. He seems agitated and worried about where this might lead tomorrow.

Manasie Maniapik, the senior carver, speaks to us in the peace of his living room through his son, Leslie, who is young enough to speak fluent English. He shows us a dancing polar bear, beautifully in motion, but our eyes involuntarily fall on a large walrus "sleeping" on the floor in the next room. The artist apologizes that this carving has not yet been polished and needs tusks...many hours of work. Sadly, we cannot have the walrus, since this is our last night on this trip.

We chat about the resettlement process that brought Manasie to Pangnirtung in the 1960s. As we move toward the door, Manasie strokes his neatly trimmed beard and thinks out loud: "I could have the walrus ready by 10 o'clock tomorrow morning, if that would be enough time for you to pack it before you catch your plane." Thrilled, we agree, and head back across the village to start organizing ourselves. It is past 11 p.m.

Promptly at 10 a.m., we hear a soft knock at our door. Manasie has been up most of the night polishing the walrus to a satin gloss, cutting and installing the tusks, and wrapping the impressive mammal—somewhat incongruously—in plastic bubble wrap and brown paper. He opens the coverings slowly, like a great unveiling in a Paris museum. There lies a walrus as real as any one could see in the fiord. His skin undulates in carefully molded wrinkles; his tail glides around in front of his flippers as if he owned the world.

This time, words fail all of us. For once, language is no barrier. Our expressions speak our joy in receiving this creature from Sedna, and his face beams with the pleasure of knowing what he has created. We hug all around, including the walrus, and say good-byes. He has tears in his eyes, as do we, though we have met only the night before.

The elders call his state of mind *Siilatujuk*: "It...allows me to see a large world which is my very own place. Here, I am not subject to unnatural forces. Here, I can create things which are beautiful and can give me great pleasure. It is a very strange place because you know that it can never be, yet when you leave it and come back to the world we know, you discover that you have created a beautiful thing which you have brought back with you. I am a carver, so I bring forth carvings—but there are songs, stories, and magical things that have been brought back by others from their own worlds."[2]

The young carver must aspire to *Siilatujuk*. He also must have a very good teacher, and the peace and courage that will allow him to bring back such beauty from the other side of his imagination.

C₂

When we queried a group of women in their mid-20s about the most serious challenges facing Inuit women of their generation, one rephrased the question as, "The front cover of the book, the first page?" Each named a different problem: Early pregnancy, poor education, a lack of jobs and opportunities, lack of skills training, lack of child support from males, gambling and bingo (among both women and men), and "women's right to speak up." The reason for this seeming disparity is that, ultimately, these challenges are intricately interwoven. Only one percent of Nunavut Inuit have completed university degrees; across Canada, the figure is closer to 20 percent.[3] In a community in which almost half of the population has received a ninth grade education or less, the braiding effects of low education, lack of jobs, and low income seem obvious: "Not much job for the woman here in Pang, especially for those who don't have education."[4] Problems in interpersonal relationships, such as male-female violence, give Inuit women great pain and cause for reflection. They see a close relationship between the two problems: Women and men are competing for livelihood in an era of rapid change and uncertainty. This causes communal and personal stress that challenges women as individuals and as a group.[5]

Lack of opportunity emerges from the difficulties in obtaining relevant skills training, although Nunavut Arctic College campuses now offer computer and secretarial skills and the Iqaluit campus offers qualifications in management, public administration, and business administration. Total enrollment is approximately 2,500 students, but not all attend full time or complete their degrees. Courses include remedial English, math, and science (since so many students are trying to catch up after dropping out of high school) and adult education classes.[6] NAC also offers professional programs in teacher training, construction, environmental technology, financial management, and community health, sometimes in starter programs that enable young women and men to take entry level jobs as teacher aides, dental assistants, nursing assistants, and social work aides. Some courses in art (drawing, printmaking, and carving) are available and a heavily subsidized law program is underway. However, staffing the campuses is a major problem, and only a handful of instructors and administrators are Inuit. Ironically, before the creation of Nunavut there were more Inuit teachers—when the new territory came into being, the best educated Inuit "got job offers they just couldn't refuse," according to the president of Nunavut Arctic College, Jonny Kusugak.[7]

Education—the key that can unlock their future—holds enticing promises and exacts a high price for Inuit women. Even the relatively generous scholarships available through the Nunavut government do not meet the real costs of attending college, especially when the student is a woman who has been working to support her family.[8] For example, when Nunavut Arctic College partnered with Dalhousie University to educate thirty nurses for local clinics, half of the students dropped out in the first year.[9] A "bridging" course that helps women transition into the regular program has since been initiated: "It's tough for students to balance family life with school."[10]

In spite of the long history of residential schools and an often-irrelevant "southern curriculum" that failed to engage the Inuit, women of all ages express enthusiasm about education—especially when it relates to breaking out of the past. They mention formal education as one of the most important changes in their own lives and as a dream for their children. A teacher confirms that at every parent-teacher meeting the mothers turn out in droves: "Every time, more women than men." Opportunities for education, training, and on-the-job experience can result in significant rewards for those Inuit who have been able to take advantage of them. However, for those who have not completed high school and/or have not been lucky enough to find employment, the blow to identity can be devastating.

Pangnirtung and other settlements began to have their own schools with more and more grade levels, but it was only a few years ago that high schools expanded to include grades eleven and twelve. Pangnirtung's first twelfth grade graduated in 1986. Almost half of all Inuit (46 percent) over 15 years of age have acquired less than a ninth grade education. Just over one percent have completed university.[11] Most of those who have gone beyond the ninth grade were born after 1960. Although Inuit women and men are less likely to complete university than other aboriginals in Canada are, women are more likely to do so than are men.[12] Using the 1995 census data, Hull showed that only about 1.3 percent of all Inuit have completed a university degree or certificate; of those who attempted higher education, only 30 percent complete their programs.[13] This educational attainment rate is about one-third that of all aboriginal youths in Canada. Canadian Ambassador to the Circumpolar North Mary May Simon pointed out that, while the former Northwest Territories had the lowest rate of literacy in Canada, the old NWT's aboriginal *il*literacy rate is highest among the Inuit, at 70 percent (the figures are 56 percent for the Dene, 52 percent for the Inuvialuit, and 31 percent for the Métis).[14]

Lack of school completion contributes to illiteracy but so do the general cultural barriers that exist for Inuit children who receive a southern education taught primarily by Qallunaat teachers. As a teacher reports, "when you get into deep discussions, the Inuit may find it difficult to understand what is being said. They have little or no concept, for example, of kingdom. They don't have a kingdom. English literature is full of that." This small example is only one of many barriers based on language. Others center on Euro-Canadian cultural traditions, customs, and practices that bear no relationship to Inuit culture. As of the mid-1990s, local schools began teaching children in Inuktitut in the early grades. The increasing presence of Inuit teachers might make a difference in future graduation rates. They tell the Inuit children that education is important for them, and "it's the only way they can get a good job." The community feels that all teachers should be Inuit, because the children need role models. On the other hand, modern technology and media help bridge the cultural gap: "The Inuit children are perfectly capable," says another teacher, "of adapting the bits they like while at the same time rejecting others by saying, 'That's not my culture.'" The last century has given the Inuit cause to test their adaptability to the outer limit.

The Gender Gap
"Some young men get depressed and lose hope"

From kindergarten through grade twelve, the hamlet schools contain about 370 children. The senior graduating class of 1988 had 14 members, most of them males. This was an unusual class, since many young men who had dropped out came back for the first offering of grade twelve in Pangnirtung. Previously, eager students had to attend residential school in Iqaluit, one hour away by plane. Now that the pent-up demand has been met among the males, the high school will return to its previous pattern: "Since then, the classes show a totally different picture. We'll have one or two boys at most and the rest will be girls." Indeed, females greatly outnumber males in graduating from high school. In the 1996 class, 17 out of 20 graduates were females.

Students, especially males, feel suspicious about what they can learn inside the four walls of school that will help them survive. A sports coach worries about the pre-teen boys on his team, because "nobody is teaching them anything." They go to school, but their generation will not know how to hunt (which is necessary for supplementing income, even if one has an education and job):

> Even when my family does not have money, we always have something to eat. My father was an alcoholic. He did not teach me how to hunt—he said, "Just go out and figure out your own way." I couldn't do that, so my grandfather taught me. We've been hunting many times. I love it.

Because doing well educationally improves one's chances of doing well occupationally, teachers point out that male resistance to female authority in high school may actually block their chances of upward mobility. Conversely, one source of power for Inuit women may be their relative conformity, as Jonah suggests: "The girl sticks to what she believes in when she's going to school, so she stays a bit longer than a boy. A few years later it pays off." Like females all over North America, Inuit girls tend to perform better in elementary and secondary school than do males. As Robin McGrath observes, "Good little Inuit girls don't make scenes or complain openly about mistreatment."[15] Studies have shown that girls respond more positively to the authority of a teacher than boys do, even if the teacher is female. Consequently, they are more likely to achieve higher grades because they complete homework and in-class assignments. They are less likely to get into trouble during school hours, which also may contribute to their lower dropout rate compared to boys. These differences tend to balance out in North America by the middle of high school. By that time, most Inuit youth have left school anyway, so the early female advantage may have a more powerful long-term effect than in other cultures.

The female advantage in the lower grades accumulates through high school and contributes to a significant differential in ultimate educational achievement.

In the Northern Skills Development Program, ten out of thirteen students were women. Women outnumber men at Nunavut Arctic College, in the Nunavut Teacher Education Program, and in social work training—out of 40-50 graduates in various programs, 75 percent are women. Even in computer skills, women head the list of enrollees, as a NAC professor says, because the courses do not seem to fit male roles:

> We have a computer lab where we teach office skills, including word processing, spreadsheets, etc.—nothing that the local culture would define as appropriate for a man. All the students are women. The man who teaches the course includes office behaviour, dress, and time-consciousness but no computer applications designed to intersect with culturally-sanctioned male roles.

A teacher reports that in Adult Basic Education, which brings people up to tenth grade level, out of ten students, at least seven are women: "One of the women just had a baby, yet she continued to come to class and has been accepted for Inuit Studies at the college in Iqaluit. Two men came until Christmas, and then just stopped."[16] In the Community Office Practices program, which includes basic accounting and computer skills such as spreadsheets, of eight students in a recent year, all were women. In Math/Science upgrading, men who had already been working in carpentry and mechanics dominate the twelve-week course. Heavy equipment training in Fort Simpson, Yellowknife, Iqaluit, or carpentry training in Fort Smith attract more men than women: "These programs are not as academic." In trying to move people from social assistance to independence, certain key skills and knowledge areas stand out: Upgrading of Inuktitut, English, and math; career development; conflict management; budgeting; child care; and the secondary layer of values toward pursuing education with a sense of discipline and organization.

Why does this gender gap exist? A teacher ventures that "most boys want the easy way out. If they can find an easy solution to it, they'll do it. If not, it's no big deal. You can boil it down to laziness in a sense." The boys would like the kind of life portrayed on the soap operas or evening sitcoms, "but they're not prepared to work for it." He acknowledges that there are many exceptions (lazy girls and motivated boys) but he also insists that females, overall, seem more oriented toward school and its meaning for their future. Roposie, a construction worker, supposes that some young men fall prey to depression and lose hope for their future. He explains the downward spiral that so many Inuit youths experience:

"HE DOESN'T HAVE A FUTURE"
Say a boy misses a day or two of school and his performance gets worse. The teacher complains that he's not coming to school regularly. This student gets pressure from the teacher and the parents. He doesn't think he can get help from them or from anyone else, so he turns to stuff that he's not supposed to do. Then he misses more school and his grades go down even more.

When he becomes a teenager, the parents can't do anything about him because he is out of control. He can't go back to school because he's too old and he would have a very low grade. That would also give him pressure. He's in the middle with a little bit of education. He doesn't have a future. He turns to those escapes—alcohol, sniffing, suicide. He thinks it's all he can do.

Although he doesn't get the education he wanted, the father would try to teach him the traditional way of life. If he starts to get behind in school, he would automatically try to learn the other direction—go out hunting.

If he has a good father, he will learn the traditional life even if he is doing well in school and attends regularly. I know what I see myself. I can't say on behalf of the woman. Fortunately, many more boys today finish off their high school. They used to leave because we didn't have high school here; now they come back. Today, if you don't have an education, you'll be like everybody else, just bumming around and asking for money, breaking in.

A homemaker who came to the settlement when she was twelve explains the gender gap:

Males were in a dark area, but now we start understanding what's happening in our lives. We were completely lost—our life goes up and down for so many years! Now more young people want to finish high school. Life will be brighter in the future. When they put us into one community, there was a lot of confusion. We don't know what to do. New things come in—schools, regulations— very new to the people. Today they start understanding it.

A teacher characterizes girls as having clearer goals and more drive to reach them: "It's remarkably noticeable. From grade ten upwards, you have very few boys; it's practically all girls—they really want to get ahead. They have definite ideas about what they want from life." Television and exchange trips south have shaped those goals and "that's what they want." Reimer also found that "Inuit women have tended to aspire toward higher levels of education than their male counterparts, and it is Inuit women who hold many of the higher level management positions."[17]

Naiomi does not know what kind of life she would like, but she knows she wants to complete twelve grades and work at the Northern Stores: "To count money. I like math in school." A civic employee who is influential in the hamlet thinks his own 16-year-old daughter will finish high school. He supports her dreams: "I'm sure she's going to university or something. We've been telling her to be fully educated, and she agrees. If she wants to go to school down south, I might let her go, to have a more solid education."

One reason for this striking gender difference in motivation toward school may lie in the fact that female role models abound, compared to male role models. Almost all of the teachers in Pangnirtung, especially in the lower grades, are women. A higher proportion of male teachers might lead the boys toward deeper engagement in the learning process. Cultural inclusion teachers include both genders, and shop teachers are male. However, at the higher levels, almost all teachers have been Qallunaat from the south. From a very early age, girls see a few professional Inuit women who have parlayed their education into a respected career path.

By contrast, boys see male role models that include a higher ratio of defeated or confusing lifestyles than those available to girls: That is, more alcohol and drug abuse, more suicide, more aggressive behaviour resulting in getting into "trouble" with the law, and more premature school leaving. Because the trend has been toward more school completion among girls since resettlement, fewer men in the community can offer the example of achievement in that realm. Furthermore, because emulating the "great hunter"—a laudable pursuit for a boy in the past—will very likely *not* result in a young man's ability to support his family completely, that role model creates confusion rather than confidence. This pattern will probably change as more young males break out of the mold of school resistance and move into wage-paying jobs. However, as indicated in the next section, *Attitudes toward School*, the link between school and work remains only very loosely drawn at this point in the transition from living on the land to living in the settlement—for both males and females.

Attitudes toward School
"Friends are worried about their education"

S ome mothers want their children to finish high school but fear they will drop out by grade ten: "They are more lazy to go to school, but we still have to push them." As mentioned earlier, the Inuit raise their children in a relatively non-directive manner, allowing them to run freely through the community at a very early age. This makes it a little harder for them to sit in classrooms all day. Unfortunately, formal schooling has not appeared especially attractive to children once they hit their teens. In fact, the dropout rate starts to swell as early as the seventh grade: "In the 1990s, only 10 percent of the students who entered the seventh grade graduated from high school."[18]

Despite encouragement from teachers, many teenagers do not see the point in completing even a high school education because so few job opportunities exist in the settlement. Jukeepa, a teacher, offers her own explanation: "The kids wonder why they should finish high school if it's not really going to do them any good. There's just not that much for them to do here." The absence of prestigious, well-paying jobs has made it difficult for young people to set high goals and aspirations for themselves. Jennie states that her "friends worry about their education and what to do with their futures because even if they get training, there aren't enough jobs to go around." Most tragically, there are few opportunities in the settlement for employment, even for those who push on through high school and achieve degrees. In fact, nationally, "Five thousand aboriginal people must enter the work force annually for the next five years in order to maintain the current low employment rate for aboriginal people (which is double the non-native rate)."[19] Inuit have been underrepresented in territorial and federal jobs, little industry exists locally, and jobs in social services or education are inherently limited. If the next crop of high school graduates were to go to college or university in the south and return home, what would they do? Some men and women work for renewable resources or for the hamlet. Unfortunately, most of the jobs go to Qallunaat; it will be important to track whether this changes under Nunavut's governmental structure. Many Inuit, both men and women, go to other settlements like Iqaluit or Nanisivik to work because they cannot find a job in Pangnirtung. For those without education, the doors open slowly, Noah points out: "The government only sees the grade level sometimes."

The lack of job opportunities heavily influences attitudes toward schooling, Noah adds: "There's more education now, but education for what? If the jobs aren't here, that creates frustration: now I have my high school, but there's nothing for me to do." When eight out of ten employable Inuit cannot translate their education into work, it is difficult to persuade teenagers to stick it out in high school. For those who want to continue schooling after high school, the chances of finding a job are slightly higher, but Noah warns there is no guarantee: "Don't expect to find a job just because you finished high school—it doesn't work that way. You have to continue and get into something that you are really interested in, and probably you will have a much better chance of getting a job when you get back." This means leaving the community for training.

Mothers observe more enthusiasm and interest among the younger children, who especially like the cultural inclusion classes on hunting and traditional skills. Women, who usually make the decisions regarding their children's education, assume that completing school will lead to better job opportunities. Like their fathers, however, many young boys prefer going out on the land, with nature and older men as their teachers, to sitting in the white-dominated, book-oriented classroom.

Older Inuit females appreciate the chance to make up for education they did not receive as children. A woman who teaches sewing in the high school explains: "For my teaching in the school, the training helps because I only had about grade seven. Sometimes it's hard for me to keep paper work, to spell words...I don't have schooling enough." Ironically, many view education as less than a boon to the Inuit community. Even children who drop out at the end of grade nine or ten are rapidly outstripping their parents in formal schooling (not necessarily in wisdom or useful learning) and sometimes act as if they "know everything." Leeta explains: "The children get a lot of education nowadays. We used to have only maybe grade six or seven. Now they are in school for the whole day. The teachers tell them so many things that when they get home, they'll say, 'We can do this on our own, you don't have to tell us.' That's not true. It seems that the teachers are kind of ruining their lives."

Many younger women have finished only grade seven or eight; they speak of early pregnancy as a primary reason for suspending their schooling. They view this not as a loss but as a fact of life. Many who never completed a high school education upgrade later to complete grades eleven and twelve. For working women, returning to school may be very difficult, Rosie admits:

> If you are working in a busy place, it's hard to upgrade during the day. When you are a full-time mother and a full-time employee, it's hard to upgrade in the evenings. You've worked all day, then you have to look after the kids—you don't want to leave them again.

The educational gap between generations may contribute to what some older Inuit see as a lack of respect and discipline among younger families. The influence of teachers starts at age five, in kindergarten: "Right at that time you can notice that your kid is changing." They make faces or resist parental authority. When corrected, they may ask for money or talk back. This new pattern serves as a deterrent even to young women in their 20s who might otherwise return to complete their education:

> I quit school when I was in grade seven. Although the kids are in school now, I don't think I'll go back. School today seems to be more of a game than a real school. When I was in school, the teachers told us what to do; you had to do it, and we respected them. Today, the kids can just make fun of their teachers, and what can the teacher do? They're only trying to do their jobs now. The children today learn a lot but not as much as we did when we were in school. They don't work as much...or the teachers are afraid to reinforce the child to learn.

Rita, 22, talks about the options she hopes might be open to her:

> "I WANT TO GO BACK TO SCHOOL"
> I've lived here all my life. My education is low. I've gone up to grade ten but no more. I want to go on a hairdressing course, take some bookkeeping or business management, then go back to school and become a businesswoman. I will start in September if they accept me in Ontario, but I haven't heard anything about it yet. I know I would be accepted but not on a regular basis.
> Last time I talked to the principal, he said there might be a possibility of going back to school for accounting, business, and typing. He knows that I want to work in an office or try to get my own business in the future. In an office, you don't work with numbers. When you do the meter tickets that the water truck men give out, you have to balance that number and put them in order.
> I've talked about upgrading with an adult educator, but I haven't thought about it that much. It will hurt me if I don't finish high school. I'm not happy about my education because I didn't finish it, but I want to go back to school now that I know how important it is. I hated school. I hated getting up in the mornings. Now, I realize that it's important that you finish grade twelve.

Many girls leave school after the 10th or 11th grade but can "upgrade" to receive their high school diploma at the local NAC branch. COP, the Community Occupational Program, involves classes in the morning and work experience in different organizations in the afternoon. Susa, 28, tried to complete the program after dropping out of high school at age 15: "I was at the hamlet office as secretary for two months and three weeks at the Parks Canada office, and then I went back to the hamlet office for six weeks. I was with the by-law officer." Susa especially enjoyed being in an office because she liked working with people who taught her new skills. Meeka also benefited from this program: "I've been working since the year after I had my first baby. I was a clerk/cashier, and then I found a job at social services. I stayed with them for almost four years. I was pregnant and didn't go back. Then I was co-op assistant manager, and once or twice hamlet councilor. After that, I worked for the hamlet in town planning. Now I'm school secretary. That's how I learned my English."

Most Inuit women agree that education has brought them into a new world. The school system in most Inuit communities is less than three decades old and has already gone through many phases. More Inuit teachers and a new curriculum based in Inuit culture are becoming popular in many settlements: "We are beginning to do things in a very short space of time." The cynicism and pessimism surrounding life after high school prompted Premier Paul Okalik to encourage new graduates to find positive role models (even in literature), to value their high school achievement, and to pursue higher education: "This honour, though, carries with it a burden. Much is expected and hoped of you. You will become the leaders of the next generation and you must be ready."[20]

Entrance into Higher Education
"They'll have something concrete"

In order to progress into college or university courses, grade twelve graduates must pass the Alberta entrance exams. So far, even the best Inuit students have found this a frustrating hurdle. The language and cultural barriers that have made schooling difficult, at best, come even more into play at this level. Many parents and teachers observe that young people have achieved fluency in neither Inuktitut nor English, thus creating a double handicap: "The kids are not literate in either language by the time they hit high school. They can't comfortably read and write in Inuktitut and they cannot read and write properly in English. So they've been left stranded between the two worlds and they're not getting enough of either one."[21] Preserving Inuktitut is critical to preserving culture and identity, both younger and older Inuit women believe.[22]

Several graduates have gone on to Nunavut Arctic College in Iqaluit and a few have been able to gain entrance to a southern university to study law. Most, however, seek more technical and vocational courses that will be useful to them and their community. Says a teacher: "We're hoping that when they come back they will be role models for other students, which right now they don't have. It's what they see on the tube or what we tell them, but when these kids come back after completing, then they'll have something concrete, something real." Some

Inuit women have attended the McGill University teacher education program in Iqaluit and returned to teach in the local school.

The complexities of a northern education have meant that the Inuit find it hard to compete with southern standards—and now many Inuit want to set their own standards rather than accepting a "southern education" as the norm. When asked how many Inuit students make it to the university level, a high school teacher replies: "They haven't made it really. They have not been exposed to the real competition of the south. Some have been pampered all along and then they flunk." By 2000, only a few had made it through the hurdles of distance and culture into higher education and professional positions.

Annie Okalik, whom we interviewed before her death a few years ago, would be proud of her son, Paul, who became not only the first Inuit lawyer in the Eastern Arctic, but Nunavut's first premier. Born in Pangnirtung rather than out on the land, and the son of a water-truck driver, Annie's son first sat at the negotiating table to create Nunavut when he was only 20 years old. It is emblematic that Paul Okalik turned to education as his personal antidote to an adolescence of drinking, breaking and entering, and bored unemployment. His own brother committed suicide (which he thought was partly due to an insensitive criminal justice system). He credits his grandmother's influence in helping him become sober and change his life, and says that his Pangnirtung classmates "could have gone a lot further...but they found other ways of living their lives that were a little bit easier."[23] Along with others who have used school as a pathway out of personal tribulations to serve their communities, he serves as a role model for female and male youths in Pangnirtung and throughout Nunavut. Similarly, Jonah travels to courses when he can—environmental science at the community college in Lethbridge, Alberta; management, accounting, and Native political science at the University of Lethbridge: "I've just been learning everyday! Nowadays, it isn't unique because everybody goes to school. Probably back in the 60s, it was unique."

Noah, a young employment counselor, emphasizes how difficult it is to go away to school for extended periods: "People are so family oriented that they don't want to leave the town or their family." Unless Inuit women and men leave their community, at least temporarily, they will find it difficult to advance. They can go to Ottawa for specialized courses, but Noah describes how the fear of leaving for the first time can paralyze them: "They're very uncertain. They've heard all kinds of advice." A nurse points out that, while women seem to adapt better to being away from home because they are used to taking care of their own needs, they can also feel caught between two powerful forces. She describes the situation of two Inuit women, one who has worked as an aide and is ready for further training as a registered nursing assistant, and the other whose husband does not support her enthusiastically.

> The year-long course takes place in Iqaluit, which isn't that far. At least in Iqaluit, you still have the same food, the same climate. For people who go

down south, it's really hard. When I went to university in Edmonton, there was an Inuk woman who had come to do a post-basic nursing program, and she had such a hard time. She had a child, lived far from the community, had to go back and forth, and she found it overwhelming. It wasn't because she was less bright.

One young woman is in Thunder Bay at Lakehead University, to do her BA in nursing. She did upgrading for a year, so she'll have been away from home for five years. She's married, she has three children; her husband is not particularly supportive. She's bright and she has potential, but the chances of her succeeding are slim.

Five years away from the community looms large. It might be easier, the nurse thinks, for women to do a two-year program, return to their settlement for a little experience, and then continue later with education toward the R.N. degree. Female students who go to Ottawa with their children often return home without completing their program because they become discouraged and cannot handle the financial burdens of studying away from home.

The thought of relocating to another place frightens many young people who have grown up in a geographically isolated community, even though airplane, television, fax, and telephone link Pangnirtung to southern society. For example, many Inuit resist going to Iqaluit because of the town's reputation for drinking, drugs, fighting, and crime. Parents are not keen on sending their children into what they see as a decadent urban setting. Mona went to school in Toronto for three years and lived in the south "quite comfortably," though she missed the North. Even a short visit south makes her homesick, "not only for the food but for sanity. Deep silence." This is a typical reaction among the older Inuit. For many, living in the south is associated with being ill with TB or polio and living in an institution. Mona elaborates: "People don't realize what a big adjustment it is to move down south. There's no one around who speaks their language; there's nobody who eats the same food; it's hot." A Qallunaat teacher explains: "We don't really have that much technical training here. The kids could go to the Arctic College or to Ottawa, but they miss home. They don't want to leave Pang. Unless they get out, though, they can't better themselves. All the qualifications they need are out there."

Inuit pay a high price for trying to educate themselves beyond high school. Extended absences from their families do not sit well. Some become depressed, even to the point of suicide. Men, especially, have a hard time adjusting to the city. Many drink too much, get into bar fights, and end up in jail. Some men and women give up and return home; then they feel like failures. The "terrible pull for home" is mentioned one way or another by many Inuit women over 30 in discussing their chances for future training or education. They say that, when they go south (to Ontario or Québec cities), they miss the peaceful landscapes, the cold climate, and—most of all—their families. Many Inuit who have ventured south find urban environments confusing, noisy, and frightening. They dislike warm weather and some have trouble adjusting to a steady diet of southern food.[24]

Some of these issues have been addressed for Inuit teachers who have completed a Bachelor of Education program offered by McGill University to learn how to teach children from Kindergarten through Grade Six in Inuktitut.[25] To ease potential teachers into this program, students study for two years in their own community and then spend two years in Iqaluit. This strategy eases the hardships involved in being away from home, eliminates the need to travel to southern Canada for higher education, and ensures the development of a cadre of professionally trained teachers. Distance learning presents another potential opportunity for earning degrees without leaving home.

Discomfort of leaving for education may be changing somewhat for teenagers, who grew up only in the settlements and with television images of southern lifestyles. Kari, in her early teens, represents the broader perspective of the youngest generation. She has lived with elders who grew up on the land in large, close-knit families—and she has visited friends in southern Canada: "My grandma has fourteen kids. I like to visit her, but when we have school vacation, we go down south sometimes. Two years ago, we went to Vancouver, British Columbia. We went with our Qallunaat friends to Florida. I like to visit my friend in Nova Scotia." This well-traveled young woman will very likely embrace the idea of attending university in a city such as Toronto or Ottawa.

Dreams can overcome the pain of being away from home. Rosemary, 18, worked in Iqaluit on a summer job and then took the leap to attend university in Nova Scotia. She wants to complete a social work degree so she can work with victims of child abuse in her own community. Thus, although Inuit women look to schooling as one of the chief engines of change in this century, it is also one of the most problematic issues.[26] Financing education presents no barriers—the government takes care of all expenses—but the wages they would lose if enrolled full time deter many women. Many females in their late teens or early 20s feel conflicted about leaving the community in order to take advantage of job training or further education. Still rooted in traditional life, women see some opportunities for success but feel caught in a period when families want them to be traditional, raise children, stay home, and be with a man: "Our parents are torn, too. They want us to succeed, but they also put pressure on us to have a family. They say, 'You should be with them.'"

The adult education center offers classes for a work release group, preparing students to give speeches. The young people who come from work release are "all forward looking, all very ambitious people," according to their teacher. Nunavut Arctic College has diversified courses:

> One young woman wants to become a teacher; another one wants to become a manager in a store. They can finish as far as grade ten, and then go for a special training called the NTEP [Nunavut Teacher's Education Program] in Iqaluit—

certification for the lower grades. After that, they can go for a BA degree at McGill University, but some don't want to leave Pang.

Women who are willing to leave their children behind with family members can attend NAC's six-month course in basic office procedures. Mary, who is thinking of taking advantage of this opportunity, says she will miss her children, "but I really want a good job, so I *have* to go to school." A well-respected artist plans to attend NAC to take up administrative studies or business management. She is happy that her mother will take care of her toddler son, "but I know that I am going to get bored without him."

A student at the main NAC campus in Iqaluit claims that the only male who entered the teacher education program left because he missed home. A few women study hairdressing or other service trades. The government sends them to Montreal or elsewhere for training. Says one young woman in weighing the balance between leaving home and becoming educated beyond high school: "Many people in the North don't appreciate the benefits we have."

"Distance education" through electronic communication will play a critical role in expanding educational opportunities for Inuit students. For example, the University of the Arctic, which involves students and faculty from the entire circumpolar region, has begun activities in Nunavut. The Arctic Council, comprised of political ministers from countries that contain Inuit peoples (e.g., Canada, U.S., Russia, Greenland, etc.), agreed at its 1998 meeting in Iqaluit to establish the University of the Arctic; it is "designed to produce a new generation of scholars with knowledge of the entire circumpolar region." Finland manages a secretariat for the initial stages of this institution that "will operate principally in cyberspace."[27] Rather than formal courses, students will have Internet access to resources, experts, and practical problem-solving projects in the field of Arctic Studies. This is an obvious solution to reducing geographic isolation.[28] As a university without a campus of its own, UArctic will borrow facilities from educational institutions that already exist. It will link students, teachers, and classrooms through distance-education, exchanges, and fieldwork.

Generally, the Inuit are taking the school system and using it to advantage, a teacher notes: "The old traditional Inuit culture is going, but they are creating a new culture for a new era. The basic values will be the same." Schools will, as always, be a critical vehicle for reshaping a culture that maintains integrity within the Canadian context; they are increasingly paying genuine attention to teaching traditional Inuit culture as well as a contemporary Canadian Inuit culture that blends the new with the old. This pattern bears the burden of hope for the future. Just as girls seem to push harder in school, they also end up with a double role that bridges home and the workplace—that carries with it the double responsibility and challenging task of balancing cultural identity demands with the stress of working outside the home. As Jean Briggs observes, "Inuit culture [is]...a mosaic of dilemmas which echo, cross-cut, confirm, and negate one another; dilemmas that are never totally resolved but have to be juggled and rearranged time after time."[29] Linking education to meaningful work within the context of geographic isolation and a history of dependency is a major dilemma facing Inuit women in this century.

Photo 16.3 Anna wearing her handmade sealskin boots with embroidered duffel socks.

Notes

1 Quoted in Hallendy, "Reflections, Shades and Shadows," p. 21.
2 Quoted in Hallendy, "Reflections, Shades and Shadows," p. 21.
3 Capozza, "Canadian Territory of Nunavut Pushes to Expand College Offerings," p. A38.
4 Department of Indian Affairs and Northern Development, *Highlights of Aboriginal Condition,* p. 77. Based on 1991 Statistics Canada data. The Inuit have lower high school graduation and university attendance rates (primarily because of the lack of schools in the region) than do other aboriginal groups.
5 John F. Burns, "Eskimo Males Said to Be Battling 'Lib' by Beating Wives," *The New York Times* (November 20, 1974), n.p.

6 Capozza, "Canadian Territory of Nunavut Pushes to Expand College Offerings," p. A39.

7 Capozza, "Canadian Territory of Nunavut Pushes to Expand College Offerings," p. A39.

8 Permanent residents of Nunavut receive $675 a month in student financial assistance, as well as help with tuition fees of up to $2550 per term and $200 per term for textbooks over a three-year period. Nunavut post-secondary students who qualify as beneficiaries of the Nunavut land claim agreement may apply to Nunavut Tunngavik for bursaries of $2500 per year toward university or $1500 per year toward college programs, if they have achieved an average of 65 percent in high school and maintain an average of 70 percent during higher education. Jane George, "Nunavut College Students Will Face More Hard Times," *Nunatsiaq News* (August 27, 1999).

9 Keeping southern nurses in the Arctic has been as problematic as retaining teachers and other professionals, which is another good reason to ensure that Inuit women and men can receive adequate training and education. See, for example, Brenda Canitz, "Health Care in Crisis: Understanding Nursing Turnover in Northern Canada," pp. 151-152 in *Circumpolar Health 90: Proceedings of the Eighth International Congress on Circumpolar Health* (Winnipeg: University of Manitoba Press, 1990); and H. E. Ferrari, "The Outpost Nurse: Role and Activities in Northern Canada," pp. 600-605 in *Circumpolar Health: Proceedings of the Third International Symposium*, edited by R. J. Shephard and S. Itoh (Toronto: University of Toronto Press, 1976).

10 Capozza, "Canadian Territory of Nunavut Pushes to Expand College Offerings," p. A39.

11 Tait, "Focus on Nunavut," p. 10; these figures were for 1996.

12 Jeremy Hull, *Aboriginal Post-Secondary Education and Labour Market Outcomes Canada, 1996* (Ottawa: Research and Analysis Directorate, Department of Indian Affairs and Northern Development, 2000), p. 12.

13 Hull, *Aboriginal Post-Secondary Education and Labour Market Outcomes Canada, 1996*, pp. 28, 42.

14 Ambassador Mary May Simon, "Children and Youth of the Arctic: A Critical Challenge of Sustainable Development," Keynote Address to Sustainable Development in the Arctic: Lessons Learned and the Way Ahead, *The Northern Review* 18 (1999), p. 74.

15 McGrath, "Circumventing the Taboos," p. 228.

16 Ken de la Barre, *The Academic Requirements Needed for Inuit Students to be Successful in Post-Secondary Education and Advanced Technical Training* (Nunavik Educational Task Force, 1990) and *Immediate Priorities and Interim Measures: School Drop-Outs and Other Youth "At Risk"* (Nunavik Educational Task Force, 1991).

17 Reimer, "Female Consciousness," p. 89.

18 Capozza, "Canadian Territory of Nunavut Pushes to Expand College Offerings," p. A38.

19 Oakes, "Climate and Cultural Barriers to Northern Economic Development," p. 91.

20 Jane George, "Go to College, Premier Okalik Urges Graduates," *Nunatsiaq News* (June 18, 1999).

21 Quoted in Griffiths, et al., *Crime, Law, and Justice among Inuit*, p. 65.

22 Jean-Philippe Chartrand, "Survival and Identity of the Inuit Ethnic Identity: The Importance of Inuktitut," pp. 241-255 in *Native People, Native Lands: Canadian Indians, Inuit and Métis*, edited by B. Alden Cox (Ottawa: Carleton University Press, 1987).

23 John Geddes, "Northern Son," *Maclean's (*April 23, 2001), p. 16.

24 For a description of Inuit experiences living in southern Canada, see Marsha Kaplansky, *Inuit in the South* (Ottawa: Department of Indian and Northern Affairs, 1981).

25 For a discussion of the importance of Inuktitut language education as a vehicle for carrying culture in Inuit schooling, see Arlene Stairs, "Beyond Language: Lessons from Eastern Canadian Inuit in the Cultural Values of Education," *Journal of Navajo Education* 7, 3 (1990): 31-36; and "The Development Context of Native Language Literacy: Inuit Children and Inuktitut Education," in *Promoting Native Writing Systems in Canada*, edited by B. Burnaby (Toronto: OISE Press, 1985).

26 Both McLean and Jennings question to what extent adult education and higher education promote southern values and perpetuate racism, cultural superiority, and dependency instead of empowering Inuit for development according to their own values and interests. Scott McLean, "Adult Education in Nunavut: Promotion of Self-Government, or the Governance of Selves?" and Michael L. Jennings, "Northern Development: The Role of the University." Both papers presented at the Third International Congress of Arctic Social Sciences, Copenhagen, Denmark, 1998.

27 Canadian Press, "Arctic Council Takes First Steps toward Action" (Iqaluit, NWT: Canadian Press, September 21, 1998); and Jane George, "University of the Arctic Takes First Baby Steps in Nunavut," *Nunatsiaq News* (February 11, 1999). Some Baffin Inuit have been using the Internet for many years: Neil Blair Christensen, "Inuit in Cyberspace: Arctic Users Networking between Past and Present," paper presented to the Eleventh Inuit Studies Conference, Nuuk, September 1998; Marianne Stenbaek-Lafon, "Inuit and Globalisation: Potential Use of the Internet in the Arctic," pp. 235-240 in *PO-LARTEC 98: International Conference on Development and Commercial Utilization of Technologies in Polar Regions*, Nuuk, June 8-14, 1998; and Barry Zellen, *Surf's up! NWT's Indigenous Communities Await a Tidal Wave of Electronic Information*, in "The Internet and Indigenous Groups," *Cultural Survival Quarterly World Report on the Rights of Indigenous Peoples and Ethnic Minorities*, QSQ 21.4 (1998). In 2002, the Bill and Melinda Gates Foundation awarded $486,000 to Nunavut for computers and Internet access in Nunavut's public libraries, as well as free training in Seattle for library personnel. Nunatsiaq News, "Nunavut Libraries Get Grant from Gates Foundation," *Nunatsiaq News* (March 23, 2001). For a discussion of the impact of higher education on Inuit lives, see F. King Alexander and Kern Alexander, eds., *The University: The Transformation of Inuit Settlement in the Central Arctic* (Montreal: McGill-Queens University Press, 2003).

28 Canada's Foreign Affairs Department has committed $400,000 for the project. Jane George, "Arctic University Grows by Degrees: UArctic to Launch on June 12," *Nunatsiaq News* (June 1, 2001).

29 Jean L. Briggs, *Inuit Morality Play: The Emotional Education of a Three-Year Old* (New Haven: Yale University Press, 1998), p. 209.

17

The Meaning of Work

For us, we call hunting independence. We're not relying on government handouts. We're not on welfare.

—Pauloosie

The Whale Hunters

Photo 17.1 Iceberg in Cumberland Sound.

It is mid-afternoon and high tide. The men have waited patiently for this moment to float their crafts safely off the beach and into the channel. Killer whales have entered the fiord further south, where it opens into Cumberland Sound. For two or three days, rumors about the whales have flown around the hamlet, but last night men who were tracking these unwelcome beasts reported good news: Beluga whales—fair game and good eating—have also been spotted.

As we walk down the gravel street on the way to the harbor for a short boat ride, six men stride along in front of us. Each carries a rifle slung casually over the right shoulder. They are off to another whale hunt, modern warriors marching with an air of nonchalance that comes only when one's purpose is deadly serious. The men are culture heroes reminiscent of a hundred years ago when the people living around Cumberland Sound worked at nearby whaling stations. At virtually every house, someone comes to the door to wish them luck or offer advice. The men nod in appreciation of the encouragement.

The atmosphere in town becomes electric with stories about who has gone hunting and when they might return. The hunt involves far more than personal achievement or the quest for food. It represents the intimate connection between hunter and nature, and "a complex of social relationships between humans, animals and spirit owners."[1] This is an important day.

Sheila Kunilusie's husband, Billy, 33, will not hunt this time. He brings his father's chestnut boat alongside a large boulder at the channel edge. It is a seaworthy wooden craft with rounded lines, suggestive of a contemporary blend of the ancient *umiak* (the "women's boat") and the *qajaq* (used more by men). As he readies the boat, we climb awkwardly across the prow on hands and knees. We sit behind Billy, his uncle Jooeelee, and 10-year-old son Charlie, who sit on the front bench, taking turns steering. The boat has seen many repairs, but it easily skims across the cold water with a seventy-horsepower motor behind it. We head north of Pangnirtung, away from the whales and toward the head of the fiord. On either side, the craggy mountains dominate the scenery. Glacial tongues—snow and ice masses that flow like lava rivers down between the highest peaks—remind us of the harsh winter the people withstand. Billy calls out the name of each mountain as we glide by, as though naming friends who live along a village street. The land, after all, is a familiar place for him. On this July afternoon, the temperature has risen to a few degrees above freezing. The wind whipping across the cabin makes us shiver in spite of long underwear and heavy jackets. We follow Billy's lead by bending low to escape the biting wind.

After an hour of exhilarating scenery, Billy searches for a place to land for a cup of tea. In true Inuit fashion, he has remembered the camp stove and kettle, but he has forgotten the cups, so we ditch the tea idea and munch on the less warming granola bars we had squirreled away in our backpacks. As we crawl off the boat onto shore, we both slip into the water and get our boots wet. This small mistake could cost a life if we were alone in this lovely but treacherous spot.

Billy refers to pools of water as "left over water" from the spring melting period, and then laughs at himself because he does not know the technical word in Inuktitut to describe this type of ice. He describes how men test the spring ice with harpoons to find soft spots or breathing holes where seals come up for air. The men wait, still as statues, sometimes for hours at a time. When the seal finally emerges, the men use harpoons or rifles to kill the seal in one swift, flawless motion. Billy adds warmly that his father is extremely nimble, able to leap from one ice floe to another much faster than other men can. Billy sees himself as very fast, too. He adds that his young son, Charlie, is *so* fast that Billy encourages him to practice to become a sports star. Charlie smiles at this praise.

After our rest, we head back toward Pangnirtung, this time with the wind against us. We become silent and rigid with cold, and spend most of the trip wishing it would quickly end. When we finally pull into the harbour, Billy's mother and other relatives await us. Once again, we clamber over the prow and jump clumsily to the rocks, this time to a chorus of giggles and good-humored jests. We walk briskly back to our cozy apartment for tea, dry socks, and a nap.

The next day we visit Andrew, who proudly tells us that he "got a whale" last night. Another man shot the whale, he explains, but the modern weapons can never finish the job. Andrew brought the huge mammal to a halt with a harpoon. Sealskin balloons at the end of the harpoon slowed the whale down; it was unable to thrash for long against the drag created by the bags of air. Andrew adds with a glint in his eye: "The old methods work best. Whales are hard to catch because they are very smart—but they're not as smart as people!"

Seven months later, Billy and young Charlie Kunilusie drowned with Henry Akulukjuk, 25, in a boating accident during an October snow squall. The newspaper reported that "...the bodies were found in a small fiord about forty km northwest of Pangnirtung, close to their overturned boat. They failed to return to Pangnirtung after starting out on the return portion of a trip to a hunting camp in a twenty-four–foot freighter canoe. Their return trip was expected to be only a four-hour journey."[2] Characteristically, the three Pangnirtung natives had taken supplies to friends in an outpost camp. Even after the official search was called off several days later, Pangnirtung men continued to look for the lost party. They found them not far from the outpost camp. The boat's rope was tied around Billy's waist. He had valiantly tried to pull it up a steep slope, out of harm's way.

ᴄ℞

Traditionally, hunting was the centerpiece of the Inuit man's ability to provide for his family, and a positive element in the self-concept of some women. Hunting the whale has been an integral part of Inuit identity for centuries, but a disastrous attempt to kill the less plentiful bowhead whale near Repulse Bay in 1996 created a negative reaction among animal-rights activists. The bullets from high-powered rifles succeeded only in sinking the giant mammal, which then rotted and had to be burned after it floated back to the surface two days later. Only about 700 bowheads live in the eastern Arctic waters around Nunavut, but in 1998, the civic leaders in Pangnirtung vowed to try another bowhead hunt. In response to critics, Eric Joamie, a leader of the Pangnirtung Hunters' Association, said: "Our ancestors were involved in harvesting any kind of animals they were able to come across, for their survival. It is our right, part of our culture, to harvest any animal within Nunavut, regardless of any regulations."[3] Permission to take one bowhead whale was granted to Pangnirtung. The endeavor constituted a major operation with a heavy sense of responsibility after the Repulse Bay fiasco. Jaco Evic thought about the elders who had whaled at Kekerten in the 1900s: "It was good to have it [the hunt] in this area and it went so well, we're so pleased about it."[4] In the aftermath of a successful hunt, the Pangnirtung group shipped some of the meat and blubber to other Nunavut communities.

Today, for men who can hunt on a regular basis, it means keeping their families off welfare, or at least providing them with significant supplements to social assistance or meager incomes from part-time or seasonal employment. The loss of hunting as a primary means of family support has had devastating effects.

Welfare: A Double-Edged Sword
"They lose their good life"

High rates of unemployment spell high rates of welfare dependency. Local estimates of the percentage of Inuit receiving some form of public assistance or social security payments run between 60 and 80 percent, depending on the season: "Welfare is high here in Pang." As in other Inuit communities, "there has been a significant increase in all forms of social assistance" during the 1980s and 1990s.[5]

The bottom line in a cash economy is money. Whether money comes from welfare may not be as important in a place characterized by little market competition, few consumer choices, and high prices as that it comes from *somewhere*. The government promised during resettlement that, absent wage-earning jobs, the fairly generous Canadian social cushion would be there to catch those who fell between the cracks of modern life and the hunting-gathering economy of old. Chabot and Duhaime have found this trend since 1950 in Nunavik: Wage earning is the major economic activity, but government funds create the "backbone of personal income"—either as salaries for government jobs or as welfare.[6]

People still remember that early social contract, but the picture is complex. First, many men who hunt still claim welfare benefits, although the rules are stricter than they previously were. Second, welfare may not be a choice but a matter of survival for many Inuit. Third, welfare may hurt people as much as it helps them keep food on the table. Some Inuit feel that the welfare cushion has weakened them, as a government employee relates: "I see welfare hurting people so much. Many people could still depend on themselves. They just rely on welfare. They lose their good life. Today, I say we are spoiled." Yet, as the next section shows, with hunting so expensive and jobs so few, welfare may be the only viable choice for many men and women—especially those who were caught in the transitional generation of relatively low schooling and little training in skills of the land. A generation dependent on welfare spins off another generation dependent on welfare when suitable work opportunities are scarce. Still, the level of support is low given the high cost of living in the North: In 1996, the welfare check was around $200 every other week for a family of four.

A Staggering Unemployment Rate
"The jobs aren't here"

With the demise of hunting and trapping, the constant backdrop behind life in this community is a high unemployment rate that mainstream society would find disastrously unacceptable. In 1994, in Pangnirtung, 400 people out of 1,419 were officially unemployed. Those between the ages of 25 and 44 experienced the highest unemployment rate (61.6 percent). Of course, different methods can be used to calculate unemployment rates. Local hamlet officials give higher rates than suggested by a Nunavut government report.[7] New jobs were created faster in Nunavut between 1994 and 1999 than in any other territory or province in Canada. The figures had improved by 1999 for the territory as a whole, but unemployment among the Inuit stood at 28 percent, "in sharp contrast to the non-Inuit unemployment rate of 2.7 percent.... This means that only 86 non-Inuit persons were unemployed during the winter of 1999 in Nunavut, compared to 2,171 Inuit who were unemployed."[8] When Inuit-only rates are examined, they are much higher than the territory as a whole. If the rate is calculated to include active job seekers who have given up looking for work, because of lack of jobs, the territorial unemployment rate is closer to 27 percent. If it is based on all people who want jobs but cannot find them, the rate is over 35 percent.[9] Rates also vary greatly by community. Furthermore, Nunavut's young population will continue to grow in the foreseeable future. This means that educating the young will undoubtedly form the centerpiece of Nunavut's development prospects.[10]

Like welfare, working in the wage economy may be the only viable choice when the subsistence economy presents so many obstacles. Mitchell saw the "indigenous mode of production" slowly transforming into a new mode of production that has many of the earmarks of capitalism and "proletarianization." Hunting and gathering takes a back seat to employment and state support through welfare, substantially altering the time-tested indigenous mode.[11] Wenzel thought that the "growth in the money sector of the economy in [Inuit] communities is less an indicator of Inuit socioeconomic well-being or satisfaction than of concerted external pressure on the cash component of modern harvesting."[12] Like welfare, wage-earning jobs may not offer the solution to economic security because they tend to be seasonal, low paying, or part time. During the summer months, employment goes up with a mini-blitz of construction, but throughout the long, bitter winter the employment rate plummets to 20 percent or lower. It is too cold to build and tourist dollars virtually disappear.

Further complicating matters, unemployment and social assistance statistics do not take into account the work of regular or occasional hunting. In the current social and economic climate, some bias surfaces toward wage-earning jobs as the only *true* employment. Ann, whose husband is a hunter, reveals: "People always ask me what he does—I say he hunts. They look at me. I see a question mark come into their eyes about what that means. Or they'll ask, 'Is he unemployed?' I'll say, no, he's not unemployed, he's hunting." The concept is very hard for some people to understand, she adds. They assume that because her husband is a hunter, he suddenly has nothing, but a good hunter contributes economically to his family and beyond: "It's always for sharing. What my husband gets, he gives to people."

Many men work sporadically as hunters, trappers, and fishermen, but just as many find that their families need some other form of income as well—either welfare or a woman's wages. In addition, as an economic activity, hunting is becoming increasingly rare because it takes both money and skill. A community leader observes that some men "now in their second generation of alcoholic families or welfare families" do not hunt. Their fathers did not hunt, either. Even if they go out occasionally, hunting is not a main part of their life: "Many townspeople simply don't know how to hunt anymore and they're dangerous. You wouldn't want to take them with you because they don't know what they should be doing. It's sad when you see that."

An element of hope emerges in the early twenty-first century, as caribou seem to be coming back to the river valley across from Pangnirtung. They live only about five miles inland, very accessible compared to previous decades since resettlement. The men take care not to hunt the caribou that venture close to the fiord, so as not to frighten them away again. Now, they can hunt in a one-day round trip. It will take years to rebuild the herds to the point of providing subsistence for a large number of families, however, and some men who want to hunt lack the equipment. Few among the younger generation have the requisite skills. In the absence of dogs and *qamutiik*, they must buy skidoos that cost several thousand dollars. For seal hunting, they must have boats, motors, and guns—a package that carries a total price tag of around $20,000. The amount of income generated is usually not enough to cover such costs. One study shows that in 1989, 5,250 Inuit (primarily men) engaged in hunting and other subsistence activities in Nunavut, generating an estimated $62.4 million in country food to their families and communities.[13] That figure could be misleading, however, because one might have ample country food but not enough cash to buy other staples like flour, milk, and fresh produce or other consumer goods (gasoline for boats, material for sewing, or ready-made clothing and shoes).

Hunting is a legitimate form of employment. As Hedican has documented, hunting and fishing do not constitute a fallback position for Inuit men: "Some of the most prolific hunters in northern Native settlements are also those with some of the higher-paying jobs."[14] The higher the per capita income, he found, the higher the consumption of country food. This finding reflects the costs of subsistence activities, since only those with wage-paying jobs can afford to engage in fishing and hunting). It also suggests that the modern economy will not necessarily supplant the traditional economy. In addition, the need to provide at least some country food gives otherwise unemployed males a sense of worth and identity. Tragically, the Inuit find it expensive to eat either way, hunting *or* buying at the stores, as a woman leader explains:

> Men are encouraged to hunt and fish because the food in the stores is poor and very expensive. I don't know how people cope. It's getting more and more expensive, and there's no end to it. I think that's why most of our children are not as healthy as they should be. Some don't eat very well. They are always eating sweets. It's not their fault. It will take a lot of education to learn how to eat better on a very limited budget. It sounds impossible. Hunting plays an important role. With sewing, or making clothing, we can't do it without the men hunting.

Men try to support each other in sharing the expenses of hunting or fishing. For example, one man who lost his job as a heavy equipment operator hunts and fishes with his father. He fishes one day and his father sells the catch; the next time, they reverse the process. They go for three-day fishing trips, fifty miles out toward the Atlantic. Some venture even further in order to catch enough to pay for the gas. Some see carving as a way to buy gas and bullets in order to hunt. Thomas Sivuraq of Baker Lake says of the early days: "Carving was a way for me to get bullets for my rifle and supplies to go hunting."[15] Many men now work in the commercial fishing industry at Pangnirtung Fisheries (started by Davidee Eevic in 1987), harvesting turbot ("Greenland halibut") and Arctic char for shipment to the south. About forty men and women work in the plant and over 120 local fishermen provide their catches throughout the season. Women work in the processing end of the operation.[16]

White Collar, Services, and the Arts
"I'd like to be a scientist..."

As with other aboriginal women, Inuit women are under-represented in the Canadian labour force.[17] They also tend to cluster in clerical, sales, service, health, and education-related occupations—all of which tend to pay less than other occupational avenues. More recently, Inuit women have become involved in the middle layers of the Nunavut government (both in Iqaluit and in the hamlets). As significant as working outside the home is for many Inuit women, only a very limited range of employment positions awaits them. In Pangnirtung, more women than men work in the hamlet office, visitor's centre, Angmarlik cultural centre, and the tapestry studio. More men than women work in construction: "They have an easier time getting jobs because they can do that." Employment tends to follow a caste-like opportunity structure, with Qallunaat controlling managerial and professional positions.

Other than the fish plant and tourism, there is no industry or production in Pangnirtung. Jobs include service or semi-professional positions in health, social services, housing, education, and the RCMP. A few sales or clerical jobs are available; some say that more jobs existed in the mid-1990s than in the 1980s, but the change seems minuscule. Jobs mentioned by women in this study include: various clerical and service jobs for the hamlet, cashier at the stores, tenant relations officer, employment outreach worker, clerk typist, secretary, assistant manager, nursing station assistant, clerk interpreter at the health center, housekeeper, cook (at the lodge), housing officer, social work assistant, teaching assistant, and custodial worker in the schools and cultural center. A few earn small amounts of cash by baby-sitting for mothers who work outside the home. Arts and crafts workshops supply a few jobs to weavers, sculptors, artists, and seamstresses; several artists work independently. Some women receive pay for teaching traditional sewing in the cultural inclusion programs. A few young girls, like 15-year-old Sandy, dream well beyond these boundaries: "I'd like to be a scientist or a cop or a nurse or a doctor."

Some women, like Eena, define their own wage-earning jobs as a mechanism for enabling their husbands to hunt: "I am working to help him follow his career. I'm quite happy to do that, because we have tried him working and being a part of this culture. He has a good education, better than most people do, but he's very unhappy when he's participating in the labour force. He tries hard, but when he's unhappy, our whole family is unhappy." Eena's employment allows her husband to do "the hunting part of his lifestyle." In the summer months, she likes to hunt with him for a month or two, living on the land, following the traditional lifestyle. She hopes their children are learning invaluable skills.

Beyond work in education and community development, the Nursing Station has always hired women. In the old days, workers received food and clothing rather than cash. Out of eleven staff members, there are five nurse practitioners (all white) and six others: clerk interpreters, housekeepers, a caretaker, and occasionally a community health representative (all Inuit). The doctor comes from Iqaluit every six weeks for a few days. Some men have complained that the station should hire more men, since they believe men would find it easier to talk with male staff about their problems.

Although they find more *consistent* employment in the wage economy, women often earn less and hold lower status positions on average than men.[18] Many Inuit women support their families, but their jobs tend to be lower status and lower income. Older women, especially, have difficulty competing in a more service and technical employment market, but younger women are unemployed and underemployed, too. This leaves a syndrome of "nothing to do" and sinking into welfare dependency. Aside from art, for those who cannot write or read English, the choices are narrow. Seasonal work and intermittent layoffs make it difficult to stay off social assistance. As an older woman confides, she and her husband, who is a trained carpenter, try hard to find work. When they do work, they work hard.

Only a few women engage in "creative work," although printmaking, weaving, sewing, and sculpture have made an enormous difference in the creative and economic life of both Inuit men and women.[19] A handful of men and women in Pangnirtung work as artists and printmakers, and a few more carve soapstone, whalebone, or caribou antler sculptures for tourists and the southern galleries.[20] A 1995 exhibit in Winnipeg of Inuit and Dene art illustrated the relatively equal productivity of Inuit women artists compared to men.[21] For the Inuit population as a whole, approximately 30 percent make some income from carving or printmaking. Some, like Pangnirtung's Manasie Maniapik, Jaco Ishulutaq, and Guyasie Veevee, have achieved national recognition, showing their work in the National Gallery of Art in Ottawa and major art outlets. Guyasie complains that carvers cannot always find suitable stone. He would like to start a "school for carvers" with his name on it. Senior carvers could have a sheltered place to work during the cold winter months and could teach young aspiring carvers.

Aside from artistic endeavors, men's jobs are not much more varied than women's and include: assistant minister, nursing station custodian, Department of Public Works employee (water delivery, sewage disposal), housing or road repair worker, self-employed building contractor ("I learned from the white men who used to come here"), Special Constable for the RCMP, working for the Government of the NWT (in the past) or for the new Nunavut government, construction worker, truck driver, heavy equipment operator, maintenance worker, settlement clerk, recreational coordinator, carpenter (for the hamlet), and heavy duty mechanic ("I went to school for that for four years, did nothing after that, then went to the hamlet office"). In addition to the government agencies, some Inuit men find employment with Parks Canada as wardens, or as private outfitters spiriting tourists from Pangnirtung into Auyuittuq National Park.

Entering the RCMP
"They want to police themselves"

The RCMP may offer some opportunities both for employment and for greater community empowerment. The RCMP employs three regular officers in Pangnirtung (all Qallunaat as of this writing) and a few cadets (including one Inuk female). Nationally, females constitute about 10 to 15 percent of RCMP officers. Up until the 1960s, RCMP recruits could not marry for five years. Lifting that restriction opened doors for females as well as for males. In the past, Inuit men (and then women) entered the force under the designation of "special constable" (a position that lacks full police status).

Several male Inuit became full RCMP in the early 1980s. Susie Nakashuk of Pangnirtung, who has participated in the RCMP cadet program, is a pioneer in becoming the first female Inuk RCMP officer: "I love this job because I like working with people. I like the uniform. Women can relate to people. I will be an example." Susie and her colleagues believe that it is significant that a woman has made this step—it is one way that Inuit women will increasingly be able to formalize their considerable influence at the community level in the twenty-first century. Says a corporal: "We have excellent aboriginal programs, but we need more Inuit here. They are great interpreters; the people like it when they see an Inuk constable. It makes our work easier and puts the community at ease. We did elder visits with the female cadets—their faces lit up."

Some characterize the RCMP as dedicated, especially in trying to round up drug dealers. Others point to success with a more subtle community-based approach that focuses on relationship building. A local teacher describes the diffuse nature of their role: "They're not just here to lay down the law; they let the kids see that they're human." To that end, the Mounties organize and participate in games: "The police here are very friendly, very nice people." At Christmas, they leave their uniforms behind and have fun with the children. An RCMP officer says the fact that the force makes it a point to recruit Inuit as local constables exemplifies this spirit:

> There are many ways of skinning a cat. The way things are happening now is very nice. The RCMP have a push on now to hire Inuit regular constables as opposed to special constables. There are thirty openings for special constables in the North, and twenty-three of them are filled. We can't fill the rest. They don't want to join the RCMP unless they can stay in their own community. They don't want to migrate to the West because they don't want to police Indians. When you tell them they will have to charge their own people, or that they might not be popular all the time, they say, "No way!" Yet, they want to police themselves. We need Inuit police officers to police themselves, so there isn't that stigma: "That's white man's law and you're doing it to the Inuit people."

In 1998, the Nunavut Interim Commissioner, Jack Anawak, and the RCMP signed a new agreement that stresses policing partnership between the people and the RCMP, and prevention instead of law enforcement. A new divisional headquarters in Iqaluit will have 112 officers, including 6 Inuit, serving the 22 Inuit communities.[22] In Pangnirtung, a summer student constable says that entering the RCMP has been "my dream all my life." She trained for three weeks in Regina, Saskatchewan, as part of the Aboriginal Cadet Development Program. After she finishes high school, doors will open for her with the RCMP. She hopes that "Inuit males will not give problems when I arrest them. I can translate and make them feel more comfortable, though."

Women as Providers
"The pattern has changed a little bit"

For some, thinking about the future is too threatening. As one woman says, "I go day by day" because the challenge of helping support one's family is not always matched by access to a paying job The creation of Nunavut was supposed to bring 1,200 new government-related and public service jobs to the territory, half of them in Iqaluit (over 400). The plan to distribute territorial functions throughout the communities means that some jobs have gone to places like Arviat, Igloolik, Pond Inlet, and Cape Dorset. Outside of the capital, Pangnirtung was slated to gain the most jobs (78 positions in health and education transferred from Yellowknife).[23]

The connection between paying jobs and education is not lost on young Inuit females. In fact, says a high school teacher, some "feel they will have to support their families, so they're getting the education. Employers see females as more reliable than men, so they're getting the jobs." Ironically, this places pressure on younger women, who face the likelihood of becoming the major provider for their families. Dorais has speculated that Inuit tend to view education (and learning English or French, math, and science) as a necessary passport to the "modern labour market."[24] Dianne says her friends often talk about the inevitable link between "our education and our future":

"MOSTLY WOMEN ARE SUPPORTING THEIR FAMILIES"
My girlfriends say, "If I don't have any education, what am I going to do?" That's their main concern. I often think about it because I'm concerned about my future. It sometimes scares me. If I don't have enough education, I won't be able to get a job. If I can't get a job, I'll end up being a bum or being a housewife—or not even a housewife, just a bum.

Some of the guys worry about it, too. They are all in school and haven't graduated yet, and they say, "I have to finish grade twelve or even further, even if I don't like school or getting up in the morning." They're really pushing themselves to have a good education.

Even if you find the right man—and he is working very hard, making good money, and you are working—it would still be the same. Mostly women are supporting their families. Women have rights, too, so why can't we do what we want to do? I want to keep on learning something new.

Similarly, the most significant event in Apea's life was getting her first job: "The highest grade here was grade eight and there weren't many jobs around here then." Her first job was working at the Bay: "Ever since, I've been working constantly. I've been off work only three or four years since I quit school. I don't like to be out of a job because I think it's boring."

One thing is certain, in spite of skepticism about Nunavut, moving to the south of Canada for work has little appeal. Pauktuutit has argued that the 4,000 or so Inuit women who have moved south (the "urban Inuit") have left Nunavut to escape "domestic strife or abuse, single motherhood, and the lack of job opportunities in the North," but have met with poverty, discrimination, and loneliness in the south. Pauktuutit wants greater priority for the employment and training options that women say are important, such as shelter workers and abuse counselors; the group also wants to see more dollars going to Inuit women in urban centers. The group is suing the federal government to obtain $800,000 a year to provide training and job opportunities for the next five years.[25]

Although a few move south, the fate of most Inuit women and men will be sealed in their beloved Nunavut. Even though living in a small community is "like an open book and everyone knows your business," the southern part of Canada is "a very different environment." As one young woman puts it, "I don't think I ever will go south to live." As women and men search for economic security and stability, they identify education and jobs as the key to a more peaceful future in their communities and homes. At the same time, opportunity revives the age-old questions of women's rights, liberation, and how to define equality between males and females.

Photo 17.2 Mother and child.

Notes

1 Nuttall, *Arctic Homeland*, p. 137.

2 "Three Missing Hunters Found Dead Near Pangnirtung," *Nunatsiaq News* (November 6, 1998).

3 Cited in David Crary, "Tradition at Stake in Hunt," *Akron Beacon Leader* (Thursday, July 16, 1998), p. A16; see also, "Canadian Inuit Set Sail on Controversial Whale Hunt," Nando.net (July 13, 1998).

4 Margaret Karpik, "A Whaler's Life: A Celebration of Harvest and Tradition (Interview with Jaco Evic), *Ittuagtuut* (Nunavut Tunngavik) 1, 1 (Winter 1998): 14-28.

5 Condon also found this in Holman, NWT. See *The Northern Copper Inuit*, p. 182.

6 Marcelle Chabot and Gerard Duhaime, "With the Help of the Crown: Trends in Personal Income in Nunavik 1950-2000," paper presented at the Third International Congress of Arctic Social Sciences, Copenhagen, Denmark, 1998.

7 http/natsiq.nunanet.com/'nic/A-6.8-A-6.9.

8 Jim Bell, "Inuit Unemployment Still High, Despite Record Job Growth," *Nunatsiaq News* (September 24, 1999).

9 Bell, "Inuit Unemployment Still High."

10 http/natsiq.nunanet.com/'nic/A-6.5a.

11 Mitchell, *From Talking Chiefs to a Native Corporate Elite*, pp. 403-404.

12 Wenzel, *Animal Rights, Human Rights Ecology, Economy and Ideology in the Canadian Arctic*, p. 173.

13 RT and Associates, *Nunavut Harvest Support Program, Background Document* (Yellowknife, N.W.T: RT and Associates, 1993).

14 Hedican, *Applied Anthropology in Canada*, p. 122; also Robert M. Bone and Donna Green, *Analysis of Responses to the Questionnaire on Economic and Social Behaviour of Hunters: Final Report for the Northern Economic Planning Directorate, Department of Indian and Northern Affairs* (Ottawa: Department of Indian and Northern Affairs, 1985).

15 Gessell, "The Art of the Matter," p. C4.

16 Michael Vlessides, "A Turbot Tale: Pangnirtung Fishery Brings Income to the Community," *Above and Beyond* (Spring 1996): 37-40.

17 Burt, "Gender and Public Policy," p. 487.

18 Deborah Hyde, in *Women, Production and Change in Inuit Society* (Thesis, Carleton University, 1980), documents the increasingly important part women play in the wage economy.

19 See Leroux, Jackson, and Freedman, eds., *Inuit Women Artists*; George Swinton, *Sculpture of the Inuit* (Toronto: McClelland and Stewart, 1992); Ann Meekitjuk Hanson, *Show Me: A Young Inuk Learns How to Carve in Canada's Arctic* (Yellowknife, NWT: Amway Environmental Foundation, 1991); Janet Catherine Berlo, "Inuit Women and Graphic Arts: Female Creativity and Its Cultural Context," *The Canadian Journal of Native Studies* 9, 2: 293-315 (1989); Nelson H. H. Graburn, "Inuit Art and the Expression of Eskimo Identity," *American Review of Canadian Studies*, 17, 1: 47-66 (1987); Pitaloosie Saila, "Pitaloosie Saila Talks about Old Age, Her First Drawing, White People and Other Things," *Inuit Art Quarterly* 2, 3 (1987): 10-12; and Josephine Withers, "Inuit Women Artists: An Art Essay," *Feminist Studies* 10, 1 (1984): 84-96.

20 Qallunaat James Houston brought Inuit printmaking and carving into the commercial gallery system of southern Canada and the United States. See his *Confessions of an Igloo Dweller* (Toronto: McClelland and Stewart, 1995) and *Eskimo Prints* (Toronto: Longman Canada, 1971). See also Nelson H. Graburn, "Commercial Inuit Art: Symbol of and Vehicle for the Economic Development of the Eskimos of Canada," pp. 177-189 in "Actes du XLIIe Congrès International des Américanistes, congrès du centenaire, paris, 2-9 septembre," 5 (1976) and also in *Inter-Nord*, 15:131-142); and Michael Shouldice, *Aspects of Social and Cultural Significance of Carving Activity at the Community Level* (Ottawa: Department of Indian and Northern Affairs, 1983).

21 Jean Blodgett (curator), *Cape Dorset: Artists and the Community* (Winnipeg: The Winnipeg Art Gallery, 1980; comments by Houston, Eber, Ryan, Pootoogook, and Blodgett). See also the Institute of American Indian Arts Museum, *Keeping Our Stories Alive: An Exhibition of the Art and Crafts from Dene and Inuit of Canada* (Santa Fe: Institute of American Indian Arts Museum, 1995).

22 Annette Bourgeois, "A New Beginning for Nunavut Inuit and the RCMP," *Nunatsiaq News* (September 3, 1998), pp. 1-2.

23 Nunatsiaq News, "The OIC's Master Plan for Nunavut: 100 More Jobs than Footprints 2," *Nunatsiaq News* (October 9, 1996), pp. 5, 9.

24 Dorais, *Quaqtaq*, p. 93.

25 The Nunavut Secretariat indicated that $150,000,000 was spent through 1999 on training and salaries to help Inuit fill the goal of 50 percent Inuit in Nunavut's government and administrative functions. Personal interview.

IX

THE ROAD TO EQUALITY

I hope my children will see our life and follow what we do. I hope I teach them by my own action, but I'm sure they'll have a different life from us.

—Geela

Photo 18.1 An elder woman at the Nunavut celebrations in Iqaluit

18

Women's Rights and Political Participation

It's going to get better.

—Ovilu

The Kitaq: More Than a Room of Her Own

Photo 18.2 The late Annie Okalik, mother of Premier Paul Okalik, at the kitaq.

At the heart of women's support in this tiny settlement is the women's *kitaq*, a group that meets in a makeshift *qammat* nestled on a rocky outcropping near the harbor. Canvas and orange plastic walls envelop a wooden frame. Men helped erect the platforms but the women built the basic structure themselves. The men built the frame and floor; the women decorated the interior by pasting white paper to the ceiling and walls. The older women wanted to "show the younger generation how they used to live."[1] Built-in benches line the room, facing an old potbelly stove. Thin pads and brightly colored quilts cover the sitting platforms. Floral patterns abound. Low shelves line the walls to make a home for Silkience, Glade Spray, raw caribou meat, and cooked Arctic char. A small "honey bucket" toilet stands in one corner, curtained off for privacy.

A kerosene lamp and an ancient *qulliq* provide the only light. One woman lights the *qulliq* and boils water "for tea in the traditional way," with the kettle hanging from a net frame above the fire. Bits of old carpeting warm the floor, on top of the old linoleum that had been acquired from the high school, which has just burned to the ground, leaving the town reeling in shock and sadness. One woman comments wryly, "That's about the only thing left from the high school." The women seem pleased that we had taped conversations with Qatsuq and other elders who have died since we interviewed them, because when the high school burned down, Daisy Dialla and other teachers lost twenty years worth of taped conversations with elders, along with their photographs.

Any woman who is a member of the association can enter the hut at any time to meet with others, to think, or to discuss issues. Children come and go as we talk, and men feel free to enter if they need something from one of the women, but they do not linger. Posters that advocate stopping child abuse and spousal assault parade across the back wall.

We enter the *kitaq* by invitation of two grandmothers in their 50s who serve as informal leaders among the women. Three women in their early 20s join us. Literally, *kitaq* means a special thread for sewing skins together in constructing a tent. This place, then, is like a thread that holds women together. For women of different generations, this interweaving proves especially important. The women agree that people were in shock during the move into Pangnirtung, and only later began to acknowledge their anger about it. We ask if they have heard that women in other communities think of Pang women as being stronger than Inuit women elsewhere. An elder woman smiles and retorts: "Pang women are more beautiful." They have a hard time identifying the most important problems facing women: "There are so many of them"—but stress education and say that unequal pay for work and domestic violence must be eliminated. Some offer praise for the healing circles that are helping a few people: "The men are just starting to go to the healing groups...but once they see that it is working for some, the others will go."

The definition of problems varies by generation. Our interpreter pauses after asking an elder to describe the problems Inuit women face today: "I couldn't really explain that question because I couldn't find an Inuktitut word for 'problem.' Then I asked her almost the same question, but I don't think she really understood, so she talked about her daughter-in-law's disobedience to her husband."

We ask what changes the young women see in their lives compared to women of earlier generations. A grandmother quietly lights a cigarette and leans forward to listen. She wears blue jeans and a flowered cotton scarf around her head. Another woman heaves a sigh, as though the answers will cover a great deal of territory. Says one, a 20-year-old who wants to be a teacher: "AIDS. We are getting our own land...Nunavut. We don't look up to whites like the older ones did. We're more equal to them now."[2] (A few Inuit women have succumbed to AIDS, some of them becoming homeless in cities like Montreal, Ottawa, or Winnipeg. Pauktuutit has received a $340,000 grant from Health Canada to launch a community-based HIV-AIDS network to reduce the number of cases and the number of deaths from the disease.) A social work student pauses, and then offers: "The ozone layer. Poverty. Women are more into work roles. We don't scrape hides and chew them so much anymore. We're losing our language. We all speak Inuktitut, but I can't understand some words my parents say. It's important not to lose our language and culture. We will be like the Labrador people—they can't speak their language. We won't understand the elders." The older women nod in agreement, especially about the loss of language.

The smoke curls toward the ceiling, where a young mother on welfare fixes her eyes in deep thought: "To be honest, in some ways we are the same as the older women. I'm a raw eater. We are hunters and gatherers. We eat raw fish, caribou, seal. We have to keep the culture because that is why we are here. We *have* to respect our ancestors. It is part of us." "But *why* is it important to respect your ancestors?" one grandmother asks slowly, as though peering with us through a window into the future. "Because they survived the winters," says one. "They were the first people...they survived," adds another. "I'm *proud* to be Inuk," puts in the third. "Our ancestors did hard work we cannot even understand. It is like a gift to us that we should pass on to our descendants." One grandmother throws her cigarette into the stove; the other looks at the floor.

Our eyes have been on the anti-abuse posters while we listen to this affirmation of culture. "What about the messages in these posters? Do women worry about these issues?" The three young women open instantly with a barrage of criticisms against young men. The mother starts: "I provided for my boyfriend. He didn't want to work. He became so dependent on me, I told him to get out because it was better for me financially." She says her married friends envy her because she is a single parent—"less stress and fewer arguments." The aspiring teacher defends the men: "They don't want to work in spring and summer because they want to go out on the land." The social work student counters: "Guys here treat you like shit. They won't take jobs that are 'for women.' They're irresponsible."

Silence descends on the hut, and we all listen to the hissing of the wood stove. The young women embark on another round of friends who have been abused, and the frustrations they have felt in relationships. One refers to her boyfriend as "the sperm bank" whenever she discusses him; she refuses to call him by name. The other two laugh at this, but their expressions reveal agreement as well as amusement. We wonder later whether they are trying to impress two white outsiders with their toughness, but this conversation is typical of other women with whom we have spoken: They are frank and seem to lack self-consciousness about their anger. Reality feeds their frustration and resentment toward men: Inuit women lack the security they need to establish viable families and raise healthy children. They want to build close, positive relationships with men—they fall in love and want men to sire babies—but they want much more than that. Like women everywhere, Inuit women want intimacy with respect and commitment with responsibility. Their feelings emanate from a deeper place than shock value.

Our efforts to change the conversation's tone fail, but the grandmothers seem unsurprised by the bitterness that laces the younger generation's words. They say that they have heard all of it inside these four walls before, and add that they will remember us next time we visit: "Come and have tea!"

ᏨᎡ

Women in their late teens and early 20s seem almost oblivious to the liberation movement, the legislation, or the important issues that absorbed their mothers and aunts. Yet, they take for granted many of the movement's principles and vaguely believe in women's equality. The older women say things have improved here but, compared to younger women, they seem acutely aware of the magnitude of their struggle. As Ovilu reflects, men have more power, "but if it was equally set, then it would be better."

The Constitutional Clause
"Men and women could have better relations"

As in many other communities, women over 30 know more than younger women do about the 1982 constitutional clause that protects women's rights in Canada. The exact language of the constitutional clause may not be so important to women as the idea that it acknowledged women's rights. Inuit women agree that the clause has affected their thinking, though the details remain blurry: "I haven't really heard that much about it, but it says that men and women could have better relations and better communication. I think it was a good idea."

Of course, the constitution does not refer to improved communication between men and women; it simply anchors the illegality of discriminating against people because of their gender (among other things). That some women interpret this to mean "better relations" between the sexes is an unintended by-product. The concept of women's rights, though sometimes blurry, has spread mostly through radio and television, which are important sources of information and opinion for women in isolated communities. The Inuit Broadcasting Corporation provides a mass communication outlet that women's organizations can harness.

The tension between male and female definitions of reality shows up very early. Teenager Carolee thinks that men make it hard for women to be equal. Typical of her age group, she has not yet heard of the women's liberation movement—"but I hope I will"—nor does she understand that the Canadian Constitution includes a guarantee for women's rights. Bonds between these girls are strong. Yet, they seem to realize even in their early teens that, for most of them, relationships with males will also be important: "We talk about being roommates and say that if we get married we won't be roommates forever. When we get married, we hope that the husband and wife will be equal—it's best." Carolee observes that the boys in her tenth grade class would say girls are equal to them. The girls would agree. Still, Carolee gets the distinct feeling that boys are better than girls are "because they have more muscles and they do more work." Boys "like to bother us in school so we just ignore them," she adds. If the girls bother them back, the boys become angry. She and her friends try to ignore the boys' teasing or "if we get in an argument, we just say let's be friends instead of fighting." Later, that perception of superior strength manifests itself in the political arena, where it is assumed that men have a superior right to lead, decide, and govern. This may be changing slowly.

For the most part, middle-aged and elderly Inuit women believe that females should receive the same pay as males for a particular job. They also agree that women should be able to enter almost all the same occupations as men. They believe in the fundamental equality of women and men, the right of young girls and women to pursue education to the extent of their desires and abilities, and the propriety of women working outside the home as long as someone responsi-

ble cares for the children. Women like Udluriak speak of a growing consciousness of their rights: "In many ways the relationship between men and women is
still good. Now people have started to realize that women have rights, especially
with the Charter of Rights. We are talking about 'women's rules.'"

For example, Ooleepeeka hears about women's liberation through letters
from friends who live in other parts of the former Northwest Territories. A single mother of five young children who sustains herself relatively well by making
coats for tourists, she likes the idea of equal opportunity and equal pay: "I don't
want to go over men. I want to be equal." Her friends agree.

Violence and Women's Liberation
"I have a right to do what I want"

Inuit feminists worry about the reactions they hear to the women's liberation
movement. Some people (including a few females) believe that women's liberation has gone too far in attempting to rebalance gender relations. Some men
feel that Inuit women and girls have over-reacted because of the protections
grounded in the Canadian Charter of Rights, which made it illegal as of 1985 to
discriminate on the basis of sex.[3] Most women disagree.

In one breath, men support the rights of women to equal opportunity and
respect. In the next, they suggest that women have gone too far. They mean that
women, in their search for independence and equality, may simultaneously and
unwittingly work against the norm of sharing. Many agree that a new emphasis
on the traditional values of sharing would help couples redefine marriage, and
face economic hardship and uncertainty. Those who champion the rights of
women to equal opportunity and respect speak of a fine balance, as Pauta contends: "Even young people should know how to share. I learned from my parents to share anything. We catch our food for the community. This is our custom. If I'm not working and my wife is working, we could support each other.
We shouldn't really be afraid of anything [like role reversal]. This is our life, the
sharing, no matter what, in the home and the family." It is a fine balance, to be
sure, but these stories also illustrate well the difficulties women everywhere
confront when they refuse to comply with men's wishes. Obviously, liberation
does not come without penalty.

Perhaps the most obvious result of women's new consciousness is that,
rather than trying to deal with spousal assault by themselves, they go to the
RCMP or to social workers, even when they know the man will end up with a
criminal record. Mark, a counselor, offers this story about conflict over bannock,
the Inuit daily bread. It typifies both the dilemmas of cultural transition and the
tension between male and female definitions of power:

> Last year a man was ready to go out hunting. He asked his wife to make ban-
> nock for him, because he would be going out for a couple of days—we have to

take bannock to eat—but she wanted to go to the bingo games. Her husband pushed her a little bit and told her, "Bingo games are not really important. I want to bring the bannock with me." The woman was angry, so she reported it to the RCMP and went to court for "spousal assault." It's not that. The girl tried to put him in jail, but the judge realized that it wasn't that serious, so they dropped the charges. That's just an example. Women never did that kind of thing before.

Clearly, the counselor's definition of what constitutes legitimate complaints of spousal assault does not match that held by most of the Inuit women we interviewed. He argued that the judge was not denying the existence of women's rights but was challenging where to draw the line between a heated disagreement and an assault. From the woman's point of view, her rights include drawing that line at whatever point makes sense to her. From the male perspective, the line seems to move. Noah claims that men today "understand that there are equal rights for women but that their work is different. We're equal for our different work. If we use equality properly, I'll agree with it, but if they go over that, I get nervous...it could be misunderstood very easily." He says that most of his friends would agree with his analysis.

Not all men are resistant toward women's liberation, of course. For example, an Inuk carpenter believes in equality for women. Some of the inspectors who check the buildings he works on are white women from Iqaluit. He respects their position and their opinions. He feels that if any woman works outside the home and "gets very little money for the work she did, it's not fair." As Madeleine Dion Stout and Gregory Kipling argue, violence between men and women cannot be separated from issues of economic development and broader community contexts. Spousal assault involves more than the perpetrator and the victim: the "web of causes and effects stretches far wider, ranging from the children whose lives are traumatized by its occurrence, to community members in general, whose views and perceptions play a crucial role in allowing the degradation of women to continue unabated.[4] For Inuit women, entering the realm of community politics is a place to start addressing these far-reaching consequences.

Women's Involvement in Community Politics
"We should be a part of it"

The transformation to equal relations between males and females is neither easy nor swift. Many factors, including the astronomical increase of domestic violence, indicate the tricky nature of attempts to change the status of women. One sign is that Inuit women in most communities have not infiltrated hamlet governance to the extent that men have, although women serve on Pangnirtung Hamlet Council. Women have served on the council for many years, shortly after the settlement became a hamlet in 1972. Recently, of eight council members, two were women; the deputy mayor is female. Meeka thinks there will soon be a woman mayor. Importantly, she can identify a woman she thinks is interested, capable, and electable: "I know one who can do it. I don't know if she still would be willing."

Some Inuit women believe that even when women manage to get on the Hamlet Council the men do not necessarily respect their ideas. They feel that men still try to run the show: "It really is maddening, but if you work hard or try to fight them, you can win." Women tend to deal with lingering sexist attitudes on an individual basis, rather than presenting a united front, which some concede may be a mistake. As in some other Inuit communities, "...women hold several prominent and powerful elective offices in the formal political structures," but the numbers are usually small and they vary from community to community.[5] It is difficult to ascertain the percentage of Inuit women serving at various levels of hamlet and territorial government.

Pauktuutit supports local women in having a local *kitaq,* a place of their own. At the local level, the *kitaq,* Pauktuutit, and church groups seem to have the most immediate impact on improving the status of women.[6] In the *kitaq* and other groups, the women organize and plan their contributions to hamlet affairs. Men do not go to these meetings, but the Women's Association welcomes men if they have something to say to the women. People assume that men and women have different views on such matters, which presents an opportunity for learning and for different action strategies. Women's political action focuses on the social and economic fronts, whereas men tend to be more involved in elected municipal offices: "Women now increasingly consider themselves the drive behind many public initiatives."[7] As an Inuk leader points out, women delve deeply into local community affairs, which she defines more broadly than just "politics":

> We don't have any set figure. We cannot say "so many women are involved" because no one has conducted a study—I hope there's one soon—but in talking to people in settlements, we always see that women are more involved in community affairs, mostly in education or social problems...like social workers, belonging to education committees, battered women's groups.
>
> Women involve themselves more in the community groups than men do. I cannot tell you what percentage, but I know for sure that more women are involved than men are! Decision-making, making more noise in social problem areas—alcohol, drugs, wife battery, childcare. It has been like that ever since I entered community affairs. Like other women, I've been in many, many groups—just about every group that existed to make better lives for people, no matter who they were.

Pangnirtung women often tell the popular story about how they took a powerful leadership role in the "pornography fight" in the early 1980s. The women banded together to stop the sale of pornographic videos in the hamlet's stores. They sought the blessing of "Christian groups" and won the battle against a force they defined as harmful to women and children. This was a defining moment in the community's history:

> It's a very masculine society, yet in Pang, the women have nearly all the say about what goes on in town. There was a flood of videos—pornography and things like that. We had a workshop in the school and invited members of the community to come in, especially the parents. When they realized what their youngsters were seeing, they were appalled.
>
> The women and some men got together, went into the stores, and said, "This is going to stop." And it did. The managers took the stuff off the shelves. They've done many other things like that.

Another battle centered on a curfew for children. Youngsters "were all over the place, all hours of the night," during the school year. They would come to school "half dead tired," recalls a teacher: "The women supported a curfew for all youngsters to be off the streets at 10:30—the siren goes off and the children are off the streets!" In a sense, this goes against the grain of Inuit culture—sleep when you feel tired and wake up when you feel refreshed. Eat when you feel like it. The curfew is "a way of adapting to clocks and bells."

Similarly, women allied to defeat another force that hurts women and children: alcohol. Although many men also favored keeping Pangnirtung dry, women worked hard to defeat a referendum on lifting the ban against alcohol. Minnie recalls: "It was a hand vote when the commissioner came to visit in the early 1970s. People were complaining about alcohol abuse in the community and the commissioner said that if you vote no by raising your hand, the community could become dry. That was the beginning."

Osuituk remarks that the work of the women and elders finished the process: "They've seen what has happened because of drink to people in places like Iqaluit. They've said, as long as we have power, it won't be here." The question of prohibition can be re-opened every two years if someone wants to raise a petition. Every time it comes up, the vote grows a little closer because, as the younger people turn 18 and the population increases, they tend to want legal distribution of alcohol—"the danger is there." Women like Kuluk and Sara, who have seen first-hand the ravages of alcohol-induced battering, fear that the town eventually will defeat prohibition: "We should be prepared for it because we're not going to always win for dry. We have to prepare for what might happen if alcohol comes to this community." She adds that women believe easier and routine access to alcohol will bring dramatic changes into their lives—especially more crime and domestic violence: "We have seen the evil things that have happened in other communities—abuse of women and children. We don't want it!"

Education about the negative effects of alcohol would be critical and is necessary even now, since there is always some black market liquor available. The Alcohol Committee does not have much influence, Kuluk laments: "People ignore them because it's a dry community. People have asked what the committee is for; everybody will understand exactly what it's trying to do if we lose prohibition. The committee has not focused on what might happen if Pangnirtung allowed alcohol, but we are deeply concerned as women. We know what alcohol can do to people if they don't control it."

Mark serves on the Alcohol Committee and believes there is a downside to prohibition. People turn to sniffing glue or other chemicals, making home brew, or using drugs more than they would if alcohol were readily available. Education and "bad experiences" can help them learn to control substance abuse, he says: "People will find a way to get high if they really want to do that. I'm also on the Hamlet Council. We want the Alcohol Committee to be more active in informing people about alcohol." Leaders who oppose alcohol believe that being a dry town has protected Pangnirtung: "When you go to Iqaluit and other communities where drink is allowed, you'll find that indigenous people seem to lose their dignity. Here it might be secret drinking; otherwise they hold their heads high. There's a different feeling of dignity in this town."

Once, when the male-dominated Hamlet Council wanted to put a gravel pit near the foot of Mount Duval, a favorite place near town for women to walk and pick berries in the summer, the women successfully negotiated its relocation. Women resisted the public ordinance that prohibits the operation of home-based businesses in public housing (in which most Inuit live) by opening their doors to tourists and other visitors for "bed and breakfast."[8] Not only is this an occasional source of income for women; it also helps many outsiders make a smooth transition into the community. A woman was the driving force behind creating the highly successful Uqqurmiut Centre, which provides a focal point for arts and crafts in Pangnirtung.

On a less formal basis, women spend a great deal of time visiting back and forth in their homes or in the open air, sometimes pausing for long chats as they pass in the settlement's gravel streets. They borrow sewing machines from each other, and tobacco and tea circulate as freely as humor and laughter.[9] Other women stay close to home and meet in church-related groups that center on issues other than equality. For example, Geela belongs to the Women's Auxiliary. She is on a committee that meets at the parish hall one night a week to sing hymns, pray, and sew. The group meets from October to May, and then breaks for the summer when so many families are out camping. This is by no means a radical feminist group, but it helps to maintain women's solidarity and commitment to each other. Women have also played a powerful role in bringing daycare into the community: "Every year there are women candidates for council, where they make decisions like this."

Women in Territorial Politics
"Women need to be recognized"

Although women comprise 51 percent of Nunavut's population and are generally better educated than men, the former NWT had the worst record in all of Canada for women's political representation: as of 1997, only two of the 24 members of the pre-Nunavut NWT Legislative Assembly were women and only one woman (Rebecca Mike) lived in what is now Nunavut.

Gender Parity

Partly in response to this historical pattern, the Nunavut Implementation Commission (NIC) proposed in 1995 a "gender parity plan" for Nunavut Territory that would help remedy this under-representation. The plan would have had voters select one person from a male slate and one from a female slate in each community. It would have resulted in a 50/50 membership in the Nunavut legislature—the first in the world. NIC "expressed a desire to do whatever it could to encourage the full participation of women in Nunavut's political life [assuming that] the people of Nunavut would be best represented if the two abiding subsets of humanity were equally represented."[10] This position seemed logical "especially in light of the disjunctive relations which exist between men and women in Nunavut today, and the scale of the social problems" facing the new government.[11]

Intense community debate ensued, with some men and women favoring the plan and others arguing against it. For example, Eeta Kanayuk spoke to a special meeting of Nunavut leaders in Iqaluit in November 1996 to voice the arguments in support of gender parity:

> If we are going to adopt a government that is similar to what we have now, I have no hope. If I'm part of a new government with gender equality…I want to work with you, very much, because without the two, hand in hand, we cannot heal what has happened over the years…. I really want it thought out in terms of women and their capabilities…. If we adopt something that is not community realistic, our children will suffer…to me, it's hope.[12]

Another eloquent argument for gender parity was cited in the NIC proposal:

> Because of our culture, we require different solutions to our problems. Because of our isolation and the smallness of our population, we require local and culturally appropriate remedies. Women need to be recognized as one of the most important pillars of our communities.[13]

Those who argued against gender parity said the proposal was demeaning, inherently unfair and undemocratic, or condescending toward women. Some women said they would prefer to get to the legislature under their own steam in order to be taken seriously. Among women, the "most vociferous opponent [was] Manitok Thompson of Rankin Inlet South, the only female member of the Nunavut Caucus and the first Minister Responsible for the Status of Women."[14] Many women, both older and younger, said that men are still "the bosses," and that gender parity would be seen as tokenism or an irritation to men: "The men have the power...and they don't want to give it up." Some were afraid that gender parity would "sow division between men and women where none currently existed" or that women "would be seen as 'affirmative action' MLAs whose opinions would be taken less seriously."[15] Other comments, cited by Hicks, were that male dominance in politics was not important because *"people think with what's between their ears, not with what's between their legs,"* and gender parity would show favoritism toward women that would *"send women back to the stone age."*[16] A few argued that justifying gender parity on the grounds that traditional gender relations were egalitarian was no more than "a romanticized retelling of history."[17] Some men and women on the "religious right" felt that "women have no business in politics."[18]

In May of 1997, 57 percent of voters defeated the referendum.[19] Many men (including then NIC chief John Amagoalik and Nunavut Tunngavik President Jose Kusugak) supported the referendum and many women voted against it. Only nine of the twenty-seven Inuit communities supported the plan.[20] Hicks identified two basic misconceptions that muddied the waters and contributed to the referendum's defeat: 1) That "men would vote for male candidates and women would vote for female candidates" and 2) That "gender parity would inflate the size of the legislature and increase the costs accordingly."[21] Essentially, however, the referendum failed because women had not won the trust of males or even of "other females who will believe that both sexes have the capacity to govern."[22] Although the "conceptualization of women as the carriers of tradition responsible for the care of the national family is central to nationalist discourse and echoes throughout the rhetoric of Inuit 'womanhood',"[23] the time apparently had not yet come to crystallize women's role in Nunavut's legislative structure.

The First Nunavut Legislative Election

Not only was the referendum defeated, but the actual legislative election results in February 1999 showed a pattern that the gender parity proposal was designed to avoid: out of nineteen elected members of the brand new Nunavut Legislative Assembly, only one was female.[24] The other ten female candidates were defeated in an 88 percent voter turnout. (In Pangnirtung, six candidates, including one woman, Meeka Kilabuk, vied for the seat won by Peter Kilabuk.) That means that even women did not support female candidates to the point of winning seats. Manitok Thompson, who opposed the gender parity proposal and defeated another woman for this seat, emerged as the only woman in Nunavut's first legislative assembly. She said that "bitter women" who had supported gender parity should have run for a seat: "There were a lot of vocal women...who were on the radio, angry; why did they not put their name in and run?" She acknowledged that some women might find it hard to compete for pubic office, because "when you have to travel long distance and be away from home a lot, you really need that support system."[25]

The fact that only one woman out of eleven female candidates was elected in this critical race for the new territory may indicate that—for whatever reasons—most Inuit men and women still perceive the public sphere as a domain in which men rightfully dominate. It will be important to monitor subsequent elections to determine the driving forces behind this seeming preference for male leaders. Another possibility looms for the new territory: rather than improving conditions for all Inuit (male and female), Hicks speculates that Nunavut may result in a "deepening of social differentiation... [a] class system" unknown in traditional Inuit society.[26] The results should come as no surprise, however. A similar situation occurred in Greenland, where Inuit women chose the path of patience in working their way into the political system while Denmark prepared to give them Home Rule. Once Home Rule was achieved, they found themselves "neglected" by Inuit males who were involved in decision-making. Rather than finding equality, they found little change in long-standing political relations between males and females.[27]

Other Political Routes

Nonetheless, in the face of what many women and men thought was a disappointing outcome in both the referendum and the legislative election, other paths to administrative and political power are opening up for women in Nunavut. For example, Meeka Kilabuk, who won the presidency of the Qikiqtani Inuit Association (QIA), argued that the organization should be open to women. She called for political bodies to become more "equally open to all" so that quotas would not be necessary: "They need a woman in there. It's been a men's organization. Women and people with disabilities have been left out. [I'm running] to make sure the organization has some kind of balance — not just men."[28]

Inuit women are creating special organizations (or revivifying branches of existing organizations) to ensure that women candidates run for every legislative and local council position. A mechanism such as "Emily's List," which raises funding and support for female political candidates in the United States, could be effective in bringing more women into the territorial political arena. The new territory established an eight-woman Status of Women Council that was to serve as an interim body while the permanent Status of Women Council was set up (after October 1, 2000).[29] The council chose to continue as *Qulliit* –the women's lamp. This "non-threatening" name was announced by then Minister Responsible for Women, Donald Havioyak:

> If you look at *Qulliit*, it can only work if both men and women take responsibilities for its maintenance. The man's job was to get the blubber for fuel. The lighting and the maintenance of the light, warmth and other uses, is the responsibility of the woman....[30]

The council members elected Rebecca Kudloo of Baker Lake as their first president, and Daisy Keenainak of Pangnirtung and Joan Kalaserk as vice presidents.[31] The council will address income security, gender equality, family violence, women's health, the birth rate, and teenage pregnancy: "Nunavut women don't see ourselves as feminists as maybe [women in the] South would...we are really in this because we care about women, children, and men too. The wellness of everyone in Nunavut...that's what our goal and mission is."[32]

Women's Involvement in National Politics
"A few key women"

Elspeth Young writes that in spite of rapid social change in the twentieth century, "aboriginal women from remote communities in Canada and Australia have maintained their roles and contributions to those activities where the environmental, economic and social spheres are most strongly combined, i.e., those which conform most closely to the core of the sustainable development model."[33] Indeed, beyond their critical contributions to development through tourism and arts and crafts, Canadian Inuit women have played a significant role in Inuit political and organizational history, including the creation of Nunavut and the development of relations among Inuit around the Circumpolar North. For example, Territorial Commissioner Helen Maksagak made history when she gave the first "speech from the throne" in October 1999, outlining Nunavut's first five-year plan. She emphasized mutual responsibility in providing for families and communities.[34]

Among many others, we can point to: Ambassador Mary May Simon, former president of the Inuit Circumpolar Conference; Mary Skillet, interim President of Inuit Tapirisat of Canada; Rosemarie Kuptana, past president of the Inuit Broadcasting Corporation, Inuit Tapirisat, and president of the Inuit Circumpolar Conference; Martha Flaherty, former president of Pauktuutit; Ann Hanson, who has served many roles, including in the NWT legislature and star of James Houston's film, *White Dawn*; Deborah Kigjugalik Webster, Northern and New Parks Archaeologist for the Inuit Heritage Trust (established by the Nunavut Land Claims Agreement); Leena Evic-Twerdin, Director of Social, Cultural and Educational Development for Nunavut Tunngavik Inc.; Pat Arnakak, manager of Kakivak association, Baffin's community economic development organization, and many, many others.[35]

Inuit women engage in projects, council work, and programs such as the Aboriginal Women's Program, the Advisory Council on the Status of Women, the Women's Secretariat, and the Northern Women's Program of the Canadian Research Institute for the Advancement of Women. John David Hamilton argued that the "number of outstanding women leaders is astounding."[36] Pauktuutit characterizes women's achievements as a "reflection of the traditional equality between the sexes that has helped give Inuit women the confidence and support necessary to be able to take such an active and productive role in these organizations."[37] Growing self-esteem will make a positive difference in women's inclination to engage in leadership roles.

The local *kitaq* sends representatives to meetings in Ottawa. Other organizations that have advocated for women's rights and interests include the Native Women's Association of Canada and Pauktuutit, discussed below. Women travel to workshops and conferences in other parts of Baffin Island and to Igloolik, Yellowknife, Edmonton, and other parts of Canada and the United States: "A few key women seem to get things rolling." Working together with other Inuit women around the circumpolar region offers another opportunity for Canadian Inuit women to improve their circumstances.

Pauktuutit

Pauktuutit, which represents all Canadian Inuit women, maintains its headquarters in Ottawa. As the "Inuit Women's Association of Canada," it was formed in 1984 to "act and be recognized as the official representative for Inuit women." It has worked on many issues, including midwifery, violence against women, child sexual abuse, substance abuse, the justice system, housing and economic development,[38] anti-smoking campaigns, fetal alcohol syndrome education, AIDS education, and healing centers. The organization believes that such programs benefit all Inuit, not just women. In recognition of its work, Inuit Tapirisat has mandated Pauktuutit to represent all Inuit in health matters and the Economic and Social Council of the United Nations has granted Pauktuutit "special consultative status." This honour means "the views and concerns of Inuit women stand a greater chance of being aired when discussions about international issues affecting northern [and aboriginal knowledge] are held."[39] John Amagoalik writes of Pauktuutit's contribution in the face of shrinking funding for the women's association, which is designed to "be there for women *and* men":

> Pauktuutit was the first organization to openly discuss the internal sources of our problems. Such taboos as child sexual abuse were being openly acknowledged. Along with acknowledgment, came the realization that only we, with the hope of God, must deal with them.

Many tears have now been shed after many years of silence, guilt and shame. Along with these tears, the weight that was crushing many of our people is beginning to lift. Only after accepting the ownership of our problems, have we been able to begin the process of healing.

Pauktuutit has also become a source of strength and pride for our young people. Many young women, and men, have had a chance to grow and mature with Pauktuutit. They have gained valuable experience in leadership and organization. Pauktuutit has strengthened the spine of the Inuit political movement.[40]

Dreams for Their Daughters
"Have a good life"

In the words of Ambassador Mary May Simon, "children and youth are the most vulnerable, the least powerful, and the most cherished members of any society." Like canaries in a mineshaft, their well being (or dis-ease) foretells the health of their community. Janet Mancini Billson and Carolyn Fluehr-Lobban in *Female Well-Being* document the many ways in which the fate of women affects the fate of a society, and vice versa.[41] In Ambassador Simon's words:

> It is the learning disabilities, the respiratory disorders, the childhood diseases that first herald the advent of environmental degradation. It is the alcohol and drug addictions, the domestic violence, and the teenage suicides that most poignantly signal the deterioration of a society, and threaten the viability and longevity of communities and cultures.[42]

Children carry forward the hopes and aspirations of their mothers but also the burdens of despair and disappointment. In their present lies the future, not to mention reparation for past disappointments. Deep in the hearts of Inuit women lie dreams of secure, family-centered futures for their daughters. No interviewee spontaneously mentioned political empowerment, although women stressed that being liberated and freed from traditional roles create the context for the younger generation's future:

> Men dominate in Inuit community. I see it here. Some men play with women's minds. I am a liberated woman. When men tell me I should do the cleaning, it pisses me off. Men say they should be head of household. My father got those ideas from the men's group. I told him I did not like those ideas and he never went again.

Women emphasize the possibility of delaying childbearing and marriage until a later age. Saila wants her daughter to "have a good life" and does not put pressure on her to be perfect. Will her dream of a good life for her daughter come true? "I don't know the future, I can't predict it, but I know if they are like me, they are not going to have a good life."

Reepa has brought her children down south twice and her oldest girl wants to go to school there: "She's always dreamt of being a dentist, so she says she'll go down south for that. If I keep doing what I'm doing today, talking to them whenever I can, understanding them when they're going through a tough time, I think their lives will be okay. They're all very good children." Geela believes that new technology will change her children's lives for the better: "Myself, I catch part of the hard time and the easy time. I'm in the middle."

Annie's dream for baby Rebecca is that she becomes an activist in women's rights and politics. She should receive a good education and become a good sewer. Dianne wants her imaginary daughter to receive a strong education in both Inuktitut and English—"even other languages"—and to be a lawyer or doctor. Theresa wants her daughter to be "happy, so she wouldn't have the unhappy times I had." For all of their children, women and men hope they avoid the destructive consequences of drug and alcohol abuse ("drugs are like cigarettes now"). They hope their children will have safe sex and avoid early pregnancy ("they should learn to use condoms"): "I was so stupid. My mother warned me not to have sex, so I did!"

Young women in high school, according to a teacher, have clear ideas of what they want for themselves, what kind of lives they want to lead, and what kind of homes they want. Their dreams seem palpably real, she says: "They're very strong in that. I'm a bit disheartened because it's southern values and goals they aspire to...very secular, southern, and materialistic. They say, 'Oh, yes, we like our culture,' but they don't want to go out on the land, and if their parents go, they'd rather be here with a summer job." Dreams of education, jobs, and comfortable homes may not pan out for young Inuit women, however. Of the older students who went through pre-vocational training in high school, the teacher says that there were not enough jobs to go around and they lacked distinct goals: "They were very bright young girls who simply lacked qualifications to pursue a particular field or find appropriate positions. We suggested all kinds of things. Some of them didn't want to go away from here. Some of them wanted to go far away, down to Ottawa, but were afraid to make a break. There was a sort of despair among them. They didn't know what life had in store."

When expectations rise but are not met by everyday realities, despair often results.[43] The teacher believes this group with high aspirations and low opportunities may be most likely to contemplate suicide: "Bright young girls, smart young people. They don't know what to do with their lives." Female aspirations for more training or their intention to leave the community to find work might frighten their boyfriends. They might be involved with young men who abuse them. Another teacher describes a 22-year-old woman who confided her suicidal thoughts: "She doesn't know what to do. She has an excellent imagination. She has a marvelous flair for writing in English. She's very advanced compared to the other students, yet she was so undecided. She lacks confidence; she doesn't know what to do with her dreams."

On a more positive note, teachers observe that a few graduates find jobs in one of the local stores: "They have some money coming in and feel a sense of dignity in their lives. They're not just sitting back and eating the parents' money." As though banking on the success of a few modern-day pioneers, Apea has one dream for her daughters: "Finish their education and try to convince them that education is important in order to get a good job." The creation of an Inuit homeland, Nunavut, may help these dreams come true.

Notes

1 Crnkovich, "Women of the Kitaq," pp. 35-36.

2 Jane George, "Pauktuutit to Create National Inuit AIDS Network," *Nunatsiaq News* (October 22, 1999).

3 For a discussion of the impact of the 1985 legislation on aboriginal women, see Sandra Burt, "Gender and Public Policy: Making Some Difference in Ottawa," in *Rethinking Canada: The Promise of Women's History*, 3rd ed., edited by Veronica Strong-Boag and Anita Clair Fellman (Toronto: Oxford University Press, 1997).

4 Madeleine Dion Stout and Gregory D. Kipling, *Aboriginal Women in Canada: Strategic Research Directions for Policy Development* (Ottawa: Status of Women Canada, 1998), p. 18.

5 J. Matthiasson, in *Living on the Land*, p. 73.

6 Andrew and Rodgers, *Women and the Canadian State*, contains several definitive articles that were originally presented at a conference to commemorate the twentieth anniversary of the release of the Report of the Royal Commission on the Status of Women; its first publication was in 1970. The impact of the Commission's report is examined from several standpoints.

7 Reimer, "Female Consciousness," p. 90.

8 Reimer, "Female Consciousness," p. 92.

9 J. Matthiasson also documents this pattern of informal gatherings in *Living on the Land*, p. 75.

10 Hicks, "The Nunavut Land Claim and the Nunavut Government," p. 35.

11 Hicks, "The Nunavut Land Claim and the Nunavut Government," p. 35.

12 Quoted in Nunavut Implementation Commission, *Footprints 2*, p. 1.

13 Cited in Canadian Government, *Inuit Women: From the Final Report on the Canadian Panel on Violence against Women* (Ottawa: Government Printing Office), p. 142.

14 Hicks, "The Nunavut Land Claim and the Nunavut Government," p. 36. Later, the council fell under the Minister Responsible for Culture, Language, Elders and Youth (Peter Kattuk in 2001). Madeleine Qumuatuq of Iqaluit was named acting president of the Nunavut Status of Women Council in 2001. She took the position "because it's always been my passion. I want to help Inuit women empower themselves for our society to get better, to balance the roles, because right there they're very unbalanced...and I do it for my [11-year-old] daughter." Quoted in Miriam Hill, "Nunavut Status of Women Council Takes Root: Chairperson Says Better Communication with Government Needed," *Nunatsiaq News* (November 30, 2001).

15 Hicks, "The Nunavut Land Claim and the Nunavut Government," p. 37.
16 Hicks, "The Nunavut Land Claim and the Nunavut Government," p. 37.
17 Hicks, "The Nunavut Land Claim and the Nunavut Government," p. 37.
18 Hicks, "The Nunavut Land Claim and the Nunavut Government," p. 38.
19 See discussions by Jens Dahl, "Gender Parity in Nunavut?" *Indigenous Affairs* (July/December 1997): 42-47; and Lisa Young, "Gender Equal Legislatures: Evaluating the Proposed Nunavut Electoral System," *Canadian Public Policy* 23, 3 (1997): 306-15. Only 39 percent of registered voters turned out for this referendum.
20 Dwane Wilkin and Annette Bourgeois, "Nunavut Voters Say No to Gender Parity Plan," *Nunatsiaq News* (May 30, 1997), p. 52.
21 Hicks, "The Nunavut Land Claim and the Nunavut Government," p. 36.
22 Elena Garces de Eder makes this observation in explaining the defeat of Noemi Sanin, a presidential candidate in Colombia during the 1990s, in *The Construction of Radical Feminist Knowledge: Women in Colombia as an Example* (PhD Thesis, The George Washington University, 2002), p. 150.
23 Elana T. Wilson, *Gender, Political Power, and Nationalism in the Circumpolar North: A Case Study of Nunavut, Canada,* MP Thesis (King's College, University of Cambridge, Scott Polar Research Institute, June 2000), p. 61. This is the most complete analysis of Nunavut as an expression of "Inuit nationalism" and of the gender parity issue that we have found.
24 Nunatsiaq News, "Look out Canada—Nunavut's Coming," *Nunatsiaq News* (February 18, 1999); and Annette Bourgeois, "The Face of Nunavut Women Still Lingers in the Shadows," *Nunatsiaq News* (February 18, 1999).
25 Annette Bourgeois, "The Face of Nunavut Women."
26 Hicks, "The Nunavut Land Claim and the Nunavut Government," p. 41.
27 Thomsen, *Ethnicity and Feminism.*
28 Michaela Rodrigue, "QIA Candidate Says Women, Handicapped Have Place in QIA," *Nunatsiaq News* (December 3, 1999).
29 Valerie G. Connell, "Nunavut Women's Council to Meet in Iqaluit Next Week," *Nunatsiaq News* (June 30, 1999).
30 Nunatsiaq News, "Women Light the Way," *Nunatsiaq News* (March 3, 2000).
31 Other members of the new council are: Elizabeth Lyall, Taloyoak; Lissie Anaviapik, Broughton Island; Kanayuk Salomonie, Cape Dorset; Elizabeth Alakariallak-Roberts, Iqaluit; Wilma Pigalak, Kugluktuk; Abigail Idlout, Iqaluit.
32 Connell, "Nunavut Women's Council to Meet in Iqaluit Next Week."
33 Elspeth Young, *Third World in the First: Development and Indigenous Peoples* (London: Routledge, 1995), p. 268.
34 Jim Bell, "Nunavut's October Throne Speech: Poetry, Dreams, but Few Specifics," *Nunatsiaq News* (October 22, 1999), p. 1.
35 The phenomenon of aboriginal women taking a more prominent role in public matters is discussed in Carol Z. Jolles, "Changing Roles of St. Lawrence Island Women: Clanswomen in the Public Sphere," in *Arctic Anthropology* 34, 1 (1997): 86-101. [Papers in Honor of Richard G. Condon, Steven L. McNabb, Alexsandr I. Pika, William W. Richards, Nikolai Galgauge, Nina Ankalina, Vera Rakhtilkon, Boris Mymykhtikak, and Nikolai Avanun, edited by Pamela R. Stern, George W. Wenzel, and Sergei Kan.]

36 John David Hamilton, *Arctic Revolution: Social Change in the Northwest Territories 1935-1994* (Toronto: Dundurn Press, 1994), p. 273.

37 Pauktuutit, *The Inuit Way.*

38 See, for example, Pauktuutit's "Inuit Women: The Housing Crisis and Violence," prepared for the Canada Mortgage and Housing Corporation (Ottawa: Pauktuutit, n.d.).

39 Dwane Wilkin, "UN Grants Inuit Women's Lobby Special Status," *Nunatsiaq News* (October 2, 1998).

40 John Amagoalik, "Pauktuutit," *Nunatsiaq News* (March 29, 1996), p. 9. See also Ovilu Goo-Doyle, "The National Inuit Women's Association of Canada," *Sixth Inuit Studies Conference, Copenhagen October 17-20, 1988: Abstracts* (Copenhagen: Institute of Eskimology, University of Copenhagen, 1988).

41 Janet Mancini Billson and Carolyn Fluehr-Lobban, *Female Well-Being: Toward a Global Theory of Social Change* (London: Zed Books, 2005).

42 Simon, "Children and Youth of the Arctic," p. 74.

43 Robert K. Merton, *Social Theory and Social Structure* (New York: The Free Press, 1957).

19

Nunavut: Defining
a New Political Identity[1]

*We're getting tired of people running our lives from down there. It's time to shout,
"We've had it!"*

—Joanasie

Capitalism, Northern Style

Photo 19.1 The Hudson's Bay Company in Pangnirtung built in 1921.

On one of our excursions into the fiord, we see an old Hudson's Bay Company (HBC) post used in the fur trapping days earlier in the century. The mountain behind the simple one-room hut a few miles from Pangnirtung rises several thousand feet, diminishing the remnants of an era long past. From a distance, the post looks like nothing more than a large rock nestled in among others along the shore, but it was both home and workplace for one extremely dedicated trader. We can only imagine what it must have been like for a person to pass the spring and summer there, far from the regular company of others.

In pre-settlement days, Inuit drove along the valley by *qamutik* and dog team in spring or rowed across the fiord in a *qajaq* to bring precious white Arctic fox and hare pelts, ptarmigan, or seal and caribou meat to the Qallunaat trader. In exchange, they took back to camp the luxuries of tea and biscuits, bullets for the rifles that had already changed their hunting style, and perhaps a bit of coffee, wool, or tobacco.[2] The exchange took place only in the warmest months, marking the rhythm of the hunter's year. Conversations about weather, wildlife, the hunt, and families must have echoed for days around the four walls of the miniature cabin.

In 1921, the cabin closed in favor of a larger structure in Pangnirtung that became more department store than trading post. Jokingly, the people say, HBC stands for "Here before Christ"—that is, even before the Anglican diocese established its mission and hospital a few years later. For 70 years, the people shopped at the "the Bay" in the growing settlement, trading cash or food coupons for powdered milk, flour, lard, and cigarettes. Over the years, the Bay added more and more of the accoutrements of southern lifestyles: All-weather, factory made jackets; duffel wool and embroidery thread; hiking boots and thick socks; cereal, apples, and chicken. In a cash economy, prices for these super-luxurious items make it hard for most families (other than Qallunaat) to put much in their shopping carts.

More recently, the Bay shut its doors, bowing out to the Northern Stores. Also a chain that had its roots in the days of fur trading, the Northern is about as far from the little HBC hut on the fiord as we can imagine.[3] When we enter the newly renovated store, the wide aisles and bright decor strike us. A superstore of the 1990s, it boasts sewing machines, duffel wool ($39.99 metre), lace, trims, and floral cotton fabric for sewing; a very southern line of jeans, T-shirts, blouses, skirts, and underwear; chesterfield suites and washing machines; soft ice cream and cartons of long-life milk; steak and pork chops; videos and Barbie dolls. Rifles and fishing gear remain, but the arts and crafts featured by the Bay have been replaced by designer watches, "Team Nunavut" windbreakers, and trinkets made somewhere on another continent.

Compared to southern stores, some items seem surprisingly similar in pricing. Others, like appliances, which are heavier and therefore more costly to transport north, seem very high. Food costs vary: Fresh fruit and vegetable prices—$6 or $7 for a small tray of grapes or a head of lettuce, $1 for an apple— put them out of reach of many families, but some dried foods seem reasonable. The store manager explains that heavy items come by boat once or twice a year. He lays in durable goods during sealift but must fly in perishables at great cost all year round.

On this day at the end of the month, long lines of women and elderly wait at the customer service counter to cash their social assistance checks. Inuit shoppers are filling their baskets with southern foods: Microwave popcorn, tinned salmon, powdered milk, and cookies at $6 a bag. Two children leave the store with contemporary treasures—a plastic toy and some bubble gum.

We follow a sign that says "Quick Stop." Here, light years from New York or Toronto, we find a small Kentucky Fried Chicken/Pizza Hut franchise. The RCMP officers have lunch here every Friday. The cost? Ten dollars for three pieces of chicken, or $30 for a "bucket." Today, the place buzzes with Inuit women and children—and a handful of men—sitting at red Formica booths, downing French fries and chicken legs. Peeona, our interpreter during an earlier visit, comes out of the kitchen and hugs us. Now, as cook for the Quick Stop, she moves her community from country food to fast food. She says more jobs have opened up since our last visit but that more people are on welfare, too. "Maybe Nunavut will mean more jobs," she responds optimistically to our query. Nunavut, Peeona hopes, will offer more Inuit families the opportunity to move from social assistance to wage-employment and greater self-sufficiency. Peeona symbolizes, as a woman in her 20s, the remarkable transition made by both the Bay and the people.

∝

Beyond these dreams of opportunity and education, what will the future hold for Inuit women and their communities? Their predictions range from pessimism to guarded optimism. "I think our traditions and our hunting—as long as we keep our language—will be alive," Meeka hopes. Perhaps this dream will become a reality if Nunavut succeeds.

The Nunavut Dream
"It's about time"

For the Inuit, the broader movement to bring more control over aboriginal political and economic destinies has crystallized into one overarching dream: *Nunavut*. Proposed since 1974, Nunavut was approved by Native constituents in 1979. The tentative agreement was signed in December of 1991 and was ratified by the people of the Northwest Territories, Native groups, and the Canadian government in late 1992. This new Canadian territory, born officially in 1999, divides the former Northwest Territories along the tree line, roughly along the boundaries of traditional Inuit and Dene Indian usage.[4] Iqaluit, with over 5,000 inhabitants the largest town in Nunavut, has been designated its capital. Iqaluit is about 40 percent Qallunaat.[5] As a symbol of its new stature, the town hosted a meeting in September 1998 of the eight-nation Arctic Council, which includes Canada, the United States, Russia, Denmark (Greenland), Finland, Iceland, Norway, and Sweden.[6] It has since held other significant meetings of Canadian Provincial and Territorial Ministers. The Nunavut Implementation Commission's report, *Footprints in New Snow*, predicted that the new territorial government, over time, should be comprised of approximately 85 percent Inuit workers, the proportion of Inuit persons in Nunavut's population.[7]

Nunavut must be placed within the context of Native Canadian history. A critical period intervened between what we call the Free Reign Period (hunting and gathering) and creation of the semi-autonomous Nunavut. As we saw in the first three chapters, the Contact Period, which peaked during the sixteenth through nineteenth centuries, and the Resettlement Period, which occurred at the mid-point of the twentieth century, have transformed Inuit lifestyles and culture, dreams and realities. The concept of Nunavut emerged from the Resettlement Period as a political and spiritual quest for freedom and independence in a modern form that will fit into the structure of Canadian federalism.

Devolution

The Canadian government has committed itself to the policy of devolution, negotiated between Canada's Native people and the Department of Indian Affairs and Northern Development. Devolution means, in this case, that the Inuit (as the majority in Nunavut) will make policy and fiscal decisions across an increasingly broad range of government and economic functions at both hamlet and territorial levels.[8] Technically, this new arrangement does not constitute "self-government" or aboriginal government, as Franks clarifies, but "public government" similar to other Canadian governments (territorial and provincial) and not specifically directed toward preserving Inuit culture.[9] Inuit leaders and the federal government concur that the new political structure, which inevitably entails writing and integrating relevant aboriginal law, must exist within the context of

Canadian sovereignty in the Arctic and Canadian constitutional traditions.[10] However, because of the strong Inuit majority in Nunavut, some believe that it essentially constitutes a form of self-government.

Using a consensus style of decision making, emphasizing sustainable resource management, conducting transactions in Inuktitut, and approaching issues with a holistic view are hallmarks of the Nunavut dream.[11] Empowerment and devolution also imply the development of case law and passing new legislation rooted more appropriately in aboriginal law and custom.[12] As Jose Kusugak, President of Nunavut Tunngavik Inc. (NTI) said, "Nunavut will be a unique jurisdiction within Canada and one where Inuit as Aboriginal People will continue to play a strong role in the social, economic and political development of the territory."[13] Strongly symbolic of this stand is the new Department of Language, Culture, Elders and Youth that will attempt to grapple with the "everpresent threat of language erosion."[14] As a Nunavut Secretariat member explained, however, "the only difference between Nunavut and any other jurisdiction in Canada is that it is almost ethnically coterminous with geography."[15] Its unique nature means that Nunavut's government will face a unique challenge to serve *all* citizens of the territory and protect their rights under Canadian and Territorial law.[16]

For Inuit women, the commitment to creating responsive policy is doubly critical. Carolyn Kenny, who conducted individual and focus group interviews with Aboriginal women (including Inuit women) for the Status of Women Canada's Policy Research Fund between 1997 and 1999, arrived at one key policy recommendation: "...[that] policymakers...conduct policy workshops in each community and create policies that are regionally based and created through a process of discourse within the communities. The policymakers must be the women themselves."[17] Kenny calls for facilitators who can help move community discussions forward in an "immersed" and inclusive manner, which, of course, would be very much in keeping with traditional Inuit values and the role of Inuit women as a strong force in their communities.

The Nunavut Settlement Area Final Agreement

The creation of Nunavut via the Nunavut Settlement Area Final Agreement[18] is the most momentous land settlement in the Americas, involving thousands of square miles and a cash settlement of over one billion dollars (Canadian) to be paid over 14 years.[19] A Native community has gained political and economic control over a substantial amount of land, about one-fifth the land/ice mass of Canada. This is especially significant because the land has been traditional Inuit hunting, fishing, and trapping grounds, not useless land that colonizers were relatively willing to forgo. Both literally and figuratively, the Inuit will no longer be "no owners of soil." The creation of Nunavut should diminish marginality and make life better for women as the social problems associated with marginality begin to dissolve.

For thousands of years, the Inuit had free reign to roam and hunt and play in this vast segment of the Canadian Arctic and sub-Arctic. Obviously, before the influx of white influence, the Inuit enjoyed political autonomy and self-government. Section 91 (24) of the Constitution Act of 1867 stated that Indians (including the Inuit) and their lands fall under the jurisdiction of the federal Parliament, but the Inuit were not governed by the Indian Act (except briefly from 1924 to 1932), which means that no significant "national legislation governing the Inuit" existed until the creation of Nunavut.[20] Land claims vis-à-vis a central government were not an issue, but control over their future was critical.[21] In Nunavut, with some negotiated exceptions, the Inuit will have improved rights to shape their destiny on this land again.

A third territory within Canada's federal system (along with Yukon and the remnants of the Northwest Territories), Nunavut is a dramatic result of the collective efforts across generations that have fired Canadian aboriginal rights initiatives of the 1980s and 1990s. Rising consciousness and awareness of the plight of Indians in Canada led the Inuit to resist signing treaties or settling land claims. It also paved the way for collecting vast lands under a new, ethnically cohesive political umbrella. In fact, when Tagak Curley initiated the land claim for Nunavut, he discovered that the concept had little meaning to most people: "They assumed the world knew the land was theirs. It had never been handed over; it had never been fought for. They wondered what in the world we were trying to do."[22] Of the significant land claims that preceded it, the Nunavut agreement is the most comprehensive (table 19.1):

The Nunavut Land Claims Agreement is the largest comprehensive claim by far and gives Eastern Arctic Inuit (in addition to the benefits shown in table 19.1) the right to share in resource royalties, hunting rights, and a key role in managing the land and the environment.[23]

The cost of establishing Nunavut administratively and legally ranges between $560 million and $632 million, and another $200 million annually has been dedicated to operating this new territorial administration. As one observer has quipped, "Canada is still a country in the making."

Inuit Impact and Benefit Agreements must be negotiated between the Inuit and potential developers: the first one was a "legally binding agreement which aboriginal communities threatened by large non-renewable resource development elsewhere in the world would find mind-boggling."[24] The agreement is complicated, but it is more than a land claims agreement; it is also constitutionally protected by Section 35 (3) of the 1982 Constitution Act, which addresses the status of the Inuit.

Table 19.1 Significant Land Claims Agreements

Agreement	Date	Number of Beneficiaries	Area in Square Kilometers	Settlement in Dollars
The Nunavut Land Claims Agreement	June 1993	Tunngavik Federation of Nunavut 17,000	2 million sq. km.	$1 billion
The James Bay and Northern Québec Agreement and Northeastern Québec Agreement	1975, 1978	Cree, Inuit, and Naskapi of Northern Québec	14,000 sq. km (compensation, ownership); 150,000 sq. km (exclusive hunting and trapping rights)	$230 million
Inuvialuit Final Agreement	June 1984	Western Arctic Inuit 2,500	91,000 sq. km.	$169 million
Gwich'in Final Agreement	April 1992	2,200	22,000 sq. km.	$75 million
Sahtu Final Agreement	September 1993	2,000	--	$75 million

Source: Based on Isaac, "Land Claims and Self-Government Developments in Canada's North," pp. 482-486.

The Nunavut Final Agreement provides not only for new jobs but also for job training, which will help to realize the dream: "Political development in Nunavut is not an end in itself; it is a means of overcoming the poverty, alcoholism, unemployment, inadequate housing, family violence and suicide, as well as the loss of culture that are all too prevalent in the central and Eastern Arctic."[25] Whether it is a blip on the statistical trend line or an aftershock of more change (creating a new territory), the suicide rate increased *after* Nunavut became a reality: "In [1999], 19 Nunavummiut died in completed suicides. In 2000, 27 people committed suicide.[26]

Preparing for Implementation

In anticipation of Nunavut's opportunities and challenges, many administrative preparations were made in the late 1990s and early part of the new century. The Nunavut Implementation Commission (NIC) was established to create the new territorial government, with its administrative branches and policies, and to facilitate the transition (it completed its work in 1997).[27] Although the transfer from Qallunaat to Inuit hegemony is planned to span a full decade, a special program (*Sivuliuqtit*) trained a contingent of Inuit senior managers to take charge as of April 1, 1999, and was slated to continue after that date.[28] *Sivuliuqtit* has been sponsored by the Nunavut Implementation Commission, Nunavut Implementation Training Committee, Nunavut Arctic College, the former Government of the Northwest Territories, the Nunavut Government, the Department of Indian Affairs and Northern Development's Nunavut Secretariat, and the Canadian Centre for Management Development. *Sivuliuqtit* means "leader, something to follow, like a lead dog." Of the first nine trainees, five were women.

The *Nunavut Sivuniksavut* training program was created to spawn new leaders from among talented Inuit youths. The eight-month program, affiliated with Algonquin College in Ottawa, gives participants a solid dose of Northern Studies, Inuit history, the Inuit land claim agreement, and "other issues essential to their future careers in Nunavut."[29] Participants have a chance to become acclimated to the "world outside the North" and to live successfully away from their home communities and families. They take college preparation courses that will help them perform well, whether they choose to pursue higher education or to work in the government. Sponsored by NTI and regional Inuit economic development corporations, *Sivuniksavut* has graduated over 130 youths since its inception in 1985. A recent meeting of program graduates suggested keeping the program in Ottawa and perhaps extending it by another year.[30] Dozens of Inuit management trainees have gone through an administrative training program in Ottawa.[31]

Pangnirtung, like many other communities, prepared for Nunavut by setting its own policies and making its own decisions through its council-mayor-secretary manager system. This "bottom up" strategy reflects the wider movements that led to the creation of Nunavut.[32] Maata Pudlat explains why Nunavut is so important now; she puts Nunavut into perspective with her memories of the way things were immediately after resettlement. In contrast to the way things were out on the land, when the Inuit made their own decisions, rules and regulations came with resettlement from the Ottawa-based federal government, "where they didn't know *anything* about us."[33] Maata says that it took over a decade for the people to begin to resist those rules.[34]

While the Inuit look to Nunavut as a doorway into a prosperous and more self-directed future, the *paradox of dependency* raises questions about the ultimate success of Nunavut. The forces that contributed to negative social change may be central in replacing enforced dependency with self-administration. The legacy of political dependency parallels the legacy of welfare dependency: those who grew up in the settlements have known life only as an administered people.[35] Despite the fact that whites comprise only 5 percent of the northern population, they head most agencies and businesses throughout the North. Most observers agree that the economic base for Nunavut is weak and the private sector is underdeveloped, which means that the new territory will have to depend on federal transfer payments for years, perhaps decades, to come.[36]

As outlined earlier, the population of Nunavut is young (about 40 percent under 15 years old, compared with 25 percent of the Canadian population as a whole). With a high birth rate, high cost of living, and low incomes, compared to the rest of

Canada, the challenges facing Nunavut are monumental.[37] As Geddes concluded, "conditions for the experiment are far from ideal. The social problems that plague the Eastern Arctic will make it a complex and costly jurisdiction to govern. The economy is weak, and its prospects uncertain."[38]

Anticipated Benefits of Nunavut
"It's been too long."

Nunavut is a creature of the twenty-first century, although its blueprints were drawn late in the twentieth century. It did not go into effect fully until 1999. Yet, the concept had already become very much a political and social force. The Inuit hope that Nunavut will allow them to regain control of their destiny. As Maata remarks, "The reason we really fought for our Nunavut is because it was about time.... We've been letting things run ignorantly, when *we* know what all the problems are."[39]

For the Inuit, the obvious benefits of Nunavut lie more in the realm of achieving a renewed sense of pride, self-worth, identity, and autonomy. Inuit view the problems mentioned earlier—alcoholism, unemployment, suicide, crime—as direct consequences of their lack of self-determination. As long as they have little or no control over the decisions that affect their lives, they will continue to experience alienation, marginality, poverty, and disenfranchisement.

The importance of Nunavut for women, in particular, resides in the hope that greater political self-determination and control of resources will lead to greater prosperity and economic stability for the Inuit. Nunavut "means the prospect for steadier employment" and a "sense of pride in people that will help ease the staggering rate of suicide, drug and alcohol addition, and domestic violence."[40] It also means renewed hope for meaningful education in Inuktitut. These gains, in turn, should help rebalance male-female power, reduce the negative impacts of role reversal, restabilize families, minimize welfare dependence, and remove the underlying reasons for violence against women: poverty, alcohol and drug abuse, and loss of cultural identity.

Women and men both look to Nunavut as an opportunity to ameliorate some of the negative impacts of resettlement on families and to generate new strategies for personal and community development: "The creation of Nunavut is not the end of the process but rather the beginning of a new and different style of government."[41]

The architects of Nunavut chose decentralization of services across the larger hamlets as one way to spread the stable jobs, wealth, and influence that many hope will come with the new territorial government. The Nunavut Secretariat estimated that 600 new full-time equivalent (FTE) positions would be created in the public sector, not to mention 1,400 construction jobs (to build territorial government buildings), and a few hundred private sector spin-off jobs spread across larger communities.[42] Hicks sees "...a decentralized government as better suited to traditional Inuit political culture" and observes that it might encourage Inuit participation (although many models of decentralization were possible).[43] He and others also worry about the cumbersome and expensive nature of operating a decentralized government across a landmass that is larger than Québec.[44] Pangnirtung, for example, hosts the Department of Tourism and the Baffin regional office of the Health Department: "Most will be office jobs, sitting at a computer, administering programs. There might be some nice salaries. Most men don't want a job like that, so most will go to females because the females are going through for further education. This could further accentuate the division between men and women."[45] While Inuit men and women are mindful of the potential costs of decentralization and ballooning of relatively new activities such as tourism, most are optimistic about the ultimate benefits for economic and cultural stability. A local Pangnirtung leader expects Nunavut "to be good for Pang and all the region."

In the past, the local government officials had to deal with government by calling "half way across the continent" to Yellowknife. Nunavut is designed to "bring government closer to people" and make it easier for local leaders: "Most are Native and it will improve communications, and result in many changes in local politics." Change has not always been easy for the Inuit, the leader observes: "When we overcome change, it will be easier in the long run. We have seen many changes in the past. The federal government, for example, dictated education. Gradually, we have had a say and we will have more control over education with Nunavut. Education will be more culturally oriented."

The first premier's words translate the Nunavut dream into a set of "achievable" objectives that will improve the lives of women and children, of men, and of communities:

> We want a Nunavut...where people can achieve their potential, where strong links exist between communities and southern Canada, where health and social conditions are equal to those enjoyed by other Canadians, where equal opportunities exist for everyone, where Nunavut enjoys growing prosperity while remaining debt free.[46]

More specifically, a local leader listed the following positive outcomes she expects from Nunavut: common empowerment, more open discussions at local and regional levels about common problems across communities (through elders' workshops, youth groups, and other meetings), improvements in wellness (control of social problems and healing sources for victims of sexual abuse, spouse abuse, alcohol and drugs, and suicide), and improved social services and availability of culturally oriented services.

Others have called for a new approach to criminal justice through culturally-sensitive corrections services, more land programs or dedicated probation officers outside Iqaluit, and stronger supervision in the community through halfway houses, minimum-security correctional or healing centers, and land camps.[47]

Anticipated Challenges
"It's like decolonization."

The reality of the Inuit dream poses the most daunting challenge any people can face: establishing a workable society within an identifiable territory, with a relatively homogeneous population, carved out of an existing and very heterogeneous larger society. As many Inuit are quick to point out, the Resettlement Period, marked by central government control, paternalism, and economic support, leaves a complicated and stubborn legacy of dependency: Nunavut is the "most fiscally dependent jurisdiction in Canada...[and] relies on federal funding as much as 90 percent."[48] As described earlier, when the government placed the Inuit into settlements, they became reliant on government policies and support. Furthermore, the former Government of the Northwest Territories took an inclusive, assimilationist stance: "Ottawa turned its oppressive bureaucracy over to a territorial government based in Yellowknife, then controlled by non-aboriginal officials whose ambition was to create a northern provincial government that ignored aboriginal identity and could have crushed aboriginal rights forever...an assimilationist ideology grew up, based on catch-phrases like "We're all northerners together."[49] A person who has lived in the Baffin region for many years offers this view:

> There [was] a wonderful celebration April 1, 1999. John Amagoalik said that when the map of Canada is redrawn, it will not occur because of the secession of Québec but because of the creation of Nunavut. We have a great deal of pride, but lives will not change dramatically, instantly. It's like decolonization, in a sense. There was great euphoria in Africa in the 60s, too, and then reality sets in.
>   The issues the Inuit are grappling with right now won't go away over-night, but it can't be any more difficult than it is right now. Maybe this for the last 30 years is good training for what will come. The leaders are realistic in struggling for the preparation of Nunavut. I hope they don't try to fool people that...there will be jobs for everyone.

Indeed, the move to autonomy may prove difficult to effect after lifetimes of government control.[50] Inuit dreams must be brought into the harsh world of Inuit realities if Nunavut is to succeed. Shattering the bonds of dependency under which two generations have lived will not be an easy task. Concerns expressed by Inuit leaders, federal government leaders, and outside observers include:

- The federal government or the Government of the Northwest Territories (GNWT) will simply "dump responsibilities onto municipalities without giving them enough money or know-how," thus making a mockery of devolution.

• The Inuit are not ready to take over the administration of agencies, distribution of funds, and decision-making processes.

• Infrastructure and governance jobs will go to Qallunaat rather than to Inuit and adequate human resources training for Inuit will not be forthcoming. The Inuit surge toward autonomy stems precisely from long-standing domination by the southern, Euro-Canadian government and business interests. Even with the new opportunities for self-administration in Nunavut, transient white professionals from southern Canada have staffed the majority of agencies. As of late 1998, more than half of all new Nunavut government staff hired were Inuit, but the recruitment process was hampered by a shortage of qualified professionals, according to then Interim Commissioner, Jack Anawak. Senior positions in finance, legal services, engineering, health, and information technology were filled by non-Inuit.[51]

• Devolution can proceed only as fast as the Inuit are ready in training and experience. One local leader comments: "It is too early for great excitement, because we are not accustomed to local power. But when we understand better what Nunavut means for local power, then we will have clearer expectations."

• In terms of the Inuit development corporations that have emerged in the last two decades, the Inuit may simply be shareholders who do not have real control over decisions.[52]

• Inuit leaders have to prove themselves to Ottawa and to their own people: "We should stand up and use our own policies and decisions. If we know what we're doing, Inuit will realize we are running it the way they want. I like the government policies—they work; but I think we should have more of our own." Many Inuit resent the doubts expressed about their capacity for self-governance.

• The Inuit may not be able to resolve inter-group conflicts and constructively administer the resources at their disposal. Umbrella, regional, and local Inuit organizations do not always agree on how to proceed.[53] Conflicts over how much Nunavut actually costs, how to build and maintain its infrastructure, how to spend funds, leadership, economic development, and intergovernmental relations lie behind much of the controversy.[54]

• Native leaders constitute an elite that will grab more than its fair share of natural and financial resources.

• Leaders carry an enormous weight on their shoulders as they try to shape a viable system out of the old political and economic structure. John Amagoalik, one of the architects of Nunavut and leader of the Nunavut Implementation Commission, acknowledges that being involved in something that so deeply affects Inuit lives is an enormous responsibility.

• The financial costs of Nunavut are extremely high. During debates on the issue, supporters of the territorial split argued that financial burdens alone should not deter the Canadian government from doing what is ethically and morally right. Others contended that bifurcation of the existing NWT carried an indefensible cost. Now that Nunavut is a reality, Canadians outside the territory might begin to resent the costs involved. As early as 2001, Nunavut government officials were warning that they were already entering a deficit spending mode.[55]

Much information about Nunavut has appeared in local and regional newspapers, a Nunavut day has been instituted in July throughout the new territory, and television and radio shows abound on the possible impacts of Nunavut. A high volume of media stories and visiting dignitaries marked the celebration of Nunavut's birth. Yet, perhaps because of the experimental nature of the new arrangement, it is difficult for people to grasp the economic and political changes that might ensue. We found that our questions on Nunavut (during 1997, 1998, and 1999 interviews) elicited contradictory or vague statements and a lack of immediate comprehension of the nature of question. Inuit seem, at best, mildly positive but uncertain about what differences *Nunavut* might make in their lives. For example, during our interviews in spring of 1997, we discovered that few had heard the term "gender parity" although it was only two months before the plebiscite. Some typical pre-1999 reactions to Nunavut included:

—*It is great. Finally, Inuit will have a say in many things. At one time, I wanted to be a politician, but the land claims study showed me that many politicians were "power people." I don't want to abuse power, so I won't be a politician.*
—*I love Nunavut, but it will be hard. Pay will change and whites won't have all the jobs.*
—*We're afraid of Nunavut. We're not ready; we don't understand it.*
—*I don't know about it and don't care about it. We are going to be poor anyway. I am happy the way things are now.*
—*Inuit teens don't know about it. It seems whites know more about it.*
—*It might make things better, but it will take time—50 years—to make the transition. Things will be hard during that "time of change."*
—*Greenland has its own government and things have not really changed as much as they should there.*
—*When I was in high school, they talked to us about the implementation. They might waste the money. Canada is trying to pay its debt. Where is the money coming from?*
—*I'm optimistic about Nunavut, but people are suspicious and cynical or at least worried because they think it will put Nunavut in debt for the first few years. That's what happened for five years when the Canadian Government gave more power to the old government of the NWT.*
—*I don't know much about it but I think it might bring more jobs.*
—*We don't see the jobs out there waiting for us. Why bother? They don't teach anything useful in school.*
—*There might be more jobs, but I don't agree with Nunavut.*

—I hope it will change education—give us more Inuktitut books.
—I wanted the capital to be farther away. With Iqaluit as capital, there will be
more alcohol here.

Interviews after Nunavut was born (in 2000 and 2001) reveal a similar mixture of hope and skepticism about the future. Undoubtedly, the mixed economy that has emerged as the Inuit have integrated traditional skills, small-scale entrepreneurship, and government employment will continue to be an important source of economic strength.[56] As the century proceeds, the realities of Nunavut's administration and policies will give the best evidence of whether Nunavut as a concept holds viable promises for Canada's Inuit people.

A Conceptual Framework for Change: Conflict, Vitality, and Marginality

Theoretically speaking, the Inuit moved from the *Gemeinschaft* end of the rural-urban continuum toward the *Gesellschaft* end when they came in from the land. "Modernizing" forces such as technology and schools imported from other cultures (in this case, southern Canada and Europe) were instrumental in spurring dramatic social change.[57] Gunnar Myrdal identified several social change processes that help describe the Baffin Inuit experience: "...the principle of interlocking circular interdependence within a process of cumulative causation has validity over the entire field of social relations."[58] In this case, cumulative causation occurred in the form of successive waves of external influence through explorers, whalers, police, traders, missionaries, and then the government administrators who implemented resettlement.

The spread effects of these influences permeated the entire Inuit system of social relations (religion, values, mores, language, work, recreation, and so forth). As each social institution was swept into the sphere of external influence, it, in turn, affected how other institutions operated on a daily basis. Thus, Myrdal's notion of "interlocking circular interdependence" played out for the Inuit. The cessation of a nomadic hunting and gathering lifestyle gave way to wage employment or welfare, which affected gender roles, the family, the interconnectivity of the family to other families in the community, which ultimately affected the interaction between the Inuit community and the larger Canadian society—which started the process of change in the first place.

The interlocking nature of these forces resulted in changes in how the Inuit make a living, how they relate to the land, and how they interact with each other. Within this circular and cumulative process, the changes in gender relations between Inuit men and women command our attention.

The Overriding Power of Gender Relations

Confusions around the key role of men and women, how to provide for one's family, and the intricate relationship between Inuit and the Canadian government all contribute to enormous challenges facing the Inuit as the century lumbers to a close. The roles of women and men inside the home are barometers of their roles outside the home, and reflect general well being or alienation, as the case may be. Relationships among family members and between generations are highly sensitive to economic and political change.[59]

As women in virtually all societies have found in their efforts to achieve equality and liberation, some men continue to interpret assertive behaviour as aggression. This holds women back from expressing their knowledge and power. Some men also continue to insist that they know what is "good for women," and to use physical force, the threat of force, or other forms of sexist coercion to get their way. This imposition of a false male superiority intimidates women and girls, and holds them back from full participation in society. Broad social change must include efforts to reduce the alienation and power differentials that Inuit women, along with their sisters in other cultures, have articulated.

The future for Inuit women and their families, and the chances of Nunavut succeeding, can best be understood within the context of social change. Many theoretical frameworks help interpret both the impact of resettlement and the changes that will likely ensue from Nunavut. We briefly explore three here: sociological conflict-functional analysis, social impact assessment, and marginality theory. Regardless of which frameworks seem most useful, future social science must construct bridges between theoretical or scholarly issues and the practical problems faced by the aboriginal peoples.[60]

Conflict-Functional Analysis

The Canadian government instigated the resettlement process with the manifest purpose of improving Inuit health, education, economic, and social conditions. No doubt, many have benefited from modern settlement living. Yet, Franks' comments about Native people in the United States and Canada ring true for the Inuit of the Eastern Arctic as well:

> The federal governments in both countries have had dominant roles in government-native relations, and are still the most important external agencies affecting native populations. Though the policies...have gone through many changes of direction and intent, the end result is similar: the native population is the most disadvantaged group in each country, with medical and health conditions that would shame a third world country, levels of poverty and economic conditions that are social disasters, problems of cultural adaptation and loss that create severe

stress and alienation in individuals and communities, and an unhealthy dependence of native populations on governments and government handouts.[61]

Merton distinguishes between *positive and negative functions* (consequences) of a social decision and between *manifest (intended) and latent (unintended) functions.* "Functions are those observed consequences which make for the adaptation or adjustment of a given system; and dysfunctions...lessen [them]."[62] This type of analysis always depends on the questions, "functional for whom?" and "what are the system's boundaries?" The conflict arising from resettlement stems from the fact that, for the government, "system" meant southern, Anglo- or Franco-European Canada with its parliamentary democracy and relatively urbanized, industrialized and/or agricultural economy. The Inuit were brought into settlements in order to make central government function more smoothly. The Inuit defined "system" in terms of their traditional culture as indigenous peoples of the Fourth World.[63] Obviously, the boundaries of these two systems have come to overlap, especially with penetration of southern social, cultural, and economic forces via the media, shipping, and air transportation. The reverse penetration—northern to southern—has been more limited, focusing primarily on the exportation of Inuit arts and crafts. Any time that two systems come into contact in such an imbalanced way, the likelihood emerges of domination and acculturation of the smaller system by the larger one.[64] It also paves the way for conflict and exploitation.

Several functions have emanated from resettlement policy. From the government point of view, manifest positive functions included improved housing, health, food supply, and education for the Inuit, and improved efficiency in delivery of services. Given the historical precedent of Indian reserves, it could be argued that the government realized it would be breaking up culture and creating a welfare economy by bringing Inuit off the land (manifest negative functions). Presumably, decision-makers judged the positive functions to outweigh probable negative consequences for both the Inuit and the national government.[65] Latent negative functions mentioned by the Inuit have been a high price to pay for the positive functions of resettlement. Women and girls in this book have spoken openly about the negatives that affect their lives—identity confusion; loss of roles, culture and language; an increase in family violence, substance abuse, and deviance; intergenerational conflict; and distrust of authorities. Economic dependency has been a frustrating consequence that is proving burdensome for everyone concerned.

Perhaps the lessons learned from the Inuit are unremarkable, but they bear repeating for countless political situations that involve marginalized people all over the world. Patriarchy, paternalism, racism, and bureaucracy are dysfunctional and dangerous to women, minority, and indigenous populations.[66] They are also hard habits to break.[67] Respect for indigenous values and beliefs must temper even the most well-intended humanitarian zeal. That means, in practical terms, making the time and effort to find out what those values and beliefs might be. Most importantly, change must be brought about with the full participation of those most immediately affected by it. For example, Grygier reflects on the ways in which the Canadian government handled the tuberculosis crisis. What seemed "functional" to officials at the time was, at least in part, very dysfunctional for the health of Inuit communities, families, and individuals:[68]

> Many of the government workers may not even have been aware, because they were so much a part of it...that it seemed entirely normal; namely, the prevailing colonial, paternalistic attitudes of the period in which they had been reared. Nowadays, such attitudes have become so unacceptable.... But in the early part of the century, there was generally the smug—and ignorant—assumption among white societies that they were superior to the local people who lived off the land that the whites coveted; and that, in the case of the Arctic, they would bring the benefits of civilization to the Inuit.

The creation of Nunavut should function to soften the collision of these two systems. Giving territorial decision-making powers back to the people within a framework of traditional lands will have more meaning than the former NWT has had for the Inuit. Though Nunavut is a "public" rather than an "aboriginal" government (because people other than Inuit live in the new territory), the new departments (including Sustainable Development; Culture, Language, Elders and Youth; Education; and Health and Social Services) provide a chance that future decisions on community building will be made more clearly and directly by the Inuit.[69] Under the old system, Hamlet Councils were not sure of their precise powers and authority: "They would try to exercise influence over aspects of settlement administration, only to find that power lay with the [southern, white] administrators. Advice that was acceptable was acted upon; otherwise it was ignored."[70] This led to the perception that the Inuit situation was one of dependency in the face of "an impenetrable wall of government authority."[71] Presumably, closer control over territorial decisions and enhanced local decision-making by communities will be able to protect and expand the Inuit political, social, cultural, and economic system, and diminish the negative consequences—intended or not—of years of southern hegemony.

Social Impact/Social Vitality Analysis

Another way to look at resettlement is through the lens of social impact theory. The typical "new town" economy has brought unexpected prosperity (through wage-paying jobs) to some individuals for short periods. However, a systematic reshaping of the economy that effectively responds to the dramatic shift from hunting and gathering to post-industrial organization has not occurred for the Inuit. The absence of a stable economic base profoundly affects the social health of any community, as has so eloquently been expressed by our consultants. Furthermore, the negative impacts on social health—such as alcoholism and violence—affect everyone in a community, but "have a particularly drastic effect on women. ...These costs have to be taken into account along with the benefits of development."[72]

Matthews, in his study of outport Newfoundland, defines "social vitality" in terms of a community's ability to:

1. Pass on values, norms, and skills necessary to survive, through family, schools, and churches (socialization)
2. Communicate within the community, through media and political bodies (communication)
3. Provide opportunities for solidarity-building interaction, through sports, entertainment, and recreation (sociation)[73]

Gibbins and Ponting add five more dimensions of a community's vitality, namely the ability to:

4. Encourage a sense of identity and collective pride
5. Preserve culture and establish boundary-maintaining mechanisms, through regulation of in- and out-migration
6. Confer legitimacy on political bodies; develop effective mechanisms for conflict resolution
7. Develop leadership and organizational expertise[74]

Especially in the case of Inuit experience, we suggest two other important criteria for measuring social vitality. A community must be able to:

8. Generate favorable, non-oppressive relations with the dominant society
9. Restructure gender relations in non-oppressive, non-violent, inclusive, and respectful forms

Although Matthews demonstrated that "a community's lack of economic viability need not entail its demise as a sociologically viable collectivity," he also found that social vitality "could not be retained over the long term in the absence of political efficacy and economic viability."[75] Economics and social life are integrally related. In the case of Pangnirtung, dependency on transfer payments has been an essential mechanism of survival. So far, social vitality has persisted, though the social problems outlined by women and men in this study threaten that vitality. Political and economic vitality obviously must be the next step if social vitality is to be renewed. For example, one obvious choice Inuit leaders face is whether to continue following the Alberta curriculum for public education. Adapting to their own needs or creating an entirely new curriculum is an important choice that has never before been possible for the people. As Pangnirtung's Eva Sowdluapik argues, "We struggle to find the words to explain to our parents what's going on at school. We don't have words [in Inuktitut] for terms in cell biology."[76]

Another choice will come in the way the Inuit handle development, especially in the areas of resource extraction and tourism. The Inuit have a history's worth of experience of living in peaceful co-existence with nature. Through the example of their stewardship of Nunavut, they can demonstrate to the rest of

Canada, North America, and the world, how humans can live productively in harmony with their environment. Managed, sustainable development, sensitively directed eco-tourism, and protection of non-renewable resources will occasion special opportunities and challenges.[77]

We also argue that Nunavut's greatest challenge lies in the ability to *"restructure gender relations in non-oppressive, non-violent forms,"* which depends heavily upon the first eight challenges. Violence and oppression harm both the victims and the perpetrators (who are usually also, themselves, victims). We agree with Bell and Klein that a healthy woman is "physically safe, economically secure, and is able to enjoy her human rights to the full."[78] That applies to the healthy man, too, of course. Nunavut carries that dream and bears that responsibility for Inuit futures.

If communities pass both female and male skills and values to the next generations, with equal respect for the contributions of both genders, that would go a long way to reducing sexism and gender conflict. Communication through the media (e.g., the Inuit Broadcasting Corporation) and policy-making by the new territorial legislature can go beyond encouraging a sense of identity and pride among the Inuit. They can also underscore the worth of female contributions to this old and complex culture.

It will be critical for future gender relations that Nunavut, the "legitimate" political body of the twenty-first century, works openly and equitably for women as well as for men. The gender parity proposal failed in 1997. However, the new legislative body can find creative ways to ensure that women's voices and preferences are respectfully heard. The political processes that elect delegates must remain equally open for both women and men.[79] Effective mechanisms for conflict resolution, leadership, and organizational expertise—tapping the old ways when they work and taking advantage of administrative training—should go a long way toward generating "favorable, non-oppressive relations" within Nunavut and with the rest of Canada.

Each of these dimensions of community vitality rests on a Nunavut-wide commitment to mutual respect and valuation between men and women, as is true for any community. In a sense, Nunavut is a utopian dream come true—but utopias must be devised to meet the needs of women, as well as men. That means integrating women into "all levels of social policy and civic participation" and a "reassessment of social and ethical values aimed at a just recognition of women's participatory activities in society."[80]

Marginality and Marginalization

In Chapter 7 we argued that the Inuit are in a classically marginal position—straddling two cultures but belonging fully to neither.[81] Resettlement succeeded in creating a structurally and culturally marginalized people. Structurally, in relation to wider Canadian society, Inuit are at the economic, political, and geographic fringe.

Yet, only as Nunavut flourishes will they move toward control of their resources or political future. Culturally, Inuit are rapidly losing the traditional life skills that ensured survival for their grandparents; yet, they have not acquired all the skills that modern society requires.

Positive social change will come when the Inuit reposition themselves within Canadian society so that they no longer live on the margins, and when they can redefine their political identity to optimize control over their future. Reducing the negative impacts of rapid social change depends on the ability to merge the old with the new in creative ways, and on the broader society's ability to change how it views aboriginal rights. Nunavut presents the opportunity to erase the marginality that has characterized Inuit society for the last few decades. As Stevenson says:

> Today, Inuit face a challenge different than that confronted by previous generations. No longer are cultural and physical survival one and the same. Once again, in order to remain Inuit, they must change. And, once again, they must do it by someone else's rules. How to preserve Inuit cultural values, customs, and traditions under such circumstances is one of the greatest challenges that Nunavut faces.[82]

In addition, as they have already demonstrated during the negotiations to create Nunavut, the leaders of Nunavut must build assertive, yet dignified relations with Canada as a whole. This will be extremely difficult, given the history of paternalism and control from Ottawa. Nunavut must tread a fine line: it must not cut itself off from the Canadian family (indeed, most Inuit view themselves as Canadians), nor must it settle for hollow representations of "autonomy."

Native peoples all over the world have found their cultures threatened and even eliminated through contact. Nunavut presents an unusual opportunity to "greenhouse" traditional Inuit culture, preserving the best and growing it into contemporary competitive economic and cultural models. That Inuit ingenuity and adaptability is already translating tradition into innovative entrepreneurial schemes. The Conference Board of Canada, in an independent study of Nunavut's likely future, warns that the new territory must commit itself to "steady improvement" in the quality of Nunavut's human capital: "The number one risk to this forecast relates to the development of Nunavut's human capital, in particular, to its youth.... An employable individual should be healthy as well as properly educated...both these public services are in desperate need of attention if the people of Nunavut are to meet all the challenges of entering the wage-based economy."[83] Ironically, improving education and health were the two main reasons the Canadian government initially gave for bringing the Inuit into settlements in the mid-twentieth century. Now, those tasks lie at the doorstep of the new Inuit leadership who, in shifting toward full control of Nunavut, must reclaim the sense of identity that was shattered during the Resettlement Period.

In the process of building communities, leaders should provide individuals and families alike with a new sense of focus that will help reduce the anxieties that, unfortunately, always accompany marginality. Tackling the most intractable symptoms of marginality—alcoholism, despair, drug addiction, suicide, unemployment, and violence—should form a central part of every policy and program. As one person warned, however, "Expectations are high that Inuit leaders are going to do things differently and solve problems creatively—but many of these problems are not solvable by governments at any level."

Nonetheless, the emergent Nunavut government has a window of opportunity to move toward vitality and away from marginality in the choices it makes for the territory. For example, the task force on Inuit *Qaujimajatuqangit* (traditional Inuit knowledge) has called for operating the government in Inuktitut: "Government programs would reflect the Inuit way of life, and Inuit culture would flourish in the workplace."[84] They said that Inuit cultural symbols should permeate daily government activities—lighting the *qulliq*, eating country food, and singing traditional songs. The task force position is that conducting business in Inuktitut, even if that means that Qallunaat employees have to take immersion language classes, would help preserve both the language and the culture. So far, the traditional symbols have been incorporated into Nunavut territorial government procedures.

If Inuit leaders approach the social, cultural, economic, and political systems as interactive, interrelated systems that make up a whole, they can break new ground. If they separate out the vibrant traditional mechanisms from the cellophane layer of Qallunaat ways imposed or unconsciously absorbed during the Resettlement Period—and discard what does not work for Inuit culture—they will succeed without losing their heritage. If the Inuit educate their children toward hope and away from despair, and simultaneously spawn new avenues of economic opportunity (for the two are intimately linked), their children will become strong leaders of the twenty-first century. If they approach decision-making with a keen awareness of their old ability to survive in a harsh environment with their new ability to juggle technology and national/international political negotiations, Nunavut will indeed become a dream worth making into reality.

Toward the Future
"This will be our biggest challenge"

Observers have long admired the Inuit for their adaptability to both natural and human conditions. Local bands could cooperate with regional groupings—or nuclear families could cooperate with extended kin—to cope with temporary shortages and long-term crises. The family and the band as the "basic socioeconomic unit" could reorganize quickly to ensure survival. In the past, the local resource base influenced the size of a settlement.[85] With artificial economic mechanisms in place in Pangnirtung and other Baffin communities, Inuit adaptability is being stretched and tested. Still, the imperative of political and social survival is no less threatening than the imperative of physical survival. In effect, Inuit have an opportunity to shape a modern-day utopia that can serve as a model for other communities, both Native and non-Native. They can avoid some of the pitfalls of the world around them. As with any effort to build or re-build a society, the Inuit must attend to all basic social institutions in order to ensure that a healthy system evolves into a coherent, positive socioeconomic system. The backbone of those institutions is the family, and the tissue that bonds the family is the nature of the relationships between men and women.

The leaders of Nunavut can construct new political mechanisms out of tradi-tional ways that *avoid* patriarchy and male domination. Before contact with Qal-lunaat, the Inuit enjoyed relatively balanced gender roles, which must be re-stored in order for both women and men to reach their potential as individuals and as community members. The Inuit have a chance with Nunavut to ensure that women have equal access to leadership positions and share decision-making opportunities. They can give high priority to issues involving the victimization of women and children. Moreover, they can imaginatively combine traditional mechanisms for supporting strong, economically self-sufficient families with modern mechanisms.

Out on the land, men and women worked hand-in-hand, and respected the value and urgent necessity of each other's skills, knowledge, and talents. This balance teetered during the Contact and Resettlement periods. If Nunavut is to thrive, the Inuit must take advantage of the wealth of wisdom and knowledge brought by both genders, rather than to slip into imported patriarchal modes. Increased political power, if shared equitably between men and women, should herald positive gains for Inuit women on economic, educational, and cultural fronts as well. Fortunately, several Inuit women—strong, dedicated leaders— already take part in that process.

The world watches this fascinating social experiment up North. There will undoubtedly be successes and failures but as the Chinese say, "In every crisis, there is an opportunity." For the Inuit, the crisis of resettlement has created op-portunities for a life style and riches unheard of out on the land. Equally, how-ever, in every opportunity there is a crisis. Threats to Inuit culture, personal self-esteem, family stability, and community vitality give credence to that proposi-tion as well. Many questions remain: Will Inuit men become the keepers of one very important part of the culture, hunting and fishing? Will men hang on to the old ways and values associated with these activities, including a negative value on indoor work? Will that influence the number and types of males who run for political office? Will women become the keepers of another part of the culture, wages gathered from various forms of paid employment outside the home?

Even carving is defined by most males as occasional work they can easily put aside when the land beckons, and then just as easily take up again when there is a specific need for money (the classic pattern of male workers in devel-oping countries). Gender roles were highly differentiated but symbiotic and bal-anced in traditional Inuit culture. Now, gender roles could remain highly differentiated but divergent in function or even antagonistic in values and priorities. Men may want to hunt seals but will women want to scrape a sealskin after working all day as a custodian or a teacher? Will increasing alienation between males and females lead to even more spousal abuse, alcohol and drug use, strained families, and suicide? Or, will the crisis of the moment force individuals, families, and communities to create new modes that will bring them closer again?

The major challenge facing the Inuit as they approach the twenty-first century is to create a new, vital culture that is theirs, not just an amalgam of traditional Inuit ways and contemporary southern ways. Nunavut, if successful, will allow the Inuit to redefine their culture to afford maximum control over their destiny, while at the same time remaining part of the Canadian family.

> If you were brought up with love and understanding and courage, no matter how hard it is, you'll strive and try to go on. We were never given the right direction, the right coordination. No one ever taught us what to do if we are caught in between, but we have managed to cope with it. We're just trying our best. We have to act together in most communities. Politicians who had never seen us were making all the regulations for us. That didn't fit at all. They made laws that were useless to us. It was not how *we* deal with people. Not long ago we started speaking up for our rights and what we wanted in our communities. That's far better than it used to be, too.

Finally, it is important to go beyond amassing data on alcohol and drug abuse, spousal assault, child abuse, unemployment, suicide, and depression—all said by the Inuit to be consequences of massive social upheaval—and to move toward understanding and empowerment. The hopes and dreams of individuals sweep along in the whirlpool of change that rushes through the community as a whole. People turn away from the way things were "at that time," as so many Inuit women and men refer to the past, and toward new and often confusing ways that come from the outside world.

Inuit women have described in these pages a rift between men and women, mirrored in spousal assault, alienation, and breakdown of the extended and nuclear family. We argue that finding ways to heal that rift is fundamental to creative social transformation. If the Inuit can rebuild solidarity between the sexes, then families, communities, and Nunavut itself will be stronger in all aspects of life. Solidarity and cohesion within a community—across genders and across generations—are the best antidotes to marginality, exploitation by dominant groups, and rapid change. Empowerment of Inuit women—and of the Inuit in general— will come through the process of recreating culture, integrating the old and the new, and redefining relationships between women and men. Elders encourage young people to "bring together the best from both cultures."[86] To that end, the gift of the elders is their keen memory and time-tested skills, which they can pass down to the younger generations. The gift of the middle, transitional generation is their frustration and pain, the sounding of the alarm that clearly warns of a time-critical situation. The gift of the young is their ability to work across generations toward a new culture that remains uniquely Inuit in its flexibility and forward-looking creativity.

IN THE ELDER'S ROOM

Elisapee, Kudloo, and Qatsuq sit in the Angmarlik Centre room that is set aside for the elders. As their leathery, gnarled fingers deftly slip wool over knitting needles, they reflect on Nunavut and the dreams held by their children, grandchildren, and great-grandchildren. "This will be our biggest challenge," Elisapee smiles, "changing the old ways but keeping them, too." Kudloo nods. Qatsuq, who lived among the whalers almost a century ago, wonders if she will still be alive when the Nunavut dream comes true, then laughs at herself: "I will be gone, but the young women will teach their children what it means to the people."

After weeks and weeks of interviewing across more than a decade, we realize that although many layers have been uncovered, many layers remain. We hope that the voices heard here will be heard as the Inuit make their way through this new century.

Photo 19.2 The authors stand on an ice floe in Pangnirtung Fiord. [Photo by P. Qappik]

Notes

1 This chapter is based in part on Janet Mancini Billson, "Inuit Dreams, Inuit Realities: Shattering the Bonds of Dependency," *American Review of Canadian Studies*, special issue on aboriginal issues, (Spring/Summer 2001): 283-299.

2 See Hantzsch, *My Life among the Eskimos*, p. 36. Hantzsch claims that the Inuit typically received one piece of tobacco for a whole seal; a hare drew one-half piece of tobacco. Nonetheless, he says, a "comradeship" developed between Inuit and whites based on reciprocal advantage and "the inborn character of the people, strengthened by the wholesome influence of Christian teaching."

3 The Bay bought out another competitor, the Northwest Company, in the nineteenth century.

4 Chris Nixon, "Land Claim Redraws Canada's Map," *The London Free Press* (December 17, 1991), p. 1; and John F. Burns, "From the Frigid North is Carved a Native Terrain," *The New York Times* (December 22, 1991), Section 4, p. 4. Nunavut's creation leaves the future of the Western Arctic and sub-Arctic portion of the Northwest Territories hanging in the balance. Unlike Nunavut, with its dominant Inuit majority, the Western Arctic contains an admixture of Dene Indians, Inuvialuit (Inuit), Métis, and whites—none of which constitutes a clear majority. These groups hold different views of how the territory should work in the twenty-first century. Even the name of this remnant of the NWT has not been determined, although the Native population at one point favored "Denendeh—The People's Land." See Darcy Henton and William Walker, "Dene Indians Set to Fight Inuit Deal," *The Toronto Star* (December 17, 1991), p. A9; Mary Williams Walsh, "Boundary Disputes with Indians Could Block Accord on New Eskimo Territory," *Los Angeles Times* (December 19, 1991), p. A4; and Scott Freschuk, "Western Arctic's Goals More Difficult to Establish," *Toronto Globe and Mail* (Saturday, July 29, 1995), p. A-6.

5 Sydney Sackett, "Iqaluit: The New Capital of Nunavut," *Above & Beyond* (Spring 1996): 11-16.

6 Mike Trickey, "Major Diplomats Bound for Iqaluit," *Ottawa Citizen* (June 5, 1998), p. A6.

7 Heather Tait, "Focus on Nunavut," *Canadian Social Trends* (Spring 1999): 10. See also Isaac, "Land Claims and Self-Government Developments in Canada's North," p. 479. The intimate links between ethnicity and territoriality seem obvious from the most cursory perusal of late twentieth century headlines: Separatists win in Québec; Yugoslavia rips apart in a war among ancient peoples; Czechoslovakia splits into Czech and Slovak Republics—and the list goes on. Furthermore, the century was a period of major transition for North American aboriginals. Starting especially in the nineteenth century, Native people were stripped of their identity and forced to adopt a new, alien identity. Welfare dependency and geographic isolation contributed greatly to the struggle for new definitions of community, self, and peoplehood. Various indigenous groups struggled (and continue to struggle) for self-determination and a land base.

8 David C. Hawkes, ed., *Aboriginal Peoples and Government Responsibility: Exploring Federal and Provincial Roles* (Ottawa: Carleton University Press, 1989).

9 C. E. S. Franks, "Nunavut and the Spirit of Sedna," paper presented at the Annual Meeting, Association for Canadian Studies in the United States, Minneapolis, November 1997, p. 21.

10 See Jim Bell, "Nunavut: The Quiet Revolution," *Arctic Circle* (January/February 1992): 13-21. See also Kirk Cameron and Graham White, *Northern Governments in Transition: Political and Constitutional Development in the Yukon, Nunavut, and the Western Northwest Territories* (Montréal: Institute for Research on Public Policy, 1995); and John Bird, Lorraine Land, and Murray Macadam, eds., *Nation to Nation: Aboriginal Sovereignty and the Future of Canada* (Toronto: Nelson, 2001). The transition to Nunavut will involve innumerable intermeshing practical issues. See, for example, John H. Hylton, ed.: *Aboriginal Self-Government in Canada: Current Trends and Issues* (Saskatoon: Purich Publishing, 1994).

11 Axtell, *The Apprenticeship of 32 Inuit Managers.*

12 See, for example, D. W. Elliott, ed., *Law and Aboriginal Peoples of Canada*, 2nd ed. (Toronto: Captus Press, 1994); and Thomas Isaac, *Aboriginal Law: Cases, Materials, and Commentary* (Saskatoon: Purich Publishing, 1995).

13 Nunatsiaq News, "NTI Calls on Standing Committee to Support Inuit Economic Development in Nunavut," *Nunatsiaq News* (May 20, 1998).

14 Dwane Wilkin, "New Culture Department Prepares to Defend Inuktitut," *Nunatsiaq News* (November 6, 1998).

15 Personal interview, 1998.

16 For a discussion of pre-Nunavut Inuit status, see Bernard Saladin d'Anglure and Francoise Morin, "The Inuit People between Particularism and Internationalism: An Overview of Their Rights and Powers in 1992," *Études/Inuit/Studies* 16, 1-2 (1992): 13-19.

17 Carolyn Bereznak Kenny, *North American Indian, Métis and Inuit Women Speak about Culture, Education and Work* (Ottawa: Status of Women Canada, 2002, http://www.swc-cfc.gc.ca/pubs/0662318978/index_e.html).

18 The key provisions of the agreement include: 1) The "Nunavut Settlement Area" covers 2.2 million square kilometers in the eastern and central Arctic, from the tree line at 60 degrees latitude to the North Pole; 2) Inuit will hold outright title to 355,842 square kilometers—about 20 percent of Nunavut—scattered in what have been traditional hunting and trapping grounds, camps, and sacred places; 3) Inuit will hold sub-surface mineral rights to 36,000 square kilometers within Inuit Owned Lands; 4) Inuit will have the right to hunt, fish, and trap in the entire Nunavut Settlement Area, whether on Crown Lands or Inuit Owned Lands; 5) Three new National Parks will be established in the Nunavut Settlement Area; 6) Inuit are guaranteed equal membership with the government on new institutions of public administration to manage land, water, offshore, and wildlife in the Nunavut Settlement Area; 7) Inuit have the right to assess the impact of future development projects on the environment; 8) Inuit will receive capital transfer payments of C$1.148 billion, payable over 14 years, with interest, in exchange for relinquishing aboriginal title to Nunavut land *not* within Inuit Owned Lands; 9) Inuit will receive a share of any royalties the Canadian government receives from oil, gas, and mineral development in the rest of Nunavut (Crown Lands); 10) Inuit have the right to negotiate with industry for economic and social benefits from non-renewable resource development on Inuit Owned Lands; and 11) Efforts will be made to increase Inuit employment in territorial government in the Nunavut Settlement area, to provide job training, and to increase Inuit

access to government contracts. The full agreement is available from Tunngavik Federation of Nunavut, Ottawa, Ontario, or the Department of Indian and Northern Affairs, Ottawa.

19 For other discussions of Nunavut, see Alan Cairns and Cynthia Williams, *Constitutionalism, Citizenship and Society in Canada* (Toronto: University of Toronto Press, 1985); Canadian Arctic Resources Committee, *Nunavut: Political Choices and Manifest Destiny* (Ottawa: Canadian Arctic Resources Committee, 1996); Bruce Clark, *Native Liberty, Crown Sovereignty: The Existing Aboriginal Right of Self-Government in Canada* (Montréal: McGill-Queen's University Press, 1990); Joe Clark, "Completing the Circle of Confederation—Aboriginal Rights," *Canada Today/d'aujourd'hui* 22, 2 (1991): 14-15 (Washington, DC: Canadian Embassy)—excerpts from a speech by the Minister Responsible for Constitutional Affairs, Queen's University, Kingston, Ontario, September 9); Mark O. Dickerson, *Whose North? Political Change, Political Development, and Self-Government in the Northwest Territories* (Vancouver: University of British Columbia Press, 1992); Duffy, *The Road to Nunavut*; Lyn Hancock, *Nunavut* (Minneapolis, MN: Lerner Publications, 1995); Inuit Committee on National Issues, *Completing Canada: Inuit Approaches to Self-Government* (Kingston: Institute of Intergovernmental Relations, 1987); Inuit Tapirisat of Canada, "Nunavut—'Our Land'," in *Two Nations, Many Cultures: Ethnic Groups in Canada*, 2nd ed., edited by Jean Leonard Elliott (Scarborough: Prentice-Hall, 1983); Inuit Tapirisat of Canada, *Agreement in Principle as to the Settlement of Inuit Land Claims in the Northwest Territories and the Yukon Territory between the Government of Canada and Inuit Tapirisat of Canada* (Ottawa: Inuit Tapirisat of Canada, 1976); E. L. Simpson, L. N. Seal, and R. L. Minion, *Nunavut: An Annotated Bibliography of the Literature since the 1930s* (Edmonton: Canadian Circumpolar Institute, 1994); and Cornelius H. W. Rémie, "The Struggle for Land among the Inuit of the Canadian Arctic," pp. 19-29 in *The Struggle for Land World-Wide*, edited by G. Peberkamp and Cornelius H. W. Rémie (Saarbrücken/Fort Lauderdale: Breitenbach Verlag, 1989).

20 The Indian Act was amended to include the Inuit in 1924, but the provision was deleted in 1932. Waldram, Herring, and Young, *Aboriginal Health in Canada*, p. 166.

21 For a comparison of Inuit status with that of other aboriginal groups in Canada, see Bruce Alden Cox, *Native People, Native Lands: Canadian Indians, Inuit and Métis* (Ottawa: Carleton University Press, 1988).

22 Andrew Duffy, "The Long, Hard Road to Nunavut," *The Ottawa Citizen* (Sunday, March 28, 1999), p. A4.

23 Government of Canada, "Inuit in Canada," http://www.inac.gc.ca/pubs/information/info16.html, p. 2.

24 Hicks, "The Nunavut Land Claim and the Nunavut Government," p. 29.

25 Cameron and White, *Northern Governments in Transition*, pp. 112-113.

26 Bell, "Anti-Suicide Campaign."

27 The Nunavut Planning Commission (NPC) was part of the co-management institutions that were designed to "give Inuit control over all activities on their settlement lands, as well as a major say in what happens in Crown [federally-owned] lands." http/natsiq.nunanet.com/'nic (Nunavut Implementation Commission, Nov. 22, 1996), p. 1.

28 Department of Indian Affairs and Northern Development, "DIAND Welcomes Nunavut Managerial Trainees," *Transition* (September 7, 1998), p. 1. See also Thomas Axtell, *The Apprenticeship of 32 Inuit Managers* (Axtell Communications and Training, 1999).

29 Murray Angus, "Nunavut Sivuniksavut Releases First Nunavut Opinion Poll," *Nunatsiaq News* (April 15, 1999).

30 Murray Angus, "Ottawa Conference Calls for Action on Post-Secondary Students," *Nunatsiaq News* (June 16, 2000).

31 Axtell, *The Apprenticeship of 32 Inuit Managers.*

32 See Neil C. Skinner, "Foundations of Aboriginal Sovereignty in North America: A Comparative Review," paper presented to the Annual Meeting of the Western Social Science Association (Albuquerque, April 1989); Inuit Committee on National Issues, *Completing Canada*; and Finn Lynge, "An International Inuit Perspective on Development in the Arctic," *The Northern Raven* VI, 1 (Summer 1986): 1-3.

33 Pudlat, "Boy, Have Things Changed," p. 19.

34 Pudlat, "Boy, Have Things Changed," p. 20.

35 For a discussion of the implications of dependency, see Diamond Jenness, "The Administration of Northern Peoples: America's Eskimos—Pawns of History," in Macdonald, ed., *The Arctic Frontier*; Peter Jull, "Aboriginal Peoples and Political Change in the North Atlantic Area," *Journal of Canadian Studies* 16, 2 (1981); and Margaret Lantis, "The Administration of Northern Peoples: Canada and Alaska," in Macdonald, ed., *The Arctic Frontier.*

36 Cameron and White, *Northern Governments in Transition*, p. 99.

37 Based on Franks, "Nunavut and the Spirit of Sedna," pp. 6-7.

38 Geddes, "Northern Dawn," p. 26.

39 Pudlat, "Boy, Have Things Changed," p. 20.

40 Janice Tibbetts, "Iqaluit: Promised Land of the Arctic," *Ottawa Citizen* (Monday, March 29, 1999), p. 1.

41 John Amagoalik, quoted in Whit Fraser, "Nunavut! What a Remarkable Chapter It Will Become in Canada's History," *Above & Beyond* (Spring 1999), p. 45.

42 Personal interview, 1998.

43 Hicks, "The Nunavut Land Claim and the Nunavut Government," p. 33.

44 Cited in Geddes, "Northern Dawn," p. 28.

45 Mark Nuttall cautions that Arctic tourism, spurred by concern for the environment and "idealised images of traditional indigenous cultures," could have the negative, unintended consequences of degrading sensitive ecosystems and commoditizing culture (*Protecting the Arctic*, pp.125-126). Nuttall observes (p. 128) that "...tourism contributes to social change and the destruction of the very things that the industry both promotes and depends upon, such as local cultures and the natural environment." He also acknowledges (p. 129) that tourism can help communities "develop strategies for self-determination and cultural survival," which is the more optimistic Inuit viewpoint we encountered. Tourism accounted for about one third of the active workforce in the former Northwest Territories, a figure that might not be far off for Nunavut as the budding industry expands. Expense and accessibility may deter some potential regular tourists but adventure tourists have already discovered areas such as Auyuittuq National Park, just 20 miles north of Pangnirtung.

46 Nunatsiaq News, "Premier Paul Okalik's Review of Nunavut's First Year: For the Record," *Nunatsiaq News* (April 7, 2000).

47 Annette Bourgeois, "Nunavut Justice: Corrections a Major Challenge for Nunavut," *Nunatsiaq News* (March 25, 1999).

48 Hicks, "The Nunavut Land Claim and the Nunavut Government," p. 46.

49 Bell, "Back Where It Began."

50 Gibbins and Ponting observe that the historical relationship between aboriginal people and the governments of Canada has been "contentious and...unsuccessful." ("An Assessment of the Probable Impact," p. 172). More optimistically, Bernard Blishen detects growing demand among Canadians in general for state recognition of group rights. "Continuity and Change in Canadian Values," in Cairns and Williams, pp. 1-26; Gurston Dacks and Kenneth Coates argue that they need to have more control over both social programs and economic conditions. *Northern Communities: The Prospects for Empowerment* (Edmonton: Canadian Circumpolar Institute, 1989).

51 Dwane Wilkin, "Anawak: Few Inuit are Qualified in Professions," *Nunatsiaq News* (November 19, 1998).

52 Mitchell, *From Talking Chiefs to a Native Corporate Elite*, p. 404.

53 Jim Bell, "Ottawa Moves on Nunavut," *Nunatsiaq News* (May 3, 1996), pp. 1, 16; "NIC Chief Lectures the GNWT," *Nunatsiaq News* (May 31, 1996), p. 3; and "MLA Warns GNWT May Impose 'Empowerment,'" *Nunatsiaq News* (June 7, 1996), pp. 1, 17. Also, Jason Van Rassel, "GNWT Wants to Manage Nunavut's Infrastructure," *Nunatsiaq News* (May 17, 1996), pp. 11-12; "Nunavut Needs More, Leaders Tell Irwin," *Nunatsiaq News* (May 17, 1996), pp. 1, 16; "Baffin Leaders to Tackle Economy in Kimmirut," *Nunatsiaq News* (June 14, 1996), p.11; and "Empower Us Carefully, Baffin Leaders Tell GNWT," *Nunatsiaq News* (June 28, 1996), pp. 1-2. Also, Nunatsiaq News, "The GNWT's Position on Nunavut," *Nunatsiaq News* (May 24, 1996), pp. 5, 9 (based on the territorial government's report, *Working Toward 1999*). Beyond Inuit Tapirisat, some of the key organizations involved in creating Nunavut to date are Nunavut Tunngavik Incorporated, Iqaluit (responsible for administering the land claim); Nunavut Implementation Commission, Iqaluit (responsible for drafting a blueprint for future Nunavut governmental structure); Keewatin Inuit Association, Rankin Inlet; Kitikmeot Inuit Association, Cambridge Bay; and Baffin Inuit Association, Iqaluit. Pauktuutit (the Inuit Women's Association) has been integrally involved throughout the process.

54 Organizations working toward economic development include Makivik Corporation, Qikiqtaaluk Corporation, Nunasi Corporation, and Kakivik Association. With the intention of swelling the ranks of Inuit-owned businesses, they stimulate growth through networking, training, and provision of small business loans and grants. Marion Soublière, "Keeping Inuit Concerns Front and Centre," *Nunatsiaq News (Parnaivik edition*, n.d., 1996), p. 6. The Department of Indian Affairs and Northern Development has announced new federal government procurement guidelines that will make it easier for aboriginal businesses to obtain contracts. It includes providing information about opportunities, creating set-asides, and mandating sub-contracting plans for aboriginal businesses.

55 Jim Bell, "Ng: Nunavut Stands at a Fiscal Turning Point," *Nunatsiaq News* (March 2, 2001). The Finance Minister, Kelvin Ng, said the Nunavut government is exceeding its financial limits, with a projected deficit of $12 million by the end of the 2001-2002 fiscal year.

56 Frances Abele, "Understanding What Happened Here: The Political Economy of Indigenous Peoples," in *Understanding Canada: Building on the New Canadian Political Economy*, edited by Wallace Clement (Montréal and Kingston: McGill-Queen's University Press, 1997).

57 George Dalton, in *Economic Anthropology and Development: Essays on Tribal and Peasant Economies* (New York: Basic Books, 1971), hypothesized that technology, schools, and exporting products or crops impact traditional culture and social organization; some features of traditional culture "make for receptivity or resistance to innovations" (p. 283).

58 Gunnar Myrdal, *Rich Lands and Poor: The Road to World Prosperity* (New York: Harper, 1957), p 23.

59 Lange documents this for the Dene in "The Relation between the Situation of Dene Women and the Changing Situation of Elders, in the Context of Colonialism."

60 Hedican, in *Applied Anthropology in Canada*, theorized that as the economic and administrative devolution gathers steam, Native Canadians should have more opportunity to set budget and other priorities and to participate in evaluating programs and policies. Within the context of Nunavut, however, this should mean training more Inuit women and men to join the ranks of the social scientists as colleagues and leaders. Marc G. Stevenson and C. G. Hickey, in *Empowering Northern and Native Communities for Social, Political, and Economic Control* (Edmonton: Canadian Circumpolar Institute, 1995, p. 7), suggest that the "positivistic instrumental/technical paradigm" and the "critical social science" paradigm both fall short of explaining northern or aboriginal relations vis a vis dominant society, nor does either paradigm serve to empower northern or native communities toward greater control. The former paradigm, used by many in the social work/human service professions, tends to blame the victims of domination for their individual frailties. The latter paradigm blames self-defeating behaviours on a lack of consciousness regarding oppression.

61 C. E. S. Franks, "Indian Self-Government: Canada and the United States Compared," paper presented to the Annual Meeting, Western Social Science Association, Albuquerque (April 1989), p. 1.

62 Robert K. Merton, *Social Theory and Social Structure* (New York: The Free Press, 1957), pp. 49-50.

63 George Manuel and Michael Posluns, "The Fourth World in Canada," in Elliott, ed., *Two Nations, Many Cultures*, pp. 15-18.

64 Billson, "No Owner of Soil."

65 Ray Funk found that government social impact studies of the construction of the Mackenzie Valley pipeline assumed that the pipeline would speed evolution from traditional to modern life for Native people and that "gains in employment, training, and social amenities would offset the unavoidable (negative) social consequences." Although one study "regretted that Natives would become a declining minority in the North," it said this was "an irreversible trend." "The Mackenzie Valley Pipeline Inquiry in Retrospect," in *Social Impact Analysis and Development Planning in the Third World* (Social Impact Assessment Series, No. 12), edited by William Derman and Scott Whiteford (Denver: Westview Press, 1985), pp. 125-26.

66 A lesson from the Inuit and Indian experiences of resettlement might be applied to current efforts to bring often-resistant homeless people into shelters. The provision of

food and shelter without simultaneous provision of opportunities for enhancing pride, self-esteem, and economic independence may create more problems than it is designed to resolve. Parallels can be drawn even more clearly with the experience of aboriginals in other parts of the world. See, for example, Armitage, *Comparing the Policy of Aboriginal Assimilation.*

67 Cornelius H. W. Rémie and Jarich G. Oosten, "The Persistent Savage: Qallunaat Perspectives on the Inuit," pp. 5-27 in *Arctic Identities: Continuity and Change in Inuit and Saami Societies,* edited by Jarich G. Oosten and Cornelius H. W. Rémie (Leiden: Universiteit Leiden, Research School of Asian, African and Amerindian Studies, CNWS 74, 1999); and Michèle Thérrien, "'All Qallunaat Predicted Our Extinction': Inuit Perspectives of Identity," pp. 28-35 in Oosten and Rémie, *Arctic Identities.*

68 Grygier, *A Long Way from Home,* p. 177.

69 Marc G. Stevenson and C. G. Hickey, *Empowering Northern and Native Communities for Social, Political, and Economic Control* (Edmonton: Canadian Circumpolar Institute, 1995); and D. E. Young and L. L. Smith, *The Involvement of Canadian Native Communities in Their Health Care Programs: Review of the Literature since the 1970s* (Edmonton: Canadian Circumpolar Institute, 1993).

70 In *The Inuit (Eskimo) of Canada,* Creery likens the situation to other colonial relationships.

71 Creery, *The Inuit (Eskimo) of Canada.*

72 Young, *Third World in the First,* p. 269.

73 Matthews, *The Creation of Regional Dependency,* p. 162.

74 Roger Gibbins and J. Rick Ponting, "An Assessment of the Probable Impact of Aboriginal Self-Government in Canada," in *The Politics of Gender, Ethnicity, and Language in Canada,* edited by Alan Cairns and Cynthia Williams (Toronto: University of Toronto Press, 1986), pp. 171-245.

75 Cited in Gibbins and Ponting, p. 182. See also Charles W. Hobart, "Impact of Resource Development Projects on Indigenous People," in *Resource Communities: A Decade of Disruption,* edited by Don D. Detomasi and John W. Gartrell (Boulder: Westview Press, 1984); and "Industrial Employment of Rural Indigenes: The Case of Canada," *Human Organization* 41, 1 (1982): 54-63.

76 Quoted in Capozza, "Canadian Territory of Nunavut Pushes to Expand College Offerings," p. A39.

77 See Freeman and Carbyn, *Traditional Knowledge and Renewable Resource Management in Northern Regions.* Tourism can bring with it a steady flow of southern influences, tends to be very seasonal (especially in the Arctic), and does not directly involve many Inuit. See also S. Nickels, S. Milne, and George W. Wenzel, "Inuit Perceptions of Tourism Development: The Case of Clyde River, Baffin Island, NWT," *Études/Inuit/Studies* 15, 1 (1991): 157-169; and Nuttall, *Protecting the Arctic,* p. 149.

78 Bell and Klein, *Radically Speaking,* p. xx.

79 Jim Bell questions whether the shape of the new Cabinet will be open enough to general oversight of Nunavut's citizens: of the nineteen members of the Nunavut Legislature, one will serve as speaker, one as premier, and seven will serve in the cabinet. That leaves only ten "ordinary members" to keep government accountable. "Is the Cabinet Too Large?" *Nunatsiaq News,* March 5 (1999).

80 Asuncion Lavrin, "Women, the Family, and Social Change in Latin America," *World Affairs* 150, 2 (1987): 109-128, p. 121.

81 Billson, "No Owner of Soil."

82 Stevenson, p. 336.

83 Bell, "Human Development Key to Nunavut's Economy." Luc Bussières led the study.

84 Denise Rideout, "Nunavut's Inuit Qaujimajatuqangit Group Gets Started: Task Force Wants 'Inuit Qaujimajatuqangit' to Prevail in GN Offices," *Nunatsiaq News* (February 2, 2001). This would be similar to the way business is conducted in the governments of Québec government (French) or, say, British Columbia (English).

85 See Sabo, *Long-Term Adaptations among Arctic Hunter-Gatherers*, pp. 47-53.

86 McDonald, Arragutainaq, and Novalinga, *Voices from the Bay*, p. 63.

REFERENCES

Abele, Frances. "The Land Claim and Nunavut: One without the Other Isn't Enough." *Arctic Circle* (January/February 1992): 20.

———. "A Time to Celebrate." *Arctic* 52 1 (1999): iii.

Abele, Frances, and Mark O. Dickerson. "The 1982 Plebiscite on Division of the Northwest Territories: Regional Government and Federal Policy." *Canadian Public Policy* 9, 1 (1985): 1-15.

Abele, Frances, Katherine A. Graham, and Allan M. Maslove. "Negotiating Canada: Changes in Aboriginal Policy over the Last Thirty Years." In *How Ottawa Spends 1999-2000: Shape Shifting—Canadian Governance toward the 21st Century*, edited by Leslie A. Pal. Ottawa: Carleton University Press, 1999.

Akulujuk, M. "Things from a Long Time Ago and Nowadays." In *Stories from Pangnirtung*, edited by Stuart Hodgson. Edmonton: Hurtig, 1976.

Albu, Karen. "Pang Print Makers Celebrate the Realization of Their Dream." *Nunatsiaq News* (June 14, 1996), p. 15.

Alexander, Bryan. *Inuit*. Austin, TX: Raintree Steck-Vaughn, 1993.

———. "The Inuit of the Canadian: Out on the Land." In *The Vanishing Arctic*, edited by Bryan Alexander and Cherry Alexander. London: Blandford Cassell, 1996.

Alexander, F. King, and Kern Alexander, eds. *The University: The Transformation of Inuit Settlement in the Central Arctic*. Montreal: McGill-Queens University Press, 2003.

Alia, Valerie. "Aboriginal Perestroika." *Arctic Circle* (November/December 1991), pp. 3-29.

———. *Names, Numbers, and Northern Policy: Inuit—Project Surname, and the Politics of Identity*. Halifax: Fernwood, 1994.

———. *Un/covering the North*. Vancouver: University of British Columbia Press, 1999.

Amagoalik, John. "Canada's Nunavut: An Indigenous Northern Territory." In *Surviving Columbus: Indigenous Peoples, Political Reform and Environmental Management in North Australia*, edited by Peter Jull, et al. Darwin: North Australia Research Unit, Australian National University, 1994.

———. "The Land Claim and Nunavut: One without the Other Isn't Enough." *Arctic Circle* (January/February 1992): 20.

———. "Pauktuutit." *Nunatsiaq News* (March 29, 1996): 9.

———. "The Road to Nunavut." *Arctic Circle* (Winter 1993): 13.

Ames, Randy, Don Axford, Peter J. Usher, Ed Weick, George W. Wenzel, and John Merritt. *Keeping on the Land: A Study of the Feasibility of a Comprehensive*

Wildlife Harvest Support Programme in the Northwest Territories. Ottawa: Canadian Arctic Resources Committee, 1989.

Anders, G., ed. *The East Coast of Baffin Island: An Area Economic Survey.* Ottawa: Industrial Division, Department of Indian Affairs and Northern Development, 1967.

Andersen, Margaret L. *Thinking about Women: Sociological Perspectives on Sex and Gender.* Boston: Allyn & Bacon, 1997.

Angmarlik, Pauloosie. "Pauloosie Angmarlik (Inuit)." In *In the Words of Elders: Aboriginal Cultures in Transition,* edited by Peter Kulchyski, Don McCaskill, and David Newhouse. Toronto: University of Toronto Press, 1999.

Angus, Murray. "Nunavut Sivuniksavut Releases First Nunavut Opinion Poll." *Nunatsiaq News* (April 15, 1999).

———. "Ottawa Conference Calls for Action on Post-Secondary Students." *Nunatsiaq News* (June 16, 2000).

Annaqtuusi, Ruth, and David F. Pelly. *Tulurialik.* Toronto: Oxford University Press, 1986.

Archibald, Linda, and Mary Crnkovich. "Intimate Outsiders: Feminist Research in a Cross-Cultural Environment." In *Changing Methods: Feminists Transforming Practice,* edited by Sandra Burt and Lorraine Code. Peterborough, ONT: Broadview Press, 1995.

Arctic Co-operatives Limited & NWT Co-operative Business Development Fund. *The Co-operative Movement in the North West Territories: An Overview 1959-1989.* Arctic Co-operatives Limited & NWT Co-operative Business Development Fund, 1990.

Arima, Eugene Y. "Views on Land Expressed in Inuit Oral Tradition." In *Inuit Land Use and Occupancy Project II,* edited by Milton M. R. Freeman. Ottawa: Department of Indian and Northern Affairs, 1976.

Armitage, Andrew. *Comparing the Policy of Aboriginal Assimilation: Australia, Canada, and New Zealand.* Vancouver: University of British Columbia Press, 1995.

Armstrong, Terrence. "The Administration of Northern Peoples: The USSR." In *The Arctic Frontier,* edited by Ronald St. J. MacDonald. Toronto: University of Toronto Press, 1966.

Asch, Michael L. *Home and Native Land: Aboriginal Rights and the Canadian Constitution.* Toronto: Methuen, 1984.

———. *Kinship and the Drum Dance in a Northern Dene Community.* Edmonton: Canadian Circumpolar Institute, 1988.

Atkin, Ronald. *Maintain the Right: The Early History of the North West Mounted Police, 1873-1900.* Toronto: Macmillan, 1973.

Axtell, Thomas. *The Apprenticeship of 32 Inuit Managers.* Axtell Communications and Training, 1999.

Baikie, Margaret. *Labrador Memories: Reflections at Mulligan.* Grand Falls, NFLD: Robinson-Blackmore, n. d.

Balikci, Asen. "Anthropological Field Work among the Arviligjuarmiut of Pelly Bay, NWT." *The Arctic Circular* 14 (1961).

———. *Development of Basic Socio-Economic Units in Two Eskimo Communities.* Ottawa: National Museum of Canada Bulletin No. 202, 1964.

————. "Ethnic Relations and the Marginal Man in Canada: A Comment." *Human Organization* 19, 4 (1960): 170-171.

————. "Female Infanticide on the Arctic Coast." *Man* 2, 4 (1967): 615-625.

————. *The Netsilik Eskimo.* Garden City, NY: (The American Museum of Natural History) The Natural History Press, 1970.

————. "The Netsilik Eskimo Today." *Études/Inuit/Studies* 2, 1 (1978): 111-119.

————. "Shamanistic Behaviour among the Netsilik Eskimos." *Southwestern Journal of Anthropology* 19, 4 (1963): 380-396.

————. "Suicidal Behaviour among the Netsilik Eskimos." In *Canadian Society: Sociological Perspectives*, edited by Bernard Blishen. New York: Free Press of Glencoe, 1961.

————. "Two Attempts at Community Organisation among the Eastern Hudson Bay Eskimos." *Anthropologica* I, 1-2 (1959): 122-135.

Barger, Ken W. "Inuit and Cree Adaptation to Northern Colonialism." In *Contemporary Political Organization of Native North Americans*, edited by E. L. Schusky. Washington: University Press of America, 1980.

Barnard, Alan, and James Woodburn. "Property, Power and Ideology in Hunter-Gathering Societies: An Introduction." In *Hunters and Gatherers*, edited by Tim Ingold, David Riches, and James Woodburn. Oxford: Berg, 1988.

Barron, W. *Old Whaling Days.* Hull, Québec: Hull Press, 1895.

Bayley, J. U. *Task Force on Spousal Assault.* Yellowknife: Government of the Northwest Territories, 1985.

Bell, Diane, and Renate Duelli Klein, eds. *Radically Speaking: Feminism Reclaimed.* London: Zed, 1996 (Spinifex, 1999).

Bell, Jim. "Anti-Suicide Campaign." *Nunatsiaq News* (February 23, 2001).

————. "Back Where It Began." *Nunatsiaq News* (March 25, 1999).

————. "Canada's Crime Capital (Part One)." *Nunatsiaq News* (October 9, 1998).

————. "Canada's Crime Capital (Part Two)." *Nunatsiaq News* (October 16, 1998).

————. "Coping with Crime in Nunavut: High Violent-Crime Rate Doesn't Surprise Justice Officials." *Nunatsiaq News* (August 3, 2001).

————. "The Crowded Arctic: The Grim Reality of the North's Housing Crisis." *Arctic Circle* (July/August 1990): 23-30.

————. "Group Will Fight Sex Abuse against NWT Children." *Nunatsiaq News* (August 16, 1996), pp. 2, 18.

————. "Human Development Key to Nunavut's Economy. Think-Tank: Health, Education in 'Desperate' Need of Attention." *Nunatsiaq News* (June 22, 2001).

————. "Inuit Unemployment Still High, Despite Record Job Growth." *Nunatsiaq News* (September 24, 1999).

————. "Is the Cabinet Too Large?" *Nunatsiaq News* (March 5, 1999).

————. "Is Violent Crime on the Rise in Nunavut? Violent Crime Exceeds Property Crime in Nunavut." *Nunatsiaq News* (July 27, 2001).

————. "MLA Warns GNWT May Impose 'Empowerment.'" *Nunatsiaq News* (June 7, 1996), pp. 1, 17.

————. "Ng: Nunavut Stands at a Fiscal Turning Point." *Nunatsiaq News* (March 2, 2001).

————. "NIC Chief Lectures the GNWT." *Nunatsiaq News* (May 31, 1996), p. 3.

―――. "Nunavut's October Throne Speech: Poetry, Dreams, But Few Specifics" *Nunatsiaq News* (October 22, 1999).

―――. "Nunavut: The Quiet Revolution." *Arctic Circle* (January/February 1992): 13-21.

―――. "Ottawa Moves on Nunavut." *Nunatsiaq News* (May 3, 1996), pp. 1, 16.

―――. "The Violating of Kitty Nowdluk." *Arctic Circle* (July/August 1991): 32-28.

―――. "Who Works for Inuit Culture?" *Nunatsiaq News* (November 6, 1998).

Bennett, Allan C., William E. Flannigan, and Marilyn P. Hladun. *Inuit Community*. Don Mills, ONT: Fitzhenry and Whiteside, 1980.

Berger, Thomas R. *A Long and Terrible Shadow: White Values, Native Rights in the Americas, 1492-1992*. Vancouver and Toronto: Douglas & McIntyre, 1991.

Berlo, Janet Catherine. "Inuit Women and Graphic Arts: Female Creativity and Its Cultural Context. *The Canadian Journal of Native Studies* 9, 2 (1989): 293-315.

Bilby, Julian W. *Among Unknown Eskimo: An Account of Twelve Years Intimate Relations with the Primitive Eskimo of Ice-Bound Baffin Land, with a Description of Their Ways of Living, Hunting, Customs and Beliefs*. London: Seeley Service, 1923 (later published as *Among Unknown Eskimos: Twelve Years in Baffin Island*. Philadelphia: J. B. Lippincott, 1923).

Billson, Janet Mancini. "'Challenging Times': Complexities of Feminism and the Women's Movement." Review Essay of *Challenging Times: The Women's Movement in Canada and the United States*, edited by Constance Backhouse and David Flaherty. [Montréal: McGill-Queen's University Press, 1992]. In *Canadian Review of American Studies* [special issue, "Reinterpreting the American Experience: Women, Gender, and American Studies," Part II] (1992): 317-325.

―――. "Daughters of Sedna," in *Keepers of the Culture: The Power of Tradition in Women's Lives*. New York: Lexington Books, 1995/Ottawa: Penumbra Press, 1999/Barrington, RI: Skywood Press, 2002.

―――. "Double Burdens, Double Roles: Jamaican Women in Toronto." Paper presented at the Annual Meeting of the Western Social Sciences Association, Portland, OR, April 1990.

―――. "Inuit Dreams, Inuit Realities. Shattering the Bonds of Dependency," *American Review of Canadian Studies*, special issue on aboriginal issues, (Spring/Summer 2001): 283-299.

―――. "Interlocking Identities: Gender, Ethnicity and Power in the Canadian Context." *International Journal of Canadian Studies* 3 (Spring 1991): 49-67.

―――. "Keepers of the Culture: Attitudes toward Women's Liberation and the Women's Movement in Canada." *Women and Politics* 14, 1 (1994): 1-34.

―――. *Keepers of the Culture: The Power of Tradition in Women's Lives*. New York: Lexington Books, 1995/Ottawa: Penumbra Press, 1999.

―――. "New Choices for a New Era." In *Gossip: A Spoken History of Women in the North*, edited by Mary Crnkovich. Ottawa: Canadian Arctic Resources Committee, 1990.

―――. "No Owner of Soil: The Concept of Marginality Revisited on its Sixtieth Birthday." *International Review of Modern Sociology* 18 (1988): 183-204.

―――. "Opportunity or Tragedy? The Impact of Resettlement Policy on Canadian Inuit Families." *The American Review of Canadian Studies* 20, 2 (Summer 1990): 187-218.

————. *Pathways to Manhood: Young Black Males Struggle for Identity.* Rutgers, NJ: Transaction, 1996.

————. *The Power of Focus Groups for Social and Policy Research: A Training Manual,* 4th ed. Barrington, RI: Skywood Press, 2004.

————. "The Progressive Verification Method: Toward a Feminist Methodology for Studying Women Cross-Culturally." *Women's Studies International Forum* 14, 3 (1991): 201-215.

————. "Recreating Canada for the 21st Century: The Social Impacts of Nunavut for the Inuit and for Canada," Association for Canadian Studies in the United States, *Canada Colloquium: North America in the 21st Century: Perspectives on Autonomy, Exchange, and Integration,* Toronto, November 1996.

————. "Social Change, Social Problems, and the Search for Identity: Canada's Northern Native Peoples in Transition." *The American Review of Canadian Studies* 18, 3 (Autumn 1988): 295-316.

————. "Standing Tradition on Its Head: Role Reversal among [Alberta] Blood Indian Couples." *Great Plains Quarterly* 11, 1 (Winter 1991): 3-21. Reprinted in David R. Millwer, Carl Beal, James Dempsey, and R. Wesley Heber, eds., *The First Ones: Readings in Indian/Native Studies,* Piapot Reserve #75: Saskatchewan Indian Federated College Press, 1992.

————. "Violence toward Inuit Women and Children." In *Gossip: A Spoken History of Women in the North,* edited by Mary Crnkovich. Ottawa: Canadian Arctic Resources Committee, 1990.

Billson, Janet Mancini, and Carolyn Fluehr-Lobban. *Female Well-Being: Toward a Global Theory of Social Change.* London: Zed Books, 2005.

Billson, Janet Mancini, and Richard Majors. *Cool Pose: Dilemmas of Black Manhood in America.* New York: Touchstone [Simon & Schuster], 1993.

Billson, Janet Mancini, and Martha Stapleton. "Accidental Motherhood: Reproductive Control and Access to Opportunity among Women in Canada." *Women's Studies International Forum* 17, 4 (July-August 1994): 357-372.

Bird, John, Lorraine Land, and Murray Macadam, eds. *Nation to Nation: Aboriginal Sovereignty and the Future of Canada.* Toronto: Nelson, 2001.

Birket-Smith, Kaj. *The Eskimos.* London, New York: Methuen, 1971 [1959, 1936].

Bjerregaard, Peter, and T. Kue Young. *The Circumpolar Inuit: Health of a Population in Transition.* Copenhagen: Munksgaard, 1998.

Blackduck, Alison. "Commentary: Exploitation of Inuit Children Must Stop." *Nunatsiaq News* (July 13, 2001).

————. "Pauktuutit to Continue Work on *Amauti* Protection: Rankin Workshop Impresses Federal Officials." *Nunatsiaq News* (June 1, 2001).

Blodgett, Jean (curator). *Cape Dorset: Artists and the Community.* Winnipeg: The Winnipeg Art Gallery. (Comments by Houston, Eber, Ryan, Pootoogook, and Blodgett), 1980.

Boas, Franz. "A Journey in Cumberland Sound and on the West Shore of Davis Strait in 1883 and 1884." *American Geographical Society Bulletin* 26 (1884): 242-272.

————. "Arctic Legend: The Myth of Sedna, Goddess of the Sea Animals" [Excerpted from an 1888 U.S. Bureau of Ethnology report, published by University of Nebraska Press]. *Canadian Geographic* (First Edition, 1998): 86.

————. *Franz Boas among the Inuit of Baffin Island, 1883-1884.* Edited by Ludger Muller-Wille. Toronto: University of Toronto Press, 1998.

————. *The Central Eskimo.* Lincoln: University of Nebraska Press, 1964 [originally published by the Bureau of American Ethnology, 6th Annual Report, Washington, DC, 1888].

————. "The Eskimo of Baffin Land and Hudson Bay." *Bulletin of the American Museum of Natural History* XV (1901).

Boas, Franz, and H. J. Rink. "Eskimo Tales and Songs." *Journal of American Folklore* 2 (1889): 123-131.

Bodenhorn, Barbara. "'I Am Not a Great Hunter, My Wife Is': Inupiat and Anthropological Models of Gender." *Études/Inuit/Studies* 14, 1-2 (1990): 55-74.

Boeri, David. *People of the Ice Whale: Eskimos, White Men, and the Whales.* New York: E. P. Dutton, 1983.

Bone, Robert M., and Donna Green. *Analysis of Responses to the Questionnaire on Economic and Social Behaviour of Hunters: Final Report for the Northern Economic Planning Directorate, Department of Indian and Northern Affairs.* Ottawa: Department of Indian and Northern Affairs, 1985.

Bonvillain, Nancy. "Gender Relations in Native North America." *American Indian Culture and Research Journal* 13, 2 (1989).

Born, David Omar. *Eskimo Education and the Trauma of Social Change.* Ottawa: Department of Indian and Northern Affairs, 1970.

Borre, Kirsten. *Dietary and Nutritional Significance of Seal and Other Country Foods in the Diet of the Inuit of Clyde River, NWT.* Technical Paper 11. Montréal: Royal Commission on Seals and the Sealing Industry in Canada, 1986.

————. "Seal Blood, Inuit Blood, and Diet: A Bio-cultural Model of Physiology and Cultural Identity." *Medical Anthropology Quarterly* 5, 1 (1991): 48-61.

Bouchard, Marie, Exhibition Curator. "Power of Thought: The Prints of Jessie Oonark." *From "Nanook" to Nunavut: The Art and Politics of Representing Inuit Culture* (Exhibition Program, St. Lawrence University Festival of the Arts, Canton, New York, February 21-March 7, 2001), pp. 6-7.

Bourgeois, Annette. "A New Beginning for Nunavut Inuit and the RCMP." *Nunatsiaq News* (September 3, 1998), pp. 1-2.

————. "The Face of Nunavut Women Still Lingers in the Shadows." *Nunatsiaq News* (February 18, 1999).

————. "Nunavut Justice: Corrections a Major Challenge for Nunavut." *Nunatsiaq News* (March 25, 1999).

Bowkett, Roy. "*Keenahvee?* (What's in a Name?)." *Anglican Journal* (May 1996), n. p.

Brannon, Linda. *Gender: Psychological Perspectives.* Needham Heights, MA: Allyn & Bacon, 1996.

Bray, D. "A Study of Youth Suicide in the Canadian Urban Arctic." Paper presented at The Fourth Annual Inuit Studies Conference, Hamilton, November 1984.

Briggs, Jean L. *Aspects of Inuit Value Socialisation.* Ottawa: National Museum of Man, Mercury Series, 1979.

————. "Eskimo Women: Makers of Men." In *Many Sisters: Women in Cross-Cultural Perspective*, edited by Carolyn J. Matthiasson, New York: Free Press, 1974.

————. "Expecting the Unexpected: Canadian Inuit Training for an Experimental Lifestyle." *Ethos* 19 (1991): 259-287.

————. *Inuit Morality Play: The Emotional Education of a Three Year Old.* New Haven and London: Yale University Press, 1998.

————. "Lines, Cycles and Transformations: Temporal Perspectives on Inuit Action." In *Contemporary Futures: Perspectives from Social Anthropology,* edited by Sandra Wallman. ASA Monographs No. 30. London: Routledge, 1992.

————. "Living Dangerously: The Contradictory Foundations of Value in Canadian Inuit Society." In *Politics and History in Band Societies,* edited by Eleanor Burke Leacock and Richard Lee. New York: Cambridge University Press, 1982, 109-131.

————. "Le modèle traditionnel d'èducation chez les Inuit." *Recherches amérindiennes au Québec* 13, 1 (1983): 13-25.

————. *Never in Anger: Portrait of an Eskimo Family.* Cambridge, MA: Harvard University Press, 1970.

————. "Playwork as a Tool in the Socialisation of an Inuit Child." *Arctic Medical Research* 49, 1 (1990): 34-38.

————. "Socialisation, Family, Conflicts and Responses to Cultural Change among Canadian Inuit." *Arctic Medical Research* 40 (1985): 40-52.

————. "From Trait to Emblem and Back: Living and Representing Culture in Everyday Inuit Life." *Arctic Anthropology* 34, 1 (1997): 227-235.

————. "Vicissitudes of Attachment: Nurturance and Dependence in Canadian Inuit Family Relationships, Old and New." *Arctic Medical Research* 54 (Supplement 1, 1995): 24-32.

————. "'Why Don't You Kill Your Baby Brother?' The Dynamics of Peace in Canadian Inuit Camps." In *The Anthropology of Peace and Nonviolence,* edited by L. Sponsel and T. Gregor. Boulder: Lynne Rienner, 1994.

Brody, Hugh. "Land Occupancy—Inuit Perceptions." In *Inuit Land Use and Occupancy Project I,* edited by Milton M. R. Freeman. Ottawa: Department of Indian and Northern Affairs, 1977.

————. *Living Arctic: Hunters of the Canadian North.* Vancouver: Douglas and MacIntyre; Boston, London: Faber & Faber, 1987.

————. *The Other Side of Eden: Hunters, Farmers, and the Shaping of the World.* New York: North Point Press, 2000.

————. *The People's Land: Inuit, Whites and the Eastern Arctic.* Vancouver: Douglas & McIntyre, 1991. [Originally published as *The People's Land: Eskimos and Whites in the Eastern Arctic.* Markham, ONT: Penguin Books, 1975.]

————. *Some Historical Aspects of the High Arctic Exiles' Experience.* Ottawa: Royal Commission on Aboriginal Peoples, 1993.

Brown, Barry. "Future Bleak as Winter for Arctic Town (Broughton Island, NWT)." *Baltimore Sun* (January 6, 1988), p. 2.

Bruemmer, Fred, et al. *Arctic Memories: Living With the Inuit.* Toronto: Key Porter, 1994.

————. *The Arctic World.* Toronto: Key Porter, 1985.

Buijs, Cunera, ed. *Continuity and Discontinuity in Arctic Cultures* (Essays in Honour of Gerti Nooter, Curator at the National Museum of Ethnology, 1970-1990). Leiden: Universiteit Leiden, Centre of Non-Western Studies, 1993.

Bunch, Charlotte. "Transforming Human Rights from a Feminist Perspective." In *Women's Rights, Human Rights,* edited by Julie Peter and Andrea Wolper. New York: Routledge, 1995.

Burch, Ernest S., Jr. *Eskimo Kinsmen: Changing Family Relations in Northwest Alaska.* New York: West, 1975.

———. "Marriage and Divorce among the North Alaskan Eskimos." In *Divorce and After,* edited by Paul Bohannon. Garden City, NY: Doubleday, 1970.

Burch, Ernest S., and T. C. Correl. "Alliance and Conflict: Inter-regional Relations in North Alaska." In *Alliance in Eskimo Society,* edited by D. L. Guemple. Seattle: University of Washington Press, 1972.

Burns, John F. "Eskimo Males Said to be Battling 'Lib' by Beating Wives." *The New York Times* (November 20, 1974), n. p.

———. "From the Frigid North is Carved a Native Terrain." *The New York Times* (December 22, 1991), p. 4.

Burt, Sandra. "Gender and Public Policy: Making Some Difference in Ottawa." In *Rethinking Canada: The Promise of Women's History, 3rd ed.,* edited by Veronica Strong-Boag and Anita Clair Fellman. Toronto: Oxford University Press, 1997.

Cairns, Alan, and Cynthia Williams. *Constitutionalism, Citizenship and Society in Canada.* Toronto: University of Toronto Press, 1985.

———. "Women's Issues and the Women's Movement in Canada since 1970." In *The Politics of Gender, Ethnicity and Language in Canada,* edited by Sandra Burt. Toronto: University of Toronto Press, 1986.

Cameron, Kirk, and Graham White. *Northern Governments in Transition: Political and Constitutional Development in the Yukon, Nunavut, and the Western Northwest Territories.* Montréal: Institute for Research on Public Policy, 1995.

Canada, Department of Northern Affairs and Natural Resources. *Northern Education: Ten Years of Progress.* Ottawa: Department of Northern Affairs and Natural Resources, 1961.

Canada, Department of Indian and Northern Affairs. *Arctic Women's Workshop.* Ottawa: Department of Indian and Northern Affairs, 1974.

Canada, Department of Indian Affairs and Northern Development. *Creating the New Territory of Nunavut.* Ottawa: Department of Indian Affairs and Northern Development, March 1996.

———. *Creating the New Territory of Nunavut.* Ottawa: Department of Indian Affairs and Northern Development, 1996.

———. "DIAND Welcomes Nunavut Managerial Trainees." *Transition* (September 7, 1998): 1.

———. *Highlights of Aboriginal Condition, 1991, 1986: Demographic, Economic and Social Characteristics.* Ottawa: Department of Indian Affairs and Northern Development, 1985.

———. *The Inuit.* Ottawa: Department of Indian Affairs and Northern Development, 1986.

———. *The Inuit.* Ottawa: Department of Indian and Northern Affairs, 1980.

———. *Native Peoples and the North: A Profile.* Ottawa: Department of Indian and Northern Affairs, 1982.

———. *The North.* Ottawa: Department of Indian Affairs and Northern Development, 1985.

Canada, Department of Indian Affairs and Northern Development and Tunngavik Federation of Nunavut. *Agreement between the Inuit of the Nunavut Settlement Area and Her Majesty the Queen in Right of Canada,* 1993.

Canada, Department of the Secretary of State. *Speaking Together: Canada's Native Women*. Ottawa: Secretary of State, 1975.

Canada, Environment Canada. *Environment Canada and the North: The Perceptions, Roles and Policies of the Department of the Environment Regarding Development North of 60*. Discussion Paper. Ottawa: Environment Canada, July 1983.

Canada, Royal Commission on Aboriginal Peoples. *The High Arctic Relocation: A Report on the 1953-55 Relocation* (3 volumes). Ottawa: Supply and Services Canada, 1994.

Canadian Embassy. "Nunavut Joins Canadian Federation on April 1." *Canada Quarterly* 7, 2 (April 1999): 1-2.

Canadian Encyclopedia Plus. Toronto: McClelland and Stewart (CD-ROM), 1995.

Canadian Geographic. "Nunavut: Canada's Youngest Population Prepares to Govern a Vast Arctic Region. Special Report on the New Territory." *Canadian Geographic* (January/February 1999).

Canadian Government. *Inuit Women: From the Final Report on the Canadian Panel on Violence against Women*. Ottawa: Government Printing Office, 1993.

Canadian Press. "Arctic Council Takes First Steps toward Action." Iqaluit, NWT[1]: Canadian Press, September 21, 1998.

Canitz, Brenda. "Health Care in Crisis: Understanding Nursing Turnover in Northern Canada." In *Circumpolar Health 90: Proceedings of the Eighth International Congress on Circumpolar Health*. Winnipeg: University of Manitoba Press, 1990, pp. 151-152.

Capozza, K. L. "Canadian Territory of Nunavut Pushes to Expand College Offerings." *The Chronicle of Higher Education* (July 27, 2001), pp. A38-A40.

Cavanagh, Beverly Anne. *Music of the Netsilik Eskimo: A Study of Stability and Change*. Ph.D. dissertation, University of Toronto, 1979. Mercury Series. National Museum of Man. Canadian Ethnology Service 82. Abstract in *Études/Inuit/Studies* 6, 2 (1979): 161-162.

Chabot, Marcelle, and Gerard Duhaime. "With the Help of the Crown: Trends in Personal Income in Nunavik 1950-2000." Paper presented at the Third International Congress of Arctic Social Sciences, Copenhagen, Denmark, 1998.

Chamberlin, J. E. *The Harrowing of Eden: White Attitudes toward North American Natives*. Toronto: Fitzhenry and Whiteside, 1975.

Chartrand, Jean-Philippe. "Survival and Identity of the Inuit Ethnic Identity: The Importance of Inuktitut." In *Native People, Native Lands: Canadian Indians, Inuit and Métis*, edited by B. Alden Cox. Ottawa: Carleton University Press, 1987, pp. 241-255.

Chaussonnet, Valérie. "Needles and Animals: Women's Magic." In *Crossroads of Continents: Cultures of Siberia and Alaska*, edited by William Fitzhugh and A. Crowell. Washington DC: Smithsonian Institution Press, 1988, pp. 209-226.

---

[1] For clarity of citation and future historical reference, all materials published in Iqaluit prior to 1999 are referenced as "Iqaluit, NWT," since Nunavut (abbreviated as NT) did not legally come into existence until April 1, 1999. References from 1999 are shown as indicated by the publisher, either as NWT or NT, depending on the month of 1999.

Cherkasov, Anatoly I. "Nunavut: The Canadian Experiment in Territorial Self-Determination for the Inuit." *Polar Geography and Geology* 17, 1 (1993): 64-71.

Chiste, Katherine Beatty, ed. *Aboriginal Small Business and Entrepreneurship in Canada.* Toronto: Captus Press, 1996.

Choinière, R., and N. Robitaille. *An Overview of Demographic and Socio-economic Conditions of the Inuit in Canada.* Ottawa: Research Branch, Corporate Policy, Indian and Northern Affairs Canada, 1985.

Christensen, Neil Blair. "Inuit in Cyberspace: Arctic Users Networking between Past and Present." Paper presented to the Eleventh Inuit Studies Conference, Nuuk, September 1998.

Clairmont, Don. *Notes on the Drinking Behaviours of the Eskimos and Indians in the Aklavik Area, Report 62-4.* Ottawa: The Northern Co-ordination and Research Centre, Department of Northern Affairs and National Resources, 1962.

———. "Review of Justice System Issues Relevant to Nunavut." In *The Nunavut Justice Research Program: Project Summaries*, prepared by Albert Currie, Tina Hattem, and John Clement. Ottawa: Department of Justice Canada, Research and Statistics Division, Policy Sector, October 1999.

Clark, Bruce. *Native Liberty, Crown Sovereignty: The Existing Aboriginal Right of Self-Government in Canada.* Montréal: McGill-Queen's University Press, 1990.

Clark, Joe. "Completing the Circle of Confederation—Aboriginal Rights." *Canada Today/d'aujourd'hui* 22, 2 (1991): 14-15. Washington, DC: Canadian Embassy. (Excerpts from a speech by the Minister Responsible for Constitutional Affairs, Queen's University, Kingston, Ontario, September 9).

Coates, Kenneth. "Best Left as Indians: The Federal Government and the Indians of the Yukon, 1894-1950." In *Out of the Background*, edited by Robin Fisher and Kenneth Coates. Toronto: Copp-Clark Pittman, 1988, pp. 236-255.

———. *Canada's Colonies: A History of the Yukon and Northwest Territories.* Toronto: James Lorimer, 1985.

Coates, Kenneth, and Judith Powell. *The Modern North: People, Politics, and the Rejection of Colonialism.* Toronto: James Lorimer, 1989.

Gary O. Coldevin. "Satellite Television and Cultural Replacement among Canadian Eskimos: Adults and Adolescents Compared." *Communication Research* VI, 5, 2 (1979): 115-133.

Comeau, Pauline, and Aldo Santin. *The First Canadians: A Profile of Canada's Native People Today.* Toronto: James Lorimer, 1990.

Connell, Valerie G. "Nunavut Women's Council to Meet in Iqaluit Next Week." *Nunatsiaq News* (June 30, 1999).

———. "Pauktuutit to Make Video on FAS [Fetal Alcohol Syndrome]." *Nunatsiaq News* (July 21, 2000).

———. "Women's March Organizer Takes Message to Nunavut." *Nunatsiaq News* (July 28, 2000).

Condon, Richard G. "Adolescence and Changing Family Relations in the Central Canadian Arctic." *Arctic Medical Research* 49 (1990): 81-92.

———. "Changing Patterns of Conflict Management and Aggression among Inuit Youth in the Canadian Arctic," *Native Studies Review* 8, 2 (1992).

———. *Inuit Behavior and Seasonal Change in the Canadian Arctic.* (Revision of 1981 Ph.D. dissertation). Studies in Cultural Anthropology, 2. Ann Arbor: UMI Research Press, 1981.

————. *Inuit Youth: Growth and Change in the Canadian Arctic.* New Brunswick, NJ: Rutgers University Press, 1987.

————. "Modern Inuit Culture and Society." In *Arctic Life: Challenge to Survive*, edited by Martina Magenau Jacobs and James B. Richardson III. Pittsburgh: Carnegie Institute, 1983.

————. *The Northern Copper Inuit: A History* (with Julia Ogina and the Holman Elders). Norman: The University of Oklahoma Press, 1996.

————. "The Rise of Adolescence: Social Change and Life Stage Dilemmas in the Central Canadian Arctic." *Human Organisation* 49, 3 (1990): 266-279.

————. "The Rise of the Leisure Class: Adolescence and Recreational Acculturation in the Canadian Arctic." *Ethos* 23, 1 (1995): 47-68.

Condon, Richard G., Peter Collings, and George W. Wenzel. "The Best Part of Life: Subsistence, Hunting, Ethnicity, and Economic Adaptation among Young Adult Inuit Males." *Arctic* 48, 1 (1995): 31-46.

Cooke, Alan. "The Eskimos and the Hudson's Bay Company." In "Le peuple esquimau aujourd'hui et demain." *Quatriéme Congrès international de l Fondation francaise d'études nordique, Bibliothèque arctique et antarctique*, edited by J. Malaurie. Paris: Mouton, 1973, pp. 209-223.

Cowan, Edward. "Canadian Eskimos are Adopting the White Man's Ways." *The New York Times* (August 8, 1978), n.p.

Cowan, Susan, ed. *We Don't Live in Snow Houses Now: Reflections of Arctic Bay.* Canadian Arctic Producers Limited, 1977.

Cox, Bruce Alden. *Native People, Native Lands: Canadian Indians, Inuit and Métis.* Ottawa: Carleton University Press, 1988.

Cox, Marlene Joan. *A Cross-Cultural Study of Sex Differences Found in Drawings by Canadian Inuit and American Children.* EdD Dissertation, Illinois State University, 1979.

Crago, Martha Borgmann, Betsy Annahatak, and Lizzie Ningiuruvik. "Changing Patterns of Language Socialisation in Inuit Homes." *Anthropology and Education Quarterly* 24, 3 (1993): 205-223.

Crary, David. "Tradition at Stake in Hunt." *Akron Beacon Record.* Thursday (July 16, 1998), p. A16.

————. "Canadian Inuit Set Sail on Controversial Whale Hunt." Nando.net (July 13, 1998).

Creery, Ian. *The Inuit (Eskimo) of Canada.* London: Minority Rights Group, 1993.

Crnkovich, Mary. "Women of the Kitaq [Pangnirtung]." In *Gossip: A Spoken History of Women in the North*, edited by Mary Crnkovich. Ottawa: Canadian Arctic Resources Committee, 1990, pp. 35-36.

Crowe, Keith J. "Claims on the land 1." *Arctic Circle* (November/December 1990): 14-23.

————. "Claims on the Land 2." *Arctic Circle* (January/February 1991): 31-35.

————. *A History of the Original Peoples of Northern Canada.* (Arctic Institute of North America). Montréal: McGill-Queen's University Press, 1991 [1974].

Cruikshank, Julia Margaret. "Matrifocal Families in the Canadian North." In *The Canadian Family*, edited by K. Ishwaran. Toronto: Holt, Rinehart and Winston of Canada, 1976.

————. *The Role of Northern Canadian Women in Social Change.* MA Thesis, University of British Columbia, 1969.

Dacks, Gurston, ed. *Devolution and Constitutional Development in the Canadian North.* Ottawa: Carleton University Press, 1990.

Dacks, Gurston. "Nunavut: Aboriginal Self-Determination through Public Government." Report prepared for the Royal Commission on Aboriginal Peoples, 1993.

Dacks, Gurston, and Kenneth Coates, eds. *Northern Communities: The Prospects for Empowerment.* Edmonton: Canadian Circumpolar Institute, 1989.

Dagenais, Huguette, and Denise Piché, eds. *Women, Feminism, and Development/Femmes, Féminisme et Dévèloppement.* Montréal: McGill-Queens University Press, 1999.

Dahl, Jens. "Gender Parity in Nunavut?" *Indigenous Affairs* (July/December 1997): 42-47.

————. *Saqqaq: An Inuit Hunting Community in the Modern World.* Toronto: University of Toronto Press, 2000.

Dalton, George. *Economic Anthropology and Development: Essays on Tribal and Peasant Economies.* New York: Basic Books, 1971.

Damas, David. "The Diversity of Eskimo Societies." In *Man the Hunter,* edited by R. E. Lee and I. Devore. Chicago: Aldine, 1968, pp. 111-117.

————. *Igluligmiut Kinship and Social Groupings: A Structural Approach.* Ottawa: National Museum of Canada, Bulletin No. 196, 1963.

————. "Domestic Group Structure among Eastern Canadian Eskimo." *Man* 1, 4 (1966): 558-559.

————. "The Problem of the Eskimo Family." In *Canadian Family: A Book of Readings,* edited by K. Ishwaran. Toronto: Holt, Rinehart and Winston Canada, 1971.

————. *Shifting Relations in the Administration of the Inuit: The Hudson Bay Company and the Canadian Government. Études/Inuit/Studies* 17, 2 (1993): 5-28.

D'Anglure, Bernard Saladin. "Man (*angut*), Son (*irniq*) and Light (*qau*): Or the Circle of Masculine Power in the Inuit of the Central Arctic." *Anthropologica* 20, 1-2 (1978): 101-144.

————. "Mythe de la famme et pouvoir de l'homme chez les Inuit de l'Arctic central (Canada)." *Anthropologie et Sociétés* 1, 3 (1977): 79-98.

————. "Rethinking the Shamanistic 'Feminine,' or the 'Third Gender' of Inuit Shamans." *Sixth Inuit Studies Conference, Copenhagen October 17-20, 1988: Abstracts.* Copenhagen: Institute of Eskimology, University of Copenhagen, 1988.

D'Anglure, Bernard Saladin, and Francoise Morin. "The Inuit People between Particularism and Internationalism: An Overview of Their Rights and Powers in 1992." *Études/Inuit/Studies* 16, 1-2 (1992): 13-19.

Davis, Robert, and Mark Zannis. *The Genocide Machine in Canada.* Montréal: Black Rose Books, 1973.

Daviss-Putt, Betty Anne. "Rights of Passage in the North: From Evacuation to the Birth of a Culture." In Mary Crnkovich, ed., *Gossip: A Spoken History of Women in the North.* Ottawa: Canadian Arctic Resources Committee, 1990.

de la Barre, Ken. *The Academic Requirements Needed for Inuit Students to be Successful in Post-Secondary Education and Advanced Technical Training.* Nunavik Educational Task Force, 1990.

————. *Immediate Priorities and Interim Measures: School Drop-Outs and Other Youth "At Risk."* Nunavik Educational Task Force, 1991.

DeMallie, Raymond J. "Male and Female in Traditional Lakota Culture." In *The Hidden Half: Studies of Plains Indian Women*, edited by Patricia Albers and Beatrice Medicine. Lanham, MD: University Press of America, 1983.

DeMarrais, Kathleen Bennett, ed. *Inside Stories: Qualitative Research Reflections*. Mahwah, NJ: Lawrence Erlbaum, 1998.

Derman, William, and Scott Whiteford. *Social Impact Analysis and Development Planning in the Third World*, (Social Impact Assessment Series, No. 12). Boulder: Westview Press, 1985.

Dewey, Kathryn. "Nutrition, Social Impact, and Development." In *Social Impact Analysis and Development in the Third World*, edited by William Derman and Scott Whiteford. Boulder: Westview Press, 1985.

Dickason, Olive Patricia. *Canada's First Nations: A History of Founding Peoples from Earliest Times*. Toronto: McClelland and Stewart, 1992.

Dickerson, Mark O. *Whose North? Political Change, Political Development, and Self-Government in the Northwest Territories*. Vancouver: University of British Columbia Press and the Arctic Institute of North America (University of Calgary), 1992.

DiSarno, Neil J., and Craig Barringer. "Otitis Media and Academic Achievement in Eskimo High School Students." *Folia Phoniatrica*, 39, 5 (1987).

Dorais, Louis-Jacques. "La situation linguistique dans l'Arctique." *Etudes/Inuit/Studies* 16, 1-2 (1992): 246-248.

———. "Language, Identity and Integration in the Canadian Arctic." *North Atlantic Studies* 3, 1 (1991): 18-24.

———. "The Canadian Inuit and Their Language." In *Arctic Languages: An Awakening*, edited by Dirmid R. F. Collis. Paris: UNESCO, 1990.

———. "Inuit Identity in Canada." *Folk* 30 (1988): 23-31.

———. "Language Revitalisation vs. Language Loss in the Canadian Arctic." *Sixth Inuit Studies Conference, Copenhagen October 17-20, 1988: Abstracts*. Copenhagen: Institute of Eskimology, University of Copenhagen, 1988.

———. *Quaqtaq: Modernity and Identity in an Inuit Community*. Toronto: University of Toronto Press, 1997.

Du Bois, Barbara. "Passionate Scholarship: Notes on Values, Knowing and Method in Feminist Social Science." In *Theories of Women's Studies*, edited by Gloria Bowles and Renate Duelli Klein. London: Routledge and Kegan Paul, 1983.

Duibaldo, R. *The Government of Canada and the Inuit 1900-1967*. Ottawa: Research Branch, Corporate Policy, Department of Indian and Northern Affairs, Canada, 1985.

Duffy, Andrew. "The Long, Hard Road to Nunavut." *The Ottawa Citizen* (March 28, 1999), p. A4.

Duffy, R. Quinn. *The Road to Nunavut: The Progress of the Eastern Arctic Inuit since the Second World War*. Montréal: McGill-Queen's University Press, 1988.

Dunning, R. W. "An Aspect of Recent Eskimo Polygyny and Wife-Lending in the Eastern Arctic." *Human Organization* 21 (1962): 17-20.

———. "An Aspect of Domestic Group Structure among Eastern Canadian Eskimo." *Man* 1, 2 (1966): 216-225.

Durst, Douglas. "The Road to Poverty is Paved with Good Intentions: Social Interventions and Indigenous Peoples." *International Social Work* 35, 2 (1992).

Duval, L., S. MacDonalds, L. Lugtig, et al. "Otitis Media as Stigma or Process: Conflicting Understandings from Inuit Culture and Biomedicine." In *Circumpolar Health 93: Proceedings of the Ninth International Congress on Circumpolar Health*" edited by G. Pétrusdottir, S. B. Sigurdsson, M. M. Karlsson, and J. Axelsson. *Arctic Medical Research* 53, 2 (1994): 676-679.

Dyck, Noel. *Indigenous Peoples and the Nation-state: World Politics in Canada, Australia and Norway.* CITTY: ISER Books, 1992.

Eber, Dorothy. *When the Whalers Were up North: Inuit Memories from the Eastern Arctic.* Montréal: McGill-Queen's University Press, 1990.

———. *Pitseolak: Pictures Out of My Life.* Montréal: Design Collaborative Books, 1972.

Eber, Dorothy, and Peter Pitseolak. *People from Our Side.* Seattle: University of Washington Press, 1975.

Eder, Elena Garces de. *The Construction of Radical Feminist Knowledge: Women in Colombia as an Example* (Ph.D. Thesis, The George Washington University, 2002)/Lexington Books (forthcoming 2006), p. 150.

Eichler, Margrit. *Family Shifts: Families, Policies, and Gender Equality.* Toronto: Oxford University Press, 1997.

———. "Sexism in Research and Its Policy Implications." In *Taking Sex into Account: The Policy Consequences of Sexist Research,* edited by Jill McCalla Vickers. Toronto: Oxford University Press, 1984.

———. "Sociology of Feminist Research in Canada." *Signs* 3, 2 (1977): 409-422.

Ekoomiak, Norman. *Arctic Memories.* Toronto: NC Press, 1988.

Elias, Peter Douglas. *Development of Aboriginal People's Communities.* North York, ONT: Centre for Aboriginal Management Education and Training and Captus Press, 1991.

Elliott, D. W., ed. *Law and Aboriginal Peoples of Canada,* 2nd ed. Toronto: Captus Press, 1994.

Engels, Friedrich. *The Origin of the Family, Private Property and the State* (Eleanor Burke Leacock, ed.). New York: International Publishers, 1985.

Engelstad, Diane, and John Bird. *Aboriginal Sovereignty and the Future of Canada.* Concord, ONT: House of Anansi Press, 1992.

Ernerk, Peter. "Inuit Culture: The Kivalliq Region." In *The Nunavut Handbook.* Iqaluit, NWT: Nortext, 1998.

Ernerk, Peter, et al. "Nunavut: Vision or Illusion?" *Canadian Parliamentary Review* (Spring 1990): 6-10.

Evic-Twerdin, Leena. *Traditional Inuit Beliefs in Stories and Legends.* Iqaluit, NWT: Baffin Divisional Board of Education, 1991.

Farnsworth, Clyde H. "The Day the Eskimos Were Cast into Darkness." *The New York Times* (April 10, 1992), p. A4.

Fenge, Terry. "Political Development and Environmental Management in Northern Canada: The Case of the Nunavut Agreement." *Études/Inuit/Studies* 16 (1992): 115-41.

Ferrari, H. E. "The Outpost Nurse: Role and Activities in Northern Canada." In *Circumpolar Health: Proceedings of the Third International Symposium,* edited by R. J. Shephard and S. Itoh. Toronto: University of Toronto Press, 1976, pp. 600-605.

Finkler, Harold W. *The Baffin Correctional Centre: A Review of Current Programs and Alternatives.* Ottawa: Department of Indian and Northern Affairs, 1981.
———. "Inuit and the Criminal Justice System: Future Strategies for Social-Legal Control and Prevention." *Études/Inuit/Studies* 9, 2 (1985): 141-152.
———. *North of 60: Inuit and the Administration of Criminal Justice in the Northwest Territories—The Case of Frobisher Bay.* Ottawa: NRD 76-3, 1976.
———. "Violence and the Administration of Criminal Justice in Northern Canada." In *Insights and Strategies for Confronting Violence,* edited by K. Johnston. Anchorage: School of Justice, University of Alaska, 1983.
Finkler, Harold W., and A. Parizeau. *Deviance and Social Control: Manifestations, Tensions and Conflict in Frobisher Bay.* Montréal: Université de Montréal, Centre International de Criminologie Comparée, 1973.
Fitzhugh, William W. *Cultures in Contact: The European Impact on Native Cultural Institutions in Eastern North America A.D. 1000-1800.* Washington: Anthropological Society of Washington Series, 1985.
Fitzhugh, William W., and Jacqueline S. Olin, eds. *Archeology of the Frobisher Voyages.* Washington, DC: Smithsonian Institution Press, 1993.
Flaherty, Martha. "Freedom of Expression or Freedom of Exploitation?" *The Northern Review* 14 (Summer 1995): 178-185.
———. "Inuit Women and Violence." In *Women and the Canadian State,* edited by Caroline Andrew and Sandra Rodgers. Montréal: McGill-Queen's University Press, 1997.
Fleischner, Jennifer. *The Inuits: People of the Arctic.* Brookfield, CT: Millbrook Press, 1995.
Fluehr-Lobban, Carolyn, ed. *Ethics and the Profession of Anthropology: Dialogue for a New Era.* Philadelphia: University of Pennsylvania Press, 1990.
Fogel-Chance, Nancy. "Living in Both Worlds: 'Modernity' and 'Tradition' among North Slope Inupiaq Women in Anchorage." *Arctic Anthropology* 30, 1 (1993): 94-108.
Fossett, Renee. *In Order to Live Untroubled: Inuit of the Central Arctic, 1550-1940.* Winnipeg: University of Manitoba Press, 2001.
Fortier, Marcel, and Francine Gauthier Jones. "Engineering Public Service Excellence for Nunavut: The Nunavut Unified Human Resources Development Strategy." *Arctic* (June 1998): 191-194.
Francis, Daniel. *Arctic Chase: A History of Whaling in Canada's North.* St John's, NFLD: Breakwater Books, 1984.
———. *Discovery of the North: The Exploration of Canada's Arctic.* Edmonton: Hurtig, 1986.
Franks, C. E. S. "Indian Self-Government: Canada and the United States Compared." Paper presented to the Annual Meeting, Western Social Science Association, Albuquerque, 1989.
———. "Nunavut and the Spirit of Sedna," paper presented at the Annual Meeting, Association for Canadian Studies in the United States, Minneapolis, November 1997.
Fraser, Whit. "Nunavut! What a Remarkable Chapter It Will Become in Canada's History." *Above & Beyond* (Spring 1999), pp. 38-45.
Freeman, Minnie Aodla. *Life among the Qallunaat.* Edmonton: Hurtig Publishers, 1978.

————. "Introduction." In *Inuit Women Artists: Voices from Cape Dorset*, edited by Odette Leroux, Marion E. Jackson, and Minnie Aodla Freeman. Vancouver: Douglas & McIntyre (Canadian Museum of Civilization and University of Washington Press), 1994.

Freeman, Milton M. R., ed. *Report of the Inuit Land Use and Occupancy Project. I-III.* Ottawa: Department of Indian and Northern Affairs, 1976-77.

————. "The Significance of Demographic Changes Occurring in the Canadian East Arctic." Anthropologica 13 (1971): 215-236.

————. "A Social and Ecological Analysis of Systematic Female Infanticide among the Netsilik Eskimo." *American Anthropologist* 73, 5 (1971): 1011-1018.

————. and L. N. Carbyn. *Traditional Knowledge and Renewable Resource Management in Northern Regions.* Edmonton: Canadian Circumpolar Institute, 1988.

————. , Lycrimila Bogosloskaya, Richard A. Caulfield, Ingmar Egede, Igor I. Krupnik, and Marc G. Stevenson. *Inuit, Whaling, and Sustainability* (Sponsored by the Inuit Circumpolar Conference.) Walnut Creek, CA: AltaMira Press, 1998.

Freschuk, Scott. "Western Arctic's Goals More Difficult to Establish." *Toronto Globe and Mail* (July 29, 1995), p. A-6.

Freuchen, Peter. *Book of the Eskimos.* New York: Fawcett, 1961.

Frideres, James S. *Native Peoples in Canada: Contemporary Conflicts*, 3rd ed. Toronto: Prentice-Hall, 1988.

Frideres, James S., and Rene R. Gadacz. *Aboriginal Peoples in Canada: Contemporary Conflicts*, 6th ed. Toronto: Prentice Hall, 2001.

Friedl, Ernestine. *Women and Men: An Anthropologist's View.* New York: Holt, Rinehart, and Winston, 1975.

Gar, Carol. "The Constitution: Why Ottawa Plan Has Natives Angry." *The Toronto Star* (September 28, 1991), p. D5.

Garber, Clark N. "Sex and the Eskimo." *Sexology* (March 1962).

————. "Eskimo Infanticide." *The Scientific Monthly* 64, 2 (February 1947): 98-102.

George, Jane. "Arctic University Grows by Degrees: UArctic to Launch on June 12." *Nunatsiaq News* (June 1, 2001).

————. "A Secure Place for Inuit Women in Distress." *Nunatsiaq News* (January 21, 2000).

————. "Babies Having Babies: An Explosion of Infants Born to Teenage Mothers." *Nunatsiaq News* (May 19, 2000).

————. "Go to College, Premier Okalik Urges Graduates." *Nunatsiaq News* (June 18, 1999).

————. "Homeless Inuk Woman in Ottawa Dying Alone of AIDS." *Nunatsiaq News* (October 8, 1999).

————. "Inuit Identity: How Do You Know You're an Inuk? Researcher Probes How Urban Inuit Define Themselves." *Nunatsiaq News* (June 15, 2001).

————. "Makivik Signs Exiles Deal." *Nunatsiaq News* (April 5, 1996), pp. 13, 19.

————. "Nunavut College Students Will Face More Hard Times." *Nunatsiaq News* (August 27, 1999).

————. "Nunavut's Teen Mothers Face Difficult Adjustments." *Nunatsiaq News* (May 19, 2000).

————. "Nunavut's Vicious Health Care Cycle: Less Money, More Sick People." *Nunatsiaq News* (September 24, 1999).

―――. "Pauktuutit to Create National Inuit AIDS Network." *Nunatsiaq News* (October 22, 1999).

―――. "Study: Smoking Sickens Baffin Babies," *Nunatsiaq News* (June 29, 2001).

―――. "Tuberculosis Stages Come-Back around the Circumpolar World." *Nunatsiaq News* (June 9, 2000).

―――. "University of the Arctic Takes First Baby Steps in Nunavut." *Nunatsiaq News* (February 11, 1999).

―――. "When They Killed the Sled Dogs in Nunavik." *Nunatsiaq News* (March 25, 1999).

Geddes, John. "Northern Dawn: The Inuit Prepare to Embrace Self-Government with Hope, Fear and Fierce Determination." *Maclean's* (February 15, 1999), pp. 26-30.

―――. "Northern Son." *Maclean's* (April 23, 2001), pp. 16-20.

Gessell, Paul. "The Art of the Matter: Inuit Art Marks 50-Year Milestone along the Rocky Road to Recognition." *The Citizen's Weekly* (March 28, 1999), pp. C3-4.

Giffen, Naomi Musmaker. *The Roles of Men and Women in Eskimo Culture.* Chicago: University of Chicago Press, 1930.

Gillies, Bruce. "The Nunavut Final Agreement and Marine Management in the North." *Northern Perspectives* 23, 1 (Spring 1995), pp. 17-19.

Goehring, Brian. *Indigenous Peoples of the World: An Introduction to Their Past, Present, and Future.* Saskatoon: Purich Publishing, 1995.

Goldhar, Harry. "Ottawa Wants Education to Aid Eskimo Integration." *The Toronto Daily Star* (June 22, 1970).

Goo-Doyle, Ovilu. "The National Inuit Women's Association of Canada." *Sixth Inuit Studies Conference, Copenhagen October 17-20, 1988: Abstracts.* Copenhagen: Institute of Eskimology, University of Copenhagen, 1988.

Goudie, Elizabeth. *Woman of Labrador.* Toronto: Peter Martin Associates, 1973.

Graburn, Nelson H. H. "Commercial Inuit Art: Symbol of and Vehicle for the Economic Development of the Eskimos of Canada." In "Actes du XLIIe Congrès International des Américanistes, congrès du centenaire, paris, 2-9 septembre," 5, 1976, pp. 177-189. (Also *Inter-Nord*, 15:131-142).

―――. *Eskimos of Northern Canada, Vols. I and II.* New Haven: Human Relations Area Files, 1972.

―――. *Eskimos without Igloos: Social and Economic Development in Sugluk.* Boston: Little Brown, 1969.

―――. *General Introduction to Lake Harbour, Baffin Island.* Ottawa: Northern Co-ordination and Research Centre, 1963.

―――. "Inuit Art and the Expression of Eskimo Identity." *American Review of Canadian Studies* 17, 1 (1987): 47-66.

―――. *Lake Harbour, Baffin Island: An Introduction to the Social and Economic Problems of a Small Eskimo Community.* Ottawa: Northern Co-ordination and Research Centre, 1963.

―――. "Severe Child Abuse among the Canadian Inuit." In *Anthropological Perspectives on the Treatment and Maltreatment of Children*, edited by Nancy Scheper-Hughes. Dordrecht, Holland: D. Reidel, 1987.

―――. "Television and the Canadian Inuit." *Études/Inuit/Studies* 6, 1 (1982): 7-17.

————. "Traditional Economic Institutions and the Acculturation of Canadian Eskimos." In *Studies in Economic Anthropology*, 7, edited by G. Dalton. Washington DC: American Anthropological Association, 1971, pp. 107-121.

Graburn, Nelson H. H., and B. Stephen Strong. *Circumpolar Peoples: An Anthropological Perspective*. Pacific Palisades, CA: Goodyear, 1973.

Graham, Bill, MP, Chair. *Canada and the Circumpolar World: Meeting the Challenges of Cooperation into the Twenty-First Century*. Report of the House of Commons Standing Committee on Foreign Affairs and International Trade. Ottawa: House of Commons, Canada, April 1997.

Grant, Shelagh D. *Sovereignty or Security: Government Policy in the Canadian North, 1936-1950*. Vancouver: University of British Columbia Press, 1989.

Green, B. L., and D. Simailak. "The Inukshuk Project: Use of TV and Satellite by Inuit Communities in the Northwest Territories." Paper presented at the American Association for the Advancement of Science Annual Meeting, Toronto, January 1981.

Griffiths, Curt Taylor, Evelyn Zellerer, Darryl S. Wood, and Gregory Saville. *Crime, Law, and Justice among Inuit in the Baffin Region, NWT, Canada*. Burnaby, BC: Criminology Research Centre, Simon Fraser University, 1995.

Grygier, Pat Sandiford. *A Long Way from Home: The Tuberculosis Epidemic among the Inuit*. Montréal: McGill-Queen's University Press, 1994.

Grzybowski, S., K. Styblo, and E. Dorken. "Tuberculosis in Eskimos." *Tubercle* 57, 4 (1976).

Guemple, D. Lee. *Inuit Adoption*. Canadian Ethnology Service Mercury Paper 47. Ottawa: National Museums of Canada, 1979.

————. "Inuit Socialization: A Study of Children as Social Actors in an Eskimo Community." In *Childhood and Adolescence in Canada*, edited by K. Ishwaran. Toronto: McGraw-Hill Ryerson, 1979, pp. 39-53.

————. *Inuit Spouse-Exchange*. Chicago: Department of Anthropology, University of Chicago, 1961.

————. "The Institutional Flexibility of Inuit Social Life." In *Inuit Land Use and Occupancy Project*, 2. Ottawa: Department of Indian Affairs and Northern Development, 1976, pp. 181-186.

————. "Men and Women, Husbands and Wives: The Role of Gender in Traditional Inuit Society." *Études/Inuit/Studies* 10, 1-2 (1986): 9-24.

————. "Teaching Social Relations to Inuit Children." In *Hunters and Gatherers, 2: Property, Power and Ideology*, edited by T. Ingold, D. Riches, and J. Woodburn. Oxford: Berg, 1988, pp. 131-139.

Gunther, M. *The 1953 Relocations of the Inukjuak Inuit to the High Arctic—A Documentary Analysis and Evaluation*. Ottawa: Department of Indian Affairs and Northern Development, 1992.

Hahn, Elizabeth. *The Inuit*. Vero Beach, FL: Rourke, 1990.

Hall, Charles Francis. *Life with the Eskimaux: A Narrative of Arctic Experience in Search of Survivors of Sir John Franklin's Expedition*. Edmonton: Hurtig, [1865] 1970.

Hall, Judy, Jill Oakes, and Sally Qimmiu'naaq Webster. *Sanatujut—Pride in Women's Work: Copper and Caribou Inuit Clothing Traditions*. Hull, Québec: Canadian Museum of Civilization, 1994.

Hallendy, Norman. "Reflections, Shades and Shadows." *Collected Papers on the Human History of the Northwest Territories, Occasional Paper 1.* Prince of Wales Northern Heritage Centre, 1982.

Haller, A. A., D. C. Foote, and P. D. Cove [edited by G. Anders]. *Baffin Island—East Coast: An Area Economic Survey.* Ottawa: Department of Indian and Northern Affairs, 1967.

Hamilton, John David. *Arctic Revolution: Social Change in the Northwest Territories 1935-1994.* Toronto: Dundurn Press, 1994.

Hamley, William. "The Nunavut Settlement: A Critical Appraisal." *International Journal of Canadian Studies* (Fall 1995): 221-234.

Hancock, Lyn. "A Good Woman in the North." *North* 22 (September-October 1975): 12-15.

———. *Nunavut.* Minneapolis, MN: Lerner Publications, 1975.

Hanley, Charles J. "Tomorrow Slowly Encroaches on Harsh, Scenic Arctic (Pond Inlet, NWT)." *Los Angeles Times* (October 11, 1987), pp. 2ff.

Hanson, Ann Meekitjuk. "Inuit Culture: The Baffin Region." *The Nunavut Handbook.* Iqaluit, NWT: Nortext, 1998.

———. *Show Me: A Young Inuk Learns How to Carve in Canada's Arctic.* Yellowknife: Amway Environmental Foundation, 1991.

Hantzsch, Bernhard. *My Life among the Eskimos: Baffin Journeys in the Years 1909 to 1911.* Edited and translated by L. G. Neatby. Institute of Northern Studies, Mawdsley Memoir 3. Saskatoon: University of Saskatchewan, 1977.

Harper, Kenn. *Give Me My Father's Body: The Life of Minik, the New York Eskimo.* Frobisher Bay [Iqaluit], NWT: Blacklead Books, 1986.

———. *Pangnirtung* (published by the author, 1972).

———. "Pangnirtung." In *The Nunavut Handbook: 1999 Commemorative Edition*, edited by Marion Soubliere. Iqaluit, NT: Nortext Multimedia, 1998.

Harrington, Lyn. *Ootook: Young Eskimo Girl.* Toronto: Thomas Nelson and Sons, n. d.

Harston, P. J. "Igloolik Mourns Again." *News/North* (July 15, 1996), p. A14.

Hawkes, David C., ed. *Aboriginal Peoples and Government Responsibility: Exploring Federal and Provincial Roles.* Ottawa: Carleton University Press, 1989.

Hedican, Edward J. *Applied Anthropology in Canada: Understanding Aboriginal Issues.* Toronto: University of Toronto Press, 1995.

Heise, Lori L., Jacqueline Pitanguy, and Adrienne Germain. *Violence against Women: The Hidden Health Burden* (Discussion Paper #255). Washington, DC: The World Bank, 1994.

Helm, Judith. *The People of Denendeh: Ethnohistory of the Indians of Canada's Northwest Territories.* Montréal: McGill-Queen's University Press, Rupert's Land Record Society Series, 2002.

Henton, Darcy, and William Walker. "Dene Indians Set to Fight Inuit Deal." *The Toronto Star* (December 17, 1991), p. A9.

Henshaw, Anne Stevens. *Central Inuit Household Economics: Zoo-archaeological, Environmental and Historical Evidence from Outer Frobisher Bay, Baffin Island, Canada.* Ph.D. dissertation, Harvard University. Abstract in *Études/Inuit/Studies* 20, 2 (1995): 145-146.

Hickey, Cliff, and Mark G. Stevenson. *Structural Variations in Traditional Canadian Inuit Marriage, Adoption, and Social Customs.* Yellowknife: Family Law Reform Commission of the NWT, 1990.

Hicks, Jack. "The Nunavut Land Claim and the Nunavut Government: Political Structures of Self-Government in Canada's Eastern Arctic." In *Dependency, Autonomy, Sustainability in the Arctic,* edited by Hanne K. Petersen and Birger Poppel. Aldershot, ONT; Brookfield, VT: Ashgate, 1999.

Hicks, Jack, and Graham White. "Nunavut: Inuit Self-Determination through a Land Claim and Public Government?" In *Nunavut,* edited by Jens Dahl, Jack Hicks, and Peter Jull. Copenhagen: International Work Group on Indigenous Affairs, 1999.

Hill, Miriam. "Breast Cancer Strikes Inuit, Too: Nunavut Women Can't Get Mammograms in the Territory, So Cancer Often Goes Undetected Until It's Too Late." *Nunatsiaq News* (September 28, 2001).

———. "Nunavut Status of Women Council Takes Root: Chairperson Says Better Communication with Government Needed." *Nunatsiaq News* (November 30, 2001).

Hobart, Charles W. "Impact of Resource Development Projects on Indigenous People." In *Resource Communities: A Decade of Disruption,* edited by Don D. Detomasi and John W. Gartrell. Boulder: Westview Press, 1984.

———. "Industrial Employment of Rural Indigenes: The Case of Canada." *Human Organization* 41, 1 (1982): 54-63.

———. "Socio-economic Correlates of Mortality and Morbidity among Inuit Infants." Pp. 452-61 in *Proceedings of the Third International Symposium on Circumpolar Health,* edited by R. J. Shephard and S. Itoh. Toronto: University of Toronto Press, 1976.

———. "Some Consequences of Residential Schooling of Eskimos in the Canadian Arctic." *Arctic Anthropology* 6 (1970): 123-135.

Hochschild, Arlie Russell. *The Managed Heart: Commercialization of Human Feeling.* Berkeley: University of California Press, 1989.

Hodgson, Stuart, ed. *Stories from Pangnirtung.* Illustrated by Germaine Arnaktauyok. Edmonton: Hurtig, 1976.

Holland, Clive. "William Penny, 1809-1892: Arctic Whaling Master." *Polar Record* 15, 94 (1970): 25-43.

Holtved, Erik. "The Eskimo Myth about the Sea-woman." *Folk* 8-9 (1966-67): 145-154.

Honigmann, John J. "Social Integration in Five Northern Canadian Communities." *Canadian Review of Sociology and Anthropology* 2, 4 (1972): 199-214.

———. "Frobisher Bay Eskimo Childhood." Reprint from *North,* Northern Administrative Branch, 1969.

———. "How Baffin Island Eskimo Have Learned to Use Alcohol." *Social Forces* (September 1965).

———. "Learning to Drink." In *Eskimo of the Canadian Arctic,* edited by Victor F. Valentine and Frank G. Vallee. Toronto: McClelland and Stewart, 1968.

———. "People under Tutelage." In *Eskimo of the Canadian Arctic,* edited by Victor F. Valentine and Frank G. Vallee. Toronto: McClelland and Stewart, 1968.

Honigmann, John J., and Irma Honigmann. *Arctic Townsmen: Ethnic Backgrounds and Modernisation.* Ottawa: Canadian Research Centre for Anthropology, St. Paul University, 1970.

Houston, James. *Confessions of an Igloo Dweller*. Toronto: McClelland and Stewart, 1995.

———. *Eskimo Prints*. Toronto: Longman Canada, 1970.

———. *The White Dawn*. San Diego: Harcourt Brace Jovanovich, 1983.

Howard, Albert, and Frances Widdowson. "The Disaster of Nunavut." *Policy Options Politiques* (July/August 1999): 58-61.

Hoyenga, Katharine Blick, and Kermit T. Hoyenga. *Gender-Related Differences: Origins and Outcomes*. Boston: Allyn & Bacon, 1993.

Hull, Jeremy. *Aboriginal Post-Secondary Education and Labour Market Outcomes Canada, 1996*. Ottawa: Research and Analysis Directorate, Department of Indian Affairs and Northern Development, 2000.

———. *Aboriginal Single Mothers in Canada 1996: A Statistical Profile*. Ottawa: Research and Analysis Directorate, Department of Indian Affairs and Northern Development, 2001.

Hunt, Constance. "Fishing Rights for Inuit Women." *Branching Out* 4 (March-April 1977): 6-7.

Hyde, Deborah. *Women, Production and Change in Inuit Society*. Thesis, Carleton University, Ottawa, Ontario, 1980.

Hylton, John H. *Aboriginal Self-Government in Canada: Current Trends and Issues*. Saskatoon: Purich Publishing, 1999.

Institute of American Indian Arts Museum. *Keeping Our Stories Alive: An Exhibition of the Art and Crafts from Dene and Inuit of Canada*. Santa Fe: Institute of American Indian Arts Museum, 1995.

Inuit Circumpolar Conference. *The Arctic Sealing Industry: A Retrospective Analysis of its Collapse and Options for Sustainable Development*. Inuit Circumpolar Conference, Nuuk, 1996.

Inuit Committee on National Issues. *Completing Canada: Inuit Approaches to Self-Government*. Kingston: Queen's University Institute of Intergovernmental Relations, 1987.

Inuit Tapirisat of Canada. "Nunavut—'Our Land'." In *Two Nations, Many Cultures: Ethnic Groups in Canada*, edited by Jean Leonard Elliott. Scarborough: Prentice-Hall, 1983.

———. *Agreement in Principle as to the Settlement of Inuit Land Claims in the Northwest Territories and the Yukon Territory between the Government of Canada and the Inuit Tapirisat of Canada*. Ottawa: Inuit Tapirisat of Canada, 1976.

Irniq, Peter. "[On Suicide] Place Faith in Inuit Culture." *Nunatsiaq News* (April 28, 2000).

———. "Let Us Care for One Another." *Nunatsiaq News* (July 14, 2000).

Irwin, Colin. "Lords of the Arctic: Wards of the State. The Growing Inuit Population, Arctic Resettlement, and Their Effects on Social and Economic Change—A Summary Report." *Northern Perspectives* 17, 1 (January-March 1989): 2-12.

Isaac, Thomas. "Land Claims and Self-Government Developments in Canada's North." In *A Passion for Identity: An Introduction to Canadian Studies*, edited by David Taras and Beverly Rasporich. Toronto: ITP Nelson, 1997.

Issenman, Betty Kobayashi. *Sinews of Survival: The Living Legacy of Inuit Clothing*. Vancouver: University of British Columbia Press, 1997.

Issenman, Betty Kobayashi, and C. Rankin. *Ivalu: Traditions of Inuit Clothing.* Montréal: McCord Museum of Canadian History, 1988.

Jenness, Diamond. "The Administration of Northern Peoples: America's Eskimos—Pawns of History." In *The Arctic Frontier*, edited by Ronald St. J. Macdonald. Toronto: University of Toronto Press, 1966.

———. *Arctic Odyssey: The Diary of Diamond Jenness, 1913-1916.* [Stuart Jenness, editor.] Hull, Québec: The Canadian Museum of Civilization, 1991.

———. "The Economic Situation of the Eskimo." In *Eskimo of the Canadian Arctic*, edited by Victor F. Valentine and Frank G. Vallee. Toronto: McClelland and Stewart, 1968.

———. *Inuit: Glimpses of an Arctic Past.* Ottawa: Canadian Museum of Civilization, 1995.

———. *The Life of the Copper Eskimos: A Report of the Canadian Arctic Expedition 1913-18, Part A, XII.* New York: Johnson Reprint Corporation, [1922] 1970.

Jennings, Michael L. "Northern Development: The Role of the University." Paper presented at the Third International Congress of Arctic Social Sciences, Copenhagen, Denmark, 1998.

Jolles, Carol Z. "Changing Roles of St. Lawrence Island Women: Clanswomen in the Public Sphere." In *Arctic Anthropology* 34, 1 (1997): 86-101. [Papers in Honor of Richard G. Condon, Steven L. McNabb, Alexsandr I. Pika, William W. Richards, Nikolai Galgauge, Nina Ankalina, Vera Rakhtilkon, Boris Mymykhtikak, and Nikolai Avanun, edited by Pamela R. Stern, George W. Wenzel, and Sergei Kan.]

Jones, H. G. "A Community's History Preserved through Art: The Case of Pangnirtung." Paper presented at the Third International Congress of Arctic Social Sciences, Copenhagen, Denmark, 1998.

Jull, Peter. "Aboriginal Peoples and Political Change in the North Atlantic Area." *Journal of Canadian Studies* 16 (1981): 2.

———. "Building Nunavut: A Story of Inuit Self-Government." *Northern Review* 1 (1988): 59-72.

———. "Nunavut Abroad." *Northern Perspectives* 21, 3 (1993): 15.

———. "Redefining Aboriginal-White Relations: Canada's Inuit." *International Journal of Canadian Studies* 3 (Spring 1991): 11-25.

Kallso, Josephine. *Taipsumane.* Nain, LAB: Torngasok Cultural Centre, 1984.

Kaplansky, Marsha. *Inuit in the South.* Ottawa: Department of Indian and Northern Affairs, 1981.

Karpik, Margaret. "A Whaler's Life: A Celebration of Harvest and Tradition (Interview with Jaco Evic)." *Ittuagtuut* (Nunavut Tunngavik) 1, 1 (Winter 1998): 14-28.

Keenleyside, D. *The Land Beyond.* Toronto: Nelson, Foster and Scott, 1975.

———. *Where the Mountain Falls.* Toronto: Nelson, Foster and Scott, 1977.

Kemp, William B. "Inuit Land Use in South and East Baffin Island." In *Inuit land Use and Occupancy Project I*, edited by Milton M. R. Freeman. Ottawa: Indian and Northern Affairs, 1976.

———. "Baffinland Eskimo." In *Handbook of North American Indians, Volume 5: Arctic*, edited by David Damas. Washington: Smithsonian Institution, 1984, pp. 463-475.

Kenny, Carolyn Bereznak. *North American Indian, Métis and Inuit Women Speak about Culture, Education and Work.* Ottawa: Status of Women Canada, 2002 (http://www.swc-cfc.gc.ca/pubs/0662318978/index_e.html).

Kilabuk, J. "The Things That the Eskimos Did." In *Stories from Pangnirtung*, edited by Stuart Hodgson. Edmonton: Hurtig, 1976.

Kirmayer, Laurence J. "Suicide among Canadian Aboriginal Peoples." *Transcultural Psychiatric Research Review* 31 (1994): 3-58.

Kirmayer, Laurence J., Chris Fletcher, Ellen Corin, and L. Boothroyd. *Inuit Concepts of Mental Health and Illness: An Ethnographic Study*. Montréal: Sir Mortimer B. Davis-Jewish General Hospital, Institute of Community and Family Psychiatry, 1994.

Kirmayer, Laurence J., M. Malus, and L. Boothroyd. "Suicide Attempts among Inuit Youth: A Community Survey of Prevalence and Risk Factors." *Acta Psychiatrica Scandinavia* 94 (1996): 8-17.

Klein, Renate Duelli. "How to Do What We Want to Do: Thoughts about Feminist Methodology." In *Theories of Women's Studies*, edited by Gloria Bowles and Renate Duelli Klein. London: Routledge and Kegan Paul, 1983.

Kleivan, Inga. "Status and Role of Men and Women as Reflected in West Greenland Petting Songs to Infants." *Folk* 18 (1976): 5-22.

Krech III, Shepard, ed. *The Subarctic Fur Trade: Native Social and Economic Adaptations*. Vancouver: University of British Columbia Press, 1984.

Krosenbrink-Gelissen, Lilianne E. *Sexual Equality as an Aboriginal Right: The Native Women's Association of Canada and the Constitutional Process on Aboriginal Matters, 1982-1987*. Fort Lauderdale, Saarbrucken: Verlag Breitenbach, 1991.

Kusugak, Jose. "Inuit Art, History, and Culture, and Today's Politics in Inuit Canada." *From "Nanook" to Nunavut: The Art and Politics of Representing Inuit Culture* (Exhibition Program, St. Lawrence University Festival of the Arts, Canton, New York, February 21-March 7, 2001), p. 12.

Kutschak, Heinrich. *Overland to Starvation Cove: With the Inuit in Search of Franklin 1878-1880*. Toronto: University of Toronto Press, 1987.

Labarge, Dorothy. "Femme traditionnelle, femme nouvelle." *North* 22 (September 1975): 8-11.

Lamphere, Louise. "The Domestic Sphere of Women and the Public World of Men: The Strengths and Limitations of an Anthropological Dichotomy." In *Gender in Cross-Cultural Perspective*, edited by Caroline B. Brettell and Carolyn F. Sargent. Englewood Cliffs, NJ: Prentice-Hall, 1993.

Lamphere, Louise, and Michelle Rosaldo, eds. *Women, Culture, and Society*. Palo Alto, CA: Stanford University Press, 1974.

Lange, Lynda. "The Relation between the Situation of Dene Women and the Changing Situation of Elders, in the Context of Colonialism: The Experience of Fort Franklin, 1945-1985." Paper presented at the Knowing the North Conference, Boreal Institute for Northern Studies, Edmonton, 1986.

Lantis, Margaret. "The Administration of Northern Peoples: Canada and Alaska." In *The Arctic Frontier*, edited by Ronald St. J. Macdonald. Toronto: University of Toronto Press, 1966.

Lavrin, Asuncion. "Women, the Family, and Social Change in Latin America." *World Affairs* 150, 2 (1987): 109-128.

Leacock, Eleanor Burke. *Myths of Male Dominance: Collected Articles on Women Cross-Culturally*. New York: Monthly Review Press, 1981.

————. "Relations of Production in Band Society." In *Politics and History in Band Societies*, edited by Eleanor Burke Leacock and Richard Lee. New York: Cambridge University Press, 1981.

Légaré, André. "Le projet Nunavut: Bilan des révindications des Inuit des Térritoires-du-Nord-Ouest." *Études/Inuit/Studies* (1993) 17, 2: 29-62.

————. "Le gouvernement du Térritoire du Nunavut (1999): Une analyse prospective." *Études/Inuit/Studies* (1996) 20, 1: 7-43.

————. "The Process Leading to a Land Claims Agreement and Its Implementation: The Case of the Nunavut Land Claims Settlement." *Canadian Journal of Native Studies* (1996) 16, 1: pp. 139-63.

————. "The Government of Nunavut (1999): A Prospective Analysis." In *First Nations in Canada: Perspectives on Opportunity, Empowerment, and Self-Determination*, edited by J. Rick Ponting. Toronto: McGraw-Hill Ryerson, 1997.

————. "An Assessment of Recent Political Development in Nunavut: The Challenges and Dilemmas of Inuit Self-Government." *Canadian Journal of Native Studies* (1998): 271-299.

Lepowsky, Maria Alexandra. *Fruits of the Motherland: Gender in an Egalitarian Society*. New York: Columbia University Press, 1993.

Leroux, Odette, Marion E. Jackson, and Minnie Aodla Freeman, eds. *Inuit Women Artists: Voices from Cape Dorset*. Vancouver: Douglas & McIntyre (Canadian Museum of Civilization and University of Washington Press), 1994.

————. "*Isumavut:* Artistic Expression of Nine Cape Dorset Women." In *Inuit Women Artists: Voices from Cape Dorset*, edited by Odette Leroux, Marion E. Jackson, and Minnie Aodla Freeman. Vancouver: Douglas & McIntyre (Canadian Museum of Civilization and University of Washington Press), 1994.

Lindsey, Linda L. *Gender Roles: A Sociological Perspective*. Englewood Cliffs, NJ: Prentice Hall, 1994.

Lopez, Barry. *Arctic Dreams: Imagination and Desire in Northern Landscape*. Toronto: Bantam Books, 1986.

Lowenstein, Tom. *Ancient Land, Sacred Whale: The Inuit Hunt and its Rituals*. New York: Farrar, Straus, and Giroux, 1994.

Lubart, J. M. *Psychodynamic Problems of Adaptation: Mackenzie Delta Eskimos*. Ottawa: Department of Indian and Northern Affairs, 1970.

Lynge, Finn. "An International Inuit Perspective on Development in the Arctic." *The Northern Raven* VI, 1 (Summer 1986): 1-3.

Mackie, Marlene. *Constructing Women and Men: Gender Socialization*. Toronto: Holt, Rinehart, and Winston, 1987.

Maclean's. "Fashion, Inuit-Style." *Maclean's* (April 23, 2001), p. 20.

Malcolmson, S., and E. Hood. "A Study of Suicide in Baffin Zone, NWT, East Canadian Arctic." Nordic Council for *Arctic Medical Research* 27 (1980).

Manuel, George, and Michael Posluns. "The Fourth World in Canada." In *Two Nations, Many Cultures: Ethnic Groups in Canada*, edited by Jean Leonard Elliott. Scarborough: Prentice-Hall, 1983.

Marcus, Alan R. "Canada's Experimental Inuit Relocation to Grise Fjord and Resolute Bay." *Polar Record* 27, 163 (1992): 285-296.

————. *Inuit Relocation Policies in Canada and Other Circumpolar Countries, 1925-60*. Report for the Royal Commission on Aboriginal Peoples, Ottawa, 1994.

————. *Out in the Cold: The Legacy of Canada's Inuit Relocation Experiment in the High Arctic.* Copenhagen: International Work Group for Indigenous Affairs, Document 71, 1992.

————. *Relocating Eden: The Image and Politics of Inuit Exile in the Canadian Arctic.* Hanover, NH: University Press of New England, 1995.

————. *Utopia on Trial: Perceptions of Canadian Government Experiments with Inuit Relocation.* Ph.D. Thesis, University of Cambridge, 1993.

Markoosie. *Harpoon of the Hunter.* Montréal: McGill-Queen's University Press, 1974.

Marsh, Donald B. *Echoes from a Frozen Land.* Edited by Winifred Marsh. Edmonton: Hurtig, 1987.

————. "A History of the Work of the Anglican Church in the Area Now Known as the Diocese of the Arctic." In *Anthropological Essays on Tutelage and Ethnicity,* edited by R. Pane. St. John's, Nfld.: Memorial University, 1977.

Marsh, Donald B., and Winifred Marsh. *Echoes into Tomorrow: A Personal Overview of a Century of Events and Endeavours Affecting the History of Canada and the Inuit.* Three Hills, AB: Prairie Graphics, 1991.

Maslove, Allen M., and David C. Hawkes. *Canada's North: A Profile.* Canadian Government Publication DDC 304.6/09729, 1991.

Mathieu, Nicole Claude. "'Woman' in Ethnology: The Other of the Other, and the Other of the Self." *Feminist Issues* 8, 1 (1988): 3-14.

Matthews, Ralph. *The Creation of Regional Dependency.* Toronto: University of Toronto Press, 1983.

Matthiasson, Carolyn J., ed. *Many Sisters: Women in Cross-Cultural Perspective.* New York: Free Press, 1974.

Matthiasson, John S. *Living on the Land: Change among the Inuit of Baffin Island.* Peterborough, ONT: Broadview Press, 1992.

————. "The Maritime Inuit: Life on the Edge," In *Native Peoples: The Canadian Experience,* edited by R. Bruce Morrison and C. Roderick Wilson. Toronto: McClelland & Stewart, 1995.

————. "Northern Baffin Island Women in Three Cultural Periods." *Western Canadian Journal of Anthropology* 6, 3 (1976): 201-212.

Mayes, Robert G. *The Creation of a Dependent People: The Inuit of Cumberland Sound, NWT.* Ph.D. Thesis, Department of Geography, McGill University, Montréal, 1978.

McAlpine, Phyllis J., and Nancy E. Simpson. "Fertility and Other Demographic Aspects of the Canadian Eskimo Communities of Igloolik and Hall Beach." *Human Biology* 48, 1 (February 1976): 113-138.

M'Closkey, Kathy. "Art of Craft: The Paradox of the Pangnirtung Weave Shop." In *Women of the First Nations: Power, Wisdom, and Strength,* edited by Christine Miller and Patricia Chuchryk with Marie Smallface Marule, Brenda Manyfingers, and Cheryl Deering. Winnipeg: The University of Manitoba Press, 1997.

McCluskey, Kerry. "Talking of Shamans and Other Things: Q&A with Salome Awa." *News/North Nunavut* (March 29, 1999), pp. A23, B9.

McComber, Louis. "Anthropologist Unearths Treasure Trove of Inuit Culture." *Nunatsiaq News* (October 16, 1998).

McCullum, Hugh, and Karmel McCullum. *This Land Is Not for Sale: Canada's Original People and Their Land—A Saga of Neglect, Exploitation, and Conflict.* Toronto: Anglican Book Centre, 1975.

McDonald, Miriam, Lucassie Arragutainaq, and Zack Novalinga. *Voices from the Bay: Traditional Ecological Knowledge of Inuit and Cree in the Hudson Bay Bioregion.* Ottawa: Canadian Arctic Resources Committee [Sanikiluaq], 1997.

McElroy, Ann. *Alternatives in Modernization: Styles and Strategies in the Acculturative Behavior of Baffin Island Inuit, Volumes I, II, and III.* New Haven, CT: Human Relations Area Files, Ethnography Series, 1977.

———. "Canadian Arctic Modernization and Change in Female Inuit Role Identification." *American Ethnologist* 2, 4 (November 1975): 662-686.

———. "The Negotiation of Sex-role Identity in Eastern Arctic Culture Change." *Western Canadian Journal of Anthropology* 6, 3 (1976): 184-200.

McGhee, Robert. "Ivory for the Sea Woman: The Symbolic Attributes of a Prehistoric Technology." *Canadian Journal of Archaeology* 1 (1977): 141-149.

———. *Ancient People of the Arctic.* Vancouver: University of British Columbia Press/Canadian Museum of Civilization (Ottawa), 1996.

McGrath, Robin. *Canadian Inuit Literature: The Development of a Tradition,* Canadian Ethnology Service Paper 94. Ottawa: Natural Museums of Canada [National Museum of Man, Mercury Series], 1984.

———. "Circumventing the Taboos: Inuit Women's Autobiographies." In *Undisciplined Women: Tradition and Culture in Canada,* edited by Pauline Greenhill and Diane Tye. Montréal: McGill-Queen's University Press, 1997.

———. "Inuit Write about Illness: Standing on Thin Ice." *Arctic Medical Research* 50 (1991): 30-36.

McLaren, Angus, and Arlene Tigar McLaren. *The Bedroom and the State: The Changing Practices and Politics of Contraception and Abortion in Canada, 1880-1980.* Toronto: McClelland and Stewart, 1980.

McLaren, Arlene Tigar, ed. *Gender and Society: Creating a Canadian Women's Sociology.* Toronto: Copp Clark Pitman, 1988.

McLean, Scott. "Adult Education in Nunavut: Promotion of Self-Government, or the Governance of Selves?" Paper presented at the Third International Congress of Arctic Social Sciences, Copenhagen, Denmark, 1998.

McKibbon, Sean. Report: "GN Doesn't Know Why Daycares [Are] Going Broke." *Nunatsiaq News* (July 7, 2000).

———. "Nunavut's Shocking Sexual Assault Rates." *Nunatsiaq News* (June 30, 2000).

McMahon, Kevin. *Arctic Twilight.* Toronto: James Lorimer, 1988.

McMillan, Alan D. *Native Peoples and Cultures of Canada: An Anthropological Overview.* Vancouver: Douglas & McIntyre, 1995.

McNiven, Jean. "La femme et la Nord." *North* 22 (October 1975): 62-63.

McRoberts, Kenneth, ed. "Aboriginal Peoples and Canada." *International Journal of Canadian Studies,* 1995.

Mead, Margaret. *The Eskimos* (based on the fieldwork of Franz Boas in Cumberland Sound, Baffin Island, NWT, 1883). (n. p.), 1959.

———. "Research with Human Beings: A Model Derived from Anthropological Field Practice." *Daedalus* 98 (1969): 361-386.

Meade, Marie. "Sewing to Maintain the Past, Present and Future." *Études/Inuit/Studies* 14, 1-2 (1990): 229-239.

Merritt, John, Terry Fenge, Randy Ames, and Peter Jull. *Nunavut: Political Choices and Manifest Destiny.* Ottawa: Canadian Arctic Resources Committee, 1989.

Merton, Robert K. *Social Theory and Social Structure.* New York: The Free Press, 1957.

Mies, Maria. "Towards a Methodology for Feminist Research." In *Theories of Women's Studies*, edited by Gloria Bowles and Renate Duelli Klein. London: Routledge and Kegan Paul, 1983.

Millman, Marcia, and Rosabeth Moss Kanter, eds. *Another Voice: Feminist Perspectives on Social Life and Social Science*. New York: Anchor Books, 1975.

Mills, C. Wright. *The Sociological Imagination*. New York: Oxford University Press, 1959.

Millward, A. E., ed. *Southern Baffin Island: An Account of Exploration, Investigation and Settlement during the Past Fifty Years*. Yellowknife: North West Territories and Yukon Branch, Department of the Interior, 1930.

Minor, Kit. *Issumatuq: Learning from the Traditional Healing Wisdom of the Canadian Inuit*. Halifax: Fernwood, 1992.

Mitchell, Marybelle. *From Talking Chiefs to a Native Corporate Elite: The Birth of Class and Nationalism among Canadian Inuit*. Montréal: McGill-Queen's University Press, 1996.

Mitchell, Marybelle, and Pat Tobin. "Nunavut: The Newest Member of Confederation." *Inuit Art Quarterly* 14, 2 (1999): 18-23.

Montcombroux, Genevieve. *The Canadian Inuit Dog: Canada's Heritage*. Inwood, Manitoba: Whippoorwill Press, 1997.

[Moravians]. *Periodical Accounts Relating to the Missions of the Church of the United Brethren Established among the Heathen*, 28 (1871): 66.

Morrison, David. *Arctic Hunters: The Inuit and Diamond Jenness*. Ottawa: Canadian Museum of Civilization, 1992.

Morrison, David, and Georges-Hebert Germain. *Inuit: Glimpses of an Arctic Past*. Hull, Québec: Canadian Museum of Civilization, 1995.

Morrison, David, and C. Roderick Smith, eds. *Native Peoples: The Canadian Experience*, 2nd ed. Toronto: McClelland and Stewart, 1995.

Morrison, William R. "Canadian Sovereignty and the Inuit of the Central and Eastern Arctic." *Études/Inuit/Studies* 10, 1 (1986): 245-259.

——. *Under the Flag: Canadian Sovereignty and the Native People in Northern Canada*. Ottawa: Department of Indian and Northern Affairs, 1984.

Mowat, Farley. *The Desperate People*. Boston: Little, Brown, 1959.

——. *The Farfarers*. Toronto: Key Porter, 1998. Excerpted as "Farley's Version" in *Canadian Geographic* 118, (September 1998), pp. 65-82.

——. *Ordeal by Ice: The Search for the Northwest Passage—1, The Top of the World Trilogy*. Toronto: McClelland and Stewart, 1960.

——. *People of the Deer*. Toronto: Seal Books, 1975.

——. *Tundra: Selections from the Great Accounts of Arctic Land Voyages*. Toronto: McClelland and Stewart, 1977.

——. *Walking on the Land*. Toronto: Key Porter, 2000.

Muckpah, James. "Remembered Childhood." *Ajurnarmat, International Year of the Child: Issue on Education*. Eskimo Point, NWT: Inuit Cultural Institute, 1979.

Munro, Mary. "Pangnirtung Women Carvers." *North* 22 (October 1975): 46-49.

Murdoch, John. *Ethnological Results of the Point Barrow Expedition*, Ninth Annual Report of the Bureau of Ethnology to the Secretary of the Smithsonian Institution, 1877-88. Washington, DC: U.S. Government Printing Office, 1892.

Myers, Marybelle. "Inuit Arts and Crafts Co-operatives in the Canadian Arctic." *Canadian Ethnic Studies* 16, 3 (1984): 132-53.

———. "Remembering (Eskimo Women's Crafts Workshop)." *North* 22 (October 1975): 26-29.

Myers, Heather, and Scott Forrest. "While Nero Fiddles: Economic Development in Pond Inlet 1987-97." Paper presented at the Third International Congress of Arctic Social Sciences, Copenhagen, Denmark, 1998.

Myrdal, Gunnar. *Rich Lands and Poor: The Road to World Prosperity.* New York: Harper, 1957.

National Archives of Canada, RG85, 1118: 1000/145-1, memo, Martin to Finnie, March 1931.

National Archives of Canada, RG85, 1872: 552/1-1, memo, A. L. Cumming to R. A. Gibson, 17 May 1937.

National Geographic Society. *The World of the American Indian.* Washington, DC: National Geographic Society, 1979.

Nickels, S., S. Milne, and George W. Wenzel. "Inuit Perceptions of Tourism Development: The Case of Clyde River, Baffin Island, NWT." *Études/Inuit/Studies* 15, 1 (1991): 157-169.

Nixon, Chris. "Land Claim Redraws Canada's Map." *The London Free Press*, December 17, 1991, p.1.

Norris, Mary Jane. "The Demography of Aboriginal People in Canada." In *Ethnic Demography: Canadian Immigrant, Racial and Cultural Variations*, edited by Shiva S. Halli, Frank Trovato, and Leo Driedger. Ottawa: Carleton University Press, 1990.

———. "Canada's Aboriginal Languages." *Canadian Social Trends* (Winter 1998): 8-16.

Nortext. *The Baffin Handbook.* Iqaluit, NWT: Nortext Publishing, 1993.

Northern Development Branch, Alberta Department of Business Development, and Alberta Department of Social Services and Community Health. *Alberta Family Planning Project 55-35070.* Edmonton: University of Alberta Press, 1970.

North West Territories Education, Culture and Employment. *The Curriculum from the Inuit Perspective.* Yellowknife: North West Territories Education, Culture and Employment, 1996.

Norwood, Robin. *Women Who Love Too Much.* New York: St. Martin's Press, 1985.

Nunatsiaq News. "GN Women's Advisor Takes Own Life." *Nunatsiaq News* (July 7, 1999).

———. "The GNWT's Position on Nunavut." *Nunatsiaq News* (May 24, 1996), pp. 5, 9 (based on the territorial government's report, *Working Toward 1999*).

———. "How Everything Had Changed." *Nunatsiaq News* (March 8, 2002).

———. "Look out Canada—Nunavut's Coming." *Nunatsiaq News* (February 18, 1999).

———. "NTI Calls on Standing Committee to Support Inuit Economic Development in Nunavut." *Nunatsiaq News* (May 20, 1998).

———. "Nunavut Libraries Get Grant from Gates Foundation." *Nunatsiaq News* (March 23, 2001).

———. "The OIC's Master Plan for Nunavut: 100 More Jobs than Footprints 2." *Nunatsiaq News* (October 9, 1996), pp. 5, 9.

———. "Premier Paul Okalik's Review of Nunavut's First Year: For the Record." *Nunatsiaq News* (April 7, 2000).

————. "Women Light the Way." *Nunatsiaq News* (March 3, 2000).

Nunavut Implementation Commission. *Footprints in New Snow: A Comprehensive Report from the Nunavut Implementation Commission to the Department of Indian Affairs and Northern Development, Government of the Northwest Territories and Nunavut Tunngavik Incorporated Concerning the Establishment of the Nunavut Government.* Iqaluit, NWT: Nunavut Implementation Commission, March 31, 1995.

————. *Footprints 2: A Second Comprehensive Report from the Nunavut Implementation Commission to the Department of Indian Affairs and Northern Development, Government of the Northwest Territories and Nunavut Tunngavik Incorporated Concerning the Establishment of the Nunavut Government.* Iqaluit, NWT: Nunavut Implementation Commission, October 21, 1996.

Nunavut Research Institute. "Negotiating Relationships: A Guide for Communities." Iqaluit, NWT: Nunavut Research Institute and Inuit Tapirisat of Canada, 1998.

Nungak, Zebedee, and Eugene Y. Arima. *Inuit Stories/Légendes Inuits: Povungnituk.* Seattle: University of Washington Press, 2001.

Nuttall, Mark. *Arctic Homeland: Kinship, Community and Development in Northwest Greenland.* Toronto: University of Toronto Press, 1992.

————. *Protecting the Arctic: Indigenous Peoples and Cultural Survival.* Amsterdam: Harwood Academic, 1998.

Oakes, Jill. "Climate and Cultural Barriers to Northern Economic Development: A Case Study from Broughton Island, NWT, Canada." *Climate Research* 5 (February 23, 1995): 91-98.

Oakes, Jill, and Rick Riewe. "Factors Influencing Decisions Made by Inuit Seamstresses in the Circumpolar Region." In *Braving the Cold, Continuity and Change in Arctic Clothing*, edited by C. Buijs and J. Oosten. Leiden: Centre of Non-Western Studies, 1996, pp. 89-104.

————, eds. *Issues in the North: Proceedings of the 1995 Lecture Series.* Edmonton: Canadian Circumpolar Institute (University of Alberta), 1996.

Odjig, Alfred (Fisher). *Aboriginal Rights in Canada.* Ottawa: National Library of Canada, 1985.

Okalik, Annie. "A Good Life" (interview by Angela Bernal, translated by Sadie Hill). In *Gossip: A Spoken History of Women in the North*, edited by Mary Crnkovich. Ottawa: Canadian Arctic Resources Committee, 1990.

O'Neil, John D. "Beyond Healers and Patients: The Emergence of Local Responsibility in Inuit Health Care." *Études/Inuit/Studies* 5, 1 (1981): 17-26.

————. "Colonial Stress in the Canadian Arctic: An Ethnography of Young Adults Changing." In *Anthropology and Epidemiology*, edited by C. R. Janes, R. Stall, and S. M. Gifford. Dordrecht: Reidel Lancaster, 1986.

————. "Health Care in the Canadian Arctic: Continuities and Change." In *Health and Canadian Society: A Sociological Perspective*, edited by D. Coburn, et al. Toronto: Fitzhenry and Whiteside, 1980.

————. "Illness in Inuit Society: Traditional Context and Acculturative Influences." *NAPAO* 9, 1-2 (1979): 40-51.

O'Neil, John D., et al. "Health Communication Problems in Canadian Inuit Communities." *Arctic Medical Research* 47, 1 (1988).

O'Neil, John D., M. E. K. Moffatt, R. B. Tate, and T. K. Young. "Suicidal Behaviour among Inuit in the Keewatin Region, NWT." *Arctic Medical Research* 2, 53 (1994): 558-561.

Oosten, Jarich Gerlof. "The Structure of the Shamanistic Complex among the Netsilik and Iglulik." *Études/Inuit/Studies* 5, 1 (1981): 83-98.

Oosten, Jarich Gerlof, and Cornelius H. W. Rémie, eds. *Arctic Identities: Continuity and Change in Inuit and Saami Societies.* Leiden: Universiteit Leiden, Research School of Asian, African and Amerindian Studies, CNWS 74, 1999.

PAC RG85/815, file 6954 [3], 14 September 1936, MacKinnon to Turner, NWT and Yukon Branch.

Paine, Robert. *The Nursery Game—Colonisers and Colonised in the Canadian Arctic. Études/Inuit/Studies* 1 (1977): 5.

———, ed. *Patrons and Brokers in the East Arctic.* St. John's, NFLD: Institute of Social and Economic Progress, Memorial University of Newfoundland, 1971.

———, ed. *The White Arctic: Anthropological Essays on Tutelage and Ethnicity.* Toronto: University of Toronto Press, 1977.

Palliser, Annie. *"Annie, jeune Inuk en transition." North* 22 (October 1975): 50-51.

Pauktuutit Inuit Women's Association of Canada. *The Inuit Way: A Guide to Inuit Culture,* edited by David Boult. Ottawa: Pauktuutit, 1991.

———. "Inuit Women: The Housing Crisis and Violence," prepared for the Canada Mortgage and Housing Corporation. Ottawa: Pauktuutit, n. d.

———. "Inuit Women's Health: A Call for Commitment. *The Canadian Women's Health Network.* (Fall/Winter 2001/2002): 1.

Peck, E. J., Rev. *The Eskimo.* Anglican Church of Canada General Synod Archives, Peck Papers, M56-1 Series, 1922.

Pelly, David F. "Dawn of Nunavut: Inuit Negotiate a Home of Their Own in Canada's Newest Territory." *Canadian Geographic* (March/April 1993): 20-9.

———. "Birth of an Inuit Nation." *Geographical Magazine* (April 1994): 23-5.

———. "Footprints in New Snow: The March toward Nunavut." *Above & Beyond* (Summer 1995): 7-10.

Pemik, Linda. "In the Same Year, Far to the South." In *Women's Changing Landscapes: Life Stories from Three Generations,* edited by Greta Hofmann Nemiroff. Toronto: Second Story Press, 1999.

Petrone, Penny. *Northern Voices: Inuit Writing in English.* Toronto: University of Toronto Press, 1988.

Petersen, Hanne K., and Birger Poppel, eds. *Dependency, Autonomy, Sustainability in the Arctic.* Aldershot, ONT: Ashgate, 1999.

Ponting, J. Rick, ed. *Arduous Journey: Canadian Indians and Decolonization.* Toronto: McClelland and Stewart, 1986.

———. *First Nations in Canada: Perspectives on Opportunity, Empowerment, and Self-Determination.* Toronto: McGraw-Hill Ryerson, 1997.

Powers, Marla N. *Oglala Women: Myth, Ritual, and Reality.* Chicago: The University of Chicago Press, 1986.

Price, Richard T. *Legacy: Indian Treaty Relationships.* Edmonton, AB.: Plains Publishing, 1991.

Pudlat, Maata. "Boy, Have Things Changed." In *Gossip: A Spoken History of Women in the North,* edited by Mary Crnkovich. Ottawa: Canadian Arctic Resources Committee, 1990.

Purich, Donald. *Our Land: Native Rights in Canada*. Toronto: James Lorimer, 1986.

——. *The Inuit and Their Land: The Story of Nunavut*. Toronto: James Lorimer, 1992.

Qitsualik, Rachel Attituq. "The Problem with Sedna: Part One." *Nunatsiaq News* (March 5, 1999).

——. "The Problem with Sedna: Part Two—The Father's Rescue." *Nunatsiaq News* (March 12, 1999).

——. "The Problem with Sedna: Part Three—The Betrayal." *Nunatsiaq News* (March 19, 1999).

——. "The Problem with Sedna: Part Four—The Mythic Being." *Nunatsiaq News* (March 25, 1999).

——. "The Problem with Sedna: Part Five—Beautiful Variation." *Nunatsiaq News* (April 8, 1999).

——. "The Problem with Sedna: Part Six—Her Influence." *Nunatsiaq News* (April 15, 1999).

——. "Suicide." *Nunatsiaq News* (June 30, 2000).

Raine, David F. *Pitseolak: A Canadian Tragedy*. Edmonton: Hurtig, 1980.

Rasing, Willem C. E. "The Case of Kolitalik: On the Encounter of Iglulingmiut Culture and Canadian Justice." In *Continuity and Discontinuity in Arctic Cultures*, edited by C. Buijs. Leiden: Universiteit Leiden, Centre of Non-Western Studies, 1993, pp. 91-107.

——. *"Too Many People": Order and Nonconformity in Iglulingmiut Social Process*. Nijmegen: Recht and Samenleving, 1994.

——. "Hunting for Identity: Thoughts on the Practice of Hunting and Its Significance for Iglulingmiut Identity." In *Arctic Identities: Continuity and Change in Inuit and Saami Societies*, edited by Jarich G. Oosten and Cornelius H. W. Rémie. Leiden: Universiteit Leiden, Research School of Asian, African and Amerindian Studies, CNWS 74, 1999.

Rasmussen, Knud. *Eskimo Songs and Stories*. Selected and translated by Edward Field. New York: Delacorte Press, 1973 [1908].

——. *Intellectual Culture of Hudson Bay Eskimos. Report of the Fifth Thule Expedition 1921-24. Volume I: Observations on the Intellectual Culture of the Iglulik Eskimos*, 1928. *Volume II: Observations on the Intellectual Culture of the Caribou Eskimos*, 1930. Volume *III: Iglulik and Caribou Eskimos*, 1930. Copenhagen: Nordisk Forlag.

——. *The Netsilik Eskimos: Cultural Life and Spiritual Culture. Report of the Fifth Thule Expedition 1921-24*, 8, 1-2:1-542, 1931. [Gyldendalske Boghandel, Nordisk Forlag.]

Rau, Dana Meachen, and Peg Magovern. *Arctic Adventure: Inuit Life in the 1800s (Smithsonian Odyssey)*. Soundprints Corp Audio, 1997.

Reimer, Gwen D. *A Case Study of an Inuit Economy: Pangnirtung, NWT*. Ottawa: Royal Commission on Aboriginal Peoples, Ottawa, 1995.

——. *Child-care Issues: A Report from Pangnirtung, NWT.* Ottawa: Royal Commission on Aboriginal Peoples, 1993.

——. *Community Participation in Research and Development: A Case Study from Pangnirtung, NWT*. Ph.D. Thesis, Department of Anthropology, McMaster University, Hamilton, Ontario, 1994.

————. "Female Consciousness: An Interpretation of Interviews with Inuit Women [Pangnirtung]." *Études/Inuit/Studies* 20, 2 (1996): 77-100.

————. "Female Consciousness and Cross-cultural Research: Reflections on Interviews with Inuit Women." (Revised version of "Female Consciousness: An Interpretation." In *Merging Trajections, New Horisons: Anthropology from the Capital*, edited by B. Cox and D. Blair. Ottawa: Carleton University Press, 1996.

Reimer, Gwen D., and Andrew Dialla. *Community Based Tourism Development in Pangnirtung, NWT: Looking Back and Looking Ahead.* Iqaluit, NWT: Report for Economic Development and Tourism, Baffin Region, Government of the Northwest Territories and the Hamlet of Pangnirtung, 1992.

Reinharz, Shulamit. "Experiential Analysis." In *Theories of Women's Studies*, edited by Gloria Bowles and Renate Duelli Klein. London: Routledge and Kegan Paul, 1983.

Rémie, Cornelius H. W. *Crime, Socio-Legal Control and Problems of Change: A Legal Anthropological Study of Igloolik, NWT.* Ottawa: Department of Indian Affairs and Northern Development, 1989.

————. "Culture, Change and Religious Continuity among the Arviligdjuarmiut of Pelly Bay, NWT, 1935-1963." *Études/Inuit/Studies* 7, 2 (1983): 53-77.

————. "Ermalik and Kukigak: Continuity and Discontinuity in Pelly Bay, Northwest Territories, Canada." In *Continuity and Discontinuity in Arctic Cultures*, edited by Cunera Buijs. Leiden: Universiteit Leiden, Centre of Non-Western Studies, 1993.

————. "Flying Like a Butterfly, or Knud Rasmussen among the Netsilingmiut." *Études/Inuit/Studies* 12 (1988): 101-27.

————. "Shifting Cultural Identities: Case Materials from Pelly Bay, NWT." In *Arctic Identities: Continuity and Change in Inuit and Saami Societies*, edited by J. G. Oosten and Cornelius H. W. Rémie. Leiden: Universiteit Leiden, Research School of Asian, African and Amerindian Studies, CNWS 74, 1999.

————. "The Struggle for Land among the Inuit of the Canadian Arctic." Pp. 19-29 in *The Struggle for Land World-Wide*, edited by G. Peberkamp and Cornelius H. W. Rémie. Saarbrücken/Fort Lauderdale: Breitenbach Verlag, 1989.

————. "Towards a New Perspective on Netsilik Inuit Female Infanticide." *Études/Inuit/Studies* 9 (1985): 67-76.

Rémie, Cornelius H. W., and J. M. Lacroix, eds. *Canada on the Threshold of the 21st Century*. Amsterdam: John Benjamins, 1991.

Rémie, Cornelius H. W., and Jarich G. Oosten. "The Persistent Savage: Qallunaat Perspectives on the Inuit." Pp. 5-27 in *Arctic Identities: Continuity and Change in Inuit and Saami Societies*, edited by J. G. Oosten and Cornelius H. W. Rémie. Leiden: Universiteit Leiden, Research School of Asian, African and Amerindian Studies, CNWS 74, 1999.

Révillon Frères. *Eskimo Life of Yesterday.* Surrey, BC: Hancock House, 1983 (1922).

Reynolds, Jan. *Frozen Land: Vanishing Cultures.* San Diego: Harcourt Brace, 1993.

Riches, David. "The Netsilik Eskimo: A Special Case of Selective Female Infanticide." *Ethnology* 13, 4 (1974): 351-362.

Rideout, Denise. "Midwives Worry Birthing Centre Is Short-Staffed: Health Officials Say Centre Isn't in Crisis." *Nunatsiaq News* (November 30, 2001).

————. "Nunavut's Inuit Qaujimajatuqangit Group Gets Started: Task Force Wants 'Inuit Qaujimajatuqangit' to Prevail in GN Offices." *Nunatsiaq News* (February 2, 2001).

————. "Racism a Reality in The Arctic, Inuit Say: Conference Calls on Aboriginals to Speak out about Bias and Bigotry," *Nunatsiaq News* (March 30, 2001).

Riewe, Rick. *Nunavut Atlas.* Edmonton: Canadian Circumpolar Institute (University of Alberta), 1992.

Rigby, Carol, ed. *Report on the Baffin Region Symposium on Family Violence and Violence against Women.* Iqaluit, NWT: Baffin Region Agvvik Society, 1986.

Robert-Lamblin, J. "Sex Ratio et Éducation des Enfants d'Ammassalik (Est Gronland): Les Enfant Changes de Sexe a la Naissance." Deuxième Congrès International sur les Sociétés de Chasseurs-Collecteurs, Québec, 1980.

Rode, Andris, and Roy J. Shepard. *Fitness and Health of an Inuit Community: 20 Years of Cultural Change.* Ottawa: Department of Indian Affairs and Northern Development, Circumpolar and Scientific Affairs, 1992.

Rodon, Thierry. "Co-Management and Self-Determination in Nunavut." *Polar Geography* 22, 2 (1998): 119-35.

Rodrigue, Michaela. "Nunavut Women Must Travel South for Mammograms." *Nunatsiaq News* (October 29, 1999).

————. "QIA Candidate Says Women, Handicapped Have Place in QIA." *Nunatsiaq News* (December 3, 1999).

Rogan, Mary. "An Epidemic of Gas Sniffing Decimates Arctic Indian Tribe." *The New York Times* (March 18, 2001).

Rosaldo, Michelle Z. "Women, Culture, and Society: A Theoretical Overview." In *Woman, Culture, and Society*, edited by Michelle Z. Rosaldo and Louise Lamphere. Stanford: Stanford University Press, 1974.

Rowland, Robyn, and Renate Duelli Klein. "Radical Feminism: History, Politics, Action." In *Radically Speaking: Feminism Reclaimed*, edited by Diane Bell and Renate Duelli Klein (London: Zed, 1996; Spinifex, 1999).

Ross, W. Gillies. *Arctic Whalers, Icy Seas, Narratives of the Davis Strait Whale Fisheries.* Toronto: Irwin, 1978.

————. "Commercial Whaling and Eskimos in the Eastern Canadian Arctic 1819-1920." In *Thule Eskimo Culture: An Anthropological Retrospective*, edited by A. P. McCartney. National Museum of Man Mercury Series, Archaeological Survey of Canada, Paper 88. Ottawa: National Museum of Man, 1979, pp. 242-266.

————. *This Distant and Unsurveyed Country: A Woman's Winter at Baffin Island, 1857-1858.* Montréal: McGill-Queen's University Press, 1997.

————. *Whaling and the Eskimos: Hudson Bay 1860-1915.* Ottawa: Publications in Ethnology 10, National Museum of Canada, 1975.

————. "Whaling, Inuit, and the Arctic Islands." In *A Century of Canada's Arctic Islands, 1880-1980*, edited by Morris Zaslow. Ottawa: The Royal Society of Canada, 1981, pp. 33-50.

Rosser, Sue V. "Good Science: Can It Ever Be Gender Free?" *Women's Studies International Forum* 11, 1 (1988): 13-19.

Roy, Gabrielle. *The Hidden Mountain.* Toronto: McClelland and Stewart, 1961.

The Royal Commission on Aboriginal Peoples. *Aboriginal Self-Government: Legal and Constitutional Issues.* Hull, Québec: Canada Communication Group, 1995.

————. *Bridging the Cultural Divide: A Report on Aboriginal People and Criminal Justice in Canada.* Hull, Québec: Canada Communication Group, 1996.

―――. *Choosing Life: Special Report on Suicide among Aboriginal People.* Hull, Québec: Canada Communication Group, 1995.

―――. *Final Report (Five Volumes):* "Looking Forward, Looking Back"; "Restructuring the Relationship"; "Gathering Strength"; "Perspectives and Realities"; "Renewal: A Twenty-Year Commitment." Hull, Québec: Canada Communication Group, 1996-97 (website).

―――. *The High Arctic Relocation: A Report on the 1953-55 Relocation (Three Volumes).* Ottawa: Supply and Services Canada, n. d.

―――. Royal Commission on Aboriginal Peoples. *The Path to Healing: Report of the National Round Table on Aboriginal Health an Social Issues.* Ottawa: Canada Communications Group, 1993.

RT and Associates. *Nunavut Harvest Support Program, Background Document.* Yellowknife, NWT: RT and Associates, 1993.

Sabo, George III. *Long Term Adaptations among Arctic Hunter-Gatherers: A Case Study from Southern Baffin Island.* New York: Garland, 1991.

Sackett, Sydney. "Iqaluit: The New Capital of Nunavut." *Above & Beyond* (Spring 1996): 1-16.

Saila, Pitaloosie. "Pitaloosie Saila Talks about Old Age, Her First Drawing, White People and Other Things." *Inuit Art Quarterly* 2, 3 (1987): 10-12.

Samek, Hana. "Evaluating Canadian Indian Policy: A Case for Comparative Historical Perspective." *American Review of Canadian Studies* 16, 3 (Autumn 1986): 293-299.

Sampath, Hugh M. "The Changing Pattern of Inuit Suicide and Attempted Suicide." In *Looking to the Future: Papers from the Seventh Inuit Studies Conference,* edited by M-J. Dufour and F. Thérien. Ste. Foy, Québec: Université Laval, 1992, pp. 141-149.

―――. "Inuit Depression in Cross Cultural Perspective." In *Sixth International Symposium on Circumpolar Health, Proceedings,* edited by B. Harvald and J. P. Hart Hansen, 1981.

―――. "Protestant Missionaries and Their Role in the Modernisation of the Inuit in the Canadian Arctic." *Sixth Inuit Studies Conference, Copenhagen October 17-20, 1988: Abstracts.* Copenhagen: Institute of Eskimology, University of Copenhagen, 1988.

Sanday, Peggy Reeves. *Female Power and Male Dominance: On the Origins of Sexual Inequality.* Cambridge: Cambridge University Press, 1981.

Saunders, Alan. "From the Editors." *Arctic Circle* (January-February 1992): 5.

Savishinsky, Joel S. *The Trail of the Hare: Environment and Stress in a Sub-Arctic Community.* Langhorne, PA: Gordon & Breach, 1994.

Schrire, Carmel, and William Lee Steiger. "A Matter of Life and Death: An Investigation into the Practice of Female Infanticide in the Arctic." *Man* 9, 2 (1974): 161-184.

Schwartz, Mildred A. "Canadian Society: Trouble in Paradise." *Current History* (December 1991): 417-421.

Schultz, J. C. *The Innuits of Our Arctic Coast.* Royal Society of Canada, Transactions, 12, 2 (1895): 113-134.

Schutz, Alfred. "On Multiple Realities." In Schutz, *Collected Papers I.* The Hague: Martinus Nijhoff, 1962.

Searles, Edmund. "The Crisis of Youth and the Poetics of Place: Juvenile Reform, Outpost Camps, and Inuit Identity in the Canadian Arctic." *Études/Inuit/Studies* (1998) 22: 2: 137-55.

Seyfrit, Carole L., and Lawrence C. Hamilton. "Social Impacts of Resource Development on Arctic Adolescents." *Arctic Research in the United States* 6 (Fall 1992): 57-61.

Shannon, Robert F. J., ed. "Salute to Women in the North!" *North* (October 1985): 1-63.

Shouldice, Michael. *Aspects of Social and Cultural Significance of Carving Activity at the Community Level.* Ottawa: Department of Indian and Northern Affairs, 1983.

Simon, Ambassador Mary May. "Children and Youth of the Arctic: A Critical Challenge of Sustainable Development," Keynote Address to Sustainable Development in the Arctic: Lessons Learned and the Way Ahead. *The Northern Review* 18 (1999): 70-78.

———. *Inuit: One Future—One Arctic.* Peterborough, ONT: Cider Press, 1996.

Simpson, E. L., L. N. Seal, and R. L. Minion. *Nunavut: An Annotated Bibliography of the Literature since the 1930s.* Edmonton: Canadian Circumpolar Institute, 1994.

Skinner, Neil C. "Foundations of Aboriginal Sovereignty in North America: A Comparative Review." Paper presented to the Annual Meeting of the Western Social Science Association, Albuquerque, 1989.

Smith, Dorothy. Women's Perspective as a Radical Critique of Sociology. *Sociological Inquiry* 44, 1974: 13.

———. "Institutional Ethnography: A Feminist Method." *Resources for Feminist Research* (May 1986): 6-13.

———. "The Everyday World as Problematic: A Feminist Methodology." In Smith, *The Everyday World as Problematic.* Boston: Northeastern University Press, 1987.

Smith, Eric Alden. *Inujjuamiut Foraging Strategies: Evolutionary Ecology of an Arctic Hunting Economy.* New York: Aldine de Gruyter, 1991.

Smith, Gordon W. "Sovereignty in the North: The Canadian Aspect of an International Problem." In *The Arctic Frontier*, edited by Ronald St. J. Macdonald. Toronto: University of Toronto Press, 1966.

Smith, Harlan I. "Notes on Eskimo Traditions." *Journal of American Folklore*, 7 (1894): 209-216.

Smith, Melvin H. *Our Home or Native Land? What Governments' Aboriginal Policy is Doing to Canada.* Victoria, BC: Crown Western, 1995.

Soberman, D. *Report to the Human Rights Commission on the Complaints of the Inuit People Relocated from Inukjuak and Point Inlet to Grise Fjord and Resolute Bay in 1953 and 1955.* Ottawa: Canadian Human Rights Commission, 1991.

Soubliere, Marion. "Keeping Inuit Concerns Front and Centre." *Nunatsiaq News (Parnaivik edition*, 1996), p. 6.

———, ed. *The Nunavut Handbook: 1999 Commemorative Edition.* Iqaluit, NWT: Nortext Multimedia, 1998.

Soubliere, Marion, and Greg Coleman, eds. *Nunavut '99: Changing the Map of Canada.* Iqaluit, NT: Nortext Multimedia and Nunavut Tunngavik, 1999.

Spindler, Louise S. *Culture Change and Modernization: Mini-Models and Case Studies.* Prospect Heights, IL: Waveland Press, 1977.

Spitzer, Aaron. " Inuk Scholar Aims to Shake Up Arctic Science." *Nunatsiaq News* (May 4, 2001).

———. "Fund Will Help Nunavut Hunters Fuel up This Spring: NTI to Offer One-Time Gas Subsidy to Nunavut Harvesters." *Nunatsiaq News* (February 23, 2001).

St. Lawrence University. "Performance by Aqsarniit Drum Dancers and Throat Singers." In St. Lawrence University, *From "Nanook" to Nunavut: The Art and Politics of Representing Inuit Culture* (Exhibition Program, St. Lawrence University Festival of the Arts, Canton, New York, February 21-March 7, 2001), p. 20.

Stairs, Arlene. "Beyond Language: Lessons from Eastern Canadian Inuit in the Cultural Values of Education." *Journal of Navajo Education* 7, 3 (1990): 31-36.

———. "The Development Context of Native Language Literacy: Inuit Children and Inuktitut Education." In *Promoting Native Writing Systems in Canada*, edited by B. Burnaby. Toronto: OISE Press, 1985.

Stanley, Liz, and Sue Wise. "'Back into the Personal' or: Our Attempt to Construct 'Feminist Research.'" In *Theories of Women's Studies*, edited by Gloria Bowles and Renate Duelli Klein. London: Routledge and Kegan Paul, 1983.

Statistics Canada. *Language, Tradition, Health, Lifestyle and Social Issues: 1991 Aboriginal Peoples Survey.* Ottawa: Statistics Canada, 1993.

———. *Profile of Canada's Aboriginal Population.* Ottawa: Statistics Canada, 1995.

———. *Projections of Population with Aboriginal Ancestry: Canada, Provinces/Regions and Territories, 1991-2016.* Ottawa: Statistics Canada, 1995.

Steele, Harwood. *Policing the Arctic. The Story of the Conquest of the Arctic by the Royal Canadian (formerly North-West) Mounted Police.* London: Jarrolds, 1995.

Stenbaek, Marianne. "The Politics of Cultural Survival: Towards a Model of Indigenous Television." *The America Review of Canadian Studies* 18, 3 (Autumn 1988): 331-340.

Stenbaek-Lafon, Marianne. "Inuit and Globalisation: Potential Use of the Internet in the Arctic." In *POLARTEC 98: International Conference on Development and Commercial Utilization of Technologies in Polar Regions*, Nuuk, June 8-14, 1998, pp. 235-240.

———. "Sustainable Development and Mass Media in the Arctic: The Case of the Inuit Circumpolar Communications Commission." In *Dependency, Autonomy, Sustainability in the Arctic*, edited by Hanne K. Petersen and Birger Poppel. Aldershot, ONT: Ashgate, 1999.

Steltzer, Ulli. *Inuit: The North in Transition.* Vancouver: Douglas and McIntyre, 1982.

Stacey, Judith. "Can There Be a Feminist Ethnography?" *Women's Studies International Forum* 11, 1 (1988): 21-27.

Steckley, John L., and Bryan D. Cummins. *Full Circle: Canada's First Nations.* Toronto: Prentice Hall, 2001.

Stern, Pamela R., and Richard G. Condon. "A Good Spouse is Hard to Find: Marriage, Spouse Exchange, and Infatuation among the Copper Inuit." In *Romantic Passion: A Universal Experience?* edited by William Jankowiak. New York: Columbia University Press, 1995.

Stevenson, A. "Then Came the Traders." *Inuit Women in Transition.* Ottawa: Department of Indian and Northern Affairs, 1975.

Stevenson, Marc G. *Inuit, Nunavut, and Government.* Ottawa: Report Prepared for the Royal Commission on Aboriginal Peoples, 1994.

————. *Inuit, Whalers, and Cultural Persistence: Structure in Cumberland Sound and Central Inuit Social Organization.* Toronto: Oxford University Press, 1997.

————. *Kekerten: Preliminary Archeology of an Arctic Whaling Station.* Yellowknife: Prince of Wales Northern Heritage Centre, Department of Justice and Public Services, GNWT, 1984.

————. "Traditional Inuit Decision-Making Structures and the Administration of Nunavut." Ottawa: Report prepared for the Royal Commission on Aboriginal Peoples, 1993.

Stevenson, Marc G., and C. G. Hickey. *Empowering Northern and Native Communities for Social, Political, and Economic Control.* Edmonton: Canadian Circumpolar Institute, 1995.

Stout, Madeleine Dion, and Gregory D. Kipling. *Aboriginal Women in Canada: Strategic Research Directions for Policy Development.* Ottawa: Status of Women Canada, 1998.

Struck, Doug. "Among the People" (Series). *The Baltimore Sun* (January 1985): 13-17.

Struzik, Edward, and Mike Beedell. *Northwest Passage: The Quest for an Arctic Route to the East.* Toronto: Key Porter, 1991.

Stuart, Donald. "Weaving at Pangnirtung, NWT." *Craftsmanslash: L'Artisan* 5 (1972): 16-17.

Swinton, George. *Sculpture of the Inuit.* Toronto: McClelland and Stewart, 1992.

Swinton, Nelda. *The Inuit Sea Goddess/La Déesse inuite de la mer.* Exhibition catalogue. Montréal: Montréal Museum of Fine Arts, 1980.

Tait, Heather. "Focus on Nunavut." *Canadian Social Trends* (Spring 1999): 10.

Tannen, Deborah. *You Just Don't Understand: Women and Men in Conversation.* New York: William Morrow, 1990.

Taylor, J. Garth. *The Canadian Eskimos.* Toronto: Royal Ontario Museum, Department of Ethnology, n. d.

Tester, Frank, and Peter Kulchyski. *Tammarniit (Mistakes): Inuit Relocation in the Eastern Arctic, 1939-1963.* Vancouver: University of British Columbia Press, 1994.

Therrien, Michèle. "'All Qallunaat Predicted Our Extinction': Inuit Perspectives of Identity." In *Arctic Identities: Continuity and Change in Inuit and Saami Societies,* edited by J. G. Oosten and Cornelius H. W. Rémie. Leiden: Universiteit Leiden, Research School of Asian, African and Amerindian Studies, CNWS 74, 1999, pp. 28-35.

Thomas, Lewis H. *The North-West Territories 1870-1905.* Ottawa: Canadian Historical Association Booklets, #26, 1970.

Thompson, Joanne. *Teaching in a Cold and Windy Place: Change in An Inuit School.* Toronto: University of Toronto Press, 1998.

Thomsen, Marianne Lykke. *Ethnicity and Feminism: Inuit Women in Greenland and Canada.* Montréal: McGill-Queens University Press, 1999.

Thorne, Barrie. *Gender Play: Girls and Boys in School.* New Brunswick, NJ: Rutgers University Press, 1993.

Thorslund, Jørgen. "Why Do They Do It? Proposal for a Theory of Inuit Suicide." Seventh Inuit Studies Conference, University of Alaska Fairbanks, 1990.

Tibbetts, Janice. "Iqaluit: Promised Land of the Arctic." *Ottawa Citizen* (March 29, 1999), pp. A1-2.

Tokolik, Sarah. "The Spence Bay Women." In *Gossip: A Spoken History of Women in the North,* edited by Mary Crnkovich. Ottawa: Canadian Arctic Resources Committee, 1990.

Trickey, Mike. "Major Diplomats Bound for Iqaluit." *Ottawa Citizen* (June 5, 1998), A6.

Tunngavik Federation. *Agreement-in-Principle between the Inuit of the Nunavut Settlement Area and Her Majesty in Right of Canada.* Ottawa: Department of Indian Affairs and Northern Development and Tunngavik Federation of Nunavut, 1990.

Turpel-Lafond, Mary Ellen (Aki-Kwe). "Patriarchy and Paternalism: The Legacy of the Canadian State for First Nations Women." In *Women and the Canadian State,* edited by Caroline Andrew and Sandra Rodgers. Montréal: McGill-Queen's University Press, 1997.

Upton, L. F. S. "The Extermination of the Beothucks of Newfoundland." In *Out of the Background: Readings on Canadian Native History,* edited by Robin Fisher and Kenneth Coates. Mississaugua, ONT: Copp Clark Pitman, 1988.

Uyarasuk, Rachael. "Rachael Uyarasuk (Inuit)." In *In the Words of Elders: Aboriginal Cultures in Transition,* edited by Peter Kulchyski, Don McCaskill, and David Newhouse. Toronto: University of Toronto Press, 1999.

Valaskakis, Gail Guthrie, and T. C. Wilson. *The Inuit Broadcasting Corporation: A Survey of Viewing Behaviour and Audience Preferences among the Inuit of Ten Communities in the Baffin and Keewatin Regions of the Northwest Territories.* Ottawa: Inuit Broadcasting Corporation, 1984.

Valentine, Victor F., and Frank G. Vallee, eds. *Eskimo of the Canadian Arctic.* Toronto: Macmillan, 1978.

Vallee, Frank G. "Differentiation among the Eskimo in Some Canadian Arctic Settlements." In *Eskimo of the Canadian Arctic,* edited by Victor F. Valentine and Frank G. Vallee. Toronto: Macmillan, 1978.

———. "The Co-operative Movement in the North." In *People of Light and Dark,* edited by Maja Van Steensel. Ottawa: Department of Indian and Northern Affairs, 1966, pp. 43-48.

Van Kirk, Sylvia. "The Role of Native Women in the Fur Trade Society of Western Canada, 1670-1830." In *Rethinking Canada: The Promise of Women's History,* 3rd ed., edited by Veronica Strong-Boag and Anita Clair Fellman. Toronto: Oxford University Press, 1997.

Van Raalte, Sharon. "Inuit Women and Their Art." *Communiqué* 8 (May 1975): 21-23.

Van Rassel, Jason. "Baffin Leaders to Tackle Economy in Kimmirut." *Nunatsiaq News* (June 14, 1996), p.11.

———. "Empower us Carefully, Baffin Leaders Tell GNWT." *Nunatsiaq News* (June 28, 1996), pp. 1-2.

———. "GNWT Wants to Manage Nunavut's Infrastructure." *Nunatsiaq News* (May 17, 1996), pp. 11-12.

———. "Nunavut Needs More, Leaders Tell Irwin." *Nunatsiaq News* (May 17, 1996), pp. 1, 16.

———. "Pauktuutit Wants a Say in Nunavut's Future." *Nunatsiaq News* (April 12, 1996), p. 10.

Van Steensel, Maja, ed. *People of Light and Dark.* Ottawa: Department of Indian and Northern Affairs, 1966.

Vanstone, James W. "Influence of European Man on the Eskimos." In *People of Light and Dark*, edited by Maja van Steensel. Ottawa: Department of Indian and Northern Affairs, 1966.

Vesilind, Priit J. "Hunters of the Lost Spirit." *National Geographic* 163, 2 (February 1983): 151-197.

Vlessides, Michael. "A Turbot Tale: Pangnirtung Fishery Brings Income to the Community." *Above and Beyond* (Spring 1996): 37-40.

Von Finckenstein, Maria, ed. *Nuvisavik: The Place Where We Weave*. Montréal: McGill-Queen's University Press and the Canadian Museum of Civilization, 2002.

Wachowich, Nancy, with Apphia Agalakti, Rhoda Kaukjak Katsak, and Sandra Pikujak Katsak. *Saqiyuq: Stories from the Lives of Three Inuit Women*. Montréal: McGill-Queen's University Press, 1999.

Waldram, James B., D. Ann Herring, and T. Kue Young. *Aboriginal Health in Canada: Historical, Cultural, and Epidemiological Perspectives*. Toronto: University of Toronto Press, 1995.

Walsh, Mary Williams. "Boundary Disputes with Indians Could Block Accord on New Eskimo Territory." *Los Angeles Times* (December 19, 1991), p. A4.

———. "Canada's Inuit Reclaiming Ancestral Land." *Los Angeles Times*, September 15, 1992, pp. C1, C4.

Warmow, M. *Extract from Br. M. Warmow's Journal of his Residence in Cumberland Inlet, During the Winter of 1857-58. Periodical Accounts Relating to the Missions of the Church of the United Brethren Established among the Heathen* 23 (1858).

Washburn, Tahoe Talbot. *Under Polaris: An Arctic Quest*. Montréal: McGill-Queens University Press, 1999.

Watts, Ronald L., and Douglas M. Brown. *Options for a New Canada*. Toronto: University of Toronto Press/Institute of Intergovernmental Relations, Queen's University and the Business Council on National Issues, 1991.

Weick, Edward. "Northern Native People and the Larger Canadian Society—Emerging Economic Relations." *American Review of Canadian Studies* 18, 3 (Autumn 1988): 317-329.

Weissling, L. "Inuit Redistribution and Development: Processes of Change in the Eastern Canadian Arctic, 1922-1968." Ph.D. thesis, Department of Geography, University of Alberta, Edmonton, 1991.

Weller, Geoffrey R. "Self-Government for Canada's Inuit: The Nunavut Proposal." *The American Review of Canadian Studies* 18, 3 (Autumn 1988): 341-358.

Wenzel, George W. *Animal Rights, Human Rights: Ecology, Economy and Ideology in the Canadian Arctic*. Toronto: University of Toronto Press, 1991.

———. "Clyde Inuit Adaptation and Ecology: The Organization of Subsistence" (Canadian Ethnology Service, Paper 77, National Museum of Man Mercury Series). Ottawa: National Museums of Canada, 1981.

———. "Inuit Sealing and Subsistence Managing after the EU Sealskin Ban." *Geographische Zeitschrift* 84, 3/4 (1996): 130-142.

———. "Niniqtuq: Resource Sharing and Generalized Reciprocity in Clyde River, Nunavut." *Geographische Zeitschrift* 84 (1995): 130-142.

———. *Subsistence, Cash and the Mixed Economy: Adaptation among Baffin Inuit*. Unpublished Report SC 257400 to the Department of Economic Development and Tourism. Iqaluit, NWT: Government of the Northwest Territories, 1985.

————. "Traditional Ecological Knowledge and Inuit: Reflections on TEK Research and Ethics." *Arctic* 52, 2 (1999): 113-124.

Westkott, Marcia. "Feminist Criticism of the Social Sciences." *Harvard Educational Review* 49, 4 (November 1979): 422-430.

Wherrett, G. J. "Arctic Survey I, Survey of Health Conditions and Medical and Hospital Services in the North West Territories." *Canadian Journal of Economics and Political Science* 11, 1 (1945).

White, Graham. "Nunavut: Challenges and Opportunities of Creating a New Government." *Public Sector Management* 9, 3 (1999): 3-7.

Whittington, Michael S. *Native Economic Development Corporations: Political and Economic Change in Canada's North*. Ottawa: Canadian Arctic Resources Committee, Conservation and the North in a Decade of Uncertainty Programme, 1986.

Wilkin, Dwane. "UN Grants Inuit Women's Lobby Special Status." *Nunatsiaq News* (October 2, 1998).

————. "Anawak: Few Inuit are Qualified in Professions." *Nunatsiaq News* (November 19, 1998).

————. "New Culture Department Prepares to Defend Inuktitut." *Nunatsiaq News* (November 6, 1998).

Wilkin, Dwane, and Annette Bourgeois. "Nunavut Voters Say No to Gender Parity Plan." *Nunatsiaq News* (May 30, 1997), p. 52.

Wilkinson, Doug. *Land of the Long Day*. New York: Henry Holt, 1965.

Williamson, Robert G. *Eskimo Underground: Socio-Cultural Change in the Canadian Central Arctic*. Uppsala, Sweden: Institutionen For Allman Och Jamforande Etnografi Vid Uppsala Universitet [Occasional Papers II], 1974.

————. "Significant Aspects of Acculturation History in the Canadian Arctic: Analysis of the Forces of Inuit and Southern White Interaction until Mid-Century. Sociocultural Background to a Government Relocation Project." Report prepared for the Royal Commission on Aboriginal Peoples, 1993.

————. "Some Aspects of the History of the Eskimo Naming System." *Folk* 30 (1988): 45-263.

————. "Value and Functional Change and Persistence in Female Role: Inuit Women in Modern Arctic Society." *Sixth Inuit Studies Conference, Copenhagen October 17-20, 1988: Abstracts*. Copenhagen: Institute of Eskimology, University of Copenhagen, 1988.

Wilson, Elana T. *Gender, Political Power, and Nationalism in the Circumpolar North: A Case Study of Nunavut, Canada*. MP Thesis, King's College, University of Cambridge, Scott Polar Research Institute, June 2000.

Wilson, S. J. *Women, Families, and Work, 3rd ed.* Toronto: McGraw-Hill Ryerson, 1991.

Withers, Josephine. "Inuit Women Artists: An Art Essay." *Feminist Studies* 10, 1 (1984): 84-96.

Wonders, William C. "Overlapping Native Land Claims in the Northwest Territories." *The American Review of Canadian Studies* 18, 3 (Autumn 1988): 359-368.

————, ed. *Knowing the North: Reflections on Tradition, Technology and Science*. Edmonton: Canadian Circumpolar Institute, 1989.

Wood, Darryl. *Violent Crime and Characteristics of Twelve Inuit Communities in the Baffin Region, NWT*. Ph.D. Dissertation, Simon Fraser University, 1997.

Wright, James V. *A History of the Native People of Canada, 1: 10,000-1,000 B.C.* Hull, Québec: Canadian Museum of Civilization, 1995.

Yama, Mark F., Stephanie L. Tovey, and Bruce S. Fogas. "Childhood Family Environment and Sexual Abuse as Predictors of Anxiety and Depression in Adult Women." *American Journal of Orthopsychiatry* 63 (1993): 136-141.

Young, D. E., and L. L. Smith. *The Involvement of Canadian Native Communities in Their Health Care Programs: Review of the Literature since the 1970s.* Edmonton: Canadian Circumpolar Institute, 1993.

Young, Elspeth. *Third World in the First: Development and Indigenous Peoples.* London: Routledge, 1995.

Young, Lisa. "Gender Equal Legislatures: Evaluating the Proposed Nunavut Electoral System." *Canadian Public Policy* 23, 3 (1997): 306-315.

Zaslow, Morris. *The Northwest Territories 1905-1980.* Ottawa: Canadian Historical Association Booklets, #38, 1984.

Zellen, Barry. *Surf's up! NWT's Indigenous Communities Await a Tidal Wave of Electronic Information.* In "The Internet and Indigenous Groups." *Cultural Survival Quarterly World Report on the Rights of Indigenous Peoples and Ethnic Minorities,* QSQ 21.4 (1998).

Websites:

The Arctic Circle Project (http://www.arcticcircle.uconn.edu).

Arctic Research Consortium (ARCUS) "People and the Arctic: A Prospectus for Research on the Human Dimensions of the Arctic System" (http://arcus.polarnet.com/HARC/>).

Canadian Arctic Resources Committee (http://www.carc.org).

Government of Nunavut (http://www.stats.gov.nu.ca and www.stats.gov.nu.ca/ Nustatinfo.html).

Inuit Broadcasting Corporation (ibcicsl@sonetis.com).

National Library of Canada, "Canadian Information by Subject" (http://www.nlc-bnc.ca/caninfo/ecaninfo.htm).

Nunatsiaq News [Iqaluit] (http://www.nunatsiaq.com).

Nunavut Implementation Commission, "Footprints in New Snow" (http://natsiq.nunanet. com/'nic).

Royal Commission on Aboriginal Peoples, "Final Report" (http://www.afn.ca/ RCAP/rcaphmpg.htm).

INDEX

Note: Page numbers in italic type indicate illustrations, figures, or tables.

activities of, 13;
attitudes toward, 17;
early, 125–27;
finger weaving introduced by,
248;
and marriage, 67;
and religious conflict, 62.
See also Christianity
Mitchell, Marybelle, xiii, 37, 55, 339–
40
Morrison, David, 58–59
Moslener, Ingo, 245–46
Mountain Sanatorium, 109–10
Mowat, Farley, 100, 219
Murdoch, John, 55
music, 251
Myrdal, Gunnar, 384

Nagliniq, Natsiapik, 108–9
Nahannee, Teressa, 300–301
Nakashuk, Susie, 344
naming of children:
gender and, 85–86, 88;
Inuit personal names, 85–86;
significance of, 86–88, 234
National Council of Women, 229
Native Women's Association of
Canada, 365
Native Women's Shelter of Montreal,
303
nature, Inuit relation to, 388–89,
398n45
ningiqtuq. See sharing, communal
nomadic life:
difficulties of, 32–34;
enjoyment of, 34–35;
gender roles in, 35–38;
social relatedness and, 31–32
non-interference, myth of, xx–xxi
Norris, Mary Jane, 133
North American Fur and Fashion
Exposition, 246
Northern Skills Development Program,
321
Northern Stores, 372–73
Northern Women's Program of the
Canadian Research Institute for the
Advancement of Women, 365

Northwest Passage, 11
Northwest Territories (NWT), 6, 381,
395n4
Nunatsiaq News, 198
Nunavut:
benefits of, 379–80;
challenges facing, 381–84, 388–
94;
cost of operating, 376, 382–83;
creation of, 6–7, 345, 374, 376,
399n53;
crime in, 289;
and cultural preservation, 390–
91;
decentralization in, 379–80;
Department of Language,
Culture, Elders and Youth,
198, 375;
dependency of, 381;
economic development in,
399n54;
employment in, 345;
first legislative election in, 362–
63;
flag of, *257*;
gender parity in politics of, 361–
62;
geography of, 7;
governance of, 374–75, 401n79;
Inuit reactions to concept of,
383–84;
land settlement in, 375–77;
maps of, *7, 9*;
politics of, 361–64;
population of, 6–7, 374, 378;
preparations for, 377–79;
social change analysis for, 384–
91
Nunavut Arctic College (NAC), 163,
318, 321, 325, 326, 329–30, 378
Nunavut Department of Health, 199
Nunavut Implementation Commission
(NIC), 361, 374, 377–78
Nunavut Implementation Training
Committee, 378
Nunavut Justice Research Program
(NJRP), 308
Nunavut Land Claims Agreement, 376

ABOUT THE AUTHORS

Janet Mancini Billson, Ph.D., Director of Group Dimensions International, is a native of Canada. She attended one-room schools in Southern Ontario and high school in British Columbia. After undergraduate work at the University of British Columbia and Baldwin-Wallace College, she received her Ph.D. in sociology from Brandeis University and was professor of sociology and women's studies at Rhode Island College for eighteen years. She is currently adjunct professor of sociology at The George Washington University. Dr. Billson is the author of *Keepers of the Culture: The Power of Tradition in Women's Lives* (1995/2006) and she co-authored *Female Well-Being: Toward a Global Theory of Social Change* with Carolyn Fluehr-Lobban (2005). She has also written *Pathways to Manhood: Young Black Males Struggle for Identity (1996);*  *Cool Pose: Dilemmas of Black Manhood in America* (with Richard Majors, 1992/1993); *Strategic Styles: Coping in the Inner City* (1980); and numerous articles, chapters, and manuals on women and identity, feminist qualitative research methods, and conducting focus group and key informant interviews. She has lectured widely on women in Canada, Native women, Inuit women and their families, and Nunavut.

Dr. Billson has conducted focus group research since 1981, focusing on social policy. For The World Bank, she has interviewed stakeholders on issues including the social dimension of development, the Bank's resettlement policy, women in Rwanda's government, Uganda's development patterns, evaluation processes, and strategies for improving girls' education in Africa. In 2003–2004, she was Visiting Scholar with the Research Group on Well-Being in Developing Countries, University of Bath, England. She received the Stuart A. Rice Career Achievement Award from the District of Columbia Sociological Society (2001), the Award for Sociological Practice, Society for Applied Sociology (2000); and Alumni of the Year Award, Baldwin-Wallace College, Ohio (1999). An avid kayaker, Dr. Billson and her husband, Norm London, live in Woolwich, Maine.

 *Kyra Mancini,* senior research associate for Group Dimensions International, has worked in social policy research since 1987. Born and educated through high school in Rhode Island, Ms. Mancini has traveled throughout Canada, Europe, and the United States. In addition to her work on *Inuit Women*, Ms. Mancini is a focus group trainer and moderator. Through Group Dimensions International, she has conducted data analysis for social policy studies on HIV/AIDS, disability, fertility clinic success rates, substance abuse prevention among adolescents and children, transitioning youth out of training schools, restructuring of nursing, affordable housing, minority perceptions of Rhode Island's court system, and many other issues in education and international development. Ms. Mancini holds an associate's degree from George Mason University and the BS/RN from the University of Southern Maine (2006). A marathon runner, she lives in Woolwich, Maine, with her sons Eamon and Stefan, and two dogs and a cat.